METHANOL PRESS

SPEEDWAY YEARBOOK

2008

Edited by Robert Bamford

First published in Great Britain by

Methanol Press
2 Tidy Street
Brighton
East Sussex BN1 4EL

For a complete catalogue of current and forthcoming publications please write to the address above, email info@methanolpress.com or visit our website at www.methanolpress.com

ISBN 978-0-9553103-5-5

A catalogue for this book is available from the British Library

Book and Cover Design: Sitting Duck@ntlworld.com
Photographs: Les Aubrey, Karen Chappell, Ian Charles, Julie Martin and
                David Valentine
Cover Photographs: Steve Dixon, Les Aubrey, Ian Charles, David Valentine

UK Distributor:
Central Books
99 Wallis Road
London E9 5LN
United Kingdom
020 8986 4854
www.centralbooks.com

Printed and bound in Great Britain by the Cromwell Press

CONTENTS

ACKNOWLEDGEMENTS

WELCOME to the *Methanol Press Speedway Yearbook*, and indeed my sixth successive term in producing such a publication. As usual, there are a number of people to thank for their help in making this possible, with much appreciation to one and all: Craig Ackroyd, Lucy Aubrey, Nick Barber, Ian Belcher, Brian Buck, Ray Collins, Graham Cooke, Richard Crowley, Gordon Day, Nick Dyer, Frank Ebdon, Matt Ford, Colin Goddard, Mike Golding, Malcolm Holloway, Mike Hunter, Jeremy Jackson, Dick Jarvis, John Jarvis, Sue Kennedy, Mark Legg, Charles McKay, Peter Oakes, Gary Patchett, Robbie Perks, Lee Poole, Andy Povey, Graham Reeve, Laurence Rogers, Alun Rossiter, Terry and Wayne Russell, John Sampford, Glynn Shailes, Mike Smillie, Rod Smith, Tony Steele, Barry Stephenson, Steve Thorn, Dominic Threlfall, Bryn Williams and Ken Wrench.

I am particularly grateful to Jeff Scott at Methanol Press for taking on this project, as well as Matt Jackson for help with numerous dates of birth and, indeed, to all the riders who were more than helpful with similar information when asked. I'm very much indebted to Chris Seaward for much assistance throughout the season and also for the superb Grand Prix and World Cup reviews, as well as the magnificent introduction to this work. Once again, statistical genius Mike Moseley has kept me on the straight and narrow as far as the accuracy of averages is concerned and I am deeply indebted for his time and trouble in cross-checking all my figures. I am grateful for the assistance of various photographers, so many thanks indeed to the following for expertly producing all the images contained herein: Les Aubrey, Karen Chappell, Ian Charles, Steve Dixon, Julie Martin and David Valentine.

The internet has proved invaluable in helping to keep right up to the minute with everything in the speedway world, so grateful thanks to all the web-masters for collectively doing such a marvellous job. I also wish to again pay tribute to *Speedway Star* magazine, which has been an excellent and invaluable reference point. For guidance purposes, please note that in the calculation of rider averages, any tactical ride and tactical substitute points are recorded as those normally given for the relevant finishing position, e.g. 1st = 3 points, 2nd = 2 points and 3rd = 1 point. Appearances are only included in a rider's statistics when he was a member of the side as per the BSPA team declarations. All other appearances are included in the total for guests. Finally, regarding Elite League averages, all rider figures are calculated with the exclusion of matches involving Oxford.

Robert Bamford

January 2008

INTRODUCTION

THE 2007 season saw British speedway's major meetings receive a makeover from King's Lynn co-promoter Jonathan Chapman, who re-branded them as the 'Super 7even' series and organised the prestigious events at neutral tracks, a thing that the public at large had wanted for a number of years. As such, the meetings got a much-needed boost and were hailed as a great success.

For the **Elite League**, the year was a turbulent one, with a huge gulf between the top and bottom of the table. Seemingly endless rainfall played havoc throughout much of June and almost all of July, not just in the top-flight but in all three tiers, and it was to the credit of everyone that all the domestic fixtures were completed in full.

Unfortunately, Oxford closed down at the end of May, although, thankfully, they were quickly resurrected under a different promotion as a Conference League side and successfully saw the season through in that sphere of racing. There was also a mid-term change of stewardship at Reading, with the Berskshire side enduring one of the most difficult campaigns in their history. Right at the top, however, Coventry swept all before them to scoop a glorious treble of top-flight trophies, winning the League Championship, Knock-Out Cup and Craven Shield.

Looking a little more deeply at history-making **Coventry**, it was a gleaming season to cherish for the Warwickshire side. Importantly, the club was able to track an unchanged line-up from the one that concluded the 2006 season and the resultant team spirit was undoubtedly a key factor in explaining the emphatic success at Brandon. It was a season when all the hard work of Avtar Sandhu, Peter Oakes and Colin Pratt paid dividends, as the loyalty they had shown to riders in the past rewarded them handsomely. Indeed, Coventry were, without doubt, the best side in British speedway in 2007.

Firstly, the Bees scooped the Elite League title after defeating Swindon in the Play-Off Grand Final. Then, they claimed the Craven Shield and, finally, survived a real scare to also register victory in the Knock-Out Cup. Captained for a third successive season by Scott Nicholls, who enjoyed a very good year on his way to a 9.83 league average, the Bees youthful septet began their domestic assault in ferocious fashion, as they soared to the top of the Elite League table. A quieter spell in the middle part of the season ensued, before a sensational record-breaking sequence of sixteen consecutive victories emphatically propelled the Bees back to the top of the standings.

Coventry made just the one change to their line-up as the year progressed and it was a decision that the experienced management team deliberated over carefully. It was decided that Danish youngster Morten Risager was to be released after some impressive scores during the early part of the campaign had been replaced by a lull of form. The Dane was ultimately replaced by popular Australian Steve Johnston, who had been out of work following the premature closure of Oxford. He settled in at the Warwickshire club impeccably and was a key component of their success, emphasized by a 6.64 average from nineteen league appearances.

It was the year when Chris Harris really shone, not just on the domestic stage but also internationally. However, the mega-popular Cornishman always put his club first and was superb value, as ever, for the Bees with his never-say-die style, as he posted a league average of 8.97. His compatriot Olly Allen was enjoying another fruitful campaign, before an injury-ravaged conclusion to the season saw him miss a majority of the Bees' final six weeks of action. Elsewhere, Billy Janniro returned to Brandon for his seventh season in succession and proved to be a real trump card, especially in the latter part of the year when the flamboyant American revelled in the reserve department. 'BJ' earned his title of the 'Bonus Point King' by recording a whopping tally of 74 such points, as he remained ever-present throughout the 36-match Elite League programme.

Australian youngster Rory Schlein was in the Coventry side for a third season and performed consistently throughout, as he registered an 8.08 average and continued to establish himself as one of the league's most improving heat leaders. German Martin Smolinski spent most of the season switching between the main body of the team and a reserve berth, but made definite progress despite occasional topsy-turvy scores. It was a stunning year for Coventry, who brilliantly clicked together as a unit to achieve their success.

Turning to **Belle Vue**, the iconic Manchester side endured a torrid 2007 season that was blighted by recurring injuries and littered with poor performances. For so long, the Aces had relied on the consistency of Jason Crump to provide a rigid structure for their side, but rumours that the Australian sought a fresh British challenge held fruition, which saw the dusty transfer market wipe away the cobwebs and creak into life as a gaggle of clubs fought for Crump's much sought-after services.

A change of management at Belle Vue did little to change the double World Champion's mind; club owner Tony Mole and his charismatic sidekick, Ian Thomas, departed from Kirkmanshulme Lane and were replaced by a high-profile new management team that included Belle Vue legend Chris Morton. The incoming promotion's late arrival left them precious little time to build a competitive side in a league that was already suffering from a shortage of top-name riders and, consequently, the Aces struggled to be competitive throughout the campaign.

Simon Stead led the side, but the British rider was niggled by injuries and bouts of poor form, which also hampered him on the international stage. This was borne out by his final league average of 7.33. His compatriot Joe Screen chipped away all season long, but lacked the speed that once saw him set alight tracks up and down the country. Meanwhile, American Ryan Fisher was unable to make the most of the lifeline offered to him by the club and departed mid-way through the season. Finnish international Kai Laukannen also failed to impress and left the club, whilst the enigmatic form of Adam Skornicki became thoroughly frustrating.

The Aces attempted to strengthen by signing Swedish international Antonio Lindback, who had initially decided to opt out of British racing in 2007, but was forced to reconsider after consultation with his Swedish team manager, Mats Olsson. Unfortunately, Lindback failed to settle into the Belle Vue camp as quickly as expected, although, after dropping to a reserve berth, he began to contribute some eye-catching scores as his confidence, which had been shattered by a succession of injuries, returned. Regrettably, Lindback's speedway season came to a premature end when he was detained by Swedish police for a drink driving offence, and it was hastily announced that he had quit the sport.

The two bright spots for the Aces came through tenacious Aussie Kevin Doolan, who enjoyed a very successful season, and also British youngster James Wright, who continued to make progress amongst the ferocity of the Elite League.

Anticipation levels were high amongst the **Oxford** fans at the start of the campaign, after it was confirmed during the close season that Colin Horton, the promoter who had played a pivotal role in

Peterborough's 2006 Championship success, was the new owner at Cowley. Horton had agreed a deal with Aaron Lanney, who was to remain with the club in a promotional capacity, and the Cheetahs quickly went about assembling a squad.

Former Oxford favourite Steve Johnston was one of the first names on the team sheet, whilst internationally experienced riders such as Jesper B. Jensen and Pepe Protasiewicz quickly followed. Eric Andersson returned for a second term, whilst Ales Dryml made an emotional return to the club less than a year since the sickening crash that nearly cost the Czech rider his life.

Unfortunately, the Oxford septet struggled to be competitive both at home and on their travels, as the team failed to gel as a unit. Huge defeats meant fans of the club quickly became disillusioned, not only with the performances, but also with the way they felt the club was being run. Then, at the end of May, news broke that Oxford were withdrawing from the Elite League with immediate effect. This came as a bombshell to the speedway world but, most of all, to many of the officials and riders at the club, who were unaware of any plans to pull the plug on the outfit. The premature closure was particularly harsh for Aaron Lanney, the man who had worked tirelessly in 2006 to communicate with the supporters and dedicated so much effort into making the club a success.

Several new promoters registered an interest in taking over the reins at Cowley and it was eventually decided that Allen Trump, the man at the forefront of Exeter's quest for a new home, was the man for the job. Trump, along with his Director of Speedway, Peter Oakes, entered Oxford in the Conference League, which kept speedway alive in the historic city. For the fans of the club it was a stressful season, but one, at least, that ended with a man at the helm who had all the credentials to succeed.

Ipswich were struck a crushing blow on the first lap of the opening race in their initial league meeting of the season, when Mark Loram went clattering through the Foxhall Heath safety fence and suffered a badly broken femur. As well as suffering the leg injury, Loram also broke his elbow and spent a considerable amount of time in hospital recuperating after numerous operations. The immensely popular 2000 World Champion was ruled out for the remainder of the season, which left Ipswich without the rider who was, undoubtedly, the most integral component of their team. From that point on, the Witches' challenge for silverware was effectively derailed and the club mainly drafted in guests or utilized the rider replacement facility for Loram.

Chris Louis captained the side throughout the year and the brilliant British stalwart rolled up his sleeves and did all he could for the club, which he is so passionate about, finishing with a league average of 7.73. New Polish recruit Zibi Suchecki performed extremely well in his debut British League season and, although his scores did tail off a tad in the latter part of the campaign, he certainly did enough to impress the Foxhall Heath supporters in the early part of the season.

The 2004 World Under-21 Champion Robert Miskowiak returned for his third successive term in the Witches' colours and once again showed signs of improvement to post a 6.94 league average. In particular, near the season's end, the Pole enjoyed a lively spell of form, both at home and away, which went some way to rewarding the loyalty the that management have shown the rider. Young German Tobias Kroner provided the Ipswich fans with most to cheer, as he built upon the foundations he had laid at the end of 2006 and enjoyed a season to remember in which he notched up some hefty hauls of points.

Kim Jansson's campaign was largely uneventful, but solid throughout; likewise, that of Marcin Rempala, who took some time to familiarise himself with British league racing. The loss of Mark Loram, such an influential rider on and off the track, meant results were hard to come by for Ipswich, however, as the team began to improve, their home record did pick up. After the unfortunate demise of Oxford, former Ipswich favourite Jesper B. Jensen was drafted in around the middle part of the campaign as a replacement for Loram, but the Dane's time with the Witches didn't run as smoothly as hoped. A shoulder injury for Jensen meant Ipswich were forced to operate the rider replacement facility.

However, most heartening was the patience of the Witches' supporters, who backed the team admirably throughout, especially at the start of the campaign when the club was struggling to halt heavy home defeats.

Under an innovative new promotion, the re-named **Lakeside** (formerly Arena-Essex) enjoyed a significantly more successful campaign than they had for several seasons. With the acclaimed movie director Stuart Douglas at the helm, the club sensationally recruited long-serving Eastbourne boss Jon Cook as co-promoter/team manager and the experienced campaigner forged a wonderful working relationship with his newly acquired side.

It was the breath of fresh air that the Essex side so desperately needed and crowds began to flock back to the circuit, which was adapted so that spectators could get closer to the racing and enjoy increased access to the pits area. The Hammers concluded their Elite League season in fifth place, reached the semi-final of the Knock-Out Cup and were unlucky not to progress to the final of the Craven Shield competition.

A highlight of the campaign came on 16 April, when the Hammers' management, thanks to a high-profile sponsorship deal, threw open the turnstiles and allowed fans in for free for the Elite League 'A' encounter against Poole. A crowd of around 6,000 responded to the offer and were rewarded by a Lakeside victory and some brilliant racing, which helped quash the myth that the technical Purfleet race-track isn't conducive to good racing.

Lakeside assembled a tasty looking side for the campaign, which included the highly-rated young Polish international Krzysztof Kasprzak, who joined on loan from Poole. And he proved to be a particularly shrewd acquisition, as he showcased his bundles of class throughout the season to finish with a league average of 8.84. After spending the previous three seasons with Eastbourne, Adam Shields linked with the Hammers on a full transfer and performed extremely well in his new environment, averaging 7.66 from the league programme. The same can also be said of the exciting Joonas Kylmakorpi, whose contract was also purchased by the Essex club from Eastbourne. The Swedish-born Finn contributed some wonderful scores, before his season was curtailed prematurely by a nasty shoulder injury.

Fans' favourite Leigh Lanham once again represented the Hammers, performing solidly in his favoured second string role, while continuing to be a formidable opponent at Purfleet. Paul Hurry's terrible luck with injuries once again came back to haunt him and, despite starting the season well, the British rider didn't appear for the club during the latter part of the campaign. Young German international Christian Hefenbrock began the season with the Hammers, but some erratic scoring saw him replaced by the rapidly improving Czech rider Lubos Tomicek mid-way through the term. Tomicek was, of course, another speedster who had been temporarily lost to the British scene following the early closure of Oxford.

Another rider to come via Oxford was the highly-rated Ricky Kling, who joined Lakeside in July and notched some encouraging scores in the closing stages of the campaign. Perhaps, most exciting was the arrival of Swedish international Andreas Jonnson, who linked with the club towards the end of the season. Whilst the Grand Prix star's appearances may have been limited due to injury, he certainly lit up every track he graced. His appearances were indicative of the professionalism of the new promotion, who endeavoured to offer their supporters an exciting and committed team to be proud of.

For **Poole**, despite reaching the Play-Offs and the final of the Craven Shield, it was a season that promised so much more for a club who plumped for a splendid blend of youth and experience. The Dorset side made no secret that Jason Crump was top of their winter shopping list, as their astute management team of Matt Ford and Mike Golding pulled out all the stops to ensure that the two-times World Champion would once again bear the skull and crossbones on his chest.

With the spearhead of Crump and Bjarne Pedersen, it left precious few points for the remaining five team places and many in the sport questioned whether Poole's top-heavy nature would be detrimental in their quest for success. As expected, Crump and Pedersen provided wonderful top-end strength, though, the Aussie scoring 410 points to yield a 10.69 league average, whilst the Dane wasn't far behind on a 9.96 figure.

After solid 2006 campaigns, two very promising Australians, Troy Batchelor and Jason Doyle, were plucked from the Premier League and joined vastly experienced compatriot Craig Boyce. Despite both suffering injuries, Batchelor and Doyle made very encouraging progress in their first full-time year amidst the hustle and bustle of Elite League racing.

Edward Kennett began the season wonderfully for the Pirates and proved to be a real match-winner during the early part of the campaign. But, as the year progressed, the scoring returns of the young Brit began to falter. It was a similar story on the international stage, as Kennett's form earned him a call to the British national squad and saw him compete in the World Cup Final at Leszno in Poland. However, the World Under-21 Championship at Ostrow, also in Poland, saw Kennett, who ranked amongst the pre-meeting favourites, fail to make his mark in his final year in the competition.

Russian thrill-merchant Sergey Darkin began the season with the Pirates, but some disappointing performances saw him quickly replaced by former Poole rider Craig Watson, who had failed to agree terms with Newport in the Premier League. Like Darkin, Watson was unable to successfully adapt to Elite League competition and, despite being given an extended run to prove himself, he was to depart from the Dorset scene and eventually ended up back in the Premier League with Glasgow.

The Pirates experimented with different riders as the season progressed, including Piotr Swist, who certainly endeared himself to the Wimborne Road faithful with some breathtaking performances. Youngsters Steve Boxall, Tai Woffinden and Adrian Gomolski were also given opportunities to impress during the latter part of the season, as the Poole management kept an eye firmly fixed on talent-spotting for the future.

The Elite League season came to an end for the Pirates at Coventry's Brandon Stadium in a rain-affected Play-Off semi-final, which the Bees won comfortably. Indeed, the Warwickshire side proved to be a real nemesis for Poole in 2007, as, along with curtailing their league title aspirations, they also dispatched them from the Knock-Out Cup and reigned victorious in the final of the Craven Shield.

After the heartbreak of losing out on the Elite League title in a last heat decider in the second leg of a dramatic Play-Off Final at Peterborough in 2006, **Reading** were on a mission to go one better in 2007. The management team of Jim Lynch and John Postlethwaite certainly put together an exciting looking side that included Reading favourite Danny Bird, who was initially part of their 2006 plans, but due to an average miscalculation had spent the year on loan with Glasgow in the Premier League.

The big four of Greg Hancock, Matej Zagar, Janusz Kolodziej and Travis McGowan all returned to the Berkshire club, who were hoping for a significant increase in their attendances after the success of 2006 wasn't necessarily matched by an increase of support on the terraces. Despite losing home and away challenge matches to local rivals Swindon, the then nicknamed Bulldogs began their league campaign extremely well and showcased the same kind of form that had seen them become such a force the previous year.

However, all was not well behind the scenes at the Berkshire outfit, as attendances fell way below the figure required to make the club profitable and rumours that the management were on the verge of putting the club up for sale began to surface. In early June, things came to a head and the future of the club looked to be in jeopardy unless a new buyer could be found.

Preceding the emergence of the financial problems was a drugs test failure for Danny Bird and a fax from Janusz Kolodziej's Polish club informing Reading that he was no longer permitted to ride in Britain. On top of that, Travis McGowan suffered a shoulder injury whilst riding in Poland, the effects of which were to hamper the popular Aussie for the remainder of the season. All in all, it was a fortnight to forget for the supporters, for whom, doubtless, it must have seemed as if there would be no way out of the predicament in which the club found itself so drastically submerged.

Thankfully, a buyer was quickly found for the Berkshire club in the shape Swindon-based businessman Mark Legg and his accomplice, Reading Speedway legend Malcolm Holloway, who stepped in to save the club from extinction and immediately reinstated the club's traditional Racers nickname. Furthermore, Tim Sugar, for so long regarded as one of the sport's greatest team managers, was placed back in charge of the side, whose league title challenge had fallen away badly.

With the new promotion came a fresh wave of optimism, which was helped by the return of Janusz Kolodziej, and crowds began to return to Smallmead. The new promotion weren't able to keep the services of Greg Hancock and, after using a number of guests for several weeks, signed Polish rider Krzysztof Buczkowski as a replacement. Although not the heat leader that the club very much needed, the youngster endeared himself to the supporters and demonstrated plenty of style, speed and dedication. Promoter Holloway was also quick to make a change to the side's No. 8 department, replacing Phil Morris with an expert of the technical-type tracks in Chris Neath, who combined the role with that of representing Rye House in the Premier League.

It certainly wasn't plain sailing for the new bosses; they seemingly endured endless problems over the availability of their commuting riders, with Matej Zagar eventually receiving a 28-day ban from the BSPA after missing the prestigious Elite League Riders' Championship at King's Lynn. This came after the Slovenian had also been absent from a number of Reading's away fixtures.

The Racers finished their league campaign in eighth place, but did manage to reach the semi-final of the Knock-Out Cup competition, where they were eventually beaten by M4 rivals, Swindon. However, great praise must be heaped on Messrs Legg and Holloway, who, in their short time in charge, ensured they communicated with the club's immediate fanbase, whilst simultaneously working towards securing the long-term future of the Smallmead-based side.

Aside from Travis McGowan, who took over the captaincy from Greg Hancock, the mainstays of the side were popular Czech Sam Simota, dependable Aussie Mark Lemon and talented Swede Jonas Davidsson, who rejoined the club in mid-May, having first ridden for the Racers at Premier League level in 2003. Janusz Kolodziej never let the side down either and, once he had returned to the fold, showed some inspired form to finish with a 7.20 average from twenty-five league appearances.

By their high standards, the form of **Wolverhampton** during the 2007 campaign was well below par and failed to either reap any silverware or bring any finals. The Wolves failed to transform their intricate raceway into a fortress and consequently Peter Adams' men inadvertently allowed too many teams to depart from Monmore Green with victories and bonus points.

The West Midlands outfit were once again led by Swedish stalwart Peter Karlsson, who enjoys legendary status amongst the club's loyal fans, and his experience was well supported by the flair of his fast-rising compatriot Fredrik Lindgren. The duo posted league averages of 9.24 and 8.35, respectively, giving the side excellent strength at the sharp end.

Indeed, Lindgren's form was a real bright spot for Wolverhampton, as he not only excelled domestically, but also on the international stage. The young Swede also romped to victory in the prestigious Banks's Olympique meeting at the end of the campaign in front of a large Monmore Green audience. Meanwhile, David Howe enjoyed one of his most consistent campaigns, as he recovered well from a disappointing 2006 at Oxford. Emphasizing his improved form, he impressively raced to second spot in the British Final, which earned him a wildcard place at the showpiece event of the year - the Millennium Stadium-staged British Grand Prix.

Elsewhere, Billy Hamill returned to the club for his second successive campaign and the American rider endured a difficult season that was laced with machinery gremlins and niggling injuries. Magnus Karlsson continued his affiliation with the team in a second string capacity and the Swede's form was somewhat enigmatic, whilst William Lawson made progress by joining the club in a full-time role from Edinburgh.

Dutchman Theo Pjper started the campaign in Wolves colours, but was replaced mid-way through the season by young Danish prospect Kenneth Hansen, who certainly rode well enough to be considered for a team place in 2008. The club's eventual sixth place league finish was indicative of a season that never really gathered any sort of momentum and, despite some flashes of brilliance in places, it couldn't be deemed as memorable. A sign that the Midlands club might opt for a more youthful looking side in 2008 came when it was announced near the close of 2007 that they had secured the services of hot Danish prospect Nicolai Klindt.

Eastbourne, under the new promotion of media guru Bob Brimson, endured a season that was heavily affected by injuries and misfortune; subsequently the Eagles' quest for silverware never really got going. Led once again by the hard-charging Nicki Pedersen, the East Sussex club were rocked by the close season departure of long-serving promoter/team manager Jon Cook and also Adam Shields, who were both lured by the newly-instated Lakeside promotion. Pedersen's form throughout the campaign was nothing short of sensational and, although he missed a number of meetings through illness and injury, the Dane went about his work in a characteristically workmanlike fashion to attain a league average of 10.55.

It wasn't just Pedersen who was forced to sit out meetings, though, as many of his team-mates were also besieged by injury, in particular the popular British pairing of David Norris and Dean Barker, both of whom missed a vast majority of the campaign. Norris was again struck by the concussion problems that had hindered his racing for sometime, whilst Barker suffered a nasty shoulder injury at Swindon. Popular Swedish campaigner Stefan Andersson was another whose season was prematurely concluded by injury, whilst quickly improving Australian youngster Cameron Woodward sustained a broken ankle at Wolverhampton's Monmore Green raceway on 14 May.

On the up-side, the talented Lewis Bridger enjoyed a solid second season in Elite League speedway and will have been pleased by the progress he made; at one stage the youngster had David Norris working alongside him as part of his pit crew. Perhaps, the brightest aspect of the Eagles' campaign was the form of exciting Australian Davey Watt, who re-joined the side after spending 2006 with Oxford. Watt's performances during the middle part of the season, after he had successfully recovered from a horrifying crash at Arlington, were sensational and earned him a call-up to the Australian national team that came third in the Speedway World Cup. Watt's season also concluded early after he suffered an injury whilst racing in Poland, which ruled him out of Eastbourne's final few fixtures. Proving just what a fine year he had put together, he finished up with an impressive 8.44 league average, having notched 272 points.

Young Dane Morten Risager was signed by the management, initially for 28 days to cover for the injured Dean Barker, having been dropped by his parent club, Coventry, mid-way through the campaign. After a sensational start to the season, Risager had struggled to maintain such impressive form, but subsequently re-established himself as one of world speedway's brightest prospects with the Eagles, deservedly securing his team spot until the end of the season.

The Eagles were forced into making some late signings and the promotion drafted in Russian thrill-merchant Roman Povazhny and also Simon Gustafsson, the son of renowned racer, Henrik. The popular Povazhny, in his fourth spell with the club, put together some good performances, whilst the young Gustafsson impressed immensely during his short end-of-term spell.

It just wasn't meant to be for **Swindon** in 2007. In a year that seemed to promise so much more, the Wiltshire outfit finished as runners-up in all three of the league's major competitions. A majority of speedway pundits had tipped the side for honours, but the Robins couldn't re-discover their splendid early-season form just when it mattered most and were defeated by Coventry in the final of the Play-Offs, Craven Shield and Knock-Out Cup. Nevertheless, it was still an excellent campaign for Swindon, who successfully carried forward their momentum from 2006 and provided their loyal supporters with plenty to cheer about.

The promotion managed to shrewdly construct a side that was rammed full of internationally recognised riders, most of whom had the potential to significantly improve their starting averages. Australian stalwart Leigh Adams represented the club for a fourth successive campaign and was simply marvellous throughout. His amazing ability to record double figure tallies in match after match saw him top the entire Elite League averages on a massive 10.80 figure, having racked-up 450.5 points from thirty-five appearances. And he also took his career tally for Swindon past 5,000 points in all competitions, leaving club legend Martin Ashby's record firmly within his reach. At times, though, Adams was left perplexed by the inconsistency of the riders around him, who often failed to click as a collective unit, particularly in some of their away meetings and also in the crunch fixtures at the season's end.

Lee Richardson was back with the club for a third successive year and was hoping to rebuild his career after a disastrous 2006 campaign had left his confidence in tatters. Thankfully, the form of the British rider did improve over the course of the year; not to the level that some would have hoped, perhaps, but a league average of 8.40 was nevertheless a significant improvement on the previous term. The campaign ended disappointingly for the club's record signing, though, as he suffered a recurrence of the groin problem that had hampered him in recent years, coupled with a pelvic injury whilst riding in the second leg of the Play-Off Grand Final at Coventry. Richardson also suffered dreadful luck with machinery, blowing a considerable number of engines during the course of the season.

Elsewhere, the likeable Mads Korneliussen began the year in scintillating style, emphatically elevating himself into the main body of the team and contributing a range of impressive hauls. However, the Dane's season was interrupted by a hand injury that kept him out of action for the best part of two months. Then, a badly broken foot unfortunately curtailed his campaign prematurely.

Polish riders Seba Ulamek and Tomasz Chrzanowski remained on board with the club and both showed flashes of brilliance, mixed with bouts of inconsistency. To be fair to Ulamek, his year was disrupted by two separate wrist injuries, which clearly sapped his confidence. Meanwhile, Chrzanowski did improve considerably on his starting green sheet average, which was rather lowly on account of the fact that he hadn't ridden sufficient meetings the year before and therefore still carried forward the figure he had achieved with Poole in 2002.

Fans' favourite Charlie Gjedde begun the season poorly, before a stint at reserve really re-ignited his racing. The Dane then enjoyed an elongated purple patch, before a heavy knock in Poland on the eve of the Play-Off Final (second leg) was clearly an unfortunate hindrance at the crucial stage of the campaign. Nevertheless, from the league programme, he registered 280 points and an 8.33 average, which were excellent figures indeed.

The Robins' bosses managed to tempt British youngster Andrew Moore out his premature retirement and the tenacious lad battled hard throughout the campaign, just about managing to cope with the ferocity of Elite League racing. Tommy Allen began the term as the club's No. 8 rider, but was replaced on 1 July by highly-rated Australian Cory Gathercole, whose bundles of enthusiasm and exciting style wasn't rewarded with bags of points. Doubtless, however, the cousin of Leigh Adams will figure prominently in the future at Swindon.

Right at the end of the season, the Robins drafted in Polish World Cup-winner Damian Balinski as a replacement for the injured Mads Korneliussen. Although the tall-in-the-saddle rider showed plenty of style and speed, it was, perhaps, expecting a little too much of him to come in and produce match-winning contributions, especially as the meetings he appeared in were the finals of the Play-Offs and Knock-Out Cup. All the same, the Pole made a very good impression with the supporters.

The 2006 Elite League Champions, **Peterborough**, had their hopes of a second successive title dashed by Swindon, when well beaten by the Wiltshire outfit at the semi-final stage of the Play-Offs. The Cambridgeshire club concluded their league campaign in third spot and were prevented from finishing further up the table by some inconsistent away form.

Nevertheless, the Panthers still enjoyed a relatively successful campaign, led by classy Danish Grand Prix rider Hans Andersen, whose performances were very solid on his way to a league average of 10.39. The side was also well served by Andersen's compatriots, Niels-Kristian Iversen and Kenneth Bjerre; the latter in particular, who significantly upped his domestic average to 8.63, compared with the figure he had achieved at Belle Vue the year before.

Czech international Lukas Dryml enjoyed a resurgent 2007 season, which also saw him qualify for the 2008 Grand Prix series. Meanwhile, in his second campaign with the club, Polish rider Piotr Swiderski yet again showed some very creditable sparkle and further endeared himself to the Panthers' supporters.

Daniel King joined the club after completing a controversial move from Ipswich in the close season and the youngster ended the campaign with a real flurry. The British hopeful notched up a number of high scores and clearly began to make real progress in his closely scrutinised career.

German international and former Lakeside teamster Christian Hefenbrock was drafted into the Peterborough septet as a replacement for the unfortunate Richard Hall, who was unable to recapture the stunning form that saw him grab the headlines at the end of the previous year. Finally, on the rider front, Ulrich Ostergaard, who was part of the title-winning side in 2006, was loaned out to the Premier League, but still maintained his affiliation with the Panthers by filling the role of the club's No. 8.

The club suffered with stadium availability at the East of England Showground, which led to them conceding their home leg of the quarter-final Knock-Out Cup tie against Swindon, having previously had two attempts to stage the meeting rained-off. They were also unable to stage their leg of the Craven Shield competition, after that too had been postponed due to inclement weather. In fact, in order to complete their league programme, they were forced to stage their final 'home' match of the campaign at King's Lynn on 26 October, when they entertained Belle Vue.

The **Premier League** generally appeared to have a much better balance than the top tier of British racing and, as in 2006, it was King's Lynn who set the pace. Right at the death, however, the Norfolk outfit were beaten by a spirited Sheffield side in the semi-final of the Play-Offs. Nevertheless, having earlier retained the Premier Trophy, the Stars went on to win the Knock-Out Cup for a remarkable third year in a row.

Ultimately, Sheffield were to lose the major prize, that of the League Championship, when they were defeated by a determined Rye House side in the Play-Off Final. During the season, the Rockets had suffered badly with injures, losing the services, in succession, of Stuart Robson, Ray Morton and Robbie Kessler. With seemingly no-one about that could come in and do a top-line job, it was shrewd team manager John Sampford who came up with the name of Stefan Ekberg. With a deal quickly completed, the acquisition of the experienced Swede proved to be a master-stroke for the Hoddesdon-based side in the crucial sector of the campaign. Meanwhile, the last piece of PL silverware refreshingly went the way of Redcar, who got the better of new boys Birmingham to lift the Young Shield.

Looking in a little more depth at **Rye House**, the Hertfordshire outfit collected their second league title in three years, as Len Silver's commitment to nurturing young British riders once again paid healthy dividends. The Rockets made the most of the Play-Off system, as they ultimately concluded their league programme in third spot; they firstly overcame the Isle of Wight and then emphatically defeated Sheffield to claim the title in front of their loyal supporters.

The Rye House line-up had a familiar look to that of 2006, but with a couple of new additions that certainly added a bit more flair to the side. The most notable of these was one of world speedway's hottest prospects, Tai Woffinden, whose form was simply breathtaking throughout the campaign, as he replicated his Conference League performances of the previous summer amidst the high-tempo of the PL to yield 219 points and a high average of 9.15; he was undoubtedly a key component of the Rockets' success. Fellow youngster Adam Roynon recovered well from a broken ankle that had curtailed his 2006 season and revelled in his role amongst the reserve department, often notching up double-point hauls on his way to an impressive league average of 7.56.

Regrettably, Stuart Robson once again endured rotten luck with injury. After recovering well from the broken wrist that had played havoc with his 2006 season, the popular British rider suffered a badly broken pelvis in a horrifying crash at Mildenhall's West Row circuit on 29 April, when the Knock-Out Cup tie against Rye House was immediately aborted. The severity of the incident ruled Robson out for the season and, as touched upon, this led to shorts spells in the side for Ray Morton and Robbie Kessler, before Stefan Ekberg arrived on the scene late in August and rode impressively to post a 9.37 average from eight league matches.

Luke Bowen, whose 2006 was ended early because of a broken leg, rode very well throughout the season and, free from injury, really found his feet in the reserve section of the side. It was also a season when Tommy Allen really came of age; in particular, the British rider's form towards the latter part of the year was sensational, embodied by his victory in the prestigious Ace of Herts Championship that brought the curtain down on the Rockets' season. Steve Boxall once again contributed a variety of points during the year and whilst the British youngster, perhaps, didn't make the significant progress of the previous season, he certainly continued to underline his undoubted potential. Of course, the cornerstone of the Rye House side was Chris Neath and, in his fourth term with the club, the diminutive rider once again went about his work with the professionalism and consistency from which many of the side's youngsters were able to learn so much.

King's Lynn enjoyed another highly successful season in which they collected the Premier Trophy and the Knock-Out Cup, and also reached the semi-final stage of the league Play-Offs. After such a superb 2006 campaign, the Stars were forced to release the Australian duo of Kevin Doolan and Troy Batchelor, both of whom linked with Elite League clubs, in order to field a team under the agreed points limit.

Stylish Czech international Tomas Topinka returned for his eleventh season with King's Lynn, having first ridden for the club way back in 1993, and once again performed excellently throughout to yield a league average of 9.70. Indeed, the thirty-three-year-old was consistently difficult to beat around the Stars' pacy Norfolk Arena raceway.

Elsewhere, the experienced Swede Daniel Nermark returned for a second term with the club and led their league averages on a terrific 10.29 figure, as he once again formed a formidable spearhead alongside Tomas Topinka. On the downside, the most unfortunate aspect of King's Lynn's season was the injury to young Australian John Oliver, who suffered a badly broken leg in a home Premier Trophy encounter with Stoke on 11 April. The reserve rider opted to fly back to his homeland in order to recuperate, missing the vast majority of the season in the process.

Chris Mills, Paul Lee and James Brundle all played their respective parts in the Stars' successes, whilst Trevor Harding hit a rich vein of form as the end of the year approached. Surprisingly, though, Brundle was to lose his team place near the season's end, as Adam Allott made an unexpected return to the sport and thrilled the crowds with his lightning quick starting ability.

Additional highlights for the season were the record-breaking 75-15 victory over Sheffield in a Premier Trophy fixture at Saddlebow Road on 28 March, along with a vast range of off-track awards as the innovative promotion were rewarded for their continued efforts to provide a fantasic product. Furthermore, facilities continued to improve at the Norfolk Arena, which was rewarded by being awarded two of the sport's most prestigious meetings, namely the Elite League Pairs Championships and the Elite League Riders' Championship.

Newcastle occupied tenth position in the final league table and their campaign saw little change in the Diamonds' top five, as the promotion remained loyal to their riders. The Tyneside club were unable to stamp any authority on the league's major competitions and were also beaten by their local arch rivals, Redcar, in the end-of-season Tyne-Tees Trophy.

It was a campaign heavily affected by injuries, especially towards the latter part of the year, but despite the lack of silverware at Brough Park, the loyal fans were treated to some exciting racing in a season when the team was beaten just twice on their own patch. However, a solitary win on their travels halted the club's attempts to progress up the table and, with only a couple of aggregate points gained all season, the Diamonds could only claim a place in the bottom half of the standings.

Newcastle continued their tradition for nurturing young Danish talent, introducing teenager Jonas Raun, who had only previously gained brief British experience with Peterborough the season before. The youngster displayed plenty of potential during the campaign, but his season ended early after he suffered breaks to both an ankle and hand in a meeting against Somerset on 9 September. Up to that point, Raun had been doing a sterling job and certainly rode well enough to suggest he has a bright future in the sport.

Popular Czech rider Josef Franc fronted the Diamonds' attack and the diminutive supporters' favourite plugged away as he contributed a characteristically workmanlike campaign to average 8.48 from the league schedule. Carl Wilkinson, who had spent the previous season with Newport, went about his work with plenty of flair and proved to be one of the highlights over the course of the season. Some poor scores from Ross Brady saw him replaced in August by experienced British rider Paul Clews, who slotted comfortably into the side.

Elsewhere, Christian Henry continued his affiliation with the club and rode well throughout despite suffering from a knee injury, which ultimately curtailed his season in September. Henry performed slightly better than Josef Franc in the league meetings in which he did appear, posting an 8.50 average. Finally, reserve Sean Stoddart proved to be the surprise package of the campaign and his rapid improvement earned considerable and deserved praise from all quarters.

Somerset took to the track under the fresh-thinking management of long-serving Poole promoter Mike Golding, who concluded a deal with club owner Peter Toogood in the winter months. As such, the Rebels enjoyed a relatively successful campaign that served up plenty of exciting racing. The Oak Tree Arena, widely regarded as one of the best tracks in domestic speedway, received a facelift, as Golding spent heavily on enhancing the facilities, including the construction of a new clubhouse that was well received by the loyal spectators.

On track, Somerset were led impeccably for a third successive campaign by their popular Swedish captain Magnus Zetterstrom, who finished second only to Chris Holder in the entire Premier League averages, having attained a 10.67 figure. Once again, Zorro proved to be one of the division's most consistent campaigners, both at home and away. However, the former Poole rider concluded his season in controversial fashion, as he was handed a 28-day ban and a £1,000 fine by the sport's governing body for choosing not to compete in the Premier League Riders' Championship, but instead opting to ride in a Polish Play-Off fixture.

A second Swede, Emil Kramer, also enjoyed a fairly successful campaign that saw him assume a heat leader role and a league average of 8.54, whilst Ritchie Hawkins re-joined the club and recovered well from the head injury that had prematurely curtailed his 2006 season with Workington. Tomas Suchanek was also drafted into the side, but his stay was short-lived and the enigmatic Czech rider was replaced in early May by Somerset favourite Stephan Katt, who eased back into the side slowly, before finishing the season with a flourish.

Simon Walker continued his association with the Rebels and the effervescent speedster generally rode well throughout; his efforts being rewarded in the latter part of the campaign when he was handed the club captaincy following Magnus Zetterstrom's ban. The reserve pairing of Danny Warwick and Jordan Frampton performed extremely well for the Rebels during the season; both riders made notable progress with their spirited and wholehearted racing styles.

Somerset's eventual sixth place league finish was, perhaps, a fair representation of their performances over the term, but with an exciting blend of youth and experience, the future certainly looks bright at the Oak Tree Arena.

It was a year when **Mildenhall** successfully established firm foundations on which to prosper. Continuity and development were high on the agenda at West Row in a season when the team's eventual twelfth place in the league standings wasn't necessarily a fair representation of the off-track progress made by the club as a whole.

The Fen Tigers pulled off a major coup when they acquired the services of hot Canadian prospect Kyle Legault on loan from Sheffield. The youngster displayed brilliant adaptability to post an 8.77 average, as he excelled on the small West Row circuit after spending the earlier part of his British career at the large Owlerton raceway. Mildenhall constructed a decent looking team around Legault, which included heat leaders Tom Madsen and flamboyant Czech rider Mario Jirout.

Second string riders Shaun Tacey and Jason King slotted into the main body of the team, whilst Mark Thompson filled one of the reserve berths. The other was occupied by the unfortunate Jamie Smith, who had successfully recovered from the broken leg that curtailed his 2006 season, but once again he was to sustain a nasty injury in 2007. The British rider was ruled out in April after being flung over the West Row safety fence in a frightening accident that left him nursing a broken lower leg and ankle.

After being released by Somerset, Tomas Suchanek was drafted in to replace Jamie Smith, whilst veteran racer Paul Fry was introduced after Mario Jirout was shown the door following a poor performance at Glasgow on 20 May. Crucially, the Fen Tigers were only able to collect a solitary win on their travels and on five occasions let other teams take victory at West Row. Whilst silverware was absent, it was, nevertheless, a productive season for Mildenhall, which saw attendance concerns ease and track preparation significantly improve.

The **Isle of Wight** enjoyed a successful campaign that saw them romp to victory in both the PL Pairs Championship and the PL Four-Team Championship, whilst also reach the semi-final stage of the Play-Offs, where they were defeated by the eventual title-winners, Rye House.

Headed for a second successive season by the awe-inspiring Chris Holder, the Islanders maintained the majority of their 2006 squad and it was this sense of established camaraderie on which much of the club's success was constructed. Holder's performances were simply impeccable throughout, as the Australian plumped for a second year in the Premier League despite plenty of interest from a gaggle of top-flight teams. Aside from topping the averages in British speedway's second tier on a 10.80 figure, the youngster surged to victory in the prestigious Pride of the East meeting at King's Lynn and also played an integral part in Australia's third place finish at the Speedway World Cup in Leszno.

Jason Bunyan also enjoyed a fantastic season, netting 251 points to yield a solid 8.44 league average; the experienced British rider consistently contributing an array of double figure hauls to the team's scorechart. The popular skipper went about his work with plenty of trademark flair and brought much cheer to the Islanders' fans when he joined forces with Chris Holder to win the Premier League Pairs title at Somerset's Oak Tree Arena on 29 June.

Elsewhere, the Islanders handed a British speedway debut to up and coming Aussie Cory Gathercole, the cousin of Leigh Adams. The youngster showed plenty of promise in his inaugural season and, despite suffering more falls than he would have wished, Gathercole certainly did enough to impress at the full-throttle Smallbrook raceway. Pole Krzysztof Stojanowski returned for a third successive campaign with the club and the hugely popular rider, affectionately nicknamed 'Stoj', once again lived up to his reputation as a thrill-merchant by posting a very respectable 7.59 average from a full-quota of twenty-eight league matches.

Glen Phillips returned to the team after spending the previous season at Somerset and he once more fulfilled his second string role admirably. Chris Johnson and Andrew Bargh occupied the reserve positions and equally made good progress throughout the campaign, proving difficult opponents on the Islanders' Smallbrook circuit. They both had their share of knocks, however, and the season finished on a particularly sad note for Johnson on 12 October, when he received serious injuries in a track crash at King's Lynn, which left him with a complicated broken thigh and a hefty spell of recovery.

Stoke endured a traumatic campaign that was besieged by a raft of serious injuries, most notably to Garry Stead, who was tragically paralysed in an abandoned league fixture at Somerset on 18 May. The speedway community brilliantly rallied round in support of Stead, who later received the proceeds of two benefit meetings and a vast number of collections across the country.

The Potters began the season with Robbie Kessler, Rusty Harrisson and Garry Stead fronting their attack, with reliable second string Ben Barker and the returning Paul Pickering providing support. Meanwhile, the reserve section of the side was occupied by Barrie Evans and Jack Hargreaves. Despite the solid-looking line-up, Stoke endured a difficult start to the campaign and a succession of poor performances wasn't helped by some early-season injuries.

After a run of seven successive defeats in the Premier Trophy, the out-of-touch Robbie Kessler was replaced by Glenn Cunningham, who had found himself without a track at the start of the season. Another change followed, as the Stoke promotion sensationally tempted Lee Complin out of retirement and the British rider was introduced as a replacement for the struggling Paul Pickering.

The young Complin had shown so much promise in his teenage years, but turned his back on the sport after the 2002 season, so it was well received when the Potters offered the Sheffield asset a team spot. He was to be the 'Comeback King' of 2007, his all-out style setting the division alight on the way to a league average of 7.42.

Stoke finally got their first win on 28 April and things gradually began to pick up from that point. Hard-working promoter David Tattum introduced youngster Claus Vissing after the horrific injuries to Garry Stead and the newly-recruited Dane wasted little time in showcasing his talents as he notched up plenty of impressive tallies.

Despite some topsy-turvy results, the Potters squad enjoyed a settled period, albeit for only a few weeks, until Jack Hargreaves lost his team spot. Jamie Smith came into the side to fill the vacant place at reserve, having recovered from the injury that had curtailed his appearances for Mildenhall at the beginning of the term. In September, having generally struggled with his machinery, Rusty Harisson announced his decision to stand down from the side and Stoke operated rider replacement in the Aussie's absence for the remaining weeks of the season.

One last injury hit the club on 5 October, when Glenn Cunningham suffered a broken femur after crashing in a Young Shield match at Somerset. This was a great shame for the Bristol-born rider, who had posted a 7.52 league average since arriving on the Loomer Road scene. Despite the loss of Cunningham, the Potters did make the semi-finals of the Young Shield competition, where they were eventually beaten by Birmingham. It was certainly a bitter-sweet year for Stoke, as the agony of Garry Stead's accident was juxtaposed against the progression made by Lee Complin and Claus Vissing.

Redcar finished ninth in the Premier League standings, but concluded their campaign on an emphatic high by reigning victorious in the Young Shield competition. It was a brilliant achievement by the Bears, being their first major trophy since the track opened in 2006. Indeed, it was just the tonic for the Teesside club in a year that saw every member of Brian Havelock's team suffer injury. The Young Shield success was quickly followed by victory in the Tyne-Tees Trophy, as Redcar retained the title they had collected the previous year by concluding a two-legged victory over local rivals Newcastle.

The Bears were led for a second successive campaign by their hugely popular skipper Gary Havelock, whose season was disrupted by two spells on the injured list. Somewhat bizarrely, the second of these was a wrist injury, which the 1992 World Champion sustained when he was competing in an all-star soccer competition! However, the tenacious British rider was able to re-join the team for the latter part of the campaign, when he re-discovered the kind of early-season form that saw him light up Premier League tracks throughout the country. In recording 232 points and a high 9.70 league average, he again proved to be a wonderful leader for Redcar.

'Havvy' was joined at the top-end of the side by James Grieves, who had spent the previous two campaigns with Newcastle. The Scotsman was recruited to add some potency in the heat-leader department and he certainly did that, posting a league average of 8.86. Indeed, Grieves proved to be a shrewd acquisition, as he became almost impossible to beat at the Bears' South Tees Motorsports Park venue.

American youngster Chris Kerr returned for a second term with the club and the all-action racer built on the foundations he laid in 2006, as he once again made solid progress. This was especially so in the later stages of the campaign, when the Californian enjoyed a rich vein of form and, despite competing with a broken bone in his hand, his double-point hauls were integral to Redcar's late season successes.

Due to the injury bug, French rider Mathieu Tresarrieu didn't enjoy a productive season, although he did start encouragingly enough. Unfortunately, he suffered a broken collarbone and then, later in the season, a badly broken leg whilst grass-tracking. His first period out of action was covered by German racer Robbie Kesseler, who had lost his place at Stoke, with Redcar subsequently operating rider replacement for Tresarrieu in the closing weeks of the season.

Delving a little deeper into the side, Daniel Giffard's year was also interrupted by injury; his two-month absence was covered by Australian youngster Arlo Bugeja, who showed plenty of dash. Jamie Courtney and Rusty Hodgson had stints in the team, while fellow Brit Jack Hargreaves came on board in August after dropping out of the Stoke side. The shining light of the campaign was the form of talented British youngster Josh Auty, who successfully negotiated the jump from Conference to Premier League in his 'doubling-up' role and impressed many with his fantastic natural ability.

In their fortieth season in speedway, **Berwick** were left marooned at the bottom of the Premier League pile, as they endured a campaign to be forgotten in which they were unable to gather any sort of home form. It was a season which saw many team changes and, at times, it was hard to keep up with just who would be lining up for the Bandits, as promoter Peter Waite was ruthless in deciding who would face the chop.

After some poor scores, John Branney was briefly replaced by Rob Grant in April. Not long afterwards, David Meldrum and Jamie Robertson were recruited at the expense of Michael Coles and Grant. However, Robertson didn't last long and was released, as Peter Waite continued to make changes in an attempt to improve the Bandits' results. At the same time, as June came to a close, it was also announced that Andreas Bergstrom and Benji Compton had also been axed, but efforts to find replacements came to nothing and the decision was reversed, albeit temporarily in the latter's case.

Into the side came Polish rider Sebastian Truminski and he was hurriedly handed the No. 1 race-jacket; understandably, he found it difficult to settle into Premier League racing from such a pressurised team position. Soon after Truminski's arrival, Australian youngster Sam Martin was also acquired to slot into Berwick's reserve department in place of Benji Compton, and the eighteen-year-old from Adelaide showed plenty of promise at the large Shielfield Park circuit.

After a very brief stint, Sebastian Truminski was released in early August to be replaced by experienced Dutch rider Theo Pijper, who had ridden for Wolverhampton and Edinburgh earlier in the season, before losing his team spot at both clubs. After a three-week period of little transfer activity, the Bandits' season just got worse, as two of their riders, Michal Makovsky and David Meldrum, suffered injury in a league encounter against Stoke on 1 September. Unfortunately, both were sufficiently injured to miss what remained of the campaign. The loss of the popular Makovsky was a huge blow, as the loyal Czech rider sat nicely on top of the club's league averages, courtesy of a solid 7.42 figure.

Following a thrashing at Rye House, Peter Waite showed the trapdoor to two more riders, dispensing with Andreas Bergstrom and Theo Pijper. Czech youngster Matej Kus was introduced, but, just two days into his British career, the new recruit, who spoke very little English, awoke in hospital speaking the language fluently after crashing in a match at Glasgow! This phenomenal tale was actually included in many of the national papers. Suffering from concussion, Kus didn't ride again and, in the same meeting, Stainslaw Burza sustained a very nasty toe injury that ruled him out for the rest of the season, leaving the Bandits relying on guests.

In a touch of irony, Matej Kus had made his debut in a home match against Newport on 8 September, when former Berwick rider Sebastian Truminski lined-up for the Wasps. The Bandits were hammered 61-32 and Truminski raced to an excellent 11+2 points, as his new side comfortably collected the league points. Then, a week later, on 15 September, the Borders club lost 55-35 at home to Edinburgh, with another former 2007 Bandit, Michael Coles, notching a tally of 12+4 points as a guest for the victorious Monarchs.

Just as the Berwick fans thought it couldn't get any worse, Sam Martin sustained damaged ligaments in his ankle whilst riding at the Isle of Wight. One final rider move saw Arlo Bugeja line-up for the Bandits in their last four league matches, following his earlier spell at Redcar. The only bright spot of the season was the third place finish from Jacek Rempala in the Premier League Riders' Championship at Swindon. Indeed, the Polish rider rode extremely well on his way to collecting the bronze medal.

Glasgow were led for a fourth successive campaign by popular Australian Shane Parker, although they will, doubtless, have been a touch disappointed not to have fared better in the Premier League, concluding the season in eighth place. The Tigers assembled a healthy looking line-up that featured Parker and George Stancl at the top-end.

Added to that was Robert Ksiezak and, before the season got underway, Tigers' fans were buoyed by the news that the Aussie youngster had been purchased from local rivals Edinburgh in an attempt to bolster the Glasgow asset base. Ksiezak's season began in an unfortunate way, as he was struck down by injury in an early encounter. Despite some flashes of brilliance upon his return, the youngster wasn't able to match his accelerated progress of 2006, although he, nevertheless, still contributed a solid campaign.

A team change in June saw Lee Smethills replaced by veteran Michael Coles, who had found himself surplus to requirements at Berwick. Another alteration was soon to follow. Having spent the previous season with Newcastle, the returning George Stancl found it hard to re-discover the form that the Glasgow supporters and management knew he was capable of. This led to the experience Czech rider being released mid-way through the season.

The departure of George Stancl paved the way for talented Australian Craig Watson to join the club after a spell in the Elite League with Poole had proved unsuccessful. Soon after Waston's arrival, he linked with compatriot Shane Parker to collect the silver medal in the Premier League Pairs Championship at Somerset on 29 June.

Of course, the main-man in the Scottish side was Shane Parker, who went about his work with the charisma that has made him a favourite with speedway enthusiasts up and down the country for many years. He again headed the Tigers' league scoring, with 316 points producing a 9.92 average. Unfortunately, Parker's campaign came to a premature conclusion in late September, when a crash in a home fixture against Redcar left the Adelaide-born racer nursing damaged knee ligaments.

After a very fruitful 2006 season on loan at Stoke, Trent Leverington made a return to Glasgow and continued his reputation as one of the Premier League's most dependable second string riders. Meanwhile, the reserve department fielded two of the division's most experienced speedsters in David McAllan and Lee Dicken, both of whom plugged away throughout the year and fulfilled their roles well. However, McAllan concluded the season on the sidelines after sustaining a nasty back injury, which required an operation as the campaign was drawing to a conclusion.

The year for **Newport** might not have been laced with silverware, but the Wasps certainly served up plenty of entertainment in a campaign that unearthed some exciting raw young talent. It was a season, though, when the Welsh club lined-up somewhat surprisingly without their long-serving Australian No.1 Craig Watson, who was unable to agree terms for a return to Queensway Meadows.

Highly-rated Aussie Tom Hedley did, however, join the club for his inaugural season in British racing. The youngster had cut his speedway teeth at Mildura's iconic Olympic Park arena and came to Newport with huge recommendations. His performances were steady, if unspectacular, and he certainly showed plenty of potential as the season unfolded, although his campaign was curtailed prematurely after he suffered a nasty knock to the head.

Elsewhere, the signature of Phil Morris was secured, but the Welsh rider was to lose his team place in a late re-shuffle, eventually re-locating to Birmingham. Meanwhile, Chris Schramm again represented the club and went about his work with plenty of his characteristic flair, whilst Tony Atkin rode tenaciously throughout the season after once more being handed the captain's armband.

Perhaps, the most encouraging aspect of the Wasps' season were the performances of Polish thrill-merchant Michal Rajkowski, who was handed a late position in the line-up after the club had been unable to conclude a deal with Craig Waston. The Pole had impressed at Queensway Meadows during January's New Year Classic and, after initially starting in the No. 1 position, he enjoyed a phenomenal spell at reserve that saw him elevated back to the top position in the riding order, from where he continued to excel. Although his scores did tend to be laced with inconsistency as the campaign wore on, there was little doubt that the youngster's early-season contributions had transformed him into a real favourite with the Newport supporters.

The late term alteration that saw the departure of Phil Morris led to a team spot for another Polish rider, Sebastian Truminski, who had lost his team spot at Berwick earlier in the campaign. This move was seen as an attempt to add some potency to the side's second string department and Truminski certainly proved to be something of a crowd-pleaser in his brief end-of-term stint.

In the final analysis, it was the lack of a true No. 1 rider that stifled Newport's ability to construct a positive period of form and, whilst the team possessed plenty of solid squad riders, they were without a leader on whom they could rely upon to contribute double-point returns week in, week out.

Edinburgh ended their league campaign occupying a disappointing thirteenth place in a season that saw numerous heat leaders come and go at Armdale. There wasn't much to cheer about in the Premier Trophy either, as the Monarchs didn't manage to progress past the group stage of the competition. There was no doubting that Edinburgh possessed some of the most potent second strings in the sport's second tier and, in addition, some lively reserves. However, in a sensational twist, the promotion made the decision to axe all three of their under-performing heat leaders. This kind of thing is not commonplace in speedway, of course, and the club must be congratulated for sticking with the backbone of their side, rather than taking the 'quick fix' option.

The Monarchs began the campaign with Ronnie Correy, Henrik Moller and William Lawson in the top three positions, but by July all three had departed the club and replacements found. Lawson went to further his career with Wolverhampton in the Elite League on a full-time basis and, after struggling in the top sphere with the West Midlands outfit, Theo Pijper returned to Edinburgh as a replacement. The Dutchman's stay was to be short-lived, though, and, following a defeat at Somerset in the Knock-Out Cup, he was released, along with Ronnie Correy and Henrik Moller.

That freed up room for George Stancl to join the club, having been released from local rivals Glasgow. Meanwhile, also linking with the Monarchs was Finnish international Kaj Laukkanen, who had been relieved of his duties at Belle Vue. The experienced rider was joined by young compatriot Kalle Katajisto, who was very much seen as a rider for the future. In the same month, the Scottish outfit announced the signing of highly-rated Australian youngster Aaron Summers, who was effectively looking to the future by getting a feel for the British racing scene whilst on holiday; consequently his stay with the club was all too brief, although he certainly did enough to impress everybody at Armadale Stadium.

Australian Matthew Wethers continued his association with Edinburgh and enjoyed a fairly decent season that saw him notch 172 points for a respectable 7.18 league average, as he comfortably held down a second string role. Italian youngster Daniele Tessari again linked with the side, but just when he looked to be making significant strides, he was struck down by injury and only made one painful appearance after 18 May.

After such a wonderful 2006 season, Scotsman Derek Sneddon once again enjoyed a campaign to savour; the reliable rider being rewarded with club captaincy following Ronnie Correy's departure in July. Andrew Tully also enjoyed a productive season in which he contributed some encouraging scores from the reserve department of the team. Indeed, the youngster from the Isle of Man was clearly beginning to reap the benefits of his success with Scunthorpe at Conference level.

Speedway roared back into Britain's second city, as **Birmingham** made a thoroughly successful return to the sport at the plush Perry Barr Stadium. Cheered on each week by large crowds, the Brummies served up plenty of excitement at their 292-metre raceway that was rapidly constructed in the winter months. The resurrection of the club was undoubtedly the success story of the British scene in 2007 and it was just reward for those who had campaigned so tirelessly to see the famous yellow and red race-jacket prevail.

In actual fact, Birmingham can count themselves unlucky not to have made the Premier League Play-Offs, as a succession of rain-offs led to the club being unable to complete all their fixtures prior to the cut-off date. As it happened, when the outstanding fixtures were completed, the Brummies ultimately finished their campaign in second spot, such was the strength of their side. They were also able to boast the best away record in their sphere of racing, having collected seven wins and a draw on their travels.

The management team of Tony Mole and Graham Drury compiled a fantastic looking side that did change quite dramatically as the season progressed, with injuries, retirements and patchy form all playing their part. However, one rider who stood firm was experienced Australian stalwart Jason Lyons, who excelled throughout the entire campaign and proved to be the perfect No. 1, posting a 9.77 average from twenty-seven league matches. The former Belle Vue racer received sturdy support from popular Argentinean Emiliano Sanchez, who was one of the first signings to be announced for the 2007 season. It proved to be a worthwhile acquisition, as the experienced campaigner fought tirelessly for points both at home and on his travels, until a track crash at Newport curtailed his season on 19 August.

It was a season to forget for Brent Werner and one that brought the curtain down on his career. Amid a great buzz of anticipation, he had been revealed as Birmingham's initial capture on 29 November 2006. Then, at the Press and Practice Day, he was handed the captain's armband. Regrettably, he subsequently found it a struggle to score points and it was announced on 2 May that Jason Lyons had taken over as skipper, so that the American could concentrate on regaining his touch. However, just six days later, Werner quit the sport with immediate effect, due to his loss of form and confidence. Shortly afterwards, he was replaced in the team by Jon Armstrong.

Aidan Collins was another rider who started the term with the Brummies, but didn't make it to the end of the campaign. The Stockport-born racer found it hard to get going and made the decision to quit the sport as June came to a close. His replacement was Austrian Manuel Hauzinger, who contributed a number of superb performances, before he ended up on the club's extended injured list.

Ulrich Ostergaard began the season in Birmingham's colours and the Danish rider started the campaign in sensational form, quickly establishing himself as one of the league's most formidable performers. However, Ostergaard was sensationally axed from the side in early August after a conflict of interests had seen him reluctant to commit himself to the club due to being nominated for a reserve position in a European Championship round in his homeland. His replacement was compatriot Henning Bager, who had been released from Elite League outfit Lakeside a few weeks previously.

Special praise must be heaped on the reserve duo of Lee Smart and Ben Powell, who both rode extremely well throughout the campaign, improving their starting averages in the process. Unluckily, Powell was sidelined by a broken wrist in the Second City Trophy on 26 September and missed the closing weeks of the season.

Other changes along the way saw Jon Armstrong replaced by Henrik Moller, whilst Phil Morris made late appearances for the club as they attempted to cover for the serious injury crisis. The Brummies reached the final in both the Premier Trophy and Young Shield competitions, but couldn't contain a rampant King's Lynn side in the former. Then, ravaged by injuries, they were unable to prevent Redcar from collecting their first trophy, as the Bears took victory in both legs of the Young Shield final. Nevertheless, it was a brilliant campaign for Birmingham, who went about their task with professionalism and lots of enthusiasm.

Workington completed their league programme in seventh position, but it was a strange old season that never really seemed to get going. Led by their rising British star James Wright, their line-up also included popular Finn Kauko Nieminen, who collected 272 points on route to a characteristically impressive 9.05 average.

Italian youngster Mattia Carpanese joined the club at the start of the season and generally struggled for points, although a series of knocks understandably drained his confidence and ultimately caused him to stand down from the team as August drew to a close. Craig Branney slotted into a second string role, whilst one of the reserve slots was filled by Charles Wright, the younger brother of James, who had also progressed through the ranks at Conference League outfit Buxton.

The Comets began the campaign with hotly-rated youngster Kenneth Hansen in their side, but an early-season injury left the Dane facing a spell on the sidelines. Sensationally, the Workington management were able to persuade club legend Carl Stonehewer back to Derwent Park and the immensely popular British campaigner took little time in once again familiarising himself with Premier League competition. Reserve rider Jamie Robertson found himself a casualty of the averages and he was replaced briefly by Scott James in order to accommodate Stonehewer's return. James' stint, in fact, lasted just one match in the Premier Trophy, before he was replaced by John Branney, the younger brother of Craig, giving the Comets two sets of siblings.

The former GP rider enjoyed three very solid months in Workington's colours, before his season was ended by injury. There was no doubting that the loyal Derwent Park fans revelled in seeing their hero back on track with his trademark spring in the step. 'Stoney' was subsequently replaced by Ulrich Ostergaard, who had been released from Birmingham and proved to be a very capable replacement.

The Comets lost just once at home during the league campaign, but were only able to muster three victories on their travels. On an individual basis, it was a wonderful year for James Wright who continued to make noteworthy progression, which was emphasised when the British rider romped to victory in the Premier League Riders' Championship at Swindon's Abbey Stadium on 30 September. As he had done since 2005, Wright also spent the season 'doubling-up' with Belle Vue in the top-flight. For the Comets, he recorded 305 points to post an excellent league average of 9.65. Meanwhile, in British speedway's highest tier, he plugged away determinedly for the Aces, appearing in twenty-seven Elite League matches and scoring 143 points to achieve an impressive 5.55 average.

For a second successive season, **Sheffield** were defeated in the Play-Off Final and had to be satisfied with the runners-up tag. Nevertheless, they did provide plenty of first class entertainment along the way. The Tigers assembled a classy line-up that, aside from Aussie Joel Parsons, was made up of British riders, all renowned for their passing ability.

The South Yorkshire side were able to inflict revenge on King's Lynn, their bogey team of 2006, as they defeated the Stars at the semi-final stage of the Play-Offs. However, the final proved to be a step too far and the Tigers were unable to defend a 9-point first leg lead against a rampant Rye House outfit at Hoddesdon.

The backbone of the Sheffield side was the British duo of Andre Compton and Ricky Ashworth, both of whom really excelled at the large Owlerton raceway and continued to be two of the league's most feared heat leaders. In particular, the experienced Compton once again sparkled in his captain's role and led by example to post a typically hefty 10.27 league average, the fourth highest in the sport's second tier. Ashworth wasn't too far behind his skipper, though, his season's work yielding an 8.79 figure from twenty-four league appearances.

Local lad James Birkinshaw slotted into the side nicely, until a shoulder injury and then a badly broken hand saw him ruled him out of action. However, Paul Cooper managed to put his injury jinx behind him, as he slotted into the Sheffield side and contributed some superb hauls; perhaps, most notably in the first leg of the Play-Off semi-final, when he tallied paid 11 in the emphatic 31-point victory over King's Lynn.

Ben Wilson continued to make notable progress and greatly improved his levels of consistency, whilst fellow young British rider James Cockle plugged away all season and will have been generally pleased with his form. After a thoroughly successful 2006 season with Newport, Joel Parsons linked with the Tigers and, once again, displayed plenty of the all-action style that makes him one of the division's most exciting riders. Sheffield will have, perhaps, been a touch disappointed not to have picked up any silverware, however, many in their side made good progress and they certainly possess a solid foundation on which to build upon in 2008.

As ever, the **Conference League** served up plenty of grass-roots entertainment, with several talented young riders making an emergence. Ten teams came to the tapes for the campaign and there were many positives to be taken from the third tier of the British racing scene.

Scunthorpe again dominated proceedings and replicated what Coventry achieved in the top-flight by collecting all three major trophies on offer. However, not only did the mighty Scorpions triumph in the Conference League, Knock-Out Cup and Conference Trophy, but they also took victory in the Four-Team Championship.

Going into the campaign, the North Lincolnshire club, one of British speedway's great success stories, once again assembled an impressive looking squad that was rammed full of young British riders. The locally-born Tai Woffinden returned for his second term with the club and the highly-rated teenager enjoyed a fabulous season in which he further enhanced his reputation as one of world speedway's hottest prospects. Woffinden finished at the top of the pile in the overall league averages on a huge 11.22 figure and also took victory in both the Conference League Riders' Championship and the British Under-18 Championship.

Looking a little more closely at the side, Josh Auty continued his rapid rise up the sport's ladder to register a 10.22 league average, while the ever-improving Andrew Tully carded a slightly higher 10.26 figure. Joe Haines enjoyed an excellent season, scorching to 168 points and an 8.83 average in only his second year at CL level, whilst Richie Dennis posted an 8.05 figure, before injury curtailed his season in late-September after seventeen league appearances.

Likeable South African Byron Bekker, in his third year with the Scorpions, once again proved difficult to beat around the continually improving Normanby Road arena. Also providing ample support to the top-end riders was Scott Richardson, who impressing greatly during the course of the campaign. Benji Compton also enjoyed several meetings for Scunthorpe, while Scott Anderson was only able to break into the team on the odd occasion.

It was announced in the latter part of the season that the club had applied to enter the Premier League; it was therefore fitting that a thrilling challenge match against Sheffield should bring the curtain down on another stunning year for the club.

For the family-run **Buxton**, the 2007 season was another term that continued the club's long and illustrious tradition of nurturing promising young riders. The Hitmen concluded their league campaign in a highly creditable seventh position and finished second, behind Scunthorpe, in the northern section of the Conference Trophy competition.

The season began in brilliant style, as Buxton narrowly defeated the touring USA Dream Team, who were making their third successive annual visit to Britain. It was a season when the highly promising Jack Roberts scored 105 league points to average 8.38 for the Hitmen, as he continued to show encouraging signs of progression.

Elsewhere, the experienced duo of Jonathan Bethell and Jon Armstrong rode well, but only had limited spells with the club at differing times. Ben Taylor also notched plenty of useful scores, as did Scott James, who increasingly collected double figure hauls at the Peak District circuit.

Australian youngster Aaron Summers also spent an all too brief spell with the club, during which time he demonstrated the talent that led Premier League outfit Edinburgh snap up his services. For yet another year, Buxton provided a wonderful platform for young riders to excel and the club continued to lead by example.

Boston enjoyed a successful campaign that saw them reign victorious in the Conference League Pairs Championship and finish fourth in the league standings. The club welcomed a new member to their promotional team, Dale Allitt, who brought a fresh new approach to the Barracudas' set-up.

A considerable amount of riders lined-up for the club in the 2007 season, with heavy-hitters James Brundle, Paul Cooper and Darren Mallett representing the side during the campaign. Brundle, in fact, headed the team's averages, posting a 9.28 figure from his ten league appearances. Meanwhile, Simon Lambert made notable progress and successfully fortified the confidence levels that had eluded him in previous seasons to attain a healthy 8.55 league average.

Overall, it was a much more harmonious season for Boston, which ended with a positive feeling rather than the uncertainty that had concluded the 2006 campaign. The club are still actively seeking a track of their own, although progress is tending to be slow. There is, however, plenty of determination and passion behind the plans to see the Barrucudas prosper at a venue that they can proudly call 'home'.

Plymouth enjoyed another successful season that saw them finish third in the league standings and reach the finals of both the Conference Trophy and Knock-Out Cup competitions. However, Scunthorpe once again proved to be a real thorn in the Devils' side, as the healthy rivalry between the two powerhouse sides continued unabated throughout the 2007 campaign.

For a second successive season, the Devon outfit were led by the fast-trapping Seemond Stephens, who maintained his position as one of the league's most consistent campaigners, courtesy of a 9.00 average. The former Exeter favourite was well supported throughout by the tenacious Tom Brown, who lit up the exciting St Boniface Arena with a variety of board-scraping passes on his way to a league average of 8.97.

Nicki Glanz proved to be a particularly shrewd acquisition and the youngster quickly endeared himself to the Plymouth faithful, while Ben Hopwood also enjoyed a hugely productive stint after linking with the club in July. Meanwhile, Adam Roynon had a brief and high-scoring early-season spell in the side, appearing in just four Conference League matches and one in the Conference Trophy.

The Devils also secured an extension on their planning permission, which will allow them to invest in spectator facilities at the St Boniface Arena. The return of the sport under promoter Mike Bowden has been well received and it was good to see healthy crowds continue to flock to the circuit each week during the summer.

Turning to the Potteries, **Stoke** didn't enjoy the best of times, as several riders came and went for various reasons. The completed league table saw the Spitfires occupying eighth position and, with three home defeats, this wasn't really surprising.

The mainstay of the side was Barrie Evans, who remained ever-present to card 217 league points and a healthy 9.05 average. He received valuable top-end support from John Branney, who ended the year with a fine 9.01 average. Sam Dore made good progress and ended the season with a flourish by hitting double figures in home and away fixtures against Buxton. Guy Kendrew was steady enough in his debut season, while Gareth Isherwood improved considerably once he was given an extended run in the side.

David Haigh, Jack Hargreaves, Kriss Irving and Gary Flint all had spells for Stoke, prior to some late-season changes that saw Jonathan Bethell and Billy Legg link with the club via Buxton and Plymouth, respectively. It was also good to note Luke Priest's return at the end of the campaign, following his horrific injuries of the previous season, sustained while representing the Spitfires in Conference League action.

The league welcomed a new club to its ranks in **Cleveland**, who had only participated in the Conference Shield the previous term. The team, based alongside Redcar at South Tees Motorsports Park, finished in ninth position and provided much in the way of entertainment during the season.

Led by veteran campaigner Buzz Burrows, the Bays used a large number of personnel that included plenty of youngsters. Burrows, who turned forty-three years of age during the season, adopted the role of rider/coach and helped nurture the team's younger element.

Greg Blair made significant strides to average 7.67 from the league programme, while Martin Emerson and Rusty Hodgson continued to head in the right diretion. The inclusion of Emerson and Hodgson, together with the likes of Jitendra Duffill and newcomer David Wallinger certainly helped to give the club a real community feel.

After the unfortunate demise of the Elite League side, a new promotion was quickly installed at **Oxford**, who saw the main priority as safeguarding the club's immediate future. Allen Trump, the man behind the continuing efforts to re-launch Exeter, took charge of the club and quickly installed Peter Oakes in the role of Director of Speedway.

It quickly became apparent that the new promotion was intent on building an attractive-looking team, which aimed to recapture the attention of the Oxford fans. Having lost his place at Glasgow, Lee Smethills led the Cheetahs side and the twenty-five-year-old British rider proved to be an extremely shrewd acquisition as the season unfolded. This was evident from a massive 10.44 average, which put him second only to Tai Woffinden in the overall league averages. Meanwhile, Danny Betson lent Smethills superb support at the top-end to post a hugely impressive 9.92 league figure.

Upcoming New Zealander Andrew Bargh performed extremely well in a campaign that was disrupted by a broken ankle, whilst Jordan Frampton enjoyed some solid scoring with the Cowley-based outfit to register a 9.00 league average. Meanwhile, Aussie Sam Martin continued to make progress, whilst Kyle Hughes and the upcoming Brendan Johnson were real crowd favourites, as the Cheetahs served up some cracking racing at their home base.

It turned out to be a thoroughly successful season for Oxford in the Conference League, which saw them just miss out on the Championship in the two-legged Play-Off Final against Scunthorpe. Despite losing out on the title, the highlight of the season was, perhaps, the way in which the Cheetahs secured their place in the showdown versus the Scorpions, when a brilliantly executed heat fifteen 5-1 against Plymouth in the second leg of the Play-Off semi-final sent Sandy Lane into delirium.

Rye House eventually finished sixth in the Conference League standings, although that wasn't really a true reflection of the progression made by the squad throughout the season. Once again, the team included a selection of young British talent and a combination of Raiders favourites.

Both Harland Cook and Barry Burchatt were associated with the Hoddesdon-based team for a fifth successive season, although neither completed the course with the side, the former re-locating to Sittingbourne, while the latter concentrated on his Premier League duties at Newport, having gained a spot in the Welsh side part-way through the campaign.

Popular Australian Ben Powell made only limited appearances for the side, but compatriot Karlis Ezergailis became one of the mainstays after first representing the Raiders in June. Daniel Halsley lined-up for his third season in the team's colours and contributed an increasing number of double figure tallies. Gary Cottham and Lee Strudwick also appeared for the side, while Luke Bowen weighed in with some big scores once his Premier League average for the senior Rye House side had dropped below 4.00, permitting him to also ride at Conference level.

Once again, a gleaming positive of the 2007 campaign was the wonderful form of promising youngster Robert Mear, who lit up tracks throughout the country with some fantastic performances. Mear hit a real purple patch towards the end of the season, when he put together a wonderful sequence of four successive unbeaten tallies, scoring 17+1, 18, 16+2 and 16+2 points, respectively. The locally-born eighteen-year-old, who hails from Welwyn Garden City, remained ever-present from the 18-match league schedule on his way to an excellent 9.58 average.

Enthusiasm levels were high at **Weymouth** ahead of the season, with the club still buoyed by the approval of full planning permission in November 2006. It allowed the promotion to spend more time selecting a competitive team, although they will have, perhaps, been a touch disappointed to have concluded their league campaign in fifth spot.

Led for a fourth season by the classy David Mason, the Wildcats assembled an attractive side beneath their long-serving skipper, whose season was disrupted by injury. Flamboyant leg-trailer Lee Smart proved to be a brilliant acquisition in his second stint with the club; the exciting British youngster posted a high 9.78 domestic average and was able to successfully combine his racing with Birmingham in the Premier League.

Delving a little deeper, Weymouth managed to sign Jay Herne in June and the young Aussie set Britain's third tier alight in his inaugural British campaign, scoring 169 points from just fifteen league matches for a superb 8.52 average. Nathan Irwin battled away in typically tenacious fashion for the club, whilst Sam Hurst settled well on the South Coast.

The Wildcats played to some very encouraging crowds during the year, with both Terry Day and Karl Mason generally performing solidly throughout the season, the latter taking over the club captaincy from his unrelated namesake, David, in June.

Sittingbourne may have finished bottom of the Conference League table, but for one of the smallest clubs in British speedway the main objective was providing opportunities for riders to improve their riding skills.

The Crusaders came to the tapes tracking a combination of youth and experience, with Dean Felton, Gordon Meakins and Andre Cross forming the old guard, whilst youngsters such as Joe Reynolds and Luke Goody, together with brothers Mark and Aaron Baseby, slotted into the side. Meakins and Goody didn't last the course, while Cross's appearances were intermittent due to injury.

Jon Stevens, Danny Warwick, Jerran Hart and Harland Cook were amongst others to sport the Sittingbourne race-jacket during the season. The club may have only been able to muster 5 points from their eighteen league matches, but it was a real credit to all those involved that the Crusaders bolstered the numbers and tracked a side in 2007.

Chris Seaward

31 October 2007

ABBREVIATIONS

GENERAL

AL	Amateur League
BSPA	British Speedway Promoters' Association
CL	Conference League
CLKOC	Conference League Knock-Out Cup
CSs	Craven Shield semi-final
SCf	Craven Shield final
CT	Conference Trophy
DNA	Did Not Arrive
DNR	Did Not Ride
EL	Elite League
ELKOC	Elite League Knock-Out Cup
FIM	Federation Internationale de Motorcyclisme
KOC/KO	Knock-Out Cup
KOs	Knock-Out Cup semi-final
KOf	Knock-Out Cup final
PL	Premier League
PLKOC	Premier League Knock-Out Cup
POs	Play-Off semi-final
POf	Play-Off final
PT	Premier Trophy
PTs	Premier Trophy semi-final
PTf	Premier Trophy final
R/R	Rider Replacement
YS	Young Shield
YSs	Young Shield semi-final
YSf	Young Shield final

LEAGUE TABLES

Mts	Matches
Won	Won
Drn	Drawn
Lst	Lost
For	For
Agn	Against
Pts	Points
AP	Aggregate Points
Tot	Total Points

AVERAGE TABLES

Mts	Matches
Rds	Rides
Pts	Points
Bon	Bonus Points
Tot	Total Points
Avge	Average
Max	Maximums

SCORE TABLES

(R)	Replay
R/R	Rider Replacement
15 (5)	Maximum. (Applies to any underlined total)

RACE POSITIONS

Ex	Excluded
F	Fell
NS	Non-starter
Rem	Remounted
Ret	Retired

RACE SCORES TABLES

F	Fell
M	Excluded, 2 minutes
N	Non-starter
R	Retired
X	Excluded
T	Excluded, tapes

THE ELITE LEAGUE
2007

Belle Vue Aces
Coventry Bees
Eastbourne Eagles
Ipswich Witches
Lakeside Hammers
Oxford Cheetahs
Peterborough Panthers
Poole Pirates
Reading Bulldogs / Racers
Swindon Robins
Wolverhampton Wolves

ELITE LEAGUE 2007

SKY SPORTS ELITE LEAGUE TABLE

Team	Mts	Won	Drn	Lst	For	Agn	Pts	AP	Tot
Coventry	36	28	1	7	1819	1463	57	16	73
Swindon	36	26	1	9	1853.5	1451.5	53	14	67
Peterborough	36	25	1	10	1757	1501	51	12	63
Poole	36	22	1	13	1761	1514	45	13	58
Lakeside	36	16	2	18	1605	1690	34	8	42
Wolverhampton	36	16	1	19	1602	1685	33	8	41
Eastbourne	36	12	2	22	1624.5	1676.5	26	7	33
Reading	36	11	1	24	1497	1779	23	3	26
Ipswich	36	9	2	25	1464	1809	20	5	25
Bele Vue	36	9	0	27	1439	1853	18	4	22
Oxford	19	3	0	16	728	991	6	1	7

NOTE: Oxford closed down at the end of May and their record was expunged from the table.

PLAY-OFFS

SEMI-FINALS

Coventry	55	Poole	38
Swindon	50	Peterborough	42

FINAL

Swindon	49	Coventry	43	
Coventry	59	Swindon	34	(Coventry won 102-83 on aggregate)

TOP 20 AVERAGES [Elite League only. Minimum qualification: 6 matches]

Rider	Mts	Rds	Pts	Bon	Tot	Avge	Max
Leigh Adams (Swindon)	35	175	450.5	22	472.5	10.80	4 full; 9 paid
Jason Crump (Poole)	33	15	410	15	425	10.69	6 full; 5 paid
Nicki Pedersen (Eastbourne)	26	131	342.5	3	345.5	10.55	10 full
Hans N. Andersen (Peterborough)	32	159	394	19	413	10.39	5 full; 5 paid
Bjarne Pedersen (Poole) *	36	171	387	39	426	9.96	2 full; 4 paid
Scott Nicholls (Coventry)	34	168	400	13	413	9.83	2 full; 1 paid
Greg Hancock (Reading)	15	73	160	12	172	9.42	Nil
Peter Karlsson (Wolverhampton)	34	164	355	24	379	9.24	2 full; 2 paid
Chris Harris (Coventry) *	36	178	356	43	399	8.97	2 paid
Krzysztof Kasprzak (Lakeside)	29	147	319	6	325	8.84	2 full
Kenneth Bjerre (Peterborough)	34	164	324	30	354	8.63	1 full; 4 paid
Davey Watt (Eastbourne)	26	136	272	15	287	8.44	1 paid
Lee Richardson (Swindon) *	36	178	346	28	374	8.40	4 full; 1 paid
Fredrik Lindgren (Wolverhampton)	30	150	288	25	313	8.35	1 full; 1 paid
Charlie Gjedde (Swindon)	34	157	280	47	327	8.33	4 paid
Rory Schlein (Coventry)	33	151	292	13	305	8.08	1 paid
Matej Zagar (Reading)	21	103	191	14	205	7.96	1 paid
Niels-Kristian Iversen (Peterborough)	27	118	217	14	231	7.83	1 paid
David Howe (Wolverhampton)	34	151	250	44	294	7.79	2 paid
Sebastian Ulamek (Swindon)	28	122	217	19	236	7.74	1 paid

* Denotes ever-present.

CRAVEN SHIELD

SEMI-FINALS

FIRST LEG (at Poole)	Poole 52	Lakeside 29	Reading 27
SECOND LEG (at Reading)	Lakeside 40	Peterborough 37	Reading 31
THIRD LEG (at Lakeside)	Peterborough 43	Lakeside 36	Poole 29
AGGREGATE:	Poole 81 (from 2 meetings: average 40.5 points)	Peterborough 80 (2 meetings: average 40)	Lakeside 105 (3 meetings: average 35), Reading 58 (2 meetings: average 29)

NOTE: Peterborough were unable to stage their home leg due to a lack of available dates at the East of England Showground.

FIRST LEG (at Ipswich)	Ipswich 43	Coventry 42	Wolverhampton 23
SECOND LEG (at Coventry)	Coventry 31	Ipswich 21	Wolverhampton 20
THIRD LEG (at Wolverhampton)	Coventry 49	Wolverhampton 35	Ipswich 24
AGGREGATE:	Coventry 122	Ipswich 88	Wolverhampton 78

FIRST LEG (at Swindon)	Swindon 48	Eastbourne 39	Belle Vue 21
SECOND LEG (at Eastbourne)	Swindon 39	Eastbourne 37	Belle Vue 32
THIRD LEG (at Belle Vue)	Eastbourne 38	Belle Vue 36	Swindon 34
AGGREGATE:	Swindon 121	Eastbourne 114	Belle Vue 89

FINAL

FIRST LEG (at Poole)	Coventry 40	Poole 35	Swindon 33
SECOND LEG (at Swindon)	Coventry 45	Swindon 35	Poole 28
THIRD LEG (at Coventry)	Swindon 50	Coventry 35	Poole 23
AGGREGATE:	Coventry 120	Swindon 118	Poole 86

KNOCK-OUT CUP

ROUND-ONE

Ipswich	52	Oxford	38	
Oxford	45	Ipswich	45	(Ipswich won 97-83 on aggregate)

Reading	56	Wolverhampton	34	
Wolverhampton	51	Reading	42	(Reading won 98-85 on aggregate)

Belle Vue	47	Lakeside	46	
Lakeside	50	Belle Vue	40	(Lakeside won 96-87 on aggregate)

QUARTER-FINALS

Swindon	63	Peterborough	27	
Peterborough	-	Swindon	-	

(Due to inclement weather, Peterborough were twice prevented from staging their leg and, being 36 points down anyway, conceded the tie.)

Coventry	53	Poole	40	
Poole	31	Coventry	44	(Coventry won 97-71 on aggregate)

Reading	53	Ipswich	40	
Ipswich	49	Reading	44	(Reading won 97-89 on aggregate)

Lakeside	59	Eastbourne	33	
Eastbourne	41	Lakeside	49	(Lakeside won 108-74 on aggregate)

SEMI-FINALS

Swindon	55	Reading	37	
Reading	38	Swindon	54	(Swindon won 109-75 on aggregate)

Coventry	52	Lakeside	41	
Lakeside	45	Coventry	45	(Coventry won 97-86 on aggregate)

FINAL

Swindon	45	Coventry	45	
Coventry	53	Swindon	40	(Coventry won 98-85 on aggregate)

ELITE SHIELD

Peterborough	53	Coventry	38	
Coventry	49	Peterborough	41	(Peterborough won 94-87 on aggregate)

BELLE VUE ACES

ADDRESS:	Belle Vue Greyhound Stadium, Kirkmanshulme Lane, Gorton, Manchester, M18 7BA.
TELEPHONE:	0161 2237720.
CLUB HOTLINE:	09068 664678 (Premium rate applies).
WEBSITE:	www.bellevuespeedway.co.uk
PROMOTERS:	Chris Morton, David Gordon & Gordon Pairman.
MAIN TEAM SPONSOR:	Channel M.
YEARS OF OPERATION:	1928 Open; 1988-1990 British League; 1991-1994 British League Division One; 1995-1996 Premier League; 1997 Elite League and Amateur League; 1998-2007 Elite League.
FIRST MEETING:	28 July 1928.
TRACK LENGTH:	285 metres.
TRACK RECORD:	57.8 seconds - Jason Crump (07/08/06).
PREVIOUS VENUE:	Zoological Gardens, Hyde Road, Manchester.
YEARS OF OPERATION:	1929 English Dirt-Track League; 1930 Northern League; 1931 Northern League and Southern League; 1932-1933 National League; 1934 National League and Reserve League; 1935-1936 National League; 1937 National League and Provincial League; 1938 National League Division One; 1939 National League Division One and National League Division Two; 1940-1945 Open; 1946 National League; 1947-1956 National League Division One; 1957-1964 National League; 1965-1967 British League; 1968-1969 British League Division One and British League Division Two; 1970-1974 British League Division One; 1975-1987 British League.

CLUB HONOURS

LEAGUE CHAMPIONS: 1930, 1931, 1933, 1934, 1935, 1936, 1963, 1970, 1971, 1972, 1982, 1993.
NOTE: The Division Two side were also crowned League Champions in 1968 and 1969.
KNOCK-OUT CUP WINNERS: 1931, 1972, 1973, 1975, 2005.
NOTE: The Division Two side also won their Knock-Out Cup competition in 1969.
NATIONAL TROPHY WINNERS: 1933, 1934, 1935, 1936, 1937, 1946, 1947, 1949, 1958.
ACU CUP WINNERS: 1934, 1935, 1936, 1937, 1946.
BRITISH SPEEDWAY CUP WINNERS: 1939.
BRITANNIA SHIELD WINNERS: 1957, 1958, 1960.
INTER-LEAGUE KNOCK-OUT CUP WINNERS: 1975.
PREMIERSHIP WINNERS: 1983.
LEAGUE CUP WINNERS: 1983.
PAIRS CHAMPIONS: 1984, 2006.
FOUR-TEAM CHAMPIONS: 1992.

Aces' skipper **Joe Screen** appeared in his nineteenth successive season of top-flight racing.

(Photo: Les Aubrey)

BELLE VUE 2007

* Denotes aggregate/bonus-point victory

NO.	DATE	OPPONENTS	VENUE	COMPETITION	RESULT	SIMON STEAD	RYAN FISHER	JOE SCREEN	ADAM SKORNICKI	KAJ LAUKKANEN	KEVIN DOOLAN	JAMES WRIGHT	JOEL PARSONS	ANTONIO LINDBACK	OTHER RIDERS
1	16/3	Oxford	A	Chal	W51-42	7+1 (4)	3 (4)	9+2 (4)	7 (4)	9 (5)	6+2 (4)	10+1 (5)	-	-	-
2	23/3	Lakeside	A	ELA	L34-58	9 (5)	0 (3)	12 (5)	2+2 (4)	3 (3)	1 (4)	7 (6)	-	-	-
3	26/3	Poole	H	ELA	W52-38	10+1 (5)	3+2 (3)	7+1 (5)	8+2 (4)	7 (4)	7+1 (4)	10+2 (5)	-	-	-
4	30/3	Oxford	A	ELA	L37-53	14 (5)	1 (3)	9 (5)	0 (3)	2 (4)	7+1 (6)	4+1 (4)	-	-	-
5	2/4	Eastbourne	H	ELA	W50-43	0 (0)	5+1 (4)	12 (5)	4+2 (4)	7 (4)	13+3 (7)	-	9+1 (6)	-	-
6	6/4	Wolverhampton	H	ELA	L42-48	-	2 (3)	8+1 (5)	6+2 (4)	8 (5)	15+2 (7)	-	-	-	3+1 (6)
7	9/4	Wolverhampton	A	ELA	L39-54	-	4+1 (3)	15 (5)	-	4 (4)	6+1 (6)	-	-	-	10 (12)
8	12/4	Swindon	A	ELA	L24-68	-	0 (3)	10 (5)	2 (4)	4 (5)	7+1 (6)	-	-	-	1 (7)
9	16/4	Coventry	H	ELA	L38-54	4+1 (3)	3+1 (4)	9 (5)	6+1 (4)	1 (4)	2 (4)	13+3 (6)	-	-	-
10	20/4	Coventry	A	ELA	L39-53	11 (5)	2 (4)	3+1 (4)	9+1 (7)	R/R	12 (6)	2+1 (4)	-	-	-
11	30/4	Lakeside	H	KO	W47-46	7 (5)	2+1 (3)	11 (5)	12+2 (6)	4 (3)	6+2 (4)	5+2 (4)	-	-	-
12	4/5	Lakeside	A	KO	L40-50	12+1 (5)	4+1 (4)	10 (5)	8 (5)	2+2 (3)	2+1 (4)	2+2 (4)	-	-	-
13	5/5	Eastbourne	A	ELA	L29-62	10 (5)	1+1 (6)	8 (5)	6+1 (6)	R/R	4+1 (5)	-	-	-	0 (3)
14	14/5	Reading	H	ELA	W55-38	11 (5)	3+1 (4)	8+2 (4)	13+2 (6)	4+1 (3)	9+1 (4)	7+2 (4)	-	-	-
15	21/5	Peterborough	H	ELA	L39-52	6 (5)	1+1 (4)	9 (5)	10+2 (6)	4 (3)	7 (4)	2+1 (3)	-	-	-
16	24/5	Peterborough	A	ELA	L31-62	4 (4)	3 (4)	11 (5)	8+1 (6)	3+2 (3)	1 (4)	1 (4)	-	-	-
17	25/5	Oxford	A	ELB	L41-49	6 (4)	6+1 (5)	10+2 (5)	0 (3)	5+1 (4)	9+1 (5)	5+1 (4)	-	-	-
18	30/5	Wolverhampton	H	ELB	L43-47	8+1 (5)	6 (4)	6 (4)	7+3 (5)	2+1 (3)	9+1 (5)	5+2 (4)	-	-	-
19	1/6	Coventry	A	ELB	L28-62	6 (5)	1 (4)	8 (5)	4+1 (5)	5+2 (4)	4 (4)	0 (3)	-	-	-
20	7/6	Ipswich	A	ELA	L25-65	1 (2)	2 (5)	R/R	6+2 (6)	6+1 (6)	6+1 (5)	4 (5)	-	-	-
21	11/6	Lakeside	H	ELA	W47-43	-	1+1 (3)	9 (4)	5+1 (5)	-	7 (4)	9+2 (5)	-	4+1 (4)	12+2 (5)
22	18/6	Poole	H	ELB	L43-50	-	0 (3)	6 (4)	7+2 (6)	-	8+1 (5)	8 (4)	-	11+2 (5)	3+1 (4)
23	4/7	Lakeside	A	ELB	L40-53	7 (4)	-	11+1 (5)	11+1 (6)	-	3+2 (4)	6 (4)	-	2+1 (4)	0 (3)
24	9/7	Swindon	H	ELA	L34-56	9 (5)	-	8+1 (4)	1+1 (4)	-	7+1 (5)	4 (4)	-	5+1 (4)	-
25	23/7	Ipswich	H	ELB	W49-40	14+1 (6)	-	12+2 (6)	8+2 (5)	-	8 (5)	7+2 (5)	-	R/R	-
26	30/7	Lakeside	H	ELB	L39-53	11+1 (6)	-	16 (6)	1 (3)	-	5 (5)	3+1 (5)	-	R/R	3+1 (5)
27	1/8	Poole	A	ELA	L43-50*	6 (4)	-	7 (5)	9+2 (5)	-	4+1 (4)	3+1 (4)	-	-	14+1 (8)
28	2/8	Swindon	A	ELB	L28-65	0 (1)	-	5 (5)	6+1 (7)	-	1 (4)	1 (4)	-	-	15 (9)
29	6/8	Coventry	H	ELB	L34-56	6 (4)	-	7+1 (5)	3+1 (4)	-	7 (4)	-	3+1 (4)	-	8+1 (5)
30	9/8	Ipswich	A	ELB	L35-55	16 (6)	-	5+1 (5)	6 (5)	-	8+1 (6)	-	-	R/R	0 (8)
31	13/8	Wolverhampton	A	ELB	L33-57	6 (4)	-	8 (5)	3 (3)	-	9+1 (5)	3+1 (4)	-	2 (4)	2+1 (5)
32	20/8	Peterborough	H	ELB	L40-52	5 (5)	-	12 (5)	5+3 (4)	-	5+3 (4)	4+1 (4)	-	4+1 (4)	5 (4)
33	22/8	Poole	A	ELB	L32-60	4+1 (5)	-	5 (4)	4+4 (4)	-	3 (4)	6 (3)	-	6 (5)	4+1 (5)
34	27/8	Reading	A	ELA	L42-48*	10+1 (6)	-	14+1 (6)	9+1 (6)	-	4+1 (4)	-	1 (3)	R/R	4 (5)
35	29/8	Reading	H	ELB	W56-37	7+2 (3)	-	9+1 (4)	8+4 (5)	-	11+1 (5)	7+1 (4)	-	-	14+1 (10)
36	3/9	Swindon	H	ELB	L35-58	8+2 (4)	-	4 (5)	4 (4)	-	6 (4)	9+1 (5)	-	1+1 (2)	3+1 (6)
37	10/9	Eastbourne	H	ELB	W60-29	11+2 (5)	-	11 (4)	6+3 (4)	-	11+2 (5)	6+1 (4)	-	9 (4)	6+2 (4)
38	17/9	Ipswich	H	ELB	W54-39	11+1 (5)	-	5 (4)	4+1 (4)	-	5+2 (4)	7 (4)	-	15 (5)	7+2 (4)
39	19/9	Reading	A	ELB	W47-46*	14+1 (5)	-	5 (4)	5 (4)	-	3+1 (4)	-	1 (3)	17+1 (7)	2+1 (3)
40	4/10	Swindon / Eastbourne	S	CSs	21-48-39	7 (4)	-	7 (4)	0 (4)	-	5 (4)	2 (4)	-	-	0 (4)
41	6/10	Eastbourne / Swindon	E	CSs	32-37-39	9 (4)	-	4+2 (4)	8 (4)	-	6 (4)	-	-	-	5+3 (8)
42	8/10	Eastbourne / Swindon	H	CSs	36-38-34	9+1 (4)	-	5 (4)	6+1 (4)	-	7+1 (4)	4 (4)	-	-	5 (4)
43	14/10	Eastbourne	A	ELB	L37-55*	8 (5)	-	0 (2)	R/R	-	13+1 (6)	3 (5)	-	-	13+2 (12)
44	26/10	Peterborough	A	ELB	L43-47	15 (6)	-	-	2 (3)	-	R/R	10 (7)	-	-	16+4 (14)

NOTE: (1) At the Elite League meetings involving Belle Vue v. Swindon (9 July) and Belle Vue v. Ipswich (23 July), as per a statement issued by the SCB on 26 July, it transpired that the Aces' line-up did not comply with the speedway regulations. New signing Billy Forsberg had been injured in his homeland and to cover his absence, the No. 8, Joel Parsons, was used to replace him in the team, contrary to the speedway regulations. As Forsberg had not yet ridden for Belle Vue, no facility was permitted as per SR 18.1.4.2, which stated: 'No facility is permitted to replace a rider, who, although declared, has not made an appearance for that team'. SR 18.1.5.3 (a) stated that if no facility is applicable, then, in the Elite League, that team's No. 8 may be used, but only if the No. 8 has a Premier League green sheet CMA of 6.00 or less. At the time, Joel Parsons' PL CMA was 6.72. As a consequence, the results of both meetings were amended, with the deduction of the points scored by Parsons. For the record, he tallied 2 points from four rides in the match versus Swindon, and 1+1 points from three outings versus Ipswich; (2) The away match against Peterborough on 26 October was ridden at King's Lynn.

Details of other riders (all guests unless **highlighted**): Match No. 6: Gary Havelock 3+1 (3); Lee Smethills 0 (3); Match No. 7: David Norris 8 (5); Jason Bunyan 2 (4); Ben Barker 0 (3); Match No. 8: David Howe 1 (4); Tai Woffinden 0 (3); Match No. 13: Jason King 0 (3); Match No. 21: Chris Harris 12+2 (5); Match No. 22: Adam Shields 3+1 (4); Match No. 23: Lee Complin 0 (3); Match No. 26: **Billy Forsberg** 3+1 (5); Match No. 27: Davey Watt 14+1 (5); Adam Roynon 0 (3); Match No. 28: Chris Harris 11 (5); **Billy Forsberg** 4 (4); Match No. 29: Adam Shields 6 (5); Adam Roynon 2+1 (4); Match No. 30: Ben Barker 0 (4); Adam Roynon 0 (4); Match No. 31: **Billy Forsberg** 2+1 (5); Match No. 32: **Billy Forsberg** 5 (4); Match No. 33: **Billy Forsberg** 4+1 (5); Match No. 34: **Billy Forsberg** 4 (5); Match No. 35: **Billy Forsberg** 14+1 (6); **Ben Wilson** 0 (4); Match No. 36: Adam Roynon 3+1 (6); Match No. 37: **Billy Forsberg** 6+2 (4); Match No. 38: **Billy Forsberg** 7+2 (4); Match No. 39: **Billy Forsberg** 2+1 (3); Match No. 40: Ben Barker 0 (4); Match No. 41: **Billy Forsberg** 4+2 (4); Shaun Tacey 1+1 (4); Match No. 42: **Billy Forsberg** 5 (4); Match No. 43: **Billy Forsberg** 10+1 (7); Jordan Frampton 3+1 (5); Match No. 44: Troy Batchelor 10+1 (5); Simon Lambert 4+2 (5); **Lukasz Jankowski** 2+1 (4).

Details of tactical rides and tactical substitute rides: Match No. 2: Screen 6 points (TR); Match No. 4: Wright 1 point (TR; not doubled); Match No. 7: Screen 6 points (TR); Match No. 8: Screen 4 points (TR); Match No. 9: Wright 4 points (TR); Match No. 10: Stead 4 points (TR); Match No. 13: Screen 4 points (TR); Match No. 15: Laukkanen 4 points (TR); Match No. 16: Screen 6 points (TR); Match No. 19: Skornicki 1 point (TR; not doubled); Match No. 20: Skornicki 0 points (TR); Match No. 22: Lindback 6 points (TR); Match No. 23: Screen 6 points (TR); Match No. 24: Screen 4 points (TR); Match No. 26: Screen 4 points (TR); Match No. 27: Watt 6 points (TR); Match No. 28: Harris 6 points (TR); Match No. 29: Skornicki 1 point (TR; not doubled); match No. 30: Doolan 1 point (TR; not doubled); Match No. 31: Doolan 0 points (TR); Match No. 32: Screen 4 points (TR); Match No. 33: Wright 4 points (TR); Match No. 36: Stead 6 points (TR); Match No. 39: Stead 6 points (TR); Match No. 43: Stead 4 points (TR).

AVERAGES

[36 Elite League; 2 Knock-Out Cup; 3 Craven Shield = 41 fixtures]

Rider	Mts	Rds	Pts	Bon	Tot	Avge	Max
Simon Stead	36	160	282	17	299	7.48	-
Joe Screen	39	181	300	15	315	6.96	-
Antonio Lindback	11	48	73	8	81	6.75	1 full
Kevin Doolan	40	186	257	34	291	6.26	-
Adam Skornicki	39	185	232	52	284	6.14	-
Billy Forsberg	13	60	70	12	82	5.47	-
James Wright	31	135	156	26	182	5.39	-
Kaj Laukkanen	15	57	62	9	71	4.98	-
Ryan Fisher	19	71	43	11	54	3.04	-

Also rode (in alphabetical order):

Lukasz Jankowski	1	4	2	1	3	3.00	-
Joel Parsons	4	16	14	2	16	4.00	-
Ben Wilson	1	4	0	0	0	0.00	-

Guests	24	99	77	12	89	3.60	-

(Ben Barker [3]; Troy Batchelor [1]; Jason Bunyan [1]; Lee Complin [1]; Jordan Frampton [1]; Chris Harris [2]; Gary Havelock [1]; David Howe [1]; Jason King [1]; Simon Lambert [1]; David Norris [1]; Adam Roynon [4]; Adam Shields [2]; Lee Smethills [1]; Shaun Tacey [1]; Davey Watt [1]; Tai Woffinden [1])

INDIVIDUAL MEETINGS

19 March: **Peter Craven Memorial Trophy**
1st Scott Nicholls 14; 2nd Joe Screen 13 (on heat wins); 3rd Andreas Jonsson 13; Chris Harris 11; Simon Stead 10; James Wright 9; Ricky Ashworth 8; Ryan Fisher 7; Gary Havelock 7; Kaj Laukkanen 6; Jason Lyons 6; Joel Parsons 5; Kevin Doolan 3; Shane Parker 3; Josh Auty (Res) 3; Adam Skornicki 1; Ben Wilson 1; Ben Hopwood (Res) 0.

18 July: **Greggs North West Junior Championship**
1st Joe Haines 15; 2nd Andrew Tully (after run-off) 13; 3rd Greg Blair 13; Simon Lambert 11; Ben Taylor 10; Byron Bekker 9; Lewis Dallaway 8; Sam Martin 8; Ben Hopwood 8; Scott Richardson 7; Aaron Summers 6; Keiran Morris 3; Kye Norton 2; Rusty Hodgson 2; Jade Mudgway 2; Phil Naylor (Res) 2; Martin Emerson 0.

Belle Vue, 2007
Back row, left to right: James Wright, Adam Skornicki, Antonio Lindback and Simon Stead.
Front row:
Billy Forsberg, Joe Screen (on bike) and Kevin Doolan.

(Photo: Ian Charles)

COVENTRY BEES

ADDRESS: Coventry International Motor Speedway, Rugby Road, Brandon, Nr Coventry, Warwickshire, CV8 3GJ.

TELEPHONE: 02476 542395.

CLUB HOTLINE: 09068 664677 (Premium rate applies).

WEBSITE: www.coventrymotorspeedway.com

PROMOTER: Colin Pratt.

MAIN TEAM SPONSOR: Buildbase.

YEARS OF OPERATION: 1928 Open; 1929-1931 Southern League; 1932-1933 National League; 1934 Open; 1936 Open; 1948 National League Division Three; 1949-1956 National League Division Two; 1957-1964 National League; 1965-1967 British League; 1968-1974 British League Division One; 1975-1990 British League; 1991-1994 British League Division One; 1995-1996 Premier League; 1997-2003 Elite League; 2004 Elite League and Conference Trophy; 2005-2007 Elite League.

FIRST MEETING: 29 September 1928.

TRACK LENGTH: 301 metres.

TRACK RECORD: 58.0 seconds - Leigh Adams (30/06/06) and Chris Harris (15/09/06).

CLUB HONOURS

LEAGUE CHAMPIONS: 1953, 1968, 1978, 1979, 1987, 1988, 2005, 2007.

KNOCK-OUT CUP WINNERS: 1967, 2006, 2007.

PAIRS CHAMPIONS: 1978 (Shared with Cradley Heath).

LEAGUE CUP WINNERS: 1981, 1985, 1987.

PREMIERSHIP WINNERS: 1986.

CRAVEN SHIELD WINNERS: 1997, 2000, 2007.

ELITE SHIELD WINNERS: 2006.

Chris 'Bomber' Harris enjoyed another terrific season with the Bees, while on the personal front he scooped the British Championship and took the Grand Prix by storm, posting a remarkable victory at Cardiff's Millennium Stadium.

(Photo: Les Aubrey)

COVENTRY 2007

* Denotes aggregate/bonus-point victory

NO.	DATE	OPPONENTS	VENUE	COMPETITION	RESULT	SCOTT NICHOLLS	BILLY JANNIRO	RORY SCHLEIN	OLLY ALLEN	CHRIS HARRIS	MORTEN RISAGER	MARTIN SMOLINSKI	STANISLAW BURZA	STEVE JOHNSTON	OTHER RIDERS
1	15/3	Peterborough	A	ES	L38-53	12 (5)	5+2 (4)	9+1 (5)	4+1 (4)	3 (4)	4+1 (4)	1+1 (4)	-	-	-
2	16/3	Peterborough	H	ES	W49-41	12 (5)	4 (4)	9 (5)	4+1 (4)	8+2 (4)	12 (5)	0 (3)	-	-	-
3	23/3	Eastbourne	H	ELA	W50-40	11+1 (5)	5+1 (4)	5+1 (4)	2+2 (4)	6+1 (4)	13 (5)	2+1 (3)	-	-	-
4	24/3	Eastbourne	A	ELA	W50-43*	8+2 (4)	10+2 (5)	7+1 (4)	6+1 (4)	11+1 (5)	3+2 (4)	5+3 (4)	-	-	-
5	30/3	Poole H	ELA		W46-44	12 (5)	4+1 (4)	9 (4)	4+3 (4)	10+1 (5)	6+1 (5)	1 (3)	-	-	-
6	2/4	Oxford	A	ELA	W64-28	14+1 (5)	8+2 (4)	11+1 (4)	0 (0)	14+1 (5)	8+2 (6)	9+1 (6)	-	-	-
7	6/4	Peterborough	H	ELA	W50-40	10 (5)	7+2 (4)	10+1 (5)	1 (3)	8+1 (4)	7+3 (4)	7 (5)	-	-	-
8	9/4	Oxford	H	ELA	W65-28*	10+1 (4)	10+4 (5)	15 (5)	R/R	13+2 (5)	8+2 (4)	7+2 (5)	-	-	2+1 (2)
9	13/4	Lakeside	H	ELA	W67-25	14 (5)	11+4 (5)	11+1 (4)	R/R	9+2 (5)	13+3 (6)	9+1 (5)	-	-	-
10	16/4	Belle Vue	H	ELA	W54-38	12 (5)	5+2 (5)	10+2 (5)	R/R	9+2 (4)	8 (5)	10 (6)	-	-	-
11	19/4	Swindon	A	ELA	L40-54	11 (5)	3 (5)	10 (5)	R/R	11+1 (5)	4+1 (6)	1 (4)	-	-	-
12	20/4	Belle Vue	H	ELA	W53-39*	14 (5)	7+2 (4)	8 (4)	4+1 (4)	13+2 (5)	4 (4)	3+1 (4)	-	-	-
13	23/4	Poole	A	ELA	L40-52	11+1 (5)	2+2 (4)	7+1 (5)	-	7 (4)	5 (4)	4+1 (4)	4+1 (4)	-	-
14	4/5	Wolverhampton	H	ELA	W47-43	-	5+2 (4)	R/R	10+1 (6)	13+1 (6)	10+1 (5)	3+2 (3)	-	-	6+2 (6)
15	7/5	Wolverhampton	A	ELA	W49-43*	R/R	8+3 (6)	15 (6)	6+1 (4)	10+1 (5)	4+2 (5)	6 (4)	-	-	-
16	14/5	Oxford	H	ELB	W57-36	R/R	8+3 (5)	14+2 (6)	8+1 (4)	15+1 (6)	1 (3)	11+1 (6)	-	-	-
17	18/5	Reading	H	ELA	D45-45	12 (5)	6+1 (4)	8 (5)	9+1 (4)	4+2 (4)	-	3 (4)	3+1 (4)	-	-
18	19/5	Eastbourne	A	ELB	W53-40	12 (5)	5+3 (5)	9+1 (4)	5+1 (4)	13+2 (6)	R/R	9+1 (6)	-	-	-
19	21/5	Swindon	H	ELA	L44-46	11 (5)	3 (4)	12 (5)	10+1 (6)	8+2 (4)	0 (3)	0 (3)	-	-	-
20	31/5	Swindon	A	ELB	L42-51	10 (5)	2+2 (4)	5 (4)	4+1 (4)	12+1 (6)	1+1 (3)	8+2 (5)	-	-	-
21	1/6	Belle Vue	H	ELB	W62-28	13+1 (5)	9+2 (5)	9 (4)	9+1 (5)	13+2 (5)	R/R	9+3 (6)	-	-	-
22	6/6	Lakeside	A	ELA	L41-52*	14 (5)	1 (4)	7 (5)	4 (4)	6+1 (4)	3 (3)	6+1 (5)	-	-	-
23	21/6	Peterborough	A	ELA	L42-48*	6 (5)	2+1 (3)	9 (4)	8+1 (5)	9+2 (5)	-	4 (4)	-	4 (4)	-
24	9/7	Poole	H	KO	W53-40	12 (5)	6+1 (4)	10+1 (5)	5 (4)	9+1 (4)	-	5 (4)	-	6+3 (4)	-
25	12/7	Ipswich	A	ELA	W56-37	14+1 (5)	1 (3)	10 (4)	6+1 (4)	11+1 (5)	-	9+1 (5)	-	5+3 (4)	-
26	13/7	Peterborough	H	ELB	W45-30	8 (4)	4+2 (3)	R/R	7+2 (4)	10 (4)	-	13+1 (5)	-	3+2 (4)	-
27	30/7	Poole	H	ELB	W49-42	9 (5)	8+2 (6)	3+1 (4)	1 (1)	12+1 (5)	-	8 (5)	-	8+1 (4)	-
28	1/8	Reading	H	ELB	W53-39*	13 (5)	8+2 (6)	11 (4)	R/R	12+1 (5)	-	8 (6)	-	1 (4)	-
29	3/8	Wolverhampton	H	ELA	W52-41	13+1 (5)	4+2 (4)	12 (5)	6 (4)	7 (4)	-	6+1 (4)	-	4 (4)	-
30	6/8	Belle Vue	A	ELB	W56-34*	15 (5)	8+3 (6)	13+1 (5)	0 (1)	10 (4)	-	6 (5)	-	4 (4)	-
31	13/8	Reading	H	ELB	W57-36	15 (5)	9+5 (7)	7+1 (4)	R/R	15+2 (6)	-	8 (4)	-	3 (4)	-
32	17/8	Ipswich	H	ELA	W57-33*	16 (6)	6+4 (5)	R/R	-	14+2 (6)	-	8 (4)	-	7+2 (4)	6+2 (5)
33	20/8	Reading	A	ELB	W49-44*	13 (5)	5+4 (5)	5 (4)	R/R	10+2 (6)	-	8+1 (5)	-	8+1 (5)	-
34	22/8	Lakeside	A	ELB	W48-42	14 (5)	14+2 (7)	7 (4)	R/R	8 (6)	-	0 (3)	-	5+3 (5)	-
35	27/8	Lakeside	H	ELB	W58-34*	11+1 (5)	8+5 (5)	6 (4)	R/R	12+2 (6)	-	11+1 (5)	-	10+3 (5)	-
36	31/8	Ipswich	H	ELB	W64-29	12+2 (5)	12+1 (5)	12 (5)	R/R	13+1 (5)	-	9+2 (5)	-	6+3 (5)	-
37	3/9	Wolverhampton	A	ELB	W51-42*	14 (5)	6 (5)	6+1 (5)	R/R	8 (5)	-	6+2 (5)	-	11+1 (5)	-
38	5/9	Poole	A	ELB	W49-43*	12 (5)	4+3 (5)	10+1 (5)	R/R	12 (5)	-	4 (5)	-	7+1 (5)	-
39	6/9	Ipswich	A	ELB	W52-41*	10 (4)	7+3 (6)	13 (6)	R/R	13+1 (5)	-	7+1 (5)	-	2+1 (4)	-
40	10/9	Swindon	H	ELB	W55-35*	12+1 (5)	11+2 (6)	9 (5)	R/R	12+1 (5)	-	3+2 (4)	-	8+2 (5)	-
41	12/9	Peterborough	H	ELB	L44-46*	12 (5)	6+2 (5)	2 (4)	R/R	4+1 (5)	-	7 (5)	-	13+1 (6)	-
42	13/9	Eastbourne	H	ELB	W49-44*	11+2 (5)	10+2 (7)	11 (5)	R/R	6+3 (5)	-	-	-	6+2 (4)	5 (4)
43	17/9	Poole	H	POs	W55-38	11+1 (5)	5+2 (5)	10 (5)	3+2 (2)	6+3 (4)	-	9+1 (4)	-	11+2 (5)	-
44	19/9	Poole	A	KO	W44-31*	7+1 (3)	7+4 (5)	10 (4)	R/R	9 (4)	-	3+1 (4)	-	8+2 (4)	-
45	24/9	Swindon	A	POf	L43-49	8+1 (5)	3+1 (4)	9 (5)	R/R	14+1 (6)	-	5 (5)	-	4 (5)	-
46	27/9	Ipswich Wolverhampton	I	CSs	42-43-23	12 (4)	5+2 (4)	11+1 (4)	-	-	-	6+1 (4)	-	4 (4)	4 (4)
47	28/9	Ipswich Wolverhampton	H	CSs	31-21-20	8 (3)	4+2 (3)	6+1 (3)	-	5+1 (2)	-	3 (3)	-	5+1 (2)	-
48	1/10	Swindon	H	POf	W59-34*	9 (5)	7+2 (5)	16+1 (6)	R/R	8+2 (4)	-	10+2 (5)	-	9+2 (5)	-
49	5/10	Lakeside	H	KOs	W52-41	11+1 (5)	7+2 (5)	13+1 (6)	R/R	11 (4)	-	8+4 (6)	-	2 (4)	-
50	6/10	Lakeside	A	KOs	D45-45*	14 (5)	8+2 (6)	8+1 (5)	R/R	9 (5)	-	5+1 (5)	-	1+1 (4)	-
51	8/10	Wolverhampton Ipswich	W	CSs	49-35-24*	10+1 (4)	6+2 (4)	10+1 (4)	-	12 (4)	-	4+1 (4)	-	7+2 (4)	-
52	17/10	Poole/Swindon	P	CSf	40-35-33	8 (4)	4+1 (4)	8 (4)	-	10+1 (4)	-	4 (4)	-	6+2 (4)	-
53	18/10	Swindon/Poole	S	CSf	45-35-28	9 (4)	5+1 (4)	10+1 (4)	-	12 (4)	-	2 (4)	-	7+2 (4)	-
54	19/10	Poole/Swindon	H	CSf	35-23-50*	11 (4)	3 (4)	4+2 (4)	-	7+1 (4)	-	4+1 (4)	-	6 (4)	-
55	25/10	Swindon	A	KOf	D45-45	7+1 (5)	7+1 (6)	9+1 (5)	R/R	11+1 (5)	-	2 (4)	-	9+1 (5)	-
56	26/10	Swindon	H	KOf	W53-40*	11+1 (4)	15+1 (7)	9+1 (6)	R/R	9+1 (5)	-	2 (3)	-	7+2 (5)	-

ADDITIONAL KEY: ES = Elite Shield.

NOTE: (1) The home ELB fixture against Peterborough on 13 July was abandoned after heat twelve, with the result permitted to stand; (2) The away Knock-Out Cup tie at Poole on 19 September was abandoned after heat twelve, with the result permitted to stand; (3) The home leg of the Craven Shield meeting against Ipswich and Wolverhampton on 28 September was abandoned after heat twelve, with the result permitted to stand.

Details of other riders (all guests unless **highlighted**): Match No. 8: Adam Roynon 2+1 (2); Match No. 14: Lee Richardson 6+2 (6); Match No. 32: Kevin Doolan 6+2 (5); Match No. 42: Tomas Topinka 5 (4); Match No. 46: Tomas Topinka 4 (4).

Details of tactical rides and tactical substitute rides: Match No. 1: Nicholls 4 points (TR); Match No. 11: Schlein 4 points (TR); Harris 4 points (TS); Match No. 13: Nicholls 4 points (TR); Match No. 20: Nicholls 1 point (TR; not doubled); Harris 6 points (TS); Match No. 22: Nicholls 6 points (TR); Match No. 45: Harris 4 points (TS); Match No. 56: Nicholls 6 points (TR).

AVERAGES

[36 Elite League; 3 Play-Offs; 6 Knock-Out Cup; 6 Craven Shield; 2 Elite Shield = 53 fixtures]

• Denotes ever-present.

Rider	Mts	Rds	Pts	Bon	Tot	Avge	Max
Scott Nicholls	51	243	567	20	587	9.66	3 full; 1 paid
Chris Harris	52	245	497	57	554	9.04	2 full; 2 paid
Rory Schlein	50	231	453	26	479	8.29	2 paid
Steve Johnston	34	148	207	46	253	6.84	-
Billy Janniro •	53	253	327	100	427	6.75	1 paid
Morten Risager	16	71	97	15	112	6.31	-
Olly Allen	23	89	118	22	140	6.29	-
Martin Smolinski	52	228	284	41	325	5.70	-

Also rode:

Stanislaw Burza	2	8	7	2	9	4.50	-

Guests	4	19	21	4	25	5.26	-

(Kevin Doolan [1]; Lee Richardson [1]; Tomas Topinka [2])

NOTE: Chris Harris was ever-present throughout the 36-match Elite League programme.

INDIVIDUAL MEETING

28 October: **Diamond Jubilee Brandonapolis**

1st Rory Schlein 13; 2nd Troy Batchelor 11; 3rd Chris Harris 10; Jason Crump 9; Steve Johnston 9; Scott Nicholls 9; Simon Stead 9; Martin Smolinski 8; Morten Risager 8; Billy Janniro 7; Eric Andersson 6; Adam Roynon 6; Leigh Lanham 5; Filip Sitera 5; Linus Sundstrom 4; Lewis Bridger 0.

Bees' skipper **Scott Nicholls** led his side from the front, finishing on top of their averages for a third successive season.

(Photo: Les Aubrey)

EASTBOURNE EAGLES

ADDRESS:	Arlington Stadium, Arlington Road West, Hailsham, East Sussex, BH27 3RE.
TELEPHONE:	01323 841642.
CLUB HOTLINE:	09068 664672 (Premium rate applies).
WEBSITE:	www.elite-eagles.com
PROMOTERS:	Bob Brimson, Trevor Geer & Bob Dugard.
MAIN TEAM SPONSOR:	Meridian Marquees.
YEARS OF OPERATION:	1929-1930 Open; 1932-1937 Open; 1938 Sunday Dirt-track League; 1939 Open; 1946 Open; 1947 National League Division Three; 1948-1953 Open; 1954-1957 Southern Area League; 1958 Open; 1959 Southern Area League; 1960-1963 Open; 1964 Metropolitan League; 1965 Training; 1969-1974 British League Division Two; 1975-1978 National League; 1979-1984 British League; 1985-1990 National League; 1991-1994 British League Division One; 1995 Premier League; 1996 Premier League and Conference League; 1997-2007 Elite League.
FIRST MEETING:	5 August 1929.
TRACK LENGTH:	275 metres.
TRACK RECORD:	55.1 seconds - Tony Rickardsson (10/05/03).

CLUB HONOURS

LEAGUE CHAMPIONS: 1938, 1947, 1959, 1971, 1977, 1986, 1987, 1995, 2000.

KNOCK-OUT CUP WINNERS: 1975, 1977, 1978, 1985, 1986, 1987, 1994, 1997, 2002.

PREMIERSHIP WINNERS: 1995, 1996.

Talented teenager **Lewis Bridger** continued his sharp rise up the speedway ladder with the Eagles in 2007.

(Photo: Les Aubrey)

EASTBOURNE 2007

Denotes aggregate/bonus-point victory

NO.	DATE	OPPONENTS	VENUE	COMPETITION	RESULT	DAVID NORRIS	DEAN BARKER	NICKI PEDERSEN	STEFAN ANDERSSON	DAVEY WATT	CAMERON WOODWARD	LEWIS BRIDGER	TREVOR HARDING	MORTEN RISAGER	OTHER RIDERS
1	17/3	Poole	H	Chal	W46-43	6+1 (4)	5+1 (4)	13 (5)	5+1 (4)	9 (5)	4 (4)	4+2 (4)	-	-	-
2	21/3	Poole	A	Chal	L41-49	4+1 (4)	5+1 (4)	10 (5)	5+1 (4)	9 (5)	3+2 (4)	5 (4)	-	-	-
3	23/3	Coventry	A	ELA	L40-50	10 (5)	4+1 (4)	10 (5)	4 (4)	7+1 (4)	3 (5)	2+1 (4)	-	-	-
4	24/3	Coventry	H	ELA	L43-50	8 (5)	3 (4)	18 (5)	3 (4)	4 (4)	5+1 (4)	2+1 (4)	-	-	-
5	31/3	Reading	H	ELA	W55-38	12+1 (5)	6+1 (4)	15 (5)	4+2 (4)	0 (0)	8+2 (6)	10+1 (6)	-	-	-
6	2/4	Belle Vue	A	ELA	L43-50	13+1 (5)	9 (5)	10 (5)	-	R/R	2 (5)	4+1 (5)	-	-	5+1 (5)
7	6/4	Poole	A	ELA	L36-52	5+1 (5)	5+1 (5)	7+1 (5)	-	R/R	7+1 (5)	8+1 (5)	-	-	4+1 (5)
8	6/4	Poole	H	ELA	W49-41	5+1 (5)	9+1 (5)	15 (5)	-	R/R	4+2 (5)	15+2 (7)	-	-	1 (3)
9	12/4	Peterborough	A	ELA	L44-49	4+1 (5)	5+1 (5)	18 (5)	5 (4)	R/R	10+1 (6)	2 (5)	-	-	-
10	14/4	Wolverhampton	H	ELA	W57-35	16+2 (6)	12+2 (5)	15 (5)	0 (2)	R/R	3 (6)	11+1 (6)	-	-	-
11	21/4	Swindon	H	ELA	W56.5-38.5	9+1 (6)	11+2 (5)	12.5 (5)	-	R/R	6+1 (4)	6+2 (5)	-	-	12+1 (5)
12	26/4	Swindon	A	ELA	L38-55*	0 (1)	5 (5)	17 (5)	-	R/R	5 (7)	8+3 (7)	-	-	3 (6)
13	4/5	Oxford	A	ELA	L34-59	R/R	-	-	5 (5)	17 (6)	2 (5)	7+2 (7)	1 (3)	-	2+1 (4)
14	5/5	Belle Vue	H	ELA	W62-29*	R/R	-	18 (6)	7+2 (4)	12+2 (5)	9+1 (5)	2+1 (4)	-	-	14+2 (6)
15	7/5	Reading	A	ELA	L38-54*	R/R	-	17 (6)	8+1 (6)	1 (3)	5 (6)	6+1 (7)	-	-	1 (3)
16	14/5	Wolverhampton	A	ELA	L42-51*	R/R	-	11 (4)	0 (1)	11 (6)	3 (2)	6 (5)	-	-	11 (6)
17	19/5	Coventry	H	ELB	L40-53	R/R	-	17 (5)	-	6+2 (5)	-	3+1 (6)	-	-	14 (14)
18	26/5	Oxford	H	ELA	W43-31	R/R	-	-	6 (3)	14 (5)	-	10 (5)	5 (5)	-	8+4 (6)
19	31/5	Ipswich	A	ELA	L30-60	R/R	-	-	1 (5)	13 (6)	-	6+1 (7)	-	-	10 (12)
20	2/6	Ipswich	H	ELA	D45-45	8+1 (5)	R/R	11 (5)	11+3 (7)	8+1 (5)	-	-	-	-	7+1 (8)
21	15/6	Lakeside	A	ELA	L36-54	4 (5)	R/R	12 (5)	6 (5)	11 (6)	-	-	2 (5)	-	1 (4)
22	16/6	Peterborough	H	ELA	L44-50	3+2 (4)	R/R	18 (5)	0 (2)	12+1 (6)	-	-	6 (7)	-	5 (5)
23	20/6	Poole	A	ELB	L46-48	R/R	-	17 (5)	7+2 (6)	12+1 (5)	-	5 (6)	-	-	5 (8)
24	28/6	Peterborough	A	ELA	L42-51	R/R	-	-	9+1 (5)	17 (6)	-	3 (5)	1+1 (4)	4 (5)	8 (5)
25	2/7	Lakeside	H	ELA	W55-38	R/R	-	15 (5)	9 (5)	15+1 (6)	4+1 (4)	6+3 (5)	-	6+2 (5)	-
26	9/7	Reading	A	ELB	L44-46	R/R	-	-	7 (6)	14+2 (6)	1+1 (3)	7+2 (5)	-	10 (6)	5+2 (4)
27	28/7	Ipswich	H	ELB	W47-46	R/R	-	-	0 (1)	16+1 (6)	9+2 (7)	4+1 (5)	-	8+1 (5)	10+1 (6)
28	4/8	Wolverhampton	H	ELB	W50-39	R/R	-	14 (5)	-	11+2 (6)	4+1 (4)	7+3 (5)	-	8+1 (5)	6+1 (5)
29	11/8	Swindon	H	ELB	W53-37	R/R	-	-	-	12 (6)	5+2 (4)	12+2 (6)	-	7+1 (5)	17+2 (9)
30	16/8	Swindon	A	ELB	L36-56	R/R	-	15 (5)	-	8 (6)	4+2 (5)	4+1 (5)	-	1 (4)	4+1 (5)
31	25/8	Lakeside	H	ELB	L43-49	R/R	-	-	-	18 (6)	5+2 (6)	4+1 (5)	-	8+1 (6)	8+2 (7)
32	27/8	Wolverhampton	A	ELB	D45-45*	R/R	-	12+1 (5)	-	12 (6)	7+2 (6)	6+1 (5)	-	5+1 (5)	3 (3)
33	1/9	Peterborough	H	ELB	L42-51	R/R	-	7+1 (4)	-	14 (6)	5 (6)	8+1 (5)	-	8+3 (6)	0 (3)
34	10/9	Belle Vue	A	ELB	L29-60	R/R	-	-	-	9 (6)	7+1 (7)	1 (4)	-	9 (6)	3+1 (7)
35	13/9	Coventry	A	ELB	L44-49	R/R	-	-	-	20 (6)	4 (6)	5 (5)	-	7+2 (6)	8 (7)
36	14/9	Lakeside	A	KO	L33-59	R/R	-	-	-	15 (6)	1 (5)	5+1 (5)	-	3 (5)	9 (9)
37	15/9	Lakeside	H	KO	L41-49	-	-	-	-	13 (5)	8 (4)	2+1 (4)	-	8+1 (5)	10+3 (12)
38	20/9	Ipswich	A	ELB	L44-46	-	-	-	-	13 (5)	7+4 (5)	3 (4)	-	3+1 (4)	18+2 (12)
39	29/9	Poole	H	ELB	W53-37*	-	-	15 (5)	-	11+1 (4)	5+3 (4)	2 (4)	-	9+1 (5)	11 (8)
40	4/10	Sw'don/B. Vue	S	CSs	39-48-21	-	-	-	-	-	5+2 (4)	5+1 (4)	-	7+1 (4)	22+3 (12)
41	6/10	B. Vue/Sw'don	H	CSs	37-32-39	-	-	-	-	-	5+2 (4)	8 (4)	-	6 (4)	18+2 (12)
42	8/10	B. Vue/Sw'don	B	CSs	38-36-34	-	-	-	-	-	4+1 (4)	10 (4)	-	7+1 (4)	17+4 (12)
43	14/10	Belle Vue	H	ELB	W55-37	-	-	-	-	R/R	12 (5)	9+3 (5)	-	5+2 (6)	29+1 (14)
44	19/10	Lakeside	A	ELB	L40-52	-	-	14 (5)	-	R/R	6+1 (5)	10+2 (6)	-	3 (5)	7+1 (9)
45	20/10	Reading	H	ELB	W58-35*	-	-	18 (6)	-	R/R	13+1 (6)	10+1 (5)	-	5+2 (5)	12+3 (8)

NOTE: (1) In the away Elite League fixture at Peterborough on 12 April, Cameron Woodward's tally was officially given as 12+1 (7), while Lewis Bridger's was shown as 0 (4). The confusion stemmed from heat nine, when Bridger took a reserve ride in place of Woodward, with the referee allegedly uninformed of the change; (2) The home match against Oxford on 26 May was abandoned after heat twelve, with the result permitted to stand.

Details of other riders (all guests unless **highlighted**): Match No. 6: Mark Lemon 5+1 (5); Match No. 7: Daniel Nermark 4+1 (5); Match No. 8: Daniel Nermark 1 (3); Match No. 11: Edward Kennett 12+1 (5); Match No. 12: Steve Johnston 3 (6); Match No. 13: Andrew Moore 2+1 (4); Match No. 14: Edward Kennett 14+2 (6); Match No. 15: Kevin Doolan 1 (3); Match No. 16: Edward Kennett 11 (6); Match No. 17: Edward Kennett 12 (6); Tom Hedley 2 (4); Tom Brown 0 (4); Match No. 18: Edward Kennett 4+2 (3); Leigh Lanham 4+2 (3); Match No. 19: Joonas Kylmakorpi 6 (4); Leigh Lanham 4 (5); Tom Hedley 0 (3); Match No. 20: Ryan Fisher 5+1 (5); Andrew Bargh 2 (3); Match No. 21: Ryan Fisher 1 (4); Match No. 22: Kim Jansson 5 (5); Match No. 23: Gary Havelock 4 (5); Rusty Harrison 1 (3); Match No. 24: Adam Shields 8 (5); Match No. 26: Gary Havelock 5+2 (4); Match No. 27: Edward Kennett 10+1 (6); Match No. 28: Leigh Lanham 6+1 (5); Match No. 29: Billy Janniro 16+1 (6); Tom Hedley 1+1 (3); Match No. 30: Jason Doyle 4+1 (5); Match No. 31: Edward Kennett 6 (4); Tom Hedley 2+2 (3); Match No. 32: **Denis Gizatullin** 3 (3); Match No. 33: Jason King 0 (3); Match No. 34: Chris Kerr 2+1 (4); Adam Shields 1 (3); Match No. 35: Simon Stead 8 (4); Shaun Tacey 0 (3); Match No. 36: Chris Harris 9 (6); Shaun Tacey 0 (3); Match No. 37: Chris Harris 8+1 (4); **Roman Povazhny** 1+1 (4); **Simon Gustafsson** 1+1 (4); Match No. 38: Simon Stead 9+1 (5); **Simon Gustafsson** 7 (4); Chris Kerr 2+1 (3); Match No. 39: **Roman Povazhny** 6 (4); **Simon Gustafsson** 5 (4); Match No. 40: **Roman Povazhny** 9+1 (4); Adam Shields 8+1 (4); **Simon Gustafsson** 5+1 (4); Match No. 41: Edward Kennett 10+1 (4); **Roman Povazhny** 4+1 (4); **Simon Gustafsson** 4 (4); Match No. 42: Edward Kennett 10+1 (4); **Simon Gustafsson** 4+1 (4); **Roman Povazhny** 3+2 (4); Match No. 43: Edward Kennett 17 (6); **Roman Povazhny** 8 (4); **Simon Gustafsson** 4+1 (4); Match No. 44: **Roman Povazhny** 5+1 (5); **Simon Gustafsson** 2 (4); Match No. 45: **Roman Povazhny** 9+2 (4); **Simon Gustafsson** 3+1 (4).

Details of tactical rides and tactical substitute rides: Match No. 4: Pedersen 6 points (TR); Match No. 6: Norris 6 points (TR); Match No. 9: Pedersen 6 points (TR); Match No. 12: Pedersen 6 points (TR); Match No. 13: Watt 6 points (TR); Match No. 15: Pedersen 6 points (TR); Match No. 16: Kennett 6 points (TR); Match No. 17: Pedersen 6 points (TR); Bridger 0 points (TS); Match No. 19: Watt 0 points (TR); Bridger 0 points (TS); Match No. 21: Watt 1 point (TS; not doubled); Pedersen 0 points (TR); Match No. 22: Pedersen 6 points (TR); Watt 2 points (TS); Match No. 23: Pedersen 6 points (TR); Bridger 2 points (TS); Match No. 24: Watt 6 points (TR); Match No. 27: Watt 6 points (TR); Kennett 0 points (TS); Match No. 30: Pedersen 6 points (TR); Match No. 31: Watt 4 points (TR); Match No. 33: Watt 6 points (TR); Match No. 34: Watt 1 point (TR; not doubled); Match No. 35: Watt 6 points (TR); Match No. 36: Watt 4 points (TR); Harris 0 points (TS); Match No. 44: Pedersen 4 points (TR).

AVERAGES

[36 Elite League; 2 Knock-Out Cup; 3 Craven Shield = 41 fixtures]

Rider	Mts	Rds	Pts	Bon	Tot	Avge	Max
Nicki Pedersen	26	131	342.5	3	345.5	10.55	10 full
Davey Watt	28	147	298	15	313	8.52	1 paid
David Norris	13	62	94	11	105	6.77	1 paid
Dean Barker	10	47	69	9	78	6.64	-
Roman Povazhny	8	33	45	8	53	6.42	-
Morten Risager	22	111	137	21	158	5.69	-
Lewis Bridger	38	194	226	41	267	5.51	-
Cameron Woodward	34	169	191	37	228	5.40	-
Stefan Andersson	17	71	81	11	92	5.18	-
Simon Gustafsson	9	36	35	5	40	4.44	-

Also rode (in alphabetical order):

Denis Gizatullin	1	3	3	0	3	4.00	-
Trevor Harding	3	16	9	1	10	2.50	-

Guests	43	187	232	22	254	5.43	-

(Andrew Bargh [1]; Tom Brown [1]; Kevin Doolan [1]; Jason Doyle [1]; Ryan Fisher [2]; Chris Harris [2]; Rusty Harrison [1]; Gary Havelock [2]; Tom Hedley [4]; Billy Janniro [1]; Kim Jansson [1]; Steve Johnston [1]; Edward Kennett [9]; Chris Kerr [2]; Jason King [1]; Joonas Kylmakorpi [1]; Leigh Lanham [2]; Mark Lemon [1]; Daniel Nermark [2]; Adam Shields [3]; Simon Stead [2]; Shaun Tacey [2])

The one and only **Nicki Pedersen** again gave sterling service to the Eagles' cause, not only on the track, but also in his role of club captain. And, of course, he also landed his second World Championship title, courtesy of a dominant display throughout the Grand Prix series.

(Photo: Les Aubrey)

IPSWICH WITCHES

ADDRESS:	Foxhall Heath Stadium, Foxhall Road, Ipswich, Suffolk, IP4 5TL.
TELEPHONE:	01473 623640.
CLUB HOTLINE:	09068 664687 (Premium rate applies).
WEBSITE:	www.ipswich-witches.com
PROMOTER:	John Louis.
MAIN TEAM SPONSOR:	Evening Star.
YEARS OF OPERATION:	1950-1951 Open; 1952-1953 Southern League; 1954-1956 National League Division Two; 1957-1958 National League; 1959 Southern Area League; 1960-1962 National League; 1964 Metropolitan League; 1965 Open; 1969-1971 British League Division Two; 1972-1974 British League Division One; 1975-1988 British League; 1989-1990 National League; 1991-1994 British League Division One; 1995-1996 Premier League; 1997 Elite League and Amateur League; 1998-2007 Elite League.
FIRST MEETING:	25 October 1950.
TRACK LENGTH:	305 metres.
TRACK RECORD:	57.5 seconds - Jaroslaw Hampel (12/09/02).

CLUB HONOURS

KNOCK-OUT CUP WINNERS: 1970, 1971, 1976, 1978, 1981, 1984, 1998.

LEAGUE CHAMPIONS: 1975, 1976, 1984, 1998.

PAIRS CHAMPIONS: 1976, 1977.

INTER-LEAGUE KNOCK-OUT CUP WINNERS: 1977.

FOUR-TEAM CHAMPIONS: 1991.

CRAVEN SHIELD WINNERS: 1998.

Mark Loram was sidelined virtually from the start of the campaign, when he suffered a badly broken left thigh in a frightening track accident in heat one of Ipswich's very first Elite League match of the season at home to Reading on 22 March.

(Photo: Karen Chappell)

IPSWICH 2007

*Denotes aggregate/bonus-point victory

NO.	DATE	OPPONENTS	VENUE	COMPETITION	RESULT	MARK LORAM	KIM JANSSON	CHRIS LOUIS	MARCIN REMPALA	ROBERT MISKOWIAK	ZIBIGNIEW SUCHECKI	TOBIAS KRONER	CHRIS SCHRAMM	JESPER B. JENSEN	OTHER RIDERS
1	15/3	Lakeside	H	SC	W51-42	14+1 (5)	5+1 (4)	11 (5)	3+3 (4)	7+1 (4)	6+1 (4)	5 (4)	-	-	-
2	16/3	Lakeside	A	SC	L28-64	10 (5)	0 (4)	10 (4)	0 (4)	4 (5)	1 (4)	3 (4)	-	-	-
3	22/3	Reading	H	ELA	L43-47	0 (0)	7+1 (4)	10 (5)	4 (4)	12 (5)	7+2 (7)	3+2 (5)	-	-	-
4	28/3	Poole	A	ELA	L34-58	-	4+1 (4)	4+1 (4)	2 (4)	8+1 (5)	5+1 (5)	1 (3)	-	-	10 (4)
5	6/4	Lakeside	H	ELA	D44-44	R/R	5+1 (5)	13 (6)	5+1 (5)	9 (6)	10 (5)	2 (3)	-	-	-
6	6/4	Lakeside	A	ELA	L33-60	R/R	0 (3)	17 (6)	3+1 (5)	3 (5)	3+1 (5)	7 (6)	-	-	-
7	12/4	Oxford	H	KO	W52-38	-	8 (4)	10 (5)	0 (3)	6 (4)	5 (4)	11+2 (5)	-	-	12+2 (5)
8	13/4	Oxford	A	KO	D45-45*	-	6+2 (4)	6 (4)	3+1 (4)	8+2 (5)	5 (4)	4+2 (4)	-	-	13 (5)
9	19/4	Poole	H	ELA	L35-58	-	8 (5)	6 (4)	2+1 (4)	8 (5)	-	1 (3)	5+1 (5)	-	5+1 (4)
10	20/4	Reading	A	ELA	L32-60	-	10+1 (5)	2 (4)	2 (4)	3 (4)	5+1 (4)	5 (4)	-	-	5 (5)
11	26/4	Wolverhampton	H	ELA	W49-43	-	7 (4)	11 (5)	4+1 (4)	8 (4)	3+1 (3)	7+3 (5)	-	-	9+1 (5)
12	30/4	Wolverhampton	A	ELA	L29-63	-	8 (6)	9 (5)	2 (7)	5 (4)	R/R	-	5+2 (7)	-	0 (1)
13	10/5	Peterborough	A	ELA	L28-46	-	7+1 (4)	1 (3)	3 (4)	7 (3)	3 (3)	2+2 (4)	-	-	5 (3)
14	17/5	Oxford	H	ELA	W53-40	-	7+1 (4)	12+1 (5)	1 (3)	10+3 (5)	3+1 (4)	12 (5)	-	-	8+1 (4)
15	24/5	Reading	H	ELB	W61-32	R/R	9+1 (5)	16+1 (6)	8+2 (4)	11 (6)	8+2 (5)	9+1 (4)	-	-	-
16	25/5	Lakeside	A	ELB	L35-58	-	4 (4)	13+1 (5)	1+1 (2)	3 (3)	0 (4)	7+1 (7)	-	-	7 (5)
17	31/5	Eastbourne	H	ELA	W60-30	-	9+2 (4)	9+1 (4)	7+2 (4)	14 (5)	5 (4)	-	6+1 (4)	-	10+3 (5)
18	2/6	Eastbourne	A	ELA	D45-45*	-	8+2 (4)	9 (4)	0 (4)	11 (5)	3+2 (4)	-	3 (4)	-	14+1 (9)
19	6/6	Poole	A	ELB	L30-63	-	1 (4)	7 (4)	2 (4)	5 (5)	7 (5)	-	3 (4)	-	5 (4)
20	7/6	Belle Vue	H	ELA	W65-25	-	8+1 (4)	12+3 (5)	4+1 (4)	15 (5)	8+1 (4)	8+1 (4)	-	-	10+2 (4)
21	21/6	Lakeside	H	ELB	W51-42	-	8+1 (5)	11+1 (5)	3+1 (4)	11+1 (5)	R/R	6+2 (6)	-	12+1 (5)	-
22	28/6	Swindon	H	ELA	W46-44	-	7+1 (4)	7+1 (4)	2 (4)	6 (4)	10+1 (5)	6+2 (4)	-	8+1 (5)	-
23	5/7	Swindon	A	ELA	L24-68	-	4+2 (5)	4 (5)	-	1 (4)	R/R	4 (6)	1 (5)	10 (5)	-
24	9/7	Peterborough	A	ELB	L30-62	-	4+1 (4)	3 (4)	2 (4)	7+1 (5)	1 (4)	1 (4)	-	12 (5)	-
25	12/7	Coventry	H	ELA	L37-56	-	3+1 (4)	14 (5)	3+1 (4)	3 (4)	3+2 (4)	4 (4)	-	7+1 (5)	-
26	13/7	Reading	A	KO	L40-53	-	9 (5)	17 (5)	6+1 (6)	0 (3)	1 (4)	7 (6)	-	-	0 (1)
27	23/7	Belle Vue	A	ELB	L40-49*	-	4+1 (4)	12 (5)	1 (3)	7 (5)	1 (3)	9 (6)	-	6+1 (4)	-
28	26/7	Wolverhampton	H	ELB	W52-41	-	2+2 (4)	12+1 (5)	6+3 (5)	8+1 (5)	R/R	17+1 (7)	-	7 (4)	-
29	28/7	Eastbourne	H	ELA	L46-47	-	7+3 (4)	9+1 (5)	-	10 (5)	0 (3)	9+2 (5)	4+2 (4)	7 (4)	-
30	4/8	Peterborough	H	ELA	L43-46	-	5+1 (4)	11+1 (5)	3 (3)	7 (5)	1+1 (3)	11 (6)	-	5+2 (4)	-
31	6/8	Reading	A	ELA	L42-50*	-	9+2 (4)	11 (5)	1+1 (4)	5 (4)	0 (3)	7+3 (5)	-	9+1 (5)	-
32	9/8	Belle Vue	H	ELB	W55-35	-	8+2 (4)	14+1 (5)	4+2 (4)	9 (5)	4 (4)	10+1 (4)	-	6+3 (4)	-
33	16/8	Reading	H	KO	W49-44	-	-	18 (6)	5+3 (4)	-	1 (3)	8+2 (6)	-	R/R	17+2 (11)
34	17/8	Coventry	A	ELA	L33-57	-	-	7+1 (5)	2 (4)	12 (6)	6 (5)	5 (6)	1 (4)	R/R	-
35	27/8	Swindon	H	ELB	L26-64	-	7 (6)	5 (5)	1 (4)	5+1 (5)	0 (4)	8 (6)	-	R/R	-
36	31/8	Coventry	A	ELB	L29-64	-	5 (5)	6 (6)	1+1 (4)	13 (6)	-	3 (5)	1 (4)	R/R	-
37	1/9	Swindon	H	ELB	L44-46	-	7+1 (5)	11+1 (6)	9+1 (5)	6+1 (6)	-	9+3 (5)	2+1 (3)	R/R	-
38	6/9	Coventry	H	ELB	L41-52	-	1 (4)	16+1 (6)	4 (4)	7+1 (5)	5+1 (5)	8+1 (6)	-	R/R	-
39	10/9	Wolverhampton	A	ELB	L38-55	-	2 (5)	18 (6)	5 (5)	11+2 (6)	1 (3)	1+1 (5)	-	R/R	-
40	13/9	Peterborough	H	ELB	L38-52	-	7 (5)	10+1 (5)	6+1 (6)	6 (4)	4+1 (4)	4+1 (4)	-	1 (3)	-
41	17/9	Belle Vue	A	ELB	L39-54*	-	6+2 (5)	12+1 (6)	7 (5)	10+1 (6)	0 (3)	4+2 (5)	-	R/R	-
42	20/9	Eastbourne	H	ELB	W46-44*	-	8 (5)	6+2 (5)	1 (4)	18 (6)	-	11+2 (6)	-	R/R	2+1 (4)
43	27/9	Coventry/Wolves	H	CSs	43-42-23	-	8 (4)	9 (4)	5+2 (4)	10 (4)	-	8+3 (4)	-	-	3+2 (4)
44	28/9	Coventry/Wolves	C	CSs	21-31-20	-	0 (1)	3 (2)	1 (5)	9 (3)	-	3 (2)	-	-	5 (3)
45	4/10	Poole	H	ELB	L41-49	-	-	11 (6)	8+1 (6)	15+1 (6)	1 (3)	4+2 (5)	-	R/R	2+1 (4)
46	8/10	Wolves/Coventry	W	CSs	24-35-49	-	-	7+1 (4)	1 (4)	7 (4)	-	5+2 (4)	0 (4)	-	4 (4)

ADDITIONAL KEY: SC = Spring Challenge.

NOTE: (1) The ELA fixture at Peterborough on 10 May was abandoned after heat twelve, with the result permitted to stand; (2) In the away ELA fixture at Belle Vue on 23 July, as per a statement issued by the SCB on 26 July, it transpired that the Aces' line-up did not comply with the speedway regulations. New signing Billy Forsberg had been injured in his homeland and to cover his absence, the No. 8, Joel Parsons, was used to replace him in the team, contrary to the speedway regulations. As Forsberg had not yet ridden for Belle Vue, no facility was permitted as per SR 18.1.4.2, which stated: 'No facility is permitted to replace a rider, who, although declared, has not made an appearance for that team'. SR 18.1.5.3 (a) stated that if no facility is applicable, then, in the Elite League, that team's No. 8 may be used, but only if the No. 8 has a Premier League green sheet CMA of 6.00 or less. At the time, Joel Parsons' PL CMA was 6.72. As a consequence, the result of the meeting was amended, with the deduction of the points scored by Parsons. For the record, he tallied 1+1 points from three rides in the match versus the Witches; (3) The away leg of the Craven Shield at Coventry on 28 September was abandoned after heat twelve, with the result permitted to stand.

Details of other riders (all guests unless **highlighted**): Match No. 4: Scott Nicholls 10 (4); Match No. 7: Scott Nicholls 12+2 (5); Match No. 8: David Norris 13 (5); Match No. 9: David Norris 5+1 (4); Match No. 10: David Norris 5 (5); Match No. 11: Adam Shields 9+1 (5); Match No. 12: David Norris 0 (1); Match No. 13: Simon Stead 5 (3); Match No. 14: Adam Shields 8+1 (4); Match No. 16: Rory Schlein 7 (5); Match No. 17: Adam Shields 10+3 (5); Match No. 18: Chris Harris 10+1 (5); Jason King 4 (4); Match No. 19: David Howe 5 (4); Match No. 20: Adam Shields 10+2 (4); Match No. 26: Adam Shields 0 (1); Match No. 33: Martin Smolinski 10+1 (6); Billy Janniro 7+1 (5); Match No. 42: Shaun Tacey 2+1 (4); Match No. 43: Kevin Doolan 3+2 (4); Match No. 44: Kevin Doolan 5 (3); Match No. 45: Jacek Rempala 2+1 (4); Match No. 46: Jacek Rempala 4 (4).

Details of tactical rides and tactical substitute rides: Match No. 2: Louis 4 points (TR); Match No. 4: Nicholls 6 points (TR); Match No. 6: Louis 6 points (TR); Match No. 9: Jansson 6 points (TR); Match No. 10: Jansson 4 points (TR); Match No. 12: Louis 4 points (TR); Match No. 13: Jansson 4 points (TR); Match No. 16: Louis 6 points (TR); Match No. 19: Louis 6 points (TR); Match No. 23: Jensen 4 points (TR); Match No. 24: Jensen 4 points (TR); Match No. 25: Louis 6 points (TR); Match No. 26: Louis 6 points (TR); Match No. 27: Miskowiak 0 points (TR); Match No. 31: Jansson 4 points (TR); Match No. 33: Louis 6 points (TR); Match No. 34: Louis 0 points (TR); Match No. 35: Kroner 0 points (TS); Match No. 36: Miskowiak 6 points (TR); Match No. 38: Louis 6 points (TR); Match No. 39: Louis 6 points (TR); Match No. 40: Miskowiak 1 point (TR; not doubled); Match No. 41: Louis 6 points (TR).

AVERAGES

[36 Elite League; 4 Knock-Out Cup; 3 Craven Shield = 43 fixtures]

• Denotes ever-present.

Rider	Mts	Rds	Pts	Bon	Tot	Avge	Max
Chris Louis •	43	209	390	21	411	7.87	2 paid
Jesper B. Jensen	12	53	86	10	96	7.25	-
Robert Miskowiak	42	200	336	13	349	6.98	2 full
Kim Jansson	39	169	221	33	254	6.01	-
Tobias Kroner	39	189	239	44	283	5.99	-
Zbigniew Suchecki	32	129	116	17	133	4.12	-
Marcin Rempala	41	175	139	29	168	3.84	-
Chris Schramm	10	44	28	7	35	3.18	-

Also rode:

Mark Loram	1	0	0	0	0	0.00	-

Guests	22	90	135	16	151	6.71	1 paid

(Kevin Doolan [2]; Chris Harris [1]; David Howe [1]; Billy Janniro [1]; Jason King [1]; Scott Nicholls [2]; David Norris [4]; Jacek Rempala [2]; Rory Schlein [1]; Adam Shields [4]; Martin Smolinski [1]; Simon Stead [1]; Shaun Tacey [1])

NOTE: Robert Miskowiak was ever-present throughout the 36-match Elite League programme.

INDIVIDUAL MEETING

11 October: 16-Lap Classic

QUALIFYING SCORES: Robert Miskowiak 11; Chris Louis 10; Troy Batchelor 9; Jacek Rempala 8; Mariusz Puszakowski 8; Krzysztof Stojanowski 6; Lubos Tomicek 6; Marcin Rempala 6; Chris Schramm 3; Kevin Wolbert 2; Martin Vaculik 2; Jerran Hart (Res) 1; Adam Shields 0.

FINAL: 1st Louis (14+2); 2nd Batchelor (12+2); 3rd Stojanowski (10); 4th Puszakowski (8); 5th Miskowiak (6+2); 6th J. Rempala (4+2); 7th Tomicek (2); 8th M. Rempala (0).

OVERALL RESULT: 1st Louis 26; 2nd Batchelor 23; 3rd Miskowiak 19; Stojanowski 16; Puszakowski 16; J. Rempala 14; Tomicek 8; M. Rempala 6.

CONSOLATION FINAL: 1st Wolbert; 2nd Schramm; 3rd Vaculik; 4th Hart.

Polish newcomer **Zibi Suchecki** proved a useful addition to the Ipswich ranks in his first season of British racing.

(Photo: Les Aubrey)

LAKESIDE HAMMERS

ADDRESS:	Arena-Essex Raceway, A1306 Arterial Road, Thurrock, Essex, RM19 1AE.
TELEPHONE:	01708 863443.
CLUB HOTLINE:	09068 664686 (Premium rate applies).
WEBSITE:	www.lakesidehammers.com
PROMOTERS:	Stuart Douglas & Jon Cook.
MAIN TEAM SPONSOR:	Duggo 7.
YEARS OF OPERATION:	1984-1990 National League; 1991 British League Division Two; 1992-1994 British League Division One; 1995 Premier League; 1996 Conference League; 1997-2003 Premier League; 2004-2007 Elite League.
FIRST MEETING:	5 April 1984.
TRACK LENGTH:	252 metres.
TRACK RECORD:	56.9 seconds - Andreas Jonsson (19/10/07).

CLUB HONOURS
LEAGUE CHAMPIONS: 1991.
KNOCK-OUT CUP WINNERS: 1991.
FOUR-TEAM CHAMPIONS: 1991.

Lakeside, 2007
Back row, left to right: Leigh Lanham, Krzysztof Kasprzak, Adam Shields, Henning Bager, Christian Hefenbrock, Joonas Kylmakorpi and Chris Neath.
Front, on bike: Paul Hurry.

(Photo: Karen Chappell)

LAKESIDE 2007

* Denotes aggregate/bonus-point victory

NO.	DATE	OPPONENTS	VENUE	COMPETITION	RESULT	JOONAS KYLMAKORPI	LEIGH LANHAM	KRZYSZTOF KASPRZAK	PAUL HURRY	ADAM SHIELDS	CHRISTIAN HEFENBROCK	HENNING BAGER	CHRIS NEATH	LUBOS TOMICEK	OTHER RIDERS
1	15/3	Ipswich	A	SC	L42-51	5 (4)	3+2 (4)	15 (5)	-	9 (5)	1+1 (4)	4 (4)	5+1 (4)	-	-
2	16/3	Ipswich	H	SC	W64-28*	10 (4)	6+3 (4)	14 (5)	-	8+1 (4)	8+1 (4)	12+3 (5)	6 (4)	-	-
3	23/3	Belle Vue	H	ELA	W58-34	12+1 (5)	3+1 (4)	15 (5)	10+2 (4)	5 (4)	5+1 (4)	8 (4)	-	-	-
4	29/3	Swindon	A	ELA	L29-63	-	2+1 (4)	10 (5)	3+1 (4)	7 (5)	2 (4)	1+1 (4)	-	-	4 (4)
5	2/4	Wolverhampton	A	ELA	L44-49	R/R	4 (4)	16 (6)	2+1 (4)	11 (6)	8+3 (6)	3+2 (4)	-	-	-
6	6/4	Ipswich	A	ELA	D44-44	10+1 (5)	4+1 (4)	8 (4)	2 (3)	11 (5)	0 (3)	9+1 (6)	-	-	-
7	6/4	Ipswich	H	ELA	W60-33*	10+3 (5)	5+3 (4)	10 (4)	6+2 (4)	10 (4)	14+1 (5)	-	5+1 (4)	-	-
8	9/4	Rye House	A	Chal	D45-45	-	11+1 (5)	-	10+1 (5)	6+2 (4)	8 (4)	-	-	-	10+2 (12)
9	13/4	Coventry	A	ELA	L25-67	R/R	3 (5)	6 (6)	0 (1)	11+1 (6)	3+1 (7)	-	2 (5)	-	-
10	16/4	Poole	H	ELA	W48-42	-	4+2 (4)	12+1 (5)	3+1 (4)	10+1 (5)	9+1 (5)	-	6 (4)	-	4+2 (4)
11	19/4	Peterborough	A	ELA	L25-65	-	1 (4)	9 (5)	0 (3)	4 (4)	4+1 (5)	-	0 (4)	-	7 (5)
12	20/4	Peterborough	H	ELA	W56-37	R/R	9+2 (5)	17 (6)	5+1 (4)	9 (6)	9+2 (5)	-	7+2 (4)	-	-
13	23/4	Reading	A	ELA	L37-55	R/R	6 (5)	14 (6)	0 (3)	7+1 (6)	2+1 (5)	-	-	-	8 (5)
14	27/4	Oxford	H	ELA	W51-42	2 (4)	13+1 (6)	15 (5)	0 (2)	11 (5)	6+2 (4)	-	4+1 (4)	-	-
15	30/4	Belle Vue	A	KO	L46-47	R/R	8 (6)	10+1 (6)	-	19 (6)	1 (3)	-	-	-	8+1 (9)
16	4/5	Belle Vue	H	KO	W50-40*	R/R	15+1 (7)	17 (6)	-	10+2 (5)	5+3 (5)	-	1+1 (3)	-	2 (4)
17	7/5	Oxford	A	ELA	W53-39*	R/R	6+1 (4)	9 (5)	-	15+1 (6)	14+1 (6)	-	1 (4)	-	8+2 (5)
18	11/5	Wolverhampton	H	ELA	L39-51	R/R	8+1 (6)	11 (6)	-	10 (6)	3+2 (5)	3+1 (4)	4 (3)	-	-
19	16/5	Poole	A	ELA	L37-56	3 (4)	3+2 (5)	16 (5)	0 (3)	10 (6)	4 (4)	-	-	-	1 (3)
20	18/5	Poole	H	ELB	L45-47	1+1 (4)	16+1 (7)	11 (5)	-	9 (5)	0 (4)	R/R	8+2 (5)	-	-
21	21/5	Reading	A	ELB	W49-41	4+2 (4)	1 (3)	11 (5)	-	12 (5)	5+2 (4)	2 (3)	14+2 (6)	-	-
22	24/5	Swindon	A	ELB	L28-62	2 (4)	0 (4)	12 (5)	-	7 (5)	3+1 (4)	2 (4)	-	-	2 (4)
23	25/5	Ipswich	H	ELB	W58-35	8+1 (4)	8+3 (5)	15 (5)	-	10 (4)	8+2 (4)	6+3 (4)	3+2 (4)	-	-
24	30/5	Poole	A	ELB	L36-57	5+1 (4)	3 (4)	13 (5)	-	7+1 (5)	1 (3)	4 (4)	3 (5)	-	-
25	6/6	Coventry	H	ELA	W52-41	7+3 (5)	12 (5)	-	8 (5)	8 (4)	0 (3)	6+1 (4)	-	-	11 (4)
26	11/6	Belle Vue	H	ELA	L43-47*	4+1 (4)	8+3 (5)	11 (5)	5 (4)	10 (5)	2+1 (3)	3+1 (4)	-	-	-
27	15/6	Eastbourne	H	ELA	W54-36	8+4 (5)	7 (4)	9 (4)	7 (4)	13 (5)	5+4 (4)	5+2 (4)	-	-	-
28	20/6	Reading	H	ELA	W52-38	11+2 (5)	5+1 (4)	-	4+2 (4)	13+1 (5)	-	5+3 (4)	-	4 (4)	10 (4)
29	21/6	Ipswich	A	ELB	L42-51*	4 (4)	3+1 (4)	-	2+1 (3)	14 (5)	-	0 (3)	-	7+2 (6)	12 (5)
30	2/7	Eastbourne	A	ELA	L38-55*	9+1 (5)	4 (4)	11 (4)	-	8+1 (5)	-	-	-	0 (4)	6 (8)
31	4/7	Belle Vue	H	ELB	W53-40	11+4 (6)	8+2 (5)	16+1 (6)	-	12 (5)	-	-	-	4 (4)	2+1 (4)
32	9/7	Wolverhampton	A	ELB	L38-52	12 (5)	8 (4)	1+1 (4)	-	7 (5)	-	-	-	2 (3)	8+3 (9)
33	11/7	Swindon	H	ELA	L41-50	8+2 (6)	9 (5)	8+2 (5)	-	14+1 (7)	-	-	-	2 (4)	0 (3)
34	30/7	Belle Vue	A	ELB	W53-39*	9+2 (6)	9+1 (5)	-	-	16 (6)	-	-	-	7+2 (4)	12+3 (9)
35	3/8	Reading	H	ELB	W53-39*	12+1 (6)	8+2 (5)	-	-	11+2 (6)	-	-	-	7+1 (4)	15+1 (9)
36	9/8	Peterborough	A	ELB	L36-54	3 (4)	4 (5)	14 (6)	-	8+1 (6)	-	-	-	2 (4)	5+2 (5)
37	10/8	Rye House	H	Chal	W67-44	15 (5)	10+2 (5)	9+1 (5)	-	13+1 (5)	-	-	-	4+2 (4)	16+2 (12)
38	17/8	Swindon	H	ELB	W52-41	-	9+4 (6)	16 (6)	-	9 (5)	-	-	-	-	18+6 (14)
39	22/8	Coventry	H	ELB	L42-48	-	6+1 (5)	16+1 (6)	-	9 (6)	-	-	-	1 (3)	10+1 (10)
40	25/8	Eastbourne	A	ELB	W49-43	-	4+2 (4)	-	-	13+1 (6)	-	-	-	-	32+4 (20)
41	27/8	Coventry	A	ELB	L34-58	R/R	2 (4)	4 (4)	-	7 (6)	-	-	-	0 (4)	21 (12)
42	31/8	Peterborough	H	ELB	D45-45	R/R	7+3 (5)	8 (4)	-	12+1 (6)	-	-	-	7+3 (7)	11 (8)
43	7/9	Wolverhampton	H	ELB	W58-35*	-	12+4 (6)	-	-	12+1 (5)	-	-	-	-	34+4 (19)
44	12/9	Poole/Reading	P	CSs	29-52-27	-	2+1 (3)	-	-	10 (4)	-	-	-	-	17+2 (17)
45	14/9	Eastbourne	H	KO	W59-33	R/R	8+2 (5)	-	-	12 (5)	-	-	-	-	39+2 (20)
46	15/9	Eastbourne	A	KO	W49-41*	R/R	5+3 (5)	-	-	15 (6)	-	-	-	-	29+5 (19)
47	5/10	Coventry	A	KOs	L41-52	R/R	4 (5)	-	-	7 (6)	-	-	-	-	30+2 (19)
48	6/10	Coventry	H	KOs	D45-45	R/R	6+1 (5)	-	-	13+1 (6)	-	-	-	-	26+2 (19)
49	8/10	Reading / Peterborough	R	CSs	40-31-37	-	7+2 (4)	11 (4)	-	10 (4)	-	-	-	-	12+2 (12)
50	12/10	Peterborough / Poole	H	CSs	36-43-29	-	7+1 (4)	11 (4)	-	-	-	-	-	-	18+4 (16)
51	19/10	Eastbourne	H	ELB	W52-40*	R/R	6+2 (5)	13 (5)	-	11 (5)	-	-	-	-	22+4 (15)

ADDITIONAL KEY: SC = Spring Challenge.

Details of other riders (all guests unless **highlighted**): Match No. 4: Simon Stead 4 (4); Match No. 8: Craig Watson 6+1 (4); Bryan Yarrow 4+1 (5); Tim Gomez 0 (3); Match No. 10: David Norris 4+2 (4); Match No. 11: Joe Screen 7 (5); Match No. 13: Dean Barker 8 (5); Match No. 15: Edward Kennett 7+1 (5); Ronnie Correy 1 (4); Match No. 16: Steve Boxall 2 (4); Match No. 17: Edward Kennett 8+2 (5); Match No. 19: Cory Gathercole 1 (3); Match No. 22: Michal Rajkowski 2 (4); Match No. 25: Peter Karlsson 11 (4); Match No. 28: Chris Louis 10 (4); Match No. 29: Davey Watt 12 (5); Match No. 30: **Ricky Kling** 6 (7); **Andreas Jonsson** 0 (1); Match No. 31: **Ricky Kling** 2+1 (4); **Andreas Jonsson** R/R; Match No. 32: **Ricky Kling** 5+2 (5); **Andreas Jonsson** 3+1 (4); Match No. 33: **Ricky Kling** 0 (3); **Andreas Jonsson** R/R; Match No. 34: Gary Havelock 8+2 (5); **Ricky Kling** 4+1 (4); **Andreas Jonsson** R/R; Match No. 35: Davey Watt 14 (5); **Ricky Kling** 1+1 (4); **Andreas Jonsson** R/R; Match No. 36: **Ricky Kling** 5+2 (5); **Andreas Jonsson** R/R; Match No. 37: Paul Hurry 10+1 (4); **Chris Mills** 6+1 (4); **Ricky Kling** 0 (4); Match No. 38: Simon Stead 9+2 (5); **Ricky Kling** 7+3 (5); **Chris Mills** 2+1 (4); **Andreas Jonsson** R/R; Match No. 39: Gary Havelock 7+1 (5); **Ricky Kling** 3 (5); **Andreas Jonsson** R/R; Match No. 40: Rory Schlein 13 (6); Billy Janniro 8+1 (5); **Ricky Kling** 7+2 (5); **Chris Mills** 4+1 (4); **Andreas Jonsson** R/R; Match No. 41: **Andreas Jonsson** 16 (5); **Ricky Kling** 5 (7); Match No. 42: **Andreas Jonsson** 10 (5); **Chris Mills** 1 (3); Match No. 43: Chris Louis 15+1 (6); Joe Screen 11+1 (5); **Ricky Kling** 6+1 (4); **Andreas Messing** 2+1 (4); **Andreas Jonsson** R/R; Match No. 44: Davey Watt 10 (4); Lewis Bridger 4 (4); **Ricky Kling** 2+1 (5);

Andreas Messing 1+1 (4); Match No. 45: **Andreas Jonsson** 15 (5); Peter Karlsson 12 (5); **Andreas Messing** 8+2 (6); **Ricky Kling** 4 (4); Match No. 46: **Andreas Jonsson** 11 (5); Peter Karlsson 9 (4); **Ricky Kling** 5+4 (7); **Andreas Messing** 4+1 (3); Match No. 47: **Andreas Jonsson** 18 (5); Simon Stead 6 (4); **Andreas Messing** 3+2 (5); **Ricky Kling** 3 (5); Match No. 48: **Andreas Jonsson** 11+1 (5); Chris Louis 9 (4); **Ricky Kling** 5+1 (5); **Andreas Messing** 1 (5); Match No. 49: **Ricky Kling** 8 (4); Phil Morris 4+2 (4); **Andreas Messing** 0 (4); Match No. 50: **Ricky Kling** 7 (4); Gary Havelock 4+1 (4); Joe Screen 4+1 (4); **Andreas Messing** 3+2 (4); Match No. 51: **Andreas Jonsson** 13+1 (5); **Andreas Messing** 5+2 (5); **Ricky Kling** 4+1 (5).

Details of tactical rides and tactical substitute rides: Match No. 1: Kasprzak 6 points (TR); Match No. 4: Kasprzak 4 points (TR); Match No. 5: Kasprzak 6 points (TR); Match No. 9: Shields 4 points (TR); Match No. 11: Screen 1 point (TR; not doubled); Match No. 13: Barker 4 points (TR); Match No. 15: Shields 6 points (TR); Match No. 19: Kasprzak 6 points (TR); Shields 1 point (TS; not doubled); Match No. 22: Kasprzak 1 point (TR; not doubled); Match No. 24: Kasprzak 6 points (TR); Match No. 29: Shields 6 points (TR); Match No. 30: Kasprzak 6 points (TR); Match No. 33: Shields 2 points (TS); Match No. 36: Shields 1 point (TR; not doubled); Match No. 41: Jonsson 4 points (TR); Match No. 47: Jonsson 6 points (TR).

AVERAGES

[36 Elite League; 6 Knock-Out Cup; 3 Craven Shield = 45 fixtures]

• Denotes ever-present.

Rider	Mts	Rds	Pts	Bon	Tot	Avge	Max
Andreas Jonsson	9	40	92	3	95	9.50	2 full
Krzysztof Kasprzak	33	167	368	7	375	8.98	2 full
Adam Shields	44	232	444	16	460	7.93	-
Joonas Kylmakorpi	21	100	153	30	183	7.32	-
Leigh Lanham •	45	211	273	54	327	6.20	-
Chris Neath	11	47	53	10	63	5.36	-
Henning Bager	14	56	57	15	72	5.14	-
Christian Hefenbrock	22	95	93	26	119	5.01	1 paid
Paul Hurry	16	57	57	11	68	4.77	1 paid
Ricky Kling	20	97	89	20	109	4.49	-
Lubos Tomicek	12	51	43	8	51	4.00	-
Andreas Messing	9	40	27	11	38	3.80	-

Also rode:

Chris Mills	3	11	7	2	9	3.27	-

Guests	29	130	214	15	229	7.05	-

(Dean Barker [1]; Steve Boxall [1]; Lewis Bridger [1]; Ronnie Correy [1]; Cory Gathercole [1]; Gary Havelock [3]; Billy Janniro [1]; Peter Karlsson [3]; Edward Kennett [1]; Chris Louis [3]; Phil Morris [1]; David Norris [1]; Michal Rajkowski [1]; Rory Schlein [1]; Joe Screen [3]; Simon Stead [3]; Davey Watt [3])

NOTE: Adam Shields was ever-present throughout the 36-match Elite League programme.

Popular Aussie **Adam Shields** followed promoter Jon Cook to the Hammers from Eastbourne and produced another season of the consistently high scoring that Elite League fans have become accustomed to.

(Photo: Karen Chappell)

OXFORD CHEETAHS

NOTE: The information below relates only to the main Oxford team. For details of the second side, please refer to the Conference League section.

ADDRESS: Oxford Stadium, Sandy Lane, Cowley, Oxford, Oxfordshire, OX4 6LJ.

TELEPHONE: 01865 396472.

CLUB HOTLINE: 09068 664680 (Premium rate applies).

WEBSITE: www.oxford-speedway.com

PROMOTERS: Colin Horton & Aaron Lanney.

MAIN TEAM SPONSOR: M4 Van Centre.

YEARS OF OPERATION: 1939-1941 Open; 1949-1950 National League Division Three; 1951-1952 National League Division Two; 1953 Southern League; 1954-1956 National League Division Two; 1957-1964 National League; 1965-1967 British League; 1968-1974 British League Division One; 1975 British League; 1976-1983 National League; 1984-1990 British League; 1991-1992 British League Division One; 1993-1994 British League Division Two; 1995-1996 Premier League; 1997 Premier League and Amateur League; 1998-2007 Elite League.

FIRST MEETING: 8 April 1939.

TRACK LENGTH: 297 metres.

TRACK RECORD: 56.2 seconds - Hans Nielsen (13/10/88).

CLUB HONOURS

LEAGUE CHAMPIONS: 1950, 1964, 1985, 1986, 1989, 2001. NOTE: The Conference League side was also crowned League Champions in 2005.

NATIONAL TROPHY (DIVISION THREE) WINNERS: 1950.

NATIONAL TROPHY WINNERS: 1964.

BRITANNIA SHIELD WINNERS: 1964.

PAIRS CHAMPIONS: 1985, 1986, 1987.

KNOCK-OUT CUP WINNERS: 1985, 1986 (Shared with Cradley Heath).

LEAGUE CUP WINNERS: 1986 (Shared with Cradley Heath).

PREMIERSHIP WINNERS: 1987.

GOLD CUP WINNERS: 1989.

FOUR-TEAM CHAMPIONS: 1994, 1996.

CRAVEN SHIELD WINNERS: 2005.

Freddie Eriksson was one of only two ever-present riders in the Cheetahs' curtailed campaign.

(Photo: Les Aubrey)

OXFORD 2007

* Denotes aggregate/bonus-point victory

NO.	DATE	OPPONENTS	VENUE	COMPETITION	RESULT	JESPER B. JENSEN	ADRIAN MIEDZINSKI	ALES DRYML	STEVE JOHNSTON	PIOTR PROTASIEWICZ	FREDDIE ERIKSSON	ERIC ANDERSSON	ANDY SMITH	LUBOS TOMICEK	OTHER RIDERS
1	16/3	Belle Vue	H	Chal	L42-51	6 (4)	2+2 (4)	5 (4)	8+2 (5)	16 (5)	3+1 (4)	2 (4)	-	-	-
2	23/3	Peterborough	H	ELA	L43-46	9+1 (5)	2+1 (3)	2 (4)	7 (4)	11 (5)	11+2 (6)	1 (3)	-	-	-
3	30/3	Belle Vue	H	ELA	W53-37	-	-	7 (4)	5 (4)	12 (5)	7+2 (4)	4+1 (4)	7+1 (4)	-	11+2 (5)
4	2/4	Coventry	H	ELA	L28-64	10 (5)	-	2+1 (4)	6 (5)	2 (4)	4 (4)	1 (4)	3+1 (4)	-	-
5	6/4	Reading	H	ELA	L40-50	8 (5)	-	2 (3)	7 (4)	11 (5)	3+2 (5)	5+1 (4)	4+1 (4)	-	-
6	6/4	Reading	A	ELA	L36-54	6+1 (4)	-	3+1 (4)	7 (5)	12 (5)	3+2 (4)	2 (4)	3 (4)	-	-
7	9/4	Coventry	A	ELA	L28-65	-	-	3 (3)	13 (6)	R/R	3+1 (6)	6+2 (7)	-	-	3 (8)
8	11/4	Poole	A	ELA	L35-57	12 (6)	-	R/R	3 (5)	-	6+1 (5)	1+1 (3)	4 (5)	-	9 (6)
9	12/4	Ipswich	A	KO	L38-52	11 (6)	-	-	3+1 (5)	R/R	10+1 (6)	0 (3)	2 (4)	-	12 (6)
10	13/4	Ipswich	H	KO	D45-45	15 (6)	-	R/R	6 (5)	-	7+2 (6)	3+1 (4)	2+1 (3)	-	12 (6)
11	17/4	Peterborough	A	ELA	L30-61	4 (4)	-	R/R	6+2 (6)	9 (5)	1+1 (4)	7+1 (7)	3+1 (4)	-	-
12	20/4	Poole	A	ELA	L34-58	9 (6)	-	R/R	4+1 (5)	6+2 (6)	7 (5)	4 (4)	4+1 (4)	-	-
13	27/4	Lakeside	A	ELA	L42-51	8+1 (5)	-	-	5+1 (4)	6 (4)	3 (4)	3+1 (2)	2+2 (6)	-	15 (5)
14	4/5	Eastbourne	H	ELA	W59-34	10+1 (5)	-	-	7+1 (4)	11+2 (5)	8+3 (4)	6+2 (4)	-	7 (4)	10+1 (4)
15	7/5	Lakeside	H	ELA	L39-53	4+1 (4)	-	-	5+2 (4)	12 (5)	1+1 (4)	0 (2)	-	8+2 (6)	9 (5)
16	14/5	Coventry	A	ELB	L36-57	16 (6)	-	R/R	5 (5)	3 (5)	5+1 (6)	3+2 (4)	-	4 (4)	-
17	17/5	Ipswich	A	ELA	L40-53	6 (4)	-	-	6 (5)	-	5+1 (4)	-	-	3+1 (6)	20 (12)
18	18/5	Swindon	H	ELA	L31-59	R/R	-	-	9+1 (6)	4 (3)	5 (5)	-	-	6+1 (6)	7+1 (10)
19	21/5	Wolverhampton	A	ELA	L32-60	0 (4)	-	-	8+2 (6)	R/R	4+1 (5)	-	-	6+2 (6)	14 (9)
20	25/5	Belle Vue	H	ELB	W49-41	R/R	-	-	9 (6)	7 (5)	4 (5)	-	-	13+1 (6)	16+4 (8)
21	26/5	Eastbourne	A	ELA	L31-43*	R/R	-	-	7+2 (4)	10 (5)	2+1 (4)	-	-	-	12+2 (12)
22	28/5	Reading	H	ELB	L42-48	-	-	-	9+2 (5)	11+1 (5)	6+1 (4)	4 (5)	-	6 (4)	6+1 (7)

NOTE: The away fixture at Eastbourne on 26 May was abandoned after heat twelve, with the result permitted to stand.

Details of other riders (all guests unless **highlighted**): Match No. 3: Niels-Kristian Iversen 11+2 (5); Match No. 7: **Henrik Moller** 2 (4); Chris Schramm 1 (4); Match No. 8: Rory Schlein 9 (6); Match No. 9: Rory Schlein 12 (6); Match No. 10: Niels-Kristian Iversen 12 (6); Match No. 13: Chris Louis 15 (5); Match No. 14: Niels-Kristian Iversen 10+1 (4); Match No. 15: Joe Screen 9 (5); Match No. 17: David Howe 15 (5); Shaun Tacey 3 (4); Chris Schramm 2 (3); Match No. 18: Chris Louis 6+1 (5); Mark Thompson 1 (5); Match No. 19: Daniel Nermark 10 (5); **Ricky Kling** 4 (4); Match No. 20: Niels-Kristian Iversen 11+1 (4); **Ricky Kling** 5+3 (4); Match No. 21: **Ricky Kling** 8+1 (6); Tom P. Madsen 2+1 (3); Shaun Tacey 2 (3); Match No. 22: Chris Holder 6+1 (4); **Ricky Kling** 0 (3).

Details of tactical rides and tactical substitute rides: Match No. 1: Protasiewicz 6 points (TR); Match No. 4: Jensen 4 points (TR); Match No. 6: Johnston 0 points (TR); Match No. 7: Johnston 6 points (TR); Match No. 8: Jensen 6 points (TR); Match No. 9: Schlein 1 point (TR; not doubled); Match No. 11: Protasiewicz 4 points (TR); Match No. 12: Eriksson 4 points (TR); Match No. 13: Louis 6 points (TR); Match No. 15: Protasiewicz 4 points (TR); Match No. 16: Jensen 6 points (TR); Match No. 17: Howe 6 points (TR); Match No. 18: Louis 1 point (TR; not doubled); Match No. 19: Nermark 4 points (TR); Match No. 21: Protasiewicz 4 points (TR).

Piotr Protasiewicz was Oxford's leading rider, prior to their premature closure.

(Photo: Les Aubrey)

REGRETTABLY, it wasn't long before storm clouds were brewing for the Cheetahs in 2007, due in the main to a series of poor on-track performances. Things reached a head on 30 May, when Reading announced that their Elite League match against the Cheetahs, which was scheduled two days later, had been cancelled at the request of the Oxford management. Within twenty-four hours, Cheetahs' co-promoter Colin Horton issued a statement, which signified the closure of the club with immediate effect.

Horton described the decision as the hardest he has ever had to make in his life, but insisted it was impossible for the struggling club to continue. He had already lost thousands of pounds since purchasing the club in 2006 and could no longer bankroll it from his own pocket. He said: 'It is with dismay that I have been forced to make the decision to pull the plug on Oxford Speedway. I have thought long and hard about this and it really is the toughest thing I have ever had to do. If I could see even the smallest glimmer of light at the end of the tunnel I would have carried on, but I can't. The club is losing several thousand pounds each and every week and that cannot continue. It has got to the stage where the club is no longer a viable business. I am not here to make money for one minute, but I do not have an endless supply of cash to keep the club going and I have to put my family first.'

Low attendances and a general lack of interest in the area had greatly hampered Horton's ambitions to turn the fortunes of Oxford Speedway around. The promoter added: 'Our crowds have been in the region of 400-500 for home meetings and we value greatly the support of every single fan to have come through the door this season. But the harsh reality is that we need attendances of double those figures to even stand a chance of breaking even and I just don't envisage that happening here.'

AVERAGES

[19 Elite League, 2 Knock-Out Cup = 21 fixtures]

• Denotes ever-present.

Rider	Mts	Rds	Pts	Bon	Tot	Avge	Max
Piotr Protasiewicz	15	72	121	5	126	7.00	-
Jesper B. Jensen	15	75	120	5	125	6.67	-
Steve Johnston •	21	103	134	15	149	5.79	-
Lubos Tomicek	8	42	53	7	60	5.71	-
Freddie Eriksson •	21	100	103	23	126	5.04	-
Andy Smith	10	42	34	8	42	4.00	-
Eric Andersson	16	64	50	12	62	3.88	-
Ales Dryml	6	22	19	2	21	3.82	-

Also rode (in alphabetical order):

Ricky Kling	4	17	17	4	21	4.94	-
Adrian Miedzinski	1	3	2	1	3	4.00	-
Henrik Moller	1	4	2	0	2	2.00	-

Guests	18	82	129	7	136	6.63	1 paid

(Chris Holder [1]; David Howe [1]; Niels-Kristian Iversen [4]; Chris Louis [2]; Tom P. Madsen [1]; Daniel Nermark [1]; Rory Schlein [2]; Chris Schramm [2]; Joe Screen [1]; Shaun Tacey [2]; Mark Thompson [1])

Due to the premature closure of the club, only the Knock-Out Cup matches counted on the career records of the team members. These were as follows:

Rider	Mts	Rds	Pts	Bon	Tot	Avge	Max
Jesper B. Jensen	2	12	26	0	26	8.67	-
Freddie Eriksson	2	12	17	3	20	6.67	-
Steve Johnston	2	10	9	1	10	4.00	-
Andy Smith	2	7	4	1	5	2.86	-
Eric Andersson	2	7	3	1	4	2.29	-

For the sake of completeness, the record for guests in the two KOC matches was as follows:

Guests	2	12	24	0	24	8.00	-

(Niels-Kristian Iversen [1]; Rory Schlein [1])

OTHER MEETINGS

18 March: **Under-21 Test**
Great Britain 55: Edward Kennett 14+1 (5); Daniel King 12+1 (5); Ben Wilson 8 (4); Lewis Bridger 7+2 (4); William Lawson 5+1 (4); Josh Auty 5+1 (4); Ben Barker 4+1 (4); Denmark 35: Klaus Jakobsen 10+1 (6); Morten Risager 8 (5); Claus Vissing 6 (4); Casper Wortmann 5+1 (5); Jonas Raun 4 (4); Peter Juul 1 (3); Kenneth Hansen 1 (3). Risager's total includes 0 points from a TR.

25 March: **Jesper B. Jensen Testimonial** (at Peterborough)
Peterborough 42, Oxford 35: Bjarne Pedersen 11 (5); Jesper B. Jensen 9 (5); Ryan Sullivan 8 (5); Steve Johnston 4+1 (5); Eric Andersson 2+2 (5); Ulrich Ostergaard 1 (5), Wolverhampton 31.

The effervescent **Steve Johnston** took over the Oxford captaincy from Jesper B. Jensen, before relocating to Coventry after the Cowley club's closedown.

(Photo: Les Aubrey)

PETERBOROUGH PANTHERS

ADDRESS:	East of England Showground, Alwalton, Peterborough, Cambridgeshire, PE2 0XE.
TELEPHONE:	07834 031895.
CLUB HOTLINE:	09068 664681 (Premium rate applies).
WEBSITE:	www.peterboroughspeedway.net
PROMOTERS:	Colin Horton & Mick Bratley.
MAIN TEAM SPONSOR:	MRI Overseas Property.
YEARS OF OPERATION:	1970-1974 British League Division Two; 1975-1990 National League; 1991-1994 British League Division Two; 1995 Premier League; 1996 Premier League and Conference League; 1997 Elite League and Amateur League; 1998 Premier League; 1999 Elite League; 2000-2003 Elite League and Conference League; 2004-2007 Elite League.
FIRST MEETING:	12 June 1970.
TRACK LENGTH:	336 metres.
TRACK RECORD:	59.1 seconds - Hans N. Andersen (06/04/07).

CLUB HONOURS

FOUR-TEAM CHAMPIONS: 1977, 1978, 1988, 1989, 1992, 1997, 1998.

LEAGUE CHAMPIONS: 1992, 1998, 1999, 2006.

NOTE: The Amateur League team won their League Championship in 1997; The Conference League side won their League Championship in 2002.

KNOCK-OUT CUP WINNERS: 1992, 1999, 2001.

PREMIERSHIP WINNERS: 1993.

PAIRS CHAMPIONS: 1998.

CRAVEN SHIELD WINNERS: 1999.

ELITE SHIELD WINNERS: 2007.

Hans N. Andersen was the undisputed No. 1 of the Peterborough side for a second successive season. The Dane was, of course, a heavy hitter in the Elite League and also on the world stage, where he occupied fifth position in the final Grand Prix standings.

(Photo: Les Aubrey)

PETERBOROUGH 2007

* Denotes aggregate/bonus-point victory

NO.	DATE	OPPONENTS	VENUE	COMPETITION	RESULT	NIELS-KRISTIAN IVERSEN	DANIEL KING	HANS N. ANDERSEN	LUKAS DRYML	KENNETH BJERRE	PIOTR SWIDERSKI	RICHARD HALL	ULRICH OSTERGAARD	CHRISTIAN HEFENBROCK	OTHER RIDERS
1	15/3	Coventry	H	ES	W53-38	9+1 (4)	3 (4)	12 (4)	2+1 (4)	12 (5)	11+1 (5)	4+1 (4)	-	-	-
2	16/3	Coventry	A	ES	L41-49*	12 (5)	1 (4)	10+1 (5)	3+1 (4)	5 (4)	4+1 (4)	6+1 (4)	-	-	-
3	19/3	Reading	A	ELA	L37-56	5+1 (4)	3 (4)	17 (5)	1 (3)	4 (4)	5+1 (5)	2 (5)	-	-	-
4	20/3	Reading	H	ELA	W52-40	10 (5)	5+2 (4)	13+2 (5)	8 (4)	5 (4)	4 (3)	7+2 (5)	-	-	-
5	23/3	Oxford	H	ELA	W46-43	3 (4)	2 (3)	14 (5)	4+3 (4)	9+1 (5)	11 (6)	3 (3)	-	-	-
6	6/4	Coventry	A	ELA	L40-50	6+1 (4)	4 (4)	14 (5)	4+1 (4)	8+1 (5)	3+1 (4)	1+1 (4)	-	-	-
7	6/4	Swindon	H	ELA	W58-35	6+2 (4)	8+2 (4)	13+2 (5)	9+1 (4)	9 (5)	6 (3)	7+1 (5)	-	-	-
8	12/4	Eastbourne	H	ELA	W49-44	13 (5)	0 (3)	9+1 (4)	5+1 (4)	9+3 (5)	7+1 (5)	6 (4)	-	-	-
9	17/4	Oxford	H	ELA	W61-30*	14+1 (5)	5+2 (4)	8+1 (4)	4 (4)	14+1 (5)	5+1 (4)	11+1 (4)	-	-	-
10	19/4	Lakeside	H	ELA	W65-25	12+1 (5)	9+1 (4)	11+2 (5)	11+1 (4)	11+1 (4)	6+2 (4)	5+2 (4)	-	-	-
11	20/4	Lakeside	A	ELA	L37-56*	6 (4)	0 (6)	15+1 (5)	R/R	10 (5)	3 (4)	3 (6)	-	-	-
12	23/4	Wolverhampton	A	ELA	L38-55	10 (5)	1 (4)	10 (5)	1 (4)	10 (5)	2+2 (3)	4 (4)	-	-	-
13	30/4	Swindon	A	ELA	L37-52*	6+1 (4)	1 (4)	13 (5)	3 (4)	8 (5)	3 (4)	3+1 (4)	-	-	-
14	2/5	Poole	A	ELA	L40-53	6 (4)	4+1 (4)	11 (5)	3+1 (4)	8 (5)	4 (4)	4+1 (4)	-	-	-
15	10/5	Ipswich	H	ELA	W46-28	10 (4)	4+2 (3)	6 (3)	5+1 (4)	8 (3)	5+1 (3)	8+1 (4)	-	-	-
16	21/5	Belle Vue	A	ELA	W52-39	10+1 (5)	6 (4)	15 (5)	6+1 (4)	7+2 (4)	4+1 (4)	4 (4)	-	-	-
17	24/5	Belle Vue	H	ELA	W62-31*	14+1 (5)	7 (4)	13+2 (5)	8+2 (4)	7+2 (4)	7+2 (4)	6 (4)	-	-	-
18	31/5	Wolverhampton	H	ELA	W53-40	11+1 (5)	4+2 (3)	11 (5)	5+1 (4)	6+1 (4)	8+1 (4)	8+1 (5)	-	-	-
19	14/6	Swindon	A	KO	L27-63	6+1 (5)	1 (4)	-	4 (4)	3 (4)	8+1 (5)	3 (4)	2+1 (4)	-	-
20	16/6	Eastbourne	A	ELA	W50-44*	10+1 (5)	7+1 (4)	-	5 (4)	9+1 (5)	7+1 (4)	4+1 (4)	-	-	8+2 (4)
21	21/6	Coventry	H	ELA	W48-42	4 (4)	7 (5)	11+1 (5)	7+2 (4)	11 (5)	6 (4)	2+1 (3)	-	-	-
22	28/6	Eastbourne	H	ELB	W51-42	8+1 (4)	6 (4)	14 (5)	7+2 (4)	10+1 (5)	5+1 (4)	1 (4)	-	-	-
23	9/7	Ipswich	H	ELB	W62-30	10+1 (5)	10 (4)	13+1 (5)	9+2 (4)	8+1 (4)	6+2 (4)	6+3 (4)	-	-	-
24	11/7	Poole	A	ELB	L44-46	6 (4)	7+1 (5)	12 (5)	4+2 (4)	8 (5)	6+1 (4)	1 (3)	-	-	-
25	12/7	Swindon	H	ELB	W51-42	11 (5)	6+2 (4)	13+1 (5)	6 (4)	5 (4)	4+2 (4)	-	6+2 (4)	-	-
26	13/7	Coventry	A	ELB	L30-45	R/R	3 (4)	-	5 (5)	-	7+1 (4)	-	2+1 (4)	-	13 (7)
27	23/7	Wolverhampton	A	ELB	W54-38	9+1 (5)	9 (4)	14+1 (5)	7 (4)	8+1 (4)	4+1 (4)	3+1 (4)	-	-	-
28	4/8	Ipswich	A	ELA	W46-43*	5 (4)	13+1 (7)	10+1 (5)	R/R	11+2 (6)	6 (5)	1+1 (3)	-	-	-
29	6/8	Swindon	A	ELB	L42-51	9 (5)	3 (4)	16+1 (5)	3+1 (4)	6 (4)	1 (4)	4 (4)	-	-	-
30	9/8	Lakeside	H	ELA	W54-36	4+1 (4)	10+1 (4)	7 (4)	12+1 (5)	12+2 (5)	6+1 (4)	3+1 (4)	-	-	-
31	13/8	Poole	H	ELA	W46-43	5 (4)	10+1 (5)	10+1 (5)	6+2 (4)	10+1 (5)	4+2 (4)	1 (3)	-	-	-
32	20/8	Belle Vue	A	ELB	W52-40	R/R	6+1 (5)	18 (6)	9+1 (5)	16+2 (6)	3 (4)	0 (4)	-	-	-
33	31/8	Lakeside	A	ELB	D45-45*	R/R	7+1 (7)	15 (5)	R/R	12+1 (6)	7 (5)	-	-	4+2 (6)	-
34	1/9	Eastbourne	H	ELB	W51-42*	R/R	4+1 (4)	15 (5)	-	17+1 (6)	10 (7)	-	-	2+1 (4)	3+1 (4)
35	3/9	Poole	H	ELB	W54-38*	R/R	4+1 (4)	18 (6)	7+3 (5)	12+2 (6)	9+1 (5)	-	-	4+1 (4)	-
36	5/9	Reading	A	ELB	L40-50	R/R	6 (5)	15 (6)	7+2 (5)	9 (6)	-	-	-	3 (4)	0 (3)
37	6/9	Wolverhampton	H	ELB	W66-24*	R/R	10+1 (5)	11+1 (4)	13+3 (6)	14+1 (5)	11+1 (5)	-	-	7+3 (5)	-
38	12/9	Coventry	H	ELB	W46-44	R/R	8+1 (5)	15 (6)	-	12+1 (6)	3+1 (5)	-	-	3 (3)	5+1 (5)
39	13/9	Ipswich	A	ELB	W52-38*	R/R	11+1 (6)	11+1 (5)	-	10+2 (5)	4 (4)	-	-	1 (4)	15+2 (6)
40	17/9	Swindon	A	POs	L42-50	3 (4)	9+1 (5)	15 (5)	2 (4)	5 (4)	5+1 (4)	-	3+2 (4)	-	-
41	20/9	Reading	H	ELB	W60-31*	11 (4)	13+2 (6)	-	R/R	15 (5)	8+2 (5)	-	-	-	13+2 (10)
42	8/10	Reading/L'side	R	CSs	37-31-40	9 (4)	6+3 (4)	-	-	8 (4)	5+4 (4)	-	5+1 (4)	-	4+1 (4)
43	12/10	Lakeside/Poole	L	CSs	43-36-29	8 (4)	6 (4)	-	-	12 (4)	5+2 (4)	-	8+1 (4)	-	4+1 (4)
44	26/10	Belle Vue	H	ELB	W47-43*	-	10 (4)	R/R	8+1 (5)	8+1 (5)	8+2 (6)	-	5+1 (5)	8 (5)	-

ADDITIONAL KEY: ES = Elite Shield.

NOTE: (1) The home ELA fixture versus Ipswich on 10 May was abandoned after heat twelve, with the result permitted to stand; (2) The away ELB fixture at Coventry on 13 July was abandoned after heat twelve, with the result permitted to stand; (3) Following the away ELB match at Swindon on 6 August, Hans N. Andersen lost an aggregate point run-off to Leigh Adams; (4) The 'home' ELB fixture versus Belle Vue on 26 October was actually staged at King's Lynn.

Details of other riders (all guests unless **highlighted**): Match No. 20: Rory Schlein 8+2 (4); Match No. 26: Simon Stead 13 (4); Shaun Tacey 0 (3); Match No. 34: Shaun Tacey 3+1 (4); Match No. 36: Shaun Tacey 0 (3); Match No. 38: Lee Complin 5+1 (5); Match No. 39: Chris Holder 15+2 (6); Match No. 41: Claus Vissing 7+1 (5); Lee Complin 6+1 (5); Match No. 42: Adam Roynon 4+1 (4); Match No. 43: Claus Vissing 4+1 (4).

Details of tactical rides and tactical substitute rides: Match No. 3: Andersen 6 points (TR); Match No. 11: Andersen 6 points (TR); Match No. 12: Andersen 6 points (TR); Iversen 1 point (TS; not doubled); Match No. 13: Swiderski 1 point (TR; not doubled); Match No. 14: Andersen 6 points (TR); Match No. 19: Iversen 0 points (TR); Match No. 26: Stead 6 points (TR); Match No. 29: Andersen 6 points (TR); Match No. 40: Andersen 4 points (TR).

AVERAGES

[36 Elite League; 1 Play-Offs; 1 Knock-Out Cup; 2 Craven Shield; 2 Elite Shield = 42 fixtures]

• Denotes ever-present.

Rider	Mts	Rds	Pts	Bon	Tot	Avge	Max
Hans N. Andersen	35	173	429	20	449	10.38	6 full; 5 paid
Kenneth Bjerre	40	189	369	30	399	8.44	2 full; 4 paid
Niels-Kristian Iversen	33	144	264	16	280	7.78	1 paid
Lukas Dryml	33	139	195	34	229	6.59	1 paid
Piotr Swiderski •	42	181	239	41	280	6.19	-
Daniel King •	42	185	252	30	282	6.10	-
Ulrich Ostergaard	7	29	31	9	40	5.52	-
Christian Hefenbrock	8	35	32	7	39	4.46	-
Richard Hall	28	114	107	20	127	4.46	-
Guests	11	47	62	10	72	6.13	-

(Lee Complin [2]; Chris Holder [1]; Adam Roynon [1]; Rory Schlein [1]; Simon Stead [1]; Shaun Tacey [3]; Claus Vissing [2])

OTHER MEETINGS

25 March: **Jesper B. Jensen** Testimonial

Peterborough 42: Hans N. Andersen 11 (5); Kenneth Bjerre 9+1 (5); Niels-Kristian Iversen 7+2 (5); Richard Hall 6+2 (5); Adam Skornicki 5+3 (5); Daniel King 4 (5), Oxford 35, Wolverhampton 31.

21 October: **Big Bang 2 Fours** (at Mildenhall)

Peterborough 38: Kenneth Bjerre 12 (4); Daniel King 11 (4); Claus Vissing 8 (4); Niels-Kristian Iversen 7 (4), East Anglian Select 27, Boston 22, Mildenhall 21.

Pole **Piotr Swiderski** followed on from where he left off in 2006, being an often-impressive performer for the defending Elite League Champions.

(Photo: Karen Chappell)

POOLE PIRATES

ADDRESS:	Poole Stadium, Wimborne Road, Poole, Dorset, BH15 2BP.
TELEPHONE:	01202 681145.
CLUB HOTLINE:	09068 664683 (Premium rate applies).
WEBSITE:	www.poolespeedway.net
PROMOTERS:	Matt Ford & Mike Golding.
MAIN TEAM SPONSOR:	Castle Cover.
YEARS OF OPERATION:	1948-1951 National League Division Three; 1952-1955 National League Division Two; 1956 National League Division One; 1957 Open; 1958-1959 National League; 1960-1963 Provincial League; 1964 Provincial League and Metropolitan League; 1965-1967 British League; 1968-1974 British League Division One; 1975-1984 British League; 1985-1990 National League; 1991-1994 British League Division One; 1995-1996 Premier League; 1997-2007 Elite League.
FIRST MEETING:	26 April 1948.
TRACK LENGTH:	299.1 metres.
TRACK RECORD:	56.91 seconds - Antonio Lindback (14/06/06).

CLUB HONOURS

LEAGUE CHAMPIONS: 1951, 1952, 1955, 1961, 1962, 1969, 1989, 1990, 1994, 2003, 2004.

NATIONAL TROPHY (DIVISION TWO) WINNERS: 1952, 1955.

KNOCK-OUT CUP WINNERS: 1990, 2003, 2004.

FOUR-TEAM CHAMPIONS: 1994.

CRAVEN SHIELD WINNERS: 2001, 2002, 2006.

BRITISH LEAGUE CUP WINNERS: 2003.

PAIRS CHAMPIONS: 2007.

Poole's big winter move saw the return of **Jason Crump** to Wimborne Road and the Australian was again a very tough man to beat in the Elite League, stringing together tall scores in the trademark style that has been so familiar to British fans for well over a decade.

(Photo: Les Aubrey)

POOLE 2007

* Denotes aggregate/bonus-point victory

NO.	DATE	OPPONENTS	VENUE	COMPETITION	RESULT	JASON CRUMP	EDWARD KENNETT	BJARNE PEDERSEN	SERGEY DARKIN	CRAIG BOYCE	JASON DOYLE	TROY BATCHELOR	CRAIG WATSON	PIOTR SWIST	OTHER RIDERS
1	17/3	Eastbourne	A	Chal	L43-46	12 (5)	6+2 (4)	11 (5)	-	6 (4)	2 (4)	6 (5)	-	-	0 (3)
2	21/3	Eastbourne	H	Chal	W49-41*	14+1 (5)	7+1 (4)	15 (5)	0 (4)	7 (4)	4 (4)	2 (4)	-	-	-
3	26/3	Belle Vue	A	ELA	L38-52	15 (5)	4 (4)	11+1 (5)	0 (3)	2 (4)	1+1 (4)	5+1 (5)	-	-	-
4	28/3	Ipswich	H	ELA	W58-34	15 (5)	8+2 (4)	14+1 (5)	0 (3)	5+2 (4)	8 (4)	8+3 (5)	-	-	-
5	30/3	Coventry	A	ELA	L44-46	11 (5)	4 (4)	11+1 (5)	-	7 (4)	7 (5)	4+1 (4)	0 (3)	-	-
6	5/4	Swindon	A	ELA	L44-46	12 (5)	3+2 (4)	13+1 (5)	-	5 (4)	5+1 (5)	5+1 (4)	1 (3)	-	-
7	6/4	Eastbourne	H	ELA	W52-36	13+1 (5)	5+1 (4)	15 (5)	-	7+3 (4)	0 (1)	9+1 (7)	3 (4)	-	-
8	6/4	Eastbourne	H	ELA	L41-49*	12 (5)	6+2 (4)	12+1 (5)	-	7+1 (4)	-	1 (5)	2 (4)	-	1+1 (3)
9	11/4	Oxford	H	ELA	W57-35	11+1 (4)	11+4 (5)	15 (5)	-	9 (4)	-	10+1 (6)	1 (3)	-	0 (3)
10	16/4	Lakeside	A	ELA	L42-48	14 (5)	2+1 (4)	11 (5)	-	6 (4)	-	8+1 (6)	0 (4)	1 (3)	-
11	18/4	Reading	H	ELA	W52-41	13+1 (5)	4+1 (4)	13+1 (5)	-	10+1 (4)	-	6+1 (4)	2 (3)	4+1 (5)	-
12	19/4	Ipswich	A	ELA	W58-35*	14 (5)	12+1 (5)	10+2 (4)	-	8+1 (4)	-	3+1 (4)	2+1 (4)	9+1 (4)	-
13	20/4	Oxford	A	ELA	W58-34*	15 (5)	9+1 (4)	13+2 (5)	-	7 (4)	-	2+1 (4)	3+1 (4)	9+1 (4)	-
14	23/4	Coventry	H	ELA	W52-40*	14+1 (5)	7+1 (4)	13 (5)	-	4 (4)	-	5 (4)	0 (3)	9 (5)	-
15	2/5	Peterborough	A	ELA	W53-40	14 (5)	8+1 (4)	12+1 (5)	-	5+1 (4)	-	8+2 (4)	1+1 (3)	5 (5)	-
16	4/5	Reading	A	ELA	W51-42*	10+1 (4)	10+1 (5)	13+2 (5)	-	8 (4)	-	7 (4)	1 (4)	2+1 (4)	-
17	9/5	Wolverhampton	H	ELA	W63-27	14+1 (5)	13+2 (5)	11+1 (4)	-	8 (4)	-	8+2 (4)	3+1 (4)	6+1 (4)	-
18	16/5	Lakeside	H	ELA	W56-37*	14 (5)	9+1 (4)	8+2 (4)	-	10 (5)	-	6+1 (4)	3+1 (4)	6+1 (4)	-
19	18/5	Lakeside	A	ELB	W47-45	15 (5)	3+1 (4)	13+1 (5)	-	6+1 (4)	-	7 (6)	2+2 (3)	1 (3)	-
20	30/5	Lakeside	H	ELB	W57-36*	-	10 (5)	10+3 (5)	-	7 (4)	4+2 (3)	9 (5)	-	8+1 (4)	9+3 (4)
21	6/6	Ipswich	H	ELB	W63-30	15 (5)	6+2 (4)	9+2 (4)	-	9+2 (4)	6 (4)	11+2 (5)	-	7+1 (4)	-
22	11/6	Swindon	H	ELA	D45-45	14 (5)	7+2 (4)	10+1 (5)	-	4+1 (4)	2 (6)	3 (2)	-	5+2 (4)	-
23	18/6	Belle Vue	A	ELB	W50-43	15 (5)	7 (4)	11+3 (5)	-	7 (4)	3 (4)	-	-	3 (4)	4+1 (4)
24	20/6	Eastbourne	H	ELB	W48-46	8+1 (5)	4+1 (4)	13 (5)	-	8+2 (4)	9+1 (5)	-	-	6 (4)	0 (3)
25	21/6	Swindon	A	ELB	L46-47	14+1 (5)	7 (4)	6+3 (5)	-	6 (4)	5 (5)	-	-	2+1 (3)	6 (4)
26	9/7	Coventry	A	KO	L40-53	18 (5)	3+1 (4)	9 (5)	-	5 (4)	1 (4)	-	-	0 (3)	4 (5)
27	11/7	Peterborough	H	ELB	W46-44	9 (5)	4 (4)	14 (5)	-	7 (4)	1+1 (3)	-	-	5+1 (4)	6 (5)
28	30/7	Coventry	H	ELB	L42-49	-	4 (4)	10 (5)	-	2 (4)	2 (2)	2+1 (4)	-	6+1 (5)	16 (6)
29	1/8	Belle Vue	H	ELA	W50-43	-	3+2 (4)	14 (5)	-	7+1 (4)	7+2 (5)	7 (4)	-	1 (3)	11+2 (5)
30	6/8	Wolverhampton	A	ELA	L43-49*	9+1 (5)	7+1 (4)	10 (5)	-	5 (4)	1 (3)	5 (4)	-	-	6+1 (5)
31	8/8	Wolverhampton	H	ELB	W56-36	14+1 (5)	8+2 (4)	11+2 (5)	-	1 (4)	12+1 (5)	7+1 (4)	-	3 (3)	-
32	13/8	Peterborough	A	ELA	L43-46*	9+1 (5)	1 (4)	13 (5)	-	4+1 (4)	9+1 (5)	5+1 (4)	-	2+2 (3)	-
33	15/8	Reading	H	ELB	W48-24	11+1 (4)	5+1 (3)	4+2 (3)	-	5+1 (3)	10+1 (4)	12 (4)	-	1+1 (3)	-
34	17/8	Reading	A	ELB	W51-39*	12+2 (5)	9+2 (4)	15 (5)	-	4 (4)	3 (4)	6 (4)	-	2+1 (4)	-
35	22/8	Belle Vue	H	ELB	W60-32*	15 (5)	9 (4)	8+3 (4)	-	5+2 (4)	8+1 (4)	13+1 (5)	-	-	2+1 (4)
36	27/8	Wolverhampton	A	ELB	L45-47*	16+1 (5)	6 (4)	10 (5)	-	5+2 (4)	3 (5)	5+1 (4)	-	-	0 (3)
37	29/8	Swindon	H	ELB	W50-43*	14+1 (5)	8 (4)	13+1 (5)	-	4 (4)	4 (5)	6 (4)	-	-	1 (3)
38	3/9	Peterborough	A	ELB	L38-54	6 (2)	1 (4)	6+1 (4)	-	9+1 (5)	6 (5)	6+1 (5)	-	-	4+1 (5)
39	5/9	Coventry	H	ELB	L43-49	13 (5)	6 (4)	8 (5)	-	6 (4)	4+2 (5)	4+1 (4)	-	-	2+1 (5)
40	12/9	L-side/Reading	H	CSs	52-29-27	12 (4)	10 (4)	11+1 (4)	-	6+4 (4)	6+2 (4)	7+2 (4)	-	-	-
41	17/9	Coventry	A	POs	L38-55	11 (5)	2 (4)	18 (5)	-	2 (4)	5 (5)	0 (4)	-	-	0 (3)
42	19/9	Coventry	H	KO	L31-44	15 (4)	2 (3)	8 (3)	-	1 (3)	2 (3)	3 (4)	-	-	0 (4)
43	29/9	Eastbourne	A	ELB	L37-53	8 (4)	6+1 (5)	11 (5)	-	-	4+2 (4)	4+1 (4)	-	-	4+2 (8)
44	3/10	Vicrown Select	H	Chal	W52-40	-	10+1 (5)	-	-	-	10+1 (5)	13+1 (5)	-	-	19+2 (15)
45	4/10	Ipswich	A	ELB	W49-41*	14 (5)	3 (4)	7+3 (4)	-	-	8 (5)	6+1 (4)	-	-	11 (8)
46	12/10	Lakeside/P'boro'	L	CSs	29-36-43	-	10+1 (4)	-	-	-	-	5+1 (4)	-	-	14+2 (16)
47	17/10	Cov'try/Swindon	H	CSf	35-40-33	6 (4)	6 (4)	12 (4)	-	-	-	2 (3)	-	-	9+2 (9)
48	18/10	Swindon/Cov'try	S	CSf	28-35-45	10 (4)	4 (4)	8 (4)	-	-	-	5+1 (4)	-	-	1+1 (8)
49	19/10	Cov'try/Swindon	C	CSf	23-35-50	8 (4)	3 (4)	9 (4)	-	-	-	3 (4)	-	-	0 (8)

NOTE: (1) The home ELB fixture versus Reading on 15 August was abandoned after heat twelve, with the result permitted to stand; (2) The home Knock-Out Cup tie against Coventry on 19 September was abandoned after heat twelve, with the result permitted to stand.

Details of other riders (all guests unless **highlighted**): Match No. 1: Brent Werner 0 (3); Match No. 8: Daniel Giffard 1+1 (3); Match No. 9: **Ritchie Hawkins** 0 (3); Match No. 20: Leigh Adams 9+3 (4); Match No. 23: **Steve Boxall** 4+1 (4); Match No. 24: **Steve Boxall** 0 (3); Match No. 25: **Steve Boxall** 6 (4); Match No. 26: **Steve Boxall** 4 (5); Match No. 27: **Steve Boxall** 6 (5); Match No. 28: Hans N. Andersen 16 (6); Match No. 29: Krzysztof Kasprzak 11+2 (5); Match No. 30: **Steve Boxall** 6+1 (5); Match No. 35: **Steve Boxall** 2+1 (4); Match No. 36: **Ritchie Hawkins** 0 (3); Match No. 37: **Steve Boxall** 1 (3); Match No. 38: **Steve Boxall** 4+1 (5); Match No. 39: **Steve Boxall** 2+1 (3); Match No. 41: **Steve Boxall** 0 (3); Match No. 42: **Tai Woffinden** 0 (4); Match No. 43: Jordan Frampton 3+1 (4); **Adrian Gomolski** 1+1 (4); Match No. 44: **Adrian Gomolski** 10+2 (5); Craig Boyce 5 (4); Chris Holder R/R; Match No. 45: **Tai Woffinden** 6 (4); **Adrian Gomolski** 5 (4); Match No. 46: Simon Stead 6 (4); **Steve Boxall** 4+1 (4); **Adrian Gomolski** 3 (4); Tomas Suchanek 1+1 (4); Match No. 48: **Adrian Gomolski** 6+1 (5); **Tai Woffinden** 3+1 (4); Match No. 48: **Adrian Gomolski** 1+1 (5); **Ritchie Hawkins** 0 (3); Match No. 49: **Adrian Gomolski** 0 (4); **Steve Boxall** 0 (4).

Details of tactical rides and tactical substitute rides: Match No. 3: Pedersen 1 point (TR; not doubled); Match No. 19: Pedersen 4 points (TR); Match No. 25: Crump 6 points (TR); Match No. 26: Crump 6 points (TR); Match No. 28: Andersen 2 points (TS); Match No. 30: Pedersen 4 points (TR); Match No. 36: Crump 6 points (TR); Match No. 38: Pedersen 4 points (TR); Match No. 39: Boyce 6 points (TR); Match No. 41: Pedersen 6 points (TR); Match No. 42: Crump 6 points (TR).

Other details: Vicrown Developments Select scorers in Match No. 44: Adam Shields 14 (5); Daniel King 10+1 (5); Tai Woffinden 7+1 (5); Andreas Messing 4 (4); Cameron Woodward 2 (4); Casper Wortmann 2 (3); Eric Andersson 1+1 (4). Shields' total includes 4 points from a TR.

AVERAGES

[36 Elite League; 1 Play-Offs; 2 Knock-Out Cup; 5 Craven Shield = 44 fixtures]

• Denotes ever-present.

Rider	Mts	Rds	Pts	Bon	Tot	Avge	Max
Jason Crump	40	189	484	15	499	10.56	9 full; 5 paid
Bjarne Pedersen	43	200	459	40	499	9.98	4 full; 5 paid
Edward Kennett •	44	179	259	33	292	6.53	1 paid
Craig Boyce	38	152	214	27	241	6.34	-
Troy Batchelor	39	167	226	30	256	6.13	1 full
Jason Doyle	30	126	146	18	164	5.21	-
Piotr Swist	23	88	94	16	110	5.00	-
Steve Boxall	13	52	39	6	45	3.46	-
Adrian Gomolski	6	26	16	3	19	2.92	-
Craig Watson	13	46	20	6	26	2.26	-

Also rode (in alphabetical order):

Sergey Darkin	2	6	0	0	0	0.00	-
Ritchie Hawkins	2	6	0	0	0	0.00	-
Tai Woffinden	3	12	9	1	10	3.33	-
Guests	7	30	46	8	54	7.20	1 paid

(Leigh Adams [1]; Hans N. Andersen [1]; Jordan Frampton [1]; Daniel Giffard [1]; Krzysztof Kasprzak [1]; Simon Stead [1]; Tomas Suchanek [1])

NOTE: Bjarne Pedersen was ever-present throughout the 36-match Elite League programme.

OTHER MEETING

18 July: **Under-21 Challenge**

Great Britain 50: Daniel King 13+1 (5); Lewis Bridger 12 (5); Tai Woffinden 8+3 (4); Adam Roynon 6+2 (4); Ben Wilson 5+1 (4); William Lawson 3 (4); Ben Barker 3 (4). Australia 40: Troy Batchelor 10 (5); Cameron Woodward 9 (5); Jason Doyle 8 (4); Cory Gathercole 6+2 (4); Tom Hedley 4+1 (5); Jay Herne 3 (4); Robert Ksiezak 0 (3).

Edward Kennett turned in many great performances for the Pirates, particularly in the early part of the campaign, and also scooped the British Under-21 Championship for a second time.

(Photo: Ian Charles)

READING RACERS

NOTE: Reading began a second season with a Bulldogs moniker, but following a mid-season takeover, the traditional Racers nickname was restored.

ADDRESS:	Smallmead Stadium, A33 Relief Road, Smallmead, Reading, Berkshire, RG2 0JL.
TELEPHONE:	0118 9867343.
CLUB HOTLINE:	09068 664662 (Premium rate applies).
WEBSITE:	www.readingspeedway.com
PROMOTERS:	Mark Legg and Malcolm Holloway, who took over from John Postlethwaite and Jim Lynch in June.
MAIN TEAM SPONSOR:	Meridian Lifts.
YEARS OF OPERATION:	1975-1990 British League; 1991-1994 British League Division One; 1995 Premier League; 1996 Premier League and Conference League; 1997 Premier League and Amateur League; 1998-2005 Premier League; 2006-2007 Elite League.
FIRST MEETING:	28 April 1975.
TRACK LENGTH:	304 metres.
TRACK RECORD:	58.1 seconds - Per Jonsson (12/10/87).
PREVIOUS VENUE:	Reading Greyhound Stadium, Oxford Road, Tilehurst, Reading, Berkshire.
YEARS OF OPERATION:	1968-1970 British League Division Two; 1971-1973 British League Division One.

CLUB HONOURS

LEAGUE CHAMPIONS: 1973, 1980, 1990, 1992, 1997.

KNOCK-OUT CUP WINNERS: 1990, 1998.

PREMIERSHIP WINNERS: 1991, 1993.

BSPA CUP WINNERS: 1992.

FOUR-TEAM CHAMPIONS: 1993.

PAIRS CHAMPIONS: 2004.

Malcolm Holloway proudly displays the Racers breastplate following Mark Legg's takeover as club owner on 20 June.

(Photo: Les Aubrey)

READING 2007

* Denotes aggregate/bonus-point victory

NO.	DATE	OPPONENTS	VENUE	COMPETITION	RESULT	GREG HANCOCK	ZDENEK SIMOTA	MATEJ ZAGAR	JANUSZ KOLODZIEJ	TRAVIS McGOWAN	MARK LEMON	DANNY BIRD	PHIL MORRIS	JONAS DAVIDSSON	OTHER RIDERS
1	15/3	Swindon	A	M4	L37-55	12 (5)	4+1 (4)	7+2 (5)	7 (4)	1 (4)	4 (5)	2+1 (3)	-	-	-
2	16/3	Swindon	H	M4	L44-49	7+1 (5)	2+2 (4)	11+1 (5)	4+1 (4)	4 (4)	10 (4)	6+1 (4)	-	-	-
3	19/3	Peterborough	H	ELA	W56-37	12 (5)	4+2 (4)	9+1 (5)	8+3 (4)	8+2 (4)	10 (4)	5 (4)	-	-	-
4	20/3	Peterborough	A	ELA	L40-52*	12+1 (5)	0 (3)	7+1 (5)	7+2 (4)	4+1 (4)	8 (5)	2+1 (4)	-	-	-
5	22/3	Ipswich	A	ELA	W47-43	12+1 (5)	0 (1)	9+1 (5)	1 (3)	3+2 (4)	14+2 (7)	8 (5)	-	-	-
6	23/3	Wolverhampton	H	ELA	W49-41	10+2 (5)	R/R	11+1 (5)	7+2 (4)	4 (5)	12+1 (6)	5+1 (5)	-	-	-
7	31/3	Eastbourne	A	ELA	L38-55	-	1 (4)	R/R	-	7+2 (6)	7 (6)	0 (3)	-	-	23+2 (11)
8	6/4	Oxford	A	ELA	W50-40	12+2 (6)	5+1 (4)	R/R	7+2 (5)	14+2 (6)	4 (3)	8+1 (6)	-	-	-
9	6/4	Oxford	H	ELA	W54-36*	15+1 (6)	4+2 (4)	R/R	8+1 (5)	16+1 (6)	-	9+2 (6)	2+1 (3)	-	-
10	8/4	Swindon	H	ELA	L39-54	9+1 (5)	5+2 (4)	6 (4)	3 (4)	8 (5)	-	0 (2)	-	-	8+2 (5)
11	8/4	Swindon	A	ELA	L28-65	13 (5)	0 (4)	5+1 (5)	2 (3)	4 (4)	-	-	-	-	4 (9)
12	13/4	Wolverhampton	H	KO	W56-34	11+3 (5)	8+1 (4)	10 (4)	7+3 (4)	12+1 (5)	4+1 (4)	4+1 (4)	-	-	-
13	16/4	Wolverhampton	A	KO	L42-51*	15 (5)	3 (4)	9+1 (5)	3 (4)	7 (4)	5+1 (4)	0 (4)	-	-	-
14	18/4	Poole	A	ELA	L41-52	3 (2)	4+2 (4)	11 (5)	7 (4)	7 (5)	4 (4)	5+2 (6)	-	-	-
15	20/4	Ipswich	H	ELA	W60-32*	-	14+1 (5)	16+2 (6)	R/R	8+2 (5)	12 (6)	2+1 (4)	-	-	8+2 (4)
16	23/4	Lakeside	H	ELA	W55-37	12+2 (5)	10+1 (5)	12 (5)	6+2 (4)	7 (4)	1 (3)	7+2 (4)	-	-	-
17	4/5	Poole	H	ELA	L42-51	9 (5)	-	11+1 (5)	10 (5)	R/R	3+1 (4)	3+1 (3)	6+1 (7)	-	-
18	7/5	Eastbourne	H	ELA	W54-38	11+1 (5)	-	13+2 (7)	11+2 (5)	9+3 (5)	R/R	6 (4)	4+2 (4)	-	-
19	14/5	Belle Vue	A	ELA	L38-55	14 (5)	3 (5)	R/R	4 (5)	-	11 (6)	-	3 (4)	-	3+2 (5)
20	17/5	Swindon	A	ELB	L36-57	15 (5)	2 (5)	4 (5)	-	R/R	8 (5)	-	-	5+3 (5)	2+1 (5)
21	18/5	Coventry	A		D45-45	13+1 (5)	11+2 (7)	12+2 (6)	-	R/R	6 (4)	-	-	0 (4)	3+1 (4)
22	21/5	Lakeside	H	ELB	L41-49	10+3 (5)	7 (7)	12 (6)	-	R/R	4+2 (4)	-	-	7 (5)	1 (3)
23	24/5	Ipswich	A	ELB	L32-61	-	14+1 (5)	-	-	R/R	1 (3)	-	6+1 (6)	-	25+1 (21)
24	28/5	Oxford	A	ELB	W48-42	-	14+1 (5)	11+1 (6)	R/R	-	3+1 (5)	-	7 (5)	-	13+4 (9)
25	11/6	Wolverhampton	A	ELA	L39-54	19 (6)	-	R/R	-	7+1 (6)	4+1 (5)	-	-	4+1 (5)	5+1 (8)
26	20/6	Lakeside	A	ELA	L38-52*	-	14 (7)	R/R	-	-	9 (5)	-	-	4 (5)	11+1 (13)
27	9/7	Eastbourne	H	ELB	W46-44	R/R	2 (3)	11+1 (6)	6+1 (5)	11 (6)	5+1 (4)	-	-	11+2 (6)	-
28	13/7	Ipswich	H	KO	W53-40	-	5+2 (4)	9 (5)	6+2 (4)	8+1 (4)	8+2 (4)	-	-	4+2 (4)	13+1 (5)
29	30/7	Wolverhampton	A	ELB	L31-59	-	5+2 (5)	R/R	2+1 (4)	7 (6)	2 (4)	-	-	11+1 (7)	4 (4)
30	1/8	Coventry	H	ELA	L39-53	-	10+1 (6)	R/R	16 (6)	3+1 (5)	2 (5)	-	-	-	8+1 (8)
31	3/8	Lakeside	A	ELA	L39-53	-	7+1 (6)	R/R	-	5 (6)	1+1 (4)	-	-	9 (5)	17 (9)
32	6/8	Ipswich	H	ELB	W50-42	-	1+1 (4)	9 (5)	8 (4)	11 (5)	7 (4)	-	-	5+1 (4)	9+1 (4)
33	13/8	Coventry	A	ELB	L36-57	-	5 (4)	11 (5)	4 (4)	5+1 (5)	6 (4)	-	-	5+2 (5)	0 (3)
34	15/8	Poole	A	ELB	L24-48	-	4 (4)	0 (1)	-	R/R	4+2 (4)	-	-	9+2 (6)	5+1 (5)
35	16/8	Ipswich	A	KO	L44-49*	-	6 (5)	-	12 (5)	9+1 (5)	1 (4)	-	-	1 (3)	15+2 (8)
36	17/8	Poole	H	ELB	L39-51	-	-	-	10+1 (5)	6 (5)	2 (4)	-	-	14+1 (7)	7+2 (9)
37	20/8	Coventry	A	ELB	L44-49	-	4 (4)	-	11+1 (5)	11 (5)	6+2 (4)	-	-	4 (4)	1 (4)
38	24/8	Wolverhampton	H	ELB	W49-33	-	-	-	10+1 (4)	10+1 (4)	3+1 (3)	-	-	6 (3)	20+3 (12)
39	27/8	Belle Vue	H	ELA	W48-42	-	7+1 (4)	12 (5)	-	4+1 (4)	8 (4)	-	-	11+1 (6)	6+1 (7)
40	29/8	Belle Vue	H	ELB	L37-56	-	9 (6)	-	-	14 (5)	3+1 (4)	-	-	2+1 (3)	5+1 (7)
41	31/8	Swindon	H	ELB	L35-57	-	-	11+1 (5)	5 (4)	7 (5)	2+1 (5)	-	-	7+1 (7)	3 (4)
42	5/9	Peterborough	H	ELB	W50-40	-	8 (5)	-	8+1 (4)	12+1 (5)	2+1 (3)	-	-	1+1 (3)	19+2 (10)
43	12/9	Poole/Lakeside	P	CSs	27-52-29	-	1+1 (4)	-	9 (4)	5 (4)	-	-	-	3+1 (4)	9+1 (8)
44	13/9	Swindon	A	KOs	L37-55	-	9+1 (6)	-	6+1 (5)	10 (6)	R/R	-	-	-	12+3 (13)
45	19/9	Belle Vue	H	ELB	L46-47	-	3+1 (5)	-	6 (4)	R/R	9+1 (6)	-	-	13+1 (6)	15+1 (9)
46	20/9	Peterborough	A	ELB	L31-60	-	6 (6)	-	11 (5)	R/R	1 (5)	-	-	6+1 (5)	7+1 (9)
47	8/10	Lakeside/P'boro	H	CSs	31-40-37	-	7+2 (4)	-	8 (4)	-	5 (4)	-	-	7 (4)	4 (8)
48	15/10	Swindon	H	KOs	L38-54	-	11+1 (6)	-	R/R	11+1 (6)	-	-	-	7+1 (5)	9+2 (13)
49	20/10	Eastbourne	A	ELB	L35-58	-	5 (6)	-	R/R	3 (5)	-	-	-	3 (5)	24+1 (14)

ADDITIONAL KEY: M4 = Don Rogers Sports M4 Trophy.

NOTE: (1) The ELB fixture at Poole on 15 August was abandoned after heat twelve, with the result permitted to stand; (2) The ELB fixture at home to Wolverhampton on 24 August was abandoned after heat thirteen, with the result permitted to stand.

Details of other riders (all guests unless **highlighted**): Match No. 7: Adam Shields 16 (5); Chris Louis 7+2 (6); Match No. 10: Jason Bunyan 8+2 (5); Match No. 11: Jason Bunyan 3 (5); Billy Legg 1 (4); Match No. 15: Lee Richardson 8+2 (5); Match No. 19: Troy Batchelor 3+2 (5); Match No. 20: **Andy Smith** 2+1 (5); Match No. 21: **Andy Smith** 3+1 (4); Match No. 22: **Andy Smith** 1 (3); Match No. 23: Rory Schlein 14+1 (5); **Andy Smith** 10 (7); Cory Gathercole 0 (3); Scott Campos 0 (3); Match No. 24: Shane Parker 10+3 (6); **Andy Smith** 3+1 (3); Match No. 25: **Andy Smith** 4 (4); Ben Barker 1+1 (4); Match No. 26: Billy Hamill 5 (4); Kevin Doolan 4+1 (5); **Andy Smith** 2 (5); Match No. 28: Lee Richardson 13+1 (5); Match No. 29: Jason Lyons 4 (4); Match No. 30: Adam Shields 6+1 (5); **Chris Neath** 2 (3); Match No. 31: Chris Louis 15 (6); Adam Skornicki 2 (3); Match No. 32: Davey Watt 9+1 (4); Match No. 33: **Krzysztof Buczkowski** 0 (3); Match No. 34: **Krzysztof Buczkowski** 5+1 (5); Match No. 35: Rory Schlein 10 (4); **Krzysztof Buczkowski** 5+2 (4); Match No. 36: Davey Watt 6+2 (4); Lee Complin 1 (5); **Krzysztof Buczkowski** R/R; Match No. 37: **Krzysztof Buczkowski** 1 (4); Match No. 38: Lee Richardson 10 (4); **Krzysztof Buczkowski** 5+2 (4); **Chris Neath** 5+1 (4); Match No. 39: **Krzysztof Buczkowski** 6+1 (4); Billy Legg 0 (3); Match No. 40: Rory Schlein 5+1 (4); **Krzysztof Buczkowski** 0 (3); Match No. 41: **Chris Neath** 3 (4); **Krzysztof Buczkowski** R/R; Match No. 42: **Krzysztof Buczkowski** 12+1 (6); Chris Louis 7+1 (4); Match No. 43: Kevin Doolan 6+1 (4); **Krzysztof Buczkowski** 3 (4); Match No. 44: Adam Shields 7+1 (4); Ben Barker 4+1 (6); Simon Walker 1+1

(3); Match No. 45: Davey Watt 9 (4); **Krzysztof Buczkowski** 6+1 (5); Match No. 46: Adam Shields 7+1 (5); **Chris Neath** 0 (4); Match No. 47: **Patrick Hougaard** 3 (4); **Krzysztof Buczkowski** 1 (4); Match No. 48: **Chris Neath** 5+2 (4); Edward Kennett 3 (5); **Patrick Hougaard** 1 (4); Match No. 49: Chris Harris 18 (6); **Patrick Hougaard** 3+1 (4); Ben Barker 3 (4).

Details of tactical rides and tactical substitute rides: Match No. 1: Hancock 4 points (TR); Match No. 2: Lemon 6 points (TR); Match No. 4: Hancock 4 points (TR); Match No. 7: Shields 6 points (TR); Match No. 10: Hancock 6 points (TR); Match No. 11: Hancock 6 points (TR); Match No. 13: Hancock 6 points (TR); Match No. 14: Kolodziej 6 points (TR); Match No. 17: Zagar 6 points (TR); Match No. 19: Lemon 6 points (TR); Match No. 20: Hancock 6 points (TR); Match No. 23: Schlein 6 points (TR); Match No. 25: Hancock 6 points (TR); Match No. 26: Lemon 2 points (TR); Match No. 29: Davidsson 0 points (TR); Match No. 30: Kolodziej 6 points (TR); Match No. 31: Louis 4 points (TR); Match No. 33: Zagar 6 points (TR); Match No. 34: McGowan 0 points (TR); Match No. 37: Kolodziej 6 points (TR); Match No. 40: Kolodziej 6 points (TR); Match No. 41: Zagar 4 points (TR); Match No. 44: Shields 4 points (TR); Match No. 46: Davidsson 2 points (TR); Match No. 48: Lemon 4 points (TR); Match No. 49: Harris 6 points (TR).

AVERAGES

[36 Elite League; 6 Knock-Out Cup; 2 Craven Shield = 44 fixtures]

Rider	Mts	Rds	Pts	Bon	Tot	Avge	Max
Greg Hancock	17	83	183	15	198	9.54	-
Matej Zagar	24	117	219	15	234	8.00	1 paid
Janusz Kolodziej	32	140	230	25	255	7.29	1 paid
Travis McGowan	30	144	206	19	225	6.25	-
Jonas Davidsson	27	132	164	24	188	5.70	-
Zdenek Simota	36	172	200	26	226	5.26	-
Mark Lemon	40	178	208	23	231	5.19	-
Danny Bird	13	54	55	10	65	4.81	-
Krzysztof Buczkowski	11	46	44	8	52	4.52	-
Andy Smith	6	28	22	2	24	3.43	-

Also rode (in alphabetical order):

Patrick Hougaard	3	12	7	1	8	2.67	-
Phil Morris	3	15	11	2	13	3.47	-
Chris Neath	5	19	15	3	18	3.79	-
Guests	35	156	204	23	227	5.82	-

(Ben Barker [3]; Troy Batchelor [1]; Jason Bunyan [2]; Scott Campos [1]; Lee Complin [1]; Kevin Doolan [2]; Cory Gathercole [1]; Billy Hamill [1]; Chris Harris [1]; Edward Kennett [1]; Billy Legg [2]; Chris Louis [3]; Jason Lyons [1]; Lee Richardson [3]; Rory Schlein [3]; Adam Shields [4]; Adam Skornicki [1]; Simon Walker [1]; Davey Watt [3])

INDIVIDUAL MEETING

22 October: **Denny Pyeatt Memorial**

QUALIFYING SCORES: Mark Lemon 14; Filip Sitera 14; Patrick Hougaard 13; Krzysztof Stojanowski 11; Ritchie Hawkins 10; Ben Barker 8; Chris Schramm 8; Cory Gathercole 8; Chris Mills 7; Robert Mear 6; Jason King 6; Luke Bowen 5; Shawn McConnell 4; Nicki Glanz 4; Billy Legg 1; Rob Smith 1; Paul Starke (Res) 0.

FINAL: 1st Lemon; 2nd Stojanowski; 3rd Sitera; 4th Hougaard.

Reading, 2007

Back row: left to right: Tim Sugar (Team Manager), Jonas Davidsson, Zdenek Simota, Matej Zagar and Mark Lemon.

Front: Janusz Kolodziej, Travis McGowan (on bike) and Krzysztof Buczkowski.

DANNY BIRD - THE SCB STATEMENTS

A STATEMENT, issued on 9 May, stated: 'As part of its continuing commitment to the SCB policy of maintaining a drug-free sport, Doping Control Officers from the UK Sports Council attended an Elite League speedway meeting at Reading on Friday 20 April.

'In addition to testing all fourteen competing riders for alcohol prior to the meeting, three (3) riders were also selected for doping control.

'The results received from the accredited laboratory shows an adverse analytical finding in respect of the Reading rider, Danny Bird, whose sample specimen contained a stimulant classified as a prohibited substance under the World Anti-Doping Rules.

'Accordingly the rider has fourteen days in which to respond to the charges, which includes his right to have the 'B' sample tested.

'However, in the meantime and in accordance with both WADA and SCB Rules, Mr. Bird is provisionally suspended from SCB competitions for a period of fifteen days.

'Mr. Bird has already informed his promoter, Mr. Jim Lynch, of the matter.

'The SCB's provisional suspension does, of course, mean that Reading will be able to utilise a facility to cover for Birds's absence during his period of suspension.

'Speedway Control Bureau referees will continue to test riders and officials for alcohol on a regular basis at meetings and, from time to time, doping control officers from UK Sport will augment these tests.

'Competitors are reminded that information regarding drugs is available on-line or by telephone from the UK Sport's Drug Free Directorate (0800-5280004 or www.uksport.gov.uk).

'The SCB Anti-Doping Rules are available in printed version from the office (01788-565603) or on the SCB section of the Auto Cycle Union website (www.acu.org.uk).

'Riders who need to take prescribed drugs on a regular basis are strongly advised to obtain a TUE (Theraputic Use Exemption), details of which are shown in the regulations.'

A further statement, issued on 23 July, said: 'The SCB Anti-Doping Tribunal was convened on Monday 16 July to hear the case against speedway rider, Mr. Danny Bird, having been charged with an offence under the WADA Anti-Doping Rules.

'The Tribunal was chaired by Mrs. Barbara Corbett (Solicitor), with Mr. Brian Bonny (ACU Finance Director & a member of the Speedway Control Bureau) and Mr. Gary Thompson (General Secretary of the ACU).

'Mr. Bird had advised the Tribunal that he was not planning to attend and the case was therefore heard in his absence.

'The Tribunal is satisfied that the tests (both 'A' and 'B') samples show that benzoylecgonine was present in Danny Bird's body on 20 April 2007. Applicable international standards for drug testing were fully complied with, and no Therapeutic Use Exemption was in place or was claimed by Mr. Bird. Danny Bird made a general denial of having taken drugs, but did not offer any explanation which could go towards mitigation of the offence.

'The Tribunal therefore found Mr. Danny Bird to be in contravention of the Anti-Doping Rules of The Speedway Control Bureau.

'Therefore, the Tribunal imposed on Mr. Danny Bird, a period of two (2) years' ineligibility. The Tribunal was satisfied that there are no exceptional circumstances which warranted a reduction or elimination of the sanction.

'Costs of £1,150 were also ordered by the Tribunal.

'The SCB will continue to order doping control tests and all riders must be aware of their responsibilities in this matter in order to maintain fairness and the safety of themselves and others.'

Danny Bird made his last appearance for the then Bulldogs at home to Eastbourne on 7 May, scoring 4+2 points from four starts.

(Photo: Les Aubrey)

SWINDON ROBINS

ADDRESS:	Swindon Stadium, Lady Lane, Blunsdon, Nr Swindon, Wiltshire, SN25 4DN.
TELEPHONE:	07003 921235.
CLUB HOTLINE:	09068 664682 (Premium rate applies).
WEBSITE:	www.swindon-speedway.co.uk
PROMOTERS:	Terry Russell, Gary Patchett & Alun Rossiter.
MAIN TEAM SPONSORS:	Pebley Beach Suzuki & Profile Shopfitting Ltd.
YEARS OF OPERATION:	1949 Open and National League Division Three; 1950-1951 National League Division Three; 1952-1953 Southern League; 1954-1956 National League Division Two; 1957-1964 National League; 1965-1967 British League; 1968-1974 British League Division One; 1975-1990 British League; 1991-1992 British League Division One; 1993-1994 British League Division Two; 1995 Premier League; 1996 Premier League and Conference League; 1997 Elite League and Amateur League; 1998 Elite League; 1999-2001 Premier League; 2002 Premier League and Conference Trophy; 2003 Premier League and Conference League; 2004 Elite League and Conference League; 2005-2007 Elite League.
FIRST MEETING:	23 July 1949.
TRACK LENGTH:	363 metres.
TRACK RECORD:	64.21 seconds - Leigh Adams (02/08/07).

CLUB HONOURS

LEAGUE CHAMPIONS: 1956, 1957, 1967.

PAIRS CHAMPIONS: 1994, 2004, 2005.

KNOCK-OUT CUP WINNERS: 2000.

YOUNG SHIELD WINNERS: 2000.

FOUR-TEAM CHAMPIONS: 2003.

Swindon, 2007

Back row, left to right: Alun Rossiter (Team Manager), Sebastian Ulamek, Tomasz Chrzanowski, Tommy Allen, Leigh Adams and Mads Korneliussen.
Front row, kneeling: Charlie Gjedde, Lee Richardson and Andrew Moore.

(Photo: Les Aubrey)

SWINDON 2007

* Denotes aggregate/bonus-point victory

NO.	DATE	OPPONENTS	VENUE	COMPETITION	RESULT	LEIGH ADAMS	TOMASZ CHRZANOWSKI	SEBASTIAN ULAMEK	CHARLIE GJEDDE	LEE RICHARDSON	ANDREW MOORE	MADS KORNELIUSSEN	TOMMY ALLEN	CORY GATHERCOLE	OTHER RIDERS
1	15/3	Reading	H	M4	W55-37	13+1 (5)	5 (4)	12+2 (5)	6+1 (4)	10+1 (4)	2 (4)	7+2 (4)	-	-	-
2	16/3	Reading	A	M4	W49-44*	11+1 (4)	5 (4)	9+1 (5)	8+1 (5)	4+1 (4)	4 (4)	8+1 (4)	-	-	-
3	22/3	Wolverhampton	H	ELA	W58-34	12+3 (5)	8+1 (4)	10 (4)	5+1 (4)	12 (5)	4+2 (3)	7+1 (5)	-	-	-
4	26/3	Wolverhampton	A	ELA	L42-51*	17 (5)	2 (4)	7 (4)	2+1 (4)	6 (5)	0 (2)	8 (5)	-	-	-
5	29/3	Lakeside	H	ELA	W63-29	10+2 (4)	9+1 (4)	12+2 (5)	12+2 (5)	12 (4)	-	8+1 (5)	0 (3)	-	-
6	5/4	Poole	H	ELA	W46-44	13 (5)	5+1 (4)	8+1 (5)	5+1 (4)	6+1 (4)	0 (3)	9+1 (5)	-	-	-
7	6/4	Peterborough	A	ELA	L35-58	14 (5)	0 (3)	7 (5)	1 (3)	0 (4)	4 (5)	9+2 (5)	-	-	-
8	8/4	Reading	A	ELA	W54-39	14+1 (5)	5+1 (4)	13+1 (5)	7+2 (4)	6 (4)	2 (4)	7 (4)	-	-	-
9	8/4	Reading	H	ELA	W65-28*	14+1 (5)	8+2 (4)	13+1 (5)	6+2 (4)	8+1 (4)	7+2 (5)	9+1 (4)	-	-	-
10	12/4	Belle Vue	H	ELA	W68-24	10+2 (4)	9+1 (4)	13+2 (5)	6+1 (3)	15 (5)	7+1 (4)	8+2 (5)	-	-	-
11	19/4	Coventry	H	ELA	W54-40	16 (6)	1+1 (4)	R/R	8+2 (5)	11+2 (6)	8+1 (4)	10+2 (5)	-	-	-
12	21/4	Eastbourne	A	ELA	L38.5-56.5	18.5 (6)	4 (4)	R/R	2+1 (4)	10+1 (7)	3+1 (5)	1 (4)	-	-	-
13	26/4	Eastbourne	H	ELA	W55-38	14+1 (6)	-	R/R	13+2 (5)	14+1 (6)	9+3 (6)	5+1 (4)	0 (3)	-	-
14	30/4	Peterborough	H	ELA	W52-37	13 (5)	11+1 (5)	5+1 (4)	10+2 (5)	9 (4)	1 (3)	3+1 (4)	-	-	-
15	17/5	Reading	H	ELB	W57-36	14 (5)	14+1 (5)	4+2 (4)	12+2 (5)	8+1 (4)	0 (3)	5+1 (4)	-	-	-
16	18/5	Oxford	A	ELA	W59-31	11+1 (4)	7 (4)	15 (6)	-	14+1 (6)	3 (5)	R/R	-	-	9+2 (5)
17	21/5	Coventry	A	ELA	W46-44*	11 (5)	17+1 (7)	5+2 (4)	3+2 (3)	5 (4)	2+2 (3)	3+2 (4)	-	-	-
18	24/5	Lakeside	A	ELB	W62-28	11+1 (4)	9+4 (5)	8+1 (4)	7+1 (4)	14 (5)	7+3 (4)	6+1 (4)	-	-	-
19	31/5	Coventry	H	ELB	W51-42	12+2 (5)	10+1 (5)	9 (4)	4+1 (4)	14 (5)	0 (3)	2 (4)	-	-	-
20	7/6	Wolverhampton	H	ELB	W57-36	12+1 (5)	12+3 (5)	9+1 (5)	6 (3)	8+1 (4)	8+2 (5)	2 (3)	-	-	-
21	11/6	Poole	A	ELA	D45-45*	9 (5)	11+1 (6)	9+1 (5)	3+1 (5)	12+1 (6)	1+1 (4)	R/R	-	-	-
22	14/6	Peterborough	H	KO	W63-27	13+1 (5)	15+3 (6)	12+1 (5)	9+3 (5)	11+1 (5)	3+1 (4)	R/R	-	-	-
23	21/6	Poole	H	ELB	W47-46	14 (5)	3+1 (6)	7 (5)	11+2 (5)	10+1 (6)	2 (3)	R/R	-	-	-
24	28/6	Ipswich	H	ELA	L44-46	11+1 (5)	-	4 (3)	9+1 (5)	9+2 (6)	8+2 (7)	R/R	3 (4)	-	-
25	5/7	Ipswich	A	ELA	W68-24*	13+2 (5)	6+1 (4)	R/R	15+3 (6)	18 (6)	7+3 (5)	-	-	-	9+1 (4)
26	9/7	Belle Vue	A	ELA	W56-34*	14 (5)	2+1 (4)	R/R	20 (7)	13+1 (6)	3+1 (4)	-	-	-	4+1 (4)
27	11/7	Lakeside	A	ELA	W50-41*	17 (6)	1+1 (4)	R/R	16+1 (7)	8 (5)	1 (3)	-	-	-	7+1 (5)
28	12/7	Peterborough	A	ELB	L42-51	18 (6)	-	R/R	8+1 (6)	11+1 (6)	0 (3)	-	-	-	5 (9)
29	2/8	Belle Vue	H	ELB	W65-28	15 (5)	13+2 (5)	7+1 (3)	6+3 (4)	9+2 (4)	9+2 (5)	6+2 (4)	-	-	-
30	6/8	Peterborough	H	ELB	W51-42*	12 (5)	5+1 (4)	8 (4)	7+3 (4)	11 (5)	4 (4)	4+1 (4)	-	-	-
31	11/8	Eastbourne	A	ELB	L37-53	-	-	R/R	8 (5)	12 (6)	4+1 (5)	7+1 (6)	5+1 (5)	-	1+1 (3)
32	16/8	Eastbourne	H	ELB	W56-36*	10+2 (5)	-	R/R	11+1 (5)	16+1 (6)	7 (5)	10+1 (5)	-	-	2+1 (4)
33	17/8	Lakeside	A	ELB	L41-52*	18 (5)	1 (4)	3 (4)	5+2 (4)	8 (6)	5 (4)	1 (3)	-	-	-
34	20/8	Wolverhampton	A	ELB	W45-44*	14 (5)	6+1 (4)	4+1 (4)	-	9 (5)	5+1 (4)	5 (5)	-	2+2 (3)	-
35	27/8	Ipswich	H	ELB	W64-26	10+2 (4)	9+1 (4)	11 (5)	11+4 (5)	12 (4)	7 (4)	4+2 (4)	-	-	-
36	29/8	Poole	A	ELB	L43-50	13 (5)	4+1 (4)	6 (4)	-	9 (5)	3+1 (3)	8+4 (6)	-	0 (3)	-
37	31/8	Reading	A	ELB	W57-35*	12 (4)	7+1 (4)	10+1 (5)	7+1 (4)	10+3 (5)	4 (4)	7 (4)	-	-	-
38	1/9	Ipswich	A	ELB	W46-44*	15 (5)	4+1 (4)	6 (4)	7 (4)	9+2 (5)	3 (4)	2+1 (4)	-	-	-
39	3/9	Belle Vue	A	ELB	W58-35*	14+1 (5)	6+2 (4)	7 (4)	14+1 (5)	9+3 (4)	4 (4)	4 (4)	-	-	-
40	10/9	Coventry	A	ELA	L35-55	14 (5)	R/R	4+1 (4)	9 (6)	3+2 (3)	2 (6)	-	-	3 (6)	-
41	13/9	Reading	H	KOs	W55-37	13+2 (5)	R/R	7+1 (4)	15+3 (6)	12 (4)	8 (7)	-	-	0 (4)	-
42	17/9	Peterborough	H	POs	W50-42	-	6 (4)	8+1 (5)	9+1 (4)	10+2 (5)	3 (4)	-	-	-	14+2 (8)
43	24/9	Coventry	H	POf	W49-43	12+2 (5)	8 (4)	3 (3)	8+1 (4)	7+3 (5)	2 (3)	-	-	-	9 (6)
44	1/10	Coventry	A	POf	L34-59	15+1 (5)	5 (5)	3 (4)	3 (4)	1+1 (2)	2 (4)	-	-	-	5 (6)
45	4/10	E'bourne/B.Vue	H	CSs	48-39-21	10+2 (4)	11 (4)	9+1 (4)	12 (4)	-	3 (4)	-	-	-	3+1 (4)
46	6/10	E'bourne/B.Vue	E	CSs	39-37-32	-	12 (4)	5+1 (4)	10 (4)	-	5+1 (4)	-	-	-	7+3 (8)
47	8/10	B.Vue/E'bourne	B	CSs	34-36-38*	7+1 (4)	2 (4)	5+1 (4)	9+1 (4)	-	4 (4)	-	-	-	7+1 (4)
48	15/10	Reading	A	KOs	W54-38	12+3 (5)	13 (6)	9+1 (5)	15+1 (6)	R/R	5+2 (5)	-	-	0 (3)	-
49	17/10	Poole/Coventry	P	CSf	33-35-40	7 (4)	5+1 (4)	10 (4)	2+1 (4)	-	3+3 (4)	-	-	-	6 (4)
50	18/10	Coventry/Poole	H	CSf	35-45-28	8 (4)	6 (4)	8+2 (4)	7+1 (4)	-	2 (4)	-	-	-	4+2 (4)
51	19/10	Coventry/Poole	C	CSf	50-35-23	12 (4)	11+1 (4)	10 (4)	4+2 (4)	-	4+1 (4)	-	-	-	9⅓ (4)
52	25/10	Coventry	H	KOf	D45-45	16+1 (6)	10+1 (6)	9 (5)	7 (5)	R/R	0 (3)	-	-	-	3 (5)
53	26/10	Coventry	A	KOf	L40-53	12+1 (7)	4+1 (5)	11+1 (6)	2+1 (4)	R/R	4 (3)	-	-	-	7 (5)

ADDITIONAL KEY: M4 = Don Rogers Sports M4 Trophy.

NOTE: (1) In the ELA meeting at Belle Vue on 9 July, as per a statement issued by the SCB on 26 July, it transpired that the Aces' line-up did not comply with the speedway regulations. New signing Billy Forsberg had been injured in his homeland and to cover his absence, the No. 8, Joel Parsons, was used to replace him in the team, contrary to the speedway regulations. As Forsberg had not yet ridden for Belle Vue, no facility was permitted to replace a rider, who, although declared, has not made an appearance for that team'. SR 18.1.5.3 (a) stated that if no facility is applicable, then, in the Elite League, that team's No. 8 may be used, but only if the No. 8 has a Premier League green sheet CMA of 6.00 or less. At the time, Joel Parsons' PL CMA was 6.72. As a consequence, the result of the meeting was amended, with the deduction of the points scored by Parsons. For the record, he tallied 2 points from four rides in the match versus the Robins; (2) Following the home ELB fixture versus Peterborough on 6 August, Leigh Adams defeated Hans N. Andersen in a run-off for the aggregate point.

Details of other riders (all guests unless **highlighted**): Match No. 16: Lewis Bridger 9+2 (5); Match No. 25: Edward Kennett 9+1 (4); Match No. 26: Shane Parker 4+1 (4); Match No. 27: Travis McGowan 7+1 (5); Match No. 28: Adam Shields 5 (4); Travis McGowan 0 (5); Match No. 31: Shaun Tacey 1+1 (3); Match No. 32: Steve Johnston 2+1 (4); Match No. 42: Davey Watt 8+1 (4); **Damian Balinski** 6+1 (4); Match No. 43: **Damian Balinski** 9 (6); Match No. 44: **Damian Balinski** 5 (6); Match No. 45: Lee Complin 3+1 (4); Match No. 46: Mark Lemon 5+2 (4); Jason King 2+1 (4); Match No. 47: Jason Lyons 7+1 (4); Match No. 49: Simon Stead 6 (4); Match No. 50: Simon Stead 4+2 (4); Match No. 51: Fredrik Lindgren 9+3 (4); Match No. 52: **Damian Balinski** 3 (5); Match No. 53: **Damian Balinski** 7 (5).

Details of tactical rides and tactical substitute rides: Match No. 4: Adams 6 points (TR); Match No. 7: Adams 6 points (TR); Match No. 12: Adams 6 points (TR); Richardson 4 points (TS); Match No. 28: Adams 6 points (TR); Match No. 31: Richardson 0 points (TS); Match No. 33: Adams 6 points (TR); Richardson 0 points (TS); Match No. 40: Richardson 1 point (TR; not doubled); Match No. 44: Adams 6 points (TR); Match No. 53: Adams 0 points (TS).

AVERAGES

[36 Elite League; 3 Play-Offs; 5 Knock-Out Cup; 6 Craven Shield = 50 fixtures]

Rider	Mts	Rds	Pts	Bon	Tot	Avge	Max
Leigh Adams	47	233	584.5	36	620.5	10.65	5 full; 12 paid
Lee Richardson	41	199	387	35	422	8.48	5 full; 1 paid
Charlie Gjedde	48	219	392	62	454	8.29	1 full; 5 paid
Sebastian Ulamek	42	183	326	29	355	7.76	1 paid
Tomasz Chrzanowski	43	192	310	41	351	7.31	1 full; 5 paid
Mads Korneliussen	28	122	158	28	186	6.10	-
Andrew Moore	49	201	192	37	229	4.56	-

Also rode (in alphabetical order):

Tommy Allen	3	10	3	0	3	1.20	-
Damian Balinski	5	26	30	1	31	4.77	-
Cory Gathercole	5	19	5	2	7	1.47	-

Guests	15	61	72	16	88	5.77	1 paid

(Lee Complin [1]; Steve Johnston [1]; Edward Kennett [1]; Jason King [1]; Mark Lemon [1]; Fredrik Lindgren [1]; Jason Lyons [1]; Travis McGowan [2]; Shane Parker [1]; Adam Shields [1]; Simon Stead [2]; Shaun Tacey [1]; Davey Watt [1])

NOTE: Lee Richardson was ever-present throughout the 36-match Elite League programme.

After a patchy start to the campaign, cheery **Charlie Gjedde** benefited greatly from a short spell at reserve, which was highlighted by a massive 20-point haul at Belle Vue in a career-best Elite League showing on 9 July.

(Photo: Les Aubrey)

WOLVERHAMPTON WOLVES

ADDRESS:	Ladbroke Stadium, Sutherland Avenue, Wolverhampton, West Midlands, WV2 2JJ.
TELEPHONE:	01902 870400.
CLUB HOTLINE:	09068 664664 (Premium rate applies).
WEBSITE:	www.wolverhampton-speedway.com
PROMOTERS:	Chris Van Straaten, Peter Adams and John Woolridge.
MAIN TEAM SPONSOR:	Parrys International.
YEARS OF OPERATION:	1928-1930 Open; 1950 Open; 1951 National League Division Three; 1952 Southern League; 1953-1954 National League Division Two; 1961-1964 Provincial League; 1965-1967 British League; 1968-1974 British League Division One; 1975-1980 British League; 1981 National League; 1984-1990 British League; 1991-1994 British League Division One; 1995-1996 Premier League; 1997 Elite League and Amateur League; 1998-2001 Elite League; 2002 Elite League and Conference Trophy; 2003 Elite League and Conference League; 2004-2007 Elite League.
FIRST MEETING:	30 May 1928.
TRACK LENGTH:	264 metres.
TRACK RECORD:	54.59 seconds - Peter Karlsson (06/08/07).

CLUB HONOURS

LEAGUE CHAMPIONS: 1963, 1991, 1996, 2002.

PREMIERSHIP WINNERS: 1992, 1997.

GOLD CUP WINNERS: 1992.

KNOCK-OUT CUP WINNERS: 1996.

David Howe enjoyed a very good year in the Elite League with the Wolves, while on the individual front he finished as runner-up in the British Final and proudly rode as the wildcard in the season's showpiece Grand Prix event at the Millennium Stadium.

(Photo: Karen Chappell)

WOLVERHAMPTON 2007

* Denotes aggregate/bonus-point victory

NO.	DATE	OPPONENTS	VENUE	COMPETITION	RESULT	PETER KARLSSON	DAVID HOWE	BILLY HAMILL	MAGNUS KARLSSON	FREDRIK LINGREN	CARL WILKINSON	THEO PIJPER	WILLIAM LAWSON	CHRIS KERR	OTHER RIDERS
1	15/3	Sheffield	A	Chal	L44-46	-	6+2 (4)	-	9+1 (4)	3+1 (4)	3+1 (4)	10+1 (5)	-	-	13+1 (9)
2	22/3	Swindon	A	ELA	L34-58	2+1 (4)	11 (5)	8 (5)	2+2 (4)	6 (4)	-	5+1 (5)	0 (3)	-	-
3	23/3	Reading	A	ELA	L41-49	11+1 (5)	5+2 (4)	10+1 (5)	6+1 (4)	3 (4)	1 (3)	5+1 (5)	-	-	-
4	26/3	Swindon	H	ELA	W51-42	12+1 (5)	8+1 (4)	8 (4)	1+1 (3)	10+1 (5)	-	7+1 (5)	5+1 (4)	-	-
5	2/4	Lakeside	H	ELA	W49-44	13+1 (5)	10+2 (5)	5+1 (4)	5 (4)	5 (4)	3 (3)	8+1 (5)	-	-	-
6	6/4	Belle Vue	A	ELA	W48-42	13 (5)	5+1 (4)	12+2 (5)	4+1 (4)	9+1 (4)	-	4 (5)	-	1+1 (3)	-
7	9/4	Belle Vue	H	ELA	W54-39*	9+2 (4)	12+1 (6)	16 (6)	3+1 (4)	R/R	-	8 (5)	6+2 (5)	-	-
8	13/4	Reading	A	KO	L34-56	8 (5)	3 (3)	11+1 (6)	6 (5)	R/R	1 (4)	5+1 (7)	-	-	-
9	14/4	Eastbourne	A	ELA	L35-57	9+1 (5)	-	7+1 (6)	6 (5)	R/R	0 (3)	6+1 (6)	-	-	7+1 (5)
10	16/4	Reading	H	KO	W51-42	14 (5)	12+3 (6)	0 (0)	10 (7)	R/R	-	8 (5)	7+2 (7)	-	-
11	23/4	Peterborough	H	ELA	W55-38	9 (4)	12+2 (5)	9 (4)	7+3 (5)	10+2 (5)	-	5+2 (4)	3 (3)	-	-
12	26/4	Ipswich	A	ELA	L43-49	R/R	16 (6)	9+1 (5)	3 (4)	11+3 (6)	3+1 (5)	1 (4)	-	-	-
13	30/4	Ipswich	H	ELA	W63-29*	11+1 (4)	10+2 (4)	13+1 (5)	6+2 (4)	13+2 (5)	5+1 (4)	5 (4)	-	-	-
14	4/5	Coventry	A	ELA	L43-47	14 (5)	7+2 (4)	9 (5)	3 (5)	8 (4)	1 (3)	1 (4)	-	-	-
15	7/5	Coventry	H	ELA	L43-49	13+1 (5)	7+1 (4)	2 (2)	5+1 (5)	13+1 (6)	-	2 (4)	1 (4)	-	-
16	9/5	Poole	A	ELA	L27-63	7+1 (6)	6+1 (5)	R/R	3 (5)	8 (6)	-	2+1 (4)	1 (4)	-	-
17	11/5	Lakeside	A	ELA	W51-39*	9+1 (4)	5+1 (4)	14 (5)	8+1 (6)	12+1 (5)	2 (3)	1+1 (3)	-	-	-
18	14/5	Eastbourne	H	ELA	W51-42	10 (5)	6+1 (3)	9 (4)	4+2 (4)	14 (5)	-	2+1 (4)	6+1 (5)	-	-
19	21/5	Oxford	H	ELA	W60-32	12 (4)	10+3 (5)	14+1 (5)	12+2 (5)	10+1 (4)	0 (3)	2+1 (4)	-	-	-
20	30/5	Belle Vue	A	ELB	W47-43	13+1 (5)	9+1 (5)	8 (4)	9 (5)	6+2 (4)	-	-	2+1 (4)	-	0 (3)
21	31/5	Peterborough	A	ELA	L40-53*	17 (5)	6+1 (4)	4 (4)	1 (4)	8+1 (5)	1 (4)	-	-	-	3 (4)
22	1/6	Edinburgh	A	Chal	L44-46	-	13+1 (5)	-	7+1 (4)	11+1 (5)	2 (4)	-	-	2 (4)	9 (8)
23	7/6	Swindon	A	ELB	L36-57	16 (6)	0 (1)	R/R	2 (5)	12 (7)	-	3 (6)	-	-	3+1 (5)
24	11/6	Reading	H	ELA	W54-39*	10+1 (4)	10+3 (5)	10 (4)	6+2 (4)	8+1 (5)	-	4+1 (5)	-	-	6+2 (4)
25	9/7	Lakeside	H	ELB	W52-38	11+1 (5)	R/R	14+1 (5)	8 (5)	11+1 (5)	-	3+1 (5)	-	-	5 (5)
26	23/7	Peterborough	H	ELB	L38-54	8 (4)	7+2 (4)	6+1 (5)	3+1 (4)	8+3 (6)	-	2 (3)	-	-	4 (5)
27	26/7	Ipswich	A	ELB	L41-52	18 (5)	4 (4)	3 (4)	4+1 (4)	9+1 (5)	-	0 (4)	-	-	3 (4)
28	30/7	Reading	H	ELB	W59-31	10+2 (4)	9+1 (4)	8+1 (5)	6+2 (4)	15 (5)	-	8 (4)	-	-	3+1 (4)
29	3/8	Coventry	A	ELB	L41-52	16 (5)	6+1 (4)	4 (4)	7+1 (4)	6 (5)	-	2 (4)	-	-	0 (4)
30	4/8	Eastbourne	A	ELB	L39-50	11+2 (5)	5 (4)	10 (5)	1+1 (4)	7+1 (4)	-	5+1 (5)	-	-	0 (2)
31	6/8	Poole	H	ELA	W49-43	12+1 (5)	7+3 (4)	5+1 (4)	5+2 (4)	13+1 (5)	-	7+2 (5)	-	-	0 (3)
32	8/8	Poole	A	ELB	L36-56	13 (5)	4+1 (4)	6 (4)	1 (4)	8+1 (5)	-	3 (4)	-	-	1 (4)
33	13/8	Belle Vue	H	ELB	W57-33*	15 (5)	9+3 (4)	9+1 (5)	7 (4)	10+1 (4)	-	2+1 (4)	-	-	5 (4)
34	20/8	Swindon	H	ELB	L44-45	0 (0)	6+1 (4)	8 (5)	1 (4)	12 (5)	-	8 (6)	-	-	9+4 (6)
35	24/8	Reading	A	ELB	L33-49*	-	5+1 (4)	2 (2)	1 (2)	13+1 (5)	-	4 (6)	-	-	8+1 (6)
36	27/8	Eastbourne	H	ELB	D45-45	6+2 (5)	13+3 (6)	R/R	1 (3)	10 (6)	-	8 (5)	-	-	7+1 (5)
37	27/8	Poole	H	ELB	W47-45	7+1 (6)	8+2 (5)	R/R	1 (3)	15 (6)	-	9+1 (5)	-	-	7 (5)
38	3/9	Coventry	H	ELB	L42-51	17+2 (6)	6+1 (5)	-	0 (4)	R/R	-	6 (6)	-	-	13 (9)
39	6/9	Peterborough	A	ELB	L24-66	5 (6)	6+1 (6)	-	0 (4)	R/R	-	2+1 (4)	-	-	11 (10)
40	7/9	Lakeside	A	ELB	L35-58	17 (6)	3 (5)	-	2 (4)	R/R	-	6 (4)	-	-	11+1 (12)
41	10/9	Ipswich	H	ELB	W55-38*	15 (6)	11+2 (6)	10+1 (5)	2+1 (4)	R/R	-	11+2 (5)	-	-	6+2 (4)
42	27/9	Ipswich / Coventry	I	CSs	23-43-42	5 (4)	8+1 (4)	5+1 (4)	-	5 (4)	-	0 (4)	-	-	0 (4)
43	28/9	Ipswich / Coventry	C	CSs	20-31-21	4 (3)	4+1 (3)	7+1 (3)	-	3 (2)	-	2 (3)	-	-	0 (2)
44	8/10	Coventry / Ipswich	H	CSs	35-49-24	11 (4)	-	6 (4)	-	9+1 (4)	-	3+1 (4)	-	-	6+1 (8)
45	22/10	Birmingham	H	WM	W55-38	11 (5)	-	9 (4)	-	13 (5)	-	7+2 (4)	-	-	15+4 (12)
46	24/10	Birmingham	A	WM	D45-45*	-	-	-	-	13+1 (5)	-	7+1 (5)	-	-	25+4 (20)

ADDITIONAL KEY: WM = BBC West Midland Shield.

NOTE: (1) The side which appeared at Edinburgh in the challenge match on 1 June was billed as Wolverhampton Select; (2) The ELB encounter at Reading on 24 August was abandoned after heat thirteen, with the result permitted to stand; (3) The away leg of the Craven Shield at Coventry on 28 September was abandoned after heat twelve, with the result permitted to stand.

Details of other riders (all guests unless **highlighted**): Match No. 1: Adam Skornicki 9+1 (5); Nicolai Klindt 4 (4); Match No. 9: Travis McGowan 7+1 (5); Match No. 20: **Kenneth Hansen** 0 (3); Match No. 21: **Kenneth Hansen** 3 (4); Match No. 22: **James Grieves** 9 (4); Arlo Bugeja 0 (4); Match No. 23: Matthew Wethers 3+1 (5); Match No. 24: **Kenneth Hansen** 6+2 (4); Match No. 25: **Kenneth Hansen** 5 (5); Match No. 26: **James Grieves** 4 (5); Match No. 27: Carl Wilkinson 3 (4); Match No. 28: **James Grieves** 3+1 (4); Match No. 29: Chris Kerr 0 (4); Match No. 30: Tom P. Madsen 0 (2); Match No. 31: **Kenneth Hansen** 1 (4); Match No. 33: **James Grieves** 5 (4); Match No. 34: **Kenneth Hansen** 9+4 (6); Match No. 35: Chris Louis 7 (4); **Kenneth Hansen** 1+1 (2); Match No. 36: **James Grieves** 7+1 (5); Match No. 37: **James Grieves** 7 (5); Match No. 38: Adam Shields 10 (6); **James Grieves** 3 (3); Match No. 39: Adam Shields 7 (5); Claus Vissing 4 (5); Match No. 40: Chris Kerr 6+1 (6); Billy Janniro 5 (6); Match No. 41: **James Grieves** 6+2 (4); Match No. 42: Tommy Allen 0 (4); Match No. 43: Tommy Allen 0 (2); Match No. 44: **Kenneth Hansen** 4+1 (4); **James Grieves** 2 (4); Match No. 45: **Kenneth Hansen** 9+1 (4); Chris Kerr 5+3 (4); Nicolai Klindt 1 (4); Match No. 46: Chris Kerr 7+2 (4); Jack Hargreaves 6 (4); **Kenneth Hansen** 5+1 (4); Nicolai Klindt 4 (4); Joe Haines 3 (4).

Details of tactical rides and tactical substitute rides: Match No. 2: Howe 4 points (TR); Match No. 8: P. Karlsson 1 point (TR; not doubled); Match No. 9: P. Karlsson 4 points (TR); Match No. 12: Howe 4 points (TR); Match No. 15: Lindgren 4 points (TS); Match No. 16: Howe 1 point (TR; not doubled); Match No. 21: P. Karlsson 6 points (TR); Match No. 23: P. Karlsson 6 points (TR); Lindgren 0 points (TS); Match No. 26: P. Karlsson 2 points (TR); Lindgren 2 points (TS); Match No. 27: P. Karlsson 6 points (TR); Match No. 29: P. Karlsson 6 points (TR); Match No. 32: P. Karlsson 6 points (TR); Match No. 35: Lindgren 4 points (TS); Louis 4 points (TR); Match No. 38: P. Karlsson 6 points (TR); Match No. 39: P. Karlsson 0 points (TR); Match No. 40: P. Karlsson 6 points (TR).

AVERAGES

[36 Elite League; 2 Knock-Out Cup; 3 Craven Shield = 41 fixtures]

Rider	Mts	Rds	Pts	Bon	Tot	Avge	Max
Peter Karlsson	39	185	397	24	421	9.10	2 full; 2 paid
Fredrik Lindgren	33	160	305	26	331	8.28	1 full; 1 paid
David Howe	38	167	277	49	326	7.81	2 paid
Billy Hamill	34	147	267	16	283	7.70	1 paid
James Grieves	8	34	37	4	41	4.82	-
Magnus Karlsson	38	161	150	26	176	4.37	-
Theo Pijper	17	79	75	11	86	4.35	-
Kenneth Hansen	9	35	29	8	37	4.23	-
William Lawson	31	139	125	18	143	4.12	-
Carl Wilkinson	9	32	17	2	19	2.38	-

Also rode:

Chris Kerr	1	3	1	1	2	2.67	-

Guests	13	58	50	3	53	3.66	-

(Tommy Allen [2]; Billy Janniro [1]; Chris Kerr [2]; Chris Louis [1]; Travis McGowan [1]; Tom P. Madsen [1]; Adam Shields [2]; Claus Vissing [1]; Matthew Wethers [1]; Carl Wilkinson [1])

NOTE: Magnus Karlsson was ever-present throughout the 36-match Elite League programme.

INDIVIDUAL MEETINGS

18 March: **Sudden Sam Ermolenko's Flaming Farewell**
QUALIFYING SCORES: Travis McGowan 6; Steve Johnston 5; Dean Barker 4; Ronnie Correy 3; Mark Lemon 3; Chris Kerr 2; Chris Neath 1; Brent Werner 0.
MAIN EVENT: Jason Crump 10; McGowan 10; Joe Screen 9; Scott Nicholls 8; Leigh Adams 8; Andreas Jonsson 8; Greg Hancock 7; Chris Harris 7; Peter Karlsson 7; Billy Hamill 6; Fredrik Lindgren 5; Billy Janniro 4; David Norris 4; Charlie Gjedde 2; Barker 1; Johnston 0.
FIRST SEMI-FINAL: 1st Crump; 2nd Hancock; 3rd Adams; 4th Screen.
SECOND SEMI-FINAL: 1st Karlsson; 2nd Nicholls; 3rd McGowan; 4th Jonsson.
FINAL: 1st Karlsson; 2nd Hancock; 3rd Crump; 4th Nicholls.

15 October: **Banks's Olympique**
1st Fredrik Lindgren 13; 2nd Scott Nicholls (after run-off) 11; 3rd Chris Harris 11; Peter Karlsson 10; Kenneth Hansen 9; Daniel Nermark 9; Jason Lyons 8; Billy Hamill 7; Chris Kerr 7; Chris Louis 6; William Lawson 6; Adam Skornicki 6; Tai Woffinden 5; Ludvig Lindgren 5; Nicolai Klindt 5; Casper Wortmann 2.

OTHER MEETING

25 March: **Jesper B. Jensen Testimonial** (at Peterborough)
Peterborough 42, Oxford 35, Wolverhampton 31: Fredrik Lindgren 11 (5); Peter Karlsson 8 (5); Billy Hamill 6+1 (5); David Howe 3 (5); Magnus Karlsson 2 (5); Theo Pijper 1 (5).

Fredrik Lindgren continued to showcase his talent with Wolverhampton and also scooped a brilliant third spot in the Swedish Grand Prix on 26 May, when he appeared as the wildcard entrant.

(Photo: Karen Chappell)

THE PREMIER LEAGUE
2007

Berwick Bandits
Birmingham Brummies
Edinburgh Monarchs
Glasgow Tigers
Isle of Wight Islanders
King's Lynn Stars
Mildenhall Fen Tigers
Newcastle Diamonds
Newport Wasps
Redcar Bears
Rye House Rockets
Sheffield Tigers
Somerset Rebels
Stoke Potters
Workington Comets

PREMIER LEAGUE 2007

PREMIER LEAGUE TABLE

Team	Mts	Won	Drn	Lst	For	Agn	Pts	AP	Tot
King's Lynn	28	20	1	7	1399	1162	41	11	52
Birmingham	28	19	1	8	1345	1215	39	9	48
Rye House	28	17	0	11	1448	1113	34	13	47
Sheffield	28	18	0	10	1356	1206	36	11	47
Isle of Wight	28	17	0	11	1385	1176	34	11	45
Somerset	28	16	0	12	1328	1233	32	10	42
Workington	28	15	1	12	1300	1251	31	8	39
Glasgow	28	16	0	12	1284	1276	32	6	38
Redcar	28	12	1	15	1252	1320	25	5	30
Newcastle	28	12	1	15	1202	1365	25	2	27
Stoke	28	10	1	17	1212	1316	21	5	26
Mildenhall	28	10	1	17	1218	1347	21	5	26
Edinburgh	28	11	0	17	1214	1350	22	4	26
Newport	28	10	0	18	1163	1369	20	5	25
Berwick	28	3	1	24	1067	1474	7	0	7

PLAY-OFFS

SEMI-FINALS

Isle of Wight	46	Rye House	44	
Rye House	61	Isle of Wight	29	(Rye House won 105-75 on aggregate)

Sheffield	62	King's Lynn	31	
King's Lynn	55	Sheffield	37	(Sheffield won 99-86 on aggregate)

FINAL

Sheffield	51	Rye House	42	
Rye House	69	Sheffield	23	(Rye House won 111-74 on aggregate)

TOP 20 AVERAGES [Premier League only. Minimum qualification: 6 matches.]

Rider	Mts	Rds	Pts	Bon	Tot	Avge	Max
Chris Holder (Isle of Wight)	26	123	317	15	332	10.80	3 full; 7 paid
Magnus Zetterstrom (Somerset)	25	129	328	16	344	10.67	2 full; 6 paid
Daniel Nermark (King's Lynn) *	28	136	338	12	350	10.29	5 full; 2 paid
Andre Compton (Sheffield)	26	127	314	12	326	10.27	6 full; 3 paid
Shane Parker (Glasgow)	26	129	316	4	320	9.92	6 full
Jason Lyons (Birmingham)	27	138	327	10	337	9.77	4 full; 1 paid
Gary Havelock (Redcar)	21	101	232	13	245	9.70	1 full; 1 paid
Tomas Topinka (King's Lynn) *	28	139	317	20	337	9.70	1 full; 4 paid
James Wright (Workington)	27	133	305	16	321	9.65	2 paid
Stefan Ekberg (Rye House)	8	35	74	8	82	9.37	1 paid
Carl Stonehewer (Workington)	17	82	177	11	188	9.17	1 full
Tai Woffinden (Rye House)	23	104	219	19	238	9.15	2 full; 2 paid
Kauko Nieminen (Workington)	26	126	272	13	285	9.05	2 full; 1 paid
James Grieves (Redcar) *	28	135	292	7	299	8.86	2 full
Ricky Ashworth (Sheffield)	24	111	226	18	244	8.79	3 paid
Chris Neath (Rye House) *	28	129	256	27	283	8.78	1 full; 2 paid
Kyle Legault (Mildenhall)	21	104	218	10	228	8.77	1 paid
Ulrich Ostergaard (Birmingham/Workington)	25	123	252	12	264	8.59	2 full; 1 paid
Craig Watson (Glasgow)	16	78	160	7	167	8.56	Nil
Emil Kramer (Somerset)	24	112	227	12	239	8.54	1 paid

* Denotes ever-present.

YOUNG SHIELD

QUARTER-FINALS

Mildenhall	43	Birmingham	47	
Birmingham	44	Mildenhall	46	(Birmingham won 91-89 on aggregate)

Redcar	49	Glasgow	41	
Glasgow	43	Redcar	47	(Redcar won 96-84 on aggregate)

Somerset	58	Stoke	34	
Stoke	59	Somerset	33	(Stoke won 93-91 on aggregate)

Workington	58	Newcastle	35	
Newcastle	46	Workington	45	(Workington won 103-81 on aggregate)

SEMI-FINALS

Birmingham	54	Stoke	38	
Stoke	46	Birmingham	43	(Birmingham won 97-84 on aggregate)

Redcar	50	Workington	40	
Workington	47	Redcar	43	(Redcar won 93-87 on aggregate)

FINAL

Redcar	49	Birmingham	41	
Birmingham	43	Redcar	46	(Redcar won 95-84 on aggregate)

KNOCK-OUT CUP

ROUND ONE

Newcastle	50	King's Lynn	40	
King's Lynn	64	Newcastle	29	(King's Lynn won 104-79 on aggregate)

Birmingham	49	Newport	41	
Newport	51	Birmingham	39	(Newport won 92-88 on aggregate)

Rye House	50	Mildenhall	41	
Mildenhall	40	Rye House	49	(Rye House won 99-81 on aggregate)

Sheffield	57	Edinburgh	36	
Edinburgh	60	Sheffield	33	(Edinburgh won 96-90 on aggregate)

Somerset	52	Glasgow	38	
Glasgow	48	Somerset	45	(Somerset won 97-86 on aggregate)

Berwick	51	Stoke	42	
Stoke	57	Berwick	35	(Stoke won 99-86 on aggregate)

Workington	50	Isle of Wight	42	
Isle of Wight	52	Workington	43	(Isle of Wight won 94-93 on aggregate)

QUARTER-FINALS

Edinburgh	48	Somerset	41	
Somerset	58	Edinburgh	32	(Somerset won 99-80 on aggregate)

Redcar	45	King's Lynn	45	
King's Lynn	59	Redcar	33	(King's Lynn won 104-78 on aggregate)

Stoke	49	Newport	41	
Newport	50	Stoke	40	(Newport won 91-89 on aggregate)

Isle of Wight	52	Rye House	40	
Rye House	50	Isle of Wight	43	(Isle of Wight won 95-90 on aggregate)

SEMI-FINALS

King's Lynn	49	Isle of Wight	44	
Isle of Wight	45	King's Lynn	45	(King's Lynn won 94-89 on aggregate)

Newport	50	Somerset	42	
Somerset	61	Newport	32	(Somerset won 103-82 on aggregate)

FINAL

Somerset	44	King's Lynn	46	
King's Lynn	59	Somerset	34	(King's Lynn won 105-78 on aggregate)

PREMIER TROPHY

PREMIER TROPHY (SOUTH) TABLE

Team	Mts	Won	Drn	Lst	For	Agn	Pts	Bon	Tot
Rye House	8	6	0	2	431	302	12	4	16
Isle of Wight	8	5	0	3	399	339	10	2	12
Mildenhall	8	4	0	4	333	391	8	2	10
Somerset	8	3	0	5	366	366	6	2	8
Newport	8	2	0	6	296	427	4	0	4

PREMIER TROPHY (MIDLANDS) TABLE

Team	Mts	Won	Drn	Lst	For	Agn	Pts	Bon	Tot
King's Lynn	8	5	2	1	447	276	12	4	16
Birmingham	8	5	1	2	358	366	11	2	13
Sheffield	8	4	1	3	382	345	9	3	12
Workington	8	4	0	4	353	375	8	1	9
Stoke	8	0	0	8	268	446	0	0	0

PREMIER TROPHY (NORTH) TABLE

Team	Mts	Won	Drn	Lst	For	Agn	Pts	Bon	Tot
Glasgow	8	6	0	2	396	330	12	3	15
Redcar	8	5	0	3	372	360	10	2	12
Newcastle	8	4	0	4	368	359	8	3	11
Edinburgh	8	3	0	5	349	355	6	2	8
Berwick	8	2	0	6	313	394	4	0	4

SEMI-FINALS

King's Lynn	55	Glasgow	39	
Glasgow	49	King's Lynn	44	(King's Lynn won 99-88 on aggregate)

Rye House	52	Birmingham	38	
Birmingham	58	Rye House	35	(Birmingham won 96-87 on aggregate)

FINAL

Birmingham	39	King's Lynn	51	
King's Lynn	58	Birmingham	35	(King's Lynn won 109-74 on aggregate)

BERWICK BANDITS

ADDRESS:	Shielfield Park Stadium, Shielfield Terrace, Tweedmouth, Berwick-upon-Tweed, Northumberland, TD15 2EF.
TELEPHONE:	01289 307707.
CLUB HOTLINE:	09068 664667 (Premium rate applies).
WEBSITE:	www.berwickspeedway.co.uk
PROMOTER:	Peter Waite.
MAIN TEAM SPONSOR:	Anderson's Butchers.
YEARS OF OPERATION:	1968-1974 British League Division Two; 1975-1980 National League; 1995 Demonstration; 1996 Conference League; 1997 Premier League and Amateur League; 1998-2007 Premier League.
FIRST MEETING:	18 May 1968.
TRACK LENGTH:	368 metres.
TRACK RECORD:	64.2 seconds - Sean Wilson (21/08/99).
PREVIOUS VENUE:	Berrington Lough Stadium, Nr Ancroft, Northumberland.
YEARS OF OPERATION:	1982-1990 National League; 1991 British League Division One; 1992 British League Division Two; 1993 Open; 1994 British League Division Three; 1995 Academy League.

CLUB HONOURS

KNOCK-OUT CUP WINNERS: 1980, 1989, 1995.

GOLD CUP WINNERS: 1991.

LEAGUE CHAMPIONS: 1994, 1995.

FOUR-TEAM CHAMPIONS: 2002.

Skipper **Michal Makovsky** remained ever-loyal to the Bandits' cause, enjoying a seventh successive season with the club.

(Photo: David Valentine)

BERWICK 2007

* Denotes aggregate/bonus-point victory

NO.	DATE	OPPONENTS	VENUE	COMPETITION	RESULT	MICHAL MAKOVSKY	ANDREAS BERGSTROM	JACEK REMPALA	MICHAEL COLES	STANISLAW BURZA	BENJI COMPTON	JOHN BRANNEY	ROB GRANT	DAVID MELDRUM	OTHER RIDERS
1	17/3	Anderson's 7	H	Chal	W52-41	11+2 (5)	10+2 (4)	5 (4)	2+1 (4)	14 (5)	6+3 (4)	4 (4)	-	-	-
2	24/3	Newcastle	H	TT	W58-31	8 (5)	9+2 (4)	9+1 (4)	7+2 (4)	13+1 (5)	8+3 (4)	4+1 (4)	-	-	-
3	29/3	Redcar	A	PT	L35-58	7 (4)	10+3 (5)	3 (4)	5 (4)	7 (5)	1 (4)	2+1 (4)	-	-	-
4	31/3	Edinburgh	H	PT	W52-38	12+2 (5)	7 (4)	9+1 (4)	8+1 (4)	13+1 (5)	2 (5)	1 (3)	-	-	-
5	1/4	Newcastle	A	TT	L42-50*	5 (4)	5+1 (4)	14 (5)	8+2 (4)	7 (5)	2 (4)	1+1 (4)	-	-	-
6	7/4	Redcar	H	PT	L44-46	6+3 (4)	8 (4)	11 (5)	4 (4)	8 (5)	5+1 (5)	2 (3)	-	-	-
7	13/4	Edinburgh	A	PT	L25-47	5 (3)	4 (4)	4 (4)	1 (3)	7 (3)	4+1 (4)	0 (3)	-	-	-
8	14/4	Glasgow	H	PT	L44-46	10+2 (5)	7+1 (4)	9 (4)	4 (4)	12 (5)	1+1 (4)	1 (4)	-	-	-
9	21/4	Newcastle	H	PT	W50-40	12 (5)	5+2 (4)	9 (4)	5+1 (4)	12+2 (5)	6+1 (4)	-	-	-	1 (4)
10	22/4	Glasgow	A	PT	L29-61	0 (3)	7 (5)	5+1 (5)	6 (4)	5 (4)	5+1 (6)	-	-	-	1 (3)
11	26/4	Sheffield	A	PL	L31-62	14 (5)	7 (5)	1 (4)	0 (3)	1+1 (4)	7 (6)	-	1 (3)	-	-
12	28/4	Sheffield	H	PL	L43-46	7+1 (5)	5+3 (4)	12 (5)	7 (4)	3+1 (4)	-	-	0 (3)	-	9+1 (5)
13	5/5	Stoke	H	KO	W51-42	12 (5)	5 (4)	9 (4)	3+1 (4)	11+2 (5)	6+2 (4)	-	5+1 (4)	-	-
14	6/5	Stoke	A	KO	L35-57	10+2 (5)	5 (4)	4 (4)	1 (3)	13 (6)	2 (5)	-	0 (3)	-	-
15	11/5	Edinburgh	A	PL	L32-60	5 (4)	7 (5)	8 (5)	-	10 (5)	1 (3)	-	-	0 (3)	1 (5)
16	14/5	Newcastle	A	PL	L34-58	4 (4)	2 (4)	14 (5)	-	4+2 (5)	2+1 (4)	-	-	1+1 (4)	7+1 (4)
17	26/5	Somerset	H	PL	L41-49	6 (4)	4 (4)	11+1 (5)	-	8+2 (5)	4+1 (4)	-	-	6 (4)	2+2 (4)
18	29/5	Isle of Wight	A	PL	L31-62	8+1 (5)	4 (4)	12 (5)	-	3 (4)	0 (4)	-	-	2+1 (4)	2 (4)
19	3/6	Newcastle	A	PL	L36-57	10 (5)	6+3 (4)	11 (6)	-	2 (4)	-	-	-	0 (4)	7+1 (7)
20	9/6	King's Lynn	H	PL	L44-46	9+1 (5)	5+2 (4)	10+1 (5)	-	7+1 (4)	-	-	-	8+2 (5)	5 (7)
21	15/6	Somerset	A	PL	L35-59	7+1 (5)	4+1 (4)	9 (4)	-	11 (6)	1+1 (4)	-	-	3+1 (4)	0 (3)
22	16/6	Glasgow	H	PL	L43-48	15+1 (6)	6+2 (5)	6 (4)	-	10+1 (5)	0 (3)	-	-	6+1 (7)	R/R
23	7/7	Newcastle	H	PL	W48-44	8 (5)	6+1 (4)	5 (4)	-	7+2 (4)	-	-	-	11+1 (5)	11+3 (8)
24	14/7	Rye House	H	PL	W51-41	11+1 (5)	7+1 (4)	8 (4)	-	11+2 (5)	-	-	-	7+2 (5)	7 (7)
25	19/7	Redcar	A	PL	L41-49	5+1 (4)	7 (4)	6 (5)	-	7 (4)	-	-	-	6+2 (5)	10+2 (8)
26	28/7	Isle of Wight	A	PL	L44-46	12 (6)	8+2 (5)	10+1 (5)	-	R/R	-	-	-	7+1 (6)	7+1 (8)
27	1/8	King's Lynn	A	PL	L28-64	7 (6)	-	9 (5)	-	R/R	-	-	-	2+2 (5)	10+1 (14)
28	4/8	Redcar	H	PL	W50-43	12 (5)	9+2 (4)	7 (4)	-	10+3 (5)	-	-	-	8+1 (4)	4+1 (8)
29	5/8	Newport	A	PL	L35-38	10 (5)	9+1 (4)	-	-	12+3 (5)	-	-	-	-	4+1 (8)
30	11/8	Birmingham	H	PL	L40-52	12 (5)	4+2 (4)	-	-	12+1 (5)	-	-	-	2+1 (5)	10+1 (11)
31	15/8	Birmingham	A	PL	L33-59	10 (5)	6 (5)	-	-	2+1 (4)	-	-	-	0 (4)	15 (12)
32	25/8	Workington	H	PL	L45-48	10 (5)	7+2 (4)	6 (4)	-	7 (5)	-	-	-	6+1 (5)	9+2 (7)
33	27/8	Workington	A	PL	L37-53	8+1 (5)	6+1 (4)	8 (5)	-	3+2 (4)	-	-	-	2+1 (3)	10+2 (9)
34	1/9	Stoke	H	PL	L42-48	4+1 (3)	-	16 (6)	-	11+2 (6)	-	-	-	3 (4)	8+1 (11)
35	7/9	Rye House	A	PL	L27-63	R/R	2 (5)	7 (5)	-	10+1 (6)	-	-	-	-	8+1 (14)
36	8/9	Newport	H	PL	L32-61	R/R	-	17 (6)	-	5+1 (6)	-	-	-	-	10+1 (18)
37	9/9	Glasgow	A	PL	L28-62	R/R	-	12 (6)	-	9+1 (5)	-	-	-	-	7+1 (18)
38	15/9	Edinburgh	H	PL	L35-55	-	-	12 (6)	-	-	-	-	-	-	23+2 (24)
39	22/9	Mildenhall	H	PL	D45-45	-	-	14 (6)	-	-	-	-	-	-	31+5 (24)
40	23/9	Mildenhall	A	PL	L39-54	-	-	4 (5)	-	-	-	-	-	-	35+2 (25)
41	26/9	Stoke	A	PL	L31-60	R/R	-	5+2 (6)	-	-	-	-	-	-	26+3 (24)

ADDITIONAL KEY: TT = Tyne-Tweed Trophy.

NOTE: (1) The away match at Edinburgh in the Premier Trophy on 13 April was abandoned after heat twelve, with the result permitted to stand; (2) The Premier League match at Newport on 5 August originally ended in a 54-38 victory for Berwick, however, the SCB subsequently ruled that the Bandits' use of facilities for absent Polish riders Sebastian Truminski and Jacek Rempala should be withdrawn. Berwick had operated rider replacement for the former, while Lee Complin had guested for the latter. The points recorded by Complin and R/R were therefore deducted to leave an amended result of 38-35 in favour of Newport. This affected four riders, whose records on the day were originally as follows: Complin 15 (5); Burza 14+4 (6); Makovsky 11+1 (6); Bergstrom 10+1 (5).

Details of other riders (all guests unless **highlighted**): Match No. 9: Byron Bekker 1 (4); Match No. 10: Rickylee Beecroft 1 (3); Match No. 12: Andrew Tully 9+1 (5); Match No. 15: **Jamie Robertson** 1 (5); Match No. 16: **Jamie Robertson** 7+1 (4); Match No. 17: **Jamie Robertson** 2+2 (4); Match No. 18: **Jamie Robertson** 2 (4); Match No. 19: **Jamie Robertson** 5+1 (4); Sam Martin 2 (3); Match No. 20: Tom Brown 3 (3); **Jamie Robertson** 2 (4); Match No. 21: **Jamie Robertson** 0 (3); Match No. 22: **Jamie Robertson** R/R; Match No. 23: **Sebastian Truminski** 9+2 (5); **Sam Martin** 2+1 (3); Match No. 24: Sebastian Truminski 6 (4); **Sam Martin** 1 (3); Match No. 25: Sebastian Truminski 9+1 (5); **Sam Martin** 1+1 (3); Match No. 26: Sebastian Truminski 7+1 (4); **Sam Martin** 0 (4); Match No. 27: **Sam Martin** 5+1 (6); **Sebastian Truminski** 3 (4); Tomas Suchanek 2 (4); Match No. 28: Sebastian Truminski 4+1 (4); **Sam Martin** 0 (4); Match No. 29: **Sam Martin** 4+1 (5); Billy Legg 0 (3); Match No. 30: **Theo Pijper** 6 (4); **Sam Martin** 3+1 (4); John MacPhail 1 (3); Match No. 31: Lee Complin 9 (4); **Theo Pijper** 5 (4); **Sam Martin** 1 (4); Match No. 32: **Theo Pijper** 7 (4); **Sam Martin** 2+2 (3); Match No. 33: **Theo Pijper** 6 (4); **Sam Martin** 4+2 (5); Match No. 34: Chris Kerr 5+1 (5); **Sam Martin** 3 (6); **Theo Pijper** R/R; Match No. 35: **Theo Pijper** 7+1 (5); Byron Bekker 1 (5); **Sam Martin** 0 (4); Match No. 36: Matej Kus 3+1 (5); Byron Bekker 3 (6); **Sam Martin** 2 (5); Joe Haines 2 (4); Match No. 37: Kalle Katajisto 4+1 (5); **Matej Kus** 2 (2); **Sam Martin** 1 (7); John MacPhail 0 (4); Match No. 38: Carl Wilkinson 10 (6); **Sam Martin** 4+2 (6); Ritchie Hawkins 4 (5); Byron Bekker 4 (4); **Arlo Bugeja** 1 (3); **Matej Kus** R/R; Match No. 39: Paul Clews 11+3 (7); Tony Atkin 10 (6); William Lawson 7 (5); **Sam Martin** 2+1 (3); **Arlo Bugeja** 1+1 (3); **Matej Kus** R/R; Match No. 40: Chris Mills 14 (6); Tommy Allen 13+1 (6); **Sam Martin** 4+1 (5); **Arlo Bugeja** 2 (4); Daniel Halsey 2 (4); **Matej Kus** R/R; Match No. 41: Chris Kerr 8+1 (5); Scott James 6+1 (4); Trent Leverington 6 (6); Jonathan Bethell 4+1 (4); **Arlo Bugeja** 2 (5).

Details of tactical rides and tactical substitute rides: Match No. 3: Bergstrom 6 points (TR); Match No. 5: Coles 4 points (TR); Match No. 7: Bergstrom 1 point (TR; not doubled); Match No. 10: Rempala 0 points (TR); Match No. 11: Makovsky 6 points (TR); Match No. 14: Makovsky 4 points (TR); Burza 1 point (TS; not doubled); Match No. 15: Burza 6 points (TR); Bergstrom 0 points (TS); Match No. 16: Rempala 4 points (TR); Match No. 18: Rempala 6 points (TR); Match No. 19: Makovsky 6 points (TR); Rempala 1 point (TS; not doubled); Match No. 21: Burza 4 points (TS); Rempala 4 points (TR); Match No. 22: Makovsky 4 points (TS); Match No. 23: Truminski 4 points (TR); Match No. 27: Rempala 4 points (TR); Match No. 30: Burza 4 points (TR); Match No. 31: Complin 4 points (TR); Match No. 35: Burza 1 point (TR; not doubled); Match No. 36: Rempala 6 points (TR); Match No. 37: Martin 0 points (TR); Match No. 38: Hawkins 0 points (TR); Match No. 40: Mills 6 points (TR); Match No. 41: Rempala 2 points (TR).

Other details: Anderson's Quality Seven scorers in Match No. 1: Adrian Rymel 11 (5); Derek Sneddon 7 (4); Theo Pijper 6+1 (5); Paul Cooper 6+1 (5); Trent Leverington 5+1 (4); Rob Grant 5 (4); Lee Smethills 1+1 (4). Rymel's total includes 6 points from a TR.

AVERAGES

[28 Premier League; 2 Knock-Out Cup; 8 Premier Trophy = 38 fixtures]

Rider	Mts	Rds	Pts	Bon	Tot	Avge	Max
Michal Makovsky	31	146	258	18	276	7.56	-
Stanislaw Burza	32	153	246	32	278	7.27	-
Jacek Rempala	35	168	290	7	297	7.07	-
Andreas Bergstrom	30	128	176	29	205	6.41	-
Sebastian Truminski	6	26	36	5	41	6.31	-
Michael Coles	11	41	44	3	47	4.59	-
David Meldrum	19	86	80	18	98	4.56	-
Benji Compton	16	69	47	10	57	3.30	-
Jamie Robertson	7	28	19	4	23	3.29	-
Sam Martin	18	80	39	13	52	2.60	-

Also rode (in alphabetical order):

Rider	Mts	Rds	Pts	Bon	Tot	Avge	Max
John Branney	5	17	6	1	7	1.65	-
Arlo Bugeja	4	15	6	1	7	1.87	-
Rob Grant	4	13	6	1	7	2.15	-
Matej Kus	2	7	5	1	6	3.43	-
Theo Pijper	5	21	31	1	32	6.10	-

Guests	28	127	137	10	147	4.63	-

(Tommy Allen [1]; Tony Atkin [1]; Rickylee Beecroft [1]; Byron Bekker [4]; Jonathan Bethell [1]; Tom Brown [1]; Paul Clews [1]; Lee Complin [1]; Joe Haines [1]; Daniel Halsey [1]; Ritchie Hawkins [1]; Scott James [1]; Kalle Katajisto [1]; Chris Kerr [2]; William Lawson [1]; Billy Legg [1]; Trent Leverington [1]; John MacPhail [2]; Sam Martin [1]; Chris Mills [1]; Tomas Suchanek [1]; Andrew Tully [1]; Carl Wilkinson [1])

INDIVIDUAL MEETING

18 August: **40th Season Bonanza**

QUALIFYING SCORES: Chris Holder 12; Kevin Doolan 11; Craig Watson 10; Josef Franc 9; Michal Makovsky 8; Jacek Rempala 7; Matej Kus 5; Casper Wortmann 4; Kozza Smith 3; Andrew Moore 1; Stanislaw Burza 1; Kalle Katajisto 1.

SEMI-FINAL: 1st Watson; 2nd Makovsky; 3rd Franc; 4th Rempala.

FINAL: 1st Doolan; 2nd Holder; 3rd Makovsky; 4th Watson.

Popular teamster **Stan Burza** spent a second term with Berwick and contributed many double figure tallies in exciting fashion.

(Photo: David Valentine)

BIRMINGHAM BRUMMIES

ADDRESS:	Perry Barr Greyhound Stadium (formerly Alexander Sports Stadium), Aldridge Road, Perry Barr, Birmingham, West Midlands, B42 2ET.
TELEPHONE:	0870 8407410.
CLUB HOTLINE:	09068 664660 (Premium rate applies).
WEBSITE:	www.birminghamspeedway.co.uk
PROMOTERS:	Anthony E. Mole & Graham Drury.
MAIN TEAM SPONSOR:	Mercom Water Products Ltd.
YEARS OF OPERATION:	1928 Open; 1946 Northern League; 1947-1948 National League Division Two; 1949-1956 National League Division One; 1957 National League; 1960 Open; 2007 Premier League.
FIRST MEETING:	12 July 1928.
TRACK LENGTH:	292 metres.
TRACK RECORD:	57.3 seconds - Jason Lyons (06/06/07).
PREVIOUS VENUES:	(1) Perry Barr Greyhound Stadium, Walsall Road, Birmingham, West Midlands, B42 1BY.
YEARS OF OPERATION:	1929 Southern League; 1930 Southern League and Open Licence; 1971-1974 British League Division Two; 1975 National League; 1976-1983 British League.
PREVIOUS VENUES:	(2) Birmingham Wheels Project, Adderley Road South, Bordesley Green, Birmingham, West Midlands, B8 1AD.
YEARS OF OPERATION:	1984 Open Licence; 1985-1986 National League.

CLUB HONOURS

ANNIVERSARY CUP (DIVISION TWO) WINNERS: 1948.

LEAGUE CHAMPIONS: 1974, 1975.

KNOCK-OUT CUP WINNERS: 1974.

Jason Lyons proved a class act, as the Brummies roared back into action following twenty years in the speedway wilderness.

(Photo: David Valentine)

BIRMINGHAM 2007

* Denotes aggregate/bonus-point victory

NO.	DATE	OPPONENTS	VENUE	COMPETITION	RESULT	ULRICH OSTERGAARD	AIDAN COLLINS	JASON LYONS	EMILIANO SANCHEZ	BRENT WERNER	LEE SMART	BEN POWELL	JON ARMSTRONG	MANUEL HAUZINGER	OTHER RIDERS
1	28/3	Stoke	H	PT	W50-34	10+2 (5)	8+1 (4)	15 (5)	-	5+1 (4)	5+3 (4)	7+1 (4)	-	-	-
2	31/3	Stoke	A	PT	W46-44*	15 (5)	1 (3)	11 (5)	5+1 (4)	5 (4)	5 (4)	4 (5)	-	-	-
3	5/4	Sheffield	A	PT	L31-62	11 (5)	1 (4)	10 (5)	4 (4)	0 (3)	3 (5)	2 (4)	-	-	-
4	6/4	Sheffield	H	PT	W52-41	9 (5)	6+3 (4)	14 (5)	8+3 (4)	7+1 (4)	2 (3)	6+3 (5)	-	-	-
5	11 /4	Workington	H	PT	W48-41	10+1 (5)	8+1 (5)	13+1 (5)	6+2 (5)	R/R	4 (5)	7 (5)	-	-	-
6	14/4	Workington	A	PT	W53-40*	11+2 (5)	6+1 (5)	11 (5)	11+2 (5)	R/R	7+3 (5)	7+1 (5)	-	-	-
7	18/4	Rye House	H	PL	L39-53	10 (5)	5 (4)	10+1 (5)	6+1 (4)	4 (4)	2 (4)	2+2 (4)	-	-	-
8	21/4	Rye House	A	PL	L39-53	12 (5)	0 (3)	11 (5)	5+1 (4)	4 (4)	3+2 (5)	4 (4)	-	-	-
9	25/4	Newport	H	KO	W49-41	12+1 (5)	0 (3)	12 (5)	6+1 (4)	6 (4)	3+1 (3)	10+1 (6)	-	-	-
10	29/4	Newport	A	KO	L39-51	R/R	3+1 (4)	15 (6)	6 (5)	4+2 (5)	3 (4)	8+1 (6)	-	-	-
11	2/5	King's Lynn	A	PT	L33-59	14+1 (6)	0 (1)	7 (5)	2 (4)	1 (3)	8+1 (7)	1+1 (4)	-	-	-
12	6/5	King's Lynn	H	PT	D45-45	9 (5)	5+1 (4)	12 (5)	7+2 (4)	7 (5)	3 (4)	2+1 (3)	-	-	-
13	16/5	Sheffield	H	PL	W47-42	15 (5)	4+1 (4)	6 (5)	8+1 (4)	-	7+1 (6)	2+1 (3)	5 (3)	-	-
14	30/5	Newport	H	PL	W62-27	15 (5)	6+1 (4)	12 (5)	9 (4)	-	7+2 (4)	8+2 (4)	5+2 (4)	-	-
15	2/6	Rye House	A	PTs	L38-52	12 (5)	0 (3)	10 (5)	3 (4)	-	2 (3)	-	1 (3)	-	10 (7)
16	6/6	Rye House	H	PTs	W58-35*	11 (5)	4+3 (4)	12 (4)	10+2 (5)	-	8+2 (4)	8+2 (4)	5+2 (4)	-	-
17	20/6	Isle of Wight	H	PL	W48-42	9+2 (5)	3 (4)	12+1 (5)	9 (4)	-	6 (4)	8+3 (5)	1 (3)	-	-
18	23/6	Workington	A	PL	D45-45	8 (5)	1+1 (3)	11+1 (5)	8+1 (4)	-	7+1 (6)	4+1 (3)	6 (4)	-	-
19	27/6	Somerset	H	PL	W49-41	11 (5)	2+1 (2)	10 (5)	4+2 (3)	-	13 (6)	7+2 (6)	2 (3)	-	-
20	6/7	Somerset	A	PL	L32-58	5 (5)	-	-	5 (4)	-	1+1 (4)	3 (3)	0 (3)	9+1 (6)	9 (5)
21	11/7	Stoke	H	PL	W53-40	12+1 (5)	-	15 (5)	6+1 (4)	-	2+1 (3)	4+1 (4)	2+1 (3)	-	12+1 (6)
22	18/7	Workington	H	PL	W46-44*	9+1 (5)	-	13 (5)	6 (4)	-	4+2 (4)	3 (4)	3+1 (3)	8+2 (5)	-
23	25/7	Glasgow	H	PL	W53-39	10 (5)	-	11+2 (5)	7 (4)	-	6+1 (4)	1 (3)	-	10+1 (5)	8+1 (4)
24	26/7	Redcar	A	PL	W53-42	12+1 (5)	-	9+1 (5)	7+2 (4)	-	9 (5)	7 (4)	-	3+2 (3)	6+1 (4)
25	27/7	Edinburgh	A	PL	L44-48	6+1 (4)	-	16 (6)	7 (5)	-	7 (5)	1 (3)	-	1 (3)	6+2 (4)
26	29/7	King's Lynn	H	PTf	L39-51	R/R	-	11 (6)	6+2 (6)	-	4+1 (3)	4+1 (3)	-	11+1 (7)	3+1 (5)
27	1/8	Newcastle	H	PL	W57-36	12+1 (5)	-	14 (5)	8+1 (4)	-	4+2 (4)	3+1 (4)	-	8+1 (4)	8+2 (4)
28	2/8	Isle of Wight	A	PL	L33-60	5 (5)	-	12 (5)	0 (3)	-	4 (5)	6 (4)	-	6 (5)	0 (3)
29	5/8	Mildenhall	A	PL	W48-42	12 (5)	-	11+1 (5)	9+2 (5)	-	0 (3)	2+1 (5)	-	14+1 (7)	R/R
30	8/8	Redcar	H	PL	W53-42*	-	-	14 (5)	7 (4)	-	2+2 (4)	5+2 (4)	-	10+1 (4)	15+3 (9)
31	11/8	Berwick	A	PL	W52-40	-	-	11+1 (4)	8 (5)	-	5+3 (4)	8+1 (4)	-	7 (4)	13+2 (9)
32	15/8	Berwick	H	PL	W59-33*	-	-	10 (4)	9+2 (4)	-	7 (4)	14+1 (6)	-	3+2 (3)	16+3 (9)
33	19/8	Newport	A	PL	W48-42*	-	-	13 (5)	8 (5)	-	3+2 (4)	6+2 (5)	-	7 (4)	11+1 (7)
34	26/8	King's Lynn	H	PL	L43-46	-	-	11 (5)	R/R	-	1 (3)	9+2 (6)	-	9 (5)	13+5 (11)
35	29/8	Mildenhall	H	PL	W58-34*	-	-	15 (5)	R/R	-	2+1 (5)	6+1 (5)	-	10 (4)	25+2 (11)
36	30/8	Sheffield	A	PL	L36-57	-	-	13 (5)	R/R	-	3+2 (4)	10 (7)	-	4 (4)	6+2 (10)
37	5/9	Edinburgh	H	PL	W63-29*	-	-	15 (5)	R/R	-	6+2 (5)	5 (4)	-	12 (5)	25+5 (11)
38	8/9	Stoke	A	PL	W48-45*	-	-	18 (6)	R/R	-	3+1 (4)	5+1 (5)	-	11 (6)	11+1 (9)
39	14/9	King's Lynn	H	PL	L44-49	-	-	16 (6)	R/R	-	-	4+1 (5)	-	0 (1)	24+6 (18)
40	15/9	Workington	A	Chal	L42-51	-	-	15 (6)	R/R	-	-	12+2 (6)	-	-	15+4 (18)
41	19/9	Stoke	H	MS	W56-37	-	-	14 (5)	-	-	12+4 (7)	10+1 (7)	-	9+1 (5)	11+2 (6)
42	22/9	Stoke	A	MS	L43-47*	-	-	17 (6)	-	-	2 (4)	10+1 (6)	-	0 (3)	14+3 (11)
43	23/9	Newcastle	A	PL	W47-43*	-	-	16+1 (6)	-	-	7+1 (5)	9+1 (6)	-	3+2 (4)	12+1 (9)
44	2/10	Mildenhall	A	YS	W47-43	-	-	15 (5)	-	-	10+3 (6)	-	-	4 (4)	18+3 (15)
45	3/10	Mildenhall	H	YS	L44-46*	-	-	14+1 (5)	-	-	4+1 (6)	-	-	4 (4)	22+1 (15)
46	5/10	King's Lynn	A	PTf	L35-58	-	-	16 (5)	-	-	5+1 (7)	-	-	0 (1)	14+1 (17)
47	10/10	Stoke	H	YSs	W54-38	-	-	17 (6)	-	-	7 (5)	-	-	R/R	30+5 (19)
48	13/10	Stoke	A	YSs	L43-46*	-	-	11 (6)	-	-	5+2 (4)	-	-	R/R	27+3 (20)
49	14/10	Glasgow	A	PL	W46-43*	-	-	15+1 (6)	-	-	2+1 (5)	-	-	R/R	29+3 (19)
50	22/10	Wolverhampton	A	WM	L38-55	-	-	3 (4)	-	-	1+1 (4)	-	-	-	34+2 (22)
51	24/10	Wolverhampton	H	WM	D45-45	-	-	15+1 (6)	-	-	5+1 (4)	-	-	-	25+2 (20)
52	25/10	Redcar	A	YSf	L41-49	-	-	13+1 (6)	-	-	4+1 (3)	-	-	R/R	24+4 (21)
53	28/10	Redcar	H	YSf	L43-46	-	-	15 (6)	-	-	4+1 (4)	-	-	R/R	24+3 (20)

ADDITIONAL KEY: MS = Midland Shield; WM = BBC West Midland Shield.

NOTE: With reference to the home fixture versus Stoke in the Premier Trophy on 28 March, the following statement was issued by the Speedway Control Bureau on 8 April: 'At the above meeting, which was declared on the night as a win by Birmingham of 56-34 against Stoke, it transpires that the Birmingham line-up did not comply with the Speedway Regulations. Emiliano Sanchez was injured the previous weekend and to cover his absence rider replacement was used. As Sanchez had not yet ridden for Birmingham, no facility was permitted as per SR 18.1.4.2 which states "No facility is permitted to replace a rider, who although declared has not made an appearance for that team". Accordingly the result of the meeting and scores of the riders who took the rider replacement rides are amended.' This affected four riders, whose records on the night were originally as follows: Ostergaard 12+3 (6); Collins 10+2 (5); Werner 7+1 (5); Jack Roberts 0 (1).

Details of other riders (all guests unless **highlighted**): Match No. 15: Tomas Suchanek 10 (7); Match No. 20: Kauko Nieminen 9 (5); Match No. 21: Tomas Suchanek 12+1 (6); Match No. 23: **Henrik Moller** 8+1 (4); Match No. 24: **Henrik Moller** 6+1 (4); Match No. 25: **Henrik Moller** 6+2 (4); Match No. 26: **Henrik Moller** 3+1 (5); Match No. 27: **Henrik Moller** 8+2 (4); Match No. 28: **Henrik Moller** 0 (3); Match No. 29: **Henrik Moller** R/R; Match No. 30: **Henning Bager** 8+2 (5); **Henrik Moller** 7+1 (4); Match No. 31: **Henning Bager**

8+1 (5); **Henrik Moller** 5+1 (4); Match No. 32: **Henning Bager** 8+1 (5); **Henrik Moller** 8+2 (4); Match No. 33: **Henning Bager** 8+1 (4); **Henrik Moller** 3 (3); Match No. 34: **Henning Bager** 8+4 (6); **Henrik Moller** 5+1 (5); Match No. 35: **Henning Bager** 15+1 (6); **Henrik Moller** 10+1 (5); Match No. 36: **Henrik Moller** 4+1 (5); **Henning Bager** 2+1 (5); Match No. 37: **Henning Bager** 15+2 (6); **Henrik Moller** 10+3 (5); Match No. 38: **Henning Bager** 8+1 (5); **Henrik Moller** 3 (4); Match No. 39: Simon Lambert 10+3 (7); **Henning Bager** 9+1 (6); Chris Schramm 5+2 (5); Match No. 40: **Henning Bager** 6+1 (5); Phil Morris 4+1 (5); Chris Kerr 3+1 (5); Scott James 2+1 (3); Match No. 41: **Phil Morris** 11+2 (6); Paul Hurry 0 (0); **Henrik Moller** R/R; Match No. 42: Chris Schramm 10+1 (6); **Phil Morris** 4+2 (5); **Henrik Moller** R/R; Match No. 43: **Phil Morris** 11+1 (6); Derek Sneddon 1 (3); **Henrik Moller** R/R; Match No. 44: **Phil Morris** 9+2 (6); Craig Branney 5+1 (5); Paul Clews 4 (4); **Henrik Moller** R/R; Match No. 45: Chris Kerr 11 (6); **Phil Morris** 9+1 (5); Paul Clews 2 (4); **Henrik Moller** R/R; Match No. 46: Shaun Tacey 7 (6); **Phil Morris** 6+1 (5); Scott James 1 (6); **Henrik Moller** R/R; Match No. 47: **Phil Morris** 12+1 (6); Chris Schramm 8+1 (5); Craig Branney 6+2 (5); Danny Warwick 4+1 (3); Match No. 48: **Phil Morris** 13 (6); Paul Clews 8+1 (6); Chris Schramm 5+2 (5); Shaun Tacey 1 (3); Match No. 49: Chris Schramm 10+2 (6); Shaun Tacey 10 (5); **Phil Morris** 6+1 (5); John Branney 3 (3); Match No. 50: Kenneth Bjerre 17 (5); Niels-Kristian Iversen 9 (5); **Phil Morris** 4+2 (4); Claus Vissing 2 (4); Shaun Tacey 2 (4); Match No. 51: Filip Sitera 13 (6); **Phil Morris** 8+1 (5); Shaun Tacey 2+1 (5); Paul Clews 2 (4); **Henrik Moller** R/R; Match No. 52: Shaun Tacey 9+1 (6); Jason King 8 (5); **Phil Morris** 4+1 (4); Barrie Evans 3+2 (6); Match No. 53: Joel Parsons 8+1 (5); Paul Clews 7 (5); Chris Schramm 6 (5); Shaun Tacey 3+2 (5).

Details of tactical rides and tactical substitute rides: Match No. 3: Lyons 6 points (TR); Match No. 7: Lyons 4 points (TR); Match No. 8: Ostergaard 4 points (TR); Match No. 11: Ostergaard 4 points (TS); Lyons 1 point (TR; not doubled); Match No. 20: Nieminen 1 point (TR; not doubled); Match No. 25: Lyons 4 points (TS); Sanchez 0 points (TR); Match No. 28: Lyons 6 points (TR); Match No. 36: Lyons 6 points (TR); Match No. 39: Lyons 6 points (TR); Match No. 40: Lyons 6 points (TR); Match No. 46: Lyons 6 points (TR); Match No. 50: Bjerre 6 points (TR).

AVERAGES

[28 Premier League; 2 Knock-Out Cup; 12 Premier Trophy; 6 Young Shield = 48 fixtures]

Rider	Mts	Rds	Pts	Bon	Tot	Avge	Max
Jason Lyons	47	243	575	13	588	9.68	7 full; 2 paid
Ulrich Ostergaard	27	135	283	14	297	8.80	3 full
Henning Bager	10	53	89	15	104	7.85	-
Phil Morris	8	43	70	8	78	7.26	-
Emiliano Sanchez	32	136	210	29	239	7.03	-
Manuel Hauzinger	23	98	154	14	168	6.86	-
Henrik Moller	15	63	86	17	103	6.54	-
Ben Powell	39	174	212	38	250	5.75	-
Lee Smart	47	208	219	48	267	5.13	-
Brent Werner	10	40	43	4	47	4.70	-
Aidan Collins	19	68	63	15	78	4.59	-
Jon Armstrong	10	33	30	6	36	4.36	-
Guests	28	142	176	22	198	5.58	-

(Craig Branney [2]; John Branney [1]; Paul Clews [4]; Barrie Evans [1]; Scott James [1]; Chris Kerr [1]; Jason King [1]; Simon Lambert [1]; Kauko Nieminen [1]; Joel Parsons [1]; Chris Schramm [5]; Derek Sneddon [1]; Tomas Suchanek [2]; Shaun Tacey [5]; Danny Warwick [1])

INDIVIDUAL MEETINGS

21 March: Alan Hunt Memorial Trophy

1st Andre Compton 15; 2nd James Wright 12; 3rd Craig Watson 11; Magnus Zetterstrom 10; Stanislaw Burza 10; Jason Lyons 10; Ronnie Correy 10; Brent Werner 8; Ulrich Ostergaard 8; Phil Morris 6; Lee Smart 5; Emiliano Sanchez 4; Aidan Collins 4; Ritchie Hawkins 4; Paul Pickering 3; Ben Powell 0.

12 September: Alan Pearce Memorial Trophy

QUALIFYING SCORES:

Lee Smart 12; Matthew Wright 9; Ben Taylor 9; Arlo Bugeja 7; Paul Starke 6; Adam McKinna 6; Karl Mason 6; Scott James 5; Luke Priest 5; Kyle Hughes 4; Scott Richardson 2; Martin Emerson 1.

FINAL:

1st Smart; 2nd Wright; 3rd Taylor; 4th Bugeja.

26 September: Second City Trophy

1st Jason Lyons 14; 2nd Rory Schlein 13; 3rd David Howe 12; Joe Screen 11; Billy Janniro 11; Kauko Nieminen 10; Cameron Woodward 10; Josef Franc 9; Phil Morris 6; Andre Compton 6; Ronnie Correy 6; Chris Schramm 5; Lee Smart 3; Henrik Moller 2; Ben Powell 1; Adam Lowe 1 (Res); Andy Smith 0.

After several impressive performances, **Lee Smart** became a fully-fledged Birmingham rider in July, when promoter Graham Drury took up the option to purchase his contract from Somerset.

(Photo: David Valentine)

EDINBURGH MONARCHS

ADDRESS:	Armadale Stadium, 2 Bathgate Road, Armadale, West Lothian, EH48 2PD.
TELEPHONE:	01501 734404.
CLUB HOTLINE:	09068 664675 (Premium rate applies).
WEBSITE:	www.edinburghspeedway.co.uk
PROMOTERS:	John Campbell & Alex Harkess.
MAIN TEAM SPONSOR:	Scotwaste Recycling.
YEARS OF OPERATION:	1997-2002 Premier League; 2003 Premier League and Conference Trophy; 2004-2005 Premier League and Conference League; 2006-2007 Premier League.
FIRST MEETING:	4 April 1997.
TRACK LENGTH:	260 metres.
TRACK RECORD:	54.6 seconds - Theo Pijper (22/09/06).
PREVIOUS VENUES:	(1) Old Meadowbank Stadium, Clockmill Road, Edinburgh.
YEARS OF OPERATION:	1948-1954 National League Division Two; 1957 Training; 1959 Open; 1960-1964 Provincial League; 1965-1967 British League; 1998 Demonstration.
PREVIOUS VENUES:	(2) Cliftonhill Stadium, Main Street, Coatbridge, ML5 3RB.
YEARS OF OPERATION:	1968-1969 British League Division One. NOTE: The team rode as Coatbridge Monarchs.
PREVIOUS VENUES:	(3) Powderhall Stadium, Beaverhall Road, Edinburgh, EH7 4JE.
YEARS OF OPERATION:	1977-1990 National League; 1991-1994 British League Division Two; 1995 Premier League.
PREVIOUS VENUES:	(4) Shawfield Stadium, Glasgow Road, Rutherglen, Glasgow, G73 1SZ.
YEARS OF OPERATION:	1996 Premier League. NOTE: The team rode under the name of Scottish Monarchs.

CLUB HONOURS

QUEEN'S CUP WINNERS: 1953.
FOUR-TEAM CHAMPIONS: 1981, 1993.
KNOCK-OUT CUP WINNERS: 1981, 1997, 1999.
PAIRS CHAMPIONS: 1986.
PREMIERSHIP WINNERS: 1998.
LEAGUE CHAMPIONS: 2003.
CONFERENCE TROPHY WINNERS : 2005.

Veteran racer **Ronnie Correy** lost his team place in a dramatic mid-season re-shuffle, which also saw Theo Pijper and Henrik Moller depart from the Monarchs' ranks.

(Photo: David Valentine)

EDINBURGH 2007

* Denotes aggregate/bonus-point victory

NO.	DATE	OPPONENTS	VENUE	COMPETITION	RESULT	RONNIE CORREY	HENRIK MOLLER	WILLIAM LAWSON	DANIELE TESSARI	MATTHEW WETHERS	DEREK SNEDDON	ANDREW TULLY	THEO PIJPER	GEORGE STANCL	OTHER RIDERS
1	23/3	Glasgow	H	ST	W37-36	6+1 (3)	8+2 (4)	10 (4)	2+1 (3)	6 (3)	4 (4)	1 (3)	-	-	-
2	25/3	Glasgow	A	ST	L39-53	5+1 (4)	5 (5)	7+1 (6)	5 (5)	R/R	14+1 (6)	3 (4)	-	-	-
3	30/3	Redcar	H	PT	L44-46	11 (5)	6+1 (4)	5+1 (5)	5+1 (4)	6+1 (4)	6 (4)	5+2 (4)	-	-	-
4	31/3	Berwick	A	PT	L38-52	3 (4)	3 (3)	12 (5)	0 (3)	4 (4)	10+1 (6)	6+2 (5)	-	-	-
5	6/4	Newcastle	H	PT	W47-42	14 (5)	8+2 (5)	7 (4)	5+2 (4)	0 (3)	12+1 (6)	1 (3)	-	-	-
6	12/4	Redcar	A	PT	L42-51	9 (5)	9+2 (4)	7 (5)	3+1 (4)	2+1 (4)	4+2 (4)	8 (4)	-	-	-
7	13/4	Berwick	H	PT	W47-25*	7 (3)	8 (4)	9 (4)	2+1 (3)	7+1 (3)	5 (3)	9+2 (4)	-	-	-
8	15/4	Newcastle	A	PT	L41-50	13 (5)	4+1 (4)	8 (5)	3+2 (3)	5 (4)	7 (6)	-	-	-	1+1 (3)
9	20/4	Glasgow	H	PT	W47-42	11+1 (5)	8 (4)	6+1 (4)	7+2 (4)	10 (5)	3 (4)	2+1 (4)	-	-	-
10	27/4	Stoke	H	PL	W58-36	14 (5)	5+1 (5)	16+2 (6)	-	8+1 (5)	R/R	7+2 (5)	-	-	8 (4)
11	29/4	Glasgow	A	PT	L43-47*	7 (5)	13+2 (6)	8 (5)	11+1 (7)	4 (5)	R/R	0 (0)	-	-	-
12	3/5	Sheffield	A	KO	L36-57	6 (5)	6 (5)	3+1 (5)	9+1 (6)	10+1 (6)	R/R	2 (3)	-	-	-
13	4/5	Sheffield	H	KO	W60-33*	12+1 (5)	7+4 (4)	11 (5)	7+1 (4)	8+1 (4)	7+1 (4)	8+3 (4)	-	-	-
14	11/5	Berwick	H	PL	W60-32	7+1 (4)	8+1 (4)	11+2 (5)	4+2 (4)	13+1 (5)	9 (4)	8+2 (4)	-	-	-
15	12/5	Workington	A	PL	L40-50	-	3+2 (4)	-	4 (3)	11+2 (6)	4+1 (4)	3+1 (4)	-	-	15 (9)
16	18/5	Isle of Wight	H	PL	W52-42	7 (4)	7 (4)	5+1 (5)	3+2 (2)	14+2 (7)	8+1 (4)	8 (4)	-	-	-
17	25/5	Somerset	H	KO	W48-41	-	6 (3)	9+1 (5)	-	15+2 (7)	5+1 (4)	6+3 (4)	-	-	7+1 (7)
18	1/6	Wolves Select	H	Chal	W46-44	-	-	10+1 (5)	-	7+1 (4)	2+2 (4)	5+1 (4)	11+1 (5)	-	11+1 (8)
19	8/6	King's Lynn	H	PL	L43-47	8+2 (5)	8+1 (4)	-	-	8+3 (5)	9 (4)	1+1 (4)	9 (5)	-	0 (3)
20	15/6	Newport	H	PL	W59-33	12+2 (5)	5+2 (3)	-	-	12 (5)	5+2 (4)	5+1 (4)	15 (5)	-	5 (4)
21	17/6	Newport	A	PL	W47-42*	12 (5)	5+1 (4)	-	-	-	5+1 (4)	0 (3)	6+1 (4)	-	19+1 (10)
22	21/6	Redcar	A	PL	L41-52	10 (5)	R/R	-	-	10+2 (7)	12+1 (5)	2+1 (4)	7 (5)	-	0 (4)
23	22/6	Redcar	H	PL	L40-50	10 (5)	R/R	-	-	11+1 (6)	7+4 (5)	4+3 (5)	8 (5)	-	0 (4)
24	3/7	Isle of Wight	A	PL	L24-67	2 (3)	8 (5)	-	-	3 (5)	0 (4)	3+1 (4)	4 (5)	-	4+1 (4)
25	11/7	Somerset	A	KO	L32-58	8 (5)	0 (1)	-	-	13+1 (7)	3+1 (4)	2+1 (4)	5 (5)	-	1+1 (4)
26	20/7	Mildenhall	H	PL	W53-40	-	-	-	-	16+1 (7)	7 (3)	4+2 (4)	-	11+2 (5)	15+2 (11)
27	27/7	Birmingham	H	PL	W48-44	-	-	-	-	16+2 (7)	8+1 (4)	4+1 (4)	-	11+1 (5)	9 (10)
28	28/7	Rye House	A	PL	L22-68	-	-	-	-	7 (5)	3 (4)	0 (4)	-	3 (4)	9 (13)
29	29/7	Mildenhall	A	PL	L41-51*	-	-	-	-	16 (7)	0 (3)	2+1 (4)	-	8+1 (5)	15 (11)
30	5/8	Newcastle	A	PL	L44-46	-	-	-	-	8+1 (4)	5+2 (4)	9+2 (6)	-	13 (5)	9+1 (11)
31	8/8	King's Lynn	A	PL	L33-60	-	-	-	-	5 (4)	4+2 (5)	4+1 (5)	-	5 (4)	15 (12)
32	9/8	Sheffield	A	PL	L31-59	-	-	-	-	7 (5)	0 (0)	8+2 (7)	-	7+1 (5)	9+1 (13)
33	10/8	Newcastle	H	PL	L43-46	-	-	1 (4)	-	10+1 (6)	R/R	14+1 (7)	-	1+1 (2)	17 (11)
34	11/8	Stoke	A	PL	L42-51*	-	-	-	-	8+1 (6)	-	6 (6)	-	R/R	28 (18)
35	17/8	Glasgow	H	PL	L41-49	-	-	-	-	13 (6)	9 (5)	3 (5)	-	R/R	16+2 (14)
36	19/8	Glasgow	A	PL	L38-55	-	-	-	-	11+1 (7)	8 (5)	1 (4)	-	R/R	18 (14)
37	24/8	Workington	H	PL	L44-49	-	-	-	-	8 (5)	9+2 (5)	11+1 (4)	-	5 (4)	11+4 (12)
38	31/8	Sheffield	H	PL	W53-40	-	-	-	-	13 (5)	10 (4)	7+1 (4)	-	8+2 (5)	15+1 (12)
39	5/9	Birmingham	A	PL	L29-63	-	-	-	-	7 (5)	5 (4)	3 (4)	-	4+1 (4)	10+1 (13)
40	14/9	Rye House	H	PL	W50-45	-	-	-	-	11 (5)	7+2 (4)	9+1 (5)	-	11+1 (4)	12+4 (12)
41	15/9	Berwick	A	PL	W55-35*	-	-	-	-	12+1 (5)	6+1 (4)	1+1 (3)	-	9 (4)	27+4 (14)
42	19/9	Somerset	A	PL	L35-57	-	-	-	-	9+1 (5)	4+1 (5)	R/R	-	6 (4)	16 (16)
43	21/9	Somerset	H	PL	W48-41	-	-	-	-	10+2 (5)	3+1 (5)	R/R	-	12 (5)	23+1 (15)
44	28/9	Finnish Select	H	Chal	W49-43	-	-	-	-	8 (5)	10+1 (6)	-	-	12 (5)	19+5 (14)
45	5/10	Glasgow	H	SC	W56-37	-	-	-	-	9+2 (4)	8+2 (5)	R/R	-	14 (5)	25+3 (16)
46	7/10	Glasgow	A	SC	L41-51*	-	-	-	-	9 (5)	6+1 (5)	R/R	-	8 (4)	18+2 (16)

ADDITIONAL KEY: ST = Spring Trophy; SC = Scottish Cup.

NOTE: (1) The home leg of the Spring Trophy versus Glasgow on 23 March was abandoned after heat twelve, with the result permitted to stand; (2) The home match against Berwick in the Premier Trophy on 13 April was abandoned after heat twelve, with the result permitted to stand.

Details of other riders (all guests unless **highlighted**): Match No. 8: Tom Brown 1+1 (3); Match No. 10: Sean Stoddart 8 (4); Match No. 15: Ricky Ashworth 10 (5); Josef Franc 5 (4); Match No. 17: Stanislaw Burza 5 (4); Gary Beaton 2+1 (3); Match No. 18: Shane Parker 6+1 (4); Daniel Nermark 5 (4); Match No. 19: Jack Roberts 0 (3); Match No. 20: Jack Roberts 5 (4); Match No. 21: Lee Complin 18+1 (7); Sam Martin 1 (3); Match No. 22: Jack Roberts 0 (4); Match No. 23: Jack Roberts 0 (4); Match No. 24: Jack Roberts 4+1 (4); Match No. 25: Aaron Summers 1+1 (4); Match No. 26: **Kaj Laukkanen** 12+1 (5); Aaron Summers 2+1 (3); **Kalle Katajisto** 1 (3); Match No. 27: **Kaj Laukkanen** 8 (4); **Aaron Summers** 1 (3); **Kalle Katajisto** 0 (3); Match No. 28: **Kaj Laukkanen** 7 (5); **Kalle Katajisto** 1 (4); **Aaron Summers** 1 (4); Match No. 29: **Kaj Laukkanen** 13 (5); **Aaron Summers** 2 (3); **Kalle Katajisto** 0 (3); Match No. 30: **Kaj Laukkanen** 8 (5); **Kalle Katajisto** 1+1 (3); John MacPhail 0 (3); Match No. 31: **Kaj Laukkanen** 15 (5); **Kalle Katajisto** 0 (4); Nathan Irwin 0 (3); Match No. 32: **Kaj Laukkanen** 5 (4); **Kalle Katajisto** 3 (4); Jack Roberts 1+1 (5); Match No. 33: Jason Lyons 14 (5); **Kalle Katajisto** 3 (5); Gary Beaton 0 (1); Match No. 34: Kyle Legault 21 (6); Robert Ksiezak 5 (5); **Kalle Katajisto** 1 (4); Scott Richardson 1 (3); Match No. 35: **Kaj Laukkanen** 13+1 (6); James Cockle 3+1 (5); **Kalle Katajisto** 0 (3); Match No. 36: **Kaj Laukkanen** 15 (6); James Cockle 3 (5); **Kalle Katajisto** 0 (3); Match No. 37: Jacek Rempala 4+2 (4); **Kalle Katajisto** 4+2 (4); Sam Martin 3 (4); Match No. 38: **Kaj Laukkanen** 11 (4); Ben Taylor 3 (5); **Kalle Katajisto** 1+1 (3); Match No. 39: **Kaj Laukkanen** 7 (5); Joe Haines 3+1 (5); **Kalle Katajisto** 0 (3); Match No. 40: **Kaj Laukkanen** 7+1 (4); Michael Coles 3+1 (4); **Kalle Katajisto** 2+2 (4); Match No. 41: **Kaj Laukkanen** 14 (5); Michael Coles 12+4 (6); **Kalle Katajisto** 1 (3); Match No. 42: **Kaj Laukkanen** 12 (5); Michael Coles 3 (6); **Kalle Katajisto** 1 (5); Match

No. 43: Paul Clews 11+1 (7); **Kaj Laukkanen** 11 (4); **Kalle Katajisto** 1 (4); Match No. 44: Sean Stoddart 9+2 (5); Gary Beaton 6+3 (5); James McBain 4 (4); Lee Complin R/R; Match No. 45: **Kaj Laukkanen** 12+1 (5); Paul Clews 12+2 (7); Daniel Giffard 1 (4); Match No. 46: **Kaj Laukkanen** 11+1 (5); Daniel Giffard 6+1 (5); Arlo Bugeja 1 (6).

Details of tactical rides and tactical substitute rides: Match No. 2: Sneddon 4 points (TR); Match No. 4: Correy 0 points (TR); Match No. 6: Moller 6 points (TR); Match No. 8: Tessari 2 points (TR); Match No. 12: Wethers 4 points (TR); Tessari 4 points (TS); Match No. 22: Sneddon 6 points (TR); Match No. 24: Moller 4 points (TR); Match No. 25: Correy 0 points (TR); Match No. 28: Wethers 0 points (TR); Match No. 29: Wethers 4 points (TR); Match No. 31: Laukkanen 6 points (TR); Match No. 32: Laukkanen 1 point (TR; not doubled); Match No. 34: Legault 6 points (TR); Match No. 36: Laukkanen 6 points (TR); Wethers 1 point (TS; not doubled); Match No. 37: Tully 6 points (TR); Match No. 39: Wethers 4 points (TR); Match No. 42: Laukkanen 4 points (TR); Match No. 46: Sneddon 4 points (TR).

Other details: Finnish Select scorers in Match No. 44: Kaj Laukkanen 14 (5); Kauko Nieminen 13 (6); Kalle Katajisto 7+1 (5); Petteri Koivunen 5+1 (4); Joni Keskinen 2+1 (4); Tero Aarnio 2 (4); Jari Makinen 0 (2) Laukkanen's total includes 6 points from a TR and Nieminen's tally includes 1 point from a TS (not doubled).

AVERAGES

[28 Premier League; 4 Knock-Out Cup; 8 Premier Trophy = 40 fixtures]

Rider	Mts	Rds	Pts	Bon	Tot	Avge	Max
Kaj Laukkanen	15	72	150	3	153	8.50	-
Ronnie Correy	20	93	183	7	190	8.17	-
George Stancl	15	65	114	10	124	7.63	1 paid
Matthew Wethers	39	206	355	31	386	7.50	-
William Lawson	14	68	117	9	126	7.41	1 paid
Henrik Moller	20	80	122	20	142	7.10	-
Theo Pijper	7	34	54	1	55	6.47	1 full
Derek Sneddon	35	147	206	29	235	6.39	-
Daniele Tessari	14	55	61	16	77	5.60	-
Andrew Tully	37	156	173	40	213	5.46	-
Kalle Katajisto	18	65	20	6	26	1.60	-

Also rode:

Aaron Summers	3	10	4	0	4	1.60	-

Guests	33	141	149	17	166	4.71	1 full

(Ricky Ashworth [1]; Gary Beaton [2]; Tom Brown [1]; Stanislaw Burza [1]; Paul Clews [1]; James Cockle [2]; Michael Coles [3]; Lee Complin [1]; Josef Franc [1]; Joe Haines [1]; Nathan Irwin [1]; Robert Ksiezak [1]; Kyle Legault [1]; Jason Lyons [1]; John MacPhail [1]; Sam Martin [2]; Jacek Rempala [1]; Scott Richardson [1]; Jack Roberts [6]; Sean Stoddart [1]; Aaron Summers [2]; Ben Taylor [1])

INDIVIDUAL MEETING

3 August: **Keyline Scottish Open**

QUALIFYING SCORES: Shane Parker 14; Tai Woffinden 12; Daniel Nermark 12; Kevin Doolan 11; Kaj Laukkanen 11; James Grieves 10; Christian Henry 9; Cameron Woodward 7; Craig Watson 7; Derek Sneddon 6; Carl Stonehewer 5; Lee Complin 5; Stanislaw Burza 4; Andrew Tully (Res) 3; Kalle Katajisto 2; Matthew Wethers 1; George Stancl 0; Daniele Tessari (Res) 0.

SEMI-FINAL: 1st Nermark; 2nd Doolan; 3rd Grieves; 4th Laukkanen.

FINAL: 1st Nermark; 2nd Doolan; 3rd Woffinden; 4th Parker.

OTHER MEETINGS

5 April: **Kevin Little Farewell** (at Redcar)

Newcastle 31, Redcar 28, Workington 23, Edinburgh 21: Rory Schlein 7 (4); Ronnie Correy 7 (3); Chris Neath 3 (3); Derek Sneddon 3 (2); William Lawson 1 (4). The total for Schelin includes 2 points from a TS.

7 September: **Challenge**

Bravehearts 47: Kaj Laukkanen 10+1 (5); Derek Sneddon 9 (5); George Stancl 9 (4); Andrew Tully 8+2 (4); James Wright 5+1 (4); Sean Stoddart 4 (4); Blair Scott 2+1 (4); Kangaroos 46: Kevin Doolan 17 (6); Shane Parker 13+1 (5); Matthew Wethers 6 (4); Kalle Katajisto 5 (4); Arlo Bugeja 5 (5); Trent Leverington 0 (3); Sam Dore 0 (3). The tally for Parker includes 6 points from a TR outing. The score for Doolan includes 2 points from a TS ride.

In the wake of all the team changes made in July, **Derek Sneddon** was delighted to become Edinburgh's captain.

(Photo: David Valentine)

GLASGOW TIGERS

ADDRESS:	Ashfield Stadium, Saracen Park, 404 Hawthorn Street, Possilpark, Glasgow, G22 6RU.
TELEPHONE:	0141 3364800.
CLUB HOTLINE:	09068 664685 (Premium rate applies).
WEBSITE:	www.glasgowspeedway.co.uk
PROMOTERS:	Alan C. Dick & Stewart Dickson.
MAIN TEAM SPONSOR:	FSM Outdoor Advertising.
YEARS OF OPERATION:	1949-1952 National League Division Two; 1953 Open; 1999-2007 Premier League. NOTE: Between 1949 and 1953, the track was home to Ashfield Giants; Ashfield Stadium also played host to a second team in the 2000 Conference League, under the banner of Lightning Ashfield Giants.
FIRST MEETING:	19 April 1949.
TRACK LENGTH:	302 metres.
TRACK RECORD:	57.3 seconds - Shane Parker (26/08/07).
PREVIOUS VENUES:	(1) White City Stadium, Paisley Road West, Ibrox, Glasgow.
YEARS OF OPERATION:	1928-1929 Open; 1930-1931 Northern League; 1939 Union Cup; 1940 Open; 1945 Open; 1946 Northern League; 1947-1953 National League Division Two; 1954 Northern Shield; 1956 Open; 1964 Provincial League; 1965-1967 British League; 1968 British League Division One. NOTE: Glasgow first acquired the Tigers moniker in 1946.
PREVIOUS VENUES:	(2) Hampden Park, Mount Florida, Glasgow, G42 9BA.
YEARS OF OPERATION:	1969-1972 British League Division One.
PREVIOUS VENUES:	(3) Cliftonhill Stadium, Main Street, Coatbridge, ML5 3RB.
YEARS OF OPERATION:	1973 British League Division One; 1974 British League Division Two; 1975-1977 National League. NOTE: The team rode as Coatbridge Tigers throughout their stay at the venue.
PREVIOUS VENUES:	(4) Blantyre Sports Stadium, Glasgow Road, Blantyre, Nr Glasgow.
YEARS OF OPERATION:	1977-1981 National League. NOTE: Coatbridge moved to Blantyre mid-way through the 1977 season, reverting back to the name of Glasgow Tigers.
PREVIOUS VENUES:	(5) Craighead Park, Forrest Street, Blantyre, Nr Glasgow.
YEARS OF OPERATION:	1982-1986 National League.
PREVIOUS VENUES:	(6) Derwent Park Stadium, Workington, Cumbria, CA14 2HG.
YEAR OF OPERATION:	1987 National League. NOTE: The side began the year as Glasgow Tigers, before becoming Workington Tigers.
PREVIOUS VENUES:	(7) Shawfield Stadium, Glasgow Road, Rutherglen, Glasgow, G73 1SZ.
YEARS OF OPERATION:	1988-1990 National League; 1991-1994 British League Division Two; 1995 Premier League; 1997-1998 Premier League. NOTE: In 1996, Shawfield Stadium was used by the Scottish Monarchs, who participated in the Premier League.

CLUB HONOURS

NATIONAL SERIES WINNERS: 1990.

LEAGUE CHAMPIONS: 1993, 1994.

KNOCK-OUT CUP WINNERS: 1993, 1994.

PAIRS CHAMPIONS: 2005, 2006.

Shane Parker again proved an inspirational leader of the Tigers in what was his fourth successive season with the Scottish side.

(Photo: David Valentine)

GLASGOW 2007

* Denotes aggregate/bonus-point victory

NO.	DATE	OPPONENTS	VENUE	COMPETITION	RESULT	GEORGE STANCL	LEE SMETHILLS	SHANE PARKER	TRENT LEVERINGTON	ROBERT KSIEZAK	LEE DICKEN	DAVID McALLAN	MICHAEL COLES	CRAIG WATSON	OTHER RIDERS
1	23/3	Edinburgh	A	ST	L36-37	8 (3)	1+1 (3)	13+1 (5)	4+1 (3)	4 (3)	3 (4)	3 (3)	-	-	-
2	24/3	Workington	A	Chal	L39-53	14 (5)	2+1 (5)	12+1 (6)	5 (5)	R/R	3 (4)	3+1 (5)	-	-	-
3	25/3	Edinburgh	H	ST	W53-39*	11+1 (5)	5+1 (5)	12+2 (5)	10+1 (5)	R/R	4+2 (5)	11+1 (5)	-	-	-
4	1/4	Workington	H	Chal	W54-39*	14 (5)	10+1 (5)	11+1 (5)	5 (5)	R/R	5+2 (5)	9+1 (5)	-	-	-
5	8/4	Newcastle	H	PT	W59-34	12+2 (5)	4 (4)	10+3 (5)	7+2 (4)	8+1 (4)	9+2 (4)	9 (4)	-	-	-
6	9/4	Newcastle	A	PT	W47-43*	12 (5)	2+1 (3)	11+1 (5)	1 (4)	6+2 (4)	6+1 (4)	9+3 (5)	-	-	-
7	14/4	Berwick	A	PT	W46-44	12 (5)	5+1 (4)	9+2 (5)	4 (4)	3+1 (4)	5+3 (4)	8+1 (4)	-	-	-
8	15/4	Redcar	H	PT	W56-37	9+2 (5)	7 (4)	14 (5)	9 (4)	6+1 (4)	7+3 (4)	4+2 (4)	-	-	-
9	20/4	Edinburgh	A	PT	L42-47	12 (5)	1+1 (3)	13+1 (5)	2+1 (3)	2 (4)	6+1 (5)	6+1 (5)	-	-	-
10	22/4	Berwick	H	PT	W61-29*	15 (5)	6+1 (4)	13+2 (5)	10+1 (4)	7+1 (4)	7+1 (4)	-	-	-	3+1 (5)
11	26/4	Redcar	A	PT	L38-53*	9 (5)	2 (4)	11+1 (5)	6+1 (4)	2+1 (4)	5 (4)	-	-	-	3+2 (4)
12	29/4	Edinburgh	H	PT	W47-43	9+1 (5)	4+1 (5)	15 (5)	8 (4)	5+1 (4)	4+1 (4)	-	-	-	2+2 (3)
13	4/5	Somerset	A	KO	L38-52	5+1 (5)	8 (5)	11+1 (6)	4+1 (4)	8+1 (4)	0 (3)	2 (3)	-	-	-
14	6/5	Somerset	H	KO	W48-45	8 (4)	6+1 (5)	12 (5)	5+2 (4)	7+1 (5)	2 (3)	8+1 (4)	-	-	-
15	20/5	Mildenhall	H	PL	W57-35	10+2 (5)	6+2 (4)	14 (5)	6+1 (4)	3 (3)	7+1 (4)	11+3 (5)	-	-	-
16	23/5	King's Lynn	A	PTs	L39-55	8 (5)	3 (4)	19 (6)	4 (4)	0 (3)	2+1 (4)	3 (4)	-	-	-
17	24/5	Sheffield	A	PL	L38-56	8 (4)	4+1 (4)	14 (6)	4+1 (4)	3+3 (5)	1+1 (4)	4 (3)	-	-	-
18	27/5	Sheffield	H	PL	W50-43	10+1 (4)	2+1 (3)	14 (5)	9 (5)	8+2 (5)	5+1 (4)	2+1 (4)	-	-	-
19	8/6	Somerset	A	PL	L36-56	5 (4)	1 (4)	15 (5)	7+1 (5)	8+1 (6)	0 (3)	0 (3)	-	-	-
20	9/6	Rye House	A	PL	L35-57	3 (4)	0 (3)	12 (5)	2+1 (4)	9 (5)	7 (5)	2 (4)	-	-	-
21	10/6	Newport	A	PL	L38-54	7+1 (4)	0 (3)	11 (5)	9+1 (5)	7+2 (6)	3+1 (4)	1 (3)	-	-	-
22	14/6	Newport	H	PL	W49-42	11 (5)	-	13 (5)	10+1 (4)	5+1 (4)	3 (4)	4+2 (4)	3+1 (4)	-	-
23	16/6	Berwick	A	PL	W48-43	10 (4)	-	15 (5)	4+2 (4)	-	2 (3)	8+3 (5)	5+1 (4)	-	4 (5)
24	17/6	Somerset	H	PL	L40-49	5 (4)	-	13 (5)	7+2 (5)	-	2 (4)	1 (2)	2+1 (4)	-	10 (6)
25	2/7	King's Lynn	H	PTs	W49-44	-	-	14 (5)	9 (4)	5+1 (4)	3+2 (5)	4+1 (4)	3 (3)	11 (5)	-
26	15/7	Rye House	H	PL	W49-40	-	-	14 (5)	6+1 (4)	5+2 (4)	7+2 (5)	2+1 (4)	3+1 (3)	12+1 (5)	-
27	21/7	Workington	A	PL	L43-47	-	-	10 (5)	5 (4)	6+1 (4)	0 (4)	5 (4)	3 (4)	14 (5)	-
28	22/7	Workington	H	PL	W49-42*	-	-	15 (5)	6 (4)	5 (4)	6+1 (4)	5 (4)	3+2 (4)	9 (5)	-
29	24/7	Isle of Wight	A	PL	L32-59	-	-	8 (5)	3 (4)	8+1 (5)	1+1 (4)	4+2 (4)	2 (4)	6 (4)	-
30	25/7	Birmingham	A	PL	L39-53	-	-	15 (5)	8 (5)	4 (4)	2 (4)	3+1 (4)	1+1 (4)	6 (4)	-
31	28/7	Stoke	A	PL	W51-43	-	-	12 (5)	9 (4)	2+1 (4)	9+1 (6)	4+2 (3)	1 (3)	14 (5)	-
32	29/7	Isle of Wight	H	PL	W52-40	-	-	12+1 (5)	14+1 (5)	5+1 (5)	2+1 (4)	R/R	7+2 (5)	12+1 (6)	-
33	17/8	Edinburgh	A	PL	W49-41	-	-	15 (5)	4 (4)	7+1 (4)	2+1 (3)	8+2 (5)	8 (5)	5+1 (4)	-
34	19/8	Edinburgh	H	PL	W55-38*	-	-	15 (5)	8 (4)	7+1 (4)	4+2 (4)	4 (4)	5+2 (4)	12+1 (5)	-
35	26/8	Newcastle	H	PL	W55-38	-	-	15 (5)	8 (4)	8+2 (4)	3+1 (4)	10+1 (5)	5+1 (4)	6 (4)	-
36	27/8	Newcastle	A	PL	L44-50*	-	-	13 (6)	6+1 (4)	5+3 (4)	9+3 (6)	2 (2)	1 (3)	8 (5)	-
37	2/9	King's Lynn	H	PL	W51-42	-	-	14 (5)	8 (4)	9+1 (5)	9+3 (6)	R/R	1 (5)	10+1 (5)	-
38	9/9	Berwick	H	PL	W62-28*	-	-	15 (5)	11 (4)	8+3 (4)	6+1 (4)	7+2 (4)	12+1 (5)	3+1 (4)	-
39	12/9	King's Lynn	A	PL	L40-52	-	-	18 (7)	11 (6)	4+2 (5)	2 (3)	4+1 (5)	1+1 (4)	R/R	-
40	13/9	Redcar	A	PL	L41-51	-	-	7+2 (5)	0 (1)	8+1 (4)	6 (7)	5+2 (4)	2 (4)	13 (5)	-
41	18/9	Mildenhall	A	PL	W47-43*	-	-	12+1 (5)	R/R	8 (5)	3 (4)	5+1 (5)	3+3 (5)	16 (6)	-
42	23/9	Redcar	H	PL	W48-47	-	-	0 (0)	7 (4)	9 (4)	11+3 (7)	7+1 (5)	5+3 (5)	9+1 (5)	-
43	4/10	Redcar	A	YS	L41-49	-	-	-	4 (4)	4+1 (4)	5+1 (5)	5+1 (4)	0 (3)	10+1 (5)	13 (5)
44	5/10	Edinburgh	A	SC	L37-56	-	-	-	3 (4)	2+1 (4)	6 (4)	5+2 (5)	1+1 (4)	4+1 (4)	16 (5)
45	7/10	Redcar	H	YS	L43-47	-	-	-	8 (5)	2+1 (3)	10+1 (5)	5+1 (4)	1+1 (4)	4+1 (4)	13 (5)
46	7/10	Edinburgh	H	SC	W51-41	-	-	-	10+1 (5)	R/R	6+2 (6)	10+1 (5)	2+1 (5)	-	23+1 (9)
47	14/10	Birmingham	H	PL	L43-46	-	-	-	5+1 (5)	8+2 (6)	5+3 (6)	9 (4)	2 (3)	R/R	14 (6)
48	14/10	Stoke	H	PL	W43-41*	-	-	-	11 (5)	-	7+1 (5)	-	0 (4)	R/R	25+3 (14)

ADDITIONAL KEY: ST = Spring Trophy; SC = Scottish Cup.

NOTE: (1) The away leg of the Spring Trophy at Edinburgh on 23 March was abandoned after heat twelve, with the result permitted to stand; (2) The home league match against Stoke on 14 October was abandoned after heat fourteen, with the result permitted to stand.

Details of other riders (all guests unless **highlighted**): Match No. 10: James Cockle 3+1 (5); Match No. 11: Tomas Suchanek 3+2 (4); Match No. 12: Gary Beaton 2+2 (3); Match No. 23: Chris Schramm 4 (5); Match No. 24: Robbie Kessler 10 (6); Match No. 38: Gary Beaton 3+1 (4); Match No. 43: Jason Lyons 13 (5); Match No. 44: James Grieves 16 (5); Match No. 45: Jason Lyons 13 (5); Match No. 46: Jason Lyons 14 (5); Gary Havelock 9+1 (4); Match No. 47: Kauko Nieminen 14 (6); Match No. 48: Kauko Nieminen 14+1 (5); John Branney 6 (4); Lee Smart 5+2 (4); Gary Beaton 0 (1).

Details of tactical rides and tactical substitute rides: Match No. 1: Parker 4 points (TS); Match No. 2: Parker 4 points (TS); Leverington 1 point (TR; not doubled); Match No. 11: Parker 4 points (TR); Match No. 13: Leverington 0 points (TR); Parker 0 points (TS); Match No. 16: Stancl 4 points (TR); Parker 4 points (TS); Match No. 17: Stancl 4 points (TR); Parker 4 points (TS); Match No. 19: Parker 4 points (TR); Match No. 20: Parker 4 points (TR); Match No. 21: Parker 4 points (TR); Match No. 29: Parker 2 points (TR); Match No. 30: Parker 4 points (TR); Match No. 36: Parker 4 points (TS); Watson 4 points (TR); Match No. 39: Parker 4 points (TS); Match No. 40: Watson 4 points (TR); Match No. 44: Grieves 6 points (TR).

AVERAGES

[28 Premier League; 2 Knock-Out Cup; 10 Premier Trophy; 2 Young Shield = 42 fixtures]

• Denotes ever-present.

Rider	Mts	Rds	Pts	Bon	Tot	Avge	Max
Shane Parker	38	191	464	15	479	10.03	7 full; 1 paid
Craig Watson	19	92	185	9	194	8.43	-
George Stancl	20	92	176	10	186	8.09	1 full
Trent Leverington	41	171	269	22	291	6.81	1 paid
Robert Ksiezak	38	164	216	41	257	6.27	-
David McAllan	36	144	179	35	214	5.94	-
Lee Dicken •	42	183	197	47	244	5.33	-
Lee Smethills	17	66	61	10	71	4.30	-
Michael Coles	25	99	74	22	96	3.88	-
Guests	13	57	90	9	99	6.95	1 paid

(Gary Beaton [3]; John Branney [1]; James Cockle [1]; Robbie Kessler [1]; Jason Lyons [2]; Kauko Nieminen [2]; Chris Schramm [1]; Lee Smart [1]; Tomas Suchanek [1])

INDIVIDUAL MEETINGS

---

21 October: **Ashfield Classic**

QUALIFYING SCORES: George Stancl 14; Kauko Nieminen 14; James Wright 11; Josef Franc 11; Jason Lyons 11; Filip Sitera 10; Derek Sneddon 9; Adam Roynon 9; Lee Dicken 8; Trent Leverington 6; Robert Ksiezak 5; Chris Kerr 5; Sean Stoddart 3; Jari Makinen 3; Gary Beaton 1; Cal McDade 0; James McBain (Res) 0.

SEMI-FINAL: 1st Lyons; 2nd Sitera; 3rd Franc; 4th Wright.

FINAL: 1st Stancl; 2nd Sitera; 3rd Nieminen; 4th Lyons.

---

28 October: **Heathersfield Golden Helmet**

QUALIFYING SCORES: Gary Beaton <u>12</u>; Adam McKinna <u>12</u>; James McBain 10; John Morrison 9; John MacPhail 5; Wayne Dunworth 5; Johnny Grey 5; Keiran Morris 4; Mark White 3; Glyn Picken (Res) 3; Cal McDade 1; Rickylee Beecroft 0; Martin Emerson 0.

FINAL: 1st Beaton; 2nd McKinna; 3rd Morrison; 4th McBain.

Aussie **Craig Watson** went a long way towards regaining his golden touch after joining Glasgow in July. This came after a disappointing spell at Elite League level with Poole.

(Photo: David Valentine)

ISLE OF WIGHT ISLANDERS

ADDRESS:	Smallbrook Stadium, Ashey Road, Ryde, Isle of Wight, PO33 4BH.
TELEPHONE:	01983 811180.
CLUB HOTLINE:	09068 664673 (Premium rate applies).
WEBSITE:	N/A.
PROMOTERS:	Dave Pavitt & Martin Newnham.
MAIN TEAM SPONSORS:	Wightlink & isleofwight.com.
YEARS OF OPERATION:	1995 Demonstration; 1996 Conference League; 1997 Amateur League and Premier League; 1998-2007 Premier League.
FIRST MEETING:	13 May 1996.
TRACK LENGTH:	385 metres.
TRACK RECORD:	66.5 seconds - Chris Holder (22/05/07).

CLUB HONOURS

YOUNG SHIELD WINNERS: 1998, 2001.

PAIRS CHAMPIONS: 2002, 2007.

KNOCK-OUT CUP WINNERS: 2003.

FOUR-TEAM CHAMPIONS: 2007.

Isle of Wight, 2007

Back row, left to right: Glen Phillips, Chris Johnson, Andrew Bargh, Cory Gathercole, Chris Holder and Krzysztof Stojanowski.

Front, on bike: Jason Bunyan.

(Photo: David Valentine)

ISLE OF WIGHT 2007

* Denotes aggregate/bonus-point victory

NO.	DATE	OPPONENTS	VENUE	COMPETITION	RESULT	CHRIS HOLDER	GLEN PHILLIPS	CORY GATHERCOLE	KRZYSZTOF STOJANOWSKI	JASON BUNYAN	ANDREW BARGH	CHRIS JOHNSON			OTHER RIDERS
1	1/4	Newport	A	PT	W48-41	6+2 (4)	8+2 (4)	7 (4)	9+2 (5)	13 (5)	2 (4)	3+1 (4)	-	-	-
2	3/4	Mildenhall	H	PT	W62-30	13+2 (5)	9+1 (4)	10+1 (4)	5 (4)	13 (5)	5+2 (4)	7+2 (4)	-	-	-
3	6/4	Somerset	A	PT	L42-52	12 (5)	5+1 (4)	7+1 (5)	5 (4)	10+1 (5)	2+1 (4)	1 (3)	-	-	-
4	7/4	Rye House	A	PT	L37-56	14+2 (5)	5 (4)	1 (4)	8 (4)	8 (5)	0 (4)	1 (4)	-	-	-
5	10/4	Somerset	H	PT	W47-43	12+1 (5)	7+1 (4)	0 (2)	9 (4)	9+1 (5)	5+2 (5)	5+1 (5)	-	-	-
6	15/4	Mildenhall	A	PT	L46-47*	13 (5)	4 (4)	2+1 (4)	12 (5)	7 (4)	0 (3)	8+2 (5)	-	-	-
7	17/4	Newport	H	PT	W62-31*	13+2 (5)	8+3 (4)	7+3 (4)	10+1 (4)	15 (5)	5 (4)	4+1 (4)	-	-	-
8	24/4	Rye House	H	PT	W55-39	15 (5)	7+1 (4)	4+1 (4)	7+2 (4)	13 (5)	3 (3)	6+1 (5)	-	-	-
9	18/5	Edinburgh	A	PL	L42-52	17 (5)	8+1 (5)	2 (4)	5+1 (4)	8+1 (5)	2+1 (4)	-	-	-	0 (3)
10	19/5	Workington	A	KO	L42-50	13 (5)	5 (4)	6 (5)	8 (4)	8+2 (5)	2+1 (4)	-	-	-	0 (3)
11	20/5	Newcastle	A	PL	L45-49	15 (5)	5+1 (4)	8 (5)	5+2 (4)	9+1 (5)	2+1 (4)	-	-	-	0 (3)
12	22/5	Workington	H	KO	W52-43*	13+1 (5)	7 (4)	7+2 (4)	8+1 (4)	12+1 (5)	1 (3)	4+1 (5)	-	-	-
13	29/5	Berwick	H	PL	W62-31	14+1 (5)	6+2 (4)	9+1 (4)	8+2 (4)	12 (5)	8+2 (4)	5 (4)	-	-	-
14	5/6	Newport	H	PL	W69-21	14+1 (5)	8+3 (4)	9+1 (4)	8+2 (4)	10+2 (5)	10+2 (4)	10+1 (4)	-	-	-
15	12/6	King's Lynn	H	PL	L42-47	5 (3)	9 (5)	5+1 (4)	2+1 (4)	12 (5)	4 (4)	5 (5)	-	-	-
16	19/6	Stoke	H	PL	W48-42	12 (5)	6+1 (4)	7+2 (4)	10 (5)	1 (2)	9+1 (7)	3 (1)	-	-	-
17	20/6	Birmingham	A	PL	L42-48	15 (5)	5 (4)	6+1 (5)	5+1 (4)	9 (4)	1 (4)	-	-	-	1 (4)
18	26/6	Rye House	H	KO	W52-40	15 (5)	5 (4)	4+1 (4)	5 (4)	13 (5)	6+1 (4)	4+1 (4)	-	-	-
19	3/7	Edinburgh	H	PL	W67-24*	13+2 (5)	11+1 (4)	13+2 (5)	12 (4)	2+1 (4)	8+2 (4)	8+2 (4)	-	-	-
20	7/7	Stoke	A	PL	L40-52	-	4+1 (4)	7+1 (5)	8+1 (4)	12 (5)	0 (4)	5 (4)	-	-	4 (4)
21	10/7	Weymouth	H	Chal	W51-39	-	-	11+1 (5)	-	-	14 (5)	11 (4)	-	-	15+2 (17)
22	13/7	Weymouth	A	Chal	W49-32*	-	-	12 (4)	11 (4)	11+1 (4)	-	4+2 (3)	-	-	11+2 (11)
23	17/7	Somerset	H	PL	W59-34	-	8+1 (4)	13+1 (5)	8+1 (4)	11+2 (5)	9+1 (5)	3+1 (3)	-	-	7+2 (4)
24	24/7	Glasgow	H	PL	W59-32	14+1 (5)	10+1 (4)	8+1 (4)	8 (4)	11+3 (5)	0 (3)	8+3 (5)	-	-	-
25	28/7	Berwick	A	PL	W46-44*	14 (5)	6+1 (4)	5+1 (4)	7 (4)	8+1 (5)	2 (4)	4+2 (4)	-	-	-
26	29/7	Glasgow	A	PL	L40-52*	5+1 (3)	5+1 (4)	6 (4)	7+1 (5)	9 (4)	0 (3)	8+2 (6)	-	-	-
27	31/7	Newcastle	H	PL	W57-35*	9+1 (4)	10+1 (4)	6+1 (4)	11+3 (5)	12+1 (5)	4+2 (4)	5+2 (4)	-	-	-
28	2/8	Birmingham	H	PL	W60-33*	12+1 (5)	9+1 (4)	10+1 (4)	9+1 (4)	12+2 (5)	3+1 (4)	5+1 (4)	-	-	-
29	4/8	Workington	A	PL	W53-42	12 (5)	8+1 (4)	7+1 (4)	7+2 (4)	12+1 (5)	2 (4)	5+2 (4)	-	-	-
30	7/8	Rye House	H	PL	W50-40	12 (5)	8+1 (4)	3+2 (4)	7+3 (4)	13+1 (5)	-	7+1 (5)	-	-	0 (3)
31	11/8	Rye House	A	KO	L43-50*	12+1 (5)	5 (4)	4 (4)	4+2 (4)	16 (5)	-	1 (3)	-	-	1 (5)
32	12/8	Mildenhall	A	PL	L43-51	14 (5)	5+1 (5)	2 (4)	6+2 (4)	13 (5)	-	2 (3)	-	-	1+1 (4)
33	16/8	Redcar	A	PL	W55-35	14+1 (5)	6+3 (4)	11+2 (5)	8 (4)	9 (4)	-	5+2 (4)	-	-	2+2 (4)
34	18/8	Mildenhall	H	PL	W60-33*	12+2 (5)	8+1 (4)	9+1 (4)	11 (5)	10+1 (4)	-	5 (4)	-	-	5+2 (4)
35	24/8	King's Lynn	A	KOs	L44-49	18 (5)	2 (4)	3 (4)	6 (4)	10 (5)	-	1+1 (4)	-	-	4+2 (4)
36	27/8	Rye House	A	PL	L21-69	8 (5)	1 (4)	2 (4)	3 (4)	6 (5)	-	0 (5)	-	-	1 (3)
37	30/8	Workington	H	PL	W56-39*	13+2 (5)	7+2 (4)	12+1 (5)	7 (4)	11 (4)	-	6+2 (4)	-	-	0 (4)
38	31/8	Somerset	A	PL	L44-46*	15 (5)	4 (4)	5+1 (4)	8+1 (4)	10+1 (5)	-	2 (5)	-	-	0 (3)
39	4/9	Sheffield	H	PL	W59-32	11+1 (5)	8+1 (4)	9 (4)	9+1 (4)	12+1 (5)	-	9+3 (5)	-	-	1 (3)
40	6/9	Sheffield	A	PL	L40-53*	17 (5)	3+1 (4)	3 (4)	4 (4)	8 (5)	-	2+1 (4)	-	-	3+1 (4)
41	11/9	Redcar	H	PL	W50-40*	15 (5)	10 (4)	6+1 (4)	8+2 (5)	0 (4)	3 (4)	8+1 (4)	-	-	-
42	18/9	King's Lynn	H	KOs	D45-45	15 (5)	7+2 (4)	2 (4)	10 (5)	6+1 (4)	2 (3)	3+2 (5)	-	-	-
43	23/9	Newport	A	PL	W50-39*	11+1 (4)	8+1 (5)	6+1 (4)	6 (4)	10 (5)	9 (6)	0 (2)	-	-	-
44	2/10	Rye House	H	POs	W46-44	12 (5)	5+1 (4)	0 (4)	11+1 (5)	10 (4)	1 (3)	7 (5)	-	-	-
45	6/10	Rye House	A	POs	L29-61	12 (5)	2+1 (4)	4 (4)	3 (3)	6 (5)	2 (5)	0 (4)	-	-	-
46	12/10	King's Lynn	A	PL	L26-61	14 (4)	1 (4)	2 (4)	2 (4)	2 (3)	0 (4)	5 (5)	-	-	-

NOTE: (1) The challenge match at Weymouth on 13 July was abandoned after heat thirteen, with the result permitted to stand; (2) The away league match at King's Lynn on 12 October was abandoned after heat fourteen, with the result permitted to stand.

Details of other riders (all guests unless **highlighted**): Match No. 9: Cal McDade 0 (3); Match No. 10: Gary Flint 0 (3); Match No. 11: Gary Flint 0 (3); Match No. 17: Sam Martin 1 (4); Match No. 20: Ulrich Ostergaard 4 (4); Match No. 21: Shane Waldron 6+1 (4); Sam Martin 5 (4); Gary Cottham 4+1 (5); Jerran Hart 0 (4); Match No. 22: Gary Cottham 10+2 (5); Harland Cook 1 (6); Karlis Ezergailis R/R; Match No. 23: Leigh Lanham 7+2 (4); Match No. 30: Gary Cottham 0 (3); Match No. 31: Tom Brown 1 (5); Match No. 32: Tom Brown 1+1 (4); Match No. 33: Ashley Johnson 2+2 (4); Match No. 34: Tom Brown 5+2 (4); Match No. 35: Simon Lambert 4+2 (4); Match No. 36: Danny Betson 1 (3); Match No. 37: Tom Brown 0 (4); Match No. 38: Daniel Halsey 0 (3); Match No. 39: Karl Mason 1 (3); Match No. 40: Simon Lambert 3+1 (4).

Details of tactical rides and tactical substitute rides: Match No. 3: Holder 6 points (TR); Bunyan 2 points (TS); Match No. 4: Holder 6 points (TR); Match No. 6: Stojanowski 6 points (TR); Match No. 9: Holder 6 points (TR); Phillips 2 points (TS); Match No. 10: Holder 4 points (TR); Gathercole 0 points (TS); Match No. 11: Holder 4 points (TR); Gathercole 4 points (TS); Match No. 20: Stojanowski 4 points (TR); Match No. 26: Stojanowski 4 points (TR); Match No. 31: Bunyan 6 points (TR); Match No. 32: Bunyan 6 points (TR); Phillips 2 points (TS); Match No. 35: Holder 6 points (TR); Match No. 36: Holder 0 points (TR); Match No. 40: Holder 6 points (TR); Match No. 45: Holder 0 points (TR); Match No. 46: Holder 6 points (TR).

AVERAGES

[28 Premier League; 2 Play-Offs; 6 Knock-Out Cup; 8 Premier Trophy = 44 fixtures]

• Denotes ever-present.

Rider	Mts	Rds	Pts	Bon	Tot	Avge	Max
Chris Holder	42	202	514	26	540	10.69	7 full; 9 paid
Jason Bunyan •	44	205	416	25	441	8.60	1 full
Krzysztof Stojanowski •	44	184	312	36	348	7.57	1 full
Glen Phillips •	44	180	276	41	317	7.04	1 paid
Cory Gathercole •	44	183	257	34	291	6.36	1 paid
Chris Johnson	40	166	180	39	219	5.28	-
Andrew Bargh	33	133	112	20	132	3.97	1 paid
Guests	17	62	30	10	40	2.58	-

(Danny Betson [1]; Tom Brown [4]; Gary Cottham [1]; Gary Flint [2]; Daniel Halsey [1]; Ashley Johnson [1]; Simon Lambert [2]; Leigh Lanham [1]; Cal McDade [1]; Sam Martin [1]; Karl Mason [1]; Ulrich Ostergaard [1])

OTHER MEETING

25 September: **Pete Redfern Memorial**
Acorn Care Service Mad Dogs 43: Krzysztof Stojanowski 13 (5); Jesper Kristiansen 8 (5); Andrew Bargh 6 (4); Chris Johnson 5 (4); Patrick Hougaard 5 (4); Daniel Halsey 3+2 (4); Joni Keskinen 2 (2); Sam Martin 1 (2), Cougars 47: Glen Phillips 14 (5); Cory Gathercole 9+1 (5); Casper Wortmann 9 (4); James Holder 7 (4); Robert Mear 5+2 (5); Tero Aarnio 3 (4); Terry Day 0 (3).

INDIVIDUAL MEETINGS

9 August: **Smallbrook Spectacular**
1st Krzysztof Stojanowski 12; 2nd Casper Wortmann 6; 3rd Jesper Kristiansen 5; James Holder 3; Cory Gathercole 2; Jason Bunyan 1.

23 October: **Island Speedway Championship**
QUALIFYING SCORES: Lewis Bridger 12; Filip Sitera 9; Cory Gathercole 7; Lee Smart 7; Krzysztof Stojanowski 7; Leigh Lanham 7; Glen Phillips 6; Chris Holder 4; Jesper Kristiansen 4; Andrew Bargh 4; Casper Wortmann 3; Danny Warwick 2.
FIRST SEMI-FINAL: 1st Bridger; 2nd Kristiansen; 3rd Stojanowski; 4th Smart.
SECOND SEMI-FINAL. 1st Sitera, 2nd Gathercole; 3rd Lanham; 4th Bargh.
FINAL: 1st Bridger; 2nd Sitera; 3rd Kristiansen; 4th Gathercole.

Cory Gathercole produced an array of impressive tallies for the Islanders in his first full season on these shores, his riding style bearing an uncanny similarity to that of his cousin, the great Leigh Adams.

(Photo: David Valentine)

KING'S LYNN STARS

ADDRESS:	Norfolk Arena, Saddlebow Road, King's Lynn, Norfolk, PE34 3AG.
TELEPHONE:	01553 771111.
CLUB HOTLINE:	09068 664690 (Premium rate applies).
WEBSITE:	www.norfolkarena.co.uk
PROMOTERS:	Keith 'Buster' Chapman & Jonathan Chapman.
MAIN TEAM SPONSOR:	The Money Centre.
YEARS OF OPERATION:	1965 Open; 1966-1967 British League; 1968 British League Division One; 1969-1970 British League Division One and Division Two; 1971-1974 British League Division One; 1975-1990 British League; 1991-1994 British League Division One; 1995 Premier League; 1996 Training; 1997 Elite League and Amateur League; 1998-1999 Elite League and Conference League; 2000-2001 Elite League; 2002 Elite League and Conference League; 2003 Premier League; 2004 Premier League and Conference Trophy; 2005-2007 Premier League. **NOTE**: In 1997, King's Lynn shared their Amateur League fixtures with Ipswich, under the banner of Anglian Angels; The track has also been occupied by Boston for their Conference League operation from 2000 to 2007.
FIRST MEETING:	23 May 1965.
TRACK LENGTH:	342 metres.
TRACK RECORD:	57.6 seconds - Nicki Pedersen (11/09/02).

CLUB HONOURS

KNOCK-OUT CUP WINNERS: 1977, 2000, 2005, 2006, 2007.

INTER-LEAGUE KNOCK-OUT CUP WINNERS: 1978, 1980.

PREMIERSHIP WINNERS: 2001.

YOUNG SHIELD WINNERS: 2005.

PREMIER TROPHY WINNERS: 2006, 2007.

LEAGUE CHAMPIONS: 2006.

Long-serving Czech ace **Tomas Topinka** was, once again, a model of absolute consistency for the Stars, scoring freely wherever the side appeared.

(Photo: David Valentine)

KING'S LYNN 2007

*Denotes aggregate/bonus-point victory

NO.	DATE	OPPONENTS	VENUE	COMPETITION	RESULT	TOMAS TOPINKA	CHRIS MILLS	DANIEL NERMARK	TREVOR HARDING	PAUL LEE	JAMES BRUNDLE	JOHN OLIVER	GRANT MacDONALD	BENJI COMPTON	OTHER RIDERS
1	16/3	A. Jones' Select	H	AJM	W46-44	8 (4)	6+1 (4)	10 (5)	-	10 (5)	3+1 (4)	9+3 (5)	-	-	0 (3)
2	28/3	Sheffield	H	PT	W75-15	14+1 (5)	9+3 (4)	14+1 (5)	9+3 (4)	8+4 (4)	10+2 (4)	11+1 (4)	-	-	-
3	9/4	Sheffield	A	PT	D45-45*	10 (5)	4+1 (4)	11 (5)	4 (4)	6+2 (4)	-	9+1 (6)	-	-	1+1 (3)
4	11/4	Stoke	H	PT	W63-27	14+1 (5)	9+3 (4)	15 (5)	8+2 (4)	11+1 (4)	-	0 (1)	-	-	6+1 (7)
5	14/4	Stoke	A	PT	W52-37*	10+1 (5)	6+1 (4)	14 (5)	7+2 (4)	4 (4)	0 (1)	-	-	-	11+1 (7)
6	18/4	Workington	H	PT	W65-27	15 (5)	9+3 (4)	13 (5)	8+2 (4)	11+1 (4)	-	-	-	-	9+1 (8)
7	21/4	Workington	A	PT	L43-47*	6+1 (5)	6+1 (4)	12 (5)	5 (4)	7 (4)	-	-	-	-	7+1 (8)
8	22/4	Newcastle	A	KO	W46-44	11 (5)	4+1 (4)	7+1 (4)	8 (5)	4 (4)	-	-	-	-	6 (8)
9	25/4	Newcastle	H	KO	W64-29*	9+2 (4)	11+2 (4)	11+1 (4)	11+3 (5)	11 (4)	5+2 (4)	-	-	-	6 (4)
10	27/4	Somerset	A	PL	W46-44	8+2 (4)	10 (5)	9 (5)	2+1 (3)	6+2 (4)	1+1 (3)	-	-	-	10+2 (6)
11	2/5	Birmingham	H	PT	W59-33	14+1 (5)	8 (4)	3+2 (4)	9+1 (4)	10+1 (5)	12+2 (5)	-	-	-	3+1 (3)
12	3/5	Redcar	A	PL	W49-44	10+1 (5)	3 (4)	17 (5)	5+1 (4)	4 (4)	8+1 (5)	-	-	-	2+2 (3)
13	6/5	Birmingham	A	PT	D45-45*	10+1 (5)	6+3 (4)	12 (5)	4+2 (4)	7 (4)	6+1 (5)	-	-	-	0 (3)
14	19/5	Rye House	A	PL	L40-50	11 (5)	3 (4)	9+1 (5)	6+1 (4)	5 (4)	4+1 (5)	-	-	-	2+1 (3)
15	23/5	Glasgow	H	PTs	W55-39	10+1 (4)	7+2 (4)	11+1 (5)	8+1 (4)	10+2 (5)	4+1 (4)	-	-	-	5+2 (4)
16	31/5	Redcar	A	KO	D45-45	9+1 (5)	6+3 (4)	12 (5)	3+2 (4)	0 (0)	3+2 (5)	-	-	-	12+1 (7)
17	6/6	Redcar	H	KO	W59-33*	13+1 (5)	5 (4)	14 (5)	7+2 (4)	9+2 (4)	8+1 (4)	-	-	-	3+1 (4)
18	8/6	Edinburgh	A	PL	W47-43	7+1 (5)	2 (3)	15 (5)	5+1 (4)	4 (4)	10 (5)	-	-	-	4 (4)
19	9/6	Berwick	H	PL	W46-44	13 (5)	6+2 (4)	11+1 (5)	9+1 (4)	3+1 (4)	4 (5)	-	-	-	0 (3)
20	12/6	Isle of Wight	A	PL	W47-42	12 (5)	5+1 (4)	12+1 (5)	6+2 (4)	6 (4)	0 (2)	-	-	-	6+1 (6)
21	17/6	Newcastle	A	PL	D45-45	6+1 (4)	5 (4)	12 (5)	8+1 (5)	5+3 (4)	8 (5)	-	1+1 (3)	-	-
22	20/6	Newport	H	PL	W56-36	12+2 (5)	7+2 (4)	7+2 (4)	8 (4)	14+1 (5)	7 (5)	-	1+1 (3)	-	-
23	22/6	Rye House	H	PL	W49-43	12 (5)	4+2 (4)	14+1 (5)	6+2 (4)	6+2 (4)	7+2 (7)	-	0 (1)	-	-
24	23/6	Stoke	A	PL	L37-53	11 (6)	1 (4)	11 (5)	6 (4)	4+2 (4)	2 (2)	-	-	-	2+1 (5)
25	27/6	Mildenhall	H	PL	W48-45	14 (5)	4+1 (4)	7+1 (4)	5+1 (4)	9 (5)	8+1 (5)	-	-	-	1 (3)
26	2/7	Glasgow	A	PTs	L44-49*	11 (4)	5+1 (4)	11 (6)	2 (3)	7+1 (5)	7+2 (5)	-	-	-	1+1 (3)
27	7/7	Mildenhall	A	PL	L42-50	10 (5)	5+2 (4)	7 (4)	6+2 (4)	10+2 (5)	3 (5)	-	-	-	1 (3)
28	11/7	Newcastle	H	PL	W55-38*	10+3 (5)	8+1 (4)	12 (5)	5+2 (4)	7+2 (4)	7+2 (4)	-	-	-	6+2 (4)
29	13/7	Sheffield	H	PL	W64-29	11+2 (5)	8+1 (4)	15 (5)	6 (4)	9+2 (4)	10+1 (4)	-	-	-	5+1 (4)
30	18/7	Redcar	H	PL	W61-32*	11 (5)	7+2 (4)	15 (5)	7+2 (4)	6 (2)	7+2 (5)	-	-	8+2 (5)	-
31	22/7	Newport	A	PL	L44-48*	16+1 (6)	3+1 (5)	17+1 (6)	6 (5)	R/R	2 (5)	-	-	0 (3)	-
32	25/7	Somerset	H	PL	W56-36*	15 (5)	7+1 (5)	14 (5)	11+1 (6)	R/R	7+2 (5)	-	-	2 (4)	-
33	29/7	Birmingham	A	PTf	W51-39	18 (6)	8+2 (5)	13+1 (5)	9+1 (5)	R/R	2 (5)	-	-	1+1 (5)	-
34	1/8	Berwick	A	PL	W64-28*	10+1 (4)	8+3 (4)	15 (5)	13 (5)	9+3 (4)	6+1 (4)	-	-	3+1 (4)	-
35	8/8	Edinburgh	H	PL	W60-33*	14 (5)	6+1 (4)	11 (4)	5 (3)	10+4 (5)	9+2 (4)	-	-	5+2 (5)	-
36	16/8	Sheffield	A	PL	L37-55*	8 (5)	2 (4)	15 (5)	1 (3)	3 (4)	5 (4)	-	-	3+1 (5)	-
37	24/8	Isle of Wight	H	KOs	W49-44	11+1 (5)	8+1 (4)	11 (5)	6+1 (4)	4+1 (4)	9 (5)	-	-	0 (3)	-
38	26/8	Birmingham	A	PL	W46-43	11 (5)	9+2 (4)	13+1 (5)	3 (4)	4+1 (4)	3+1 (4)	-	-	3 (5)	-
39	1/9	Workington	A	PL	L40-53	12 (6)	2 (4)	15+1 (5)	6 (4)	1 (4)	2+1 (4)	-	-	2 (3)	-
40	2/9	Glasgow	A	PL	L42-51	11 (5)	7 (4)	12 (5)	0 (3)	2+1 (4)	8+1 (6)	-	-	2 (3)	-
41	5/9	Stoke	H	PL	W64-26*	13+2 (5)	10+2 (4)	13+2 (5)	6+1 (4)	6+1 (4)	-	-	-	6+3 (4)	10 (4)
42	12/9	Glasgow	H	PL	W52-40*	14+1 (5)	5 (4)	14 (5)	4 (4)	6+1 (4)	6 (4)	-	-	3+2 (4)	-
43	14/9	Birmingham	H	PL	W49-44*	14+1 (5)	8+2 (4)	14 (5)	5 (4)	3+1 (4)	4 (4)	-	-	1 (4)	-
44	18/9	Isle of Wight	A	KOs	D45-45*	4+1 (4)	6+1 (5)	12 (5)	1+1 (3)	7 (4)	-	-	-	2 (3)	13+3 (6)
45	19/9	Workington	H	PL	W52-41	13+2 (5)	7+1 (4)	15 (5)	7+1 (4)	7 (4)	-	-	-	0 (1)	3+1 (7)
46	3/10	Leicester	H	Chal	W46-44	11 (5)	6+1 (4)	12 (5)	4+1 (4)	4+1 (4)	-	-	-	4+3 (4)	5 (4)
47	4/10	Sheffield	H	POs	L31-62	8 (5)	5 (4)	10 (5)	4 (4)	2 (4)	-	-	-	0 (3)	2 (5)
48	5/10	Birmingham	H	PTf	W58-35*	11 (4)	7+1 (4)	10 (4)	11+3 (5)	10+3 (5)	-	-	-	3+1 (4)	6 (4)
49	10/10	Sheffield	H	POs	W55-37	15 (5)	5 (4)	10 (4)	10+4 (5)	2 (4)	-	-	-	-	13+3 (8)
50	12/10	Isle of Wight	H	PL	W61-26*	11 (4)	9+1 (4)	11 (4)	6+3 (4)	8+2 (4)	-	-	-	-	16+5 (8)
51	19/10	Somerset	A	KOf	W46-44	12+1 (5)	7+1 (4)	14 (5)	5+1 (4)	5+2 (4)	-	-	-	-	3+2 (8)
52	24/10	Somerset	H	KOf	W59-34*	15 (5)	0 (1)	10+2 (5)	10+2 (4)	6+3 (4)	-	-	-	-	18+2 (11)

ADDITIONAL KEY: AJM = Ashley Jones Memorial.

NOTE: The home league match versus the Isle of Wight on 12 October was abandoned after heat fourteen, with the result permitted to stand.

Details of other riders (all guests unless **highlighted**): Match No. 1: Darren Mallett 0 (3); Match No. 3: Simon Lambert 1+1 (3); Match No. 4: Simon Lambert 6+1 (7); Match No. 5: Andrew Tully 11+1 (7); Match No. 6: Simon Lambert 7+1 (4); Grant MacDonald 2 (4); Match No. 7: Lee Dicken 5 (5); Grant MacDonald 2+1 (3); Match No. 8: Andrew Tully 6 (5); Byron Bekker 0 (3); Match No. 9: Simon Lambert 6 (4); Match No. 10: Michal Rajkowski 10+2 (6); Match No. 11: Simon Lambert 3+1 (3); Match No. 12: Jack Hargreaves 2+2 (3); Match No. 13: Simon Lambert 0 (3); Match No. 14: Nicki Glanz 2+1 (3); Match No. 15: Simon Lambert 5+2 (4); Match No. 16: Michal Rajkowski 12+1 (7); Match No. 17: Shane Waldron 3+1 (4); Match No. 18: Tomas Suchanek 4 (4); Match No. 19: Adam McKinna 0 (3); Match No. 20: Tomas Suchanek 6+1 (6); Match No. 24: Simon Lambert 2+1 (5); Match No. 25: Simon Lambert 1 (3); Match No. 26: Cal McDade 1+1 (3); Match No. 27: Simon Lambert 1 (3); Match No. 28: Simon Lambert 6+2 (4); Match No. 29: Benji Compton 5+1 (4); Match No. 41: Chris Schramm 10 (4); Match No. 44: Chris Schramm 13+3 (6); Match No. 45: **Adam Allott** 3+1 (7); Match No. 46: **Adam Allott** 5 (4); Match No. 47: **Adam Allott** 2 (5); Match No. 48: **Adam Allott** 6 (4); Match No. 49: **Adam Allott** 8+1 (4); Simon Lambert 5+2 (4); Match No. 50: Simon Lambert 8+4 (4); **Adam Allott** 8+1 (4); Match No. 51: Simon Lambert 2+1 (4); **Adam Allott** 1+1 (4); Match No. 52: Simon Lambert 11+1 (6); **Adam Allott** 7+1 (5).

Details of tactical rides and tactical substitute rides: Match No. 12: Nermark 6 points (TR); Match No. 24: Topinka 0 points (TS); Match No. 26: Topinka 4 points (TR); Nermark 2 points (TS); Match No. 27: Nermark 6 points (TR); Match No. 31: Nermark 4 points (TS); Match No. 36: Nermark 6 points (TR); Match No. 39: Nermark 6 points (TR); Topinka 1 point (TS; not doubled); Match No. 40: Topinka 6 points (TR); Match No. 47: Nermark 6 points (TR).

Other details: Ashley Jones' Select scorers in Match No. 1: Troy Batchelor 13+2 (5); Cameron Woodward 11 (5); Craig Watson 6+1 (4); Shaun Tacey 5+1 (4); Simon Lambert 4+1 (4); Mark Jones 4 (4); James Cockle 1 (4).; Leicester scorers in Match No. 46: Chris Holder 13 (5); Lewis Bridger 9+1 (4); Kevin Doolan 8+1 (5); Sergey Darkin 6 (4); Chris Schramm 5+1 (4); Simon Lambert 3+1 (4); James Holder 0 (4).

AVERAGES

[28 Premier League; 2 Play-Offs; 8 Knock-Out Cup; 12 Premier Trophy = 50 fixtures]

• Denotes ever-present.

Rider	Mts	Rds	Pts	Bon	Tot	Avge	Max
Daniel Nermark •	50	242	584	21	605	10.00	6 full; 4 paid
Tomas Topinka •	50	245	565	34	599	9.78	5 full; 7 paid
Paul Lee	47	190	298	54	352	7.41	5 paid
Trevor Harding •	50	204	312	56	368	7.22	2 paid
Chris Mills •	50	202	302	58	360	7.13	4 paid
James Brundle	36	158	204	32	236	5.97	1 paid
Adam Allott	7	33	35	5	40	4.85	-
Benji Compton	18	68	44	13	57	3.35	-

Also rode (in alphabetical order):

Grant MacDonald	3	7	2	2	4	2.29	-
John Oliver	3	11	20	2	22	8.00	1 paid

Guests	33	141	158	32	190	5.39	1 paid

(Byron Bekker [1]; Benji Compton [1]; Lee Dicken [1]; Nicki Glanz [1]; Jack Hargreaves [1]; Simon Lambert [15]; Grant MacDonald [2]; Cal McDade [1]; Adam McKinna [1]; Michal Rajkowski [2]; Chris Schramm [2]; Tomas Suchanek [2]; Andrew Tully [2]; Shane Waldron [1])

INDIVIDUAL MEETING

17 October: **Pride of the East**

QUALIFYING SCORES: Tomas Topinka 15; Chris Holder 14; Daniel Nermark 13; Kevin Doolan 12; Lewis Bridger 11; Josef Franc 9; Chris Mills 8; Chris Schramm 7; Mark Lemon 6; Leigh Lanham 6; Shaun Tacey 5; Adam Allott 4; Cameron Woodward 4; Darren Mallett 3; Simon Lambert 2; Kozza Smith 0.

FINAL: 1st Holder; 2nd Topinka; 3rd Nermark; 4th Doolan.

Daniel Nermark enjoyed a second terrific term with King's Lynn, while on the individual front he took victory in the prestigious Scottish Open at Edinburgh.

(Photo: David Valentine)

MILDENHALL FEN TIGERS

ADDRESS:	Mildenhall Stadium, Hayland Drove, West Row Fen, Mildenhall, Suffolk, IP28 8QU.
TELEPHONE:	01638 711777.
CLUB HOTLINE:	09068 664674 (Premium rate applies).
WEBSITE:	www.mildenhallspeedway.com
PROMOTERS:	Mick Horton & Simon Barton.
MAIN TEAM SPONSOR:	ASL Freight.
YEARS OF OPERATION:	1973 Training; 1974 Open and Training; 1975-1989 National League; 1990-1991 Training; 1992 British League Division Two; 1994 British League Division Three; 1995 Academy League; 1996 Conference League; 1997 Amateur League; 1998-2005 Conference League; 2006 Premier League and Conference League; 2007 Premier League.
FIRST MEETING:	18 May 1975.
TRACK LENGTH:	260 metres.
TRACK RECORD:	49.81 seconds - Kenneth Bjerre (21/10/07).

CLUB HONOURS

LEAGUE CHAMPIONS: 1979, 2003, 2004.
FOUR-TEAM CHAMPIONS: 1984, 1987, 2004.
PAIRS CHAMPIONS: 1987.
LEAGUE CUP WINNERS: 2000.
CONFERENCE TROPHY WINNERS: 2002, 2004.
KNOCK-OUT CUP WINNERS: 2003, 2004.

Canadian **Kyle Legault** continued his sharp rise up the speedway ladder with the Fen Tigers, impressing everyone fortunate enough to witness his exciting brand of racing.

(Photo: David Valentine)

MILDENHALL 2007

* Denotes aggregate/bonus-point victory

NO.	DATE	OPPONENTS	VENUE	COMPETITION	RESULT	MARIO JIROUT	SHAUN TACEY	KYLE LEGAULT	JAMIE SMITH	TOM P. MADSEN	JASON KING	MARK THOMPSON	PAUL FRY	TOMAS SUCHANEK	OTHER RIDERS
1	18/3	Sheffield	H	TTT	D45-45	6+1 (4)	8+1 (5)	6 (4)	7+1 (4)	5+1 (4)	10+1 (5)	3+1 (4)	-	-	-
2	22/3	Sheffield	A	TTT	L31-59	5+1 (5)	7 (5)	4 (4)	2 (4)	2+1 (4)	6 (4)	5 (4)	-	-	-
3	25/3	Somerset	H	PT	W54-38	7+1 (4)	8+2 (5)	13 (5)	6+2 (4)	10+1 (4)	9+1 (5)	1 (3)	-	-	-
4	31/3	Rye House	A	PT	L23-66	5 (5)	2+1 (4)	1 (4)	7 (5)	3+1 (4)	5 (4)	0 (4)	-	-	-
5	1/4	Rye House	H	PT	W45-44	8+1 (4)	10+1 (5)	8 (4)	0 (4)	10+1 (5)	6+2 (4)	3+1 (4)	-	-	-
6	3/4	Isle of Wight	A	PT	L30-62	7 (4)	2 (4)	7+1 (5)	4+1 (4)	7 (5)	2+1 (4)	1+1 (4)	-	-	-
7	7/4	Newport	H	PT	W52-34	8 (4)	7+2 (4)	9 (4)	5+1 (4)	10+2 (4)	11 (4)	2+1 (4)	-	-	-
8	8/4	Newport	A	PT	L41-49*	11 (5)	4 (4)	9 (4)	R/R	10+1 (5)	5 (7)	2+1 (5)	-	-	-
9	15/4	Isle of Wight	H	PT	W47-46	R/R	8+1 (5)	15+1 (6)	-	11+1 (5)	8+2 (5)	3 (5)	-	-	2+1 (4)
10	20/4	Somerset	A	PT	L41-52*	5 (3)	10 (5)	9+1 (5)	-	5+1 (4)	6 (4)	0 (3)	-	-	6+1 (6)
11	22/4	Somerset	H	PL	L45-48	7 (4)	7+1 (4)	4 (4)	-	9 (5)	13+1 (5)	3+1 (4)	-	-	2+1 (4)
12	30/4	Rye House	A	KO	L41-50	5+1 (4)	3+1 (4)	13 (5)	-	8 (5)	2+1 (4)	1+1 (3)	-	-	9+1 (5)
13	6/5	Redcar	H	PL	W47-45	8+1 (4)	9 (5)	7+2 (4)	-	6+3 (4)	10+1 (5)	6+1 (7)	-	-	1+1 (1)
14	12/5	Stoke	A	PL	W50-40	11 (5)	6+1 (4)	13 (5)	-	6 (4)	6+1 (4)	0 (3)	-	-	8+2 (5)
15	19/5	Newcastle	H	PL	W53-40	7+2 (4)	9+1 (5)	11+2 (5)	-	8 (4)	6+1 (4)	5+4 (4)	-	-	7 (4)
16	20/5	Glasgow	A	PL	L35-57	1 (3)	5+2 (4)	9 (5)	-	10+1 (5)	6+1 (4)	3 (5)	-	-	1 (4)
17	3/6	Rye House	H	KO	L40-49	-	3 (4)	9+1 (5)	-	3 (1)	4+1 (4)	3 (5)	6+1 (4)	12+1 (7)	-
18	7/6	Sheffield	A	PL	L38-52	-	5+1 (4)	10 (5)	-	4+1 (4)	6+1 (4)	4+1 (4)	9+1 (5)	0 (4)	-
19	9/6	Workington	A	PL	L35-57	-	5+2 (4)	8 (5)	-	10 (5)	5+2 (4)	1 (3)	4 (4)	2+1 (5)	-
20	10/6	Stoke	H	PL	W49-44*	-	2+1 (4)	15 (5)	-	11+1 (5)	8+1 (4)	1 (3)	4 (4)	8+2 (5)	-
21	27/6	King's Lynn	A	PL	L45-48	-	4 (4)	9 (5)	-	0 (2)	5+2 (4)	0 (3)	13+1 (5)	14+1 (7)	-
22	7/7	King's Lynn	H	PL	W50-42*	-	9+2 (5)	-	-	8+1 (4)	10 (4)	-	3 (4)	14+1 (6)	6+2 (7)
23	8/7	Newport	A	PL	L42-48	-	4+1 (4)	-	-	10+1 (5)	4 (3)	-	3 (4)	10 (6)	11 (8)
24	20/7	Edinburgh	A	PL	L40-53	-	8+1 (5)	16 (5)	-	6+1 (4)	1 (4)	-	3+2 (4)	5 (5)	1 (3)
25	22/7	Newcastle	A	PL	L42-48*	-	1 (3)	12 (5)	-	4 (4)	5+1 (4)	-	8 (5)	8+1 (5)	4+3 (4)
26	29/7	Edinburgh	H	PL	W51-41	-	8+1 (4)	13+1 (5)	-	6+2 (4)	10 (5)	-	4 (4)	10+1 (5)	0 (3)
27	3/8	Somerset	A	PL	L39-50	-	4 (4)	6 (4)	-	4+2 (4)	5+1 (4)	-	5+2 (4)	11 (6)	4+1 (4)
28	5/8	Birmingham	H	PL	L42-48	-	4+3 (4)	12+1 (5)	-	7 (5)	2 (4)	-	6 (4)	9 (5)	2+1 (3)
29	9/8	Redcar	A	PL	L42-51	-	4+1 (4)	14 (5)	-	4 (4)	6 (4)	-	7+2 (5)	6+2 (5)	1 (3)
30	12/8	Isle of Wight	H	PL	W51-43	-	6+1 (4)	13 (5)	-	7+2 (4)	8 (4)	-	6+1 (4)	7+2 (5)	4+1 (4)
31	21/8	Isle of Wight	A	PL	L33-60	-	3 (4)	7 (5)	-	0 (3)	5 (4)	-	14 (5)	4+1 (5)	0 (4)
32	26/8	Sheffield	H	PL	L43-46	-	10+1 (5)	7+1 (4)	-	3 (3)	6 (4)	-	9+1 (5)	4+1 (5)	4+1 (4)
33	29/8	Birmingham	A	PL	L34-58	-	2 (3)	-	-	0 (1)	6 (5)	-	2+2 (4)	11+2 (7)	13 (10)
34	2/9	Workington	H	PL	W47-44	-	8+1 (5)	-	-	R/R	8+1 (5)	-	11+1 (6)	8+2 (6)	12+2 (8)
35	4/9	Newport	H	PL	W54-39*	-	11 (5)	15+3 (6)	-	R/R	6+1 (4)	-	10+1 (6)	11+1 (6)	1 (4)
36	8/9	Rye House	A	PL	L25-65	-	5 (5)	9 (6)	-	R/R	3 (5)	-	3+1 (4)	5 (6)	0 (4)
37	9/9	Rye House	H	PL	L44-49	-	4+2 (5)	20 (6)	-	R/R	2 (4)	-	9+1 (6)	9+1 (6)	0 (3)
38	18/9	Glasgow	H	PL	L43-47	-	10 (5)	-	-	R/R	6+1 (5)	-	6+2 (5)	9+2 (6)	12+1 (9)
39	22/9	Berwick	A	PL	D45-45	-	11+1 (6)	-	-	R/R	9 (5)	-	5 (4)	2+1 (5)	18+2 (10)
40	23/9	Berwick	H	PL	W54-39*	-	11+1 (6)	-	-	R/R	6+2 (4)	-	10+2 (6)	9+1 (5)	18+2 (9)
41	2/10	Birmingham	H	YS	L43-47	-	8+1 (5)	-	-	R/R	6+2 (5)	-	9+1 (5)	7+1 (6)	13 (9)
42	3/10	Birmingham	A	YS	W46-44	-	7+2 (5)	-	-	R/R	7+1 (4)	-	10+1 (6)	9+2 (6)	13+1 (9)

ADDITIONAL KEY: TTT = Top Tigers Trophy.

NOTE: The home match versus Newport in the Premier Trophy on 7 April was abandoned after heat fourteen, with the result permitted to stand.

Details of other riders (all guests unless **highlighted**): Match No. 9: Ben Barker 2+1 (3); Nicki Glanz 0 (1); Match No. 10: Ben Barker 6+1 (6); Match No. 11: Paul Cooper 2+1 (4); Match No. 12: Tomas Suchanek 9+1 (5); Match No. 13: Chris Johnson 1+1 (1); Match No. 14: Daniel Giffard 8+2 (5); Match No. 15: James Cockle 7 (4); Match No. 16: Jamie Robertson 1 (4); Match No. 22: Theo Pijper 3+1 (4); **Mark Baseby** 3+1 (3); Match No. 23: Rusty Harrison 10 (5); **Mark Baseby** 1 (3); Match No. 24: **Mark Baseby** 1 (3); Match No. 25: **Mark Baseby** 4+3 (4); Match No. 26: Daniel Halsey 0 (3); Match No. 27: **Mark Baseby** 4+1 (4); Match No. 28: **Mark Baseby** 2+1 (3); Match No. 29: **Mark Baseby** 1 (3); Match No. 30: **Mark Baseby** 4+1 (4); Match No. 31: Jay Herne 0 (4); Match No. 32: **Mark Baseby** 4+1 (4); Match No. 33: Lee Complin 11 (5); Karl Mason 2 (5); Match No. 34: Ricky Ashworth 10+1 (5); Matthew Wright 2+1 (3); Match No. 35: **Mark Baseby** 1 (4); Match No. 36: Karl Mason 0 (4); Match No. 37: Ricky Ashworth 9+1 (6); Matthew Wright 3 (3); Match No. 39: Josef Franc 14+2 (6); Scott James 4 (4); Match No. 40: Steve Boxall 14+1 (6); Joe Haines 4+1 (3); Match No. 41:Ricky Ashworth 13 (6); Matthew Wright 0 (3); Match No. 42: Lee Complin 12+1 (6); Scott James 1 (3).

Details of tactical rides and tactical substitute rides: Match No. 2: Tacey 0 points (TS); Match No. 4: Jirout 1 point (TR; not doubled); Match No. 6: Jirout 4 points (TR); Match No. 10: Tacey 6 points (TR); Match No. 11: King 6 points (TR); Match No. 12: Legault 4 points (TR); Match No. 16: Madsen 4 points (TR); Match No. 17: King 0 points (TR); Match No. 18: King 1 point (TR; not doubled); Match No. 19: Madsen 4 points (TR); Match No. 20: Legault 6 points (TR); Match No. 21: Fry 6 points (TR); Match No. 24: Legault 6 points (TR); Match No. 27: Tacey 0 points (TR); Match No. 29: Legault 6 points (TR); Match No. 31: Fry 6 points (TR); Match No. 33: Complin 4 points (TR); Match No. 36: Legault 1 point (TR); Match No. 37: Legault 6 points (TR).

AVERAGES

[28 Premier League; 2 Knock-Out Cup; 8 Premier Trophy; 2 Young Shield = 40 fixtures]

• Denotes ever-present.

Rider	Mts	Rds	Pts	Bon	Tot	Avge	Max
Kyle Legault	31	151	309	14	323	8.56	1 paid
Mario Jirout	13	53	88	6	94	7.09	-
Tom P. Madsen	31	125	196	23	219	7.01	1 paid
Paul Fry	26	122	173	23	196	6.43	-
Tomas Suchanek	26	145	204	27	231	6.37	-
Shaun Tacey •	40	178	244	36	280	6.29	-
Jason King •	40	173	241	29	270	6.24	-
Mark Baseby	10	35	25	8	33	3.77	-
Mark Thompson	19	76	39	12	51	2.68	-

Also rode:

Jamie Smith	5	21	22	4	26	4.95	-
Guests	29	120	146	16	162	5.40	-

(Ricky Ashworth [3]; Ben Barker [2]; Steve Boxall [1]; James Cockle [1]; Lee Complin [2]; Paul Cooper [1]; Josef Franc [1]; Daniel Giffard [1]; Nicki Glanz [1]; Joe Haines [1]; Daniel Halsey [1]; Rusty Harrison [1]; Jay Herne [1]; Scott James [2]; Chris Johnson [1]; Karl Mason [3]; Theo Pijper [1]; Jamie Robertson [1]; Tomas Suchanek [1]; Matthew Wright [3])

INDIVIDUAL MEETING

14 October: Shareholders' Junior Trophy

QUALIFYING SCORES: Joe Haines 13; Jan Gravesen 12; Daniel Halsey 12; Darren Mallett 10; Matthew Wright 10; James Holder 10; Rob Smith 9; Jerran Hart 9; Karl Mason 9; Nicki Glanz 7; Aaron Baseby 7; Mark Thompson 3; Jaimie Pickard 3; Adam Lowe (Res) 2; Shane Henry 2; Keiran Morris 1; Henning Loof 0; Wayne Dunworth 0.

SEMI-FINAL: 1st Wright; 2nd Mallett; 3rd Holder; 4th Halsey.

FINAL: 1st Wright; 2nd Gravesen; 3rd Mallett; 4th Haines.

OTHER MEETING

21 October: Big Bang 2 Fours

Peterborough 38, East Anglian Select 27 (Chris Schramm 12 (4); Leigh Lanham 11 (4); James Holder 2 (4); Nicki Glanz 2 (4), Boston 22, Mildenhall 21 (Shaun Tacey 9 (4); Jason King 8 (4); Ritchie Hawkins 2 (4); Tomas Suchanek 2 (4). For Mildenhall, Tacey's total includes 6 points from a TR, whilst King's includes 4 points from a TR. For the East Anglian Select, Schramm's score includes 6 points from a TR, whilst Lanham's includes 4 points from a TR.

Czech racer **Mario Jirout** found consistency hard to obtain after almost three years away from British racing and was eventually axed by Mildenhall following a poor performance at Glasgow on 20 May.

(Photo: David Valentine)

NEWCASTLE DIAMONDS

ADDRESS:	Newcastle Greyhound Stadium, Brough Park, The Fossway, Byker, Newcastle-upon-Tyne, Tyne and Wear, NE6 2XJ.
TELEPHONE:	0191 2656581.
CLUB HOTLINE:	09068 664679 (Premium rate applies).
WEBSITE:	www.newcastlediamonds.com
PROMOTERS:	Darryl Illingworth, George English & Barry Wallace.
MAIN TEAM SPONSOR:	Warburtons.
YEARS OF OPERATION:	1929 English Dirt-Track League; 1930 Open; 1938-1939 National League Division Two; 1945 Open; 1946 Northern League; 1947-1951 National League Division Two; 1961-1964 Provincial League; 1965-1967 British League; 1968-1970 British League Division One; 1975-1983 National League; 1984 British League; 1986-1987 National League; 1989-1990 National League; 1991-1994 British League Division Two; 1997-2001 Premier League; 2002-2004 Premier League and Conference League; 2005-2007 Premier League.
FIRST MEETING:	17 May 1929.
TRACK LENGTH:	300 metres.
TRACK RECORD:	62.1 seconds - Kenneth Bjerre (20/07/03).

CLUB HONOURS

LEAGUE CHAMPIONS: 1964, 1976, 1982, 1983, 2001.

PAIRS CHAMPIONS: 1975.

FOUR-TEAM CHAMPIONS: 1976, 1982, 1983.

KNOCK-OUT CUP WINNERS: 1976, 1982.

SUPERNATIONAL WINNERS: 1982, 1983.

GOLD CUP WINNERS: 1991, 1992.

When fit, **Christian Henry** served up more of his spectacular brand of never-say-die racing, making him an extremely popular member of the Newcastle team.

(Photo: David Valentine)

NEWCASTLE 2007

* Denotes aggregate/bonus-point victory

NO.	DATE	OPPONENTS	VENUE	COMPETITION	RESULT	JOSEF FRANC	ROSS BRADY	JONAS RAUN	CARL WILKINSON	CHRISTIAN HENRY	ADAM MCKINNA	SEAN STODDART	ASHLEY JOHNSON	SAM DORE	OTHER RIDERS
1	18/3	Workington	H	Chal	L42-47	8+2 (5)	6 (4)	-	7+1 (4)	5+1 (4)	2 (1)	3 (7)	-	-	11+1 (5)
2	24/3	Berwick	A	TT	L31-58	9 (5)	1 (4)	1 (4)	4 (4)	10 (5)	-	4 (5)	-	-	2+2 (4)
3	25/3	Redcar	H	Chal	W53-37	11+2 (5)	7+1 (4)	9 (4)	4+2 (4)	9 (5)	-	12+3 (5)	-	-	1+1 (3)
4	31/3	Redcar	A	Chal	L39-53*	11 (5)	8+2 (5)	5 (4)	4 (4)	4 (4)	-	6+2 (4)	-	-	1 (4)
5	1/4	Berwick	H	TT	W50-42	12+2 (5)	7 (4)	7+1 (4)	6 (4)	11 (5)	-	7+1 (5)	-	-	0 (3)
6	6/4	Edinburgh	A	PT	L42-47	4+1 (5)	9 (4)	6 (4)	2+1 (4)	13 (5)	-	7+1 (5)	-	-	1 (3)
7	8/4	Glasgow	A	PT	L34-59	13 (5)	4 (4)	0 (4)	7 (4)	6 (5)	-	3+1 (5)	-	-	1 (3)
8	9/4	Glasgow	H	PT	L43-47	13+1 (5)	8+1 (4)	2+1 (4)	4 (4)	10 (5)	-	6 (5)	-	-	0 (3)
9	15/4	Edinburgh	H	PT	W50-41*	8+2 (5)	7 (4)	6 (4)	9+1 (4)	13+1 (5)	-	-	-	-	7+2 (8)
10	19/4	Redcar	A	PT	W48-42	7+2 (4)	4+2 (4)	14 (5)	9+1 (4)	7+1 (5)	-	6+1 (5)	-	-	1 (3)
11	21/4	Berwick	A	PT	L40-50	7 (5)	8 (4)	4+1 (4)	6 (4)	10 (5)	-	5+1 (5)	-	-	0 (3)
12	22/4	King's Lynn	H	KO	W50-40	8+1 (4)	9+1 (4)	10+1 (4)	7+1 (4)	9+1 (5)	-	6 (6)	-	-	1+1 (3)
13	25/4	King's Lynn	A	KO	L29-64	13 (5)	0 (4)	6 (5)	4 (4)	4 (4)	-	2 (4)	-	-	0 (4)
14	28/4	Stoke	A	PL	L38-55	3+2 (4)	0 (3)	12 (4)	9+1 (5)	6 (4)	-	7+1 (6)	-	-	1+1 (3)
15	29/4	Redcar	H	PT	W53-39*	11+1 (5)	7+1 (4)	10+1 (5)	8+2 (4)	9 (4)	-	5+1 (5)	-	-	3+2 (3)
16	6/5	Sheffield	H	PL	W48-43	8 (4)	5 (4)	11+2 (5)	9+1 (4)	12 (5)	-	2 (5)	1+1 (3)	-	-
17	10/5	Sheffield	A	PL	L36-57	11 (5)	4 (4)	6 (5)	5+1 (4)	5 (4)	-	4 (5)	1 (3)	-	-
18	14/5	Berwick	H	PT	W58-34*	9+2 (4)	10+1 (4)	12 (5)	10 (4)	10+3 (5)	-	6+1 (4)	1 (4)	-	-
19	19/5	Mildenhall	A	PL	L40-53	12 (5)	0 (1)	4 (4)	5+2 (4)	14 (5)	-	5+1 (6)	0 (5)	-	-
20	20/5	Isle of Wight	H	PL	W49-45	11 (5)	3 (3)	8 (4)	2+2 (4)	11 (5)	-	10+2 (6)	4+2 (3)	-	-
21	27/5	Newport	H	PL	W50-40	9 (4)	6 (4)	13+1 (5)	3+1 (4)	14+1 (5)	-	4+1 (5)	1 (3)	-	-
22	2/6	Workington	A	PL	L39-51	10+2 (5)	7 (4)	7 (4)	5+2 (4)	7 (5)	-	3 (5)	0 (3)	-	-
23	3/6	Berwick	H	PL	W57-36	13+1 (5)	7+2 (4)	6+1 (4)	8+1 (4)	12+1 (5)	-	10+1 (5)	1 (3)	-	-
24	10/6	Workington	H	PL	W49-41	R/R	10+1 (5)	8 (5)	9+1 (6)	16+1 (6)	-	6+1 (5)	0 (3)	-	-
25	17/6	King's Lynn	H	PL	D45-45	9 (5)	6 (4)	4 (4)	6 (4)	10+1 (5)	1 (3)	9+2 (5)	-	-	-
26	7/7	Berwick	A	PL	L44-48*	13+1 (5)	1 (1)	6 (4)	13+2 (5)	6 (3)	0 (5)	5 (7)	-	-	-
27	11/7	King's Lynn	A	PL	L38-55	17 (5)	R/R	1 (4)	7 (5)	-	-	1 (5)	-	-	12+3 (11)
28	15/7	Stoke	H	PL	W50-43	8+4 (4)	4+2 (3)	6 (4)	7+2 (5)	-	-	8+3 (6)	3 (3)	-	14+1 (5)
29	22/7	Mildenhall	H	PL	W48-42	11+2 (5)	6 (4)	5 (4)	11+3 (5)	12 (4)	-	3 (5)	0 (3)	-	-
30	31/7	Isle of Wight	A	PL	L35-57	7 (5)	0 (2)	2 (4)	5+1 (4)	14 (5)	-	7+1 (6)	-	-	0 (4)
31	1/8	Birmingham	A	PL	L36-57	15 (5)	2 (4)	6 (4)	5 (5)	3 (4)	-	4 (4)	-	-	1+1 (5)
32	5/8	Edinburgh	H	PL	W46-44	13+1 (5)	0 (3)	3+1 (4)	8 (4)	11 (5)	-	8 (6)	-	-	3 (3)
33	10/8	Edinburgh	A	PL	W46-43*	R/R	8 (5)	3+2 (5)	7 (6)	17 (6)	-	8+1 (5)	-	3 (3)	-
34	12/8	Redcar	H	PL	L38-55	11 (5)	-	R/R	3+1 (5)	8 (5)	-	16 (7)	-	0 (4)	0 (5)
35	26/8	Glasgow	A	PL	L38-55	8+1 (6)	-	5 (4)	4+1 (4)	13+1 (5)	-	5 (6)	-	1+1 (3)	2 (3)
36	27/8	Glasgow	H	PL	W50-44	13+1 (5)	-	2 (4)	14 (5)	9 (4)	-	6 (5)	-	0 (3)	6+2 (4)
37	30/8	Redcar	A	PL	L40-53	9+1 (5)	-	5+1 (4)	9 (5)	2 (2)	-	12+2 (6)	-	1+1 (4)	2 (4)
38	1/9	Rye House	A	PL	L26-65	3 (4)	-	6 (5)	4 (4)	-	-	2+1 (5)	-	0 (3)	11+1 (9)
39	2/9	Rye House	H	PL	W47-43	11 (5)	-	8+1 (4)	10 (5)	-	-	8+1 (5)	-	0 (3)	10+2 (8)
40	9/9	Somerset	H	PL	W48-41	12+1 (5)	-	2+1 (2)	11+1 (5)	5 (4)	-	R/R	-	1+1 (7)	17+1 (7)
41	16/9	Newport	A	PL	L40-52	11+2 (5)	-	R/R	4+2 (5)	-	-	3 (5)	-	0 (3)	22 (12)
42	19/9	Somerset	A	PL	L38-55	5 (4)	-	R/R	10 (6)	-	-	2+1 (5)	-	1+1 (4)	20 (11)
43	23/9	Birmingham	H	PL	L43-47	6 (4)	-	R/R	14 (6)	-	-	3+1 (5)	-	1 (2)	19+2 (12)
44	6/10	Workington	A	YS	L35-58	9 (5)	-	R/R	12 (6)	-	-	2+2 (5)	-	0 (3)	12+3 (11)
45	7/10	Workington	H	YS	W46-45	12 (5)	-	R/R	12 (5)	-	-	5 (5)	-	1 (3)	16+3 (12)
46	14/10	Redcar	H	TTT	D45-45	11+2 (5)	-	R/R	9 (5)	-	-	7+1 (5)	-	1+1 (3)	17+1 (12)
47	29/10	Redcar	A	TTT	L40-53	10 (5)	-	-	14 (6)	-	-	2+2 (5)	-	2+2 (5)	12 (9)

ADDITIONAL KEY: TT = Tyne-Tweed Trophy; TTT = Tyne-Tees Trophy.

Details of other riders (all guests unless **highlighted**): Match No. 1: George Stancl 11+1 (5); Match No. 2: Ashley Johnson 2+2 (4); Match No. 3: Ashley Johnson 1+1 (3); Match No. 4: Ashley Johnson 1 (4); Match No. 5: Ashley Johnson 0 (3); Match No. 6: Ashley Johnson 1 (3); Match No. 7: Ashley Johnson 1 (3); Match No. 8: Ashley Johnson 0 (3); Match No. 9: Ben Powell 7+2 (5); Ashley Johnson 0 (3); Match No. 10: Ashley Johnson 1 (3); Match No. 11: Ashley Johnson 0 (3); Match No. 12: Ashley Johnson 1+1 (3); Match No. 13: Robert Mear 0 (4); Match No. 14: Ashley Johnson 1+1 (3); Match No. 15: Ashley Johnson 3+2 (3); Match No. 27: Kyle Legault 8+1 (5); Benji Compton 4+2 (6); Match No. 28: George Stancl 14+1 (5); Match No. 30: Simon Lambert 0 (4); Match No. 31: Simon Lambert 1+1 (5); Match No. 32: Sam Dore 3 (3); Match No. 34: **Paul Clews** 0 (5); Match No. 35: **Paul Clews** 2 (3); Match No. 36: **Paul Clews** 6+2 (4); Match No. 37: **Paul Clews** 2 (4); Match No. 38: Craig Watson 9+1 (5); Match No. 39: George Stancl 7+1 (4); **Paul Clews** 3+1 (4); Match No. 40: **Paul Clews** 17+1 (7); Match No. 41: George Stancl 14 (5); **Paul Clews** 8 (7); Match No. 42: Ricky Ashworth 14 (5); **Paul Clews** 6 (6); Match No. 43: George Stancl 11+1 (5); **Paul Clews** 8+1 (7); Match No. 44: **Paul Clews** 7+3 (7); George Stancl 5 (4); Match No. 45: Ricky Ashworth 8+2 (5); **Paul Clews** 8+1 (7); Match No. 46: George Stancl 12 (5); **Paul Clews** 5+1 (7); Match No. 47: George Stancl 8 (4); **Paul Clews** 4 (5); Robert Ksiezak R/R.

Details of tactical rides and tactical substitute rides: Match No. 2: Franc 1 point (TR; not doubled); Match No. 4: Franc 4 points (TR); Match No. 7: Franc 6 points (TR); Match No. 13: Franc 6 points (TR); Match No. 14: Raun 6 points (TR); Match No. 17: Franc 6 points (TR); Match No. 19: Henry 6 points (TR); Match No. 27: Franc 6 points (TR); Match No. 30: Henry 4 points (TR); Match No. 31: Franc 6 points (TR); Match No. 34: Franc 6 points (TR); Match No. 35: Henry 6 points (TR); Franc 1 point (TS; not doubled); Match No. 37: Wilkinson 6 points (TR); Match No. 38: Watson 2 points (TR); Match No. 41: Stancl 4 points (TR); Match No. 42: Ashworth 6 points (TR); Match No. 44: Wilkinson 6 points (TR); Match No. 47: Wilkinson 6 points (TR).

AVERAGES

[28 Premier League; 2 Knock-Out Cup; 8 Premier Trophy; 2 Young Shield = 40 fixtures]

• Denotes ever-present.

Rider	Mts	Rds	Pts	Bon	Tot	Avge	Max
Josef Franc	38	181	355	26	381	8.42	-
Christian Henry	31	144	290	11	301	8.36	1 full; 1 paid
Carl Wilkinson •	40	183	291	31	322	7.04	1 paid
Jonas Raun	34	144	206	14	220	6.11	-
Ross Brady	27	98	135	11	146	5.96	-
Sean Stoddart	38	200	214	28	242	4.84	-
Paul Clews	12	65	69	9	78	4.80	-
Ashley Johnson	11	36	12	3	15	1.67	-
Sam Dore	13	45	9	4	13	1.16	-

Also rode:

Adam McKinna	2	8	1	0	1	0.50	-

Guests	24	97	107	16	123	5.07	1 paid

(Ricky Ashworth [2]; Benji Compton [1]; Sam Dore [1]; Ashley Johnson [9]; Simon Lambert [2]; Kyle Legault [1]; Robert Mear [1]; Ben Powell [1]; George Stancl [5]; Craig Watson [1])

OTHER MEETING

5 April: **Kevin Little Farewell** (at Redcar)
Newcastle 31: Kenneth Bjerre 11 (4); Stuart Robson 8 (4); George Stancl 7 (4); Richard Hall 5 (4), Redcar 28, Workington 23, Edinburgh 21.

After losing his early-season sparkle, **Ross Brady's** confidence deserted him and he was released by the Diamonds in August, with Paul Clews taking his place in the team.

(Photo: David Valentine)

NEWPORT WASPS

ADDRESS:	Hayley Stadium, Plover Close, Nash Mead, Queensway Meadows, Newport, South Wales, NS19 4SU.
TELEPHONE:	N/A.
CLUB HOTLINE:	09068 664676.
WEBSITE:	www.newportspeedway.org
PROMOTER:	Tim Stone.
YEARS OF OPERATION:	1997 Premier League and Amateur League; 1998-2006 Premier League and Conference League; 2007 Premier League.
FIRST MEETING:	4 May 1997.
TRACK LENGTH:	285 metres.
TRACK RECORD:	58.38 seconds - Craig Watson (03/08/03).
PREVIOUS VENUE:	Somerton Park Stadium, Somerton Park, Newport, Gwent, South Wales.
YEARS OF OPERATION:	1964 Provincial League; 1965-1967 British League; 1968-1974 British League Division One; 1975-1976 British League; 1977 National League.

CLUB HONOURS

PREMIER NATIONAL TROPHY WINNERS: 1999.

Newport signed newcomer **Michal Rajkowski** after being unable to agree a deal with Craig Watson. The Pole began the campaign at No. 1, before dropping to reserve, but produced some breathtaking performances thereafter, eventually regaining his position at the head of the side.

(Photo: David Valentine)

NEWPORT 2007

* Denotes aggregate/bonus-point victory

NO.	DATE	OPPONENTS	VENUE	COMPETITION	RESULT	MICHAL RAJKOWSKI	CHRIS SCHRAMM	TOM HEDLEY	TONY ATKIN	PHIL MORRIS	NICK SIMMONS	KARL MASON	BARRY BURCHATT	SEBASTIAN TRUMINSKI	OTHER RIDERS
1	25/3	Rye House	H	PT	L36-57	2 (4)	4 (4)	11 (5)	4+1 (4)	9 (5)	6+1 (5)	0 (3)	-	-	-
2	1/4	Isle of Wight	H	PT	L41-48	4 (4)	6+2 (4)	5+1 (5)	6+1 (4)	10 (5)	9 (5)	1 (3)	-	-	-
3	7/4	Mildenhall	A	PT	L34-52	4+1 (4)	7 (4)	3 (4)	5 (4)	10+1 (4)	5+2 (5)	0 (3)	-	-	-
4	8/4	Mildenhall	H	PT	W49-41	9+1 (5)	6+1 (4)	7 (4)	6+2 (4)	12+1 (5)	3 (2)	6+2 (6)	-	-	-
5	13/4	Somerset	A	PT	L25-65	3 (4)	6 (5)	5+1 (5)	4 (4)	1 (4)	5+1 (5)	1 (3)	-	-	-
6	14/4	Rye House	H	PT	L27-65	1 (4)	6 (5)	1 (4)	3 (4)	8 (5)	4+1 (3)	-	-	-	4+1 (5)
7	15/4	Somerset	H	PT	W53-37	10+1 (5)	11+2 (5)	4+1 (4)	6+1 (4)	7+1 (4)	7 1 2 (4)	-	-	-	8+1 (4)
8	17/4	Isle of Wight	A	PT	L31-62	1 (4)	9 (6)	13 (6)	3+1 (5)	R/R	5+1 (6)	0 (3)	-	-	-
9	22/4	Stoke	H	PL	W49-44	13+1 (7)	12+3 (6)	4 (4)	4+2 (4)	15 (6)	R/R	1 (3)	-	-	-
10	25/4	Birmingham	A	KO	L41-49	11+2 (7)	7+2 (6)	6+1 (4)	7+1 (4)	8+1 (6)	R/R	2 (3)	-	-	-
11	29/4	Birmingham	H	KO	W51-39*	19 (7)	13+1 (6)	4+1 (4)	6+1 (4)	8+3 (6)	R/R	1+1 (3)	-	-	-
12	10/5	Redcar	A	PL	L42-48	14 (7)	3+1 (5)	7 (5)	7+2 (5)	9 (5)	R/R	2 (3)	-	-	-
13	20/5	Workington	H	PL	W51-42	15+1 (6)	6+3 (5)	10+1 (5)	9+2 (4)	4+1 (4)	3 (3)	-	4+1 (3)	-	-
14	27/5	Newcastle	A	PL	L40-50	8 (6)	8+1 (5)	4+1 (4)	4+2 (4)	9 (4)	4+1 (3)	-	3+1 (3)	-	-
15	30/5	Birmingham	A	PL	L27-62	2 (4)	8 (5)	4 (4)	7+1 (5)	3+3 (4)	1+1 (4)	-	2 (4)	-	-
16	2/6	Stoke	A	KO	L41-49	10+1 (6)	7 (5)	11 (5)	4+2 (4)	7+1 (4)	0 (3)	-	2+1 (3)	-	-
17	3/6	Stoke	H	KO	W50-40*	9 (6)	12 (5)	2 (2)	8+1 (4)	11+2 (5)	1 (3)	-	7+1 (5)	-	-
18	5/6	Isle of Wight	A	PL	L21-69	-	6+1 (5)	6 (5)	2 (4)	3 (4)	0 (4)	-	1 (4)	-	3 (4)
19	9/6	Stoke	A	PL	L43-46*	19 (7)	4+1 (5)	9+1 (5)	6+1 (4)	4+1 (4)	1 (4)	-	0 (0)	-	-
20	10/6	Glasgow	H	PL	W54-38	12+1 (6)	6+1 (4)	12 (4)	4 (4)	11+1 (5)	3+1 (3)	-	6+1 (4)	-	-
21	14/6	Glasgow	A	PL	L42-49*	5 (6)	8+1 (5)	4 (4)	11+2 (5)	6+2 (4)	4 (3)	-	4+1 (3)	-	-
22	15/6	Edinburgh	A	PL	L33-59	11 (7)	5 (5)	2 (4)	2+1 (2)	10 (5)	1 (3)	-	2 (4)	-	-
23	17/6	Edinburgh	H	PL	L42-47	12+1 (7)	7+1 (5)	12 (6)	R/R	8+2 (5)	1 (3)	-	2 (4)	-	-
24	20/6	King's Lynn	A	PL	L36-56	18 (7)	8+2 (6)	4 (6)	R/R	2 (4)	0 (3)	-	-	-	4+2 (4)
25	7/7	Workington	A	PL	L37-55	6 (4)	6 (4)	6+2 (5)	11+1 (5)	5+2 (4)	2 (4)	-	1+1 (4)	-	-
26	8/7	Mildenhall	H	PL	W48-42	12 (5)	7 (4)	6+1 (4)	6+2 (4)	10 (5)	6+1 (4)	-	1 (4)	-	-
27	22/7	King's Lynn	H	PL	W48-44	8 (4)	8+1 (4)	8+1 (5)	6+3 (5)	8 (4)	5 (4)	-	5+2 (4)	-	-
28	4/8	Rye House	A	PL	L23-68	1 (4)	1 (4)	7+2 (5)	2 (4)	7 (5)	2 (4)	-	3 (4)	-	-
29	5/8	Berwick	H	PL	W38-35	8+2 (5)	4 (5)	R/R	11 (6)	1+1 (4)	8 (6)	-	6+2 (4)	-	-
30	10/8	Somerset	A	PL	L29-61	6+1 (5)	7 (5)	3+1 (4)	4+1 (4)	2 (4)	3 (4)	-	4 (4)	-	-
31	12/8	Rye House	H	PL	L43-50	8+1 (5)	8+1 (5)	8+2 (4)	6+1 (4)	4+1 (4)	3+1 (3)	-	6+3 (5)	-	-
32	19/8	Birmingham	H	PL	L42-48	3 (4)	8+1 (5)	9+1 (5)	7+1 (4)	11+1 (5)	0 (3)	-	4 (4)	-	-
33	26/8	Somerset	H	PL	W48-42	12+1 (5)	9 (4)	2+1 (4)	11 (5)	6+2 (4)	5+2 (4)	-	3+2 (4)	-	-
34	2/9	Redcar	H	PL	W55-38*	8+1 (4)	9+2 (4)	2+1 (4)	11 (5)	6+2 (4)	8+3 (4)	-	11+1 (5)	-	-
35	4/9	Mildenhall	A	PL	L39-54	6+1 (5)	12+1 (5)	4 (4)	6 (4)	4+1 (3)	5 (4)	-	2+1 (5)	-	-
36	8/9	Berwick	A	PL	W61-32*	11+1 (5)	6 (4)	8+2 (4)	10+1 (4)	-	8+1 (4)	-	7+4 (4)	11+2 (5)	-
37	9/9	Sheffield	H	PL	L43-46	8+1 (5)	10 (5)	6 (4)	8+1 (4)	-	6+2 (4)	-	4+1 (4)	1 (4)	-
38	16/9	Newcastle	H	PL	W52-40*	6+1 (4)	12 (5)	5+2 (4)	5+1 (4)	-	7+2 (4)	-	6 (4)	11 (5)	-
39	20/9	Sheffield	A	PL	L38-54	8+1 (5)	7+1 (5)	6+1 (4)	11 (4)	-	3 (5)	-	1 (3)	2+2 (4)	-
40	23/9	Isle of Wight	H	PL	L39-50	4+1 (4)	9+1 (6)	R/R	4+2 (4)	-	14+2 (7)	-	3 (3)	5 (5)	-
41	7/10	Somerset	H	KOs	W50-42	2 (4)	12+1 (5)	R/R	13+1 (5)	-	9+1 (6)	-	3 (5)	11+2 (5)	-
42	12/10	Somerset	A	KOs	L32-61	6+1 (5)	13 (5)	R/R	5 (5)	-	1 (4)	-	4 (7)	3 (4)	-

NOTE: (1) The away match at Mildenhall in the Premier Trophy on 7 April was abandoned after heat fourteen, with the result permitted to stand; (2) The home Premier League versus Berwick on 5 August originally ended in a 54-38 victory for Berwick, however, the SCB subsequently ruled that the Bandits' use of facilities for absent Polish riders Sebastian Truminski and Jacek Rempala should be withdrawn. Berwick had operated rider replacement for the former, while Lee Complin had guested for the latter. The points recorded by Complin and R/R were therefore deducted to leave an amended result of 38-35 in favour of the Wasps.

Details of other riders (all guests unless **highlighted**): Match No. 6: Daniel Halsey 4+1 (5); Match No. 7: Barry Burchatt 8+1 (4); Match No. 18: Danny Warwick 3 (4); Match No. 24: Simon Lambert 4+2 (4).

Details of tactical rides and tactical substitute rides: Match No. 1: Hedley 6 points (TR); Match No. 3: Morris 4 points (TR); Match No. 5: Rajkowski 0 points (TR); Match No. 6: Schramm 4 points (TR); Match No. 8: Hedley 6 points (TR); Match No. 15: Atkin 0 points (TR); Match No. 18: Schramm 1 point (TR; not doubled); Match No. 21: Morris 2 points (TR); Match No. 22: Morris 6 points (TR); Match No. 24: Rajkowski 4 points (TR); Match No. 25: Atkin 4 points (TR); Match No. 28: Hedley 2 points (TR); Match No. 29: Rajkowski 4 points (TR); Match No. 30: Atkin 1 point (TR; not doubled); Match No. 32: Morris 2 points (TR); Match No. 35: Schramm 6 points (TR); Match No. 39: Atkin 4 points (TR); Match No. 40: Simmons 4 points (TR); Match No. 42: Schramm 6 points (TR).

AVERAGES

[28 Premier League; 6 Knock-Out Cup; 8 Premier Trophy = 42 fixtures]

• Denotes ever-present.

Rider	Mts	Rds	Pts	Bon	Tot	Avge	Max
Phil Morris	34	153	232	30	262	6.85	-
Tony Atkin	40	170	251	39	290	6.82	-
Chris Schramm •	42	204	315	32	347	6.80	-
Michal Rajkowski	41	212	331	23	354	6.68	-
Sebastian Truminski	7	32	44	6	50	6.25	-
Tom Hedley	38	168	223	25	248	5.90	1 full
Nick Simmons	38	152	156	26	182	4.79	-
Barry Burchatt	29	114	107	23	130	4.56	-
Karl Mason	10	33	14	3	17	2.06	-
Guests	4	17	19	4	23	5.41	-

(Barry Burchatt [1]; Daniel Halsey [1]; Simon Lambert [1]; Danny Warwick [1])

INDIVIDUAL MEETINGS

14 January: **New Year Classic**
QUALIFYING SCORES: Chris Harris 13; David Howe 13; Leigh Lanham 11; Chris Neath 10; Glenn Cunningham 10; Brent Werner 9; Richard Hall 7; Phil Morris 7; Ricky Ashworth 4; Michal Rajkowski 4; Nicki Glanz 2; David Mason 0.   **FINAL**: 1st Howe; 2nd Harris; 3rd Lanham; 4th Neath.

18 March: **Prince of Wales Trophy**
QUALIFYING SCORES: Glenn Cunningham 13; David Howe 12; Stanislaw Burza 10; Nick Simmons 9; Ritchie Hawkins 8; Jason Doyle 8; Tony Atkin 8; Sam Hurst (Res) 7; Chris Schramm 6; Phil Morris 5; Danny Warwick 3; Andrew Bargh 1.   **FINAL**: 1st Howe; 2nd Burza; 3rd Cunningham; 4th Simmons.

6 May: **The Celebration** (10-Year Anniversary)
QUALIFYING SCORES: Michal Rajkowski 12; Steve Boxall 11; Tony Atkin 11; Tom Hedley 10; Chris Neath 9; Kauko Nieminen 9; Phil Morris 8; Jason Bunyan 7; Chris Schramm 7; Emil Lindqvist 3; Scott Pegler 2; Karl Mason 1; Sam Hurst (Res) 0.   **FINAL**: 1st Rajkowski; 2nd Boxall; 3rd Atkin; 4th Hedley.

1 July: **Welsh Open**
QUALIFYING SCORES: Leigh Lanham 12; David Howe 12; Adam Shields 12; Chris Holder 10; Mark Lemon 9; Krzysztof Stojanowski 9; Lubos Tomicek 8; Ricky Ashworth 7; Phil Morris 7; Andre Compton 6; Jason Bunyan 6; Eric Andersson 5; Ryan Fisher 5; Marek Mroz 4; Ronnie Correy 2; Josef Franc 0.   **FINAL**: 1st Holder; 2nd Howe; 3rd Lanham; 4th Shields.

Tony Atkin initially joined the Wasps in 2003 and has long since become a club legend. Having celebrated his forty-first birthday in April, the veteran racer was as solid as ever for the Welsh side in 2007.

(Photo: David Valentine)

REDCAR BEARS

NOTE: The information below relates only to the main Redcar team. For details of the second side, Cleveland Bays, please refer to the Conference League section.

ADDRESS:	South Tees Motorsports Park, Dormer Way, South Bank Road, Middlesbrough, Cleveland, TS6 6XH.
TELEPHONE:	07796 441850.
CLUB HOTLINE:	09068 664665 (Premium rate applies).
WEBSITE:	www.redcarspeedway.co.uk
PROMOTERS:	Chris Van Straaten, Gareth Rogers & Glyn Taylor.
YEARS OF OPERATION:	2006-07 Premier League.
FIRST MEETING:	13 April 2006.
TRACK LENGTH:	266 metres.
TRACK RECORD:	53.0 seconds - Gary Havelock (31/08/06).

CLUB HONOURS
YOUNG SHIELD WINNERS: 2007.

Having overcome an injury earlier in the season, Redcar's popular Frenchman **Mathieu Tresarrieu** suffered a further blow in September, when he crashed during practice for the European Grass-track Championship at Swingfield in Kent, suffering a broken fibula and smashed knee socket.

(Photo: David Valentine)

REDCAR 2007

* Denotes aggregate/bonus-point victory

NO.	DATE	OPPONENTS	VENUE	COMPETITION	RESULT	GARY HAVELOCK	DANIEL GIFFARD	JAMES GRIEVES	CHRIS KERR	MATHIEU TRESARRIEU	JAMIE COURTNEY	RUSTY HODGSON	JOSH AUTY	ROBBIE KESSLER	OTHER RIDERS
1	17/3	Rye House	A	Chal	L39-53	11 (5)	3+1 (4)	4+1 (4)	9+1 (4)	9+1 (5)	1 (4)	2+1 (4)	-	-	-
2	25/3	Newcastle	A	Chal	L37-53	13 (5)	R/R	5+1 (4)	10+2 (6)	1 (5)	3+1 (4)	5 (6)	-	-	-
3	29/3	Berwick	H	PT	W58-35	12+2 (5)	4+1 (4)	8+1 (4)	8+2 (4)	12+1 (5)	7 (4)	-	7+1 (4)	-	-
4	30/3	Edinburgh	A	PT	W46-44	13+1 (5)	4 (4)	15 (5)	6+1 (4)	7 (4)	0 (4)	1 (4)	-	-	-
5	31/3	Newcastle	H	Chal	W53-39	12+2 (5)	7 (4)	9 (4)	8+2 (4)	13+1 (5)	4 (4)	0 (4)	-	-	-
6	7/4	Berwick	A	PT	W46-44*	14 (5)	3 (4)	7+1 (4)	10 (5)	5 (4)	2+1 (3)	-	5+2 (5)	-	-
7	12/4	Edinburgh	H	PT	W51-42*	11 (4)	5+2 (4)	13+1 (5)	10+2 (5)	10 (4)	1 (4)	1 (4)	-	-	-
8	15/4	Glasgow	A	PT	L37-56	10 (4)	1 (4)	16 (5)	2+1 (5)	2 (2)	-	2+1 (4)	-	-	4 (6)
9	19/4	Newcastle	H	PT	L42-48	-	6+2 (5)	11 (6)	3 (5)	R/R	6+1 (4)	-	6 (6)	-	10 (5)
10	26/4	Glasgow	H	PT	W53-38	-	6+2 (4)	11 (5)	10 (4)	-	6 (5)	0 (3)	-	6+3 (4)	14 (5)
11	29/4	Newcastle	A	PT	L39-53	-	3+1 (4)	8+1 (5)	6+1 (4)	-	1 (4)	1+1 (4)	-	8+1 (4)	12 (5)
12	3/5	King's Lynn	H	PL	L44-49	-	5+1 (4)	10 (5)	6 (4)	-	3 (4)	4 (4)	-	9+1 (5)	7+1 (4)
13	6/5	Mildenhall	A	PL	L45-47	-	6 (5)	18+1 (6)	R/R	-	0 (1)	5+1 (7)	-	12+2 (6)	4 (4)
14	10/5	Newport	H	PL	W48-42	-	2+1 (5)	16+1 (6)	R/R	-	-	1 (3)	10+2 (6)	6+1 (5)	13 (5)
15	17/5	Sheffield	A	PL	L41-52	-	1 (4)	13 (5)	9 (4)	-	-	0 (4)	-	9+3 (5)	9+2 (8)
16	18/5	Sheffield	H	PL	W45-43	-	2 (2)	6 (4)	9+1 (5)	-	-	2+1 (5)	-	7+1 (4)	19+2 (10)
17	24/5	Rye House	H	PL	W47-43	-	-	10 (5)	5+1 (4)	6+3 (4)	-	1 (3)	11 (5)	-	14+2 (9)
18	31/5	King's Lynn	H	KO	D45-45	8 (4)	-	14 (5)	7 (5)	4+1 (4)	-	-	11+3 (7)	-	1 (5)
19	6/6	King's Lynn	A	KO	L33-59	13 (5)	-	7 (5)	4 (4)	4+1 (4)	-	1+1 (4)	-	-	4 (7)
20	7/6	Stoke	H	PL	D45-45	13+1 (5)	-	12+1 (5)	8+1 (4)	6 (4)	-	3+1 (4)	-	-	3 (8)
21	21/6	Edinburgh	H	PL	W52-41	14 (5)	-	12+1 (5)	8+2 (4)	3+1 (4)	-	-	11+2 (5)	-	4 (7)
22	22/6	Edinburgh	A	PL	W50-40*	14+1 (5)	-	15 (5)	3+1 (4)	6+1 (4)	-	-	11 (6)	-	1+1 (6)
23	1/7	Rye House	A	PL	L42-49	12 (5)	-	13 (5)	6+2 (4)	DNA	-	1+1 (3)	10+2 (7)	-	0 (3)
24	12/7	Somerset	H	PL	W47-46	11+2 (5)	-	14 (6)	4+2 (5)	R/R	-	-	14 (6)	-	4 (8)
25	18/7	King's Lynn	A	PL	L32-61	15 (5)	-	4 (5)	3 (5)	2+1 (4)	-	-	5+2 (4)	-	3 (7)
26	19/7	Berwick	H	PL	W49-41	13+1 (5)	-	9+1 (4)	7 (4)	11+1 (5)	-	-	5 (4)	-	4+1 (8)
27	21/7	Stoke	A	PL	L44-45	12 (5)	7+1 (6)	9+2 (5)	10+1 (6)	R/R	-	-	-	-	6+1 (8)
28	26/7	Birmingham	H	PL	L42-53	8+1 (4)	2 (5)	10 (5)	3+2 (4)	17 (6)	-	-	-	-	2+1 (6)
29	28/7	Workington	A	PL	L36-56	7 (4)	4 (4)	8 (5)	7 (4)	6+1 (6)	-	-	-	-	4+1 (7)
30	4/8	Berwick	A	PL	L43-50*	8 (5)	6+1 (4)	17 (5)	2+2 (4)	6+1 (4)	-	-	-	-	4+3 (7)
31	8/8	Birmingham	A	PL	L42-53	12 (4)	0 (4)	11 (5)	2+2 (4)	12+1 (6)	-	-	-	-	5 (7)
32	8/8	Mildenhall	H	PL	W51-42*	13 (5)	7+2 (4)	8 (4)	10+3 (5)	6 (4)	-	-	5+1 (4)	-	2 (5)
33	12/8	Newcastle	A	PL	W55-38	12+2 (5)	5+1 (5)	14 (5)	5+2 (4)	9+1 (4)	-	-	8+2 (4)	-	2+2 (3)
34	16/8	Isle of Wight	H	PL	L35-55	9+1 (5)	5+2 (4)	2 (4)	9 (5)	8 (5)	-	-	2 (4)	-	0 (3)
35	30/8	Newcastle	H	PL	W53-40*	5 (4)	9 (6)	14 (5)	11+2 (6)	R/R	-	-	12 (5)	-	2 (4)
36	2/9	Newport	A	PL	L38-55	9+1 (5)	4 (6)	21 (6)	2 (5)	R/R	-	-	-	-	2 (8)
37	6/9	Workington	H	PL	W48-42	12 (5)	4+1 (5)	11 (5)	5+1 (4)	6+1 (4)	-	-	7+1 (4)	-	3 (3)
38	11/9	Isle of Wight	A	PL	L40-50	DNA	2 (4)	13 (5)	2 (4)	10 (4)	-	-	9+1 (5)	-	4 (5)
39	13/9	Glasgow	H	PL	W51-41	12+2 (5)	2+2 (4)	13 (5)	4+1 (4)	10+1 (4)	-	-	6 (4)	-	4 (4)
40	14/9	Somerset	A	PL	L40-53	15+1 (5)	2+1 (4)	5 (4)	6+1 (4)	10 (5)	-	-	-	-	2 (9)
41	23/9	Glasgow	A	PL	L47-48*	18 (5)	5+2 (7)	0 (1)	11+1 (6)	R/R	-	-	-	-	13+1 (11)
42	4/10	Glasgow	H	YS	W49-41	9+1 (5)	8+1 (6)	14+1 (6)	8+2 (5)	R/R	-	-	9+1 (5)	-	1+1 (3)
43	7/10	Glasgow	A	YS	W47-43*	10+2 (5)	8+3 (6)	17 (6)	8+1 (5)	R/R	-	-	-	-	4 (8)
44	11/10	Workington	H	YSs	W50-40	14 (5)	2 (4)	10+1 (5)	9+1 (6)	R/R	-	-	9+1 (5)	-	6+3 (5)
45	14/10	Newcastle	A	TTT	D45-45	8+1 (5)	6+1 (4)	14 (5)	6+1 (4)	-	-	-	3+2 (4)	-	8+1 (8)
46	20/10	Workington	A	YSs	L43-47*	12+1 (5)	5 (5)	12 (5)	9+1 (6)	R/R	-	-	-	-	5+1 (9)
47	25/10	Birmingham	H	YSf	W49-41	11+3 (5)	6+2 (5)	15 (6)	13 (5)	R/R	-	-	-	-	4 (9)
48	28/10	Birmingham	A	YSf	W46-43*	9+2 (5)	5 (5)	12+1 (5)	11 (6)	R/R	-	-	-	-	9+1 (9)
49	29/10	Newcastle	H	TTT	W53-40*	11 (5)	7+2 (4)	14 (5)	10+1 (4)	-	-	-	-	-	11+2 (12)

ADDITIONAL KEY: TTT = Tyne-Tees Trophy.

NOTE: (1) Prior to Hodgson taking a TS ride in Match No. 8, Havelock had been nominated for the TS outing in the original running of the race (heat fourteen), but crashed, without exclusion, and was unable participate in the re-run; (2) Regarding Match No. 23, Tresarrieu was delayed returning from a World Long-track Championship meeting and, as such, the rules did not permit Redcar the use of the rider replacement facility.

Details of other riders (all guests unless **highlighted**): Match No. 8: Lee Smart 4 (6); Match No. 9: Daniel Nermark 10 (5); Match No. 10: Jason Lyons 14 (5); Match No. 11: James Wright 12 (5); Match No. 12: Jason Lyons 7+1 (4); Match No. 13: Ronnie Correy 4 (4); Match No. 14: Chris Holder 13 (5); Match No. 15: Magnus Karlsson 7+1 (4); Mark Thompson 2+1 (4); Match No. 16: Carl Stonehewer 11+2 (5); Benji Compton 8 (5); Match No. 17: Carl Stonehewer 12+1 (5); **Arlo Bugeja** 2+1 (4); Match No. 18: **Arlo Bugeja** 1 (3); Benji Compton 0 (2); Match No. 19: Karlis Ezergailis 3 (3); **Arlo Bugeja** 1 (4); Match No. 20: **Arlo Bugeja** 3 (4); Karlis Ezergailis 0 (4); Match No. 21: **Arlo Bugeja** 2 (4); Benji Compton 2 (3); Match No. 22: Benji Compton 1+1 (3); **Arlo Bugeja** 0 (3); Match No. 23: **Arlo Bugeja** 0 (3); Match No. 24: **Arlo Bugeja** 2 (4); Benji Compton 2 (4); Match No. 25: **Arlo Bugeja** 2 (3); Darren Mallett 1 (4); Match No. 26: Greg Blair 4+1 (5); **Arlo Bugeja** 0 (3); Match No. 27: Karlis Ezergailis 4+1 (5); Shane Waldron 2 (3); Match No. 28: Shane Waldron 1+1 (3); Simon Lambert 1 (3); Match No. 29: Byron Bekker 4+1 (4); Ben Taylor 0 (3); Match No. 30: Byron Bekker 3+2 (4); **Jack Hargreaves** 1+1 (3); Match No. 31: **Jack Hargreaves** 5 (4); Byron Bekker 0 (3); Match No. 32: **Jack Hargreaves** 2 (5); Match No. 33: **Jack Hargreaves** 2+2 (3); Match No. 34: **Jack Hargreaves** 0 (3); Match No. 35: **Jack Hargreaves** 2 (4); Match No. 36: Kyle Hughes 1 (3); **Jack Hargreaves** 1 (5); Match No. 37: **Jack Hargreaves** 3 (3); Match No. 38: **Jack Hargreaves** 4 (5); Match No. 39:

Jack Hargreaves 4 (4); Match No. 40: **Jack Hargreaves** 2 (5); Karlis Ezergailis 0 (4); Match No. 41: Paul Cooper 12+1 (6); Adam McKinna 1 (5); Match No. 42: **Jack Hargreaves** 1+1 (3); Match No. 43: **Jack Hargreaves** 4 (5); Jitendra Duffill 0 (3); Match No. 44: **Jack Hargreaves** 6+3 (5); Match No. 45: Adam Roynon 6+1 (4); **Jack Hargreaves** 2 (4); Match No. 46: Joe Haines 5+1 (5); **Jack Hargreaves** 0 (4); Match No. 47: **Jack Hargreaves** 4 (6); Joe Haines 0 (3); Match No. 48: **Jack Hargreaves** 5+1 (4); Simon Lambert 4 (5); Match No. 49: Adam Roynon 5+1 (4); **Jack Hargreaves** 5+1 (4); Martin Emerson 1 (4).

Details of tactical rides and tactical substitute rides: Match No. 1: Kerr 4 points (TR); Match No. 2: Havelock 1 point (TR; not doubled); Match No. 8: Grieves 6 points (TR); Hodgson 1 point (TS; not doubled); Match No. 11: Wright 4 points (TR); Match No. 13: Grieves 6 points (TR); Match No. 15: Grieves 6 points (TR); Match No. 19: Havelock 4 points (TR); Match No. 23: Grieves 4 points (TR); Match No. 24: Auty 6 points (TS); Match No. 25: Havelock 6 points (TR); Kerr 0 points (TS); Match No. 28: Tresarrieu 6 points (TS); Grieves 4 points (TR); Match No. 29: Kerr 4 points (TR); Tresarrieu 0 points (TS); Match No. 30: Grieves 6 points (TR); Match No. 31: Havelock 6 points (TR); Tresarrieu 4 points (TS); Match No. 34: Tresarrieu 1 point (TS; not doubled); Grieves 0 points (TR); Match No. 36: Grieves 6 points (TR); Match No. 38: Tresarrieu 6 points (TR); Match No. 40: Havelock 6 points (TR); Match No. 41: Havelock 6 points (TR); Cooper 6 points (TS).

AVERAGES

[28 Premier League; 2 Knock-Out Cup; 8 Premier Trophy; 6 Young Shield = 44 fixtures]

• Denotes ever-present.

Rider	Mts	Rds	Pts	Bon	Tot	Avge	Max
Gary Havelock	34	163	376	25	401	9.84	1 full; 1 paid
James Grieves •	44	217	479	14	493	9.09	3 full
Robbie Kessler	7	33	57	12	69	8.36	-
Josh Auty	21	105	170	21	191	7.28	-
Mathieu Tresarrieu	24	104	170	16	186	7.15	-
Chris Kerr	42	194	279	40	319	6.58	-
Daniel Giffard	34	157	146	29	175	4.46	-
Jamie Courtney	9	33	26	2	28	3.39	-
Jack Hargreaves	17	71	46	8	54	3.04	-
Rusty Hodgson	14	56	23	7	30	2.14	-
Arlo Bugeja	10	35	13	1	14	1.60	-
Guests	36	147	150	15	165	4.49	-

(Byron Bekker [3]; Greg Blair [1]; Benji Compton [5]; Paul Cooper [1]; Ronnie Correy [1]; Jitendra Duffill [1]; Karlis Ezergailis [4]; Joe Haines [2]; Chris Holder [1]; Kyle Hughes [1]; Magnus Karlsson [1]; Simon Lambert [2]; Jason Lyons [2]; Adam McKinna [1]; Darren Mallett [1]; Daniel Nermark [1]; Lee Smart [1]; Carl Stonehewer [2]; Ben Taylor [1]; Mark Thompson [1]; Shane Waldron [2]; James Wright [1])

OTHER MEETING

5 April: **Kevin Little Farewell**

Newcastle 31, Redcar 28: Chris Harris 13 (4); Gary Havelock 7 (4); Chris Kerr 6 (4); Daniel Giffard 2 (4), Workington 23, Edinburgh 21. Harris' total includes 6 points from a TR.

INDIVIDUAL MEETING

18 October: **South Tees Silver Helmet**

1st Peter Karlsson 15; 2nd Chris Holder 13; 3rd Daniel Nermark 11; James Grieves 10; Gary Havelock 10; Josef Franc 10; Lewis Bridger 9; Jason Lyons 7; Fredrik Lindgren 6; Daniel Giffard 6; Chris Kerr 6; Ludvig Lindgren 5; Casper Wortmann 5; Nicolai Klindt 4; Kenneth Hansen 1; Joe Haines (Res) 1; Josh Auty 0.

Californian **Chris Kerr** made good progress in his second full season of British racing, a highlight being a return of 11+2 points against the Bears' local rivals, Newcastle, in a memorable Premier League encounter at the South Tees Motorpark on 30 August.

(Photo: David Valentine)

RYE HOUSE ROCKETS

NOTE: The information below relates only to the main Rye House team. For details of the second side, please refer to the Conference League section.

ADDRESS:	Rye House Stadium, Rye Road, Hoddesdon, Hertfordshire, EN11 0EH.
TELEPHONE:	01992 440400.
CLUB HOTLINE:	09066 555948.
WEBSITE:	www.ryehouse.com
PROMOTERS:	Len Silver & Hazal Naylor.
MAIN TEAM SPONSOR:	Silver Ski.
YEARS OF OPERATION:	1958 Open; 1959 Southern Area League; 1960-1966 Open and Training; 1967 Training; 1969-1973 Open and Training; 1974 British League Division Two; 1975-1990 National League; 1991-1993 British League Division Two; 1999-2001; Conference League; 2002-2007 Premier League. NOTE: In 1999, Rye House staged their home matches at Eastbourne, King's Lynn and Mildenhall.
FIRST MEETING:	3 August 1958.
TRACK LENGTH:	262 metres.
TRACK RECORD:	55.6 seconds - Tai Woffinden (29/09/07).
PREVIOUS VENUE:	Hoddesdon Stadium, Rye Road, Hoddesdon, Hertfordshire.
YEARS OF OPERATION:	1935 Open and Training; 1936-37 Open; 1938 Sunday Dirt-Track League; 1939-43 Open; 1945-53 Open; 1954-57 Southern Area League.

CLUB HONOURS

KNOCK-OUT CUP WINNERS: 1979.
LEAGUE CHAMPIONS: 1980, 2005, 2007.
PREMIER TROPHY WINNERS: 2005.

Teenage hotshot **Tai Woffinden** put together a blistering first full term in the Premier League, plundering big scores countrywide. He was certainly kept busy during the season, as he also represented Scunthorpe in the Conference League and enjoyed a late-season stint 'doubling up' for top-flight Poole. During a wonderful year for the youngster, he also scooped a memorable individual double, taking victory in the Conference League Riders' Championship and also the British Under-18 Championship.

(Photo: David Valentine)

RYE HOUSE 2007

* Denotes aggregate/bonus-point victory

NO.	DATE	OPPONENTS	VENUE	COMPETITION	RESULT	CHRIS NEATH	LUKE BOWEN	STEVE BOXALL	TOMMY ALLEN	STUART ROBSON	ADAM ROYNON	TAI WOFFINDEN	RAY MORTON	ROBBIE KESSLER	OTHER RIDERS
1	17/3	Redcar	H	Chal	W53-39	14 (5)	3+1 (4)	9 (5)	6 (4)	1 (4)	10+1 (5)	10+2 (4)	-	-	-
2	24/3	Somerset	H	PT	W55-38	13+1 (5)	6+1 (4)	10+1 (5)	7+3 (4)	7 (4)	4+1 (4)	8 (4)	-	-	-
3	25/3	Newport	A	PT	W57-36	9 (4)	4+1 (4)	6+2 (4)	8 (4)	10+1 (5)	6+2 (4)	14+1 (5)	-	-	-
4	30/3	Somerset	A	PT	W49-41*	6+1 (4)	1 (3)	8 (4)	5+2 (4)	11 (5)	6+2 (4)	12+1 (6)	-	-	-
5	31/3	Mildenhall	H	PT	W66-23	14+1 (5)	4+2 (4)	15 (5)	6+2 (4)	10+2 (4)	8+2 (4)	9 (4)	-	-	-
6	1/4	Mildenhall	A	PT	L44-45*	11 (5)	2 (4)	7 (4)	3+1 (4)	10 (5)	11 (7)	0 (1)	-	-	-
7	7/4	Isle of Wight	H	PT	W56-37	10+1 (5)	3 (4)	8+1 (4)	7 (4)	11 (5)	5+2 (4)	12 (4)	-	-	-
8	9/4	Lakeside	H	Chal	D45-45	5 (4)	0 (3)	9+2 (5)	9 (4)	8 (4)	2+1 (3)	12 (7)	-	-	-
9	14/4	Newport	H	PT	W65-27*	9+1 (4)	3 (4)	11+1 (4)	12+3 (5)	9+1 (4)	-	14+1 (5)	-	-	7+2 (4)
10	18/4	Birmingham	A	PL	W53-39	11+1 (5)	0 (3)	8+1 (4)	6+1 (4)	9 (4)	-	-	-	-	19 (10)
11	21/4	Birmingham	H	PL	W53-39*	8+3 (5)	9+2 (5)	9 (4)	7+1 (4)	11+1 (5)	-	9+1 (4)	-	-	0 (3)
12	24/4	Isle of Wight	A	PT	L39-55*	0 (3)	0 (0)	13 (5)	8 (4)	10 (6)	-	2+2 (4)	-	-	6 (7)
13	30/4	Mildenhall	H	KO	W50-41	18 (6)	4+1 (4)	7+1 (5)	-	R/R	5+1 (5)	5 (4)	-	-	11+2 (6)
14	5/5	Workington	A	PL	L37-53	6 (4)	-	9 (5)	R/R	-	7+1 (7)	7 (5)	7 (5)	-	1+1 (4)
15	19/5	King's Lynn	H	PL	W50-40	11+1 (5)	1 (3)	5+1 (4)	2+1 (3)	-	15+1 (7)	12 (5)	4 (4)	-	-
16	24/5	Redcar	A	PL	L43-47	11 (5)	4 (5)	8 (4)	7+1 (4)	-	3+2 (5)	8 (4)	2 (3)	-	-
17	31/5	Sheffield	A	PL	L37-56	6 (4)	2 (4)	6 (5)	3 (4)	-	3+2 (4)	13 (5)	4+1 (4)	-	-
18	2/6	Birmingham	H	PTs	W52-38	8 (4)	5+1 (4)	12+1 (5)	9 (4)	-	8+1 (5)	8+2 (5)	2+1 (3)	-	-
19	3/6	Mildenhall	A	KO	W49-40*	6 (4)	5+1 (5)	17 (6)	5+1 (5)	-	6+1 (5)	10 (5)	R/R	-	-
20	6/6	Birmingham	A	PTs	L35-58	3 (2)	6 (7)	16+1 (6)	0 (1)	-	10 (7)	0 (0)	R/R	-	-
21	9/6	Glasgow	H	PL	W57-35	12+3 (5)	2+1 (5)	13+1 (5)	6+1 (4)	-	5 (4)	-	-	8 (4)	11 (4)
22	22/6	King's Lynn	A	PL	L43-49*	10 (5)	2+1 (3)	6 (4)	3 (3)	-	2+1 (4)	-	-	6+1 (5)	14+1 (6)
23	26/6	Isle of Wight	A	KO	L40-52	13 (6)	0 (3)	R/R	7+1 (5)	-	2+1 (5)	-	-	10+1 (6)	8 (5)
24	1/7	Redcar	H	PL	W49-42*	13 (5)	2 (3)	5+1 (5)	9 (4)	-	11+1 (5)	-	-	4+2 (4)	5+2 (4)
25	1/7	Workington	H	PL	W58-37*	13 (5)	6+1 (4)	8+3 (5)	11 (4)	-	11+3 (5)	-	-	6+1 (4)	3 (3)
26	7/7	Sheffield	A	PL	W55-37	8+1 (4)	2 (2)	14 (5)	9+2 (4)	-	12+3 (7)	9 (5)	-	1 (3)	-
27	14/7	Berwick	A	PL	L41-51	6+3 (5)	1+1 (3)	14 (6)	R/R	-	6 (6)	4+1 (4)	-	9 (5)	1 (1)
28	15/7	Glasgow	A	PL	L40-49*	6 (5)	4+1 (7)	10+1 (6)	R/R	-	9 (7)	10 (4)	-	1 (2)	-
29	28/7	Edinburgh	H	PL	W68-22	15 (5)	5+3 (4)	10+1 (4)	11+4 (5)	-	7 (4)	12 (4)	-	8+4 (4)	-
30	4/8	Newport	H	PL	W68-23	9+1 (4)	10+1 (6)	11+1 (5)	12 (4)	-	15+3 (6)	11+4 (5)	-	0 (0)	-
31	7/8	Isle of Wight	A	PL	L40-50	7 (5)	3+1 (6)	9 (5)	8+1 (5)	-	11+2 (7)	2 (2)	-	R/R	-
32	10/8	Lakeside	A	Chal	L44-67	6+1 (5)	4 (4)	2+1 (4)	1+1 (4)	-	3+2 (4)	8 (5)	-	-	20 (10)
33	11/8	Isle of Wight	H	KO	W50-43	6 (4)	8+2 (5)	10+1 (5)	6+2 (5)	-	10+2 (6)	10 (5)	-	R/R	-
34	12/8	Newport	A	PL	W50-43*	13+2 (5)	1+1 (6)	5 (4)	0 (3)	-	10+2 (6)	21 (6)	-	R/R	-
35	17/8	Somerset	A	PL	L42-51	3+1 (4)	3 (5)	1 (3)	9+1 (6)	-	14 (7)	12+1 (5)	-	R/R	-
36	25/8	Stoke	A	PL	L43-47	3 (4)	2+1 (3)	10+1 (5)	3 (4)	-	6 (5)	8+1 (4)	-	-	11 (5)
37	27/8	Isle of Wight	H	PL	W69-21*	13+1 (5)	6+3 (4)	12+1 (5)	9+3 (4)	-	10+2 (4)	10 (4)	-	-	9+3 (4)
38	1/9	Newcastle	H	PL	W65-26	9+2 (4)	8+1 (4)	11+1 (4)	13+1 (5)	-	7+2 (4)	9+3 (5)	-	-	8+1 (4)
39	2/9	Newcastle	H	PL	L43-47*	10 (5)	4 (4)	9+1 (5)	2 (3)	-	7+1 (5)	5 (4)	-	-	6+1 (4)
40	7/9	Berwick	H	PL	W63-27*	8+2 (4)	8 (4)	8+2 (5)	8+2 (4)	-	8+3 (4)	9+2 (4)	-	-	14 (5)
41	8/9	Mildenhall	H	PL	W65-25	8+3 (4)	10+1 (4)	12+1 (5)	5+2 (4)	-	7+3 (4)	13+1 (5)	-	-	10+1 (4)
42	9/9	Mildenhall	A	PL	W49-44*	8+1 (4)	2+1 (3)	10 (5)	6 (4)	-	9+3 (5)	5+1 (4)	-	-	9+1 (5)
43	14/9	Edinburgh	A	PL	L45-50*	4+1 (4)	3 (2)	6+1 (5)	4 (5)	-	12+2 (7)	16 (6)	-	-	R/R
44	16/9	Stoke	H	PL	W66-26*	12 (5)	8+1 (4)	8+2 (4)	11+1 (4)	-	11+1 (4)	12+3 (5)	-	-	4+1 (4)
45	22/9	Somerset	H	PL	W56-37*	13+1 (5)	8+2 (4)	3+1 (4)	6+2 (4)	-	6 (4)	13+1 (5)	-	-	7+1 (4)
46	2/10	Isle of Wight	A	POs	L44-46	5+1 (4)	2+1 (3)	9+1 (5)	8 (4)	-	4+1 (5)	4+2 (4)	-	-	12 (5)
47	6/10	Isle of Wight	H	POs	W61-29*	11 (4)	7+3 (4)	8+1 (4)	12+2 (5)	-	8+2 (4)	12+2 (5)	-	-	3+2 (4)
48	18/10	Sheffield	A	POf	L42-51	4+1 (4)	1 (3)	4 (4)	1 (3)	-	11+1 (6)	10 (5)	-	-	11 (5)
49	20/10	Sheffield	H	POf	W69-23*	9+1 (4)	7+3 (4)	10+1 (4)	14+1 (5)	-	7+2 (4)	12+3 (5)	-	-	10+2 (4)

Details of other riders (all guests unless **highlighted**): Match No. 9: Barry Burchatt 7+2 (4); Match No. 10: Chris Holder 13 (5); Joel Parsons 6 (5); Match No. 11: Chris Kerr 0 (3); Match No. 12: Barry Burchatt 6 (7); Match No. 13: Rusty Harrison 11+2 (6); Match No. 14: Byron Bekker 1+1 (4); Match No. 21: Daniel King 11 (4); Match No. 22: Leigh Lanham 14+1 (6); Match No. 23: Daniel King 8 (5); Match No. 24: Christian Henry 5+2 (4); Match No. 25: Christian Henry 3 (3); Match No. 27: Karlis Ezergailis 1 (1); Match No. 32: Edward Kennett 15 (5); Shane Parker 5 (5); Match No. 36: **Stefan Ekberg** 11 (5); Match No. 37: **Stefan Ekberg** 9+3 (4); Match No. 38: **Stefan Ekberg** 8+1 (4); Match No. 39: **Stefan Ekberg** 6+1 (4); Match No. 40: **Stefan Ekberg** 14 (5); Match No. 41: **Stefan Ekberg** 10+1 (4); Match No. 42: **Stefan Ekberg** 9+1 (5); Match No. 43: **Stefan Ekberg** R/R; Match No. 44: Robert Mear 4+1 (4); Match No. 45: **Stefan Ekberg** 7+1 (4); Match No. 46: **Stefan Ekberg** 12 (5); Match No. 47: **Stefan Ekberg** 3+2 (4); Match No. 48: **Stefan Ekberg** 11 (5); Match No. 49: **Stefan Ekberg** 10+2 (4).

Details of tactical rides and tactical substitute rides: Match No. 12: Boxall 6 points (TR); Robson 2 points (TS); Match No. 17: Woffinden 6 points (TR); Match No. 20: Boxall 6 points (TR); Match No. 22: Lanham 4 points (TS); Match No. 23: Neath 4 points (TR); Match No. 27: Kessler 4 points (TR); Match No. 32: Kennett 6 points (TR); Match No. 34: Woffinden 6 points (TS); Match No. 35: Woffinden 6 points (TR); Match No. 43: Roynon 6 points (TR); Woffinden 4 points (TS); Match No. 48: Ekberg 6 points (TR).

AVERAGES

[28 Premier League; 4 Play-Offs; 4 Knock-Out Cup; 10 Premier Trophy = 46 fixtures]

• Denotes ever-present.

Rider	Mts	Rds	Pts	Bon	Tot	Avge	Max
Tai Woffinden	40	175	361	33	394	9.01	3 full; 5 paid
Stefan Ekberg	12	53	107	12	119	8.98	2 paid
Stuart Robson	10	47	97	5	102	8.68	1 paid
Chris Neath •	46	206	409	35	444	8.62	2 full; 3 paid
Steve Boxall	45	209	405	33	438	8.38	1 full; 2 paid
Tommy Allen	42	172	288	42	330	7.67	1 full; 5 paid
Adam Roynon	42	216	332	59	391	7.24	3 paid
Robbie Kessler	10	37	51	9	60	6.49	1 paid
Luke Bowen	45	179	184	39	223	4.98	-

Also rode:

Ray Morton	5	19	19	2	21	4.42	-

Guests	14	61	88	9	97	6.36	-

(Byron Bekker [1]; Barry Burchatt [2]; Karlis Ezergailis [1]; Rusty Harrison [1]; Christian Henry [2]; Chris Holder [1]; Chris Kerr [1]; Daniel King [2]; Leigh Lanham [1]; Robert Mear [1]; Joel Parsons [1])

NOTE: Steve Boxall was ever-present throughout the 28-match Premier League programme.

INDIVIDUAL MEETINGS

29 September: **Robbo's Champions Chase** (Stuart Robson Benefit)

ELIMINATED RIDERS (ROUND ONE): Joe Screen, Luke Bowen, Chris Schramm; Daniel Giffard, Jason King, Paul Lee, Tommy Allen, Shaun Tacey.

(ROUND TWO): Robert Mear, Trevor Harding; Daniel Halsey, Chris Neath, Stefan Ekberg, Karlis Ezergailis, Niels-Kristian Iversen, Brent Werner, Leigh Lanham, Paul Clews, Jason Bunyan, Emil Kramer.

(ROUND THREE): Tai Woffinden, Chris Holder, Joe Haines.

FIRST SEMI-FINAL: 1st Chris Harris; 2nd Daniel Nermark; 3rd Billy Janniro; 4th Ritchie Hawkins.

SECOND SEMI-FINAL: 1st Adam Roynon; 2nd Steve Johnston; 3rd Rory Schlein; 4th Steve Boxall.

FINAL: 1st Harris; 2nd Johnston; 3rd Roynon; 4th Nermark.

NOTE: Piotr Swiderski had qualified for the first semi-final, but was replaced by Hawkins after blowing his engine as he crossed the line in heat fifteen.

27 October: **Ace of Herts Championship**

QUALIFYING SCORES: Daniel King 13; Chris Neath 12; Edward Kennett 11; Tai Woffinden 10; Lewis Bridger 8; Steve Boxall 7; Tommy Allen 7; Leigh Lanham 7; Robert Mear 5; Luke Bowen 4; Adam Roynon 4; Karlis Ezergailis 2.

FIRST SEMI-FINAL: 1st Allen; 2nd Kennett; 3rd King; 4th Bridger.

SECOND SEMI-FINAL: 1st Neath; 2nd Woffinden; 3rd Boxall; 4th Lanham.

FINAL: 1st Allen; 2nd Neath; 3rd Woffinden; 4th Kennett.

After being released by Stoke, **Robbie Kessler** had a spell with Redcar, prior to joining Rye House. Unfortunately, his time with the Rockets was short-lived, as he suffered complicated ligament damage to his shoulder after crashing in the opening heat of a home league fixture against Newport on 4 August.

(Photo: David Valentine)

SHEFFIELD TIGERS

ADDRESS: Owlerton Sports Stadium, Penistone Road, Owlerton, Sheffield, South Yorkshire, S6 2DE.

TELEPHONE: 0114 2853142.

CLUB HOTLINE: 09068 664670 (Premium rate applies).

WEBSITE: www.sheffieldspeedway.com

PROMOTERS: Neil Machin & David Hoggart.

MAIN TEAM SPONSOR: Sheffield Window Centre.

YEARS OF OPERATION: 1929 English Dirt-Track League; 1930-1931 Northern League; 1932 Speedway National Association Trophy; 1933 National League; 1938-1939 National League Division Two; 1945 Open; 1946 Northern League; 1947-1950 National League Division Two; 1951-1952 Open; 1960-1964 Provincial League; 1965-1967 British League; 1968-1974 British League Division One; 1975-1988 British League; 1991-1994 British League Division Two; 1995 Premier League; 1996 Premier League and Conference League; 1997-1999 Premier League; 2000-2003 Premier League and Conference League; 2004 Premier League and Conference Trophy; 2005-2007 Premier League.

FIRST MEETING: 30 March 1929.

TRACK LENGTH: 361 metres.

TRACK RECORD: 59.3 seconds - Chris Holder (06/09/07).

CLUB HONOURS

BRITISH SPEEDWAY CUP (DIVISION TWO) WINNERS: 1947.

KNOCK-OUT CUP WINNERS: 1974, 2002.

FOUR-TEAM CHAMPIONS: 1999, 2000.

LEAGUE CHAMPIONS: 1999, 2002.

YOUNG SHIELD WINNERS: 1999, 2002.

PREMIERSHIP WINNERS: 2000.

PREMIER TROPHY WINNERS: 2001.

Aussie **Joel Parsons** made notable progress in the sport's second tier with Sheffield during the 2007 campaign, making many significant on-track contributions for the South Yorkshire club.

(Photo: David Valentine)

SHEFFIELD 2007

* Denotes aggregate/bonus-point victory

NO.	DATE	OPPONENTS	VENUE	COMPETITION	RESULT	RICKY ASHWORTH	JOEL PARSONS	ANDRE COMPTON	JAMES COCKLE	BEN WILSON	PAUL COOPER	JAMES BIRKINSHAW			OTHER RIDERS
1	15/3	Wolverhampton	H	Chal	W46-44	11+1 (5)	2 (4)	15 (5)	1 (4)	9+1 (4)	2+1 (4)	6 (4)	-	-	-
2	18/3	Mildenhall	A	TTT	D45-45	11+2 (6)	9+1 (5)	15 (5)	3 (4)	R/R	4 (4)	2 (5)	-	-	1+1 (1)
3	22/3	Mildenhall	H	TTT	W59-31*	10 (4)	7+2 (4)	15 (5)	2 (4)	10+4 (5)	8+1 (4)	7 (4)	-	-	-
4	28/3	King's Lynn	A	PT	L15-75	0 (4)	4 (5)	0 (1)	2 (4)	6 (6)	0 (4)	3 (6)	-	-	-
5	31/3	Workington	A	PT	L41-49	8+2 (5)	3 (4)	-	4 (4)	4+1 (4)	5 (4)	5+2 (4)	-	-	12 (5)
6	5/4	Birmingham	H	PT	W62-31	13+1 (5)	7+1 (4)	15 (5)	5+1 (4)	6+3 (4)	7+1 (4)	9+1 (4)	-	-	-
7	6/4	Birmingham	A	PT	L41-52*	5+1 (5)	11 (5)	13 (4)	1+1 (4)	7 (4)	0 (4)	4 (4)	-	-	-
8	9/4	King's Lynn	H	PT	D45-45	10+1 (5)	6 (4)	13+1 (5)	2 (3)	2 (4)	6+2 (5)	6 (4)	-	-	-
9	12/4	Workington	H	PT	W66-26*	13+1 (5)	9+2 (4)	14+1 (5)	6+1 (4)	11+1 (4)	7+3 (4)	6+1 (4)	-	-	-
10	19/4	Stoke	H	PT	W65-25	10+2 (5)	7 (4)	15 (5)	6+3 (4)	10 (4)	8+3 (4)	9+3 (4)	-	-	-
11	21/4	Stoke	A	PT	W47-42*	5+3 (4)	9 (4)	14 (5)	3 (3)	10+2 (5)	4+1 (5)	2+2 (4)	-	-	-
12	26/4	Berwick	H	PL	W62-31	10+1 (4)	7 (4)	13+2 (5)	3+2 (4)	12+1 (5)	8+3 (4)	9+2 (4)	-	-	-
13	28/4	Berwick	A	PL	W46-43*	11+1 (6)	R/R	10 (4)	2+1 (4)	-	12+2 (7)	3 (3)	-	-	8+2 (6)
14	3/5	Edinburgh	H	KO	W57-36	14+1 (5)	5 (4)	14+1 (5)	4+1 (4)	9+1 (4)	11+3 (5)	0 (1)	-	-	-
15	4/5	Edinburgh	A	KO	L33-60	2 (4)	7 (6)	17 (5)	3 (5)	1 (5)	3+1 (5)	R/R	-	-	-
16	6/5	Newcastle	A	PL	L43-48	12 (5)	6 (4)	7 (4)	1 (4)	9 (6)	8+4 (7)	R/R	-	-	-
17	10/5	Newcastle	H	PL	W57-36*	13+1 (5)	8+1 (4)	15 (5)	2+1 (4)	9 (5)	10+3 (7)	R/R	-	-	-
18	16/5	Birmingham	A	PL	L42-47	7 (4)	6+1 (4)	9+3 (5)	0 (3)	11+1 (5)	4+1 (4)	5+1 (4)	-	-	-
19	17/5	Redcar	H	PL	W52-41	8+1 (5)	7+1 (4)	13 (5)	4+1 (3)	6 (4)	9+2 (5)	5+2 (4)	-	-	-
20	18/5	Redcar	A	PL	L43-45*	4+1 (4)	7 (4)	10+2 (5)	1+1 (4)	9+1 (5)	5+1 (4)	7 (4)	-	-	-
21	24/5	Glasgow	H	PL	W56-38	9 (4)	12+1 (5)	12 (5)	4 (3)	7+2 (4)	6+1 (5)	6 (4)	-	-	-
22	27/5	Glasgow	A	PL	L43-50*	11 (5)	4 (4)	15 (5)	-	2+2 (4)	8+2 (6)	1+1 (3)	-	-	2+1 (3)
23	31/5	Rye House	H	PL	W56-37	8+1 (4)	7+2 (4)	15 (5)	-	11+4 (5)	8+1 (5)	7+1 (4)	-	-	0 (3)
24	7/6	Mildenhall	H	PL	W52-38	6 (4)	6+2 (4)	13 (5)	5+2 (4)	10+1 (5)	6+4 (4)	6 (4)	-	-	-
25	7/7	Rye House	A	PL	L37-55*	8 (5)	3+1 (4)	14 (5)	5 (4)	2+1 (4)	2 (4)	3+1 (4)	-	-	-
26	13/7	King's Lynn	A	PL	L29-64	R/R	3 (6)	16 (6)	3 (5)	4 (6)	2 (4)	1+1 (3)	-	-	-
27	14/7	Workington	A	PL	L41-49	R/R	4 (5)	10+1 (6)	1 (3)	12 (6)	9+3 (7)	5 (3)	-	-	-
28	19/7	Somerset	H	PL	W55-37	R/R	6+1 (5)	17+1 (6)	8 (5)	17+1 (6)	5+1 (4)	2+1 (4)	-	-	-
29	2/8	Stoke	H	PL	W51-39	1+1 (2)	8 (4)	15 (5)	7 (5)	9+1 (5)	7+1 (5)	4+2 (4)	-	-	-
30	4/8	Stoke	A	PL	L35-55	R/R	8+1 (5)	11 (6)	3+1 (4)	10+1 (6)	3 (6)	0 (3)	-	-	-
31	9/8	Edinburgh	H	PL	W59-31	16+2 (6)	9+1 (5)	15 (5)	6+1 (7)	R/R	13+3 (7)	0 (0)	-	-	-
32	16/8	King's Lynn	H	PL	W55-37	9+2 (5)	8 (5)	15 (5)	7+2 (5)	10+1 (4)	6+1 (6)	R/R	-	-	-
33	24/8	Somerset	A	PL	W53-41*	12+1 (5)	7+1 (5)	12+3 (5)	5+1 (4)	4+1 (4)	13+2 (7)	R/R	-	-	-
34	26/8	Mildenhall	A	PL	W46-43*	12+1 (5)	6+1 (5)	13 (5)	5 (5)	6+2 (4)	4+1 (6)	R/R	-	-	-
35	30/8	Birmingham	H	PL	W57-36*	14+1 (5)	10+1 (5)	2 (1)	2+1 (2)	11+1 (5)	17+2 (7)	R/R	-	-	1 (2)
36	31/8	Edinburgh	A	PL	L40-53*	12 (5)	7 (5)	-	-	2+1 (4)	9+1 (7)	R/R	-	-	10+1 (9)
37	4/9	Isle of Wight	A	PL	L32-59	3+1 (4)	3 (4)	-	-	8 (5)	3 (4)	-	-	-	15+2 (13)
38	6/9	Isle of Wight	H	PL	W53-40	11 (5)	4+1 (4)	11 (4)	-	8+1 (4)	8+2 (5)	11+2 (6)	-	-	0 (1)
39	9/9	Newport	A	PL	W46-43	11 (5)	7+1 (4)	11 (5)	2+1 (4)	5+1 (4)	3+2 (4)	-	-	-	7+1 (5)
40	13/9	Workington	H	PL	W61-32*	8+1 (4)	6+2 (4)	15 (5)	4 (4)	12+1 (5)	8+2 (4)	-	-	-	8+1 (4)
41	15/9	Stoke	A	SST	L41-49	14+1 (6)	4+1 (5)	10 (5)	6+2 (5)	6 (5)	R/R	-	-	-	1 (4)
42	20/9	Newport	H	PL	W54-38*	13+2 (5)	4 (4)	14 (5)	7 (4)	9+1 (4)	4+1 (4)	-	-	-	3+1 (4)
43	27/9	Stoke	H	SST	W49-41	7 (4)	7+1 (4)	15 (5)	3+1 (4)	8 (4)	8+2 (5)	-	-	-	1 (4)
44	4/10	King's Lynn	H	POs	W62-31	13+2 (5)	7 (4)	14+1 (5)	6+1 (4)	10 (4)	8+3 (4)	-	-	-	4+3 (4)
45	10/10	King's Lynn	A	POs	L37-55*	10 (5)	6 (4)	8+1 (4)	0 (4)	4+1 (4)	6+1 (5)	-	-	-	3+1 (4)
46	18/10	Rye House	H	POf	W51-42	12+3 (5)	6 (4)	14 (5)	1+1 (3)	11+1 (4)	2 (4)	-	-	-	5 (5)
47	20/10	Rye House	A	POf	L23-69	2 (4)	4 (5)	11 (5)	4 (4)	2 (4)	0 (4)	-	-	-	0 (4)
48	30/10	Scunthorpe	A	HT	W45-44	R/R	10+2 (5)	13 (6)	-	-	9+3 (6)	-	-	-	13+2 (13)

ADDITIONAL KEY: TTT = Top Tigers Trophy; SST = Sunday Sport Trophy; HT = Hallowe'en Trophy.

Details of other riders (all guests unless **highlighted**): Match No. 2: Ben Hopwood 1+1 (1); Match No. 5: George Stancl 12 (5); Match No. 13: Chris Kerr 8+2 (6); Match No. 22: Cal McDade 2+1 (3); Match No. 23: Ben Hopwood 0 (3); Match No. 35: Ben Hopwood 1 (2); Match No. 36: Lee Complin 10+1 (5); David Speight 0 (4); Match No. 37: Lee Complin 11+1 (5); Ben Powell 3 (5); Karlis Ezergailis 1+1 (3); Match No. 38: Byron Bekker 0 (1); Match No. 39: Ben Powell 7+1 (5); Match No. 40: Ben Powell 8+1 (4); Match No. 41: Luke Priest 1 (4); Ben Hopwood 0 (0); Match No. 42: Simon Lambert 3+1 (4); Match No. 43: Ben Hopwood 1 (4); Match No. 44: Jordan Frampton 4+3 (4); Match No. 45: Jordan Frampton 3+1 (4); Match No. 46: Jordan Frampton 5 (5); Match No. 47: Jordan Frampton 0 (4); Match No. 48: Simon Lambert 8+1 (5); Luke Priest 3 (4); Ricky Scarboro 2+1 (4).

Details of tactical rides and tactical substitute rides: Match No. 4: Parsons 1 point (TR; not doubled); Wilson 1 point (TS; not doubled); Match No. 7: Compton 6 points (TR); Match No. 15: Compton 6 points (TR); Parsons 0 points (TS); Match No. 16: Compton 2 points (TR); Match No. 22: Compton 6 points (TR); Match No. 25: Compton 4 points (TR); Match No. 26: Compton 6 points (TR); Wilson 0 points (TS); Match No. 30: Compton 1 point (TR; not doubled); Match No. 36: Ashworth 6 points (TR); Match No. 37: Complin 4 points (TR); Match No. 45: Ashworth 4 points (TR); Match No. 47: Compton 4 points (TR).

AVERAGES

[28 Premier League; 4 Play-Offs; 2 Knock-Out Cup; 8 Premier Trophy = 42 fixtures]

• Denotes ever-present.

Rider	Mts	Rds	Pts	Bon	Tot	Avge	Max
Andre Compton	39	186	468	17	485	10.43	8 full; 6 paid
Ricky Ashworth	38	177	341	35	376	8.50	6 paid
Ben Wilson	40	184	308	36	344	7.48	4 paid
Joel Parsons	41	181	264	22	286	6.32	-
Paul Cooper •	42	210	267	64	331	6.30	-
James Birkinshaw	26	96	119	23	142	5.92	1 paid
James Cockle	37	148	134	24	158	4.27	-
Guests	18	72	76	13	89	4.94	-

(Byron Bekker [1]; Lee Complin [2]; Karlis Ezergailis [1]; Jordan Frampton [4]; Ben Hopwood [2]; Chris Kerr [1]; Simon Lambert [1]; Cal McDade [1]; Ben Powell [3]; David Speight [1]; George Stancl [1])

INDIVIDUAL MEETINGS

12 July: **Top Gun Championship**
QUALIFYING SCORES: Adam Roynon 14; James Cockle 14; Simon Lambert 14; Jack Roberts 11; Greg Blair 9; David Speight 9; Byron Bekker 8; Shane Waldron 8; Scott Richardson 8; Joe Haines 5; Karlis Ezergailis 5; Scott Anderson 4; Ben Taylor 4; Gary Flint 2; Adam Chandler 2; Andrew Blackburn (Res) 2; Ben Hopwood 0.
SEMI-FINAL: 1st Lambert; 2nd Roberts; 3rd Blair; 4th Speight.
FINAL: 1st Roynon; 2nd Lambert; 3rd Cockle; 4th Roberts.

23 August: **Garry Stead Benefit**
QUALIFYING SCORES: Fredrik Lindgren 11; Lee Complin 10; Jason Lyons 9; Simon Stead 9; Andre Compton 8; Tai Woffinden 8; Steve Johnston 7; Magnus Zetterstrom 5; Ricky Ashworth 5; Gary Havelock 4; Chris Kerr 4; Rusty Harrison 4; Joel Parsons 4; Paul Cooper 3; George Stancl 2; Ben Barker (Res) 2; Richard Hall 0.
FIRST SEMI-FINAL: 1st Compton; 2nd Lindgren; 3rd Johnston; 4th Stead.
SECOND SEMI-FINAL: 1st Complin; 2nd Lyons; 3rd Ashworth; 4th Woffinden.
FINAL: 1st Complin; 2nd Lindgren; 3rd Compton; 4th Lyons.

Genuine British prospect **Ben Wilson** was a heavy hitter and an exciting talent for Sheffield in 2007. No doubt, he will be looking to make the transition to Elite League racing in the fullness of time.

(Photo: David Valentine)

SOMERSET REBELS

ADDRESS:	Oak Tree Arena, Bristol Road, Edithmead, Nr Highbridge, Somerset, TA9 4HA.
TELEPHONE:	01278 780993.
CLUB HOTLINE:	09068 664684 (Premium rate applies).
WEBSITE:	www.somerset-rebels.co.uk
PROMOTERS:	Mike Golding & Peter Toogood.
MAIN TEAM SPONSOR:	Sharp Retail Systems.
YEARS OF OPERATION:	2000-2001 Conference League; 2002-2007 Premier League.
FIRST MEETING:	2 June 2000.
TRACK LENGTH:	300 metres.
TRACK RECORD:	56.08 seconds - Leigh Adams (23/03/07).

CLUB HONOURS

CONFERENCE TROPHY WINNERS: 2001.

KNOCK-OUT CUP WINNERS: 2001.

FOUR-TEAM CHAMPIONS: 2005.

Swedish ace **Magnus Zetterstrom** enjoyed another fruitful campaign with the Rebels. His season ended with a 28-day ban, however, after he missed his defence of the PLRC in order to appear for Gorzow in the Polish Play-Offs.

(Photo: David Valentine)

SOMERSET 2007

* Denotes aggregate/bonus-point victory

NO.	DATE	OPPONENTS	VENUE	COMPETITION	RESULT	MAGNUS ZETTERSTROM	SIMON WALKER	EMIL KRAMER	TOMAS SUCHANEK	RITCHIE HAWKINS	JORDAN FRAMPTON	DANNY WARWICK	STEPHAN KATT		OTHER RIDERS
1	16/3	Czestochowa	H	Chal	W51-40	15 (5)	5 (4)	10 (5)	8+1 (4)	5 (3)	4 (5)	4+1 (4)	-	-	-
2	24/3	Rye House	A	PT	L38-55	16 (5)	1 (3)	2 (4)	9+1 (5)	4 (4)	5+1 (6)	1 (3)	-	-	-
3	25/3	Mildenhall	A	PT	L38-54	11 (6)	3 (4)	14+1 (5)	1 (3)	1 (3)	4+1 (5)	4+1 (4)	-	-	-
4	30/3	Rye House	H	PT	L41-49	12 (4)	5 (4)	12 (5)	1 (4)	7+1 (5)	3 (4)	1 (4)	-	-	-
5	6/4	Isle of Wight	H	PT	W52-42	15 (5)	7+1 (4)	11+1 (5)	1 (4)	7+1 (4)	7 (4)	4+1 (4)	-	-	-
6	10/4	Isle of Wight	A	PT	L43-47*	14 (5)	4 (4)	10+2 (5)	4 (4)	5 (4)	4+3 (4)	2 (4)	-	-	-
7	13/4	Newport	H	PT	W65-25	14+1 (5)	6+2 (4)	15 (5)	6+2 (4)	11+1 (4)	9+1 (4)	4+2 (4)	-	-	-
8	15/4	Newport	A	PT	L37-53*	13 (5)	0 (3)	4+2 (4)	4 (4)	7 (5)	9 (7)	0 (2)	-	-	-
9	20/4	Mildenhall	H	PT	W52-41	14 (5)	6+1 (4)	14+1 (5)	-	8+1 (4)	5+1 (4)	3 (5)	-	-	2+1 (3)
10	22/4	Mildenhall	A	PL	W48-45	11+1 (5)	4 (4)	12 (5)	5+1 (4)	8 (4)	6+1 (4)	2+1 (4)	-	-	-
11	27/4	King's Lynn	H	PL	L44-46	14+1 (5)	3+1 (4)	13 (5)	1+1 (4)	6 (4)	3+1 (4)	4 (4)	-	-	-
12	4/5	Glasgow	H	KO	W52-38	15 (5)	7+2 (4)	10 (5)	2 (3)	8 (4)	4+2 (4)	6+2 (5)	-	-	-
13	6/5	Glasgow	A	KO	L45-48*	16+1 (5)	3+1 (4)	9 (5)	1+1 (3)	6 (4)	3 (4)	7 (5)	-	-	-
14	19/5	Stoke	A	PL	W48-42	11+1 (5)	5+2 (5)	12 (5)	-	9 (5)	R/R	8+1 (6)	3 (4)	-	-
15	25/5	Edinburgh	A	KO	L41-48	14+1 (5)	4 (6)	12 (5)	-	5 (5)	R/R	6+2 (6)	-	-	0 (3)
16	26/5	Berwick	A	PL	W49-41	14+1 (5)	0 (5)	10+1 (4)	-	13 (6)	R/R	11+1 (7)	-	-	1 (3)
17	1/6	Sharp Select	H	Chal	W46-44	-	8+2 (4)	14+1 (6)	-	R/R	4+1 (4)	6 (5)	3+3 (5)	-	11 (6)
18	8/6	Glasgow	H	PL	W56-36	12+2 (5)	9+1 (4)	12 (5)	-	9+1 (4)	4+3 (4)	4+2 (4)	6+1 (4)	-	-
19	15/6	Berwick	H	PL	W59-35*	15 (5)	6+1 (4)	14+1 (5)	-	8+1 (4)	5+1 (4)	5 (4)	6+1 (4)	-	-
20	17/6	Glasgow	A	PL	W49-40*	15 (5)	6+1 (4)	10 (5)	-	4 (4)	6+3 (4)	6 (4)	5+1 (4)	-	-
21	22/6	Workington	H	PL	W52-41	17 (6)	13+2 (6)	R/R	-	4 (4)	3 (4)	9 (5)	6+1 (5)	-	-
22	27/6	Birmingham	A	PL	L41-49	14 (5)	6+1 (5)	8 (5)	-	4+1 (4)	5 (4)	1 (3)	3 (4)	-	-
23	6/7	Birmingham	H	PL	W58-32*	14+1 (5)	10+1 (5)	10+1 (4)	-	9 (5)	5+2 (4)	5+1 (3)	5 (4)	-	-
24	11/7	Edinburgh	H	KO	W58-32*	13+2 (5)	11+1 (5)	14 (5)	-	6+2 (4)	2+1 (4)	9 (4)	3 (3)	-	-
25	12/7	Redcar	A	PL	L46-47	11+1 (5)	9+2 (6)	11 (5)	-	8 (4)	3+1 (5)	4+2 (5)	R/R	-	-
26	17/7	Isle of Wight	A	PL	L34-59	16+1 (5)	4 (5)	5 (4)	-	2 (4)	0 (3)	2+1 (4)	5 (5)	-	-
27	19/7	Sheffield	A	PL	L37-55	12 (6)	4+1 (4)	R/R	-	9+1 (7)	5+2 (5)	2 (3)	5+2 (5)	-	-
28	25/7	King's Lynn	A	PL	L36-56	-	5+1 (4)	9+1 (5)	-	3 (4)	0 (4)	2+1 (4)	4+1 (4)	-	13 (5)
29	3/8	Mildenhall	H	PL	W50-39*	13+2 (5)	6 (4)	12 (5)	-	7 (4)	3+1 (4)	6 (4)	3 (4)	-	-
30	10/8	Newport	H	PL	W61-29	11+1 (4)	8+1 (4)	8+1 (4)	-	10+2 (5)	8+1 (4)	10+2 (5)	6 (4)	-	-
31	11/8	Workington	A	PL	L44-51*	18 (6)	0 (3)	10 (5)	-	4 (4)	7+2 (5)	2 (3)	3 (4)	-	-
32	17/8	Rye House	H	PL	W51-42	10+1 (5)	7+1 (4)	8+1 (5)	-	4+1 (4)	3+1 (4)	13 (5)	6+1 (4)	-	-
33	24/8	Sheffield	H	PL	L41-53	10+1 (5)	9 (5)	10+1 (5)	-	6 (4)	2 (3)	4+1 (5)	0 (3)	-	-
34	26/8	Newport	A	PL	L42-48*	-	7 (4)	10+2 (5)	-	10 (5)	13+2 (7)	1 (3)	1 (4)	-	0 (2)
35	31/8	Isle of Wight	H	PL	W46-44	-	8 (5)	8 (5)	-	3 (3)	13 (5)	6+4 (5)	3+1 (3)	-	5+2 (4)
36	7/9	Stoke	H	PL	W52-38*	14+1 (5)	7 (4)	11 (4)	-	8 (5)	4 (4)	4 (4)	4+2 (4)	-	-
37	9/9	Newcastle	A	PL	L41-48	13 (5)	2 (3)	4 (4)	-	7 (5)	3 (2)	7+3 (7)	5+1 (4)	-	-
38	14/9	Redcar	H	PL	W53-40*	17 (6)	9+1 (5)	R/R	-	9+1 (5)	10+2 (6)	4+2 (4)	4+2 (4)	-	-
39	19/9	Edinburgh	H	PL	W57-35	13+1 (5)	8+1 (4)	10 (4)	-	10 (5)	7 (5)	4+2 (4)	5+1 (4)	-	-
40	19/9	Newcastle	H	PL	W55-38*	14 (5)	6+1 (4)	7+2 (4)	-	5 (4)	8+3 (4)	5+1 (4)	10+2 (5)	-	-
41	21/9	Edinburgh	A	PL	L41-48*	17 (6)	1 (3)	R/R	-	6+1 (6)	14+1 (7)	2+1 (5)	1 (3)	-	-
42	22/9	Rye House	A	PL	L37-56	12 (5)	R/R	10+1 (5)	-	6 (5)	6+1 (6)	3+2 (5)	0 (4)	-	-
43	5/10	Stoke	H	YS	W58-34	-	5+1 (4)	13+1 (5)	-	6 (4)	5+2 (4)	9+1 (4)	8+1 (4)	-	12 (5)
44	6/10	Stoke	A	YS	L33-59	-	3 (4)	14 (6)	-	5 (5)	1 (4)	0 (3)	4 (5)	-	6 (3)
45	7/10	Newport	A	KOs	L42-50	-	3 (3)	9 (5)	-	12 (5)	6+1 (4)	0 (3)	8+1 (6)	-	4+1 (4)
46	12/10	Newport	H	KOs	W61-32*	-	11+1 (4)	9+1 (4)	-	11+2 (5)	4+2 (4)	10 (5)	7+2 (4)	-	9+2 (4)
47	19/10	King's Lynn	H	KOf	L44-46	-	6+1 (4)	8 (5)	-	4 (4)	2 (4)	6+4 (4)	9 (4)	-	9 (5)
48	24/10	King's Lynn	A	KOf	L34-59	-	R/R	5 (4)	-	5+2 (5)	1+1 (3)	3 (5)	9+1 (7)	-	11 (5)
49	26/10	Int. Select	H	Chal	W49-44	-	R/R	12 (5)	-	6+1 (5)	9+3 (6)	4+1 (3)	12+3 (7)	-	6+1 (4)

Details of other riders (all guests unless **highlighted**): Match No. 9: Andrew Bargh 2+1 (3); Match No. 15: Jay Herne 0 (3); Match No. 16: Jay Herne 1 (3); Match No. 17: Jason Bunyan 11 (6); Match No. 28: Chris Holder 13 (5); Match No. 34: Karl Mason 0 (2); Match No. 35: Tai Woffinden 5+2 (4); Match No. 43: Jason Doyle 12 (5); Match No. 44: Jason Doyle 6 (3); Match No. 45: Lee Complin 4+1 (4); Match No. 46: Chris Neath 9+2 (4); Match No. 47: Chris Holder 9 (5); Match No. 48: Ricky Ashworth 11 (5); Match No. 49: Ricky Ashworth 6+1 (4).

Details of tactical rides and tactical substitute rides: Match No. 2: Zetterstrom 6 points (TR); Match No. 3: Kramer 6 points (TR); Zetterstrom 0 points (TS); Match No. 8: Kramer 1 point (TR; not doubled); Match No. 13: Zetterstrom 6 points (TR); Match No. 26: Zetterstrom 6 points (TR); Match No. 27: Zetterstrom 4 points (TS); Hawkins 6 points (TR); Match No. 28: Holder 4 points (TR); Match No. 31: Kramer 6 points (TR); Zetterstrom 4 points (TS); Match No. 33: Zetterstrom 6 points (TR); Kramer 2 points (TS); Match No. 42: Kramer 6 points (TR); Match No. 44: Kramer 4 points (TS); Doyle 0 points (TR); Match No. 45: Hawkins 4 points (TR); Match No. 48: Ashworth 6 points (TR).

Other details: Czestochowa scorers in Match No. 1: Edward Kennett 17 (6); Mateusz Szczepaniak 11 (7); Lewis Bridger 9 (5); Marcin Piekarski 2+1 (6); Mateusz Kowalczyk 1+1 (4); Borys Miturski 0 (1); Slawomir Drabik R/R. Kennett's total included 6 points from a TR.; Sharp Retail Systems Select scorers in Match No. 17: Craig Boyce 13+2 (5); Jason Doyle 11+1 (4); Tom Hedley 9+1 (5); Craig Watson 7 (4); Jay Herne 2+1 (4); Andrew Bargh 2 (4); Robert Mear 0 (4).; International League Select scorers in Match No. 49: Bjarne Pedersen 15 (5); Filip Sitera 13 (5); Mark Lemon 9 (5); Luke Bowen 5 (5); Tomas Suchanek 1 (3); Mattie Bates 1 (4); Casper Wortmann 0 (3). Sitera's total includes 6 points from a TS.

AVERAGES

[28 Premier League; 8 Knock-Out Cup; 8 Premier Trophy; 2 Young Shield = 46 fixtures]

• Denotes ever-present.

Rider	Mts	Rds	Pts	Bon	Tot	Avge	Max
Magnus Zetterstrom	37	189	489	21	510	10.79	5 full; 9 paid
Emil Kramer	42	199	407	21	428	8.60	1 full; 2 paid
Ritchie Hawkins •	46	205	307	19	326	6.36	1 paid
Simon Walker	44	185	244	30	274	5.92	1 paid
Jordan Frampton	43	188	220	44	264	5.62	-
Stephan Katt	31	130	147	22	169	5.20	-
Danny Warwick •	46	197	211	41	252	5.12	-
Tomas Suchanek	11	42	35	6	41	3.90	-
Guests	12	46	67	6	73	6.35	-

(Ricky Ashworth [1]; Andrew Bargh [1]; Lee Complin [1]; Jason Doyle [2]; Jay Herne [2]; Chris Holder [2]; Karl Mason [1]; Chris Neath [1]; Tai Woffinden [1])

INDIVIDUAL MEETING

23 March: **Paul Fry Testimonial**
QUALIFYING SCORES: Leigh Adams <u>15</u>; Magnus Zetterstrom 14; Mads Korneliussen 12; Chris Neath 10; Glenn Cunningham 10; Tommy Allen 9; Charlie Gjedde 8; Ritchie Hawkins 8; Garry Stead 7; Craig Watson 7; Simon Walker 5; Brent Werner 4; Jamie Smith 3; Sergey Darkin 3; Neil Collins 2; Paul Pickering 1; Jordan Frampton (Res) 1; Adam Roynon (Res) 1.
FINAL: 1st Adams; 2nd Zetterstrom; 3rd Korneliussen; 4th Neath.

Bristol-born **Simon Walker** made great strides with the Rebels in 2007, culminating in him being handed the club captaincy when Magnus Zetterstrom was served with a ban after pulling out of the Premier League Riders' Championship.

(Photo: David Valentine)

STOKE POTTERS

NOTE: The information below relates only to the main Stoke team. For details of the second side, please refer to the Conference League section.

ADDRESS: Chesterton Stadium, Loomer Road, Chesterton, Newcastle-under-Lyme, Staffordshire, ST5 7LB.

TELEPHONE: 01782 566779 / 01782 562184.

CLUB HOTLINE: 09068 664669.

WEBSITE: N/A.

PROMOTER: David Tattum

MAIN TEAM SPONSOR: Easy Rider.

YEARS OF OPERATION: 1972 Training; 1973-1974 British League Division Two; 1975-1990 National League; 1991-1992 British League Division Two; 1994 British League Division Three; 1995 Academy League; 1996-2007 Premier League. NOTE: The team rode under the name of Chesterton in 1973; The team rode under the name of Cradley Heath & Stoke in 1996.

FIRST MEETING: 12 April 1973.

TRACK LENGTH: 312 metres.

TRACK RECORD: 60.6 seconds - Lee Complin (08/09/07).

PREVIOUS VENUE: Hanley Stadium, Sun Street, Hanley, Staffordshire.

YEARS OF OPERATION: 1929 English Dirt-Track League and Open; 1939 National League Division Two; 1947-1949 National League Division Three; 1950-1953 National League Division Two; 1960-1963 Provincial League.

CLUB HONOURS

LEAGUE CHAMPIONS: 1949.

PAIRS CHAMPIONS: 1984, 1988, 1989.

FOUR-TEAM CHAMPIONS: 1990.

Following some five years out of the sport, **Lee Complin** proved to be the 'Comeback King' of 2007 after linking with Stoke in April. In fact, the points simply flowed from his wheels and he ended the campaign occupying second spot in the team's averages.

(Photo: David Valentine)

STOKE 2007

* Denotes aggregate/bonus-point victory

NO.	DATE	OPPONENTS	VENUE	COMPETITION	RESULTS	ROBBIE KESSLER	BEN BARKER	GARRY STEAD	PAUL PICKERING	RUSTY HARRISON	BARRIE EVANS	JACK HARGREAVES	GLENN CUNNINGHAM	LEE COMPLIN	OTHER RIDERS
1	17/3	Polish Select	H	Chal	L43-47	6 (4)	6+1 (4)	10+2 (5)	6 (4)	-	2+1 (3)	8+2 (6)	-	-	5+1 (4)
2	24/3	Danish Select	H	Chal	L37-55	4+1 (5)	4 (4)	14 (5)	3 (4)	4 (4)	3+1 (4)	5+1 (4)	-	-	-
3	28/3	Birmingham	A	PT	L34-50	5 (4)	9+1 (5)	8 (5)	3 (4)	4+1 (4)	3 (4)	2 (4)	-	-	-
4	31/3	Birmingham	H	PT	L44-46	3+1 (4)	6+1 (4)	10+1 (5)	2 (3)	6+3 (5)	7+2 (4)	10+1 (5)	-	-	-
5	6/4	Workington	A	PT	L24-68	7 (5)	2 (5)	7 (3)	2 (5)	3 (4)	3 (6)	0 (1)	-	-	-
6	7/4	Workington	H	PT	L35-55	5 (4)	8 (5)	2+1 (4)	3 (4)	7+2 (5)	9 (5)	-	-	-	1 (3)
7	11/4	King's Lynn	A	PT	L27-63	5 (4)	2 (4)	6 (5)	4+1 (4)	4 (4)	5+2 (6)	-	-	-	1 (3)
8	14/4	King's Lynn	H	PT	L37-52	-	5 (4)	10 (5)	2+1 (4)	6+2 (4)	5+1 (5)	-	9 (5)	-	0 (3)
9	19/4	Sheffield	A	PT	L25-65	-	1+1 (4)	6 (4)	0 (2)	6+1 (5)	1 (5)	-	9 (5)	-	2 (5)
10	21/4	Sheffield	H	PT	L42-47	-	3+1 (4)	12 (5)	-	7 (4)	2+2 (5)	-	11 (5)	4 (4)	3+1 (3)
11	22/4	Newport	A	PL	L44-49	-	4 (4)	6 (5)	-	5 (4)	6+1 (4)	-	15 (5)	5+2 (4)	3+2 (4)
12	27/4	Edinburgh	A	PL	L36-58	-	4+1 (4)	6 (5)	-	14 (6)	0 (3)	4 (4)	7+1 (4)	1 (4)	-
13	28/4	Newcastle	H	PL	W55-38	-	R/R	7 (4)	-	15+2 (6)	12+3 (6)	5 (4)	10 (5)	6+1 (5)	-
14	5/5	Berwick	A	KO	L42-51	-	3 (4)	9 (4)	-	9 (5)	5+1 (6)	0 (2)	6 (4)	10+2 (5)	-
15	6/5	Berwick	H	KO	W57-35*	-	8+1 (4)	11+2 (5)	-	11 (5)	4+2 (4)	7+2 (4)	7+1 (4)	9+1 (4)	-
16	12/5	Mildenhall	H	PL	L40-50	-	R/R	9 (5)	-	7+1 (5)	5+1 (6)	1+1 (4)	11+1 (5)	7+2 (5)	-
17	19/5	Somerset	H	PL	L42-48	-	-	R/R	-	7 (5)	1 (3)	5+2 (5)	-	8+1 (6)	21+3 (11)
18	26/5	Workington	H	PL	L34-56	-	6+1 (5)	-	-	9+1 (6)	1 (3)	4 (5)	R/R	9 (6)	5+1 (5)
19	28/5	Workington	A	PL	L32-40	-	3+1 (4)	-	-	7+1 (4)	2+1 (4)	3 (3)	R/R	5+2 (4)	12 (5)
20	2/6	Newport	H	KO	W49-41	-	-	-	-	8 (4)	5+1 (5)	1+1 (3)	14 (5)	10 (5)	11+2 (8)
21	3/6	Newport	A	KO	L40-50	-	R/R	-	-	6+2 (5)	10+1 (6)	3+1 (5)	6 (4)	8 (5)	7+2 (5)
22	7/6	Redcar	A	PL	D45-45	-	6+1 (4)	-	-	1 (3)	9+1 (5)	4+1 (4)	10+1 (5)	7+1 (4)	8+2 (5)
23	9/6	Newport	H	PL	W46-43	-	11+3 (5)	-	-	9+1 (4)	3 (6)	0 (1)	12 (5)	6 (4)	5 (4)
24	10/6	Mildenhall	A	PL	L44-49	-	5+1 (4)	-	-	5+3 (4)	7 (4)	-	8 (5)	5+1 (4)	14+2 (9)
25	19/6	Isle of Wight	A	PL	L42-48	-	6 (4)	-	-	9 (5)	7+4 (5)	1+1 (3)	6 (4)	10 (5)	3+1 (4)
26	23/6	King's Lynn	H	PL	W53-37	-	13 (5)	-	-	8 (4)	10+4 (6)	4+3 (5)	0 (0)	13+1 (5)	5+2 (4)
27	7/7	Isle of Wight	H	PL	W52-40*	-	6+3 (4)	-	-	10+1 (5)	7 (5)	2+2 (3)	-	14 (5)	13+3 (8)
28	11/7	Birmingham	A	PL	L40-53	-	13 (5)	-	-	4 (4)	3 (5)	-	-	6 (4)	14+3 (12)
29	15/7	Newcastle	A	PL	L43-50*	-	7+1 (4)	-	-	10+1 (5)	1 (5)	-	-	5+1 (4)	20 (12)
30	21/7	Redcar	H	PL	W45-44*	-	8+1 (5)	-	-	7 (4)	4+2 (4)	-	-	5+1 (4)	21+4 (13)
31	28/7	Glasgow	H	PL	L43-51	-	11 (6)	-	-	5 (4)	7+1 (5)	-	6+1 (4)	13+1 (5)	1 (6)
32	2/8	Sheffield	A	PL	L39-51	-	6 (4)	-	-	11+2 (5)	4+1 (5)	-	5+3 (4)	6 (4)	7 (8)
33	4/8	Sheffield	H	PL	W55-35*	-	11+1 (5)	-	-	12+2 (5)	7+3 (5)	-	9+2 (4)	10 (4)	6 (7)
34	11/8	Edinburgh	H	PL	W51-42	-	11+1 (6)	-	-	9+3 (5)	10+2 (5)	-	7 (4)	9+2 (5)	5+2 (5)
35	25/8	Rye House	H	PL	W47-43	-	6+2 (5)	-	-	6+2 (4)	6+2 (5)	-	5+1 (4)	12 (5)	12+1 (7)
36	1/9	Berwick	A	PL	W48-42	-	13 (5)	-	-	4+2 (4)	4+1 (4)	-	6+2 (4)	10 (5)	11+3 (8)
37	5/9	King's Lynn	A	PL	L26-64	-	8 (5)	-	-	5 (4)	-	-	2 (4)	3 (4)	8+1 (13)
38	7/9	Somerset	A	PL	L38-52	-	6 (4)	-	-	2+2 (3)	-	-	11 (5)	7+3 (6)	12+2 (12)
39	8/9	Birmingham	H	PL	L45-48	-	6+1 (4)	-	-	6+2 (4)	-	-	8+1 (5)	17 (6)	8+1 (11)
40	15/9	Sheffield	H	SST	W49-41	-	12 (5)	-	-	2+1 (3)	-	-	13 (5)	7+2 (4)	15+2 (13)
41	16/9	Rye House	A	PL	L26-66	-	11 (5)	-	-	2+1 (4)	3 (5)	-	3 (4)	0 (2)	7+2 (10)
42	19/9	Birmingham	A	MS	L37-56	-	5+1 (5)	-	-	1 (3)	4 (5)	-	3 (4)	16+1 (5)	8 (8)
43	22/9	Birmingham	H	MS	W47-43	-	12+3 (6)	-	-	R/R	5 (5)	-	9 (4)	10+2 (6)	11+2 (9)
44	26/9	Berwick	H	PL	W60-31*	-	10+1 (5)	-	-	R/R	3 (4)	-	8+1 (4)	16+2 (6)	23+3 (11)
45	27/9	Sheffield	A	SST	L41-49	-	-	-	-	R/R	5+1 (6)	-	-	10+1 (6)	26+3 (18)
46	5/10	Somerset	A	YS	L34-58	-	8 (5)	-	-	R/R	1 (5)	-	10+1 (5)	5+1 (5)	10 (10)
47	6/10	Somerset	H	YS	W59-33*	-	10+2 (5)	-	-	R/R	12+1 (6)	-	-	13+2 (6)	24+6 (13)
48	10/10	Birmingham	A	YSs	L38-54	-	15 (6)	-	-	R/R	7+2 (7)	-	-	6+1 (5)	10+2 (12)
49	13/10	Birmingham	H	YSs	W46-43	-	8 (5)	-	-	R/R	10+2 (6)	-	-	12+2 (6)	16 (13)
50	14/10	Glasgow	A	PL	L41-43	-	5 (5)	-	-	R/R	10+2 (6)	-	-	10 (5)	16+5 (12)

ADDITIONAL KEY: SST = Sunday Sport Trophy; MS = Midland Shield.

NOTE: (1) With reference to the away fixture at Birmingham in the Premier Trophy on 28 March, the following statement was issued by the Speedway Control Bureau on 8 April: 'At the above meeting, which was declared on the night as a win by Birmingham of 56-34 against Stoke, it transpires that the Birmingham line-up did not comply with the Speedway Regulations. Emiliano Sanchez was injured the previous weekend and to cover his absence rider replacement was used. As Sanchez had not yet ridden for Birmingham, no facility was permitted as per SR 18.1.4.2 which states "No facility is permitted to replace a rider, who although declared has not made an appearance for that team". Accordingly the result of the meeting and scores of the riders who took the rider replacement rides are amended.'; (2) The Premier League fixture at Workington on 28 May was abandoned after heat twelve, with the result permitted to stand; (3) The away league match at Glasgow on 14 October was abandoned after heat fourteen, with the result permitted to stand.

Details of other riders (all guests unless **highlighted**): Match No. 1: Paul Clews 5+1 (4); Match No. 6: Simon Lambert 1 (3); Match No. 7: Tom Brown 1 (3); Match No. 8: Tom Brown 0 (3); Match No. 9: David Speight 2 (5); Match No. 10: Jonathan Bethell 3+1 (3); Match No. 11: Tom Brown 3+2 (4); Match No. 17: Tony Atkin 11+2 (5); Ricky Ashworth 10+1 (6); Match No. 18: **Claus Vissing** 5+1 (5); Match No. 19: **Claus Vissing** 12 (5); Match No. 20: **Claus Vissing** 7+1 (4); Lee Smethills 4+1 (4); Match No. 21: **Claus Vissing** 7+2 (5); Match No. 22: **Claus Vissing** 8+2 (5); Match No. 23: **Claus Vissing** 5 (4); Match No. 24: **Claus Vissing** 7+1 (5); Lee Smart 7+1 (4); Match No. 25: **Claus Vissing** 3+1 (4); Match No. 26: **Claus Vissing** 5+2 (4); Match No. 27: Emiliano Sanchez 9+1 (4); **Claus Vissing** 4+2 (4); Match No. 28: Krzysztof Stojanowski 6+2 (4); **Claus Vissing** 6+1 (5); Nick Simmons 2 (3); Match No. 29: **Claus Vissing** 15 (5); Matthew

Wethers 5 (4); Jonathan Bethell 0 (3); Match No. 30: **Claus Vissing** 9 (5); Emiliano Sanchez 8+2 (4); **Jamie Smith** 4+2 (4); Match No. 31: **Jamie Smith** 1 (4); **Claus Vissing** 0 (2); Match No. 32: **Claus Vissing** 7 (5); **Jamie Smith** 0 (3); Match No. 33: **Claus Vissing** 6 (4); **Jamie Smith** 0 (3); Match No. 34: **Jamie Smith** 5+2 (5); **Claus Vissing** R/R; Match No. 35: **Claus Vissing** 9 (4); **Jamie Smith** 3+1 (3); Match No. 36: **Claus Vissing** 7 (4); **Jamie Smith** 4+3 (4); Match No. 37: **Claus Vissing** 6+1 (5); **Jamie Smith** 1 (4); Simon Lambert 1 (4); Match No. 38: **Claus Vissing** 6+1 (4); **Jamie Smith** 4+1 (5); Benji Compton 2 (3); Match No. 39: **Claus Vissing** 6 (4); **Jamie Smith** 2+1 (4); Benji Compton 0 (3); Match No. 40: Jon Armstrong 9 (5); **Jamie Smith** 3+2 (4); **Claus Vissing** 3 (4); Match No. 41: **Claus Vissing** 4+1 (5); **Jamie Smith** 3+1 (5); Match No. 42: **Claus Vissing** 7 (5); **Jamie Smith** 1 (3); Match No. 43: **Claus Vissing** 8 (5); **Jamie Smith** 3+2 (4); Match No. 44: **Claus Vissing** 14+1 (6); **Jamie Smith** 9+2 (5); Match No. 45: Jason Bunyan 13 (6); **Claus Vissing** 6+1 (5); Mark Burrows 4+1 (3); **Jamie Smith** 3+1 (4); Match No. 46: **Claus Vissing** 10 (7); **Jamie Smith** 0 (3); Match No. 47: **Claus Vissing** 14+3 (6); Tony Atkin 7+2 (4); **Jamie Smith** 3+1 (3); Match No. 48: Tony Atkin 5+2 (6); **Claus Vissing** 3 (2); **Jamie Smith** 2 (4); Match No. 49: **Claus Vissing** 11 (6); Tony Atkin 5 (4); **Jamie Smith** 0 (3); Match No. 50: Chris Schramm 7+2 (5); Shaun Tacey 6+3 (4); Luke Priest 3 (3).

Details of tactical rides and tactical substitute rides: Match No. 2: Stead 6 points (TR); Match No. 3: Harrison 0 points (TR); Match No. 5: Stead 4 points (TR); Barker 0 points (TS); Match No. 6: Harrison 0 points (TR); Match No. 7: Harrison 1 point (TR; not doubled); Match No. 8: Barker 1 point (TR; not doubled); Match No. 9: Cunningham 1 point (TR; not doubled); Match No. 11: Cunningham 6 points (TR); Match No. 12: Cunningham 4 points (TR); Harrison 4 points (TS); Match No. 14: Stead 6 points (TR); Match No. 16: Complin 1 point (TR; not doubled); Match No. 18: Complin 1 point (TR; not doubled); Match No. 28: Barker 6 points (TR); Match No. 29: Vissing 6 points (TR); Match No. 31: Complin 4 points (TR); Barker 4 points (TS); Match No. 37: Complin 0 points (TR); Match No. 38: Barker 0 points (TR); Complin 0 points (TS); Match No. 39: Complin 6 points (TR); Match No. 41: Barker 4 points (TR); Match No. 42: Complin 6 points (TR); Barker 1 point (TS; not doubled); Match No. 46: Cunningham 4 points (TR); Vissing 0 points (TS); Match No. 48: Barker 4 points (TR); Atkin 0 points (TS).

Other details: Polish Select scorers in Match No. 1: Sebastian Ulamek 18 (6); Andy Smith 10+1 (5); Mateusz Szczepaniak 10 (7); Robert Ksiezak 4+1 (4); Mateusz Kowalczyk 4 (5); Marcin Piekarski 0 (3); Slawomir Drabik R/R; Danish Select scorers in Match No. 2: Niels-Kristian Iversen 15 (5); Henning Bager 11+1 (5); Ulrich Ostergaard 8+1 (4); Mads Korneliussen 8 (4); Claus Vissing 6 (4); Tom P. Madsen 5+2 (4); Henrik Moller 2+1 (4).

AVERAGES

[28 Premier League; 4 Knock-Out Cup; 8 Premier Trophy; 4 Young Shield = 44 fixtures]

Rider	Mts	Rds	Pts	Bon	Tot	Avge	Max
Glenn Cunningham	28	121	214	16	230	7.60	-
Lee Complin	37	175	297	30	327	7.47	1 paid
Rusty Harrison	38	170	264	38	302	7.11	-
Claus Vissing	27	124	193	20	213	6.87	-
Garry Stead	14	64	104	4	108	6.75	-
Ben Barker	39	180	275	26	301	6.69	-
Barrie Evans	41	203	221	46	267	5.26	-
Jack Hargreaves	18	65	56	15	71	4.37	-
Jamie Smith	16	62	41	14	55	3.55	-
Paul Pickering	7	26	16	2	18	2.77	-

Also rode:

Robbie Kessler	5	21	25	1	26	4.95	-

Guests	25	98	108	22	130	5.31	-

(Ricky Ashworth [1]; Tony Atkin [4]; Jonathan Bethell [2]; Tom Brown [3]; Benji Compton [2]; Simon Lambert [2]; Luke Priest [1]; Emiliano Sanchez [2]; Chris Schramm [1]; Nick Simmons [1]; Lee Smart [1]; Lee Smethills [1]; David Speight [1]; Krzysztof Stojanowski [1]; Shaun Tacey [1]; Matthew Wethers [1])

NOTE: Lee Complin was ever-present throughout the 28-match Premier League programme.

INDIVIDUAL MEETING

27 October: **Garry Stead Benefit**
1st Rory Schlein 15; 2nd Ben Barker 13; 3rd George Stancl 11; James Wright 10; Mark Lemon 10; Tony Atkin 9; Emil Kramer 7; Barrie Evans 7; Lee Dicken 7; Trent Leverington 7; Rob Grant 6; Adam Allott 6; Luke Priest 5; Jonathan Bethell 4; Gareth Isherwood 1; Alan Grahame (Res) 1; Aidan Collins 0.

Having found himself out in the cold with no team berth, **Glenn Cunningham** made a belated start to the season at Stoke in April. The 'Bristol Bomber' helped turn around the club's fortunes and did well to head their averages, despite several spells on the sidelines through injury.

(Photo: David Valentine)

WORKINGTON COMETS

ADDRESS:	Derwent Park Stadium, Workington, Cumbria, CA14 2HG.
TELEPHONE:	01900 608071.
CLUB HOTLINE:	09068 664671 (Premium rate applies).
WEBSITE:	www.workingtonspeedway.com
PROMOTERS:	Anthony E. Mole, Redvers Mole & Ian Thomas.
MAIN TEAM SPONSOR:	Thomas Armstrong Ltd.
YEARS OF OPERATION:	1970-1974 British League Division Two; 1975-1981 National League; 1985 Open; 1987 National League; 1994 Demonstration; 1999-2007 Premier League. NOTE: In 1987, the track was occupied by Glasgow Tigers, who later that year became known as Workington Tigers.
FIRST MEETING:	3 April 1970.
TRACK LENGTH:	364 metres.
TRACK RECORD:	63.2 seconds - Simon Stead (23/09/06).

CLUB HONOURS

PAIRS CHAMPIONS: 1999, 2000, 2001, 2003.
FOUR-TEAM CHAMPIONS: 2001, 2004, 2006.

Young Englishman **James Wright** continued to hone his skills in the Premier League with Workington, whilst 'doubling up' for Belle Vue in the top-flight.

(Photo: David Valentine)

WORKINGTON 2007

* Denotes aggregate/bonus-point victory

NO.	DATE	OPPONENTS	VENUE	COMPETITION	RESULT	JAMES WRIGHT	MATTIA CARPANESE	KENNETH HANSEN	CRAIG BRANNEY	KAUKO NIEMINEN	CHARLES WRIGHT	JAMIE ROBERTSON	CARL STONEHEWER	JOHN BRANNEY	OTHER RIDERS
1	18/3	Newcastle	A	Chal	W47-42	14+1 (5)	4+1 (4)	-	1 (2)	6+2 (5)	3+2 (4)	12 (6)	-	-	7+1 (4)
2	24/3	Glasgow	H	Chal	W53-39	11 (5)	5+1 (4)	7+1 (4)	7 (4)	11+2 (5)	3+1 (4)	9+3 (4)	-	-	-
3	31/3	Sheffield	H	PT	W49-41	2 (1)	4+1 (4)	8+1 (5)	7+1 (4)	14 (5)	3 (4)	11+1 (7)	-	-	-
4	1/4	Glasgow	A	Chal	L39-54	R/R	2+1 (5)	11 (6)	2+1 (5)	18 (6)	4 (5)	2+1 (3)	-	-	-
5	6/4	Stoke	H	PT	W68-24	-	9+3 (4)	12+2 (5)	8+3 (4)	10 (4)	9+1 (4)	5+1 (4)	-	-	15 (5)
6	7/4	Stoke	A	PT	W55-35*	-	7+1 (4)	12 (5)	10+3 (5)	12 (4)	4+1 (5)	2+1 (3)	-	-	8+2 (4)
7	11/4	Birmingham	A	PT	L41-48	-	5+1 (4)	4+1 (4)	9 (4)	9 (5)	3+1 (5)	1 (3)	-	-	10+1 (5)
8	12/4	Sheffield	A	PT	L26-66	-	0 (4)	2 (4)	3+1 (4)	6 (5)	4 (5)	1+1 (3)	-	-	10 (5)
9	14/4	Birmingham	H	PT	L40-53	16+1 (5)	2 (4)	5 (4)	5+2 (4)	6 (5)	3+1 (4)	3 (4)	-	-	-
10	18/4	King's Lynn	A	PT	L27-65	12 (6)	0 (4)	R/R	6+1 (6)	3 (5)	2+1 (4)	4 (5)	-	-	-
11	21/4	King's Lynn	H	PT	W47-43	12 (5)	3 (4)	-	5+1 (4)	12+1 (5)	5+1 (5)	-	10+1 (4)	-	0 (3)
12	5/5	Rye House	H	PL	W53-37	12+1 (5)	1 (3)	-	7+3 (4)	10 (4)	9+1 (6)	-	13 (5)	1 (3)	-
13	12/5	Edinburgh	H	PL	W50-40	14 (5)	1 (4)	-	4+2 (4)	13+2 (5)	7 (5)	-	11 (4)	0 (3)	-
14	19/5	Isle of Wight	H	KO	W50-42	12 (5)	2+1 (4)	-	3 (4)	8 (4)	8+2 (6)	-	13 (5)	4+2 (3)	-
15	20/5	Newport	A	PL	L42-51	7 (4)	6+1 (4)	-	4+2 (4)	15 (5)	1 (4)	-	8 (5)	1+1 (4)	-
16	22/5	Isle of Wight	A	KO	L43-52	11+1 (5)	1 (3)	-	3 (4)	16 (6)	6+2 (4)	-	-	1+1 (4)	5 (4)
17	26/5	Stoke	H	PL	W56-34	13+1 (5)	11 (4)	-	5+2 (4)	15 (5)	1 (4)	-	5+2 (4)	6 (4)	-
18	28/5	Stoke	H	PL	W40-32*	14 (5)	5+1 (4)	-	7+2 (4)	R/R	5 (4)	-	5 (3)	4+2 (4)	-
19	2/6	Newcastle	H	PL	W51-39	-	3+1 (3)	-	7+1 (4)	15 (5)	3 (5)	-	12+1 (5)	5+2 (4)	6 (4)
20	9/6	Mildenhall	H	PL	W57-35	14+1 (5)	R/R	-	9+2 (5)	9+2 (4)	3 (6)	-	14 (5)	8+3 (5)	-
21	10/6	Newcastle	A	PL	L41-49*	13+1 (5)	R/R	-	5 (5)	9 (5)	3+1 (6)	-	8+1 (4)	3+2 (5)	-
22	22/6	Somerset	H	PL	L41-52	12+2 (6)	1+1 (3)	-	2 (4)	15 (5)	2 (4)	-	7+1 (4)	2 (4)	-
23	23/6	Birmingham	H	PL	D45-45	13 (5)	1 (2)	-	6+3 (4)	10 (5)	6 (6)	-	7 (4)	2+1 (4)	-
24	1/7	Rye House	A	PL	L37-58	13 (5)	4 (4)	-	0 (4)	6 (4)	1 (4)	-	12 (6)	1 (3)	-
25	7/7	Newport	H	PL	W55-37*	14+1 (5)	R/R	-	7+2 (5)	5+2 (4)	11+2 (7)	-	15 (5)	3 (4)	-
26	14/7	Sheffield	H	PL	W49-41	16+1 (6)	1+1 (1)	-	1 (2)	R/R	8+1 (7)	-	15+1 (6)	7+1 (7)	1 (1)
27	18/7	Birmingham	A	PL	L44-46	8 (4)	-	-	R/R	13+1 (5)	4+1 (7)	-	14 (6)	0 (3)	5 (5)
28	21/7	Glasgow	H	PL	W47-43	12 (5)	-	-	R/R	12 (5)	7+1 (5)	-	10+2 (5)	3+1 (5)	3 (5)
29	22/7	Glasgow	A	PL	L42-49	9 (4)	-	-	R/R	14+1 (6)	0 (1)	-	12+1 (6)	1 (7)	6 (6)
30	28/7	Redcar	H	PL	W56-36	12+2 (5)	-	-	R/R	13 (5)	-	-	11+2 (5)	6+2 (5)	14+2 (10)
31	4/8	Isle of Wight	H	PL	L42-53	14 (5)	-	-	-	18 (7)	0 (4)	-	R/R	5+1 (4)	-
32	11/8	Somerset	H	PL	W51-44	13+1 (5)	4+1 (3)	-	6+1 (4)	7+1 (4)	7+1 (6)	-	-	5 (3)	9 (5)
33	24/8	Edinburgh	A	PL	W49-44*	12+1 (5)	1 (3)	-	3 (4)	12 (5)	10+1 (6)	-	-	3+1 (3)	8+1 (4)
34	25/8	Berwick	A	PL	W48-45	10+1 (5)	0 (3)	-	5+1 (4)	7 (4)	9+1 (6)	-	-	1 (3)	16+1 (5)
35	27/8	Berwick	H	PL	W53-37*	11 (4)	0 (3)	-	6+3 (4)	13 (5)	4 (4)	-	-	5 (5)	14+1 (5)
36	30/8	Isle of Wight	A	PL	L39-56	11 (5)	R/R	-	4 (5)	14+1 (6)	1 (5)	-	-	4+1 (5)	5+1 (4)
37	1/9	King's Lynn	H	PL	W53-40	12+1 (5)	-	-	9 (5)	12+1 (6)	7+2 (6)	-	-	3+2 (4)	10+1 (4)
38	2/9	Mildenhall	A	PL	L44-47*	9 (4)	R/R	-	3 (5)	13+1 (5)	0 (5)	-	-	3 (5)	16+1 (6)
39	6/9	Redcar	A	PL	L42-48*	8 (5)	R/R	-	8 (5)	6+1 (4)	6+1 (6)	-	-	3+2 (5)	11 (5)
40	13/9	Sheffield	H	PL	L32-61	10+1 (5)	R/R	-	2 (4)	3 (4)	6 (6)	-	-	1+1 (6)	10 (5)
41	15/9	Birmingham	H	Chal	W51-42	7+1 (4)	R/R	-	11+1 (5)	14+1 (5)	5 (6)	-	-	-	14 (10)
42	19/9	King's Lynn	A	PL	L41-52*	15+1 (6)	R/R	-	7+1 (5)	4 (4)	4+1 (5)	-	-	5+2 (5)	6 (5)
43	6/10	Newcastle	H	YS	W58-35	14+1 (5)	R/R	-	8+1 (5)	15 (5)	5+1 (3)	-	-	5+1 (7)	11+1 (5)
44	7/10	Newcastle	A	YS	L45-46*	15 (6)	R/R	-	9+2 (5)	4 (4)	-	-	-	6 (6)	11+1 (9)
45	11/10	Redcar	A	YSs	L40-50	7 (4)	R/R	-	3+1 (5)	10 (5)	3+1 (5)	-	-	8+2 (6)	9 (5)
46	20/10	Redcar	H	YSs	W47-43	13 (5)	-	-	9+2 (5)	14 (6)	3 (5)	-	-	7 (6)	1 (3)

NOTE: The home Premier League fixture against Stoke on 28 May was abandoned after heat twelve, with the result permitted to stand.

Details of other riders (all guests unless **highlighted**): Match No. 1: Stuart Robson 7+1 (4); Match No. 5: George Stancl 15 (5); Match No. 6: Josef Franc 8+2 (4); Match No. 7: Josef Franc 10+1 (5); Match No. 8: Michal Makovsky 10 (5); Match No. 11: **Scott James** 0 (3); Match No. 16: Michal Rajkowski 5 (4); Match No. 19: Ricky Ashworth 6 (4); Match No. 26: David Haigh 1 (1); Match No. 27: Chris Johnson 5 (5); Match No. 28: Lee Smart 3 (5); Match No. 29: Simon Walker 6 (5); David Haigh 0 (1); Match No. 30: Tomas Suchanek 7+1 (5); Barry Burchatt 7+1 (5); Match No. 31: Robert Ksiezak 4+1 (6); Benji Compton 1 (4); Match No. 32: **Ulrich Ostergaard** 9 (5); Match No. 33: **Ulrich Ostergaard** 8+1 (4); Match No. 34: **Ulrich Ostergaard** 16+1 (5); Match No. 35: **Ulrich Ostergaard** 14+1 (5); Match No. 36: **Ulrich Ostergaard** 5+1 (4); Match No. 37: Danny Warwick 10+1 (4); **Ulrich Ostergaard** R/R; Match No. 38: **Ulrich Ostergaard** 13 (5); Match No. 39: **Ulrich Ostergaard** 11 (5); Match No. 40: **Ulrich Ostergaard** 10 (5); Match No. 41: **Ulrich Ostergaard** 16+1 (5); Match No. 42: **Ulrich Ostergaard** 6 (5); Match No. 43: **Ulrich Ostergaard** 11+1 (5); Scott James 0 (1); Match No. 44: **Ulrich Ostergaard** 10+1 (5); Scott James 1 (4); Match No. 45: **Ulrich Ostergaard** 9 (5); Match No. 46: Andrew Bargh 1 (3); **Ulrich Ostergaard** R/R.

Details of tactical rides and tactical substitute rides: Match No. 4: Nieminen 6 points (TR); Match No. 8: Makovsky 4 points (TR); Match No. 9: J. Wright 6 points (TR); Match No. 10: J. Wright 4 points (TR); Match No. 15: Nieminen 6 points (TR); Match No. 16: J. Wright 6 points (TR); Nieminen 4 points (TS); Match No. 22: Nieminen 2 points (TR); J. Wright 2 points (TS); Match No. 24: J. Wright 6 points (TR); Stonehewer 4 points (TS); Match No. 29: Nieminen 2 points (TS); Match No. 31: J. Wright 6 points (TR); Nieminen 4 points (TS); Match No. 34: Ostergaard 6 points (TR); Match No. 36: J. Wright 6 points (TR); Nieminen 4 points (TS); Match No. 38: Ostergaard 2 points (TR); Match No. 40: J. Wright 6 points (TR); Match No. 42: J. Wright 6 points (TS); Match No. 44: J. Wright 2 points (TS).

AVERAGES

[28 Premier League; 2 Knock-Out Cup; 8 Premier Trophy; 4 Young Shield = 42 fixtures]

Rider	Mts	Rds	Pts	Bon	Tot	Avge	Max
James Wright	37	180	410	19	429	9.53	3 paid
Carl Stonehewer	19	91	200	12	212	9.32	1 full
Ulrich Ostergaard	12	58	121	7	128	8.83	2 paid
Kauko Nieminen	40	194	409	14	423	8.72	4 full; 1 paid
Kenneth Hansen	6	27	43	4	47	6.96	-
Craig Branney	37	161	205	43	248	6.16	-
Jamie Robertson	7	29	27	4	31	4.28	-
Charles Wright	40	199	183	26	209	4.20	-
Mattia Carpanese	24	83	72	13	85	4.10	1 paid
John Branney	34	154	122	31	153	3.97	-

Also rode

| Scott James | 1 | 3 | 0 | 0 | 0 | 0.00 | - |

| Guests | 19 | 76 | 98 | 7 | 105 | 5.53 | 1 full |

(Ricky Ashworth [1]; Andrew Bargh [1]; Barry Burchatt [1]; Benji Compton [1]; Josef Franc [2]; David Haigh [2]; Scott James [2]; Chris Johnson [1]; Robert Ksiezak [1]; Michal Makovsky [1]; Michal Rajkowski [1]; Lee Smart [1]; George Stancl [1]; Tomas Suchanek [1]; Simon Walker [1]; Danny Warwick [1])

NOTE: John Branney was ever-present throughout the 28-match Premier League programme.

OTHER MEETING

5 April: **Kevin Little Farewell** (at Redcar)
Newcastle 31, Redcar 28, Workington 23: Joe Screen 12 (4); Billy Janniro 6 (3); Paul Lee 3 (4); Kauko Nieminen 1 (3); Jamie Robertson 1 (2), Edinburgh 21.

INDIVIDUAL MEETINGS

23 September: **British Under-15 Championship** (Round Two; staged at Northside)
QUALIFYING SCORES: James Sarjeant 11; Dan Greenwood 8; Dale Lamb 8; Richard Franklin 8; Jack Hirst 7; Jason Garrity 6; Shane Hazelden 4; Kye Norton 4; Cameron Hoskins 4; Montana Jowett 4; Scott Meakins 3; Jack Butler 1; Nathan Stoneman (Res) 0.
QUARTER-FINAL: 1st Hazelden; 2nd Hoskins; 3rd Garrity; 4th Norton.
SEMI-FINAL: 1st Franklin; 2nd Hazelden; 3rd Hirst; 4th Lamb.
FINAL: 1st Sarjeant; 2nd Greenwood, 3rd Franklin; 4th Hazelden.

29 September: **Cumberland Classic**
1st Simon Stead <u>15</u>; 2nd Ulrich Ostergaard 14; 3rd Kauko Nieminen 13; Kevin Doolan 10; Kaj Laukkanen 10; James Wright 9; Tomas Topinka 9; Josef Franc 8; Charles Wright 8; Josh Auty 4; David Howe 4; Tero Aarnio 4; Peter Juul 4; Chris Kerr 4; John Branney 3; Craig Branney 1.

INFORMATION ON NORTHSIDE

ADDRESS: Northside Arena, Allerdale Motor Project, Oldside, Workington, Cumbria.

YEARS OF OPERATION: 2002-2006 Training; 2007 Open.

TRACK LENGTH: 138 metres (2002-2007).

BERNARD O'Neill and a band of enthusiasts joined forces to construct the training track on a former caravan site. By March 2002, a base consisting of 900 tons of hardcore had been laid as the racing strip began to take shape. A further 600 tons of shale were laid on top, creating a circuit with 13-metre wide straights and different shaped bends of 20 metres in width. A 2-metre high chain-link safety fence was added, complete with tyres to cushion the uprights.

The directors of the company behind the project, which is limited by guarantee, were listed as Greg Irving, Chris Irving, Jacko Irving, Brian Jenkinson and Judith Lomas. Bikes first took to the track on 6 August 2002, when Carl Stonehewer performed the official opening. Afterwards, a dozen youngsters participated in Northside's first training session, held under the watchful eye of Louis Carr from 6.00 p.m. until 8.00 p.m.

The track staged its first fully licensed meeting on 23 September 2007, when James Sarjeant took victory in round two of the British Under-15 Championship. During the event, Mancunian Jason Garrity established a track record of 47.4 seconds for the mini circuit, which had seen the white line purposely extended out to produce a bigger-than-normal lap distance of 165 metres.

Local boy **Craig Branney** enjoyed a steady season with the Comets, his best official performance being a return of 10+3 points from an away trip to Stoke in the Premier Trophy.

(Photo: David Valentine)

CONFERENCE LEAGUE
2007

Boston Barracudas
Buxton Hitmen
Cleveland Bays
Oxford Lions / Cheetahs
Plymouth Devils
Rye House Raiders
Scunthorpe Scorpions
Sittingbourne Crusaders
Stoke Spitfires
Weymouth Wildcats

CONFERENCE LEAGUE

CONFERENCE LEAGUE TABLE

Team	Mts	Won	Drn	Lst	For	Agn	Pts	AP	Tot
Scunthorpe	18	16	0	2	993	637	32	9	41
Oxford	18	13	1	4	921	729	27	8	35
Plymouth	18	11	0	7	872	769	22	6	28
Boston	18	10	1	7	842	801	21	5	26
Weymouth	18	9	1	8	841	801	19	5	24
Rye House	18	8	0	10	844	794	16	6	22
Buxton	18	8	0	10	762	887	16	1	17
Stoke	18	7	1	10	758	898	15	2	17
Cleveland	18	3	1	14	719	910	7	3	10
Sittingbourne	18	2	1	15	653	979	5	0	5

PLAY-OFFS

SEMI-FINALS

Plymouth	54	Oxford	37	
Oxford	56	Plymouth	38	(Oxford won 93-92 on aggregate)

Scunthorpe	63	Boston	30	
Boston	36	Scunthorpe	56	(Scunthorpe won 119-66 on aggregate)

FINAL

Oxford	42	Scunthorpe	47	
Scunthorpe	61	Oxford	31	(Scunthorpe won 108-73 on aggregate)

TOP 20 AVERAGES [Conference League only. Minimum qualification: 6 matches.]

Rider	Mts	Rds	Pts	Bon	Tot	Avge	Max
Tai Woffinden (Scunthorpe)	8	41	113	2	115	11.22	2 full; 2 paid
Lee Smethills (Oxford) *	18	90	213	22	235	10.44	1 full; 5 paid
Andrew Tully (Scunthorpe)	9	39	91	9	100	10.26	1 paid
Josh Auty (Scunthorpe)	13	63	150	11	161	10.22	1 full; 3 paid
Danny Betson (Oxford)	16	79	186	10	196	9.92	2 full; 2 paid
Lee Smart (Weymouth)	13	65	153	6	159	9.78	3 full; 2 paid
Robert Mear (Rye House) *	18	104	235	14	249	9.58	2 full; 5 paid
Jon Armstrong (Boston/Buxton)	6	30	71	0	71	9.47	Nil
Benji Compton (Scunthorpe)	7	31	63	10	73	9.42	Nil
James Brundle (Boston)	10	50	110	6	116	9.28	1 paid
Luke Bowen (Rye House)	8	45	93	9	102	9.07	1 full
Barrie Evans (Stoke) *	18	99	217	7	224	9.05	1 full; 2 paid
John Branney (Stoke)	15	79	170	8	178	9.01	2 paid
Jordan Frampton (Oxford)	10	48	99	9	108	9.00	2 paid
Seemond Stephens (Plymouth)	16	76	159	12	171	9.00	1 paid
Tom Brown (Plymouth) *	18	87	182	13	195	8.97	2 paid
Joe Haines (Scunthorpe) *	18	87	168	24	192	8.83	1 full; 2 paid
Simon Lambert (Boston) *	18	94	185	16	201	8.55	2 paid
Jay Herne (Weymouth)	15	85	169	12	181	8.52	1 paid
Jack Roberts (Buxton)	10	52	105	4	109	8.38	1 paid

* Denotes ever-present.

KNOCK-OUT CUP

ROUND ONE

Rye House	61	Sittingbourne	29	
Sittingbourne	32	Rye House	59	(Rye House won 120-61 on aggregate)

Stoke	50	Weymouth	40	
Weymouth	54	Stoke	32	(Weymouth won 94-82 on aggregate)

QUARTER FINALS

Weymouth	51	Buxton	45	
Buxton	43	Weymouth	50	(Weymouth won 101-88 on aggregate)

Scunthorpe	59	Rye House	31	
Rye House	52	Scunthorpe	41	(Scunthorpe won 100-83 on aggregate)

Boston	49	Cleveland	40	
Cleveland	35	Boston	35	(Boston won 84-75 on aggregate)

Oxford	45	Plymouth	44	
Plymouth	45	Oxford	44	(Aggregate result: 89-89)

REPLAY

Oxford	61	Plymouth	29	
Plymouth	63	Oxford	30	(Plymouth won 92-91 on aggregate)

SEMI-FINALS

Plymouth	51	Weymouth	39	
Weymouth	45	Plymouth	45	(Plymouth won 96-84 on aggregate)

Scunthorpe	51	Boston	45	
Boston	30	Scunthorpe	62	(Scunthorpe won 113-75 on aggregate)

NOTE: Boston's 'home' leg of the semi-final tie was raced at Scunthorpe.

FINAL

Plymouth	49	Scunthorpe	44	
Scunthorpe	58	Plymouth	35	(Scunthorpe won 102-84 on aggregate)

CONFERENCE TROPHY

CONFERENCE TROPHY (SOUTH) TABLE

Team	Mts	Won	Drn	Lst	For	Agn	Pts	Bon	Tot
Plymouth	4	4	0	0	214	154	8	2	10
Oxford	4	1	0	3	174	192	2	1	3
Weymouth	4	1	0	3	164	206	2	0	2

CONFERENCE TROPHY (NORTH) TABLE

Team	Mts	Won	Drn	Lst	For	Agn	Pts	Bon	Tot
Scunthorpe	6	6	0	0	353	197	12	3	15
Buxton	6	3	0	3	247	301	6	1	7
Boston	6	2	0	4	275	278	4	2	6
Stoke	6	1	0	5	224	323	2	0	2

FINAL

Plymouth	33	Scunthorpe	59	
Scunthorpe	65	Plymouth	28	(Scunthorpe won 124-61 on aggregate)

BOSTON BARRACUDAS

ADDRESS:	Norfolk Arena, Saddlebow Road, King's Lynn, Norfolk, PE34 3AG.
TELEPHONE:	01553 771111.
CLUB HOTLINE:	09066 555969 (Premium rate applies).
WEBSITE:	www.boston-barracudas.co.uk
CLUB CHAIRMEN:	Malcolm Vasey, Mick Smith & Dale Allitt.
MAIN TEAM SPONSOR:	Staffsmart.
TRACK LENGTH:	342 metres.
CL TRACK RECORD:	60.0 seconds - Trevor Harding (15/06/03).
FIRST MEETING:	1 April 2000.
YEARS OF OPERATION:	2000-2007 Conference League.
PREVIOUS VENUE:	Boston Sports Stadium, New Hammond Beck Road, Boston, Lincolnshire.
YEARS OF OPERATION:	1970-1974 British League Division Two; 1975-1984 National League; 1986-1987 National League.

CLUB HONOURS

LEAGUE CHAMPIONS: 1973.

KNOCK-OUT CUP WINNERS: 1973, 2000.

PAIRS CHAMPIONS: 1977, 2007.

CONFERENCE TROPHY WINNERS: 2003.

James Brundle was invariably a big scorer for the Barracudas, when his Premier League commitments with King's Lynn permitted him to appear.

(Photo: Ian Charles)

BOSTON 2007

* Denotes aggregate/bonus-point victory

NO.	DATE	OPPONENTS	VENUE	COMPETITION	RESULT	JON ARMSTRONG	ROB SMITH	DARREN MALLETT	SIMON LAMBERT	MATTHEW WRIGHT	BEN JOHNSON	CAL McDADE	KEIRAN MORRIS	ADAM LOWE	OTHER RIDERS
1	25/3	Scunthorpe	A	LC	L41-55	13 (5)	1 (3)	4+1 (4)	15+1 (6)	2 (4)	2+1 (4)	4 (4)	-	-	-
2	6/4	Scunthorpe	H	LC	L41-54	18 (6)	-	0 (4)	13 (5)	6 (4)	0 (3)	4 (4)	0 (4)	-	-
3	13/4	Stoke	H	CT	W55-37	13 (5)	7+3 (4)	10+2 (5)	6+2 (4)	7+1 (4)	-	12+1 (6)	0 (2)	-	-
4	20/4	Buxton	H	CT	W56-36	14+1 (5)	6+2 (4)	6+1 (4)	11+1 (5)	11+1 (4)	-	8+1 (5)	0 (1)	-	-
5	22/4	Buxton	A	CT	L46-48*	17 (5)	3 (4)	2+2 (4)	11 (5)	8+1 (5)	-	-	-	-	5+2 (7)
6	29/4	Scunthorpe	A	CT	L35-58	17 (5)	1+1 (4)	1 (4)	7 (5)	5 (4)	-	4 (4)	-	0 (4)	-
7	4/5	Scunthorpe	H	CT	L40-52	12 (5)	4+1 (4)	5+2 (4)	12+1 (6)	3 (4)	-	3+1 (4)	-	1 (3)	-
8	5/5	Cleveland	A	CL	W47-46	13 (5)	3 (4)	5+2 (4)	13 (5)	7 (4)	-	3+2 (4)	-	3+1 (4)	-
9	25/5	Plymouth	H	CL	W49-43	-	5+1 (4)	8+2 (4)	11+1 (5)	7+1 (4)	-	4 (5)	-	5+1 (4)	9 (5)
10	29/6	Weymouth	A	CL	L34-59	-	2 (4)	4 (4)	4 (4)	15+1 (5)	-	3 (4)	-	0 (3)	6+1 (6)
11	1/7	Weymouth	H	CL	W47-42	-	2+1 (4)	8+1 (4)	11 (5)	7 (4)	-	3+1 (4)	-	3+1 (4)	13 (5)
12	6/7	Cleveland	H	CL	W56-33*	-	5+1 (4)	12+1 (5)	11+3 (5)	10 (4)	-	-	-	4 (4)	14+3 (8)
13	6/7	Cleveland	H	KO	W49-40	-	5+1 (4)	9+2 (5)	9+1 (4)	8+1 (4)	-	-	-	3+1 (4)	15+1 (9)
14	14/7	Stoke	A	CT	L43-47*	-	-	3+1 (5)	13+1 (6)	-	-	-	2+2 (3)	6+1 (6)	19 (10)
15	20/7	Plymouth	A	CL	L40-51	-	-	R/R	3+2 (5)	-	-	-	1+1 (4)	2 (3)	34+3 (18)
16	27/7	Sittingbourne	H	CL	W55-38	-	-	10+1 (5)	11+2 (5)	7+2 (4)	-	-	5 (4)	6+2 (4)	16+3 (8)
17	28/7	Cleveland	A	KO	D35-35*	-	-	7+2 (4)	9 (3)	7 (3)	-	-	0 (4)	3+1 (3)	9 (4)
18	3/8	Stoke	H	CL	W52-44	-	-	10 (6)	13+1 (6)	12+1 (5)	-	7+3 (4)	-	4+2 (4)	6+3 (5)
19	5/8	Scunthorpe	A	CL	L31-50	-	-	R/R	10 (5)	3+1 (4)	-	0 (4)	-	1 (3)	17 (10)
20	8/8	Stoke	A	CL	D46-46*	-	-	R/R	11+1 (6)	8+3 (5)	-	-	1+1 (3)	5+1 (5)	21+1 (11)
21	10/8	Oxford	H	CL	L44-48	-	-	R/R	19+1 (7)	5+1 (5)	-	2 (4)	-	1+1 (3)	17+2 (11)
22	12/8	Buxton	A	CL	L43-47	-	-	R/R	11+1 (6)	7+1 (5)	-	2+2 (4)	-	2 (4)	21+1 (11)
23	17/8	Scunthorpe	H	CL	W46-43	-	-	R/R	12 (6)	8 (5)	-	2+2 (5)	-	3 (3)	21 (11)
24	31/8	Oxford	A	CL	L43-50	-	-	-	11 (4)	13 (5)	-	5+2 (4)	-	3+1 (4)	11+2 (13)
25	7/9	Rye House	H	CL	W65-26	-	-	8 (4)	14+1 (5)	10+2 (5)	-	8+2 (4)	-	6+1 (4)	19+3 (8)
26	7/9	Buxton	H	CL	W58-34*	-	-	13+2 (5)	11+1 (4)	12+1 (5)	-	4 (5)	-	8+3 (6)	10 (5)
27	9/9	Sittingbourne	A	CL	W53-40*	-	-	6 (4)	9+1 (5)	13+1 (5)	-	7+1 (5)	-	4+1 (5)	14+2 (6)
28	30/9	Scunthorpe	A	KOs	L45-51	-	-	5 (4)	15+1 (6)	2 (4)	-	2+1 (4)	-	1+1 (3)	20+1 (9)
29	5/10	Scunthorpe	H	KOs	L30-62	-	-	6 (5)	7 (5)	3 (4)	-	0 (3)	-	1+1 (4)	13+1 (9)
30	7/10	Scunthorpe	A	POs	L30-63	-	-	2 (4)	10 (6)	0 (4)	-	1 (3)	2 (4)	-	15 (9)
31	12/10	Scunthorpe	H	POs	L36-56	-	-	7 (5)	9 (5)	3 (4)	-	0 (5)	-	0 (1)	17+1 (9)
32	13/10	Rye House	A	CL	L33-61*	-	-	3 (4)	5+1 (6)	10+2 (6)	-	4 (4)	0 (3)	3+1 (3)	8 (4)

ADDITIONAL KEY: LC = Lincolnshire Cup.

NOTE: (1) The Knock-Out Cup tie at Cleveland on 28 July was abandoned after heat twelve, with the result permitted to stand; (2) The Conference League match at Scunthorpe on 5 August was abandoned after heat thirteen, with the result permitted to stand; (3) Boston's 'home' leg of the Knock-Out Cup tie on 5 October was actually raced at Scunthorpe.

Details of other riders (all guests unless **highlighted**): Match No. 5: Phil Naylor 3+1 (4); Adam Lowe 2+1 (3); Match No. 9: **James Brundle** 9 (5); Match No. 10: **James Brundle** 6+1 (6); Match No. 11: **James Brundle** 13 (5); Match No. 12: **James Brundle** 11+1 (4); Jerran Hart 3+2 (4); Match No. 13: **James Brundle** 14 (5); Jerran Hart 1+1 (4); Match No. 14: **Shane Waldron** 16 (6); **Wayne Dunworth** 3 (4); **Sean Stoddart** R/R; Match No. 15: **Paul Cooper** 14+2 (7); **Shane Waldron** 11+1 (6); **Sean Stoddart** 9 (5); Match No. 16: **Paul Cooper** 9 (4); **Shane Waldron** 7+3 (4); Match No. 17: **Paul Cooper** 9 (3); **Shane Waldron** 0 (1); Match No. 18: **Adam McKinna** 6+3 (5); **Paul Cooper** R/R; Match No. 19: **Paul Cooper** 12 (5); **Adam McKinna** 5 (5); Match No. 20: **Paul Cooper** 12 (6); **Adam McKinna** 9+1 (5); Match No. 21: **James Brundle** 13+2 (6); **Adam McKinna** 4 (5); Match No. 22: **James Brundle** 13 (6); **Adam McKinna** 8+1 (5); Match No. 23: **James Brundle** 17 (6); **Adam McKinna** 4 (5); Match No. 24: **Adam McKinna** 9 (5); Jaimie Pickard 2+2 (5); **Wayne Dunworth** 0 (3); Match No. 25: **James Brundle** 10+1 (4); **Adam McKinna** 9+2 (4); Match No. 26: **James Brundle** 9 (4); **Adam McKinna** 1 (1); Match No. 27: **James Brundle** 12+1 (4); **Adam McKinna** 2+1 (2); Match No. 28: **Paul Cooper** 16 (5); **Adam McKinna** 4+1 (4); Match No. 29: **Paul Cooper** 12+1 (5); **Adam McKinna** 1 (4); Match No. 30: **Paul Cooper** 13 (5); **Adam McKinna** 2 (4); Match No. 31: **James Brundle** 13 (4); **Adam McKinna** 4+1 (5); Match No. 32: **Adam McKinna** 8 (4); **James Brundle** R/R.

Details of tactical rides and tactical substitute rides: Match No. 1: Armstrong 6 points (TR); Lambert 6 points (TS); Match No. 2: Armstrong 6 points (TS); Lambert 6 points (TR); Match No. 5: Armstrong 6 points (TR); Lambert 4 points (TS); Match No. 6: Armstrong 6 points (TR); Match No. 7: Lambert 4 points (TS); Match No. 10: Wright 6 points (TR); Brundle 0 points (TS); Match No. 15: Cooper 2 points (TS); Match No. 19: Cooper 6 points (TR); Match No. 21: Lambert 4 points (TR); Match No. 24: Lambert 6 points (TR); Match No. 27: Brundle 6 points (TR); Match No. 28: Cooper 6 points (TR); Lambert 6 points (TS); Match No. 29: Cooper 6 points (TR); Lambert 0 points (TS); Match No. 30: Cooper 6 points (TR); Lambert 1 point (TS; not doubled); Match No. 31: Brundle 6 points (TR); Lambert 0 points (TS); Match No. 32: McKinna 4 points (TR); Wright 4 points (TS).

AVERAGES

[18 Conference League; 2 Play-Offs; 4 Knock-Out Cup; 6 Conference Trophy = 30 fixtures]

• Denotes ever-present.

Rider	Mts	Rds	Pts	Bon	Tot	Avge	Max
Jon Armstrong	6	30	80	1	81	10.80	1 paid
James Brundle	12	59	134	6	140	9.49	1 paid
Paul Cooper	8	40	84	3	87	8.70	-
Simon Lambert •	30	154	297	23	320	8.31	2 paid
Matthew Wright	28	124	206	21	227	7.32	1 paid
Darren Mallett	23	102	150	21	171	6.71	1 paid
Adam McKinna	15	63	74	10	84	5.33	-
Rob Smith	11	44	43	11	54	4.91	-
Cal McDade	22	94	84	19	103	4.38	-
Adam Lowe	26	98	78	21	99	4.04	-
Keiran Morris	9	28	11	4	15	2.14	-

Also rode (in alphabetical order):

Wayne Dunworth	2	7	3	0	3	1.71	-
Sean Stoddart	1	5	9	0	9	7.20	-
Shane Waldron	4	17	34	4	38	8.94	-

Guests	5	20	11	7	18	3.60	-

(Jerran Hart [2]; Adam Lowe [1]; Phil Naylor [1]; Jaimie Pickard [1])

NOTE: Adam Lowe was ever-present throughout the 18-match Conference League programme.

OTHER MEETING

21 October: **Big Bang 2 Fours** (staged at Mildenhall)

Peterborough 38, East Anglian Select 27, Boston 22: Lewis Bridger 11 (4); Carl Wilkinson 5 (4); James Brundle 3 (4); Kevin Doolan 3 (4), Mildenhall 21. Bridger's tally includes 4 points from a TR, whilst Doolan's includes 0 points from a TR.

Boston, 2007

Back row, left to right: Mick Smith (Co-Chairman), Rob Smith, Matthew Wright, Simon Lambert, Phil Naylor and Malcolm Vasey (Co-Chairman/Team Manager).

Front, kneeling: Jon Armstrong, Adam Lowe and Darren Mallett.

(Photo: Ian Charles)

BUXTON HITMEN

ADDRESS:	Buxton Raceway, Dale Head Lane, Axe Edge, Nr Buxton, Derbyshire.
TELEPHONE:	01298 72271.
CLUB HOTLINE:	N/A.
WEBSITE:	www.hitmen2000.co.uk
CLUB CHAIRMEN:	Richard Moss & Jayne Moss.
MAIN TEAM SPONSORS:	University of Derby - Buxton & Wayside Farm Holidays.
TRACK LENGTH:	240 metres.
TRACK RECORD:	52.9 seconds - James Wright (27/06/04).
FIRST MEETING:	19 May 1996.
YEARS OF OPERATION:	1996 Conference League; 1997 Amateur League; 1998-2007 Conference League.
PREVIOUS VENUE:	Buxton Stadium, off A53 Leek-to-Buxton Road, Buxton, Derbyshire.
YEARS OF OPERATION:	1994 British League Division Three; 1995 Academy League.

Buxton, 2007

Back row, left to right: Jack Lee (Team Manager), Ben Taylor, Carl Belfield, Jonathan Bethell, Jack Roberts, Scott James and Danny Hodgson.

Front, kneeling: Lewis Dallaway, Josh Moss (Mascot) and Andy Braithwaite.

(Photo: Ian Charles)

BUXTON 2007

* Denotes aggregate/bonus-point victory

NO.	DATE	OPPONENTS	VENUE	COMPETITION	RESULT	SCOTT JAMES	JACK ROBERTS	BEN TAYLOR	CARL BELFIELD	JONATHAN BETHELL	ANDY BRAITHWAITE	LEWIS DALLAWAY	GARETH ISHERWOOD	PAUL STARKE	OTHER RIDERS
1	15/4	US Dream Team	H	Chal	W46-44	R/R	11+1 (6)	8+2 (5)	4+2 (3)	12+1 (6)	1+1 (3)	10+1 (7)	-	-	-
2	20/4	Boston	A	CT	L36-56	8 (5)	6+3 (6)	R/R	11 (6)	3 (5)	3 (3)	5+2 (5)	-	-	-
3	22/4	Boston	H	CT	W48-46	4+1 (4)	9+1 (4)	11+3 (5)	7 (4)	11 (5)	-	6+1 (5)	-	-	0 (3)
4	29/4	Stoke	H	CT	W52-39	8+1 (4)	12+3 (5)	5+2 (4)	5+1 (4)	14 (5)	-	4 (4)	4+1 (4)	-	-
5	5/5	Rye House	A	CL	L35-57	6+2 (6)	12 (6)	R/R	1 (4)	5 (3)	-	6+1 (6)	5+1 (5)	-	-
6	6/5	Scunthorpe	H	CT	L37-52	5+1 (4)	9+1 (5)	-	9+1 (5)	6+1 (4)	-	6+1 (5)	2+1 (4)	-	0 (3)
7	7/5	Scunthorpe	A	CT	L28-64	4 (5)	13 (6)	R/R	7 (6)	2 (5)	-	0 (4)	2 (4)	-	-
8	20/5	Cleveland	H	CL	W50-42	6+3 (5)	12+1 (6)	R/R	12+2 (6)	11 (5)	-	7 (5)	2 (3)	-	-
9	1/6	Weymouth	A	KO	L45-51	3 (5)	20+1 (7)	R/R	1 (4)	16 (6)	-	2 (4)	3+1 (4)	-	-
10	10/6	Sittingbourne	A	CL	W48-42	7+2 (6)	14 (6)	R/R	-	11+1 (5)	0 (3)	5 (3)	11+2 (6)	-	-
11	17/6	Rye House	H	CL	W47-43	10 (4)	13+2 (5)	6+2 (4)	-	14 (5)	0 (3)	0 (4)	4 (5)	-	-
12	1/7	Oxford	A	CL	L23-67	9 (6)	R/R	2 (6)	-	7 (4)	1 (4)	4 (6)	-	-	0 (4)
13	8/7	Weymouth	H	KO	L43-50	6+1 (4)	15+1 (5)	7+1 (5)	-	8 (4)	0 (3)	5 (5)	-	-	2+1 (4)
14	29/7	Sittingbourne	H	CL	W56-31*	10+2 (4)	7+1 (4)	14+1 (5)	-	12 (5)	-	9+3 (5)	-	-	4 (7)
15	1/8	Stoke	A	CT	W46-44*	6+2 (6)	R/R	7 (5)	-	8+1 (5)	-	5+3 (4)	-	-	20+1 (10)
16	3/8	Plymouth	A	CL	L26-64	10+1 (6)	DNA	8+1 (6)	-	R/R	-	5 (7)	-	3 (5)	0 (3)
17	5/8	Weymouth	H	CL	W55-35	16 (6)	R/R	15+3 (6)	-	11 (5)	-	0 (1)	-	4 (7)	9+2 (5)
18	11/8	Cleveland	A	CL	L41-50	6 (4)	11 (5)	8+1 (5)	-	8 (4)	-	7 (6)	-	1+1 (3)	0 (3)
19	12/8	Boston	H	CL	W47-43	5+1 (4)	8 (4)	13 (5)	-	10 (5)	-	9+3 (6)	-	1 (3)	1 (3)
20	24/8	Weymouth	A	CL	L37-58	7 (5)	20 (7)	6+2 (6)	-	-	-	4 (6)	-	0 (3)	0 (3)
21	26/8	Scunthorpe	H	CL	L38-54	6 (4)	7 (6)	12+1 (5)	-	-	-	2+1 (4)	-	0 (3)	11 (8)
22	27/8	Scunthorpe	A	CL	L35-58	1 (4)	5 (3)	8 (5)	-	-	-	2+2 (5)	-	2 (4)	17 (9)
23	7/9	Boston	A	CL	L34-58	5+1 (5)	R/R	7 (6)	-	-	-	5+2 (4)	-	0 (4)	17+2 (11)
24	9/9	Oxford	H	CL	W59-36	15+1 (6)	R/R	14+3 (6)	-	-	-	10+1 (6)	-	5+2 (4)	15+2 (9)
25	30/9	Plymouth	H	CL	W53-42	12+1 (5)	R/R	13+3 (6)	-	-	-	7 (5)	-	5+2 (5)	16 (9)
26	20/10	Stoke	A	CL	L39-53	17 (6)	-	9 (6)	-	-	-	2 (5)	-	2+1 (5)	9+1 (8)
27	21/10	Stoke	H	CL	L39-54	20 (6)	-	7 (5)	-	-	-	-	-	5 (5)	7+4 (14)

Details of other riders (all guests unless **highlighted**): Match No. 3: Ben Hannon 0 (3); Match No. 6: **Charles Wright** 0 (3); Match No. 12: Ben Hannon 0 (4); Match No. 13: **Aaron Summers** 2+1 (4); Match No. 14: Paul Starke 4 (4); Tom Hill 0 (3); Match No. 15: **Danny Hodgson** 1+1 (3); **Aaron Summers** 19 (7); Match No. 16: Cecil Forbes 0 (3); Match No. 17: **Danny Hodgson** 9+2 (5); Match No. 18: **Danny Hodgson** 0 (3); Match No. 19: **Danny Hodgson** 1 (3); Match No. 20: Olly Gay 0 (3); **Jon Armstrong** R/R; Match No. 21: **Jon Armstrong** 9 (4); **Danny Hodgson** 2 (4); Match No. 22: **Jon Armstrong** 16 (5); **Danny Hodgson** 1 (4); Match No. 23: **Jon Armstrong** 11 (5); **Danny Hodgson** 6+2 (6); Match No. 24: **Jon Armstrong** 11 (5); **Danny Hodgson** 4+2 (4); Match No. 25: **Jon Armstrong** 16 (6); Shane Henry 0 (3); Match No. 26: **Danny Hodgson** 8+1 (5); Scott Whittington 1 (3); **Jon Armstrong** R/R; Match No. 27: **Danny Hodgson** 7+4 (6); Scott Whittington 0 (4); Adam Chandler 0 (4); **Jon Armstrong** R/R.

Details of tactical rides and tactical substitute rides: Match No. 2: James 4 points (TR); Belfield 4 points (TS); Match No. 5: Bethell 4 points (TR); Match No. 6: Wright 0 points (TR); Match No. 7: Roberts 6 points (TR); Match No. 9: Bethell 6 points (TS); Match No. 12: James 1 point (TR; not doubled); Match No. 13: Roberts 6 points (TR); Match No. 16: Taylor 1 point (TR; not doubled); Match No. 18: Roberts 2 points (TR); Match No. 20: Roberts 6 points (TS); James 4 points (TR); Match No. 21: Taylor 4 points (TR); Roberts 0 points (TS); Match No. 22: Armstrong 6 points (TR); Match No. 23: Armstrong 4 points (TR); Match No. 26: James 6 points (TR); Match No. 27: James 6 points (TR).

Other details: USA Dream Team scorers in Match No. 1: Bryan Yarrow 13+1 (5); Tommy Hedden 12 (5); Dale Facchini 6+1 (4); Tim Gomez 4+1 (4); Kenny Ingalls 4+1 (4); J.T. Mabry 3+1 (4); Neil Facchini 2 (4).

AVERAGES

[18 Conference League; 2 Knock-Out Cup; 6 Conference Trophy = 26 fixtures]

• Denotes ever-present.

Rider	Mts	Rds	Pts	Bon	Tot	Avge	Max
Jack Roberts	17	90	180	14	194	8.62	2 paid
Jonathan Bethell	17	80	152	3	155	7.75	-
Ben Taylor	19	101	170	23	193	7.64	2 paid
Scott James •	26	129	202	20	222	6.88	1 paid
Carl Belfield	8	39	51	4	55	5.64	-
Danny Hodgson	10	43	39	12	51	4.74	-
Lewis Dallaway	25	120	117	20	137	4.57	-
Gareth Isherwood	8	35	33	6	39	4.46	-
Paul Starke	12	51	28	6	34	2.67	-

Also rode (in alphabetical order):

Jon Armstrong	5	25	58	0	58	9.28	-
Andy Braithwaite	5	16	4	0	4	1.00	-
Aaron Summers	2	11	21	1	22	8.00	-
Charles Wright	1	3	0	0	0	0.00	-
Guests	10	34	5	0	5	0.59	-

(Adam Chandler [1]; Cecil Forbes [1]; Olly Gay [1]; Ben Hannon [2]; Shane Henry [1]; Tom Hill [1]; Paul Starke [1]; Scott Whittington [2])

Hereford-born **Paul Starke** officially came into Buxton's declared squad on 3 August, having impressed at Academy League level with both Swindon and Birmingham.

(Photo: Ian Charles)

CLEVELAND BAYS

ADDRESS:	South Tees Motorsports Park, Dormer Way, South Bank Road, Middlesbrough, Cleveland, TS6 6XH.
TELEPHONE:	07796 441850.
CLUB HOTLINE:	09068 664665 (Premium rate applies).
WEBSITE:	www.redcarspeedway.co.uk
CLUB CHAIRMEN:	Chris Van Straaten, Gareth Rogers & Glyn Taylor.
MAIN TEAM SPONSOR:	Burnt Tree Vehicle Solutions.
YEARS OF OPERATION:	2006 Conference Shield; 2007 Conference League.
FIRST MEETING:	24 August 2006.
TRACK LENGTH:	266 metres.
TRACK RECORD:	54.2 seconds - Tai Woffinden (02/08/07).

Despite reaching 43 years of age during the season, veteran racer **Buzz Burrows** was the entertainer-in-chief for Cleveland throughout the 2007 campaign.

(Photo: Ian Charles)

CLEVELAND 2007

* Denotes aggregate/bonus-point victory

NO.	DATE	OPPONENTS	VENUE	COMPETITION	RESULT	MARK BURROWS	GARY BEATON	STEVEN JONES	MARTIN EMERSON	JAMIE COURTNEY	RUSTY HODGSON	GREG BLAIR	PAUL BURNETT	ADAM McKINNA	OTHER RIDERS
1	21/4	Plymouth	H	CL	L43-47	4 (4)	9+2 (5)	5+1 (4)	6+2 (4)	6 (4)	6+3 (4)	7+1 (5)	-	-	-
2	22/4	Sittingbourne	A	CL	W54-38	10 (5)	14+1 (6)	10+2 (5)	-	-	5+3 (6)	13+2 (5)	R/R	-	2+1 (3)
3	5/5	Boston	H	CL	L46-47	11 (6)	3+1 (4)	2 (2)	7+1 (4)	-	13+1 (7)	10+1 (6)	-	-	0 (1)
4	20/5	Buxton	A	CL	L42-50	17 (7)	7+1 (5)	R/R	3+1 (4)	-	-	11+2 (7)	3 (4)	-	1 (3)
5	2/6	Rye House	H	CL	L41-48	12+1 (6)	8+1 (5)	R/R	4+2 (6)	-	4 (4)	10 (6)	-	3+3 (3)	-
6	22/6	Plymouth	A	CL	L40-48	9+1 (5)	5+1 (4)	-	2+1 (3)	-	2 (4)	12 (7)	-	10+1 (4)	0 (4)
7	23/6	Weymouth	A	CL	L33-57	13 (5)	3 (4)	-	0 (3)	-	4 (4)	9 (6)	-	4 (5)	0 (3)
8	28/6	Stoke	H	CL	W57-36	14 (5)	7 (4)	-	6+3 (4)	-	5 (4)	11+1 (5)	-	7 (4)	7+3 (4)
9	6/7	Boston	A	CL	L33-56	6+1 (4)	6+1 (4)	2 (5)	8 (4)	-	-	4 (4)	-	-	7+1 (9)
10	6/7	Boston	A	KO	L40-49	11 (5)	9 (5)	3+2 (3)	3 (4)	-	2 (4)	9+1 (5)	-	-	3+1 (4)
11	26/7	Stoke	A	CL	L35-51*	2 (4)	8 (5)	-	-	-	-	-	5+2 (4)	-	20+3 (17)
12	28/7	Weymouth	H	CL	L44-46	11+1 (5)	5+2 (4)	4+1 (4)	-	-	-	13 (6)	-	-	11+2 (11)
13	28/7	Boston	H	KO	D35-35	4 (2)	6+1 (3)	-	-	-	-	13 (6)	1+1 (3)	-	11+2 (7)
14	2/8	Scunthorpe	H	CL	L34-57	1 (3)	1 (4)	3 (3)	-	-	-	8 (3)	-	-	21+3 (17)
15	11/8	Buxton	H	CL	W50-41*	7 (5)	7 (5)	8+2 (5)	-	-	-	R/R	-	-	23+6 (14)
16	17/8	Oxford	A	CL	L18-70	5 (4)	-	-	-	-	3 (4)	R/R	4 (6)	-	6 (16)
17	25/8	Sittingbourne	H	CL	D45-45*	13 (5)	7+1 (5)	6 (4)	4+2 (4)	-	7+2 (6)	-	-	-	8+1 (6)
18	9/9	Scunthorpe	A	CL	L28-64	13 (7)	R/R	3+1 (5)	3 (4)	-	1 (4)	-	-	-	8+1 (9)
19	20/9	Oxford	H	CL	L43-49	18 (7)	7+1 (6)	8 (5)	6+1 (5)	-	2+1 (3)	-	-	-	2+2 (4)
20	22/9	Rye House	A	CL	L33-60	8 (5)	11 (6)	-	4+1 (4)	-	-	-	4+1 (4)	-	6+1 (11)

NOTE: The home Knock-Out Cup tie versus Boston on 28 July was abandoned after heat twelve, with the result permitted to stand.

Details of other riders (all guests unless **highlighted**): Match No. 2: Lee Lingham 2+1 (3); Match No. 3: **Danny Norton** 0 (1); Match No. 4: Kye Norton 1 (3); Match No. 6: **Jitendra Duffill** 0 (4); Match No. 7: **Jitendra Duffill** 0 (3); Match No. 8: Ashley Johnson 7+3 (4); Match No. 9: **Ashley Johnson** 5 (4); **David Wallinger** 2+1 (5); Match No. 10: **Ashley Johnson** 3+1 (4); Match No. 11: **Ashley Johnson** 10 (5); Adam Chandler 6 (4); **David Wallinger** 3+2 (4); Kye Norton 1+1 (4); Match No. 12: **Ashley Johnson** 8+1 (4); Kye Norton 2+1 (4); **David Wallinger** 1 (3); Match No. 13: **David Wallinger** 6+2 (4); **Ashley Johnson** 5 (3); Kye Norton DNR; Match No. 14: **Sean Stoddart** 12 (5); **Ashley Johnson** 8+2 (6); **David Wallinger** 1+1 (6); Match No. 15: **David Wallinger** 12+2 (6); **Ashley Johnson** 9+2 (5); Kye Norton 2+2 (3); Match No. 16: **David Wallinger** 6 (7); Ben Reade 0 (7); Ben Hannon 0 (1); Chris Baldwin 0 (1); Match No. 17: **David Wallinger** 5 (3); **Ashley Johnson** 3+1 (3); Match No. 18: **Jack Hargreaves** 7 (6); Kye Norton 1+1 (3); Match No. 19: **Michael Pickering** 2+2 (4); **Jack Hargreaves** R/R; Match No. 20: Shane Henry 3 (4); **Michael Pickering** 2 (4); Ben Reade 1+1 (3).

Details of tactical rides and tactical substitute rides: Match No. 3: Burrows 6 points (TS); Match No. 4: Burrows 4 points (TS); Burnett 0 points (TR); Match No. 7: Blair 0 points (TR); McKinna 0 points (TS); Match No. 9: Blair 0 points (TR); Match No. 11: Beaton 0 points (TR); Match No. 14: Stoddart 4 points (TR); Match No. 16: Burrows 1 point (TR; not doubled); Wallinger 0 points (TS); Match No. 18: Burrows 4 points (TS); Match No. 19: Burrows 4 points (TS); Match No. 20: Burrows 4 points (TR); Beaton 4 points (TS).

AVERAGES

[18 Conference League; 2 Knock-Out Cup = 20 fixtures]

• Denotes ever-present.

Rider	Mts	Rds	Pts	Bon	Tot	Avge	Max
Greg Blair	13	71	130	8	138	7.77	1 paid
Mark Burrows •	20	100	183	4	187	7.48	-
Ashley Johnson	9	38	58	10	68	7.16	-
Gary Beaton	18	84	121	13	134	6.38	-
Steven Jones	11	45	54	9	63	5.60	-
Martin Emerson	13	53	56	14	70	5.28	-
Rusty Hodgson	12	54	54	10	64	4.74	-
David Wallinger	8	38	36	8	44	4.63	-

Also rode (in alphabetical order):

Paul Burnett	5	21	17	4	21	4.00	-
Jamie Courtney	1	4	6	0	6	6.00	-
Jitendra Duffill	2	7	0	0	0	0.00	-
Jack Hargreaves	1	6	7	0	7	4.67	-
Adam McKinna	4	16	24	4	28	7.00	-
Danny Norton	1	1	0	0	0	0.00	-
Michael Pickering	2	8	4	2	6	3.00	-
Sean Stoddart	1	5	10	0	10	8.00	-

Guests	12	40	19	7	26	2.60	-

(Chris Baldwin [1]; Adam Chandler [1]; Ben Hannon [1]; Shane Henry [1]; Lee Lingham [1]; Kye Norton [5]; Ben Reade [2])

Cleveland, 2007

Back row, left to right: Jason Pipe (Team Manager), Kye Norton, Mark Burrows and Gary Beaton.

Front, kneeling: Martin Emerson, Greg Blair and Paul Burnett.

(Photo: Ian Charles)

OXFORD CHEETAHS

NOTE: The information below relates only to the second Oxford team. For details of the main side, please refer to the Elite League section. The Conference League side began the season with a Lions moniker, but shortly after the club had resumed under new management, it was decided to revert to the Cheetahs nickname.

ADDRESS: Oxford Stadium, Sandy Lane, Cowley, Oxford, OX4 6LJ.

TELEPHONE: 01865 396472.

CLUB HOTLINE: 09068 664680 (Premium rate applies).

WEBSITE: www.oxford-cheetahs.com

CLUB CHAIRMAN: Allen Trump, who took over in June, following the collapse of the previous Oxford management, which was headed by Colin Horton and Aaron Lanney.

MAIN TEAM SPONSOR: LCD Publishing.

TRACK LENGTH: 297 metres.

CL TRACK RECORD: 60.72 seconds - Danny Betson (17/08/07).

FIRST MEETING: 25 May 1997.

YEARS OF OPERATION: 1997 Amateur League; 2003-05 Conference League; 2007 Conference League.

CLUB HONOURS
LEAGUE CHAMPIONS: 2005.

Jordan Frampton sports Oxford's early-season Lions race-jacket. The Poole-born youngster came on in leaps and bounds during the 2007 campaign, both at Conference level with the Cowley-based club and in the Premier League with Somerset.

(Photo: www.juliemartinphotography.co.uk)

OXFORD 2007

* Denotes aggregate/bonus-point victory

NO.	DATE	OPPONENTS	VENUE	COMPETITION	RESULT	ANDREW BARGH	SAM MARTIN	GRANT MacDONALD	KYLE HUGHES	JORDAN FRAMPTON	BEN HOPWOOD	LEWIS BLACKBIRD	LEE SMETHILLS	DANNY BETSON	OTHER RIDERS
1	8/4	Weymouth	H	CT	W57-34	7+2 (5)	10 (4)	11+1 (4)	8+1 (4)	13 (5)	8+2 (7)	-	-	-	0 (1)
2	22/4	Plymouth	H	CT	L42-48	11 (6)	7+3 (5)	11+1 (6)	4+2 (5)	R/R	6+1 (5)	3+1 (3)	-	-	-
3	27/4	Weymouth	A	CT	L41-52*	16 (6)	4+2 (5)	10+1 (6)	3 (5)	R/R	4 (3)	4+2 (5)	-	-	-
4	1/7	Buxton	H	CL	W67-23	11+1 (4)	9+2 (4)	-	12+3 (5)	-	-		15 (5)	8+2 (4)	12+1 (8)
5	8/7	Plymouth	H	KO	W45-44	13+1 (6)	5 (2)	-	1+1 (3)	R/R	-		11+3 (6)	7 (3)	8 (10)
6	15/7	Weymouth	H	CL	W49-44	12+2 (5)	-	-	9 (4)	-	-		13+2 (5)	9 (4)	6 (12)
7	20/7	Weymouth	A	CL	D45-45*	13 (5)	3 (4)	-	7+1 (5)	-	-		7+1 (4)	7+1 (4)	8+2 (9)
8	27/7	Plymouth	A	KO	L44-45	11+1 (5)	9+2 (5)	-	6+1 (4)	-	-		13 (5)	3 (4)	2 (7)
9	29/7	Stoke	H	CL	W57-35	R/R	8+1 (5)	-	15+1 (6)	-	-		13+2 (5)	13 (6)	8+2 (8)
10	3/8	Rye House	H	CL	W50-43	14+2 (6)	9+2 (5)	-	R/R	-	-		15 (6)	9+2 (5)	3 (8)
11	5/8	Sittingbourne	A	CL	L44-45	11 (5)	-	-	-	9 (4)	-		7+2 (4)	11 (5)	6+1 (11)
12	10/8	Boston	A	CL	W48-44	-	8 (6)	-	5+2 (6)	R/R	-		10+3 (5)	15 (5)	10 (8)
13	12/8	Sittingbourne	H	CL	W71-21*	-	15 (5)	-	10 (4)	10+2 (4)	-		10+2 (4)	12+3 (5)	14+4 (8)
14	17/8	Cleveland	H	CL	W70-18	-	12+3 (5)	-	11+2 (5)	R/R	-		17+1 (6)	17+1 (6)	13+4 (8)
15	25/8	Rye House	A	CL	W54-37*	R/R	-	-	5+3 (5)	12+1 (5)	-		11+2 (5)	15 (6)	11+3 (9)
16	27/8	Plymouth	H	KO	W61-29	R/R	-	-	7+1 (5)	15+1 (6)	-		17+1 (6)	14+1 (5)	8+2 (8)
17	31/8	Boston	H	CL	W50-43*	R/R	14+2 (6)	-	3+1 (4)	-	-		16 (6)	-	17+4 (14)
18	7/9	Plymouth	A	KO	L30-63	R/R	-	-	9 (7)	-	-		15 (6)	-	6+1 (14)
19	9/9	Buxton	A	CL	L36-59*	R/R	-	-	13+1 (7)	-	-		18 (6)	-	5+1 (17)
20	14/9	Scunthorpe	H	CL	W47-45	5+1 (4)	10+1 (4)	-	5 (4)	-	-		9+2 (5)	13 (5)	5 (8)
21	20/9	Cleveland	A	CL	W49-43*	6 (4)	8 (4)	-	-	11 (5)	-		12+2 (5)	9 (4)	3 (8)
22	21/9	Plymouth	A	CL	L41-51	1 (3)	5 (4)	-	7+2 (4)	-	-		15 (5)	11+1 (5)	2 (9)
23	23/9	Plymouth	H	CL	W53-38*	R/R	-	-	8+2 (5)	4+1 (5)	-		16+2 (6)	18 (6)	7+1 (8)
24	24/9	Scunthorpe	A	CL	L35-58	1 (4)	6 (6)	-	-	13 (5)	-		6 (4)	6 (4)	3+1 (7)
25	29/9	Stoke	A	CL	W55-37*	6 (4)	8 (4)	-	10+3 (5)	-	-		9+1 (4)	13 (5)	9+2 (8)
26	5/10	Plymouth	A	POs	L37-54	4 (4)	5+1 (5)	-	7+1 (5)	-	-		7+1 (4)	11 (5)	3 (7)
27	12/10	Plymouth	A	CT	L34-58	-	8+1 (6)	-	13 (6)	-	-		R/R	-	13+2 (18)
28	15/10	Plymouth	H	POs	W56-38*	10+1 (4)	6+1 (4)	-	-	9+2 (4)	-		12+1 (5)	15 (5)	4 (8)
29	19/10	Scunthorpe	A	POf	L42-47	9+1 (5)	5 (4)	-	7+2 (4)	-	-		10+1 (5)	7+1 (4)	4 (8)
30	21/10	Scunthorpe	A	POf	L31-61	3+1 (4)	-	-	4+1 (4)	6 (5)	-		12 (5)	3 (4)	3 (8)

Details of other riders (all guests unless **highlighted**): Match No. 1: **Adam Wrathall** 0 (1); Match No. 4: Brendan Johnson 8 (5); **Dan Blake** 4+1 (3); Match No. 5: Brendan Johnson 7 (7); **Dan Blake** 1 (3); Match No. 6: Brendan Johnson 5 (6); **Dan Blake** 1 (3); Jerran Hart 0 (3); Match No. 7: **Dan Blake** 1+1 (3); **Brendan Johnson** 7+1 (6); Match No. 8: Olly Gay 1 (3); **Brendan Johnson** 1 (4); Match No. 9: **Brendan Johnson** 5+1 (4); **George Piper** 3+1 (4); Match No. 10: **Brendan Johnson** 2 (4); **George Piper** 1 (4); Match No. 11: **Brendan Johnson** 6+1 (7); **Mattie Bates** 0 (4); **George Piper** 0 (3); Match No. 12: **Brendan Johnson** 10 (7); **George Piper** 0 (1); Match No. 13: **Brendan Johnson** 8+2 (4); **Mattie Bates** 6+2 (4); Match No. 14: **Brendan Johnson** 8+2 (4); **Mattie Bates** 5+2 (4); Match No. 15: **Brendan Johnson** 9+2 (5); **Scott Campos** 2+1 (4); Match No. 16: **Brendan Johnson** 6+1 (5); **Scott Campos** 2+1 (3); Match No. 17: **Brendan Johnson** 9+2 (7); **Scott Campos** 6 (4); **Darren Andrews** 2+2 (3); Match No. 18: Dakota North 3 (5); **Brendan Johnson** 2+1 (6); Jaimie Pickard 1 (3); Bob Charles DNA; Match No. 19: **Scott Campos** 5+1 (7); Jason Newitt 0 (3); **Darren Andrews** 0 (3); **Brendan Johnson** 0 (4); Match No. 20: Brendan Johnson 1 (4); Dakota North 4 (4); Match No. 21: **Brendan Johnson** 3 (5); Kye Norton 0 (3); Match No. 22: **Brendan Johnson** 1 (5); Alex McLeod 1 (4); Match No. 23: **Brendan Johnson** 6 (5); Niall Strudwick 1+1 (3); Match No. 24: Kye Norton 2+1 (3); **Brendan Johnson** 1 (4); Match No. 25: **Brendan Johnson** 5+2 (4); **Scott Campos** 4 (4); Match No. 26: **Scott Campos** 2 (3); **Brendan Johnson** 1 (4); Match No. 27: **Brendan Johnson** 7+1 (6); Paul Starke 3+1 (5); Scott Meakins 2 (4); Alex McLeod 1 (3); Match No. 28: **Scott Campos** 2 (3); **Brendan Johnson** 2 (5); Match No. 29: **Scott Campos** 4 (4); **Brendan Johnson** 0 (4); Match No. 30; **Brendan Johnson** 2 (4); **Scott Campos** 1 (4).

Details of tactical rides and tactical substitute rides: Match No. 3: Bargh 6 points (TR); Match No. 8: Martin 2 points (TS); Match No. 18: Smethills 6 points (TR); Hughes 1 point (TS; not doubled); Match No. 19: Smethills 6 points (TR); Hughes 4 points (TS); Match No. 22: Smethills 6 points (TR); Match No. 24: Frampton 6 points (TR); Martin 0 points (TS); Match No. 26: Smethills 4 points (TR); Martin 0 points (TS); Match No. 27: Hughes 6 points (TR); Match No. 30: Smethills 6 points (TR).

AVERAGES

[18 Conference League; 4 Play-Offs; 4 Knock-Out Cup; 4 Conference Trophy = 30 fixtures]

Rider	Mts	Rds	Pts	Bon	Tot	Avge	Max
Lee Smethills	26	132	302	29	331	10.03	1 full; 6 paid
Danny Betson	23	109	246	12	258	9.47	3 full; 3 paid
Jordan Frampton	15	72	148	13	161	8.94	2 paid
Andrew Bargh	19	89	161	13	174	7.82	1 paid
Sam Martin	22	102	173	21	194	7.61	1 full; 1 paid
Kyle Hughes	20	97	135	25	160	6.60	-
Brendan Johnson	24	117	102	16	118	4.03	-
Scott Campos	9	36	28	3	31	3.44	-

Also rode (in alphabetical order):

Darren Andrews	2	6	2	2	4	2.67	-
Mattie Bates	3	9	11	4	15	6.67	-
Dan Blake	4	12	7	2	9	3.00	-
Grant MacDonald	3	16	32	3	35	8.75	1 paid
George Piper	4	12	4	1	5	1.67	-
Adam Wrathall	1	1	0	0	0	0.00	-

Guests	16	64	39	3	42	2.63	-

(Olly Gay [1]; Jerran Hart [1]; Brendan Johnson [3]; Alex McLeod [2]; Scott Meakins [1]; Jason Newitt [1]; Dakota North [2]; Kye Norton [2]; Jaimie Pickard [1]; Paul Starke [1]; Niall Strudwick [1])

NOTE: Lee Smethills was ever-present throughout the 18-match Conference League programme.

INDIVIDUAL MEETINGS

7 October: **New Era Trophy**

QUALIFYING SCORES: Tai Woffinden <u>15</u>; Josh Auty 14; Andrew Tully 13; Scott Richardson 10; Benji Compton 9; Jamie Courtney 9; Joe Haines 9; James Cockle 8; Richie Dennis 8; Sean Stoddart 7; Simon Lambert 5; Kriss Irving 4; Gary Beaton 3; Ben Hannon (Res) 2; Jerran Hart (Res) 2; Darren Mallett 1; Charles Wright 0.

SEMI-FINAL: 1st Compton; 2nd Courtney; 3rd Richardson; 4th Tully.

FINAL: 1st Woffinden; 2nd Auty; 3rd Courtney; 4th Compton.

26 October: **British Under-15 Championship** (Round Three)

QUALIFYING SCORES: Dan Greenwood 14; James Sarjeant 14; Kye Norton 13; Brendan Johnson 12; Shane Hazelden 12; Richard Franklin 10; Danny Stoneman 8; John Resch 8; Scott Meakins 8; Jake Knight 6; Jack Hirst 4; Chris Bint 4; Cameron Hoskins 3; Montana Jowett 2.

FINAL: 1st Greenwood; 2nd Sarjeant; 3rd Johnson; 4th Norton.

TITLE RUN-OFF: 1st Greenwood; 2nd Sarjeant.

OVERALL SERIES STANDINGS: 1st Greenwood 32 (15+17); 2nd Sarjeant 32 (17+15); 3rd Johnson 31 (17+14); Norton 26 (13+13); Franklin 26 (15+11); Hazelden 25 (13+12); Stoneman 19 (9+10); Hirst 18 (12+6); Resch 17 (7+10); Meakins 16 (6+10); Hoskins 14 (10+4); Jowett 13 (10+3); Bint 11 (5+6); Dale Lamb 11 (11+DNR); Jason Garrity 9 (9+DNR); Jack Butler 8 (8+DNR); Knight 7 (DNR+7); Michael Bovis 4 (4+DNR); Nathan Stoneman 4 (4+DNR).

NOTE: Overall result calculated by adding each competitor's best score from the opening two rounds at Weymouth and Northside to their tally at Oxford.

Oxford, 2007

Back row, left to right: Jason Newitt, Darren Andrews, Scott Campos and Allen Trump (Club Chairman/Team Manager).

Front, kneeling: Lee Smethills, Kyle Hughes and Brendan Johnson.

(Photo: Ian Charles)

PLYMOUTH DEVILS

ADDRESS:	St Boniface Arena, Coypool Road, Marsh Mills, Plymouth, Devon, PL7 4NW.
TELEPHONE:	01752 345146.
CLUB HOTLINE:	09068 664668 (Premium rate applies).
WEBSITE:	www.plymouthdevils.co.uk
CLUB CHAIRMAN:	Mike Bowden.
MAIN TEAM SPONSORS:	GT Motorcycles & Silverline Taxis.
TRACK LENGTH:	260 metres.
TRACK RECORD:	51.07 - Tai Woffinden (18/05/07).
FIRST MEETING:	21 April 2006.
YEARS OF OPERATION:	2006-2007 Conference League.
PREVIOUS VENUE:	Pennycross Stadium, Pennycross, Plymouth, Devon.
YEARS OF OPERATION:	1931 Open; 1932-1934 National League; 1935 Open; 1936 Provincial League; 1937 Open; 1947-1949 National League Division Three; 1950 National League Division Two; 1951 National League Division Three; 1952-1953 Southern League; 1954 National League Division Two; 1959-1960 Open; 1961-1962 Provincial League; 1968-1969 British League Division Two; 1970 Open.

CLUB HONOURS

NATIONAL TROPHY (SOUTHERN LEAGUE) WINNERS: 1952.

Plymouth, 2007
Back row, left to right: Tom Brown, Seemond Stephens, Rob Smith and Nicki Glanz.
Front, kneeling: Jaimie Pickard, Ben Hopwood and Tim Webster.

(Photo: Ian Charles)

PLYMOUTH 2007

* Denotes aggregate/bonus-point victory

NO.	DATE	OPPONENTS	VENUE	COMPETITION	RESULT	SEEMOND STEPHENS	TIM WEBSTER	TOM BROWN	BILLY LEGG	JAIMIE PICKARD	DAN BLAKE	NICKI GLANZ	ADAM ROYNON	SHANE WALDRON	OTHER RIDERS
1	13/4	US Dream Team	H	Chal	W49-44	13 (5)	2 (4)	10 (4)	4+2 (4)	1 (3)	1 (3)	18+1 (7)	-	-	-
2	21/4	Cleveland	A	CL	W47-43	10 (4)	1 (4)	8+1 (5)	12+1 (5)	0 (3)	2+1 (3)	14+1 (6)	-	-	-
3	22/4	Oxford	A	CT	W48-42	17 (6)	1+1 (4)	13 (6)	2+1 (5)	-	1 (3)	14+2 (6)	R/R	-	-
4	27/4	Rye House	H	CL	W47-40	13 (6)	4 (4)	14 (6)	-	0 (4)	0 (3)	16 (6)	R/R	-	0 (1)
5	4/5	Weymouth	H	CT	W60-34	14 (5)	5+1 (4)	8+2 (4)	-	2 (3)	4+1 (3)	17+2 (7)	10+2 (4)	-	-
6	5/5	Weymouth	A	CT	W48-44*	15 (6)	-	14 (5)	-	3 (4)	1 (4)	14+3 (7)	R/R	-	1 (4)
7	25/5	Boston	A	CL	L43-49	10 (5)	4+1 (6)	7 (4)	2 (4)	2 (3)	-	-	15 (5)	3 (3)	-
8	1/6	Scunthorpe	H	CL	L43-46	8+1 (5)	2+1 (3)	7 (4)	2+2 (3)	-	-	15 (6)	3+2 (5)	6+2 (4)	-
9	8/6	Stoke	H	CL	W67-25	12+2 (5)	6+2 (4)	11+1 (4)	7+1 (4)	-	-	9+1 (4)	14 (5)	8+2 (4)	-
10	16/6	Weymouth	A	CL	L44-48	10+1 (5)	5+2 (4)	1 (3)	2+1 (3)	-	-	6+2 (5)	16+1 (6)	4 (4)	-
11	22/6	Cleveland	H	CL	W48-40*	12+1 (5)	2+1 (4)	13 (5)	3+2 (4)	-	-	8+1 (4)	-	4+1 (4)	6 (4)
12	8/7	Oxford	A	KO	L44-45	11 (5)	1+1 (4)	14 (5)	3+1 (4)	-	-	6 (4)	-	-	9+4 (9)
13	20/7	Boston	H	CL	W51-40*	13 (5)	-	10+1 (4)	3 (4)	-	-	10+2 (5)	-	-	15+4 (12)
14	27/7	Oxford	H	KO	W45-44	9 (5)	4+3 (4)	9+1 (4)	3+2 (4)	-	-	6+1 (5)	-	-	14+2 (8)
15	3/8	Buxton	H	CL	W64-26	11+1 (4)	4 (3)	9+3 (4)	-	-	-	9+1 (4)	-	-	31+5 (15)
16	5/8	Rye House	A	CL	L33-60	R/R	0 (4)	14 (6)	-	-	-	5 (5)	-	-	14+3 (15)
17	17/8	Sittingbourne	H	CL	W64-28	10+1 (5)	6+2 (4)	12+2 (5)	-	-	-	8 (3)	-	-	28+6 (13)
18	24/8	Scunthorpe	H	CTf	L33-59	5 (4)	5 (4)	9 (5)	-	-	-	4 (4)	-	-	10+6 (14)
19	27/8	Oxford	A	KO	L29-61	1 (2)	1+1 (5)	8+1 (6)	-	-	-	5 (4)	-	-	14+3 (13)
20	31/8	Weymouth	H	CL	W50-43*	R/R	6+2 (5)	16+1 (6)	-	-	-	10+2 (6)	-	-	18+2 (14)
21	2/9	Scunthorpe	A	CTf	L28-65	-	2 (5)	5 (4)	-	1 (4)	-	13 (5)	-	-	7+2 (12)
22	7/9	Oxford	H	KO	W63-30*	12+2 (5)	1+1 (2)	7+4 (4)	-	-	-	13+2 (5)	-	-	30+3 (14)
23	9/9	Sittingbourne	A	CL	W51-38*	12 (5)	-	10+2 (5)	-	2 (4)	-	6+1 (4)	-	-	21+3 (12)
24	12/9	Stoke	A	CL	W49-44*	9 (4)	-	10 (4)	-	3 (4)	-	6+3 (5)	-	-	21+6 (13)
25	14/9	Wimbledon	H	Chal	W56-37	12+3 (5)	2+2 (4)	11 (5)	-	6 (5)	-	14 (5)	-	-	11+3 (6)
26	16/9	Oxford	A	CL	L40-52	6+1 (5)	-	18 (6)	-	-	-	5+1 (5)	-	-	11+3 (14)
27	21/9	Oxford	H	CL	W51-41	6+3 (4)	-	9+1 (5)	-	4+1 (3)	-	12+1 (5)	-	-	20+2 (10)
28	23/9	Oxford	A	CL	L38-53	6 (4)	-	9+1 (5)	-	3+1 (4)	-	7 (5)	-	-	13+4 (12)
29	28/9	Weymouth	H	KOs	W51-39	10+1 (4)	4+1 (4)	9 (5)	-	3 (4)	-	10+1 (5)	-	-	15+2 (8)
30	29/9	Weymouth	A	KOs	D45-45*	9+1 (4)	1+1 (4)	12 (4)	-	2 (4)	-	10+1 (5)	-	-	11+2 (9)
31	30/9	Buxton	A	CL	L42-53*	13+1 (5)	0 (3)	15 (6)	-	1+1 (4)	-	7 (4)	-	-	6+1 (8)
32	5/10	Oxford	H	POs	W54-37	10 (4)	4+2 (4)	9+2 (5)	-	3 (3)	-	12 (5)	-	-	16+2 (9)
33	12/10	Oxford	H	CT	W58-34*	12 (4)	3 (5)	11+1 (4)	-	8+1 (5)	-	7+2 (4)	-	-	17+3 (8)
34	15/10	Oxford	A	POs	L38-56	10 (5)	0 (3)	10 (6)	-	2+1 (4)	-	6 (4)	-	-	10+4 (8)
35	26/10	Scunthorpe	H	KOf	W49-44	8+1 (4)	-	9+3 (5)	-	6+1 (4)	-	11 (5)	-	-	13+4 (9)
36	28/10	Scunthorpe	A	KOf	L35-58	6 (4)	1 (4)	13 (5)	-	2+1 (4)	-	6+1 (5)	-	-	7+2 (8)

Details of other riders (all guests unless **highlighted**): Match No. 4: **Danny Stoneman** 0 (1); Match No. 6: Nick Mallett 1 (4); Match No. 11: **Jamie Westacott** 6 (4); Match No. 12: **Jamie Westacott** 6+4 (5); Match No. 13: **Ben Hopwood** 8+2 (5); **Jamie Westacott** 7+2 (4); **Rob Smith** 0 (3); Match No. 14: **Jamie Westacott** 7+2 (4); **Ben Hopwood** 7 (4); Match No. 15: **Jamie Westacott** 12+1 (5); **Ben Hopwood** 10+2 (5); **Rob Smith** 9+2 (5); Match No. 16: **Rob Smith** 7 (6); **Ben Hopwood** 6+2 (5); **Jamie Westacott** 1+1 (4); Match No. 17: **Jamie Westacott** 11+1 (4); **Rob Smith** 9+3 (4); **Ben Hopwood** 8+2 (5); Match No. 18: **Jamie Westacott** 5+3 (5); **Ben Hopwood** 3+2 (5); **Rob Smith** 2+1 (4); Match No. 19: **Rob Smith** 6 (5); **Jamie Westacott** 5+1 (4); **Ben Hopwood** 3+2 (4); Match No. 20: **Jamie Westacott** 9 (5); **Rob Smith** 5 (5); **Ben Hopwood** 4+2 (4); Match No. 21: **Rob Smith** 3+2 (4); **Jamie Westacott** 2 (4); **Ben Hopwood** 2 (4); Match No. 22: **Ben Hopwood** 15+2 (6); **Rob Smith** 10+1 (4); **Jamie Westacott** 5 (4); Match No. 23: **Rob Smith** 11+1 (4); **Jamie Westacott** 6+1 (4); **Ben Hopwood** 4+1 (4); Match No. 24: **Ben Hopwood** 11 (4); **Rob Smith** 7+4 (5); **Jamie Westacott** 3+2 (4); Match No. 25: **Ben Hopwood** 11+3 (6); **Jamie Westacott** R/R; Match No. 26: **Rob Smith** 5+2 (5); **Ben Hopwood** 5+1 (6); Nigel Knott 1 (3); **Jamie Westacott** R/R; Match No. 27: **Ben Hopwood** 15+1 (6); **Rob Smith** 5+1 (4); Match No. 28: **Ben Hopwood** 6+2 (5); **Rob Smith** 6+1 (4); Danny Stoneman 1+1 (3); Match No. 29: **Rob Smith** 8+1 (4); **Ben Hopwood** 7+1 (4); Match No. 30: **Ben Hopwood** 6+1 (5); **Rob Smith** 5+1 (4); Match No. 31: **Ben Hopwood** 5+1 (5); **Rob Smith** 1 (3); Match No. 32: **Ben Hopwood** 9+1 (5); **Rob Smith** 7+1 (4); Match No. 33: **Rob Smith** 9+1 (4); **Ben Hopwood** 8+2 (4); Match No. 34: **Rob Smith** 5+2 (4); **Ben Hopwood** 5+2 (4); Match No. 35: **Ben Hopwood** 7+3 (5); **Rob Smith** 6+1 (4); Match No. 36: **Ben Hopwood** 5+1 (4); **Rob Smith** 2+1 (4).

Details of tactical rides and tactical substitute rides: Match No. 1: Glanz 6 points (TR); Match No. 7: Roynon 6 points (TR); Match No. 10: Roynon 4 points (TS); Match No. 16: Brown 6 points (TR); Match No. 18: Brown 4 points (TR); Match No. 19: Brown 1 point (TS; not doubled); Match No. 21: Glanz 6 points (TR); Match No. 26: Brown 6 points (TR); Match No. 28: Brown 4 points (TR); Match No. 31: Brown 6 points (TS); Stephens 4 points (TR); Match No. 34: Brown 4 points (TS); Stephens 4 points (TR); Match No. 36: Brown 6 points (TR).

Other details: USA Dream Team scorers in Match No. 1: Tommy Hedden 13 (5); Bryan Yarrow 9+1 (5); Dale Facchini 6+2 (4); Neil Facchini 6 (4); Kenny Ingalls 4+2 (4); Tim Gomez 3+2 (4); J.T. Mabry 3 (4).; Wimbledon scorers in Match No. 25: Mark Burrows 15 (6); Dean Felton 6 (5); Nathan Irwin 5 (5); Terry Day 4+1 (5); Rob Smith 4 (5); Jon Stevens 3+1 (5); Ray Morton R/R. The total for Burrows includes 6 points from a TR.

AVERAGES

[18 Conference League; 2 Play-Offs; 8 Knock-Out Cup; 6 Conference Trophy = 34 fixtures]

• Denotes ever-present.

Rider	Mts	Rds	Pts	Bon	Tot	Avge	Max
Seemond Stephens	31	143	306	17	323	9.03	1 full; 1 paid
Tom Brown •	34	164	335	27	362	8.83	1 full; 3 paid
Nicki Glanz	33	162	304	31	335	8.27	1 paid
Ben Hopwood	24	113	165	37	202	7.15	-
Rob Smith	22	93	128	26	154	6.62	2 paid
Jamie Westacott	14	59	82	14	96	6.51	1 paid
Billy Legg	10	40	39	11	50	5.00	-
Tim Webster	27	107	75	25	100	3.74	-
Jaimie Pickard	18	68	47	7	54	3.18	-

Also rode (in alphabetical order):

Dan Blake	5	16	8	2	10	2.50	-
Adam Roynon	5	25	53	5	58	9.28	1 paid
Danny Stoneman	1	1	0	0	0	0.00	-
Shane Waldron	5	19	25	5	30	6.32	-

Guests	3	10	3	1	4	1.60	-

(Nigel Knott [1]; Nick Mallett [1]; Danny Stoneman [1])

INDIVIDUAL MEETINGS

6 April: **British Under-21 Championship** (Qualifying Round)

QUALIFYING SCORES: Steve Boxall 15; Adam Roynon 14; Jack Roberts 11; Luke Bowen 11; Nicki Glanz 9; Jamie Westacott 8; Billy Legg 8; Ben Taylor 8; Rob Smith 7; Sam Martin 7; Kyle Hughes 7; Dan Blake 4; Jaimie Pickard 3; Tim Webster (Res) 3; Gary Cottham 2; Bob Charles (Res) 1; Harland Cook 0; George Piper 0.

SEMI-FINAL: 1st Bowen; 2nd Glanz; 3rd Roberts; 4th Westacott.

FINAL: 1st Boxall; 2nd Bowen; 3rd Roynon; 4th Glanz.

6 July: **Devils' Summer Classic**

QUALIFYING SCORES: Ben Barker 15; Seemond Stephens 12; Tom Brown 11; Nicki Glanz 10; Ben Hopwood 9; Jamie Westacott 7; Ben Taylor 6; Kyle Hughes 6; Tim Webster 5; Jaimie Pickard 4; Billy Legg 4; Jason Prynne 0.

FINAL: 1st Brown; 2nd Barker; 3rd Stephens; 4th Glanz.

PAIRS MEETING

25 May: **Silverline Perpetual Trophy**

1st Ben Hopwood (15+3) & Kyle Hughes (15+1) = 30; 2nd Jamie Westacott (17) & Jason Prynne (9+3) = 26; 3rd Jack Roberts (15) & Nick Mallett (6+1) = 21; Dean Felton (14) & Gordon Meakins (6+3) = 20; Michael Coles (18) & Danny Stoneman (0) = 18; Ben Barker (16) & Bob Charles (0) = 16; Russell Barnett (Res) 2; James White-Williams (Res) 0.

Nicki Glanz, the son of former rider Peter, showed great promise in only his second term of British racing, netting a hatful of double figure tallies for the Devils.

(Photo: Ian Charles)

RYE HOUSE RAIDERS

NOTE: The information below relates only to the second Rye House team. For details of the main side, please refer to the Premier League section.

ADDRESS: Rye House Stadium, Rye Road, Hoddesdon, Hertfordshire, EN11 0EH.

TELEPHONE: 01992 440400.

CLUB HOTLINE: 09066 555948.

WEBSITE: www.ryehouse.com

CLUB CHAIRMEN: Len Silver & Hazal Naylor.

MAIN TEAM SPONSOR: Elmside.

TRACK LENGTH: 271 metres.

FIRST MEETING: 1 April 2002

CL TRACK RECORD: 56.4 seconds - Tai Woffinden (27/07/07).

YEARS OF OPERATION: 2002-2007 Conference League.

CLUB HONOURS
FOUR-TEAM CHAMPIONS: 2003.

Robert Mear enjoyed a terrific season with the Raiders, highlighted by his third-place finish in the Conference League Riders' Championship at Rye House on 15 September.

(Photo: Ian Charles)

RYE HOUSE 2007

* Denotes aggregate/bonus-point victory

NO.	DATE	OPPONENTS	VENUE	COMPETITION	RESULT	BEN POWELL	GARY COTTHAM	HARLAND COOK	ROBERT MEAR	BARRY BURCHATT	LEE STRUDWICK	DANIEL HALSEY	KARLIS EZERGAILIS	LUKE BOWEN	OTHER RIDERS
1	9/4	Sittingbourne	H	KO	W61-29	8+1 (4)	10+2 (4)	2 (4)	12 (5)	11+1 (5)	8+1 (4)	10+2 (4)	-	-	-
2	22/4	Sittingbourne	A	KO	W59-32*	R/R	9+1 (5)	7+1 (4)	14 (5)	12 (4)	3 (4)	8+2 (4)	-	-	6+2 (4)
3	27/4	Plymouth	A	CL	L40-47	4 (3)	1+1 (3)	7+2 (4)	6+1 (5)	11 (5)	3+2 (4)	8+2 (6)	-	-	-
4	5/5	Buxton	H	CL	W57-35	R/R	11+1 (5)	7 (4)	17+1 (6)	10 (5)	5+1 (4)	7+2 (4)	-	-	0 (2)
5	2/6	Cleveland	A	CL	W48-41	R/R	3 (4)	1 (3)	14 (6)	-	10+1 (6)	9+1 (6)	11+1 (5)	-	-
6	10/6	Scunthorpe	A	CL	L31-59	R/R	2+1 (5)	-	9+1 (6)	-	1 (4)	7+1 (5)	11 (6)	-	1 (4)
7	16/6	Scunthorpe	H	KO	W52-41	R/R	4 (3)	-	12+2 (6)	10 (5)	3 (4)	13+4 (7)	10 (5)	-	-
8	17/6	Buxton	A	CL	L43-47*	7+1 (5)	-	-	6+2 (5)	-	3 (3)	14+1 (7)	R/R	-	13+1 (10)
9	6/7	Weymouth	A	CL	L46-47	R/R	0 (3)	-	7+1 (5)	-	1+1 (3)	18+2 (7)	13 (6)	7+2 (6)	-
10	14/7	Sittingbourne	H	CL	W61-28	-	6+1 (3)	-	17+1 (6)	14+1 (6)	6 (3)	7+4 (6)	R/R	-	11+3 (6)
11	27/7	Scunthorpe	H	CL	L43-48	-	1 (3)	-	13+1 (6)	5+2 (4)	-	7 (6)	R/R	15 (7)	2 (4)
12	3/8	Oxford	A	CL	L43-50	R/R	11+1 (6)	-	9+1 (5)	-	-	6 (5)	5 (5)	10 (6)	2 (3)
13	5/8	Plymouth	H	CL	W60-33*	R/R	11 (5)	-	13 (5)	-	-	10+4 (6)	9+3 (5)	15 (5)	2 (4)
14	12/8	Scunthorpe	A	CL	L28-61	R/R	-	-	12 (6)	-	-	-	5 (7)	-	11+2 (14)
15	25/8	Oxford	H	CL	L37-54	R/R	1 (4)	-	21 (6)	-	-	7 (6)	6+1 (5)	-	2 (7)
16	2/9	Sittingbourne	A	CL	L39-49*	R/R	0 (1)	-	11+1 (6)	-	-	7 (5)	14 (6)	-	7+2 (11)
17	7/9	Boston	A	CL	L26-65	R/R	-	-	13 (6)	-	-	9+1 (6)	3+1 (4)	-	1 (14)
18	8/9	Weymouth	H	CL	W58-33*	R/R	-	-	17+1 (6)	-	-	12+3 (6)	13+1 (5)	12+2 (5)	4 (8)
19	16/9	Stoke	H	CL	W54-38	R/R	-	-	18 (6)	-	-	7+1 (5)	10 (5)	14+1 (6)	5+1 (8)
20	22/9	Cleveland	H	CL	W60-33*	R/R	-	-	16+2 (6)	-	-	13+1 (6)	8+1 (3)	13+1 (5)	10+2 (10)
21	13/10	Boston	H	CL	W61-33	R/R	-	-	16+2 (6)	-	-	13+2 (5)	18 (6)	8+3 (5)	6+2 (8)
22	17/10	Stoke	A	CL	L40-52*	R/R	-	-	19 (7)	-	-	10+1 (6)	5 (3)	-	6+1 (14)

NOTE: Gary Cottham was present for the Conference League match at Scunthorpe on 12 August, but did not ride due to machinery problems. This is therefore not counted as an appearance in Cottham's record for the season.

Details of other riders (all guests unless **highlighted**): Match No. 2: Jerran Hart 6+2 (4); Match No. 4: Jerran Hart 0 (2); Match No. 6: Jerran Hart 1 (4); Match No. 8: Brendan Johnson 10+1 (7); Jerran Hart 3 (3); Match No. 10: Brendan Johnson 11+3 (6); Match No. 11: Nick Laurence 2 (4); Match No. 12: Nick Laurence 2 (3); Match No. 13: Nick Laurence 2 (4); Match No. 14: Kye Norton 8+1 (7); Nick Laurence 3+1 (6); Aaron Vale 0 (1); Match No. 15: Nick Laurence 2 (5); Kye Norton 0 (2); Match No. 16: Kye Norton 5+1 (7); Nick Laurence 2+1 (4); Match No. 17: Nick Laurence 1 (5); Shane Henry 0 (5); Kye Norton 0 (4); Match No. 18: Dakota North 3 (4); Nick Laurence 1 (4); Match No. 19: Nick Laurence 4+1 (4); Dakota North 1 (4); Match No. 20: Nick Laurence 7+1 (5); Adam Filmer 3+1 (5); Match No. 21: Kyle Newman 6+2 (5); Adam Filmer 0 (3); Match No. 22: Adam Filmer 6+1 (7); Scott Whittington 0 (3); Adam Chandler 0 (4).

Details of tactical rides and tactical substitute rides: Match No. 6: Ezergailis 1 point (TR; not doubled); Match No. 9: Halsey 6 points (TR); Match No. 11: Bowen 2 points (TS); Match No. 12: Mear 6 points (TR); Match No. 14: Ezergailis 0 points (TS); Norton 0 points (TR); Match No. 15: Mear 6 points (TR); Match No. 17: Mear 4 points (TR); Match No. 22: Mear 4 points (TS).

AVERAGES

[18 Conference League; 4 Knock-Out Cup = 22 fixtures]

• Denotes ever-present.

Rider	Mts	Rds	Pts	Bon	Tot	Avge	Max
Robert Mear •	22	126	282	17	299	9.49	2 full; 5 paid
Luke Bowen	8	45	93	9	102	9.07	1 full
Barry Burchatt	7	34	73	4	77	9.06	1 full
Daniel Halsey	21	118	199	34	233	7.90	2 paid
Karlis Ezergailis	15	76	141	8	149	7.84	1 full
Gary Cottham	14	54	70	8	78	5.78	1 paid
Lee Strudwick	10	39	43	6	49	5.03	-

Also rode (in alphabetical order):

	Mts	Rds	Pts	Bon	Tot	Avge	Max
Harland Cook	5	19	24	3	27	5.68	-
Ben Powell	3	12	19	2	21	7.00	-
Guests	30	131	89	16	105	3.21	-

(Adam Chandler [1]; Adam Filmer [3]; Jerran Hart [4]; Shane Henry [1]; Brendan Johnson [2]; Nick Laurence [10]; Kyle Newman [1]; Dakota North [2]; Kye Norton [4]; Aaron Vale [1]; Scott Whittington [1])

Rye House, 2007

Back row, left to right: Jerran Hart, Robert Mear, Daniel Halsey and John Sampford (Team Manager).

Front row: Lee Strudwick, Brendan Johnson and Ben Powell.

(Photo: Ian Charles)

SCUNTHORPE SCORPIONS

ADDRESS:	Normanby Road, Scunthorpe, North Lincolnshire, DN15 8QZ.
TELEPHONE:	01724 848899.
CLUB HOTLINE:	09066 555923 (Premium rate applies).
WEBSITE:	www.scunthorpespeedway.com
CLUB CHAIRMEN:	Norman Beeney & Robert Godfrey.
MAIN TEAM SPONSORS:	Henderson Insurance Brokers & Lincs FM.
TRACK LENGTH:	285 metres.
TRACK RECORD:	56.92 seconds - Tai Woffinden (07/10/07).
FIRST MEETING:	27 March 2005.
YEARS OF OPERATION:	2004 Training; 2005-2007 Conference League.
PREVIOUS VENUES:	(1) Quibell Park, Brumby Wood Lane, Scunthorpe, North Lincolnshire, DN17 1ST.
YEARS OF OPERATION:	1971 Open; 1972-1974 British League Division Two; 1975-1978 National League.
PREVIOUS VENUES:	(2) Ashby Ville Stadium, off Queensway, Ashby, Scunthorpe, North Lincolnshire.
YEARS OF OPERATION:	1979-1985 National League.

CLUB HONOURS

PAIRS CHAMPIONS: 2006. NOTE: The side that took the plaudits of victory were Scunthorpe 'B'.

CONFERENCE SHIELD WINNERS: 2006.

KNOCK-OUT CUP WINNERS: 2006, 2007.

LEAGUE CHAMPIONS: 2006, 2007.

CONFERENCE TROPHY WINNERS: 2006, 2007.

FOUR-TEAM CHAMPIONS: 2007.

Scott Anderson enjoyed only a handful of outings with the Scorpions in 2007, his best performance being a return of 4+2 points from the side's massive 68-24 league victory at Sittingbourne on 17 June.

(Photo: www.juliemartinphotography.co.uk)

SCUNTHORPE 2007

* Denotes aggregate/bonus-point victory

NO.	DATE	OPPONENTS	VENUE	COMPETITION	RESULT	RICHIE DENNIS	BYRON BEKKER	JOSH AUTY	BENJI COMPTON	TAI WOFFINDEN	SCOTT RICHARDSON	JOE HAINES	ANDREW TULLY	SCOTT ANDERSON	OTHER RIDERS
1	25/3	Boston	H	LC	W55-41	11+2 (5)	9+2 (4)	14+1 (6)	10+1 (6)	R/R	2+1 (4)	9+1 (5)	-	-	-
2	6/4	Boston	A	LC	W54-41*	6+1 (4)	6+2 (4)	10+1 (5)	9 (4)	12 (5)	7 (4)	4+2 (4)	-	-	-
3	8/4	US Dream Team	H	Chal	W62-31	4+2 (3)	10+1 (4)	6+3 (4)	-	6 (4)	9+4 (5)	13 (5)	14 (5)	-	-
4	29/4	Boston	H	CT	W58-35	11+1 (5)	12+2 (6)	14+2 (6)	9+1 (5)	R/R	4+2 (4)	8+1 (4)	-	-	-
5	4/5	Boston	A	CT	W52-40*	7 (4)	5+1 (3)	10 (5)	8+1 (4)	14 (5)	3+1 (5)	5 (4)	-	-	-
6	6/5	Buxton	A	CT	W52-37	4+2 (4)	3 (4)	12 (4)	-	9 (4)	3+1 (5)	11+1 (5)	10+1 (4)	-	-
7	7/5	Buxton	H	CT	W64-28*	8+3 (4)	9+1 (4)	7+2 (4)	12+1 (5)	-	5+2 (4)	9+2 (4)	14 (5)	-	-
8	19/5	Weymouth	A	CL	W48-44	7+3 (5)	10 (6)	17 (6)	-	R/R	5+1 (5)	8+1 (5)	-	1 (3)	-
9	20/5	Stoke	H	CT	W69-21	10+2 (4)	7 (4)	13+2 (5)	-	15 (5)	6+3 (4)	8+2 (4)	10+2 (4)	-	-
10	23/5	Stoke	A	CT	W58-36*	10+1 (5)	7+1 (4)	9 (4)	-	13+1 (5)	5+1 (4)	4 (4)	10+2 (4)	-	-
11	1/6	Plymouth	A	CL	W46-43	7 (4)	0 (3)	13+1 (5)	-	15 (5)	-	8 (5)	-	3+2 (5)	DNA
12	10/6	Rye House	H	KO	W59-31	8+1 (5)	9+2 (5)	16+2 (6)	-	R/R	2 (3)	9 (5)	15+3 (6)	-	-
13	16/6	Rye House	A	KO	L41-52*	10 (6)	7+1 (5)	12+1 (6)	-	R/R	1 (3)	7+1 (5)	-	-	4+1 (5)
14	17/6	Sittingbourne	A	CL	W68-24	11 (4)	7+3 (4)	14+1 (5)	-	-	8+2 (4)	15 (5)	-	4+2 (4)	9+3 (4)
15	23/6	Sittingbourne	H	CL	W60-29*	11+1 (5)	6+1 (4)	11+1 (4)	-	-	6+3 (4)	10+4 (5)	8+1 (4)	-	8+1 (4)
16	8/7	Stoke	H	CL	W67-23	9+2 (4)	13+1 (5)	10+2 (4)	8+2 (4)	-	10+3 (5)	8+1 (4)	9+2 (4)	-	-
17	27/7	Rye House	A	CL	W48-43	8+2 (4)	7 (4)	-	8+1 (4)	12 (5)	1+1 (4)	5+1 (5)	-	-	7 (4)
18	29/7	Weymouth	H	CL	W54-37*	14+1 (5)	6+1 (4)	-	-	9 (4)	5 (4)	13+2 (5)	-	2 (4)	5+1 (4)
19	2/8	Cleveland	A	CL	W57-34	7+1 (5)	7+1 (4)	R/R	-	17+1 (6)	4+1 (4)	8+1 (5)	14+1 (6)	-	-
20	5/8	Boston	H	CL	W50-31	7+2 (5)	7+1 (4)	R/R	6+2 (4)	14 (5)	5+3 (4)	11+1 (4)	-	-	-
21	12/8	Rye House	H	CL	W61-28*	12+2 (5)	10+2 (4)	-	10+1 (4)	-	5 (4)	9+1 (4)	13+1 (5)	2+1 (4)	-
22	17/8	Boston	A	CL	L43-46*	6+2 (6)	9+1 (5)	0 (3)	14+1 (6)	R/R	0 (4)	14 (6)	-	-	-
23	24/8	Plymouth	A	CTf	W59-33	13+2 (5)	5+1 (5)	14+4 (6)	-	18 (6)	0 (4)	9 (4)	R/R	-	-
24	26/8	Buxton	A	CL	W54-38	5 (4)	8+1 (4)	5+1 (4)	-	14 (5)	3+1 (4)	7+2 (4)	12+1 (5)	-	-
25	27/8	Buxton	H	CL	W58-35*	11 (5)	6 (4)	912 (4)	11+2 (5)	-	3+1 (4)	8+2 (4)	10+1 (4)	-	-
26	29/8	Stoke	A	CL	W60-32*	7 (4)	5+2 (4)	8+1 (4)	-	15 (5)	6+2 (4)	11+5 (5)	8+1 (4)	-	-
27	2/9	Plymouth	H	CTf	W65-28*	12 (5)	10+2 (5)	14+1 (5)	-	R/R	6+4 (5)	10+2 (5)	13+2 (5)	-	-
28	9/9	Cleveland	H	CL	W54-28*	R/R	6+3 (4)	18 (6)	6+1 (4)	-	7+2 (5)	10+3 (5)	17+1 (6)	-	-
29	14/9	Oxford	A	CL	L45-47	5+1 (5)	8+2 (5)	17 (6)	-	R/R	1 (3)	6+3 (6)	-	-	8+1 (5)
30	16/9	Plymouth	H	CL	W52-40*	8+3 (6)	13+1 (6)	15+1 (6)	R/R	-	5+2 (6)	11+1 (5)	0 (1)	-	-
31	24/9	Oxford	H	CL	W58-35*	0 (1)	12 (6)	15+1 (6)	-	17+1 (6)	8+3 (6)	6 (5)	R/R	-	-
32	30/9	Boston	H	KOs	W51-45	-	8 (6)	11+3 (6)	6 (3)	R/R	5+2 (4)	14 (6)	-	-	7+2 (5)
33	5/10	Boston	A	KOs	W62-30	-	10+2 (5)	16+2 (6)	-	14+1 (6)	7+3 (4)	10 (5)	R/R	-	5 (4)
34	7/10	Boston	H	POs	W63-30	-	9+3 (5)	10 (4)	7 (3)	13+2 (5)	5+3 (4)	12+1 (5)	-	-	7+2 (4)
35	12/10	Boston	A	POs	W56-36*	-	8+2 (4)	13+1 (5)	6 (4)	15 (5)	4+2 (4)	7+1 (4)	-	-	3+1 (4)
36	19/10	Oxford	A	POf	W47-42	-	10 (6)	R/R	5+1 (5)	17+1 (6)	1+1 (3)	10+2 (6)	-	-	4+1 (4)
37	21/10	Oxford	H	POf	W61-31*	-	14+3 (6)	R/R	11 (5)	15+3 (6)	4+1 (3)	14+1 (6)	-	-	3+1 (4)
38	26/10	Plymouth	A	KOf	L44-49	-	13+1 (6)	R/R	5 (5)	17 (6)	0 (4)	8+1 (6)	-	1 (3)	-
39	28/10	Plymouth	H	KOf	W58-35*	-	13+1 (5)	R/R	8+3 (5)	18 (6)	9+1 (4)	10+3 (6)	-	0 (4)	-
40	30/10	Sheffield	H	HT	L44-45	-	6+2 (5)	R/R	7 (5)	6 (3)	3+1 (5)	-	-	-	22 (12)

ADDITIONAL KEY: LC = Lincolnshire Cup; HT = Hallowe'en Trophy.

NOTE: (1) Josh Auty is not credited with a full maximum in the Conference Trophy fixture at Buxton on 6 May, as he was nominated to appear in heat fifteen, but fell and was unable to participate in the re-run; (2) The home Conference League match versus Boston on 5 August was abandoned after heat thirteen, with the result permitted to stand; (3) The away leg of the Knock-Out Cup semi-final versus Boston was actually staged at Scunthorpe.

Details of other riders (all guests unless **highlighted**): Match No. 11: Bob Charles DNA; Match No. 13: **James Cockle** 4+1 (5); Match No. 14: **James Cockle** 9+3 (4); Match No. 15: **James Cockle** 8+1 (4); Match No. 17: **James Cockle** 7 (4); Match No. 18: **James Cockle** 5+1 (4); Match No. 29: **James Cockle** 8+1 (5); Match No. 32: **James Cockle** 7+2 (5); Match No. 33: **James Cockle** 5 (4); Match No. 34: **James Cockle** 7+2 (4); Match No. 35: **James Cockle** 3+1 (4); Match No. 36: **James Cockle** 4+1 (4); Match No. 37: **James Cockle** 3+1 (4); Match No. 40: Adam Roynon 11 (6); Carl Wilkinson 11 (6).

Details of tactical rides and tactical substitute rides: Match No. 13: Dennis 6 points (TR); Match No. 29: Auty 4 points (TR); Match No. 38: Woffinden 6 points (TR).

Other details: USA Dream Team scorers in Match No. 3: Bryan Yarrow 11 (5); Tommy Hedden 8 (5); Neil Facchini 6 (4); Tim Gomez 3 (4); J.T. Mabry 2 (4); Kenny Ingalls 1 (4); Dale Facchini 0 (4). Yarrow's tally includes 6 points from a TR; Hedden's total includes 1 point from a TS (not doubled).

AVERAGES

[18 Conference League; 4 Play-Offs; 6 Knock-Out Cup; 8 Conference Trophy = 36 fixtures]

• Denotes ever-present.

Rider	Mts	Rds	Pts	Bon	Tot	Avge	Max
Tai Woffinden	20	106	288	10	298	11.25	6 full; 5 paid
Andrew Tully	15	67	163	19	182	10.87	5 paid
Josh Auty	27	135	321	31	352	10.43	1 full; 8 paid
Joe Haines •	36	175	333	42	375	8.57	1 full; 2 paid
Benji Compton	17	75	140	17	157	8.37	-
Richie Dennis	27	124	225	32	257	8.29	3 paid
Byron Bekker •	36	168	299	43	342	8.14	1 paid
James Cockle	12	51	70	14	84	6.59	1 paid
Scott Richardson	35	145	152	52	204	5.63	-
Scott Anderson	7	27	13	5	18	2.67	-

INDIVIDUAL MEETINGS

1 April: Wayne Carter Farewell

1st Garry Stead (after run-off) 10; 2nd Simon Lambert 10; 3rd Robbie Kessler (after run-off) 9; Chris Kerr 9; Ben Wilson 9; Andrew Tully 9; Josh Auty 8; Peter Carr 8; Byron Bekker 8; Ronnie Correy 7; Paul Cooper 6; Daniel Nermark 6; Derek Sneddon 5; Jack Hargreaves 5; Lee Complin 4; Richie Dennis 3; Joe Haines (Res) 2; Scott Richardson (Res) 2.

18 April: British Under-21 Championship (Qualifying Round)

QUALIFYING SCORES: Tai Woffinden 15; Josh Auty 14; Andrew Tully 13; Scott Richardson 10; Benji Compton 9; Jamie Courtney 9; Joe Haines 9; James Cockle 8; Richie Dennis 8; Sean Stoddart 7; Simon Lambert 5; Kriss Irving 4; Gary Beaton 3; Ben Hannon (Res) 2; Jerran Hart (Res) 2; Darren Mallett 1; Charles Wright 0.

SEMI-FINAL: 1st Compton; 2nd Courtney; 3rd Richardson; 4th Tully.

FINAL: 1st Woffinden; 2nd Auty; 3rd Courtney; 4th Compton.

3 June: Henderson Insurance Trophy

QUALIFYING SCORES: Andrew Tully 11; Joe Haines 10; Josh Auty 10; Greg Blair 9; Scott Richardson 7; Simon Lambert 5; Byron Bekker 5; Rusty Hodgson 4; Jonathan Bethell 4; Jack Roberts 2; Richie Dennis 1; Scott Anderson 1.

FIRST SEMI-FINAL: 1st Tully; 2nd Bethell; 3rd Hodgson; 4th Blair.

SECOND SEMI-FINAL: 1st Auty; 2nd Bekker; 3rd Lambert; 4th Haines.

FINAL: 1st Auty; 2nd Tully; 3rd Bekker; 4th Bethell.

23 September: David Nix Memorial Trophy

QUALIFYING SCORES: Adam Roynon 15; Tero Aarnio 11; Simon Lambert 11; Darren Mallett 11; Byron Bekker 10; Benji Compton 9; Mark Thompson 9; Jonathan Bethell 9; Joni Keskinen 8; Karl Mason 7; Scott Richardson 7; Martin Emerson 4; Nathan Irwin 3; Ricky Scarboro 3; Mark Richardson (Res) 2; Adam Lowe 1; Wayne Dunworth 0.

SEMI-FINAL: 1st Compton; 2nd Bekker; 3rd Mallett; 4th Lambert.

FINAL: 1st Roynon; 2nd Compton; 3rd Aarnio; 4th Bekker.

Scunthorpe, 2007

Back row, left to right: Byron Bekker, Scott Richardson, Richie Dennis, Andrew Tully and Kenny Smith (Team Manager).

Front row: Joe Haines, Tai Woffinden and Josh Auty.

(Photo: Ian Charles)

SITTINGBOURNE CRUSADERS

ADDRESS:	The Old Gun Site, Raspberry Hill Lane, Iwade, Nr Sittingbourne, Kent, ME9 8SP.
TELEPHONE:	01795 430014.
CLUB HOTLINE:	07857 849551 (Premium rate applies).
WEBSITE:	www.sittingbournespeedway.co.uk
CLUB CHAIRMAN:	Graham Arnold.
MAIN TEAM SPONSOR:	Spray-Tex.
TRACK LENGTH:	251 metres.
TRACK RECORD:	58.0 seconds - Paul Hurry (30/10/05).
FIRST MEETING:	5 November 1972.
YEARS OF OPERATION:	1971 Training; 1972-1993 Open and Training; 1994 British League Division Three; 1995 Academy League; 1996 Conference League; 1997-2003 Open and Training; 2004 Conference League Knock-Out Cup, Open and Training; 2005 Conference League; 2006 Conference Shield; 2007 Conference League.

Dean Felton was the mainstay of the Sittingbourne side in 2007, appearing in all twenty of their official matches.

(Photo: Ian Charles)

SITTINGBOURNE 2007

* Denotes aggregate/bonus-point victory

NO.	DATE	OPPONENTS	VENUE	COMPETITION	RESULT	DEAN FELTON	JOE REYNOLDS	ANDRE CROSS	MARK BASEBY	GORDON MEAKINS	AARON BASEBY	LUKE GOODY	JON STEVENS	DANNY WARWICK	OTHER RIDERS
1	9/4	Rye House	A	KO	L29-61	8 (5)	3+2 (4)	0 (4)	9+1 (5)	1+1 (3)	5 (5)	3 (4)	-	-	-
2	22/4	Cleveland	H	CL	L38-54	16+1 (5)	2+1 (4)	3 (4)	8 (5)	0 (3)	6+1 (5)	3+1 (4)	-	-	-
3	22/4	Rye House	H	KO	L32-59	7 (4)	3 (3)	-	14 (5)	-	3 (4)	3 (5)	2+1 (5)	-	0 (4)
4	13/5	Stoke	H	CL	L44-49	6+1 (4)	3+1 (3)	-	11 (5)	3 (3)	8+1 (6)	3 (4)	-	10 (5)	-
5	30/5	Stoke	A	CL	L43-52	8 (5)	4+2 (4)	3 (4)	10+1 (5)	-	2 (3)	-	-	14 (5)	2+1 (4)
6	10/6	Buxton	H	CL	L42-48	6 (4)	2+2 (4)	4 (4)	9 (5)	-	6 (5)	2+1 (4)	-	13 (5)	-
7	17/6	Scunthorpe	H	CL	L24-68	6 (5)	0 (3)	0 (4)	8 (4)	2+1 (4)	6 (6)	-	2 (5)	-	-
8	23/6	Scunthorpe	A	CL	L29-60	5 (4)	1+1 (3)	0 (4)	10 (5)	-	2 (4)	-	-	5 (4)	6+1 (6)
9	14/7	Rye House	A	CL	L28-61	7 (5)	1 (5)	2+1 (4)	8 (5)	-	2+1 (4)	-	-	3 (2)	5 (5)
10	27/7	Boston	A	CL	L38-55	4 (4)	2 (3)	-	8 (5)	-	2 (4)	-	-	18 (5)	4+1 (9)
11	29/7	Buxton	A	CL	L31-56	8 (5)	0 (2)	-	3 (4)	-	5+1 (4)	-	-	5 (4)	10+3 (11)
12	5/8	Oxford	H	CL	W45-44	9+1 (5)	-	-	R/R	-	7 (4)	-	2+1 (2)	14 (6)	13+4 (12)
13	10/8	Weymouth	A	CL	L27-62	7 (5)	2 (4)	-	6 (6)	-	4+1 (6)	-	-	R/R	8 (9)
14	12/8	Oxford	A	CL	L21-71	9 (6)	1 (4)	-	-	-	-	-	0 (3)	R/R	11 (17)
15	17/8	Plymouth	A	CL	L28-64	14 (6)	2 (6)	0 (1)	R/R	-	-	-	-	-	12+1 (17)
16	25/8	Cleveland	A	CL	D45-45	10 (5)	1 (3)	-	15 (5)	-	3+2 (4)	-	-	-	16+1 (14)
17	2/9	Weymouth	H	CL	L43-47	4+2 (4)	-	-	8+2 (4)	-	5+3 (4)	-	-	2 (4)	24+1 (14)
18	2/9	Rye House	H	CL	W49-39	10 (4)	1 (3)	-	14 (5)	-	5+1 (4)	-	-	3+1 (4)	16+2 (10)
19	9/9	Plymouth	H	CL	L38-51	6+1 (5)	0 (3)	4+1 (4)	R/R	-	5+2 (6)	-	-	-	23+3 (13)
20	9/9	Boston	H	CL	L40-53	12+2 (6)	4 (4)	4 (4)	R/R	-	3+2 (5)	-	-	-	17 (11)

Details of other riders (all guests unless **highlighted**): Match No. 3: **Martin Elliott** 0 (4); Match No. 5: Jerran Hart 2+1 (4); Match No. 8: Jerran Hart 6+1 (6); Match No. 9: Jerran Hart 5 (5); Match No. 10: **Jerran Hart** 3+1 (5); **James Theobald** 1 (4); Match No. 11: **Jerran Hart** 8+2 (7); **Harland Cook** 2+1 (4); Match No. 12: **Jerran Hart** 10+1 (6); **Harland Cook** 3+3 (4); **James Theobald** 0 (2); Match No. 13: **Jerran Hart** 8 (6); **Harland Cook** 0 (3); Match No. 14: **Jerran Hart** 7 (7); **Harland Cook** 3 (4); **James Theobald** 1 (5); Alex McLeod 0 (1); Match No. 15: **Harland Cook** 6 (6); **Jerran Hart** 3 (6); Jaimie Pickard 3+1 (5); Match No. 16: **Jerran Hart** 9 (6); **Harland Cook** 4+1 (4); **James Theobald** 3 (4); Match No. 17: **Jerran Hart** 12 (6); **Harland Cook** 10+1 (5); **James Theobald** 2 (3); Match No. 18: **Jerran Hart** 12+2 (6); **Harland Cook** 4 (4); Match No. 19: **Jerran Hart** 16 (7); **Harland Cook** 6+2 (5); Rikki Mullins 1+1 (1); Match No. 19: **Harland Cook** 11 (5); **Jerran Hart** 6 (5); Rikki Mullins 0 (1).

Details of tactical rides and tactical substitute rides: Match No. 1: M. Baseby 1 point (TR; not doubled); Match No. 2: Felton 6 points (TR); Match No. 3: M. Baseby 4 points (TR); Match No. 4: M. Baseby 6 points (TR); Match No. 5: Warwick 6 points (TS); Felton 4 points (TR); Match No. 7: M. Baseby 4 points (TR); Match No. 8: M. Baseby 1 point (TR; not doubled); Match No. 9: M. Baseby 6 points (TR); Match No. 10: Warwick 6 points (TR); Match No. 11: M. Baseby 1 point (TR; not doubled); Match No. 13: Felton 4 points (TR); Match No. 14: Felton 4 points (TR); Match No. 15: Felton 4 points (TR).

AVERAGES

[18 Conference League; 2 Knock-Out Cup = 20 fixtures]

• Denotes ever-present.

Rider	Mts	Rds	Pts	Bon	Tot	Avge	Max
Danny Warwick	10	44	81	1	82	7.45	1 full
Mark Baseby	15	73	131	4	135	7.40	1 full
Dean Felton •	20	96	151	8	159	6.63	-
Jerran Hart	11	67	94	6	100	5.97	-
Harland Cook	10	44	49	8	57	5.18	-
Aaron Baseby	18	83	79	15	94	4.53	-
Joe Reynolds	18	65	32	9	41	2.52	-
Andre Cross	10	37	20	2	22	2.38	-

Also rode (in alphabetical order):

Martin Elliott	1	4	0	0	0	0.00	-
Luke Goody	5	21	14	2	16	3.05	-
Gordon Meakins	4	13	6	2	8	2.46	-
Jon Stevens	4	15	6	2	8	2.13	-
James Theobald	5	18	7	0	7	1.56	-
Guests	7	23	17	4	21	3.65	-

(Jerran Hart [3]; Alex McLeod [1]; Rikki Mullins [2]; Jaimie Pickard [1])

OTHER MEETING

21 October: **Spray-Tex Fours**
Wimbledon 29: Barry Burchatt 17 (6); Alex McLeod 6 (5); Richard Sar-Butt 6 (5); Andre Cross 0 (0), Spray-Tex Crusaders 27: Dean Felton 10 (4); Aaron Baseby 9 (4); Shane Henry 5 (4); Andy Garner 3 (4), Duggo 7 Hammers 20: Jerran Hart 11 (5); Rikki Mullins 7 (4); Cecil Forbes 2 (3); Chris Neame 0 (4), BTS Mouldings 18: Jack Swann 8 (5); Harland Cook 7 (4); Michael Bovis 3 (6); Marc Andrews 0 (1).

Sittingbourne, 2007

Back row, left to right: Aaron Baseby, Dean Felton, Harland Cook, Mark Baseby and Chris Hunt (Team Manager).

Front row: Joe Reynolds, Danny Warwick, Jerran Hart and Marc Owen (Mascot).

(Photo: Ian Charles)

STOKE SPITFIRES

NOTE: The information below relates only to the second Stoke team. For details of the main side, please refer to the Premier League section.

ADDRESS:	Chesterton Stadium, Loomer Road, Chesterton, Newcastle-under-Lyme, Staffordshire, ST5 7LB.
TELEPHONE:	01782 566799 / 01782 562184.
CLUB HOTLINE:	09068 664669 (Premium rate applies).
WEBSITE:	N/A.
CLUB CHAIRMAN:	David Tattum.
MAIN TEAM SPONSOR:	SAS Securities.
TRACK LENGTH:	312 metres.
CL TRACK RECORD:	62.0 seconds - Andrew Tully (29/08/07).
FIRST MEETING:	13 April 2003.
YEARS OF OPERATION:	2003 Conference Trophy; 2004-2007 Conference League.

CLUB HONOURS
FOUR-TEAM CHAMPIONS: 2006.

Barrie Evans enjoyed a great campaign with the Spitfires, top scoring in virtually every match.

(Photo: Ian Charles)

STOKE 2007

*Denotes aggregate/bonus-point victory

NO.	DATE	OPPONENTS	VENUE	COMPETITION	RESULT	BARRIE EVANS	DAVID HAIGH	JACK HARGREAVES	KRISS IRVING	GARETH ISHERWOOD	SAM DORE	GUY KENDREW	JOHN BRANNEY	GARY FLINT	OTHER RIDERS
1	13/4	Boston	A	CT	L37-55	20 (6)	0 (3)	R/R	3+1 (5)	2 (3)	7 (6)	5 (6)	13+1 (6)	-	0 (1)
2	18/4	Weymouth	H	KO	W50-40	15 (6)	1 (3)	R/R	7+2 (5)	-	14+1 (7)	0 (3)	-	-	-
3	20/4	Weymouth	A	KO	L32-54	12 (5)	1 (3)	R/R	4 (5)	-	2 (3)	1+1 (7)	12 (5)	-	-
4	13/5	Sittingbourne	A	CL	W49-44	16 (6)	5+1 (4)	R/R	2+1 (4)	-	7+2 (6)	-	12+1 (6)	-	7+1 (4)
5	29/4	Buxton	A	CT	L39-52	15+1 (6)	2 (4)	9 (5)	2 (5)	-	11+1 (7)	0 (3)	-	-	R/R
6	20/5	Scunthorpe	A	CT	L21-69	6 (6)	1 (3)	6 (6)	0 (4)	-	4+2 (5)	-	R/R	-	4 (6)
7	23/5	Scunthorpe	H	CT	L36-58	8 (6)	2 (4)	4 (4)	3 (4)	-	6+1 (4)	1+1 (3)	12 (5)	-	-
8	25/5	Weymouth	A	CL	L40-51	13 (6)	2 (3)	R/R	2+1 (5)	-	10+1 (5)	-	12 (6)	-	1+1 (5)
9	30/5	Sittingbourne	H	CL	W52-43*	10 (4)	-	11+2 (5)	2 (4)	-	6+1 (3)	8 (5)	12+1 (5)	3 (4)	-
10	8/6	Plymouth	A	CL	L25-67	13 (6)	-	R/R	-	-	4 (6)	0 (3)	5 (4)	3 (7)	0 (2)
11	28/6	Cleveland	A	CL	L36-57	13 (6)	-	12 (5)	-	2 (3)	3+1 (4)	1 (4)	4 (4)	1+1 (4)	-
12	8/7	Scunthorpe	A	CL	L23-67	11 (6)	-	5 (5)	-	2 (4)	2 (4)	1 (3)	-	0 (4)	2 (4)
13	14/7	Boston	H	CT	W47-43	16+1 (6)	-	-	-	13+4 (7)	9+1 (6)	1+1 (3)	R/R	3 (4)	5+1 (4)
14	26/7	Cleveland	H	CL	W51-35	17+1 (6)	-	R/R	-	0 (1)	-	9+1 (7)	17+1 (6)	4 (5)	4 (5)
15	29/7	Oxford	A	CL	L35-57	13 (7)	-	R/R	-	-	6+1 (5)	0 (3)	9 (6)	2+1 (4)	5+1 (5)
16	1/8	Buxton	H	CT	L44-46	13+1 (5)	-	-	-	2+1 (4)	7+2 (4)	1+1 (4)	14 (5)	2 (4)	5 (4)
17	3/8	Boston	A	CL	L44-52	19 (6)	-	-	-	1 (5)	5+1 (4)	0 (3)	16+1 (5)	0 (4)	3 (4)
18	8/8	Boston	H	CL	D46-46	15 (5)	-	-	-	5 (4)	4+1 (4)	0 (4)	16+1 (5)	-	6 (9)
19	22/8	Weymouth	H	CL	W47-43	13+1 (5)	-	-	-	4+2 (4)	3+1 (4)	4+1 (4)	12+1 (5)	-	11 (8)
20	29/8	Scunthorpe	H	CL	L32-60	4+1 (4)	-	-	-	3+1 (3)	0 (3)	4+1 (5)	12 (6)	-	9 (9)
21	12/9	Plymouth	A	CL	L44-49	16+1 (5)	-	-	-	2 (4)	6 (4)	2+1 (6)	14+1 (5)	-	4+1 (7)
22	16/9	Rye House	A	CL	L38-54	5+1 (5)	-	-	-	7+1 (5)	-	4+3 (4)	15 (6)	-	7 (10)
23	29/9	Oxford	H	CL	L37-55	14 (7)	-	-	-	5 (5)	-	1 (4)	R/R	-	17+1 (14)
24	17/10	Rye House	H	CL	W52-40	14+1 (5)	-	-	-	8+1 (4)	5+2 (4)	4+1 (4)	12+1 (5)	-	9+2 (8)
25	20/10	Buxton	H	CL	W53-39	13 (6)	-	-	-	6+1 (4)	10+1 (5)	5+2 (4)	R/R	-	19+4 (11)
26	21/10	Buxton	A	CL	W54-39*	8+1 (4)	-	-	-	7+2 (4)	10+2 (5)	3+2 (4)	13 (5)	-	13+1 (8)

NOTE: The Knock-Out Cup tie at Weymouth on 20 April was abandoned after heat fourteen, with the result permitted to stand.

Details of other riders (all guests unless **highlighted**): Match No. 1: Jerran Hart 0 (1); Match No. 4: Jerran Hart 7+1 (4); Match No. 5: **Rob Grant** R/R; Match No. 6: Scott Anderson 4 (6); Match No. 8: Olly Gay 1+1 (5); Match No. 10: Sam Wyatt 0 (2); Match No. 12: Jerran Hart 2 (4); Match No. 13: Jaimie Pickard 5+1 (4); Match No. 14: Jaimie Pickard 4 (5); Match No. 15: Jaimie Pickard 5+1 (5); Match No. 16: Jaimie Pickard 5 (4); Match No. 17: Jaimie Pickard 3 (4); Match No. 18: Jaimie Pickard 4 (5); Billy Legg 2 (4); Match No. 19: Jonathan Bethell 8 (4); Billy Legg 3 (4); Match No. 20: **Jonathan Bethell** 4 (4); Billy Legg 5 (5); Match No. 21: **Billy Legg** 2+1 (3); **Jonathan Bethell** 2 (4); Match No. 22: **Jonathan Bethell** 6 (4); Chris Widman 1 (3); Dan Blake 0 (3); Match No. 23: **Jonathan Bethell** 12 (5); Billy Legg 5+1 (6); Adam Chandler 0 (3); Match No. 24: **Jonathan Bethell** 7+1 (4); **Billy Legg** 2+1 (4); Match No. 25: **Jonathan Bethell** 10+2 (6); **Billy Legg** 9+2 (5); Match No. 26: **Billy Legg** 7+1 (4); **Luke Priest** 6 (4).

Details of tactical rides and tactical substitute rides: Match No. 1: Evans 6 points (TR); Match No. 3: Branney 6 points (TR); Match No. 5: Evans 6 points (TR); Match No. 6: Evans 1 point (TR; not doubled); Match No. 7: Branney 6 points (TR); Evans 2 points (TS); Match No. 8: Dore 4 points (TR); Match No. 10: Evans 4 points (TR); Match No. 11: Hargreaves 4 points (TR); Evans 2 points (TS); Match No. 12: Hargreaves 1 point (TR; not doubled); Evans 1 point (TS; not doubled); Match No. 15: Branney 2 points (TS); Evans 2 points (TS); Match No. 17: Branney 6 points (TR); Evans 6 points (TS); Match No. 18: Branney 6 points (TR); Match No. 20: Branney 4 points (TS); Evans 0 points (TR); Match No. 21: Evans 6 points (TR); Match No. 22: Branney 4 points (TS); Evans 0 points (TR); Match No. 23: Bethell 4 points (TR); Evans 0 points (TS).

AVERAGES

[18 Conference League; 2 Knock-Out Cup; 6 Conference Trophy = 26 fixtures]

• Denotes ever-present.

Rider	Mts	Rds	Pts	Bon	Tot	Avge	Max
Barrie Evans •	26	145	315	10	325	8.97	1 full; 2 paid
John Branney	19	100	215	9	224	8.96	2 paid
Jack Hargreaves	6	30	45	2	47	6.27	-
Jonathan Bethell	6	27	39	3	42	6.22	-
Sam Dore	23	108	139	22	161	5.96	-
Gareth Isherwood	16	64	69	13	82	5.13	-
Guy Kendrew	23	96	55	16	71	2.96	-
Kriss Irving	9	41	25	5	30	2.93	-
David Haigh	8	27	14	1	15	2.22	-
Gary Flint	9	40	18	2	20	2.00	-

Also rode (in alphabetical order):

Billy Legg	5	22	25	6	31	5.64	-
Luke Priest	1	4	6	0	6	6.00	-
Guests	19	75	59	4	63	3.36	-

(Scott Anderson [1]; Jonathan Bethell [1]; Dan Blake [1]; Adam Chandler [1]; Olly Gay [1]; Jerran Hart [3]; Billy Legg [3]; Jaimie Pickard [6]; Chris Widman [1]; Sam Wyatt [1])

Stoke, 2007

Back row, left to right: John Woolridge (Team Manager), Barrie Evans, Kriss Irving and Guy Kendrew.

Front row, kneeling: Jack Hargreaves, David Haigh and Sam Dore.

(Photo: Ian Charles)

WEYMOUTH WILDCATS

ADDRESS:	Wessex Stadium (2), Radipole Lane, Weymouth, Dorset, DT4 9XJ.
TELEPHONE:	01305 773399.
CLUB HOTLINE:	09068 664663 (Premium rate applies).
WEBSITE:	www.wildcatsweymouth.co.uk
CLUB CHAIRMAN:	Phil Bartlett.
MAIN TEAM SPONSOR:	Doonans Building Materials Ltd.
TRACK LENGTH:	223 metres.
TRACK RECORD:	52.2 seconds - Lewis Bridger (11/05/07).
FIRST MEETING:	15 August 2003.
YEARS OF OPERATION:	2003 Open; 2004-2005 Conference League; 2006 Conference Shield; 2007 Conference League.
PREVIOUS VENUE:	Wessex Stadium (1), Radipole Lane, Weymouth, Dorset.
YEARS OF OPERATION:	1954 Open; 1955 National League Division Two; 1962-1963 Open; 1964 Metropolitan League; 1965 Open; 1966-1967 Training; 1968 British League Division 2; 1969-1970 Training; 1971-1973 Open & Training; 1974 British League Division Two; 1975-1984 National League; 1985 Open & Training.

CLUB HONOURS

PAIRS CHAMPIONS: 1982, 1983.

FOUR-TEAM CHAMPIONS: 2005.

KNOCK-OUT CUP WINNERS: 2005.

Weymouth, 2007

Back row, left to right: Jem Dicken (Club Director), Karl Mason, Adam Filmer, Terry Day, George Piper, Jamie Westacott and Phil Bartlett (Club Chairman).

Front row: Sam Hurst, David Mason (on bike), Callum Gordon (Mascot) and Nathan Irwin.

(Photo: www.juliemartinphotography.co.uk)

WEYMOUTH 2007

* Denotes aggregate/bonus-point victory

NO.	DATE	OPPONENTS	VENUE	COMPETITION	RESULT	DAVID MASON	NATHAN IRWIN	KARL MASON	SAM HURST	LEE SMART	ADAM FILMER	TERRY DAY	GEORGE PIPER	JAY HERNE	OTHER RIDERS
1	6/4	US Dream Team	H	Chal	L44-45	7 (5)	8+2 (6)	16 (6)	4+1 (4)	R/R	3+1 (4)	6 (5)	-	-	-
2	8/4	Oxford	A	CT	L34-57	8+1 (5)	3 (4)	6+1 (4)	3 (4)	10 (5)	-	3+1 (5)	1+1 (3)	-	-
3	18/4	Stoke	A	KO	L40-50	10 (5)	4+1 (4)	7 (5)	5 (4)	-	3+2 (4)	4+1 (4)	-	-	7 (4)
4	20/4	Stoke	H	KO	W54-32*	8+2 (4)	10+1 (4)	6+2 (4)	8 (4)	11+1 (4)	1+1 (3)	10+2 (5)	-	-	-
5	27/4	Oxford	H	CT	W52-41	14+1 (5)	5+1 (4)	7+1 (4)	4+1 (4)	9+1 (4)	-	12 (6)	1 (3)	-	-
6	4/5	Plymouth	A	CT	L34-60	9 (4)	2+2 (4)	6 (5)	4 (4)	12 (6)	1 (6)	0 (1)	-	-	-
7	5/5	Plymouth	H	CT	L44-48	5+1 (4)	6+1 (4)	7 (5)	4+2 (4)	17 (6)	0 (3)	5+1 (4)	-	-	-
8	11/5	Exeter Select	H	Chal	W45-44	5+2 (4)	8 (4)	10 (5)	4+1 (4)	11 (5)	-	5+1 (2)	2+1 (3)	-	-
9	19/5	Scunthorpe	H	CL	L44-48	14 (5)	6 (4)	6 (5)	2+2 (4)	7 (4)	-	7+2 (5)	2+1 (3)	-	-
10	25/5	Stoke	H	CL	W51-40	10+1 (5)	8 (4)	10+1 (4)	6 (4)	8+1 (5)	-	9+1 (7)	0 (1)	-	-
11	1/6	Buxton	H	KO	W51-45	7+1 (5)	7+1 (4)	6+1 (4)	6 (4)	10+1 (5)	1 (1)	14+3 (7)	-	-	-
12	16/6	Plymouth	H	CL	W48-44	5+1 (4)	3+1 (3)	6+1 (5)	0 (3)	14+1 (5)	-	0 (3)	-	20+1 (7)	-
13	23/6	Cleveland	H	CL	W57-33	12+3 (6)	9+3 (5)	11+1 (5)	4+2 (4)	R/R	-	7+1 (4)	-	14+1 (6)	-
14	29/6	Boston	H	CL	W59-34	8 (4)	5+1 (3)	7+1 (4)	4+3 (3)	12+2 (5)	-	8+1 (4)	-	15+3 (7)	-
15	1/7	Boston	A	CL	L42-47*	8+1 (5)	3 (4)	7+1 (4)	5+1 (4)	7 (5)	-	6+4 (4)	-	6 (4)	-
16	6/7	Rye House	H	CL	W47-46	7+1 (5)	4 (4)	11+2 (6)	7+1 (4)	R/R	-	5+1 (4)	-	13 (7)	-
17	8/7	Buxton	A	KO	W50-43*	8 (4)	3 (3)	5+1 (4)	7+3 (5)	11+1 (4)	-	7+1 (5)	-	9+4 (5)	-
18	10/7	Isle of Wight	A	Chal	L39-51	4+1 (4)	1 (3)	5+1 (5)	5+1 (4)	12 (5)	-	5+1 (4)	-	7+2 (5)	-
19	13/7	Isle of Wight	H	Chal	L32-49	5 (4)	0 (3)	10 (4)	2+2 (3)	6 (4)	-	3+1 (4)	-	6+3 (4)	-
20	15/7	Oxford	A	CL	L44-49	-	-	4 (3)	4+1 (4)	12+1 (5)	-	2 (4)	-	17 (7)	5+1 (7)
21	20/7	Oxford	H	CL	D45-45	-	3+2 (3)	4+1 (4)	3 (4)	15 (5)	-	1 (3)	-	14 (7)	5+1 (4)
22	28/7	Cleveland	A	CL	W46-44*	-	3+1 (4)	6 (4)	5 (4)	12 (5)	-	3+2 (4)	-	11+1 (6)	6 (4)
23	29/7	Scunthorpe	A	CL	L37-54	-	7+2 (5)	9 (5)	6+1 (5)	R/R	-	3+1 (5)	-	5+2 (5)	7 (5)
24	3/8	Newport Select	H	Chal	L44-46	-	5 (5)	-	-	17 (6)	-	10+1 (6)	-	R/R	12+1 (13)
25	5/8	Buxton	A	CL	L35-55	-	14 (6)	1+1 (1)	0 (0)	R/R	-	14+1 (7)	-	-	6 (7)
26	10/8	Sittingbourne	H	CL	W62-27	-	6 (4)	6+3 (5)	13+4 (7)	15 (5)	-	0 (1)	-	10 (4)	12 (4)
27	22/8	Stoke	A	CL	L43-47*	-	5 (4)	7 (4)	-	13 (5)	-	3 (5)	-	4+2 (4)	11+1 (8)
28	24/8	Buxton	H	CL	W58-37*	-	5+1 (5)	11 (5)	-	17+1 (6)	-	10+3 (5)	-	13 (6)	2+1 (3)
29	31/8	Plymouth	A	CL	L43-50	-	2+1 (4)	5+1 (4)	2 (4)	12 (5)	-	2 (4)	-	11 (5)	9+1 (4)
30	2/9	Sittingbourne	A	CL	W47-43*	-	4 (6)	6+1 (5)	6+1 (5)	15 (5)	-	5+1 (5)	-	11 (5)	0 (1)
31	7/9	Wimbledon	H	Chal	W57-38	8 (5)	-	8+2 (4)	8+1 (5)	16+1 (6)	-	-	-	13+1 (5)	4+3 (5)
32	8/9	Rye House	A	CL	L33-58	13 (6)	3+1 (5)	5 (5)	2+1 (4)	R/R	-	5 (5)	-	5+2 (5)	0 (1)
33	28/9	Plymouth	A	KOs	L39-51	5 (4)	2 (4)	1 (4)	6+1 (4)	12 (5)	-	4 (4)	-	9+1 (5)	-
34	29/9	Plymouth	H	KOs	D45-45	5+1 (4)	4 (4)	7 (5)	15+3 (7)	14 (5)	-	-	-	0 (1)	0 (3)

NOTE: (1) The Knock-Out Cup tie versus Stoke on 20 April was abandoned after heat fourteen, with the result permitted to stand; (2) The challenge match at home to the Isle of Wight on 13 July was abandoned after heat thirteen, with the result permitted to stand.

Details of other riders (all guests unless **highlighted**): Match No. 3: **Jamie Westacott** 7 (4); Match No. 20: Mark Thompson 4+1 (4); Kyle Newman 1 (3); Match No. 21: **Mark Thompson** 5+1 (4); Match No. 22: **Mark Thompson** 6 (4); Match No. 23: **Mark Thompson** 7 (5); Match No. 24: **Daniel Giffard** 11+1 (6); Chris Glanville 1 (4); **Kyle Newman** 0 (3); Match No. 25: **Kyle Newman** 6 (7); Match No. 26: **Daniel Giffard** 12 (4); Match No. 27: **Daniel Giffard** 10+1 (5); **Kyle Newman** 1 (3); Match No. 28: **Kyle Newman** 2+1 (3); **Daniel Giffard** R/R; Match No. 29: **Daniel Giffard** 9+1 (4); Match No. 30: **Kyle Newman** 0 (1); **Daniel Giffard** R/R; Match No. 31: **Kyle Newman** 4+3 (5); **Daniel Giffard** R/R; Match No. 32: **Kyle Newman** 0 (1); Match No. 34: **Kyle Newman** 0 (3).

Details of tactical rides and tactical substitute rides: Match No. 2: Smart 4 points (TR); Match No. 6: Smart 4 points (TS); D. Mason 4 points (TR); Match No. 7: Smart 4 points (TS); Match No. 9: D. Mason 4 points (TR); Match No. 18: Day 1 point (TR; not doubled); Match No. 19: K. Mason 4 points (TR); Herne 2 points (TS); Match No. 20: Smart 6 points (TR); Match No. 23: Hurst 4 points (TR); Match No. 25: Irwin 6 points (TR); Match No. 29: Smart 6 points (TR); Match No. 32: D. Mason 4 points (TR); Match No. 33: Day 0 points (TR).

Other details: USA Dream Team scorers in Match No. 1: Bryan Yarrow 10 (4); Tim Gomez 9+2 (5); Tommy Hedden 9+1 (4); Neil Facchini 9 (4); Kenny Ingalls 4 (4); J.T. Mabry 3+2 (5); Dale Facchini 1 (4).; Exeter Select scorers in Match No. 8: Lewis Bridger 18 (6); Tom Brown 12 (6); Andre Cross 8+1 (5); Rob Smith 5 (5); Adam Filmer 1 (5); Jamie Westacott R/R. Bridger's total includes 6 points from a TR.; Newport Select scorers in Match No. 24: Jon Armstrong 13 (5); Mark Burrows 11+1 (6); Sam Hurst 9+2 (6); Karl Mason 5 (4); Billy Legg 5 (5); Alex McLeod 3+1 (4). The Newport side also operated rider replacement at No. 2.; Wimbledon scorers in Match No. 31: Mark Burrows 16 (7); Terry Day 15 (7); Nathan Irwin 6+1 (6); Alex McLeod 1 (4); Martin Elliott 0 (4); Dean Garrod 0 (3); Ray Morton R/R. Day's tally includes 6 points from a TR, while Burrows' total includes 4 points from a TS.

AVERAGES

[18 Conference League; 6 Knock-Out Cup; 4 Conference Trophy = 28 fixtures]

• Denotes ever-present.

Rider	Mts	Rds	Pts	Bon	Tot	Avge	Max
Lee Smart	22	109	253	10	263	9.65	3 full; 4 paid
Jay Herne	18	96	187	17	204	8.50	1 paid
David Mason	18	84	150	14	164	7.81	1 paid
Karl Mason •	28	122	180	20	200	6.56	-
Terry Day	27	120	149	27	176	5.87	-
Sam Hurst	26	107	129	27	156	5.83	-
Nathan Irwin	27	112	133	20	153	5.46	-
Kyle Newman	6	18	9	1	10	2.22	-

Also rode (in alphabetical order):

Adam Filmer	5	17	6	3	9	2.12	-
Daniel Giffard	3	13	31	2	33	10.15	1 full
George Piper	4	10	4	2	6	2.40	-
Mark Thompson	3	13	18	1	19	5.85	-
Jamie Westacott	1	4	7	0	7	7.00	-
Guests	2	7	5	1	6	3.43	-

(Kyle Newman [1]; Mark Thompson [1])

NOTE: Terry Day was ever-present throughout the 18-match Conference League programme.

INDIVIDUAL MEETINGS

13 April: **British Under-21 Championship** (Qualifying Round)

QUALIFYING SCORES: Lee Smart 13; Ben Barker 13; Mark Baseby 13; Robert Mear 12; Daniel Halsey 11; Barry Burchatt 9; Chris Johnson 7; Sam Hurst 7; Lee Strudwick 6; Lewis Dallaway 6; Ben Hopwood 6; Aaron Baseby 5; Adam Filmer 4; George Piper (Res) 3; Joe Reynolds 2; Luke Goody 1.

SEMI-FINAL: 1st Mear; 2nd M. Baseby; 3rd Burchatt; 4th Halsey.

FINAL: 1st Barker; 2nd Smart; 3rd M. Baseby; 4th Mear.

1 September: **British Under-15 Championship** (Round One)

QUALIFYING SCORES: Brendan Johnson 12; James Sarjeant 9; Richard Franklin 7; Dan Greenwood 6; Kye Norton 6; Shane Hazelden 6; Danny Stoneman 6; Montana Jowett 5; John Resch 4; Jack Butler 4; Scott Meakins 3; Chris Bint 2, Michael Bovis (Res) 0.

QUARTER-FINAL: 1st Hazelden; 2nd Jowett; 3rd Stoneman; 4th Butler.

SEMI-FINAL: 1st Norton; 2nd Franklin; 3rd Hazelden; 4th Greenwood.

FINAL: 1st Johnson; 2nd Franklin; 3rd Sarjeant; 4th Norton.

OTHER MEETINGS

8 June: **Wessex Best Pairs**

1st Weymouth 'B' 21 (Lee Smart 12+2; Nathan Irwin 9+2); 2nd Isle of Wight Select 18 (Andrew Bargh 12; Sam Martin 6+1); 3rd Kangaroos 18 (Jay Herne 10+2; Kyle Hughes 8+1); Newport Select 13 (Karl Mason 10; Sam Hurst 3+1); Weymouth 'A' (David Mason 7; Brendan Johnson 3+2); Wimbledon 10 (Terry Day 9; Andre Cross 1+1). Third Place Run-Off: 1st Bargh; 2nd Herne; 3rd Hughes; 4th Martin.

17 August: **MOT Stop Carnival Trophy Four-Team Tournament**

Weymouth 33: Lee Smart 12 (4); Karl Mason 9 (4); Kyle Newman 8 (6); David Mason 4 (2), Wimbledon 24: Daniel Giffard 14 (4); Gary Cottham 7 (4); Martin Elliott 2 (4); Nathan Irwin 1 (4), Poole 24: Jay Herne 11 (4); Terry Day 7 (4); Alex McLeod 5 (4); Chris Glanville 1 (4), Newport 21: Karlis Ezergailis 13 (5); Billy Legg 6 (4); Olly Gay 2 (6); Sam Hurst 0 (1). Three riders took TR outings in the meeting, scoring the following points: Giffard 6, Ezergailis 4 and Herne 2.

Jay Herne, the son of former rider Phil, proved something of a sensation after joining the Wildcats in June.

(Photo: Ian Charles)

MAJOR MEETINGS
2007

MAJOR BRITSH MEETINGS

ELITE LEAGUE PAIRS CHAMPIONSHIP

BRITISH UNDER-21 CHAMPIONSHIP

CONFERENCE LEAGUE FOUR-TEAM CHAMPIONSHIP

BRITISH CHAMPIONSHIP

PREMIER LEAGUE PAIRS CHAMPIONSHIP

PREMIER LEAGUE FOUR-TEAM CHAMPIONSHIP

CONFERENCE LEAGUE PAIRS CHAMPIONSHIP

ELITE LEAGUE RIDERS' CHAMPIONSHIP

CONFERENCE LEAGUE RIDERS' CHAMPIONSHIP

BRITISH UNDER-18 CHAMPIONSHIP

PREMIER LEAGUE RIDERS' CHAMPIONSHIP

SPEEDWAY GRAND PRIX

MAJOR INTERNATIONAL MEETINGS

SPEEDWAY WORLD CUP

WORLD UNDER-21 TEAM CUP

WORLD UNDER-21 CHAMPIONSHIP

EUROPEAN CHAMPIONSHIP

EUROPEAN UNDER-19 CHAMPIONSHIP

MAJOR BRITISH MEETINGS 2007

ELITE LEAGUE PAIRS CHAMPIONSHIP 2007

(SUPER 7EVEN SERIES: EVENT ONE)

7 APRIL, KING'S LYNN

Scoring system: 4-3-2-0

1st   POOLE
2nd READING
3rd PETERBOROUGH
4th SWINDON

GROUP 'A'	QUALIFYING SCORES				TOTALS
READING 22					
Greg Hancock	4	3*	2*	4	13 (2)
Travis McGowan	2	4	3	0	9
POOLE 21					
Jason Crump	3	2*	4	4	13 (1)
Bjarne Pedersen	R	3	2	3*	8 (1)
COVENTRY 21					
Scott Nicholls	2	3*	3	3	11 (1)
Rory Schlein	4	4	0	2*	10 (1)
EASTBOURNE 18					
Nicki Pedersen	3	4	4	4	15
Lewis Bridger	0	0	0	3*	3 (1)
IPSWICH 8					
Chris Louis	0	2	0	N	2
Kim Jansson	2	0	2	2	6

GROUP 'B'	QUALIFYING SCORES				TOTALS
PETERBOROUGH 24					
Hans N. Andersen	4	4	4	4	16
Niels-Kristian Iversen	3*	0	3*	2	8 (2)
SWINDON 23					
Leigh Adams	3	3	4	4	14
Sebastian Ulamek	2*	2*	2	3*	9 (3)
LAKESIDE 19					
Joonas Kylmakorpi	3*	N	2*	0	5 (2)
Adam Shields	4	4	3	3	14

WOLVERHAMPTON 12					
Peter Karlsson	0	4	2	2	8
Billy Hamill	2	2	R	0	4

OXFORD 12					
Jesper B. Jensen	2	3	4	3	12
Freddie Eriksson	0	0	0	0	0

HEAT DETAILS

Ht 1:	Schlein, N. Pedersen, Nicholls, Bridger, 59.5
Ht 2:	Shields, Kylmakorpi, Hamill, Karlsson, 60.2
Ht 3:	Hancock, Crump, McGowan, B. Pedersen (ret), 59.4
Ht 4:	Andersen, Iversen, Jensen, Eriksson, 60.0
Ht 5:	Schlein, Nicholls, Jansson, Louis, 60.3
Ht 6:	Shields, Adams, Ulamek, Kylmakorpi (ns), 60.3 (3 riders only)
Ht 7:	N. Pedersen, B. Pedersen, Crump, Bridger, 60.1
Ht 8:	Karlsson, Jensen, Hamill, Eriksson, 61.7
Ht 9:	McGowan, Hancock, Louis, Jansson, 61.3
Ht 10:	Andersen, Adams, Ulamek, Iversen, 60.8
Ht 11:	Crump, Nicholls, B. Pedersen, Schlein, 60.1
Ht 12:	Jensen, Shields, Kylmakorpi, Eriksson, 61.5
Ht 13:	N. Pedersen, McGowan, Hancock, Bridger, 60.7
Ht 14:	Andersen, Iversen, Karlsson, Hamill (ret), 61.7
Ht 15:	Crump, B. Pedersen, Jansson, Louis, 61.7
Ht 16:	Adams, Jensen, Ulamek, Eriksson, 61.6
Ht 17:	Hancock, Nicholls, Schlein, McGowan, 61.2
Ht 18:	Andersen, Shields, Iversen, Kylmakorpi, 62.1
Ht 19:	N. Pedersen, Bridger, Jansson, Louis (ns), 61.8 (3 riders only)
Ht 20:	Adams, Ulamek, Karlsson, Hamill, 61.6

First semi-final:	McGowan, Adams, Hancock, Ulamek, 61.4
Second semi-final:	Crump, Iversen, B. Pedersen, Andersen, 61.1
Consolation Final:	Adams, Iversen, Andersen, Ulamek, 61.3
Grand Final:	Crump, Hancock, B. Pedersen, McGowan, 62.6

ROLL OF HONOUR

NOTE: Known as the British League Pairs Championship from 1976-1978 and the British Open Pairs Championship from 1984-1987.

YEAR	FIRST	SECOND
1976	Ipswich (John Louis & Billy Sanders)	Coventry (Ole Olsen & Mitch Shirra)
1977	Ipswich (Billy Sanders & John Louis)	King's Lynn (Michael Lee & David Gagen)
1978	Cradley Heath (Steve Bastable & Bruce Penhall) & Coventry (Ole Olsen & Mitch Shirra) [shared]	
1979-83	Not staged	
1984	Belle Vue (Peter Collins & Chris Morton)	Reading (Mitch Shirra & Tim Hunt)
1985	Oxford (Hans Nielsen & Simon Wigg)	Reading (John Davis & Mitch Shirra)
1986	Oxford (Simon Wigg & Hans Nielsen)	Coventry (Kelvin Tatum & John Jorgensen)
1987	Oxford (Hans Nielsen & Andy Grahame)	Swindon (Mitch Shirra & Jimmy Nilsen)
1988-2003	Not staged	
2004	Swindon (Leigh Adams & Charlie Gjedde)	Belle Vue (Jason Crump & Joe Screen)
2005	Swindon (Leigh Adams & Lee Richardson)	Belle Vue (Jason Crump & Joe Screen)
2006	Belle Vue (Jason Crump & Simon Stead)	Swindon (Leigh Adams & Sebastian Ulamek)
2007	Poole (Jason Crump & Bjarne Pedersen)	Reading (Greg Hancock & Travis McGowan)

BRITISH UNDER-21 CHAMPIONSHIP FINAL 2007

(SUPER 7EVEN SERIES: EVENT TWO)

28 APRIL, EASTBOURNE

1st EDWARD KENNETT
2nd WILLIAM LAWSON
3rd TAI WOFFINDEN
4th BEN BARKER

RIDER	QUALIFYING SCORES					TOTAL
Edward Kennett	3	3	3	2	3	14
Ben Barker	2	3	3	1	3	12
Tai Woffinden	3	1	2	3	3	12
Lewis Bridger	3	2	2	3	2	12
Daniel King	3	3	3	2	R	11
William Lawson	2	0	3	3	2	10
Adam Roynon	2	2	1	1	3	9
Steve Boxall	1	3	F	2	2	8
Ben Wilson	1	1	2	3	X	7
James Wright	F	R	2	2	1	5
Lee Smart	2	X	1	0	1	4
Jamie Courtney	1	1	0	1	1	4
Mark Baseby	0	2	1	0	0	3
Nicki Glanz	1	2	0	0	0	3
Luke Bowen	F	0	1	0	2	3
Josh Auty	0	X	X	1	X	1
Benji Compton (Reserve)	-	-	-	-	-	-
Robert Mear (Reserve)	-	-	-	-	-	-

HEAT DETAILS

Qualifier:	Glanz, Compton, Mear (f, rem), 60.1 (3 riders only)
Ht 1:	King, Barker, Glanz, Bowen (fell), 57.8
Ht 2:	Kennett, Roynon, Courtney, Auty, 58.4
Ht 3:	Woffinden, Smart, Wilson, Wright (fell), 59.5
Ht 4:	Bridger, Lawson, Boxall, Baseby, 58.3
Ht 5:	Kennett, Bridger, Woffinden, Bowen, 57.2
Ht 6:	(Re-Run) Boxall, Glanz, Auty (ex, delaying start), Smart (f, ex), 60.3
Ht 7:	Barker, Baseby, Courtney, Wright (ret), 60.4
Ht 8:	King, Roynon, Wilson, Lawson (f, rem), 50.3
Ht 9:	(Re-Run) Lawson, Wright, Bowen, Auty (f, ex), 58.2
Ht 10:	Kennett, Wilson, Baseby, Glanz, 57.9
Ht 11:	Barker, Woffinden, Roynon, Boxall (fell), 59.5
Ht 12:	King, Bridger, Smart, Courtney, 57.8
Ht 13:	Wilson, Boxall, Courtney, Bowen, 59.5
Ht 14:	Bridger, Wright, Roynon, Glanz, 58.0
Ht 15:	Lawson, Kennett, Barker, Smart, 58.1
Ht 16:	Woffinden, King, Auty, Baseby (f, rem), 59.0
Ht 17:	Roynon, Bowen, Smart, Baseby (f, rem), 60.6
Ht 18:	Woffinden, Lawson, Courtney, Glanz, 58.9
Ht 19:	(Re-Run twice) Barker, Bridger, Wilson (f, ex), Auty (f, ex), 58.8
Ht 20:	Kennett, Boxall, Wright, King (ret), 58.8

Semi-final:	(Re-Run; Awarded) Woffinden and Lawson seeded, Bridger (ex, foul riding), King (ex, foul riding), No Time
Final:	Kennett, Lawson, Woffinden, Barker, 58.6

ROLL OF HONOUR

NOTE: Became known as the British Under-21 Championship in 1987, having previously been called the Junior Championship of Great Britain.

YEAR	FIRST	SECOND	THIRD
1969	Graham Plant	Geoff Ambrose	Mick Bell
1970	Barry Thomas	Dave Jessup	Mick Bell
1971	Ian Turner	Dave Jessup	Peter Ingram
1972	Allen Emmett	Gordon Kennett	Tony Davey
1973	Peter Collins	Barney Kennett	David Gagen
1974	Chris Morton	Steve Bastable	Neil Middleditch
1975	Neil Middleditch	Steve Weatherley	Joe Owen
1976	Michael Lee	Steve Weatherley	Colin Richardson
1977	Les Collins	Phil Collins	Colin Richardson
1978	Phil Collins	Ian Gledhill	Bob Garrad
1979	Kenny Carter	Nigel Flatman	Mel Taylor
1980	Mark Courtney	Kevin Smith	John Barker
1981	Rob Lightfoot	Peter Carr	Neil Evitts
1982	Peter Carr	Martin Hagon	Simon Cross
1983	Keith Millard	Simon Cross	Kenny McKinna
1984	Marvyn Cox	Simon Cross	Andy Smith
1985	Carl Blackbird	David Mullett	Andy Smith
1986	Gary Havelock	Andrew Silver	Daz Sumner
1987	Daz Sumner	David Biles	Mark Loram
1988	Mark Loram	Andy Phillips	Martin Dugard
1989	Martin Dugard	Chris Louis	Dean Barker
1990	Joe Screen	Mark Loram	Chris Louis
1991	Not staged		
1992	Scott Smith	Mark Loram	Joe Screen
1993	Joe Screen	Carl Stonehewer	David Norris
1994	Paul Hurry	Ben Howe	James Grieves
1995	Ben Howe	Paul Hurry	Savalas Clouting
1996	Savalas Clouting	Scott Nicholls	Paul Hurry
1997	Leigh Lanham	Lee Richardson	Scott Nicholls
1998	Scott Nicholls	Lee Richardson	Paul Lee
1999	Scott Nicholls	Lee Richardson	David Howe
2000	David Howe	Lee Richardson	Paul Lee
2001	Simon Stead	David Howe	Paul Lee
2002	Simon Stead	Ross Brady	Olly Allen
2003	Simon Stead	Olly Allen	Edward Kennett
2004	Ritchie Hawkins	Steve Boxall	Edward Kennett
2005	Edward Kennett	Chris Schramm	Richard Hall
2006	Ben Wilson	Daniel King	Lewis Bridger
2007	Edward Kennett	William Lawson	Tai Woffinden

CONFERENCE LEAGUE FOUR-TEAM CHAMPIONSHIP 2007

18 MAY, PLYMOUTH

1st SCUNTHORPE
2nd PLYMOUTH
3rd WEYMOUTH
4th BUXTON

FIRST SEMI-FINAL   **QUALIFYING SCORES TOTAL**

SCUNTHORPE 20			
Tai Woffinden	3	3	6
Byron Bekker	3	3	6
Josh Auty	3	3	6
Richie Dennis	2	R	2

OXFORD 11			
Sam Martin	2	1	3
Michael Coles	1	2	3
Kyle Hughes	0	2	2
Ben Hopwood	2	1	3

QUALIFYING SCORES TOTAL

BUXTON 14			
Scott James	2	2	4
Jack Roberts	3	2	5
Lewis Dallaway	1	1	2
Jonathan Bethell	R	3	3

SITTINGBOURNE 3			
Dean Felton	1	0	1
Joe Reynolds	0	1	1
Luke Goody	1	0	1
Gordon Meakins	0	0	0

HEAT DETAILS

Ht 1:	Roberts, Dennis, Felton, Hughes, 53.11
Ht 2:	Woffinden, Hopwood, Dallaway, Reynolds, 51.07 (Track Record)
Ht 3:	Bekker, Martin, Goody, Bethell (ret), 54.69
Ht 4:	(Re-Run) Auty, James, Coles (15 met), Meakins, 52.96
Ht 5:	Woffinden, James, Martin, Felton, 52.59
Ht 6:	Bekker, Roberts, Hopwood, Meakins, 54.25
Ht 7:	Auty, Hughes, Dallaway, Goody, 53.06
Ht 8:	Bethell, Coles, Reynolds, Dennis (ret), 54.28

SECOND SEMI-FINAL   **QUALIFYING SCORES TOTAL**

PLYMOUTH 22			
Seemond Stephens	3	2	5
Tom Brown	2	3	5
Adam Roynon	3	3	6
Nicki Glanz	3	3	6

CLEVELAND 8			
Mark Burrows	3	1	4
Martin Emerson	0	X	0
Greg Blair	1	1	2
Gary Beaton	1	1	2

QUALIFYING SCORES TOTAL

WEYMOUTH 11			
Lee Smart	2	3	5
Sam Hurst	2	2	4
Nathan Irwin	0	0	0
Karl Mason	1	1	2

BOSTON 7			
Matthew Wright	0	0	0
Rob Smith	2	2	4
Darren Mallett	0	2	2
Simon Lambert	1	0	1

HEAT DETAILS

Ht 1:	Burrows, Brown, Mason, Mallett, 53.60
Ht 2:	Roynon, Smart, Lambert, Emerson, 51.66
Ht 3:	Glanz, Hurst, Blair, Wright, 53.66
Ht 4:	(Re-Run) Stephens, Smith, Beaton, Irwin (15 met), 53.81
Ht 5:	Smart, Stephens, Burrows, Wright, 53.10
Ht 6:	Brown, Hurst, Beaton, Lambert, 54.65
Ht 7:	Roynon, Mallett, Blair, Irwin, 53.28
Ht 8:	(Awarded) Glanz, Smith, Mason, Emerson (f, ex), No Time

FINAL — **QUALIFYING SCORES TOTAL**   **QUALIFYING SCORES TOTAL**

SCUNTHORPE 19			
Tai Woffinden	3	3	6
Byron Bekker	0	3	3
Josh Auty	2	2	4
Richie Dennis	3	3	6

PLYMOUTH 16			
Seemond Stephens	1	2	3
Tom Brown	2	2	4
Adam Roynon	3	3	6
Nicki Glanz	3	X	3

WEYMOUTH 8			
Lee Smart	2	1	3
Sam Hurst	1	1	2
Nathan Irwin	0	1	1
Karl Mason	1	1	2

BUXTON 5			
Scott James	0	0	0
Jack Roberts	2	2	4
Lewis Dallaway	0	X	0
Jonathan Bethell	1	0	1

HEAT DETAILS

Ht 1:	Woffinden, Brown, Mason, Dallaway, 52.03
Ht 2:	(Re-Run) Roynon, Smart, Bethell, Bekker, 51.97
Ht 3:	Glanz, Auty, Hurst, James, 51.84
Ht 4:	Dennis, Roberts, Stephens, Irwin, 52.72
Ht 5:	Woffinden, Stephens, Smart, James, 52.06
Ht 6:	Dennis, Brown, Hurst, Bethell, 53.15
Ht 7:	(Re-Run; Awarded) Roynon, Auty, Irwin (15 met), Dallaway (f, ex), No Time
Ht 8:	(Re-Run) Bekker, Roberts, Mason, Glanz (ex, foul riding), 53.81

ROLL OF HONOUR

YEAR	FIRST	SECOND	THIRD	FOURTH
2003	Rye House	Mildenhall	Peterborough	Boston
2004	Mildenhall	Newcastle & Wimbledon	-	Stoke
2005	Weymouth	Oxford	Armadale	Boston
2006	Stoke	Plymouth	Mildenhall	Scunthorpe
2007	Scunthorpe	Plymouth	Weymouth	Buxton

BRITISH CHAMPIONSHIP FINAL 2007

(SUPER 7EVEN SERIES: EVENT THREE)

4 JUNE, WOLVERHAMPTON

1st   CHRIS HARRIS
2nd DAVID HOWE
3rd SCOTT NICHOLLS
4th EDWARD KENNETT

RIDER	QUALIFYING SCORES					TOTAL
Chris Harris	3	3	3	3	2	14
David Howe	2	3	3	3	3	14
Edward Kennett	3	3	2	3	2	13
Scott Nicholls	2	3	2	3	3	13
Daniel King	3	2	2	2	0	9
Olly Allen	1	2	1	2	3	9
Lewis Bridger	2	2	1	X	3	8
Simon Stead	3	1	2	1	1	8
Chris Louis	R	1	3	1	2	7
Lee Richardson	1	0	3	2	1	7
William Lawson	1	0	0	2	1	4
Richard Hall	2	1	R	0	1	4
Joe Screen	1	2	1	R	-	4
Gary Havelock	0	1	1	1	R	3
James Wright	0	0	0	1	2	3
Tai Woffinden	X	-	-	-	-	0
Ben Wilson (Reserve)	0	0	0	-	-	0
Adam Roynon (Reserve)	0	R	-	-	-	0

HEAT DETAILS

Ht 1:	(Re-Run) Kennett, Nicholls, Allen, Wright, 55.8
Ht 2:	Harris, Howe, Lawson, Louis (ret), 55.6
Ht 3:	King, Bridger, Screen, Havelock, 56.2
Ht 4:	(Awarded) Stead, Hall, Richardson, Woffinden (f, ex), No Time
Ht 5:	Kennett, Bridger, Louis, Richardson, 56.3
Ht 6:	Harris, King, Hall, Wright, 55.3
Ht 7:	Nicholls, Screen, Stead, Lawson, 55.9
Ht 8:	Howe, Allen, Havelock, Wilson, 56.3
Ht 9:	Harris, Kennett, Screen, Roynon, 55.2
Ht 10:	Louis, Stead, Havelock, Wright, 57.0
Ht 11:	Howe, Nicholls, Bridger, Hall (ret), 56.2
Ht 12:	Richardson, King, Allen, Lawson, 56.9
Ht 13:	Kennett, Lawson, Havelock, Hall (f, rem), 57.3
Ht 14:	Howe, Richardson, Wright, Screen (ret), 56.0
Ht 15:	Nicholls, King, Louis, Wilson, 56.5
Ht 16:	(Re-Run) Harris, Allen, Stead, Bridger (f, ex), 56.2
Ht 17:	Howe, Kennett, Stead, King, 57.0
Ht 18:	Bridger, Wright, Lawson, Roynon (ret), 58.3
Ht 19:	Nicholls, Harris, Richardson, Havelock (ret), 57.1
Ht 20:	Allen, Louis, Hall, Wilson, 57.9

Semi-final:	Kennett, Nicholls, King, Allen (fell), 56.9
Final:	(Re-Run) Harris, Howe, Nicholls, Kennett, 56.7

ROLL OF HONOUR

NOTE: Was known as the Championship of Great Britain from 2002 to 2006 inclusive, before reverting back to its original title in 2007.

YEAR	FIRST	SECOND	THIRD
1961	Barry Briggs	Peter Craven	Ronnie Moore
1962	Peter Craven	Barry Briggs	Ronnie Moore
1963	Peter Craven	Barry Briggs	Leo McAuliffe
1964	Barry Briggs	Ken McKinlay	Ron How
1965	Barry Briggs	Nigel Boocock	Ken McKinlay
1966	Barry Briggs	Ivan Mauger	Colin Pratt
1967	Barry Briggs	Ivan Mauger	Eric Boocock
1968	Ivan Mauger	Barry Briggs	Eric Boocock
1969	Barry Briggs	Nigel Boocock	Ronnie Moore
1970	Ivan Mauger	Ronnie Moore	Roy Trigg
1971	Ivan Mauger	Barry Briggs	Tony Lomas
1972	Ivan Mauger	Nigel Boocock	Barry Briggs
1973	Ray Wilson	Bob Valentine	Peter Collins
1974	Eric Boocock	Terry Betts	Dave Jessup
1975	John Louis	Peter Collins	Malcolm Simmons
1976	Malcolm Simmons	Chris Morton	Doug Wyer
1977	Michael Lee	Dave Jessup	Doug Wyer
1978	Michael Lee	Dave Jessup	Malcolm Simmons
1979	Peter Collins	Michael Lee	Dave Jessup
1980	Dave Jessup	Michael Lee	Phil Collins
1981	Steve Bastable	Kenny Carter	John Louis
1982	Andy Grahame	Alan Grahame	Kenny Carter
1983	Chris Morton	Michael Lee	Andy Grahame
1984	Kenny Carter	Andy Grahame	Dave Jessup
1985	Kenny Carter	John Davis	Kelvin Tatum
1986	Neil Evitts	Phil Collins	Jeremy Doncaster
1987	Kelvin Tatum	Neil Evitts	Simon Wigg
1988	Simon Wigg	Kelvin Tatum	Chris Morton
1989	Simon Wigg	Kelvin Tatum	Alan Grahame
1990	Kelvin Tatum	Simon Cross	Jeremy Doncaster
1991	Gary Havelock	Kelvin Tatum	Chris Louis
1992	Gary Havelock	Martin Dugard	Andy Smith
1993	Andy Smith	Joe Screen	Gary Havelock
1994	Andy Smith	Joe Screen	Steve Schofield
1995	Andy Smith	Joe Screen	Dean Barker
1996	Joe Screen	Chris Louis	Carl Stonehewer
1997	Mark Loram	Chris Louis	Sean Wilson
1998	Chris Louis	Joe Screen	Paul Hurry
1999	Mark Loram	Joe Screen	Chris Louis
2000	Chris Louis	Paul Hurry	Martin Dugard
2001	Mark Loram	Stuart Robson	Martin Dugard
2002	Scott Nicholls	Lee Richardson	David Howe
2003	Scott Nicholls	Dean Barker	David Norris
2004	Joe Screen	David Norris	Mark Loram
2005	Scott Nicholls	Chris Harris	Joe Screen
2006	Scott Nicholls	Joe Screen	Simon Stead
2007	Chris Harris	David Howe	Scott Nicholls

PREMIER LEAGUE PAIRS CHAMPIONSHIP 2007

(SUPER 7EVEN SERIES: EVENT FOUR)

29 JUNE, SOMERSET

Scoring system: 4-3-2-0

1st   ISLE OF WIGHT
2nd GLASGOW
3rd NEWCASTLE
4th WORKINGTON

GROUP 'A'	QUALIFYING SCORES				TOTALS
ISLE OF WIGHT 24					
Chris Holder	4	4	4	4	16
Jason Bunyan	3*	2	0	3*	8 (2)
GLASGOW 22					
Shane Parker	3	3	3	3*	12 (1)
Craig Watson	2*	2*	2*	4	10 (3)
SOMERSET 21					
Magnus Zetterstrom	4	3	3*	3*	13 (2)
Emil Kramer	0	0	4	4	8
RYE HOUSE 15					
Tommy Allen	0	3*	2	0	5 (1)
Chris Neath	4	4	0	2	10
SHEFFIELD 8					
Andre Compton	2	0	0	0	2
Ricky Ashworth	0	2	2	2	6

GROUP 'B'	QUALIFYING SCORES				TOTALS
WORKINGTON 24					
James Wright	2	3*	2*	2	9 (2)
Kauko Nieminen	4	4	3	4	15
NEWCASTLE 21					
Christian Henry	4	0	4	0	8
Josef Franc	3*	3	3*	4	13 (2)
KING'S LYNN 17					
Daniel Nermark	3*	3	0	3	9 (1)
Tomas Topinka	4	0	2	2*	8 (1)
BIRMINGHAM 16					
Emiliano Sanchez	0	2	2*	0	4 (1)
Ulrich Ostergaard	2	4	3	3	12
REDCAR 12					
Gary Havelock	2	0	4	4	10
James Grieves	0	2	0	0	2

HEAT DETAILS

Ht 1:	Zetterstrom, Parker, Watson, Kramer, 56.95
Ht 2:	Topinka, Nermark, Ostergaard, Sanchez, 57.77
Ht 3:	Holder, Bunyan, Compton, Ashworth, 57.33
Ht 4:	(Re-Run) Henry, Franc, Havelock (15 met), Grieves, 58.42
Ht 5:	Neath, Parker, Watson, Allen, 57.21
Ht 6:	Nieminen, Nermark, Wright, Topinka, 57.44
Ht 7:	Holder, Zetterstrom, Bunyan, Kramer, 57.16
Ht 8:	Ostergaard, Franc, Sanchez, Henry, 58.19
Ht 9:	Neath, Allen, Ashworth, Compton, 57.88
Ht 10:	Nieminen, Wright, Grieves, Havelock, 57.67
Ht 11:	Holder, Parker, Watson, Bunyan, 58.60
Ht 12:	Henry, Franc, Topinka, Nermark, 58.99
Ht 13:	Kramer, Zetterstrom, Ashworth, Compton, 57.87
Ht 14:	Havelock, Ostergaard, Sanchez, Grieves, 58.25
Ht 15:	Holder, Bunyan, Allen, Neath, 58.83
Ht 16:	Franc, Nieminen, Wright, Henry, 58.86
Ht 17:	Watson, Parker, Ashworth, Compton, 59.15
Ht 18:	Havelock, Nermark, Topinka, Grieves, 58.73
Ht 19:	Kramer, Zetterstrom, Neath, Allen, 58.99
Ht 20:	Nieminen, Ostergaard, Wright, Sanchez, 58.51

First semi-final:	Franc, Holder, Bunyan, Henry, 58.26
Second semi-final:	Nieminen, Parker, Watson, Wright, 57.80
Consolation Final:	Henry, Nieminen, Franc, Wright, 58.22
Grand Final:	Holder, Parker, Bunyan, Watson, 58.71

ROLL OF HONOUR

NOTE: Became known as the Premier League Pairs Championship in 1997, having previously been known as the National League Pairs Championship (1975-1990) and Division Two Pairs Championship (1994).

YEAR	FIRST	SECOND
1975	Newcastle (Tom Owen & Brian Havelock)	Ellesmere Port (John Jackson & Colin Goad)
1976	Ellesmere Port (John Jackson & Chris Turner)	Newcastle (Joe Owen & Tom Owen)
1977	Boston (Robert Hollingworth & Colin Cook)	Newport (Jim Brett & Brian Woodward)
1978	Ellesmere Port (John Jackson & Steve Finch)	Newcastle (Tom Owen & Robbie Blackadder)
1979	Milton Keynes (Andy Grahame & Bob Humphreys)	Ellesmere Port (John Jackson & Steve Finch)
1980	Middlesbrough (Mark Courtney & Steve Wilcock)	Boston (Robert Hollingworth & Gary Guglielmi)
1981	Canterbury (Mike Ferreira & Denzil Kent)	Berwick (Wayne Brown & Steve McDermott)
1982	Weymouth (Martin Yeates & Simon Wigg)	Long Eaton (Alan Molyneux & Dave Perks)
1983	Weymouth (Martin Yeates & Simon Cross)	Glasgow (Jim McMillan & Steve Lawson)
1984	Stoke (Nigel Crabtree & Tom Owen)	Berwick (Bruce Cribb & Steve McDermott)
1985	Ellesmere Port (Joe Owen & Louis Carr)	Poole (Martin Yeates & Stan Bear)
1986	Edinburgh (Les Collins & Doug Wyer)	Hackney (Barry Thomas & Andy Galvin)
1987	Mildenhall (Dave Jessup & Mel Taylor)	Peterborough (Ian Barney & Kevin Hawkins)
1988	Stoke (Graham Jones & Steve Bastable)	Poole (Steve Schofield & David Biles)
1989	Stoke (Nigel Crabtree & Eric Monaghan)	Mildenhall (Preben Eriksen & Peter Glanz)
1990	Hackney (Steve Schofield & Andy Galvin)	Exeter (Steve Regeling & Peter Jeffery)
1991-93	Not staged	
1994	Swindon (Tony Olsson & Tony Langdon)	Glasgow (Nigel Crabtree & David Walsh)
1995-96	Not staged	
1997	Long Eaton (Martin Dixon & Carl Stonehewer)	Reading (David Mullett & Lee Richardson)
1998	Peterborough (Glenn Cunningham & Brett Woodifield)	Exeter (Frank Smart & Michael Coles)
1999	Workington (Carl Stonehewer & Brent Werner)	Arena-Essex (Colin White & Leigh Lanham)
2000	Workington (Carl Stonehewer & Mick Powell)	Isle of Wight (Ray Morton & Danny Bird)
2001	Workington (Carl Stonehewer & Peter I. Karlsson)	Newcastle (Bjarne Pedersen & Jesper Olsen)
2002	Isle of Wight (Adam Shields & Danny Bird)	Newport (Frank Smart & Craig Watson)
2003	Workington (Carl Stonehewer & Simon Stead)	Newport (Frank Smart & Niels-Kristian Iversen)
2004	Reading (Danny Bird & Phil Morris)	Stoke (Paul Pickering & Alan Mogridge)
2005	Glasgow (Shane Parker & George Stancl)	Somerset (Magnus Zetterstrom & Glenn Cunningham)
2006	Glasgow (Danny Bird & Shane Parker)	Sheffield (Ben Wilson & Ricky Ashworth)
2007	Isle of Wight (Chris Holder & Jason Bunyan)	Glasgow (Shane Parker & Craig Watson)

PREMIER LEAGUE FOUR-TEAM CHAMPIONSHIP 2007

(SUPER 7EVEN SERIES: EVENT FIVE)

8 JULY, PETERBOROUGH

1st   ISLE OF WIGHT
2nd SOMERSET
3rd   KING'S LYNN
4th   RYE HOUSE

FIRST SEMI-FINAL   QUALIFYING SCORES TOTAL   QUALIFYING SCORES TOTAL

KING'S LYNN 16			
Daniel Nermark	2	3	5
Tomas Topinka	1	3	4
Paul Lee	0	3	3
Chris Mills	1	3	4

SOMERSET 15			
Magnus Zetterstrom	3	1	4
Emil Kramer	3	1	4
Ritchie Hawkins	2	2	4
Jordan Frampton	1	2	3

GLASGOW 11			
Craig Watson	3	2	5
Shane Parker	3	0	3
Lee Dicken	0	0	0
David McAllan	2	1	3

SHEFFIELD 6			
Andre Compton	1	0	1
Ricky Ashworth	X	-	0
Joel Parsons	0	1	1
Ben Wilson	2	2	4
Paul Cooper (Res)	0	-	0

HEAT DETAILS

Ht 1:	Zetterstrom, Wilson, Topinka, Dicken, 60.0
Ht 2:	Kramer, McAllan, Compton, Lee, 60.8
Ht 3:	(Re-Run) Watson, Hawkins, Mills, Ashworth (f, ex), 61.9
Ht 4:	Parker, Nermark, Frampton, Parsons, 61.8
Ht 5:	Nermark, Watson, Zetterstrom, Compton, 61.5
Ht 6:	Topinka, Frampton, McAllan, Cooper, 62.8
Ht 7:	Lee, Hawkins, Parsons, Dicken, 63.1
Ht 8:	Mills, Wilson, Kramer, Parker, 63.3

SECOND SEMI-FINAL   QUALIFYING SCORES TOTAL   QUALIFYING SCORES TOTAL

ISLE OF WIGHT 16			
Chris Holder	2	3	5
Jason Bunyan	3	3	6
Krzysztof Stojanowski	1	3	4
Glen Phillips	1	0	1

RYE HOUSE 13			
Tai Woffinden	3	0	3
Chris Neath	2	1	3
Tommy Allen	0	-	0
Steve Boxall	2	3	5
Adam Roynon (Res)	2	-	2

BIRMINGHAM 11			
Jason Lyons	3	2	5
Ulrich Ostergaard	3	2	5
Emiliano Sanchez	0	1	1
Jon Armstrong	0	-	0
Ben Powell (Res)	0	-	0

WORKINGTON 8			
Carl Stonehewer	1	1	2
James Wright	2	1	3
Charles Wright	0	0	0
Craig Branney	1	2	3

HEAT DETAILS

Ht 1:	Woffinden, J. Wright, Stojanowski, Armstrong, 61.3
Ht 2:	Lyons, Neath, Phillips, C. Wright, 61.4
Ht 3:	Ostergaard, Holder, Branney, Allen, 61.0
Ht 4:	Bunyan, Boxall, Stonehewer, Sanchez, 61.9
Ht 5:	Holder, Lyons, Stonehewer, Woffinden, 62.2
Ht 6:	Boxall, Ostergaard, J. Wright, Phillips, 61.8
Ht 7:	Stojanowski, Roynon, Sanchez, C. Wright, 62.4
Ht 8:	Bunyan, Branney, Neath, Powell, 63.5

FINAL	RACE SCORES				TOTAL
ISLE OF WIGHT 38					
Chris Holder	3	3	3	3	12
Jason Bunyan	3	0	3	3	9
Krzysztof Stojanowski	3	-	-	-	3
Glen Phillips	2	0	2	3	7
Cory Gathercole (Res)	3	1	3	-	7
SOMERSET 22					
Magnus Zetterstrom	2	3	3	0	8
Emil Kramer	0	0	3	1	4
Ritchie Hawkins	1	1	1	2	5
Jordan Frampton	1	2	2	0	5
KING'S LYNN 21					
Daniel Nermark	3	2	2	2	9
Tomas Topinka	2	1	0	2	5
Paul Lee	2	1	2	0	5
Chris Mills	0	0	2	-	2
Trevor Harding (Res)	R	-	-	-	0
RYE HOUSE 15					
Tai Woffinden	0	3	1	1	5
Chris Neath	R	2	0	0	2
Tommy Allen	1	-	-	-	1
Steve Boxall	1	2	0	1	4
Adam Roynon (Res)	1	1	1	-	3

HEAT DETAILS

Ht 1:	Nermark, Phillips, Frampton, Neath (ret), 63.1
Ht 2:	Gathercole, Topinka, Hawkins, Woffinden, 64.1
Ht 3:	Bunyan, Zetterstrom, Allen, Mills, 63.4
Ht 4:	Holder, Lee, Boxall, Kramer, 62.9
Ht 5:	Zetterstrom, Boxall, Topinka, Phillips, 62.7
Ht 6:	Stojanowski, Nermark, Roynon, Kramer, 63.8
Ht 7:	Woffinden, Frampton, Lee, Bunyan, 63.6
Ht 8:	Holder, Neath, Hawkins, Mills, 65.6
Ht 9:	Kramer, Phillips, Woffinden, Harding (ret), 63.4
Ht 10:	Zetterstrom, Lee, Gathercole, Neath, 63.6
Ht 11:	Bunyan, Nermark, Hawkins, Boxall, 63.6
Ht 12:	Holder, Frampton, Roynon, Topinka, 63.7
Ht 13:	Gathercole, Mills, Boxall, Frampton, 65.5
Ht 14:	Phillips, Hawkins, Roynon, Lee, 65.1
Ht 15:	Bunyan, Topinka, Kramer, Neath, 64.5
Ht 16:	Holder, Nermark, Woffinden, Zetterstrom, 64.0

ROLL OF HONOUR

NOTE: Became known as the Premier League Four-Team Championship in 1997, having previously been known as the National League Four-Team Championship (1976-1990) and the Division Two Four-Team Championship (1991-1994).

YEAR	FIRST	SECOND	THIRD	FOURTH
1976	Newcastle	Eastbourne	Ellesmere Port	Workington
1977	Peterborough	Canterbury	Eastbourne	Stoke
1978	Peterborough	Stoke	Canterbury	Ellesmere Port
1979	Ellesmere Port	Mildenhall	Peterborough	Berwick
1980	Crayford	Rye House	Ellesmere Port	Stoke
1981	Edinburgh	Newcastle	Middlesbrough	Wolverhampton
1982	Newcastle	Mildenhall	Middlesbrough	Rye House
1983	Newcastle	Mildenhall	Milton Keynes	Long Eaton
1984	Mildenhall	Stoke	Milton Keynes	Boston
1985	Middlesbrough	Peterborough	Hackney	Stoke
1986	Middlesbrough	Arena-Essex	Hackney	Mildenhall
1987	Mildenhall	Arena-Essex	Eastbourne	Wimbledon
1988	Peterborough	Mildenhall	Eastbourne	Poole
1989	Peterborough	Stoke	Exeter	Eastbourne
1990	Stoke	Poole	Hackney	Ipswich
1991	Arena-Essex	Long Eaton	Edinburgh	Milton Keynes
1992	Peterborough	Edinburgh	Rye House	Glasgow
1993	Edinburgh	Swindon	Long Eaton	Rye House
1994	Oxford	Long Eaton	Peterborough	Edinburgh
1995-96	Not staged			
1997	Long Eaton	Edinburgh	Oxford	Berwick
1998	Peterborough	Edinburgh	Hull	Reading
1999	Sheffield	Newport	Isle of Wight	Arena-Essex
2000	Sheffield	Isle of Wight	Swindon	Berwick
2001	Workington	Newcastle	Sheffield	Isle of Wight
2002	Berwick	Arena-Essex	Newport	Hull
2003	Swindon	Trelawny	Newport	Glasgow
2004	Workington	Stoke	Glasgow	Rye House
2005	Somerset	Workington	Exeter	Rye House
2006	Workington	Somerset	Sheffield	King's Lynn
2007	Isle of Wight	Somerset	King's Lynn	Rye House

CONFERENCE LEAGUE PAIRS CHAMPIONSHIP 2007

22 JULY, SCUNTHORPE

Scoring system: 4-3-2-0

1st BOSTON

2nd OXFORD

3rd SCUNTHORPE

4th BUXTON

GROUP ONE	QUALIFYING SCORES				TOTALS
BOSTON 25					
Paul Cooper	3*	4	2*	4	13 (2)
Simon Lambert	4	3*	3	2	12 (1)
SCUNTHORPE 23					
Andrew Tully	2	2	0	4	8
Tai Woffinden	4	4	4	3*	15 (1)
WEYMOUTH 19					
Jay Herne	2	0	3*	0	5 (1)
Lee Smart	4	3	4	3	14
RYE HOUSE 10					
Karlis Ezergailis	0	0	3	0	3
Robert Mear	3	2	X	2	7
CLEVELAND 9					
Greg Blair	X	-	-	-	0
Mark Burrows	N	3	4	2	9

GROUP TWO	QUALIFYING SCORES				TOTALS
OXFORD 27					
Jordan Frampton	3*	3*	4	4	14+2
Lee Smethills	4	4	3*	2	13 (1)
BUXTON 18					
Jonathan Bethell	0	4	0	4	8
Jack Roberts	2	3*	3	2	10 (1)
STOKE 17					
Sam Dore	2	2	2	-	6
Barrie Evans	F	4	4	3	11
SITTINGBOURNE 16					
Dean Felton	0	0	2	0	2
Danny Warwick	4	3	4	3	14
PLYMOUTH 12					
Ben Hopwood	2*	2	0	0	4 (1)
Jamie Westacott	3	0	2	3	8

HEAT DETAILS

Ht 1:	(Re-Run) Lambert, Cooper, Blair (f, ex), Burrows (f, ns), 60.32
Ht 2:	Smethills, Frampton, Roberts, Bethell, 60.56
Ht 3:	Woffinden, Mear, Tully, Ezergailis, 60.73
Ht 4:	Warwick, Westacott, Hopwood, Felton, 62.67
Ht 5:	Smart, Burrows, Herne, 59.46 (3 riders only)
Ht 6:	Smethills, Frampton, Dore, Evans (fell), 60.23
Ht 7:	Cooper, Lambert, Mear, Ezergailis, 60.27
Ht 8:	Bethell, Roberts, Hopwood, Westacott, 61.40
Ht 9:	Woffinden, Smart, Tully, Herne, 58.09
Ht 10:	Evans, Warwick, Dore, Felton, 60.34
Ht 11:	(Re-Run) Burrows, Ezergailis, Mear (f, ex), 61.51 (3 riders only)
Ht 12:	Frampton, Smethills, Westacott, Hopwood, 60.53
Ht 13:	Woffinden, Lambert, Cooper, Tully, 58.59
Ht 14:	Warwick, Roberts, Felton, Bethell, 60.45
Ht 15:	Smart, Herne, Mear, Ezergailis, 59.69
Ht 16:	Evans, Westacott, Dore, Hopwood, 60.78
Ht 17:	Tully, Woffinden, Burrows, 60.93 (3 riders only)
Ht 18:	Frampton, Warwick, Smethills, Felton, 60.73
Ht 19:	Cooper, Smart, Lambert, Herne, 60.36
Ht 20:	Bethell, Evans, Roberts, 60.81 (3 riders only)

Consolation Final:	Woffinden, Tully, Bethell, Roberts, 60.17
Grand Final:	Cooper, Lambert, Smethills, Frampton (ret), 60.15

ROLL OF HONOUR

YEAR	FIRST	SECOND
2004	Wimbledon (Mark Burrows & Barrie Evans)	Mildenhall (Ritchie Hawkins & Jon Armstrong)
2005	Wimbledon (Scott James & Mark Burrows)	Oxford (Chris Mills & Craig Branney)
2006	Scunthorpe 'B' (Paul Cooper & Benji Compton)	Stoke (Ben Barker & Adam Allott)
2007	Boston (Paul Cooper & Simon Lambert)	Oxford (Jordan Frampton & Lee Smethills)

ELITE LEAGUE RIDERS' CHAMPIONSHIP 2007

(SUPER 7EVEN SERIES: EVENT SIX)

30 AUGUST, KING'S LYNN

1st NICKI PEDERSEN
2nd CHRIS HARRIS
3rd LEIGH ADAMS
4th DAVEY WATT

RIDER	QUALIFYING SCORES					TOTAL
Nicki Pedersen	3	3	3	3	2	14
Leigh Adams	3	3	2	2	3	13
Davey Watt	3	1	2	3	3	12
Chris Harris	X	2	3	2	3	10
Bjarne Pedersen	1	3	1	3	2	10
Krzysztof Kasprzak	2	2	0	1	3	8
Troy Batchelor	2	0	3	1	2	8
Hans N. Andersen	2	3	0	0	2	7
Scott Nicholls	0	2	1	3	1	7
Travis McGowan	3	2	M	0	1	6
Rory Schlein	1	1	3	1	0	6
Adam Shields	R	1	2	2	1	6
Tomas Topinka	2	X	2	1	0	5
Fredrik Lindgren	X	1	1	2	1	5
Chris Louis	0	0	1	0	0	1
Chris Mills	1	0	0	0	0	1

HEAT DETAILS

Ht 1:	(Re-Run) Watt, Batchelor, Harris (f, ex), Lindgren (f, ex), 62.65
Ht 2:	Adams, Topinka, Schlein, Shields (f, rem, ret), 61.09
Ht 3:	N. Pedersen, Kasprzak, B. Pedersen, Louis, 62.38
Ht 4:	McGowan, Andersen, Mills, Nicholls (f, rem), 61.54
Ht 5:	(Re-Run twice) Andersen, Kasprzak, Lindgren, Topinka (f, ex), 62.33
Ht 6:	B. Pedersen, Nicholls, Shields, Batchelor, 60.64
Ht 7:	N. Pedersen, Harris, Schlein, Mills, 59.59
Ht 8:	Adams, McGowan, Watt, Louis, 59.91
Ht 9:	N. Pedersen, Shields, Lindgren, McGowan (ex, 2 mins) (3 riders only), 59.62
Ht 10:	Batchelor, Topinka, Louis, Mills (f, rem), 59.69
Ht 11:	Harris, Adams, Nicholls, Kasprzak, 59.62
Ht 12:	Schlein, Watt, B. Pedersen, Andersen, 60.52
Ht 13:	Nicholls, Lindgren, Schlein, Louis, 60.00
Ht 14:	N. Pedersen, Adams, Batchelor, Andersen, 60.22
Ht 15:	B. Pedersen, Harris, Topinka, McGowan, 60.63
Ht 16:	Watt, Shields, Kasprzak, Mills, 60.52
Ht 17:	Adams, B. Pedersen, Lindgren, Mills, 60.40
Ht 18:	Kasprzak, Batchelor, McGowan, Schlein, 60.00
Ht 19:	Harris, Andersen, Shields, Louis, 61.78
Ht 20:	Watt, N. Pedersen, Nicholls, Topinka, 60.82

Semi-final:	Watt, Harris, B. Pedersen, Kasprzak, 60.93
Final:	N. Pedersen, Harris, Adams, Watt, 61.02

ROLL OF HONOUR

NOTE: Became known as the Elite League Riders' Championship in 1997, having previously been known as British League Riders' Championship (1965-1967 and 1975-1990), Division One Riders' Championship (1968-1974 and 1991-1994) and Premier League Riders' Championship (1995-1996).

YEAR	FIRST	SECOND	THIRD
1965	Barry Briggs	Jimmy Gooch	Cyril Maidment
1966	Barry Briggs	Olle Nygren	Norman Hunter
1967	Barry Briggs	Nigel Boocock	Ray Wilson
1968	Barry Briggs	Eric Boocock	Ivan Mauger
1969	Barry Briggs	Ivan Mauger	Jim Airey
1970	Barry Briggs	Anders Michanek	Eric Boocock
1971	Ivan Mauger	Barry Briggs	Jim McMillan
1972	Ole Olsen	Martin Ashby	Ronnie Moore
1973	Ivan Mauger	Ray Wilson	Anders Michanek
1974	Peter Collins	Ivan Mauger	Phil Crump
1975	Peter Collins	Phil Crump	Martin Ashby
1976	Ole Olsen	Peter Collins	John Louis
1977	Ole Olsen	Peter Collins	Michael Lee
1978	Ole Olsen	Peter Collins	Steve Bastable
1979	John Louis	Bruce Penhall	Michael Lee
1980	Les Collins	Bruce Penhall	Larry Ross
1981	Kenny Carter	Chris Morton	Shawn Moran
1982	Kenny Carter	Shawn Moran	Hans Nielsen
1983	Erik Gundersen	Michael Lee	Hans Nielsen
1984	Chris Morton	Hans Nielsen	Erik Gundersen
1985	Erik Gundersen	Peter Collins	Chris Morton
1986	Hans Nielsen	Erik Gundersen	Shawn Moran
1987	Hans Nielsen	Chris Morton	Kelly Moran
1988	Jan O.Pedersen	Erik Gundersen	Hans Nielsen
1989	Shawn Moran	Hans Nielsen	Brian Karger
1990	Hans Nielsen	Kelly Moran	Ronnie Correy
1991	Sam Ermolenko	Hans Nielsen	Joe Screen
1992	Joe Screen	Per Jonsson	Gary Havelock
1993	Per Jonsson	Henrik Gustafsson	Chris Louis
1994	Sam Ermolenko	Hans Nielsen	Martin Dugard
1995	Gary Havelock	Billy Hamill	Jason Crump
1996	Sam Ermolenko	Jason Crump	Leigh Adams
1997	Greg Hancock	Tony Rickardsson	Chris Louis
1998	Tony Rickardsson	Jason Crump	Joe Screen
1999	Jason Crump	Todd Wiltshire	Jason Lyons
2000	Ryan Sullivan	Greg Hancock	Nicki Pedersen
2001	Jason Crump	Scott Nicholls	Nicki Pedersen
2002	Tony Rickardsson	Nicki Pedersen	Jason Crump
2003	Lee Richardson	Andreas Jonsson	Scott Nicholls
2004	Bjarne Pedersen	Ryan Sullivan	Hans N. Andersen
2005	Nicki Pedersen	Scott Nicholls	Peter Karlsson
2006	Jason Crump	Nicki Pedersen	Greg Hancock
2007	Nicki Pedersen	Chris Harris	Leigh Adams

CONFERENCE LEAGUE RIDERS' CHAMPIONSHIP 2007

15 SEPTEMBER, RYE HOUSE

1st TAI WOFFINDEN
2nd JOSH AUTY
3rd ROBERT MEAR
4th JAY HERNE

RIDER	RACE SCORES					TOTAL
Tai Woffinden	3	3	3	3	3	15
Josh Auty	2	3	2	3	3	13
Robert Mear	3	1	3	2	3	12
Jay Herne	1	3	1	2	3	10
Danny Warwick	2	2	3	1	1	9
Barrie Evans	3	R	0	3	2	8
Lee Smart	2	2	2	0	2	8
Ben Taylor	1	2	2	2	1	8
Mark Burrows	1	1	X	3	2	7
John Branney	2	0	1	2	2	7
Tom Brown	0	2	2	1	1	6
Daniel Halsey	X	1	3	0	1	5
Andrew Bargh	3	0	1	1	X	5
Lee Smethills	1	1	1	1	0	4
Nicki Glanz	0	3	0	0	0	3
Simon Lambert	0	0	0	0	0	0

HEAT DETAILS

Ht 1:	Woffinden, Auty, Herne, Lambert, 56.7
Ht 2:	(Re-Run) Mear, Warwick, Taylor, Halsey (f, ex), 57.8
Ht 3:	Bargh, Branney, Smethills, Brown, 58.4
Ht 4:	Evans, Smart, Burrows, Glanz, 58.7
Ht 5:	Auty, Warwick, Burrows, Bargh, 57.8
Ht 6:	Herne, Smart, Mear, Branney, 59.6
Ht 7:	Glanz, Taylor, Smethills, Lambert, 60.2
Ht 8:	Woffinden, Brown, Halsey, Evans (f, rem, ret), 56.8
Ht 9:	Mear, Auty, Smethills, Evans, 59.7
Ht 10:	Warwick, Brown, Herne, Glanz, 59.8
Ht 11:	Halsey, Smart, Bargh, Lambert, 60.6
Ht 12:	(Re-Run) Woffinden, Taylor, Branney, Burrows (f, ex), 58.9
Ht 13:	Auty, Taylor, Brown, Smart, 59.0
Ht 14:	Burrows, Herne, Smethills, Halsey, 60.2
Ht 15:	Evans, Branney, Warwick, Lambert, 59.5
Ht 16:	Woffinden, Mear, Bargh, Glanz, 58.4
Ht 17:	Auty, Branney, Halsey, Glanz, 60.1
Ht 18:	(Re-Run) Herne, Evans, Taylor, Bargh (f, ex), 60.2
Ht 19:	Mear, Burrows, Brown, Lambert, 59.7
Ht 20:	Woffinden, Smart, Warwick, Smethills, 59.2

ROLL OF HONOUR

NOTE: Previously known as the Division Three Riders' Championship (1994), Academy League Riders' Championship (1995) and Amateur League Riders' Championship (1997).

YEAR	FIRST	SECOND	THIRD
1994	Andy Howe	Kevin Little	Colin Earl
1995	Kevin Little	Chris Cobby	Andre Compton
1996	Mike Hampson	Justin Elkins	Graeme Gordon
1997	Jon Armstrong	Bobby Eldridge	David Howe
1998	Steve Bishop	Andrew Appleton	Seemond Stephens
1999	Jonathan Swales	Steve Camden	Scott Courtney
2000	Scott Pegler	Steve Bishop	Adam Allott
2001	David Mason	Scott Pegler	Simon Wolstenholme
2002	James Birkinshaw	Edward Kennett	Jamie Robertson
2003	Barrie Evans	Jamie Robertson	Trevor Harding
2004	James Wright	Mark Burrows	Richard Hall
2005	Steve Boxall	Barrie Evans	Blair Scott
2006	Adam Roynon	Seemond Stephens	Lee Smart
2007	Tai Woffinden	Josh Auty	Robert Mear

BRITISH UNDER-18 CHAMPIONSHIP 2007

17 SEPTEMBER, WOLVERHAMPTON

1st TAI WOFFINDEN
2nd LEWIS BRIDGER
3rd JOE HAINES
4th JOSH AUTY

RIDER	RACE SCORES					TOTAL
Tai Woffinden	3	3	3	3	3	15
Lewis Bridger	3	3	3	2	3	14
Joe Haines	2	2	2	3	3	12
Josh Auty	3	2	3	3	X	11
Ben Taylor	2	3	2	1	2	10
Robert Mear	3	0	3	2	2	10
Nicki Glanz	M	1	2	2	3	8
Jerran Hart	2	X	1	3	1	7
Brendan Johnson	2	3	1	0	0	6
Simon Lambert	1	2	X	2	1	6
Kyle Hughes	1	X	2	1	2	6
Jaimie Pickard	1	2	0	X	2	5
Kyle Newman	1	1	0	1	1	4
Richard Franklin	0	1	F	0	1	2
Joe Reynolds	0	X	1	1	0	2
Adam Lowe	X	X	1	0	0	1
James Sarjeant (Res)	0	-	-	-	-	0

HEAT DETAILS

Ht 1:	Bridger, Taylor, Pickard, Sarjeant, Glanz (ex, 2 mins), 59.64
Ht 2:	(Re-Run) Woffinden, Hart, Lambert, Lowe (f, ex), 57.17
Ht 3:	Auty, Haines, Hughes, Reynolds, 59.89
Ht 4:	Mear, Johnson, Newman, Franklin, 60.13
Ht 5:	Woffinden, Haines, Glanz, Mear, 56.76
Ht 6:	(Re-Run) Taylor, Lambert, Franklin, Hughes (f, ex), 60.61
Ht 7:	(Re-Run) Bridger, Auty, Newman, Hart (f, ex), 57.72
Ht 8:	(Re-Run) Johnson, Pickard, Lowe (f, ex), Reynolds (f, ex), 61.59
Ht 9:	(Re-Run) Auty, Glanz, Johnson, Lambert (f, ex), 59.07
Ht 10:	Woffinden, Taylor, Reynolds, Newman, 57.52
Ht 11:	Bridger, Haines, Lowe, Franklin (fell), 58.38
Ht 12:	Mear, Hughes, Hart, Pickard, 59.63
Ht 13:	Hart, Glanz, Reynolds, Franklin, 60.30
Ht 14:	Auty, Mear, Taylor, Lowe, 59.29
Ht 15:	Woffinden, Bridger, Hughes, Johnson, 57.33
Ht 16:	(Re-Run) Haines, Lambert, Newman, Pickard (f, ex), 59.77
Ht 17:	Glanz, Hughes, Newman, Lowe, 60.56
Ht 18:	Haines, Taylor, Hart, Johnson, 60.27
Ht 19:	Bridger, Mear, Lambert, Reynolds, 59.43
Ht 20:	(Re-Run) Woffinden, Pickard, Franklin, Auty (f, ex), 58.44

ROLL OF HONOUR

YEAR	FIRST	SECOND	THIRD
2004	Daniel King	James Wright	Edward Kennett
2005	William Lawson	Lewis Bridger	Jack Hargreaves
2006	Lewis Bridger	Tai Woffinden	Ben Barker
2007	Tai Woffinden	Lewis Bridger	Joe Haines

PREMIER LEAGUE RIDERS' CHAMPIONSHIP 2007

(SUPER 7EVEN SERIES: EVENT SEVEN)

30 SEPTEMBER, SWINDON

1st   JAMES WRIGHT
2nd JASON LYONS
3rd   JACEK REMPALA
4th   DANIEL NERMARK

RIDER	QUALIFYING SCORES					TOTAL
James Wright	3	3	2	3	3	14
Jason Lyons	3	3	2	2	3	13
Daniel Nermark	2	2	3	3	3	13
Chris Holder	2	3	3	1	2	11
Tomas Topinka	1	3	2	3	1	10
Jacek Rempala	0	1	3	2	3	9
Kaj Laukkanen	3	2	R	2	T	7
Tai Woffinden	1	1	3	1	1	7
Josef Franc	2	1	1	1	2	7
Chris Kerr	1	0	R	3	2	6
Chris Schramm (Res)	3	0	2	1	0	6
Lee Complin	1	2	X	0	2	5
Michal Rajkowski	2	2	0	0	0	4
Andre Compton	0	0	1	2	1	4
Emil Kramer	0	1	0	0	1	2
Trent Leverington	0	0	1	0	0	1

NOTE: Jason King was due to participate, but failed to arrive after being stuck in gridlocked traffic on the M4, following an accident that had unfortunately claimed the life of a baby girl. King was replaced by the meeting reserve, Schramm, throughout.

HEAT DETAILS

Ht 1:	Wright, Holder, Woffinden, Rempala, 67.08
Ht 2:	Lyons, Nermark, Topinka, Compton, 66.52
Ht 3:	Laukkanen, Rajkowski, Kerr, Kramer, 66.93
Ht 4:	Schramm, Franc, Complin, Leverington, 68.15
Ht 5:	Topinka, Rajkowski, Rempala, Leverington, 67.21
Ht 6:	Lyons, Laukkanen, Woffinden, Schramm, 66.86
Ht 7:	Holder, Nermark, Franc, Kerr, 66.96
Ht 8:	(Re-Run) Wright, Complin, Kramer, Compton, 67.71
Ht 9:	(Re-Run) Rempala, Lyons, Complin (f, ex), Kerr (ex, not under power), 68.05
Ht 10:	Woffinden, Topinka, Franc, Kramer, 67.43
Ht 11:	Holder, Schramm, Compton, Rajkowski, 68.05
Ht 12:	Nermark, Wright, Leverington, Laukkanen (ret), 67.99
Ht 13:	Nermark, Rempala, Schramm, Kramer, 66.92
Ht 14:	Kerr, Compton, Woffinden, Leverington, 68.65
Ht 15:	Topinka, Laukkanen, Holder, Complin, 67.80
Ht 16:	Wright, Lyons, Franc, Rajkowski, 67.95
Ht 17:	(Re-Run) Rempala, Franc, Compton, Laukkanen (ex, tapes), 68.83 (3 riders only)
Ht 18:	Nermark, Complin, Woffinden, Rajkowski, 67.08
Ht 19:	Lyons, Holder, Kramer, Leverington, 67.83
Ht 20:	Wright, Kerr, Topinka, Schramm, 68.24

Semi-final:	Nermark, Rempala, Topinka, Holder, 66.52
Final:	Wright, Lyons, Rempala, Nermark, 66.27

ROLL OF HONOUR

NOTE: Became known as the Premier League Riders' Championship in 1997, having previously been known as the Division Two Riders' Championship (1968-1974 and 1991-1994) and National League Riders' Championship (1975-1990).

YEAR	FIRST	SECOND	THIRD
1968	Graham Plant	Ken Eyre	Graeme Smith
1969	Geoff Ambrose	Mick Bell	Ross Gilbertson
1970	Dave Jessup	Barry Crowson	Gary Peterson
1971	John Louis	Malcolm Shakespeare	Hugh Saunders
1972	Phil Crump	Arthur Price	Bob Coles
1973	Arthur Price	Bobby McNeil	Lou Sansom
1974	Carl Glover	Ted Hubbard	Phil Herne
1975	Laurie Etheridge	Brian Collins	Arthur Browning
1976	Joe Owen	John Jackson	Ted Hubbard
1977	Colin Richardson	Martin Yeates	Tom Owen
1978	Steve Koppe	John Jackson	Ted Hubbard
1979	Ian Gledhill	Steve Wilcock	Andy Grahame
1980	Wayne Brown	Martin Yeates	Steve Finch
1981	Mike Ferreira	Simon Wigg	Bruce Cribb
1982	Joe Owen	Steve Lomas	Bob Garrad
1983	Steve McDermott	Richard Knight	Martin Yeates
1984	Ian Barney	Dave Perks	Martin Yeates
1985	Neil Middleditch	Kevin Hawkins	Trevor Banks
1986	Paul Thorp	Steve Schofield	Les Collins
1987	Andrew Silver	Nigel Crabtree	David Blackburn
1988	Troy Butler	Mark Loram	Kenny McKinna
1989	Mark Loram	Kenny McKinna	David Blackburn
1990	Andy Grahame	Chris Louis	Craig Boyce
1991	Jan Staechmann	David Bargh	Troy Butler
1992	Robert Nagy	Mick Poole	Richard Green
1993	Gary Allan	Mick Poole	Tony Langdon
1994	Paul Bentley	Tony Olsson	Tony Langdon
1995-96	Not staged		
1997	Peter Carr	Glenn Cunningham	Robert Eriksson
1998	Glenn Cunningham	Carl Stonehewer	Peter Carr
1999	Sean Wilson	Jesper Olsen	Craig Watson
2000	Carl Stonehewer	Peter Carr	Paul Pickering
2001	Carl Stonehewer	Sean Wilson	Bjarne Pedersen
2002	Adam Shields	Craig Watson	Phil Morris
2003	Sean Wilson	Adam Shields	Carl Stonehewer
2004	Andre Compton	Mark Lemon	Simon Stead
2005	Sean Wilson	Alan Mogridge	Tomas Topinka
2006	Magnus Zetterstrom	Jason Lyons	Gary Havelock
2007	James Wright	Jason Lyons	Jacek Rempala

SPEEDWAY GRAND PRIX 2007

KEY: 1 = Italy; 2 = Europe; 3 = Sweden; 4 = Denmark; 5 = Britain; 6 = Czech Republic; 7 = Scandinavia; 8 = Latvia; 9 = Poland; 10 = Slovenia; 11 = Germany.

RIDER	1	2	3	4	5	6	7	8	9	10	11	TOTAL
NICKI PEDERSEN (Denmark)	24	23	11	16	12	24	16	19	19	23	9	196
LEIGH ADAMS (Australia)	12	10	21	18	14	8	19	22	9	9	11	153
JASON CRUMP (Australia)	12	13	4	9	15	11	15	10	7	13	15	124
TOMASZ GOLLOB (Poland)	10	3	9	11	3	1	19	14	21	10	7	108
HANS N. ANDERSEN (Denmark)	9	13	20	12	13	8	12	5	3	3	9	107
GREG HANCOCK (USA)	19	15	9	7	17	6	5	3	5	4	16	106
RUNE HOLTA (Poland)	2	6	9	5	5	16	5	7	10	16	10	91
SCOTT NICHOLLS (Great Britain)	4	6	4	7	9	12	8	13	4	16	8	91
CHRIS HARRIS (Great Britain)	7	15	9	5	20	5	6	7	5	8	4	91
ANDREAS JONSSON (Sweden)	7	5	5	16	5	7	-	8	11	6	20	90
WIESLAW JAGUS (Poland)	14	6	6	3	0	9	12	11	5	9	6	81
BJARNE PEDERSEN (Denmark)	5	8	3	5	7	6	7	8	8	9	11	77
JAROSLAW HAMPEL (Poland)	8	6	5	7	8	16	-	-	11	6	-	67
MATEJ ZAGAR (Slovenia)	5	7	7	1	5	8	3	2	4	6	6	54
ANTONIO LINDBACK (Sweden)	3	0	3	9	7	0	3	0	5	1	-	31
FREDRIK LINDGREN (Sweden)	-	-	14	-	-	-	7	-	-	-	-	21
KRZYSZTOF KASPRZAK (Poland)	-	-	-	-	-	-	-	-	17	-	-	17
PETER KARLSSON (Sweden)	-	-	-	-	-	-	5	-	-	-	8	13
KENNETH BJERRE (Denmark)	-	-	-	10	-	-	-	-	-	-	-	10
GRIGORY LAGUTA (Russia)	-	-	-	-	-	-	-	8	-	-	-	8
SEBASTIAN ULAMEK (Poland)	-	6	-	-	-	-	-	-	-	-	-	6
JONAS DAVIDSSON (Sweden)	-	-	5	-	-	-	-	-	-	-	-	5
JURICA PAVLIC (Croatia)	-	-	-	-	-	-	-	-	-	5	-	5
KAJ LAUKKANEN (Finland)	-	-	-	-	-	-	2	3	-	-	0	5
DAVID HOWE (Great Britain)	-	-	-	-	4	-	-	-	-	-	-	4
LUBOS TOMICEK (Czech Republic)	-	-	-	-	-	4	-	-	-	-	-	4
CHRISTIAN HEFENBROCK (Germany)	-	-	-	-	-	-	-	-	-	-	4	4
JOSFF FRANC (Czech Republic)	-	-	-	-	-	3	-	-	-	-	-	3
MATTIA CARPANESE (Italy)	2	-	-	-	-	-	-	-	-	-	-	2
MORTEN RISAGER (Denmark)	-	-	-	2	-	-	-	-	-	-	-	2
MAKSIMS BOGDANOVS (Latvia)	-	-	-	-	-	-	-	2	-	-	-	2
TOMASZ GAPINSKI (Poland)	-	1	-	-	-	-	-	-	-	-	-	1
KJASTAS PUODZHUKS (Latvia)	-	-	-	-	-	-	-	1	-	-	-	1
DANIELE TESSARI (Italy)	0	-	-	-	-	-	-	-	-	-	-	0
CHRISTIAN MIOTELLO (Italy)	0	-	-	-	-	-	-	-	-	-	-	0
ERIC ANDERSSON (Sweden)	-	-	0	-	-	-	-	-	-	-	-	0
JESPER B. JENSEN (Denmark)	-	-	-	0	-	-	-	-	-	-	-	0
MATEJ KUS (Czech Republic)	-	-	-	-	-	0	-	-	-	-	-	0

GRAND PRIX OF ITALY (ROUND ONE)

DATE: 28 April.

VENUE: Motorclub Lonigo, Vicenza.

1st   NICKI PEDERSEN
2nd GREG HANCOCK
3rd WIESLAW JAGUS
4th JASON CRUMP

SCORECHART

RIDER	1	2	3	4	5	S/F	Final	Total
Nicki Pedersen	3	3	3	3	3	3	6	24
Greg Hancock	3	3	2	2	2	3	4	19
Wieslaw Jagus	0	3	3	3	1	2	2	14
Jason Crump	3	1	2	3	1	2	0	12
Leigh Adams	2	2	1	3	3	1	-	12
Tomasz Gollob	1	3	3	0	2	1	-	10
Hans N. Andersen	2	1	1	2	3	0	-	9
Jaroslaw Hampel	3	0	1	2	2	0	-	8
Andreas Jonsson	2	2	2	0	1	-	-	7
Chris Harris	2	2	0	1	2	-	-	7
Matej Zagar	1	0	1	0	3	-	-	5
Bjarne Pedersen	T	R	3	1	1	-	-	5
Scott Nicholls	1	1	2	X	0	-	-	4
Antonio Lindback	1	1	0	1	0	-	-	3
Rune Holta	X	0	X	2	0	-	-	2
Mattia Carpanese (Wildcard)	0	2	M	X	0	-	-	2
Daniele Tessari (Reserve)	0	-	-	-	-	-	-	0
Christian Miotello (Reserve)	0	-	-	-	-	-	-	0

RACE DETAILS

Ht 1:	(Re-Run) Hampel, Andersen, Gollob, Holta (f, ex), 66.09
Ht 2:	(Re-Run) Crump, Jonsson, Zagar, Tessari, B. Pedersen (ex, tapes), 66.16
Ht 3:	Hancock, Harris, Lindback, Carpanese, 66.41
Ht 4:	N. Pedersen, Adams, Nicholls, Jagus, 66.63
Ht 5:	N. Pedersen, Carpanese, Andersen, B. Pedersen (ret), 67.20
Ht 6:	Hancock, Adams, Crump, Hampel, 66.75
Ht 7:	Gollob, Harris, Nicholls, Zagar, 67.01
Ht 8:	Jagus, Jonsson, Lindback, Holta, 67.40
Ht 9:	Jagus, Crump, Andersen, Harris, 66.87
Ht 10:	B. Pedersen, Nicholls, Hampel, Lindback, 67.46
Ht 11:	Gollob, Jonsson, Adams, Miotello, Carpanese (ex, 2 mins), 67.51
Ht 12:	(Re-Run) N. Pedersen, Hancock, Zagar, Holta (f, ex), 67.49
Ht 13:	Adams, Andersen, Lindback, Zagar, 69.30
Ht 14:	N. Pedersen, Hampel, Harris, Jonsson, 69.17
Ht 15:	Jagus, Hancock, B. Pedersen, Gollob, 68.70
Ht 16:	(Re-Run) Crump, Holta, Nicholls (f, ex), Carpanese (ex, not under power), 68.74
Ht 17:	Andersen, Hancock, Jonsson, Nicholls, 68.70
Ht 18:	Zagar, Hampel, Jagus, Carpanese, 68.66
Ht 19:	N. Pedersen, Gollob, Crump, Lindback, 68.80
Ht 20:	Adams, Harris, B. Pedersen, Holta, 68.37

First semi-final:	N. Pedersen, Jagus, Gollob, Andersen, 67.83
Second semi-final:	Hancock, Crump, Adams, Hampel, 68.39
Grand Final:	N. Pedersen, Hancock, Jagus, Crump, 67.92

NICKI Pedersen sent out a fierce signal of intent by scorching to a majestic 24-point maximum at the pacy Lonigo circuit, as the 2007 Grand Prix series got underway amongst the humidity of the Italian countryside. The Danish rider performed brilliantly on a track that favoured the white line and rewarded those who were able to produce quick starts.

In truth, Pedersen was rarely troubled throughout the evening and his endless reserves of straight line speed meant he was nigh impossible to catch once he headed the chasing pack. The only competitor who looked like challenging Pedersen was Greg Hancock who, especially in the early part of the meeting, was able to match the Dane's blistering pace. It was a solid performance from Hancock, which netted him a very tasty 19 points and provided him with a solid platform on which to launch his 2007 World Championship assault.

Elsewhere, Wieslaw Jagus rode exceptionally well, as he romped to a podium finish in his first meeting as a fully-fledged Grand Prix rider and the diminutive Polish rider showcased plenty of track craft on route to a hefty 14-point tally. His third place finish denied Jason Crump a spot on the rostrum and the double World Champion was clearly disappointed not to have made more of his appearance in the final. The absence of a wider racing line hampered the Australian's chances, although he also seemed to lack some of the speed on which the foundations of his 2006 success had been constructed.

Britain's Chris Harris also impressed in his maiden outing as a permanent member of the series; the popular Coventry rider narrowly missed out on a place in the semi-finals, but conveyed clear signs that he had the necessary to skill to compete on the international stage. His compatriot, Scott Nicholls, endured a night to forget, as he clattered into the back straight safety fence in his fourth outing in what was an exceptionally frightening looking smash.

It was also a dismal evening for the Swedish contingent of Antonio Lindback and Andreas Jonsson, both of whom failed to collect a race win and never realistically appeared likely to challenge for a spot in the last eight. The other Poles in the field, Tomasz Gollob and Jaroslaw Hampel, were unable to progress past the semi-final stage, likewise Leigh Adams, who, on his thirty-sixth birthday, couldn't forge a route into the all-important showdown race.

Chris Seaward

GRAND PRIX OF EUROPE (ROUND TWO)

DATE: 12 May.

VENUE: Olympic Stadium, Wroclaw, Poland.

1st NICKI PEDERSEN
2nd HANS N. ANDERSEN
3rd CHRIS HARRIS
4th JASON CRUMP

SCORECHART

RIDER	1	2	3	4	5	S/F	Final	Total
Nicki Pedersen	3	2	3	3	3	3	6	23
Greg Hancock	2	3	3	3	3	1	-	15
Chris Harris	1	1	3	3	3	2	2	15
Jason Crump	3	2	2	2	2	2	0	13
Hans N. Andersen	0	3	1	0	2	3	4	13
Leigh Adams	2	3	2	X	3	0	-	10
Bjarne Pedersen	3	1	0	2	1	1	-	8
Matej Zagar	0	3	1	2	1	0	-	7
Sebastian Ulamek (Wildcard)	0	0	3	1	2	-	-	6
Jaroslaw Hampel	3	F	1	F	2	-	-	6
Rune Holta	1	F	2	3	X	-	-	6
Wieslaw Jagus	2	2	0	2	0	-	-	6
Scott Nicholls	1	1	2	1	1	-	-	6
Andreas Jonsson	2	2	1	X	-	-	-	5
Tomasz Gollob	1	1	R	1	0	-	-	3
Tomasz Gapinski (Reserve)	1	-	-	-	-	-	-	1
Antonio Lindback	0	0	0	0	0	-	-	0
Tomasz Jedrzejak (Reserve)	-	-	-	-	-	-	-	-

RACE DETAILS

Ht 1:	N. Pedersen, Hancock, Harris, Ulamek, 66.35
Ht 2:	Hampel, Adams, Holta, Andersen, 65.88
Ht 3:	B. Pedersen, Jagus, Gollob, Lindback, 65.97
Ht 4:	Crump, Jonsson, Nicholls, Zagar, 65.59
Ht 5:	Adams, Crump, Harris, Lindback, 64.25
Ht 6:	Hancock, Jagus, Nicholls, Holta (fell), 65.34
Ht 7:	Zagar, N. Pedersen, Gollob, Hampel (fell), 66.22
Ht 8:	Andersen, Jonsson, B. Pedersen, Ulamek, 65.50
Ht 9:	Harris, Holta, Jonsson, Gollob (ret), 64.88
Ht 10:	Hancock, Adams, Zagar, B. Pedersen, 65.77
Ht 11:	N. Pedersen, Nicholls, Andersen, Lindback, 65.84
Ht 12:	Ulamek, Crump, Hampel, Jagus, 66.22
Ht 13:	Harris, B. Pedersen, Nicholls, Hampel (fell), 66.00
Ht 14:	Hancock, Crump, Gollob, Andersen (f, rem), 65.12
Ht 15:	(Re-Run twice) N. Pedersen, Jagus, Jonsson (f, ex), Adams (f, ex), 66.81
Ht 16:	Holta, Zagar, Ulamek, Lindback, 66.65
Ht 17:	Harris, Andersen, Zagar, Jagus, 66.06
Ht 18:	Hancock, Hampel, Gapinski, Lindback, 66.41
Ht 19:	(Re-Run) N. Pedersen, Crump, B. Pedersen, Holta (f, ex), 66.96
Ht 20:	Adams, Ulamek, Nicholls, Gollob, 67.22

First semi-final:	N. Pedersen, Crump, B. Pedersen, Zagar, 66.44
Second semi-final:	Andersen, Harris, Hancock, Adams, 67.13
Grand Final:	N. Pedersen, Andersen, Harris, Crump, 65.85

AFTER a somewhat tame start in the humidity of the beautiful Italian countryside, the Grand Prix series really sprung into life amongst the red hot atmosphere of Wroclaw's Olympic Stadium, where the world's best gathered for the European GP. Italy was a quaint, albeit low key, location to begin the series in front of a modest crowd of 10,000, who clapped politely in appreciation as the stars of shale put on an entertaining show. In stark contrast, the second round of the 2007 series was fiercely contested, engulfed by passion and staged in front of 25,000 extremely vocal Polish fans. If the Italian GP was a chilled glass of white wine, then the European Grand Prix was a large bottle of Poland's finest vodka.

The vast change in atmosphere made no difference to Nicki Pedersen, who cruised to his second successive Grand Prix win of the season on a night of frantic action and high drama. The 2003 World Champion took his tally to a phenomenal 47 points out of a possible 48 from the two opening rounds, as he continued a simply breathtaking assault on the Grand Prix series.

This wasn't a Grand Prix for the faint hearted, that's for sure. It featured a number of nasty crashes and board-scraping passes on a track that became heavily rutted as the night progressed. However, the wet Polish weather that preceded the meeting ensured that the Wroclaw racetrack had a variety of different racing lines, which subsequently created an array of classic racing.

The GP really sprung to life after the first round of heats had been completed, when the wet shale had been blasted away from the top surface and the world's best began to utilize the pockets of grip located in the circuit's wider outposts. Pedersen's compatriot Hans Andersen collected second spot, whilst Britain's Chris Harris rode superbly to grab the final podium positiont. In doing so, the exciting youngster silenced some critics within the sport, having ridden wonderfully in a crackerjack second semi-final race.

In an uncanny resemblance to the Italian Grand Prix two weeks earlier, Leigh Adams again faltered at the semi-final stage, whilst Jason Crump failed to stamp his authority on the final, running a second successive last in the showdown race. The qualifying heats saw Adams recover from a nasty looking fall in his fourth outing to collect 10 points and progress through to the semi-finals. However, the Mildura-born racer, despite at one stage occupying second spot, was squeezed out and eventually came home in fourth spot.

Meanwhile, Crump went one better than his fellow countryman by progressing through to the final, but, having come from row three on the grid, he never fully recovered from an aggressive first corner shove from Andersen. In comparison to the lightning quick pace of Pedersen, the 2006 World Champion looked uncharacteristically sluggish and his performances in the first couple of rounds did not live up to expectation.

Chris Seaward

GRAND PRIX OF SWEDEN (ROUND THREE)

DATE: 26 May.

VENUE: Smed Stadium, Eskilstuna.

1st LEIGH ADAMS
2nd HANS N. ANDERSEN
3rd FREDRIK LINDGREN
4th NICKI PEDERSEN

SCORECHART

RIDER	1	2	3	4	5	S/F	Final	Total
Leigh Adams	3	3	2	3	1	3	6	21
Hans N. Andersen	3	2	3	3	2	3	4	20
Fredrik Lindgren (Wildcard)	2	2	2	3	1	2	2	14
Nicki Pedersen	0	3	3	X	3	2	0	11
Greg Hancock	3	1	3	2	0	0	-	9
Rune Holta	3	1	1	1	3	0	-	9
Tomasz Gollob	1	1	1	2	3	1	-	9
Chris Harris	1	2	1	2	2	1	-	9
Matej Zagar	1	3	2	1	0	-	-	7
Wieslaw Jagus	0	3	3	N	-	-	-	6
Jonas Davidsson (Reserve)	2	3	-	-	-	-	-	5
Jaroslaw Hampel	1	0	0	3	1	-	-	5
Andreas Jonsson	2	1	0	0	2	-	-	5
Scott Nicholls	2	0	0	0	2	-	-	4
Jason Crump	2	2	0	F	-	-	-	4
Bjarne Pedersen	0	0	2	1	0	-	-	3
Antonio Lindback	0	0	1	1	1	-	-	3
Eric Andersson (Reserve)	0	-	-	-	-	-	-	0

RACE DETAILS

Ht 1:	Holta, Jonsson, Hampel, B. Pedersen, 61.7
Ht 2:	Andersen, Nicholls, Harris, Jagus, 61.1
Ht 3:	Hancock, Crump, Gollob, N. Pedersen, 61.5
Ht 4:	Adams, Lindgren, Zagar, Lindback, 61.6
Ht 5:	N. Pedersen, Andersen, Holta, Lindback, 59.8
Ht 6:	Jagus, Lindgren, Hancock, Hampel, 60.7
Ht 7:	Adams, Crump, Jonsson, Nicholls, 60.7
Ht 8:	Zagar, Harris, Gollob, B. Pedersen, 61.2
Ht 9:	Jagus, Zagar, Holta, Crump, 60.5
Ht 10:	Andersen, Adams, Gollob, Hampel, 61.1
Ht 11:	N. Pedersen, Lindgren, Harris, Jonsson, 61.0
Ht 12:	Hancock, B. Pedersen, Lindback, Nicholls, 61.5
Ht 13:	Lindgren, Gollob, Holta, Nicholls, 61.2
Ht 14:	Hampel, Harris, Lindback, Crump (fell), 60.9
Ht 15:	Andersen, Hancock, Zagar, Jonsson, 61.0
Ht 16:	(Re-Run) Adams, Davidsson, B. Pedersen, N. Pedersen (f, ex), Jagus (f, ns), 61.2
Ht 17:	Holta, Harris, Adams, Hancock, 61.0
Ht 18:	N. Pedersen, Nicholls, Hampel, Zagar, 61.7
Ht 19:	Gollob, Jonsson, Lindback, Andersson, 61.8
Ht 20:	Davidsson, Andersen, Lindgren, B. Pedersen, 62.0

First semi-final:	Andersen, N. Pedersen, Gollob, Holta, 61.4
Second semi-final:	Adams, Lindgren, Harris, Hancock, 61.4
Grand Final:	Adams, Andersen, Lindgren, N. Pedersen, 61.4

LEIGH Adams conjured a breathtaking last gasp pass on Hans Andersen to take an emphatic victory in round three of the speedway Grand Prix in Eskilstuna, Sweden. It was just what the popular Australian required to kick-start his 2007 World Championship campaign, having failed to progress past the semi-final stage in the opening two rounds of the tournament.

On a night of high drama, many of the big-guns in the series left Eskilstuna nursing injuries, including Jason Crump and Nicki Pedersen, who both fell heavily in unrelated incidents. The most dramatic of these occurred in heat sixteen, when Pedersen, together with his namesake, Bjarne, and Wieslaw Jagus tangled awkwardly on the apex of turn one. Remarkably, Nicki Pedersen continued in the meeting, whilst Jagus, suffering from heavy concussion, was deemed unfit to continue by the track doctor.

Previously, in heat fourteen, Crump had hit the home straight safety fence after a lump of grit had thrown him from his steed exiting turn four of the circuit. Crump was able to haul himself from the track, but was later placed on a stretcher and taken to hospital, having taken knocks to the shoulder and collarbone.

Combined with all the drama was some fantastic racing on a track that provided an array of differing lines. Whilst permanent Swedish Grand Prix riders Andreas Jonsson and Antonio Lindback proved to be a disappointment, the home crowd were very much entertained by the exploits of wildcard Fredrik Lindgren, who further enhanced his reputation as one of the sport's hottest young prospects. Lindgren comfortably negotiated a route through to the final, where he was joined by Adams, Andersen and also Nicki Pedersen, who had done remarkably well to recover after his earlier fall.

Andersen looked to have the final sewn up, as he made a commanding start from gate one to lead Adams by two or three bike lengths for a majority of the race. However, the nine times Australian Champion had other ideas and cleverly discovered a cushion of grip on the exit of the second bend on the fourth lap to nip inside Andersen in the coolest of fashion. Adams' victory propelled him to joint second place alongside Greg Hancock in the standings, 15 points adrift of Pedersen. It was a result which proved that the fiery Dane was beatable and provided Adams with a much needed confidence boost.

Chris Seaward

GRAND PRIX OF DENMARK (ROUND FOUR)

DATE: 9 June.

VENUE: Parken, Copenhagen.

1st   ANDREAS JONSSON
2nd NICKI PEDERSEN
3rd   LEIGH ADAMS
4th   TOMASZ GOLLOB

SCORECHART

RIDER	1	2	3	4	5	S/F	Final	Total
Andreas Jonsson	0	2	1	3	2	2	6	16
Nicki Pedersen	T	3	3	1	2	3	4	16
Leigh Adams	2	3	3	2	3	3	2	18
Tomasz Gollob	1	0	3	2	3	2	0	11
Hans N. Andersen	3	3	1	2	3	R	-	12
Kenneth Bjerre (Wildcard)	1	1	2	3	2	1	-	10
Antonio Lindback	3	2	0	3	1	X	-	9
Jason Crump	3	1	2	1	2	0	-	9
Greg Hancock	3	X	1	3	0	-	-	7
Jaroslaw Hampel	2	0	2	0	3	-	-	7
Scott Nicholls	2	1	2	1	1	-	-	7
Rune Holta	0	2	3	F	0	-	-	5
Bjarne Pedersen	X	3	1	0	1	-	-	5
Chris Harris	2	2	R	0	1	-	-	5
Wieslaw Jagus	1	1	0	1	0	-	-	3
Morten Risager (Reserve)	0	2	-	-	-	-	-	2
Matej Zagar	1	-	-	-	-	-	-	1
Jesper B. Jensen (Reserve)	0	0	0	-	-	-	-	0

RACE RESULTS

Ht 1:	Lindback, Harris, Jagus, Holta, 56.6
Ht 2:	(Re-Run) Hancock, Hampel, Gollob, Jensen, N. Pedersen (ex, tapes), 56.7
Ht 3:	(Re-Run) Andersen, Adams, Zagar, B. Pedersen (ex, foul riding), 56.0 (Equalled Track Record)
Ht 4:	Crump, Nicholls, Bjerre, Jonsson, 55.5 (New Track Record)
Ht 5:	Andersen, Harris, Nicholls, Hampel, 55.9
Ht 6:	N. Pedersen, Lindback, Crump, Risager, 56.0
Ht 7:	(Re-Run) B. Pedersen, Jonsson, Jagus, Hancock (f, ex), 56.4
Ht 8:	Adams, Holta, Bjerre, Gollob, 56.6
Ht 9:	N. Pedersen, Bjerre, B. Pedersen, Harris (ret), 56.0
Ht 10:	Adams, Hampel, Jonsson, Lindback, 55.7
Ht 11:	Gollob, Crump, Andersen, Jagus, 56.1
Ht 12:	Holta, Nicholls, Hancock, Jensen, 56.7
Ht 13:	Hancock, Adams, Crump, Harris, 55.5 (Equalled Track Record)
Ht 14:	(Re-Run twice) Lindback, Gollob, Nicholls, B. Pedersen, 56.1
Ht 15:	Bjerre, Risager, Jagus, Hampel, 56.0
Ht 16:	Jonsson, Andersen, N. Pedersen, Holta (fell), 56.9
Ht 17:	Gollob, Jonsson, Harris, Jensen, 56.8
Ht 18:	Andersen, Bjerre, Lindback, Hancock, 57.0
Ht 19:	Adams, N. Pedersen, Nicholls, Jagus, 56.1
Ht 20:	Hampel, Crump, B. Pedersen, Holta, 56.5

First semi-final:	Adams, Gollob, Bjerre, Crump, 56.0
Second semi-final:	(Re-Run) N. Pedersen, Jonsson, Andersen (ret), Lindback (f, ex), 56.4
Grand Final:	Jonsson, N. Pedersen, Adams, Gollob, 56.8

SWEDEN'S Andreas Jonsson tore up the meticulously planned script in dramatic fashion as he rock 'n' rolled to victory on a night of high drama at a sun-drenched Parken. The Speedway Grand Prix made a welcome return to Denmark's national stadium for a fifth successive year and served up a twenty-three heat thriller in front of a passionate 30,000-strong audience. Jonsson's victory was the perfect remedy to kick-start his 2007 GP campaign, which, previously, had been distinctly under par and lacked the characteristic flair he had in the past exuded with such regularity.

The bustling streets of Copenhagen, renowned for their sublime architecture and quirky cafes is home of the intimidating Parken arena, an overflowing cauldron of emotion. The beer flowed freely in the bars outside the stadium as the atmosphere steadily increased, with a sea of Danish flags quickly dominating the sunny landscape.

Jonsonn's victory looked distinctly unlikely, as the stylish Swede stuttered through the qualifying stages after failing to score in his opening race. However, Jonsson did engineer a route into the top eight and inadvertently aroused the passionate home crowd as he barged past local hero Hans Andersen on the back straight of the second semi final, removing the Dane's chain in the process. The stadium erupted into a chorus of boos and whistles as a furious Andersen retired on the centre green, realising his dream of reigning victorious at his home GP for a second successive year were over.

As the stadium morphed into a fully-fledged amphitheatre, Jonsson conjured an impeccable start from the generally undesirable gate four and clamped his opponents on the white line to take victory in a ferocious final. Cue intense annoyance from the home crowd, whose jeering certainly curbed Jonsson's post victory celebrations. Even Nicki Pedersen's second place couldn't prevent the Danes from directing their passionate anger at Jonsson, as his Swedish national anthem was drowned out by a wave of dissatisfaction.

It had appeared as if Leigh Adams would collect his second Grand Prix victory in succession, as he notched up a hefty 13 points in his qualifying heats. Adams breezed through the semi final, but uncharacteristically made a minor mistake from the start in the big showdown, which allowed Jonsson to complete his phenomenal sweep from the outside grid. Nevertheless, Adams still top-scored on the night with 18 points and closed the gap on World Championship leader Nicki Pedersen to 13 points.

Pedersen himself clearly felt the immense pressure from his expectant home fans and was excluded from his first ride for clattering into the tapes. The current World Champion, Jason Crump, yet again continued his lull in form and, despite some very impressive league scores, was still seen to be under-achieving on the world stage. After negotiating a safe route to the first semi-final, Crump nestled into second spot behind Adams before surprisingly drifting off-line on the entry to the first bend of lap two. That momentary slip cost him dearly and provided a passage for Tomasz Gollob to exploit and move into second place.

Chris Seaward

GRAND PRIX OF GREAT BRITAIN (ROUND FIVE)

DATE: 30 June.

VENUE: Millennium Stadium, Cardiff.

1st CHRIS HARRIS
2nd GREG HANCOCK
3rd JASON CRUMP
4th LEIGH ADAMS

SCORECHART

RIDER	1	2	3	4	5	S/F	Final	Total
Chris Harris	3	2	2	2	3	2	6	20
Greg Hancock	0	3	2	3	3	2	4	17
Jason Crump	1	1	3	2	3	3	2	15
Leigh Adams	1	2	3	3	2	3	0	14
Hans N. Andersen	3	3	3	2	1	1	-	13
Nicki Pedersen	2	3	2	3	2	X	-	12
Scott Nicholls	1	1	2	2	3	0	-	9
Jaroslaw Hampel	0	0	3	3	1	1	-	8
Antonio Lindback	3	2	1	1	0	-	-	7
Bjarne Pedersen	2	3	1	1	0	-	-	7
Rune Holta	3	1	0	1	0	-	-	5
Matej Zagar	2	0	1	0	2	-	-	5
Andreas Jonsson	2	1	1	X	1	-	-	5
David Howe (Wildcard)	0	2	0	1	1	-	-	4
Tomasz Gollob	1	0	0	0	2	-	-	3
Wieslaw Jagus	0	0	0	0	0	-	-	0
Edward Kennett (Reserve)	-	-	-	-	-	-	-	-
Daniel King (Reserve)	-	-	-	-	-	-	-	-

RACE RESULTS

Ht 1:	Andersen, Jonsson, Nicholls, Howe, 57.5
Ht 2:	Holta, Zagar, Gollob, Jagus, 57.4
Ht 3:	(Re-Run) Harris, N. Pedersen, Crump, Hampel, 56.6 (Track Record)
Ht 4:	Lindback, B. Pedersen, Adams, Hancock, 57.7
Ht 5:	N. Pedersen, Lindback, Jonsson, Jagus, 56.8
Ht 6:	Andersen, Adams, Crump, Gollob, 56.8
Ht 7:	B. Pedersen, Howe, Holta, Hampel, 57.5
Ht 8:	Hancock, Harris, Nicholls, Zagar, 57.6
Ht 9:	Hampel, Hancock, Jonsson, Gollob, 56.9
Ht 10:	Andersen, Harris, B. Pedersen, Jagus, 56.9
Ht 11:	Adams, N. Pedersen, Zagar, Howe, 56.9
Ht 12:	Crump, Nicholls, Lindback, Holta, 57.4
Ht 13:	(Re-Run) Adams, Harris, Holta, Jonsson (f, ex), 57.2
Ht 14:	Hampel, Andersen, Lindback, Zagar, 57.5
Ht 15:	Hancock, Crump, Howe, Jagus, 57.5
Ht 16:	(Re-Run) N. Pedersen, Nicholls, B. Pedersen, Gollob, 58.0
Ht 17:	Crump, Zagar, Jonsson, B. Pedersen, 57.7
Ht 18:	Hancock, N. Pedersen, Andersen, Holta, 58.1
Ht 19:	(Re-Run) Harris, Gollob, Howe, Lindback, 58.2
Ht 20:	Nicholls, Adams, Hampel, Jagus, 58.1

First semi-final:	(Re-Run) Crump, Hancock, Andersen, Nicholls, 57.8
Second semi-final:	(Re-Run) Adams, Harris, Hampel, N. Pedersen (f, ex), 58.4
Grand Final:	(Re-Run) Harris, Hancock, Crump, Adams, 57.6

FOOTBALL has the last minute penalty, rugby has the last gasp try and cricket has the final over decider. But, as dramatic climaxes go, nothing comes remotely close to rivalling speedway's version of a breathtaking conclusion; a passing manoeuvre on the final bend, which seals victory.

Imagine, then, the euphoria as Britain's Chris Harris cleverly sold Greg Hancock the most sublime of dummies exiting the fourth bend of the final lap, allowing him to nip inside the American to take victory and send 42,000 fans into pandemonium at a bustling Millennium Stadium. However, it wasn't just the heroics of Britain's brightest star that lit up world speedway's most prestigious event, as an array of classic racing made the seventh annual staging of the Cardiff weekend the best yet.

The timing of Harris's surge to the front couldn't have been better and provoked an intensely passionate reaction from a British crowd, which had been starved of a Grand Prix winner for seven long years. From the moment Harris crossed the line to take victory in heat three it became apparent that the unique atmosphere of the much-anticipated British Grand Prix hadn't been dampened by the pouring rain that was relentlessly sweeping through the streets of Cardiff. With the roof bolted shut, the buzz of air horns cannoned off the walls and merged with the beautiful musk of 500cc speedway machines to create the most fantastic of ambiences.

It was a modern day amphitheatre that didn't faze Harris in the slightest, as he spectacularly leg-trailed a route to victory and the super-quick twenty-four-year-old was roared on every inch of the way by the vocal chords of a record crowd. On the Sunday morning, doubtless, forty thousand voice boxes sounded slightly funky, a fair few heads pounded and eighty thousand eardrums were still complaining. It was the best hangover British speedway had ever had!

It could have been so much different though, especially for Leigh Adams who was left cursing Greg Hancock's premature reactions when the initial staging of the final was stopped after the over-zealous American had moved at the start. Adams had made a fast getaway at the first time of asking, but, almost inevitably, the second time the tapes rose he found himself languishing at the rear. It was cruel luck for Adams, who had secured a reasonably comfortable route through the qualifying races and then blitzed the field in the second semi-final.

It was the first time Adams had made three consecutive finals in his Grand Prix career and the Australian was able to claw a further 2 points into Nicki Pedersen's overall lead, reducing the margin to a tantalisingly close 11 points. The most fascinating and tactical speedway seemed to occur when the top two in the standings emerged on track. Adams would settle into his armchair style and think about which line to adopt, before breezing past his opponents, whilst Pedersen would buck, rear and barge his way through the field.

The Dane's night came to a premature conclusion when he struck a rut on the first corner in the second semi-final and was unable to keep hold of his machine. In typical Pedersen style, he hunted for a scapegoat on which he could place the blame, but his half-hearted excuse that Jaroslaw Hampel had pushed him wide quite rightly fell on deaf ears. Pedersen's two frighteningly dominant performances at Italy and Poland at the start of the 2007 campaign had quickly become fading memories and over the last three rounds Adams had collected 14 more points than the Championship leader.

Jason Crump collected his highest tally of the Grand Prix season thus far and his third place on the night was well deserved. The World Champion was slowly but surely regaining his form of 2006 and there were definite signs inside the Millennium Stadium that Crump had re-established the mental tenacity of which much of his success has been constructed upon. Take heat twelve for example, when the Aussie engaged in an absorbing battle with Scott Nicholls and eventually took victory on the line, thanks to an unbelievably brave effort.

The night belonged to Harris, though, and the Cornishman's all-out style added a new dimension of excitement to a series that after two relatively calm campaigns enjoyed a vintage year in 2007. Whether it was the wave of enthusiasm provoked by the arrival of IMG or the re-designed points system, the GP series was most certainly touring Europe with a beaming smile on its pretty little face.

Chris Harris was another walking around with a permanent grin and a spring in his step. Even the most optimistic of speedway pundits couldn't have predicted Harris's meteoritic rise to top spot of the podium in just his fifth event as a fully-fledged Grand Prix rider. The Truro-born racer made British speedway immensely proud by collecting a well deserved third spot in Wroclaw, but his barnstorming performance at Cardiff further conveyed what a wonderful young talent this country really has. It was the perfect tonic to help revive a beleaguered league structure that finds itself wrought with an extensive catalogue of problems. Chris Harris was the hero the Brits had so desperately craved since Mark Loram lost his crown in 2001.

For twenty-six years the World Final of 1981 had been widely regarded as the greatest speedway contest in the history of the sport. Time to budge up and share the mantelpiece, Wembley, there's a new kid on the block; Cardiff 2007 - you will be remembered eternally.

Chris Seaward

GRAND PRIX OF CZECH REPUBLIC (ROUND SIX)

DATE: 28 July.

VENUE: Marketa Stadium, Prague.

1st   NICKI PEDERSEN
2nd JAROSLAW HAMPEL
3rd   RUNE HOLTA
4th   SCOTT NICHOLLS

SCORECHART

RIDER	1	2	3	4	5	S/F	Final	Total
Nicki Pedersen	3	3	3	3	3	3	6	<u>24</u>
Jaroslaw Hampel	1	0	3	3	3	2	4	16
Rune Holta	1	2	3	2	3	3	2	16
Scott Nicholls	0	3	2	3	2	2	0	12
Jason Crump	1	2	2	3	2	1	-	11
Wieslaw Jagus	1	3	1	0	3	1	-	9
Matej Zagar	3	3	1	0	1	0	-	8
Leigh Adams	2	2	2	2	0	0	-	8
Hans N. Andersen	2	1	2	2	1	-	-	8
Andreas Jonsson	3	1	3	X	-	-	-	7
Bjarne Pedersen	3	1	0	0	2	-	-	6
Greg Hancock	0	2	1	2	1	-	-	6
Chris Harris	2	0	1	1	1	-	-	5
Lubos Tomicek (Wildcard)	2	1	0	1	0	-	-	4
Josef Franc (Reserve)	1	2	-	-	-	-	-	3
Tomasz Gollob	0	0	R	1	0	-	-	1
Antonio Lindback	0	0	R	-	-	-	-	0
Matej Kus (Reserve)	0	-	-	-	-	-	-	0

RACE RESULTS

Ht 1:	B. Pedersen, Tomicek, Hampel, Lindback, 64.89
Ht 2:	N. Pedersen, Harris, Jagus, Hancock, 63.82
Ht 3:	Zagar, Adams, Holta, Nicholls, 64.74
Ht 4:	Jonsson, Andersen, Crump, Gollob, 63.85
Ht 5:	Nicholls, Crump, B. Pedersen, Harris, 64.37
Ht 6:	Zagar, Hancock, Tomicek, Gollob, 63.35
Ht 7:	N. Pedersen, Holta, Jonsson, Hampel, 64.84
Ht 8:	Jagus, Adams, Andersen, Lindback, 64.84
Ht 9:	Holta, Andersen, Hancock, B. Pedersen, 65.56
Ht 10:	Jonsson, Adams, Harris, Tomicek, 64.29
Ht 11:	Hampel, Nicholls, Jagus, Gollob (ret), 65.31
Ht 12:	N. Pedersen, Crump, Zagar, Lindback (ret), 65.53
Ht 13:	N. Pedersen, Adams, Gollob, B. Pedersen, 65.02
Ht 14:	Crump, Holta, Tomicek, Jagus, 66.71
Ht 15:	Hampel, Andersen, Harris, Zagar, 65.89
Ht 16:	(Re-Run) Nicholls, Hancock, Franc, Jonsson (f, ex), 66.79
Ht 17:	Jagus, B. Pedersen, Zagar, Kus, 66.74
Ht 18:	N. Pedersen, Nicholls, Andersen, Tomicek, 66.16
Ht 19:	Hampel, Crump, Hancock, Adams, 66.75
Ht 20:	Holta, Franc, Harris, Gollob, 66.71

First semi-final:	N. Pedersen, Nicholls, Jagus, Zagar, 66.69
Second semi-final:	Holta, Hampel, Crump, Adams, 65.69
Grand Final:	N. Pedersen, Hampel, Holta, Nicholls, 65.75

A HEAVY and severely rutted Prague track meant entertainment levels were well below par at round six of the Speedway Grand Prix. Nevertheless, Nicki Pedersen was imperious, as he grabbed conditions by the scruff of the neck and romped to his third victory of the season on a night when the challenge from his main title rivals severely faltered.

For the second time in 2007, the lightning quick Dane didn't drop a point on route to victory, as he comfortably reigned victorious in all seven of his races. Much of his work was done in the first corner, as he shuffled his opponents aside and made the most of a clear, if very rutted, circuit.

Perhaps, even sweeter for Pedersen was the strange occurrence that the three riders who joined him in the final all held positions outside of the top eight in the standings. Therefore, all of those who had posed a threat before the meeting lost serious points to Pedersen, who was naturally elated with his victory. There wasn't much racing to enthuse about, though, with passing usually occurring due to riders making mistakes as they attempted to negotiate the tricky conditions.

Leigh Adams and Jason Crump failed to make it past the semi-finals and were eliminated in heat twenty-two, whilst Greg Hancock endured a miserable night that saw him fail to progress past the qualifying heats. Once again, there was disappointment for the Swedish contingent, as both Antonio Lindback and Andreas Jonsson withdrew from the meeting because of injury. Most spectacularly, it was Jonsson who clattered heavily into the air safety barrier on bend four of heat sixteen and aggravated an already troublesome shoulder complaint.

The final saw Pedersen and Jaroslaw Hampel jostle for top spot in the early stages, with the Dane eventually getting the better of the Polish rider. Meanwhile, Scott Nicholls and Rune Holta induldged in a real ding-dong battle that saw Holta prevail and relegate the British rider to fourth spot. Pedersen's win, combined with the failure of his closest rivals, meant he enjoyed a substantial overall lead of 27 points in the title race, not to mention and a significant psychological advantage.

Chris Seaward

GRAND PRIX OF SCANDINAVIA (ROUND SEVEN)

DATE: 11 August.

VENUE: G & B Arena, Malilla, Sweden.

1st LEIGH ADAMS
2nd TOMASZ GOLLOB
3rd JASON CRUMP
4th HANS N. ANDERSEN

SCORECHART

RIDER	1	2	3	4	5	S/F	Final	Total
Leigh Adams	2	3	2	2	1	3	6	19
Tomasz Gollob	3	3	2	3	2	2	4	19
Jason Crump	2	2	1	2	3	3	2	15
Hans N. Andersen	3	1	1	3	2	2	0	12
Nicki Pedersen	3	3	3	3	3	1	-	16
Wieslaw Jagus	2	3	3	1	3	0	-	12
Scott Nicholls	1	1	1	3	1	1	-	8
Fredrik Lindgren (Wildcard)	1	0	3	1	2	X	-	7
Bjarne Pedersen	0	1	2	2	2	-	-	7
Chris Harris	0	2	3	0	1	-	-	6
Rune Holta	0	0	1	1	3	-	-	5
Peter Karlsson	3	1	0	1	0	-	-	5
Greg Hancock	1	2	0	2	0	-	-	5
Antonio Lindback	1	2	0	0	0	-	-	3
Matej Zagar	0	0	2	0	1	-	-	3
Kaj Laukkanen	2	0	X	R	0	-	-	2
Jonas Davidsson (Reserve)	-	-	-	-	-	-	-	-
Sebastian Alden (Reserve)	-	-	-	-	-	-	-	-

RACE RESULTS

Ht 1:	Gollob, Crump, Lindgren, Zagar, 59.5
Ht 2:	Andersen, Adams, Nicholls, B. Pedersen, 60.6
Ht 3:	N. Pedersen, Laukkanen, Lindback, Holta, 59.3
Ht 4:	Karlsson, Jagus, Hancock, Harris, 60.0
Ht 5:	Adams, Lindback, Karlsson, Zagar, 59.7
Ht 6:	Jagus, Crump, Nicholls, Holta, 60.3
Ht 7:	Gollob, Hancock, B. Pedersen, Laukkanen, 60.8
Ht 8:	N. Pedersen, Harris, Andersen, Lindgren, 60.3
Ht 9:	(Re-Run) Harris, Zagar, Nicholls, Laukkanen (f, ex), 60.9
Ht 10:	N. Pedersen, Adams, Crump, Hancock, 59.6
Ht 11:	Jagus, Gollob, Andersen, Lindback, 59.9
Ht 12:	Lindgren, B. Pedersen, Holta, Karlsson, 61.0
Ht 13:	N. Pedersen, B. Pedersen, Jagus, Zagar, 59.4
Ht 14:	Andersen, Crump, Karlsson, Laukkanen (ret), 60.6
Ht 15:	Gollob, Adams, Holta, Harris, 60.6
Ht 16:	Nicholls, Hancock, Lindgren, Lindback, 60.3
Ht 17:	Holta, Andersen, Zagar, Hancock, 59.7
Ht 18:	Crump, B. Pedersen, Harris, Lindback, 59.9
Ht 19:	N. Pedersen, Gollob, Nicholls, Karlsson, 60.1
Ht 20:	Jagus, Lindgren, Adams, Laukkanen, 59.8

First semi-final:	(Re-Run) Crump, Andersen, N. Pedersen, Lindgren (f, ex), 59.8
Second semi-final:	Adams, Gollob, Nicholls, Jagus, 59.1
Grand Final:	Adams, Gollob, Crump, Andersen, 59.3

LEIGH Adams kept his World Championship aspirations well and truly alive with a much-needed victory at the serenely located Malilla racetrack, set deep in the dense forests of central Sweden. It was just what the doctor ordered for Adams, whose quest to become Speedway World Champion was under real threat of fizzling out after a disastrous previous round in Prague had left series leader Nicki Pedersen fondling a hefty 27-eight point cushion.

But the man from Mildura, who enjoyed the best Grand Prix season of his career, provided the Dane with a timely reminder that the 2007 title race was far from over by taking 3 points out of his lead in front of 12,000 fans at a thoroughly absorbing round seven. It was a marvellous evening for Australian speedway, as Jason Crump demonstrated bundles of the speed that had been so frustratingly absent in 2007 on route to grabbing third place on the rostrum.

Unfazed by the chilling form of Pedersen, Adams set about his work quietly in the five qualifying races and then flicked off the cruise control switch, took a deep breath and reigned victorious in a straightforward second semi-final. The Australian then emphatically conjured a sublime start from gate two to ease away from a vintage Tomasz Gollob, a resurgent Crump and a typically aggressive Hans Andersen to collect a tapes-to-flag win in the final. It provided Adams with his second Grand Prix victory of the year, following up his triumph at Ekilstuna back in May. Sweden was certainly kind to the Australian in 2007.

Whilst Adams maintained his composure impeccably all night long, Pedersen dramatically lost his after an imperious succession of twelve Grand Prix race wins that began in Prague two weeks earlier had come to an end in the first semi-final at Malilla. In a tub-thumping race, reigning World Champion Crump and the tenacious Andersen landed an unlikely body blow on Pedersen, which concluded his evening prematurely and handed Adams a wonderful opportunity to eat into the Dane's lead. It was one of those pulsating races that will be labelled as a classic in years to come; not just because it was utterly breathtaking, but because of the way in which it threw the 2007 title-race wide open.

After those aforementioned twelve successive GP race wins it was a case of unlucky thirteen and an unwelcome reality check for Pedersen, who spent his post race semi-final slow down lap directing his anger at compatriot Andersen, who had driven hard inside the Championship leader in a thoroughly boisterous dash to the chequered flag. Pedersen protested to the referee on his return to the pits, but his heartfelt pleas were dismissed and the Dane was left to contemplate just why he had allowed Andersen the opportunity to charge past him in a manner Pedersen himself would have been distinctly proud of. As the two Danish heavyweights indulged in pantomime fun and frolics, it allowed a resurgent Crump to secure a safe passage into a final.

The Aussie's miraculous recovery from the much documented keyhole surgery on his broken kneecap was a huge bonus for Adams, who desperately needed his fellow countryman to maintain that sort of form in order to provide Pedersen with ferocious competition from every possible angle. Crump, himself, would have been content with his night's work that in total netted him 15 points and elevated him to fourth place in the overall standings. The World Champion was slowly allowing a smile to creep back on to his face and was focused on collecting enough points in the four remaining rounds to forge a route into the top three of the standings.

On a Malilla track that was far superior to the horrendously rutted surface in Prague some fourteen days earlier, the world's best made the most of the perfect conditions at Sweden's finest speedway complex. However, the Scandinavian GP was a poorer place due to the absence of injured duo Andreas Jonsson and Jaroslaw Hampel, in particular Jonsson, who is regarded as a local hero in Malilla and was victorious at the venue in 2006. Without his presence, the home fans had very little to cheer as Antonio Lindback's poor form continued, whilst the highly-rated Fredrik Lndgren crashed out spectacularly in the initial semi-final.

It was the Swede's crash that caused the race to be stopped whilst Nicki Pedersen was leading the race, the re-run saw Pedersen unexpectedly miss out. Elsewhere in the field Tomasz Gollob went about his nights work with a touch of the old dash that has lit up dozens of speedway tracks on his way to a second spot on the night that significantly enhances his chances of making the all important top eight come the end of the season. Britain's Scott Nicholls failed to progress past the semi final stages whilst Chris Harris's six points was a far cry from his heroics in Cardiff some two rounds previous. On that night at the Millennium stadium Leigh Adams failed to capitalise on Nicki Pedersen's inability to make the final, in Sweden however the Australian hit the series leader where it hurt, right in the precious points bank.

If Adams is going to win the World Championship this season he requires the sort of luck he enjoyed in Mallila. He also needs oodles of composure and unremitting determination but perhaps most of all he could do with a helping hand from his old chum Jason Crump.

Chris Seaward

GRAND PRIX OF LATVIA (ROUND EIGHT)

DATE: 25 August.

VENUE: Latvian Speedway Centre, Daugavpils.

1st   LEIGH ADAMS
2nd NICKI PEDERSEN
3rd TOMASZ GOLLOB
4th SCOTT NICHOLLS

SC\ORECHART

RIDER	1	2	3	4	5	S/F	Final	Total
Leigh Adams	2	2	3	3	3	3	6	22
Nicki Pedersen	3	3	1	3	2	3	4	19
Tomasz Gollob	3	1	3	2	1	2	2	14
Scott Nicholls	1	3	2	3	2	2	0	13
Wieslaw Jagus	1	3	1	2	3	1	-	11
Jason Crump	0	2	3	2	2	1	-	10
Grigory Laguta (Wildcard)	3	1	3	0	1	0	-	8
Andreas Jonsson	3	2	0	1	2	0	-	8
Bjarne Pedersen	2	2	2	1	1	-	-	8
Rune Holta	1	1	2	3	0	-	-	7
Chris Harris	2	1	1	F	3	-	-	7
Hans N. Andersen	X	3	2	X	R	-	-	5
Greg Hancock	R	0	0	0	3	-	-	3
Kaj Laukkanen	1	0	0	2	0	-	-	3
Matej Zagar	2	0	0	0	0	-	-	2
Maksims Bogdanovs (Reserve)	1	1	-	-	-	-	-	2
Kjastas Puodzhuks (Reserve)	0	1	-	-	-	-	-	1
Antonio Lindback	X	-	-	-	-	-	-	0

RACE RESULTS

Ht 1:	Jonsson, Zagar, Laukkanen, Hancock (ret), 69.0
Ht 2:	Gollob, Harris, Jagus, Crump, 69.0
Ht 3:	(Re-Run) N. Pedersen, Adams, Nicholls, Andersen (f, ex), 70.0
Ht 4:	(Re-Run) Laguta, B. Pedersen, Holta, Lindback (f, ex), 70.0
Ht 5:	Nicholls, Jonsson, Harris, Puodzhuks, 70.0
Ht 6:	Andersen, Crump, Laguta, Hancock, 70.0
Ht 7:	N. Pedersen, B. Pedersen, Gollob, Laukkanen, 70.0
Ht 8:	Jagus, Adams, Holta, Zagar, 70.0
Ht 9:	Crump, Holta, N. Pedersen, Jonsson, 70.0
Ht 10:	Adams, B. Pedersen, Harris, Hancock, 69.0
Ht 11:	Laguta, Nicholls, Jagus, Laukkanen, 70.0
Ht 12:	Gollob, Andersen, Bogdanovs, Zagar, 70.0
Ht 13:	Adams, Gollob, Jonsson, Laguta, 70.0
Ht 14:	N. Pedersen, Jagus, Puodzhuks, Hancock, 70.2
Ht 15:	(Re-Run) Holta, Laukkanen, Harris (fell), Andersen (f, ex), 71.0
Ht 16:	Nicholls, Crump, B. Pedersen, Zagar, 70.0
Ht 17:	Jagus, Jonsson, B. Pedersen, Andersen (ret), 71.0
Ht 18:	Hancock, Nicholls, Gollob, Holta, 71.0
Ht 19:	Adams, Crump, Bogdanovs, Laukkanen, 70.0
Ht 20:	Harris, N. Pedersen, Laguta, Zagar, 70.0

First semi-final:	Adams, Gollob, Crump, Laguta, 70.0
Second semi-final:	N. Pedersen, Nicholls, Jagus, Jonsson, 70.2
Grand Final:	Adams, N. Pedersen, Gollob, Nicholls, 70.0

LEIGH Adams rode superbly to take his second successive Grand Prix victory, his third of the season, at the plush Daugavpils venue, set deep into the Latvian countryside. A wonderfully competitive round eight saw a scattering of brilliant racing on a track that, despite a little dust, was highly conducive to very good racing.

Adams was closely followed home in second spot by the consistent Nicki Pedersen, who managed to prevent his main title rival from extracting a major chunk from his series lead. Adams breezed through the five qualifying races, dropping just 2 points. He then eased to victory in the first semi-final, before making a sublime start from gate one in the major race of the evening to take victory. Cue scenes of intense celebration from the Australian's pit crew and Adams himself, who experienced back-to-back Grand Prix wins for the first time in his illustrious career.

After a point-less opening ride, Jason Crump collected 9 points in the qualifying heats but, as so often became the case in 2007, failed to progress past the semi-final stage. Elsewhere, Tomasz Gollob rode a typically gutsy meeting to grab a well-deserved third spot in the showdown race, whilst Britain's Scott Nicholls was fourth overall.

Antonio Lindback's miserable season continued, as he withdrew from the meeting through an injury sustained when he fell in his first scheduled outing of night. Hans Andersen also suffered a nasty crash in his fourth ride, which halted his chances of claiming a semi-final slot.

On the Friday preceding the meeting, it was announced that IMG had signed a contract to keep the Grand Prix at Daugavpils until 2009. The already impressive complex would be receiving a substantial makeover rumoured to be costing around £600,000.

Chris Seaward

GRAND PRIX OF POLAND (ROUND NINE)

DATE: 8 September.

VENUE: Polonia Stadium, Bydgoszcz.

1st TOMASZ GOLLOB
2nd KRZYSZTOF KASPRZAK
3rd NICKI PEDERSEN
4th ANDREAS JONSSON

SCORECHART

RIDER	1	2	3	4	5	S/F	Final	Total
Tomasz Gollob	2	3	2	2	3	3	6	21
Krzysztof Kasprzak (Wildcard)	3	0	3	3	2	2	4	17
Nicki Pedersen	2	3	3	3	3	3	2	19
Andreas Jonsson	1	3	0	3	2	2	0	11
Jaroslaw Hampel	3	2	3	0	2	1	-	11
Rune Holta	0	3	2	2	3	0	-	10
Leigh Adams	3	1	1	0	3	1	-	9
Bjarne Pedersen	3	1	3	1	0	0	-	8
Jason Crump	1	2	1	2	1	-	-	7
Antonio Lindback	0	0	1	3	1	-	-	5
Greg Hancock	1	2	0	2	0	-	-	5
Chris Harris	0	2	2	1	F	-	-	5
Wieslaw Jagus	2	1	0	1	1	-	-	5
Scott Nicholls	0	R	2	0	2	-	-	4
Matej Zagar	1	1	1	0	1	-	-	4
Hans N. Andersen	2	X	0	1	0	-	-	3
Krzysztof Buczkowski (Reserve)	-	-	-	-	-	-	-	-
Adrian Miedzinski (Reserve)	-	-	-	-	-	-	-	-

RACE RESULTS

Ht 1:	Adams, Andersen, Hancock, Harris, 64.97
Ht 2:	Hampel, Jagus, Zagar, Lindback, 64.53
Ht 3:	B. Pedersen, Gollob, Jonsson, Holta, 65.22
Ht 4:	Kasprzak, N. Pedersen, Crump, Nicholls, 64.56
Ht 5:	Jonsson, Hancock, Jagus, Kasprzak, 64.44
Ht 6:	Gollob, Harris, Zagar, Nicholls (ret), 64.38
Ht 7:	Holta, Crump, Adams, Lindback, 64.69
Ht 8:	(Re-Run) N. Pedersen, Hampel, B. Pedersen, Andersen (ex, foul riding), 65.07
Ht 9:	N. Pedersen, Holta, Zagar, Hancock, 64.78
Ht 10:	B. Pedersen, Harris, Crump, Jagus, 65.35
Ht 11:	Hampel, Nicholls, Adams, Jonsson, 64.53
Ht 12:	Kasprzak, Gollob, Lindback, Andersen, 64.75
Ht 13:	Lindback, Hancock, B. Pedersen, Nicholls, 66.59
Ht 14:	Kasprzak, Holta, Harris, Hampel, 66.13
Ht 15:	N. Pedersen, Gollob, Jagus, Adams, 65.00
Ht 16:	Jonsson, Crump, Andersen, Zagar, 64.81
Ht 17:	Gollob, Hampel, Crump, Hancock, 65.72
Ht 18:	N. Pedersen, Jonsson, Lindback, Harris (fell), 65.75
Ht 19:	Adams, Kasprzak, Zagar, B. Pedersen, 65.09
Ht 20:	Holta, Nicholls, Jagus, Andersen, 65.29

First semi-final:	N. Pedersen, Jonsson, Adams, Holta, 64.25
Second semi-final:	Gollob, Kasprzak, Hampel, B. Pedersen, 64.69
Grand Final:	Gollob, Kasprzak, N. Pedersen, Jonsson, 64.17

ALL hail the 'King of Bydgoszcz', who majestically regained his crown in front of a characteristically rapturous Polish crowd at round nine of the Speedway Grand Prix. Tomasz Gollob, the hometown hero, the icon of Polish speedway and, arguably, one of the best riders never to be crowned World Champion, conjured a breathtaking manoeuvre in the final race to clinch victory in a typically feisty Bydgoszcz affair.

Gollob's first lap, third bend surge to the front involved magnificently dissecting a route through the middle of Nicki Pedersen and Krzysztof Kasprzak, as he pampered his rear wheel with phenomenal amounts of grip by riding the kind of jaw-dropping racing lines only he dare discover. His audacious move wasn't received well by Pedersen, who spent his post-race time directing his anger at the highly-talented Pole. Pedersen felt strongly that Gollob's barnstorming move had hampered his race, but the Bydgoszcz boy couldn't have cared less, as he revelled in the glory and lapped up the vast amounts of affection the home crowd typically afforded him.

The Polonia Stadium might be a touch dusty and tired in places, but it proudly boasts the best atmosphere of any worldwide speedway event. Cardiff has the unrelenting barrage of a thousand air horns, Copenhagen has a family feel, but the brilliant Bydgoszcz arena has an electric atmosphere that is made up of constant chants, immense passion and colossal alcohol consumption. It's seedy, it's gritty and it's utterly absorbing!

Gollob revels in such an environment, he knows every single drop of the sacred Bydgoszcz shale personally and shares a wonderful affiliation with a race-track that consistently serves up crackerjack action. There's no doubt it was a sublime night for Polish speedway, as one of their brightest young prospects, Kasprzak, followed Gollob home to collect second spot. The performance further underlined the ability and determination of Kasprzak, whose worldwide form was certainly very impressive in 2007. If Gollob is the craggy King, there is no doubt that Kasprzak is the handsome Prince waiting patiently to lay claim to the throne.

Speedway can break language barriers, no more so than in Poland, where simply uttering the words 'Tomasz Gollob' to the most taciturn of locals will induce a beaming smile and bundles of national pride. This was Gollob's sixth Grand Prix success amongst the familiar surroundings of his hometown circuit, but his victory was far from predictable as a gaggle of riders all seemed capable of taking top spot on the night. These included the aforementioned Pedersen, who significantly strengthened his grasp on the World Championship by recovering from a frightening heat eight spill to collect 19 vital GP points.

Pedersen may have been nursing a sore shoulder from the crash, but the performance of Leigh Adams, whose poor record at Bydgoszcz continued, will have helped ease the Dane's pain. The Australian couldn't discover the elusive bike set-up he required to compete win the top four and, despite scraping his way to semi-finals, he never really looked to possess the speed to progress any further. The well-documented successes in Sweden and Latvia suddenly seemed like faint memories for the Aussie, whose lack-lustre performance was, perhaps, his most disappointing of the 2007 campaign. It meant that Pedersen nurtured a hefty 31-point lead overall and needed just 18 points, if Adams was to collect a maximum tally of 48 from the final two rounds in Slovenia and Germany, to be World Champion again.

Meanwhile, Jason Crump elevated himself to third spot in the overall standings by collecting a 7-point haul, which proved just 1-point shy of gaining him a semi-final slot. Nevertheless, the 2006 World Champion moved his total tally on to 96 points, one ahead of Hans Andersen, whose lack of Grand Prix form saw him collectively gain 8 points from the Polish round and the previous one in Latvia. Dogged by a recurring knee-cap injury, Crump was far from his best and the Grand Prix was a poorer place without the two times World Champion throwing his machine around in the scintillating style many had come to expect. Elsewhere in the field, Andreas Jonsson rode well to earn a creditable fourth spot, whilst Greg Hancock's woes continued as the charismatic American was only able to muster a lowly 5 points.

Gollob is a well-chronicled enigma, but, once on the sacred shale of his beloved hometown raceway, his performances reflect what a sensational campaigner he really is. The Pole celebrated his victory with a vast array of tricks, before bowing to the crowd on the home straight. The thirty-six-year-old undoubtedly found some eye-catching form entering the latter part of the season and three consecutive podiums saw him climb comfortably into the top eight of the standings. The Polish King clearly wasn't ready to vacate his throne and the huge support from the patriotic public suggested that he might well wear his crown proudly for a few years yet.

Chris Seaward

GRAND PRIX OF SLOVENIA (ROUND TEN)

DATE: 22 September.

VENUE: Matije Gubca Stadium, Krsko.

1st   NICKI PEDERSEN
2nd SCOTT NICHOLLS
3rd   RUNE HOLTA
4th   JASON CRUMP

SCORECHART

RIDER	1	2	3	4	5	S/F	Final	Total
Nicki Pedersen	3	2	3	3	3	3	6	23
Scott Nicholls	2	1	2	3	2	2	4	16
Rune Holta	2	3	3	2	2	2	2	16
Jason Crump	3	2	1	1	3	3	0	13
Tomasz Gollob	2	2	2	1	2	1	-	10
Leigh Adams	3	3	1	0	2	0	-	9
Bjarne Pedersen	0	0	2	3	3	1	-	9
Wieslaw Jagus	1	3	3	1	1	0	-	9
Chris Harris	3	1	0	3	1	-	-	8
Andreas Jonsson	1	3	2	0	0	-	-	6
Jaroslaw Hampel	0	1	0	2	3	-	-	6
Matej Zagar	R	1	3	1	1	-	-	6
Jurica Pavlic (Wildcard)	2	0	0	2	1	-	-	5
Greg Hancock	1	2	1	0	0	-	-	4
Hans N. Andersen	1	0	0	2	R	-	-	3
Antonio Lindback	0	0	1	0	0	-	-	1
Izak Santej (Reserve)	-	-	-	-	-	-	-	-
Jernej Kolenko (Reserve)	-	-	-	-	-	-	-	-

RACE RESULTS

Ht 1:	Crump, Nicholls, Jonsson, Hampel, 66.36
Ht 2:	Harris, Pavlic, Andersen, Lindback, 66.16
Ht 3:	Adams, Gollob, Hancock, B. Pedersen, 66.14
Ht 4:	N. Pedersen, Holta, Jagus, Zagar (ret), 66.66
Ht 5:	Holta, Crump, Harris, B. Pedersen, 65.95
Ht 6:	Adams, N. Pedersen, Nicholls, Pavlic, 65.81
Ht 7:	Jagus, Gollob, Hampel, Andersen, 66.09
Ht 8:	Jonsson, Hancock, Zagar, Lindback, 66.89
Ht 9:	Zagar, Gollob, Crump, Pavlic, 66.81
Ht 10:	Jagus, Nicholls, Hancock, Harris, 67.45
Ht 11:	N. Pedersen, B. Pedersen, Lindback, Hampel, 67.77
Ht 12:	Holta, Jonsson, Adams, Andersen, 66.76
Ht 13:	N. Pedersen, Andersen, Crump, Hancock, 66.79
Ht 14:	Nicholls, Holta, Gollob, Lindback, 67.38
Ht 15:	Harris, Hampel, Zagar, Adams, 67.70
Ht 16:	B. Pedersen, Pavlic, Jagus, Jonsson, 67.91
Ht 17:	Crump, Adams, Jagus, Lindback, 67.27
Ht 18:	B. Pedersen, Nicholls, Zagar, Andersen (ret), 67.91
Ht 19:	Hampel, Holta, Pavlic, Hancock, 68.04
Ht 20:	N. Pedersen, Gollob, Harris, Jonsson, 68.27

First semi-final:	N. Pedersen, Nicholls, Gollob, Jagus, 67.88
Second semi-final:	Crump, Holta, B. Pedersen, Adams, 67.88
Grand Final:	N. Pedersen, Nicholls, Holta, Crump, 67.55

NICKI Pedersen completed the formalities to ensure his second World Championship title and then went on to brilliantly win the Slovenian Grand Prix at Krsko. It was a sheer master-class from the Danish rider, who thoroughly deserved the 2007 crown, which he had worked so hard in the winter months to prepare for.

Pedersen entered the penultimate meeting of the series needing just 18 points from the remaining two rounds, even if Leigh Adams collected a maximum 48-point haul. The Australian began the meeting superbly, but as it progressed his challenge started to fizzle, which left Pedersen requiring just 1-point from heat twenty to clinch the title. The Dane conjured a brilliant start and eased to a comfortable win to secure the Championship and then continued to impress by winning the final from Scott Nicholls, Rune Holta and Jason Crump.

In a meeting scattered with good racing, the Slovenian audience was less vocal than usual due to the continuance of Matej Zagar's disappointing run of form; the local favourite being only able to muster 6 points. Meanwhile, Croatian wonder-kid Jurica Pavlic rode extremely well as the wildcard entrant, showcasing his array of potential on the way to a 5-point haul.

The battle for the top eight places in the series began to intensify as Tomasz Gollob shot up the standings to fourth spot, whilst Hans Andersen and Greg Hancock both slipped down the leaderboard to fifth and sixth place, respectively. Indeed, the form of Hancock since round five could be described as poor, as the popular American continued to be plagued by a lack of speed.

As Pedersen celebrated his title, Leigh Adams was left wondering what might have been. The same could also be said of Jason Crump, who, despite strengthening his grip on third spot in the standings, must surely have been pondering just how he allowed his 2006 title to slip away so easily.

Chris Seaward

GRAND PRIX OF GERMANY (ROUND ELEVEN)

DATE: 13 October.

VENUE: Veltins Arena, Gelsenkirchen.

1st ANDREAS JONSSON
2nd GREG HANCOCK
3rd JASON CRUMP
4th LEIGH ADAMS

SCORECHART

RIDER	1	2	3	4	5	S/F	Final	Total
Andreas Jonsson	3	1	3	3	2	2	6	20
Greg Hancock	3	3	0	1	2	3	4	16
Jason Crump	2	2	1	3	3	2	2	15
Leigh Adams	0	3	1	1	3	3	0	11
Bjarne Pedersen	0	3	2	2	3	1	-	11
Rune Holta	1	2	3	1	2	1	-	10
Hans N. Andersen	3	2	3	0	1	X	-	9
Nicki Pedersen	1	1	1	3	3	R	-	9
Peter Karlsson	2	1	2	3	0	-	-	8
Scott Nicholls	2	1	2	2	1	-	-	8
Tomasz Gollob	1	0	3	2	1	-	-	7
Wieslaw Jagus	1	3	0	2	0	-	-	6
Matej Zagar	2	2	1	0	1	-	-	6
Christian Hefenbrock (Wildcard)	3	0	0	1	0	-	-	4
Chris Harris	0	0	2	0	2	-	-	4
Kaj Laukkanen	0	0	0	0	0	-	-	0
Martin Smolinski (Reserve)	-	-	-	-	-	-	-	-
Tobias Kroner (Reserve)	-	-	-	-	-	-	-	-

RACE RESULTS

Ht 1:	Hefenbrock, Zagar, Gollob, Harris, 59.6 (Track Record)
Ht 2:	Andersen, Crump, N. Pedersen, Adams, 58.6 (Track Record)
Ht 3:	Jonsson, Karlsson, Jagus, B. Pedersen, 58.4 (Track Record)
Ht 4:	Hancock, Nicholls, Holta, Laukkanen, 58.2 (Track Record)
Ht 5:	Adams, Zagar, Jonsson, Laukkanen, 57.4 (Track Record)
Ht 6:	Hancock, Andersen, Karlsson, Hefenbrock, 58.1
Ht 7:	Jagus, Holta, N. Pedersen, Harris, 57.6
Ht 8:	B. Pedersen, Crump, Nicholls, Gollob, 58.7
Ht 9:	Andersen, Nicholls, Zagar, Jagus, 58.3
Ht 10:	Holta, B. Pedersen, Adams, Hefenbrock, 58.0
Ht 11:	Jonsson, Harris, Crump, Hancock, 58.3
Ht 12:	Gollob, Karlsson, N. Pedersen, Laukkanen, 58.7
Ht 13:	N. Pedersen, B. Pedersen, Hancock, Zagar, 58.5
Ht 14:	Crump, Jagus, Hefenbrock, Laukkanen, 58.3
Ht 15:	Karlsson, Nicholls, Adams, Harris, 58.0
Ht 16:	Jonsson, Gollob, Holta, Andersen, 58.2
Ht 17:	Crump, Holta, Zagar, Karlsson, 58.1
Ht 18:	N. Pedersen, Jonsson, Nicholls, Hefenbrock, 57.8
Ht 19:	B. Pedersen, Harris, Andersen, Laukkanen, 58.5
Ht 20:	Adams, Hancock, Gollob, Jagus, 57.9

First semi-final:	Hancock, Jonsson, Holta, N. Pedersen (ret), 56.9 (Track Record)
Second semi-final:	(Re-Run) Adams, Crump, B. Pedersen, Andersen (f, ex), 57.5
Run off for seventh and eighth position overall:	Holta, Nicholls, Harris (fell), 57.7
Grand Final:	Jonsson, Hancock, Crump, Adams, 56.9 (Equalled Track Record)

THE prestigious IMG beacon shone more intensely than it had all season as the Speedway Grand Prix made a welcome return to Germany in the plush Veltins Arena at Gelsenkirchen. Ever since it was announced that the final round of the 2007 series, the 100th in the history of the competition, would be held at the 61,482-capacity venue there was a genuine excitement amongst supporters.

Not only was the series making a welcome to Germany, a nation that had for some time been screaming out for international speedway recognition, but the winner of the event would scoop a cool $100,000. The series organizers had given Germany a wide berth after an ill-fated Grand Prix round at Berlin in 2001 was almost obliterated by wet weather; six years later and the threat of rain was taken out of the equation by every speedway supporters dream, a retractable roof.

The meeting was extensively marketed as the 'Richest Minute in Motor Sport' and a healthy crowd, somewhere around the 25,000 mark, seemed to suggest that the event had successfully captured the imagination. Sixteen past World Champions were paraded around the track and received a rapturous reception on a night when the sport of speedway revelled in past glories.

All of this at the state-of-the-art Gelsenkirchen venue, the home of soccer club FC Schalke, who ply their trade in the Germany's top division, the Bundesliga. The particularly impressive place boasts the aforementioned retractable roof, but most intriguing of all is the soccer pitch itself that actually resides outside the stadium and is rolled into the arena by a series of conveyors when it is required.

That allowed a speedway track to be constructed inside the venue in just five days, with shale that had been imported all the way from Denmark using a network or roads and canals. The colossal construction process was captured by a stadium webcam and broadcast live to the waiting world, monitoring the arena transform to a speedway venue was like watching a piece of art being sketched on a blank canvas.

Of course, the $100,000 top prize kept the series alive after Nicki Pedersen had sewn up his second World Championship title in Slovenia some three weeks earlier. But the Dane could do little to stop Andreas Jonsson further demonstrating his liking for temporary speedway surfaces, as he firmly put his 2007 injury woes behind him and filled his boots with cash. The Swede's victory came after he took top spot at Copenhagen back in June and surely guaranteed him a wildcard inclusion in the 2008.

It was just the boost Swedish speedway required after one of their brightest young stars, Antonio Lindback, announced just days earlier that he was taking a hiatus from the sport after being caught drink driving in his homeland. Jonsson's win in the final earned him around $1,700 per second and only for about four of those seconds did the Swedish rider have to work particularly hard; for the most part he simply sat back and enjoyed the ride. Afterwards, he demonstrated his modesty by quickly pledging to use some of the money to take his mother on holiday.

Jason Crump's third place managed to secure the double World Champion the overall bronze medal in the 2007 series. The Australian looked on course to finish his season on a high as he performed well in the qualifying races, before following Leigh Adams home in the second semi-final. But, he was unable to conjure a good start in the final. It was a familiar tale for Adams himself, whose attempt to anticipate the start in the concluding race effectively curtailed his chances of collecting the pot of cash.

Perhaps the most dramatic moment of the evening came in an unscheduled race that preceded the final and was hastily organized to decide who would finish in the top eight. Three riders, Scott Nicholls, Chris Harris and Rune Holta all shared 91 points, and, with only room for two of them in next season's series, it was quickly decided to include a run-off. Holta and Nicholls made the start, before Harris charged under his Coventry team-mate on the final lap, only for Nicholls to audaciously come back underneath Harris on the second bend, resulting in the exciting youngster hitting the deck. The referee failed to hit the red stoppage lights and Nicholls got away with daylight robbery, as Harris waved his arms wildly in the direction of the officials.

The razzmatazz and barrage of hype leading up to the meeting certainly wasn't matched by the racing, which was mostly processional and wholly unsympathetic to those who dared stray off the white line. It was unfortunate that the shale, which had been meticulously transported from Denmark after its impeccable performance at Copenhagen earlier in the season, on this occasion failed to deliver.

As a spectacle the 100th Speedway Grand Prix was simply unbeatable and the post-meeting awards ceremonies were rammed full of glamour, with a huge gaggle of photographers clambering for shots. However, the Gelsenkirchen event once again illustrated the ongoing tug of war transition between temporary and permanent racing circuits. The indoor tracks offer wonderful facilities, comfortable seating and great viewing, but fail to compete in terms of racing quality. Outdoor strips produce outstanding racing and allow the riders a platform on which to showcase their true talents. The key for the Speedway Grand Prix is combining the best aspects of both temporary and permanent events; that means extensively researching better ways of transporting breathtaking racing into the best sporting venues the world has to offer.

Chris Seaward

GRAND PRIX RECORDS (1995-2007)

TOTAL ROUNDS STAGED: 100

MOST GP APPEARANCES	MOST GP WINS	MOST GP POINTS
100 Greg Hancock	20 Tony Rickardsson	1,401 Tony Rickardsson
96 Tomasz Gollob	16 Jason Crump	1,324 Jason Crump
93 Leigh Adams	11 Tomasz Gollob	1,268 Greg Hancock
89 Jason Crump	8 Greg Hancock, Nicki Pedersen	1,182 Tomasz Gollob
84 Tony Rickardsson	6 Hans Nielsen, Billy Hamill, Leigh Adams	1,072 Leigh Adams

WORLD CHAMPIONSHIP ROLL OF HONOUR

NOTE: Run as a one-off World Final from 1936-1994 and as the Grand Prix from 1995-2007.

YEAR	FIRST	SECOND	THIRD
1936	Lionel Van Praag	Eric Langton	Bluey Wilkinson
1937	Jack Milne	Wilbur Lamoreaux	Cordy Milne
1938	Bluey Wilkinson	Jack Milne	Wilbur Lamoreaux
1939-48	Not staged		
1949	Tommy Price	Jack Parker	Louis Lawson
1950	Freddie Williams	Wally Green	Graham Warren
1951	Jack Young	Split Waterman	Jack Biggs
1952	Jack Young	Freddie Williams	Bob Oakley
1953	Freddie Williams	Split Waterman	Geoff Mardon
1954	Ronnie Moore	Brian Crutcher	Olle Nygren
1955	Peter Craven	Ronnie Moore	Barry Briggs
1956	Ove Fundin	Ronnie Moore	Arthur Forrest
1957	Barry Briggs	Ove Fundin	Peter Craven
1958	Barry Briggs	Ove Fundin	Aub Lawson
1959	Ronnie Moore	Ove Fundin	Barry Briggs
1960	Ove Fundin	Ronnie Moore	Peter Craven
1961	Ove Fundin	Bjorn Knutsson	Gote Nordin
1962	Peter Craven	Barry Briggs	Ove Fundin
1963	Ove Fundin	Bjorn Knutsson	Barry Briggs
1964	Barry Briggs	Igor Plechanov	Ove Fundin
1965	Bjorn Knutsson	Igor Plechanov	Ove Fundin
1966	Barry Briggs	Sverre Harrfeldt	Antoni Woryna
1967	Ove Fundin	Bengt Jansson	Ivan Mauger
1968	Ivan Mauger	Barry Briggs	Edward Jancarz
1969	Ivan Mauger	Barry Briggs	Soren Sjosten
1970	Ivan Mauger	Pawel Waloszek	Antoni Woryna
1971	Ole Olsen	Ivan Mauger	Bengt Jansson
1972	Ivan Mauger	Bernt Persson	Ole Olsen
1973	Jerzy Szczakiel	Ivan Mauger	Zenon Plech
1974	Anders Michanek	Ivan Mauger	Soren Sjosten
1975	Ole Olsen	Anders Michanek	John Louis

YEAR	FIRST	SECOND	THIRD
1976	Peter Collins	Malcolm Simmons	Phil Crump
1977	Ivan Mauger	Peter Collins	Ole Olsen
1978	Ole Olsen	Gordon Kennett	Scott Autrey
1979	Ivan Mauger	Zenon Plech	Michael Lee
1980	Michael Lee	Dave Jessup	Billy Sanders
1981	Bruce Penhall	Ole Olsen	Tommy Knudsen
1982	Bruce Penhall	Les Collins	Dennis Sigalos
1983	Egon Muller	Billy Sanders	Michael Lee
1984	Erik Gundersen	Hans Nielsen	Lance King
1985	Erik Gundersen	Hans Nielsen	Sam Ermolenko
1986	Hans Nielsen	Jan O. Pedersen	Kelvin Tatum
1987	Hans Nielsen	Erik Gundersen	Sam Ermolenko
1988	Erik Gundersen	Hans Nielsen	Jan O. Pedersen
1989	Hans Nielsen	Simon Wigg	Jeremy Doncaster
1990	Per Jonsson	Shawn Moran	Todd Wiltshire
1991	Jan O. Pedersen	Tony Rickardsson	Hans Nielsen
1992	Gary Havelock	Per Jonsson	Gert Handberg
1993	Sam Ermolenko	Hans Nielsen	Chris Louis
1994	Tony Rickardsson	Hans Nielsen	Craig Boyce
1995	Hans Nielsen	Tony Rickardsson	Sam Ermolenko
1996	Billy Hamill	Hans Nielsen	Greg Hancock
1997	Greg Hancock	Billy Hamill	Tomasz Gollob
1998	Tony Rickardsson	Jimmy Nilsen	Tomasz Gollob
1999	Tony Rickardsson	Tomasz Gollob	Hans Nielsen
2000	Mark Loram	Billy Hamill	Tony Rickardsson
2001	Tony Rickardsson	Jason Crump	Tomasz Gollob
2002	Tony Rickardsson	Jason Crump	Ryan Sullivan
2003	Nicki Pedersen	Jason Crump	Tony Rickardsson
2004	Jason Crump	Tony Rickardsson	Greg Hancock
2005	Tony Rickardsson	Jason Crump	Leigh Adams
2006	Jason Crump	Greg Hancock	Nicki Pedersen
2007	Nicki Pedersen	Leigh Adams	Jason Crump

NOTE: In 1990, Shawn Moran was subsequently stripped of second place, having tested positive in a drugs test at the Overseas Final.

GRAND PRIX QUALIFICATION

(FOR THE 2008 GRAND PRIX SERIES)

ROUND ONE; 23 JUNE, TERENZANO, ITALY

1st Niels-Kristian Iversen <u>15</u>; 2nd Jurica Pavlic 12+3; 3rd Rafal Dobrucki 12+2; Richard Hall 12+R; Kyle Legault 11; Niklas Klingberg 10; Steve Johnston 10; David Howe 8+3; Henrik Moller 8+2; Matej Ferjan 5; Andrea Maida 4; Denis Stojs 3; Guglielmo Franchetti 3; Josef Franc 3; Marco Greganin 3; Maks Gregoric 1.

ROUND TWO: 23 JUNE, MSENO, CZECH REPUBLIC

1st Krzysztof Kasprzak <u>15</u>; 2nd Renat Gafurov 13; 3rd Ales Dryml 11; Tobias Kroner 10; Izak Santej 9; Jaroslaw Hampel 9; Lukas Dryml 8+3; Lewis Bridger 8+2; Daniel King 8+1; Adrian Rymel 6; Martin Vaculik 6; Thomas Stange 6; Hynck Stichauer (Res) 3; Henk Bos 3; Friedrich Wallner 3; Kaj de Jong 1; Manuel Hauzinger 0; Richard Wolff (Res) 0.

ROUND THREE: 24 JUNE, MISKOLC, HUNGARY

1st Rory Schlein 14; 2nd Piotr Protasiewicz 12+3; 3rd Charlie Gjedde 12+2; Sebastian Ulamek 10; Chris Holder 10; Denis Gizatullin 9; Lubos Tomicek 8+3; Zdenek Simota 8+2; Norbert Magosi 7; Joonas Kylmakorpi 7; Jozsef Tabaka 6; Ruslan Gatiyatov 5; Maksims Bogdanovs 5; Kjastas Puodzhuks 5; Magnus Karlsson 1; Jaroslav Polyuhovich 1.

ROUND FOUR: 30 JUNE, MOTALA, SWEDEN

1st Damian Balinski 12+3; 2nd Kenneth Bjerre 12+2; 3rd Mikael Max 12+1; Tomasz Gapinski 11; Fredrik Lindgren 11; Kaj Laukkanen 11; Jonas Davidsson 10; Kauko Nieminen 9; Jesper B. Jensen 8; Simon Stead 6; Martin Smolinski 6; Christian Hefenbrock 5; Daniel Davidsson 3; Olly Allen 2; Rune Sola 2; Matt Browne 0.

FIRST SEMI-FINAL: 7 JULY, LONIGO, ITALY

1st Bjarne Pedersen 11+3; 2nd Krzysztof Kasprzak 11+2; 3rd Damian Balinski 10+3; Denis Gizatullin 10+2; Tobias Kroner 10+1; Lukas Dryml 9; Kyle Legault 8+3; Steve Johnston 8+2; Charlie Gjedde 8+1; Chris Holder 7; Jaroslaw Hampel 7; Jurica Pavlic 7; Mikael Max 6; Tomasz Gapinski 4; Richard Hall 2; Zdenek Simota (Res) 1; Mattia Carpanese 0; David Howe (Res) 0.

SECOND SEMI-FINAL: 8 JULY, LJUBLJANA, SLOVENIA

1st Fredrik Lindgren 11+3; 2nd Renat Gafurov 11+2; 3rd Kenneth Bjerre 11+1; Rory Schlein 10; Niels-Kristian Iversen 10; Rafal Dobrucki 9; Lubos Tomicek 8+3; Jonas Davidsson 8+2; Piotr Protasiewicz 8+1; Grzegorz Walasek 7; Niklas Klingberg 7; Kaj Laukkanen 6; Jernej Kolenko 5; Sebastian Ulamek 4; Izak Santej 4; Ales Dryml 1; Kauko Nieminen (Res) 0.

GRAND FINAL

15 SEPTEMBER, VOJENS, DENMARK

1st   NIELS-KRISTIAN IVERSEN

2nd   LUKAS DRYML

3rd   BJARNE PEDERSEN

4th   LUBOS TOMICEK

RIDER	RACE SCORES					TOTAL
Niels-Kristian Iversen	3	3	3	3	2	14
Lukas Dryml	1	3	2	3	3	12
Bjarne Pedersen	3	1	3	1	3	11
Lubos Tomicek	3	2	2	3	1	11
Kenneth Bjerre	2	3	3	X	2	10
Rafal Dobrucki	1	3	3	2	1	10
Jonas Davidsson	0	2	1	3	2	8
Krzysztof Kasprzak	1	1	1	2	3	8
Renat Gafurov	3	2	0	2	0	7
Fredrik Lindgren	2	1	2	2	X	7
Denis Gizatullin	2	0	0	1	3	6
Damian Balinski	2	2	1	R	N	5
Rory Schlein	0	0	1	1	2	4
Steve Johnston	0	1	2	0	0	3
Tobias Kroner	1	0	0	R	1	2
Kyle Legault	X	0	0	1	0	1
Charlie Gjedde (Res)	1	-	-	-	-	1
Piotr Protasiewicz (Res)	-	-	-	-	-	-

HEAT DETAILS

Ht 1:	Pedersen, Balinski, Kroner, Davidsson, 59.4
Ht 2:	Iversen, Bjerre, Dryml, Schlein, 59.4
Ht 3:	Tomicek, Lindgren, Dobrucki, Johnston, 59.7
Ht 4:	(Re-Run) Gafurov, Gizatullin, Kasprzak, Legault (f, ex), 60.0
Ht 5:	Bjerre, Balinski, Johnston, Legault, 59.4
Ht 6:	Dryml, Gafurov, Johnston, Kroner, 59.4
Ht 7:	Dobrucki, Davidsson, Kasprzak, Schlein, 60.0
Ht 8:	Iversen, Tomicek, Pedersen, Gizatullin, 60.2
Ht 9:	Dobrucki, Dryml, Balinski, Gizatullin, 61.0
Ht 10:	Bjerre, Tomicek, Kasprzak, Kroner, 59.8
Ht 11:	Iversen, Johnston, Davidsson, Gafurov, 60.6
Ht 12:	Pedersen, Lindgren, Schlein, Legault, 60.3
Ht 13:	Tomicek, Gafurov, Schlein, Balinski (ret), 60.5
Ht 14:	Iversen, Dobrucki, Legault, Kroner (ret), 60.6
Ht 15:	(Re-Run) Davidsson, Lindgren, Gizatullin, Bjerre (f, ex), 60.2
Ht 16:	Dryml, Kasprzak, Pedersen, Johnston, 60.7
Ht 17:	(Re-Run) Kasprzak, Iversen, Gjedde, Lindgren (f, ex), Balinski (ns), 60.3
Ht 18:	Gizatullin, Schlein, Kroner, Johnston, 60.7
Ht 19:	Dryml, Davidsson, Tomicek, Legault, 61.3
Ht 20:	Pedersen, Bjerre, Dobrucki, Gafurov, 60.5

Run-off:	Pedersen, Tomicek, 61.1

NOTE: Niels-Kristian Iversen, Lukas Dryml and Bjarne Pedersen qualified for the 2008 GP series.

SPEEDWAY WORLD CUP 2007

QUALIFYING ROUND ONE	28 MAY, ABENSBERG, GERMANY
FINLAND 43	Kaj Laukkanen 14; Joonas Kylmakorpi 13; Kauko Nieminen 8; Juha Hautamaki 6; Tero Aarnio 2
GERMANY 40	Martin Smolinski 13; Christian Hefenbrock 9; Thomas Stange 9; Tobias Kroner 5; Mathias Schultz 4
LATVIA 37	Kjastas Puodzhuks 14; Maksim Bogdanov 9; Viatcheslav Giruckis 7; Leonid Paura 6; Aleksandrs Ivanov 1
SLOVENIA 29	Matej Zagar 16; Izak Santej 8; Denis Stojs 3; Jernej Kolenko 2; Maks Gregoric 0

QUALIFYING ROUND TWO	10 JUNE, LONIGO, ITALY
RUSSIA 59	Emil Sajfutdinov 15; Denis Gizatullin 12; Roman Povazhny 12; Renat Gafurov 11; Roman Ivanov 9
CZECH REPUBLIC 46	Lukas Dryml 13; Ales Dryml 10; Zdenek Simota 9; Lubos Tomicek 7; Josef Franc 7
ITALY 31	Mattia Carpanese 12; Guglielmo Franchetti 8; Marco Gregnanin 7; Andrea Maida 3; Alessandro Milanese 1
HUNGARY 12	Norbert Magosi 4; Jozsef Tabaka 4; Attila Stefani 2; Sandor Tihanyi 1; Zsolt Bencze 1

ROUND ONE

14 JULY, VOJENS, DENMARK

COUNTRY	RACE SCORES						TOTAL
DENMARK 60							
Nicki Pedersen	2	3	2	3	3	-	13
Niels-Kristian Iversen	3	2	1	3	2	-	11
Hans N. Andersen	3	1	3	3	2	-	12
Kenneth Bjerre	2	3	3	1	2	-	11
Bjarne Pedersen	1	3	3	3	3	-	13
POLAND 44							
Tomasz Gollob	1	2	1	2	0	-	6
Jaroslaw Hampel	0	1	2	3	-	-	6
Rune Holta	2	0	1	2	3	-	8
Grzegorz Walasek	3	3	4	1	2	2	15
Krzysztof Kasprzak	2	2	2	3	0	-	9
AUSTRALIA 39							
Jason Crump	3	2	3	1	1	-	10
Chris Holder	1	1	2	1	-	-	5
Rory Schlein	1	1	X	1	1	-	4
Ryan Sullivan	0	3	F	1	3	-	7
Leigh Adams	3	1	3	4	1	1	13
FINLAND 11							
Juha Hautamaki	0	0	1	0	0	-	1
Joonas Kylmakorpi	2	0	2	0	2	-	6
Kauko Nieminen	0	0	0	0	1	-	1
Kaj Laukkanen	1	2	0	0	0	-	3
Tero Aarnio	0	0	0	0	0	-	0

RACE DETAILS

Ht 1:	Crump, N. Pedersen, Gollob, Hautamaki, 60.5
Ht 2:	Iversen, Kylmakorpi, Holder, Hampel, 60.4
Ht 3:	Andersen, Holta, Schlein, Nieminen, 60.7
Ht 4:	Walasek, Bjerre, Laukkanen, Sullivan, 60.3
Ht 5:	Adams, Kasprzak, B. Pedersen, Aarnio, 60.2
Ht 6:	Sullivan, Kasprzak, Andersen, Hautamaki, 61.6
Ht 7:	Bjerre, Gollob, Adams, Kylmakorpi, 60.5
Ht 8:	B. Pedersen, Crump, Hampel, Nieminen, 60.7
Ht 9:	N. Pedersen, Laukkanen, Holder, Holta, 60.2
Ht 10:	(Re-Run) Walasek, Iversen, Schlein, Aarnio, 60.6
Ht 11:	Bjerre, Walasek (tactical joker), Hautamaki, Schlein (ex, crossed white line), 60.0
Ht 12:	B. Pedersen, Kylmakorpi, Holta, Sullivan (fell), 60.7
Ht 13:	Adams, N. Pedersen, Walasek, Nieminen, 60.0
Ht 14:	Crump, Kasprzak, Iversen, Laukkanen, 60.8
Ht 15:	(Re-Run) Andersen, Adams (tactical joker), Gollob, Aarnio, 60.7
Ht 16:	(Re-Run) Iversen, Holta, Adams, Hautamaki, 60.6
Ht 17:	Andersen, Walasek, Crump, Kylmakorpi, 60.5
Ht 18:	(Re-Run) Kasprzak, Holder, Bjerre, Nieminen, 60.5
Ht 19:	B. Pedersen, Gollob, Schlein, Nieminen, 60.8
Ht 20:	N. Pedersen, Hampel, Sullivan, Aarnio, 60.5
Ht 21:	B. Pedersen, Walasek, Holder, Hautamaki, 60.9
Ht 22:	N. Pedersen, Kylmakorpi, Schlein, Kasprzak, 60.8
Ht 23:	Sullivan, Iversen, Nieminen, Gollob, 61.1
Ht 24:	Hampel, Andersen, Adams, Laukkanen, 60.9
Ht 25:	Holta, Bjerre, Crump, Aarnio, 60.4

THE Speedway World Cup is renowned for superb racing, top notch entertainment and spine-tingling unpredictability. Indeed, some of the best racing in the last decade has been provided by the hotly-anticipated SWC, which gathers more momentum with each passing season. Passions run high when the world's best national squads come together and do battle in four events that span the best part of a week.

Yet, just fourteen days after the sport had revelled in the ecstasy of a mind-blowing British Grand Prix, the opening round of the 2007 World Cup at Vojens was a bland and uninspiring twenty-five-heat procession. A slick track, the bane of many a speedway enthusiast, ensured that the Danish quintet comfortably progressed to the final of the competition, whilst the three other teams were left wondering why all the loose shale had disappeared.

The Danish team hugged the white line as the Aussies, Poles and Finns tried courageously to squeeze a morsel of speed from the outside. When the world's best gather, all they require to showcase their talents is a well prepared track but, on this occasion, the riders were not in the luxury zone of enjoying a half decent surface to race on.

Track conditions aside, this was an event that saw an Australian team with an exciting new inclusion in their prestigious ranks. Chris Holder, one of the hottest prospects in world speedway, was chosen by team manager Craig Boyce to take his place in the five-man line-up. Holder's breathtaking youth, juxtaposed against the wise head of Leigh Adams and combined with the all-out style of Jason Crump, guaranteed action. But, when Adams made a deliberate point of asking Race Director Ole Olsen to pepper a painfully dry outside line with moisture, it became apparent that the first round of the 2007 competition wasn't exactly going to be a classic.

A frustratingly slick, tyre-packed 300-metre circuit was far from conducive to fulfil the criteria which speedway fans have come to expect of this usually spectacular week-long tournament. Everyone is aware that the Danes revel on slick surfaces, but this was the most warped home track advantage world speedway had seen for many years.

Watching the all-action styles of Crump, Tomasz Gollob and Joonas Kylmakorpi - who clearly possessed more speed than their opponents - being punished when they dared move of the white line was painful. Take heat twelve for example, when Ryan Sullivan's rear wheel simply refused to grip on bend three of lap one and sent the Australian tumbling; it was ludicrous. Even the most extensively coined speedway cliché - 'It's the same for everyone' - didn't even begin to make up for it.

By heat fifteen, it was all over; the Danes had eased away from the chasing pack of Poland and Australia, who already had their thoughts on the Race-Off in Leszno. The host nation's sheer consistency proved to be the decisive factor as all five of their riders contributed double-point hauls. It was a familiar tale for the Finnish team; plenty of bravery, lashings of speed, but not the competitive edge to cut it in the sheer ferocity of this type of meeting.

Chris Seaward

ROUND TWO

16 JULY, COVENTRY

COUNTRY	RACE SCORES						TOTAL
GREAT BRITAIN 60							
Lee Richardson	0	3	3	2	3	-	11
Simon Stead	2	3	2	2	1	-	10
Edward Kennett	3	2	1	3	1	-	10
Chris Harris	3	3	3	2	3	-	14
Scott Nicholls	3	3	3	3	3	-	15
SWEDEN 49							
Fredrik Lindgren	1	2	3	1	2	3	12
Peter Karlsson	3	1	0	3	2	-	9
Antonio Lindback	2	F	-	-	-	-	2
Mikael Max	2	1	2	2	1	-	8
Jonas Davidsson	2	3	6	3	2	-	16
Magnus Karlsson (Res)	0	2	-	-	-	-	2
RUSSIA 27							
Denis Gizatullin	2	1	2	3	1	2	11
Sergey Darkin	1	0	1	N	-	-	2
Emil Sajfutdinov	0	2	2	X	2	-	6
Roman Ivanov	1	1	1	1	0	-	4
Renat Gafurov	1	R	0	1	-	-	2
Danil Ivanov (Res)	1	1	-	-	-	-	2
USA 20							
Greg Hancock	3	2	4	2	1	3	15
Charlie Venegas	0	0	0	0	-	-	0
Chris Kerr	1	1	X	X	0	0	2
Tommy Hedden	0	0	0	-	-	-	0
Billy Janniro	0	2	1	0	X	0	3

RACE DETAILS

Ht 1:	(Re-Run) Hancock, Gizatullin, Lindgren, Richardson, 59.81
Ht 2:	P. Karlsson, Stead, Darkin, Venegas, 59.90
Ht 3:	Kennett, Lindback, Kerr, Sajfutdinov (f, rem), 60.34
Ht 4:	Harris, Max, R. Ivanov, Hedden, 59.68
Ht 5:	Nicholls, Davidsson, Gafurov, Janniro, 59.92
Ht 6:	Richardson, Janniro, R. Ivanov, Lindback (fell), 59.92
Ht 7:	(Re-Run) Stead, Hancock, Max, Gafurov (ret), 59.73
Ht 8:	Davidsson, Kennett, Gizatullin, Venegas, 60.48
Ht 9:	Harris, Lindgren, Kerr, Darkin, 60.00
Ht 10:	Nicholls, Sajfutdinov, P. Karlsson, Hedden, 60.45
Ht 11:	Richardson, Max, Sajfutdinov (tactical joker), Venegas, 60.15
Ht 12:	(Re-Run) Davidsson (tactical joker), Stead, R. Ivanov, Kerr (f, ex), 60.37
Ht 13:	Lindgren, Hancock (tactical joker), Kennett, Gafurov, 61.84
Ht 14:	(Re-Run) Harris, Gizatullin, Janniro, P. Karlsson, 61.68
Ht 15:	Nicholls, Hancock, Darkin, M. Karlsson, 61.58
Ht 16:	(Re-Run) P. Karlsson, Richardson, Gafurov, Kerr (f, ex), 61.42
Ht 17:	Gizatullin, Stead, Lindgren, Janniro, 62.46
Ht 18:	(Re-Run) Kennett, Max, D. Ivanov, Janniro (ex, impeding opponent), Darkin (f, ns), 62.78
Ht 19:	(Re-Run) Davidsson, Harris, Hancock, Sajfutdinov (f, ex), 61.65
Ht 20:	Nicholls, Lindgren, R. Ivanov, Kerr, 62.60
Ht 21:	Richardson, Davidsson, Gizatullin, Hedden, 61.75
Ht 22:	Lindgren, Sajfutdinov, Stead, Janniro, 63.00
Ht 23:	Hancock, P. Karlsson, Kennett, R. Ivanov, 62.39
Ht 24:	Harris, M. Karlsson, D. Ivanov, Venegas, 62.98
Ht 25:	Nicholls, Gizatullin, Max, Kerr, 62.80

IN front of a large and patriotic crowd at Coventry's plush Brandon Stadium, Great Britain romped to an emphatic victory that secured them a direct route through to the World Cup Final at Leszno. Neil Middleditch's squad certainly had a younger look about it, with Simon Stead and Edward Kennett joining the more experienced internationals, Chris Harris, Scott Nicholls and Lee Richardson. Completing the line-up, Olly Allen was chosen to fill the reserve berth and the much lamented blend of youth and experienced reaped definite rewards.

Indeed, the British side certainly went about their work with a spring in their step and, led by an impeccable 15-point, excellently acquired, maximum from their skipper Scott Nicholls, were in control throughout the majority of the meeting. Every team member collected a double figure score and the performances of Kennett and Stead, both of whom tallied 10 points, were particularly satisfying for the GB boss. Meanwhile, Harris typically demonstrated a rich vein of form with an array of trademark passing manoeuvres, whilst Richardson went about his work quietly but extremely effectively.

It quickly became apparent that two separate battles would ensue as Great Britian and Sweden indulged in a clash for the top spot, whilst Russia and the United States fiercely contested third spot and the chance to appear in the Race-Off meeting. After initially falling behind, the Brits struck back with great determination and dropped just a solitary point between races three and eleven, which provided them with a lead that they never relinquished.

However, an injury-struck Swedish outfit did mount a strong challenge in the middle part of the meeting as Jonas Davidsson, nominated for a joker ride, conjured a truly superb heat twelve victory, passing Stead majestically in the process. That was as good as it got for Mats Olsson's side, though.

They were already without Andreas Jonsson because of a shoulder problem and lost Antonio Lindback in heat six through an innocuous turn two fall. The enigmatic Davidsson did, however, excel in the face of adversity and his 16-point return was the largest tally notched up by any rider throughout the evening.

Only Greg Hancock provided the severely under-strength Americans with any sort of fire-power, as the much-loved Californian romped to a well deserved 15 points. Support, though, proved to be particularly thin on the ground for Hancock, who notched three-quarters of his team's points, whilst Billy Janniro and Chris Kerr could only muster 5 between them. The Americans will surely have been bitterly disappointed not to have progressed past this first hurdle in the competition.

Undoubtedly, the most entertaining aspect of the night was the fantastic performances of the Russian riders, many of them youngsters, who combined plenty of speed with endless reserves of bravery. For most, it would have been the first time that they had set eyes on the Brandon track and whilst they may have finished the night some 33 points behind the Brits, they certainly showed plenty of raw potential. Denis Gizatullin top scored for the Russian squad and his 11-point haul was excellently acquired, as he managed to successfully master the Brandon circuit. The highly-rated rising star Emil Sajfutdinov displayed wonderful skill, speed and tenacity on his way to collecting a 6-point total that wasn't necessarily a fair reflection of the youngster's brilliant efforts.

Chris Seaward

RACE-OFF

19 JULY, LESZNO, POLAND

COUNTRY	RACE SCORES						TOTAL
AUSTRALIA 53							
Ryan Sullivan	3	1	2	3	3	-	12
Chris Holder	2	3	1	1	1	-	8
Leigh Adams	3	3	1	3	3	-	13
Rory Schlein	1	1	1	1	2	-	6
Jason Crump	3	2	3	3	3	-	14
POLAND 52							
Tomasz Gollob	1	2	3	3	2	-	11
Damian Balinski	3	2	2	2	1	-	10
Jaroslaw Hampel	2	1	3	3	3	-	12
Grzegorz Walasek	0	2	3	2	2	-	9
Krzysztof Kasprzak	1	1	3	2	3	-	10
SWEDEN 40							
Jonas Davidsson	2	2	1	2	1	1	9
Andreas Jonsson	0	1	1	1	-	-	3
Mikael Max	0	3	2	0	0	-	5
Fredrik Lindgren	2	3	2	4	2	-	13
Peter Karlsson	2	3	2	1	2	-	10
RUSSIA 7							
Denis Gizatullin	0	0	0	R	R	-	0
Danil Ivanov	1	0	0	0	1	-	2
Emil Sajfutdinov	1	0	0	0	0	-	1
Roman Ivanov	3	0	0	1	0	-	4
Renat Gafurov	0	0	0	0	0	-	0

RACE DETAILS

Ht 1:	Sullivan, Davidsson, Gollob, Gitatullin, 59.35
Ht 2:	Balinski, Holder, D. Ivanov, Jonsson, 60.55
Ht 3:	Adams, Hampel, Sajfutdinov, Max, 58.51
Ht 4:	R. Ivanov, Lindgren, Schlein, Walasek, 60.53
Ht 5:	Crump, Karlsson, Kasprzak, Gafurov, 59.72
Ht 6:	Lindgren, Crump, Hampel, Gizatullin, 59.47
Ht 7:	Karlsson, Walasek, Sullivan, D. Ivanov, 61.25
Ht 8:	Holder, Davidsson, Kasprzak, Sajfutdinov, 60.53
Ht 9:	Adams, Gollob, Jonsson, R. Ivanov, 59.20
Ht 10:	Max, Balinski, Schlein, Gafurov, 60.12
Ht 11:	Walasek, Max, Holder, Gizatullin, 62.13
Ht 12:	Kasprzak, Lindgren, Adams, D. Ivanov, 61.55
Ht 13:	Gollob, Karlsson, Schlein, Sajfutdinov, 61.83
Ht 14:	Crump, Balinski, Davidsson, R. Ivanov, 61.73
Ht 15:	Hampel, Sullivan, Jonsson, Gafurov, 60.62
Ht 16:	Adams, Balinski, Karlsson, Gizatullin (ret), 61.60
Ht 17:	Hampel, Davidsson, Schlein, D. Ivanov, 60.28
Ht 18:	Crump, Walasek, Jonsson, Sajfutdinov, 60.47
Ht 19:	Sullivan, Kasprzak, R. Ivanov, Max, 61.98
Ht 20:	Gollob, Lindgren (tactical joker), Holder, Gafurov, 61.75
Ht 21:	Kasprzak, Schlein, Davidsson, Gizatullin (ret), 61.44
Ht 22:	Crump, Gollob, D. Ivanov, Max, 61.15
Ht 23:	Sullivan, Lindgren, Balinski, Sajfutdinov, 62.63
Ht 24:	Hampel, Karlsson, Holder, R. Ivanov (tactical joker), 63.05
Ht 25:	Adams, Walasek, Davidsson, Gafurov, 61.82

'A BIG track with plenty of dirt, and very hot weather. It feels just like home,' quipped Leigh Adams in an interview moments before the hotly-anticipated World Cup Race-Off roared into life. Appropriate then that the Aussie captain and his well drilled troops rode just like they were on the sweet shale of Australia and comfortably secured themselves a harmonious route to the World Cup Final.

Their professional approach sent out a forceful message of intent to the watching speedway world on what was a night of pulsating racing at the fabulous Leszno arena, played out in front of 15,000 rowdy Polish fans. It wasn't just what the Aussies did, it was the highly efficient manner in which they went about their task right from the moment the tapes sprung up for heat one.

From the outset, it became clear that this was Australia at their delightful best, with a fascinating blend of youth and experience coming to the fore. It was somehow fitting that the enigmatic Ryan Sullivan, the forgotten man of world speedway, got proceedings underway with a comfortable race victory in the opener. That set the tone for the night, with the big three of Adams, Sullivan and a rejuvenated Jason Crump nurturing the less experienced duo of Rory Schlein and Chris Holder.

The Australians held the lead until heat twenty and then successfully fended off a spirited Polish challenge to regain top spot in heat twenty-three. The much fancied host nation started the meeting poorly and found themselves in an unlikely battle with Sweden up to the half-way stage for second spot. The seriously under-strength Swedish quintet began to falter in the last two batchs of races and began to lose touch with the Poles, who duly set about chasing the Australians.

The post-Tony Rickardsson era looked to have hit Swedish international speedway hard and, with recurrent injuries to Andreas Jonsson along with the poor form of Antonio Lindback, the Swedes had plenty to ponder after this disappointing World Cup exit. It's not all doom and gloom for Sweden, though, and the superb performances of Fredrik Lindgren and Jonas Davidsson served as a welcome reminder that there are plenty of talented youngsters just waiting to step into Rickardsson's illustrious footsteps.

In fact, it was a race meeting in which speedway's future stars shone vibrantly, as Poland's Krzysztof Kasprzak yet again demonstrated his immense potential in the ferocity of international competition by contributing 10 points. However, both Kasprzak and Davidsson were well beaten by Australia's rising star Holder in heat eight, as the youngster showed experience beyond his then nineteen years to claim his first World Cup race victory. Holder's 8-point eventual haul was well earned and yet again underlined the frightening potential of the unassuming rider.

Holder's third spot in heat twenty-four meant that the scores were tied between Australia and Poland entering the concluding race. However, Adams' splendid final heat victory ensured that Craig Boyce's side had triumphed in the impossible, by inflicting defeat on Poland in their own extremely intimidating backyard. Last heat deciders are kids play to a seasoned campaigner like Adams and his race victory typified his whole-hearted performance for the sake of his team; that familiar theme - it wasn't what he did, it was the way in which he did it - once again held immense relevance.

Exiting the fourth corner of lap one, Adams engineered a breathtaking route underneath Poland's Grzegorz Walasek in the sublime way in which only he could. It was the kind of move that makes your head shake and eyes bulge simultaneously, it was magic. Cue scenes of passionate celebrations, a crowded top spot on the rostrum, the Australian national anthem and a shower of champagne. As the Polish fans left moderately satisfied with their team's performance, a blow-up kangaroo was waved with gusto in the emptying stadium. For Boyce's team, the town of Leszno felt closer to home than ever before.

Chris Seaward

FINAL

21 JULY, LESZNO, POLAND

COUNTRY	RACE SCORES						TOTAL
POLAND 55							
Krzysztof Kasprzak	3	3	2	3	3	-	14
Jaroslaw Hampel	3	3	3	2	2	-	13
Tomasz Gollob	3	3	3	0	3	-	12
Rune Holta	3	2	2	2	3	-	12
Grzegorz Walasek	0	0	-	-	-	-	0
Damian Balinski (Res)	X	2	2	-	-	-	4
DENMARK 52							
Hans N. Andersen	2	2	2	3	1	-	10
Kenneth Bjerre	1	2	3	3	1	-	10
Niels-Kristian Iversen	2	3	2	1	1	-	9
Nicki Pedersen	2	3	2	3	2	-	12
Bjarne Pedersen	2	1	3	2	3	-	11

AUSTRALIA 29							
Ryan Sullivan	1	1	1	1	3	-	7
Jason Crump	2	T	3	3	1	-	9
Chris Holder	1	2	0	-	-	-	3
Leigh Adams	1	2	1	1	0	-	5
Davey Watt	3	1	0	0	0	-	4
Rory Schlein (Res)	0	1	-	-	-	-	1

GREAT BRITAIN 15							
Lee Richardson	0	1	R	1	2	-	4
Simon Stead	0	0	1	0	-	-	1
Edward Kennett	0	0	0	-	-	-	0
Chris Harris	0	0	1	2	0	-	3
Scott Nicholls	1	1	1	2	0	2	7
Olly Allen (Res)	0	R	-	-	-	-	0

RACE DETAILS

Ht 1:	Kasprzak, Andersen, Sullivan, Richardson, 60.50
Ht 2:	Hampel, Crump, Bjerre, Stead, 60.91
Ht 3:	Gollob, Iversen, Holder, Kennett, 60.30
Ht 4:	Holta, N. Pedersen, Adams, Harris, 61.12
Ht 5:	Watt. B. Pedersen, Nicholls, Walasek, 62.01
Ht 6:	N. Pedersen, Holder, Richardson, Walasek, 62.21
Ht 7:	Kasprzak, Adams, B. Pedersen, Stead, 61.65
Ht 8:	Hampel, Andersen, Watt, Kennett, 61.51
Ht 9:	Gollob, Bjerre, Sullivan, Harris, 61.19
Ht 10:	(Re-Run) Iversen, Holta, Nicholls, Crump (tactical joker, ex, tapes), 63.01
Ht 11:	Hampel, Iversen, Adams, Richardson (ret), 62.99
Ht 12:	Gollob, N. Pedersen, Stead, Watt, 62.96
Ht 13:	B. Pedersen, Holta, Sullivan, Kennett, 62.80
Ht 14:	(Re-Run) Crump, Andersen, Harris, Balinski (f, ex), 63.18
Ht 15:	Bjerre, Kasprzak, Nicholls, Holder, 63.53
Ht 16:	Crump, B. Pedersen, Richardson, Gollob, 62.41
Ht 17:	Andersen, Holta, Nicholls (tactical joker), Schlein, 63.02
Ht 18:	Bjerre, Balinski, Adams, Allen, 62.22
Ht 19:	Kasprzak, Harris, Iversen, Watt, 62.37
Ht 20:	N. Pedersen, Hampel, Sullivan, Nicholls, 62.78
Ht 21:	Holta, Richardson, Bjerre, Wall, 63.23
Ht 22:	Sullivan, Balinski, Iversen, Stead, 63.44
Ht 23:	Kasprzak, N. Pedersen, Crump, Allen (ret), 63.48
Ht 24:	B. Pedersen, Hampel, Schlein, Harris, 63.69
Ht 25:	Gollob, Nicholls, Andersen, Adams, 63.97

POLAND sent their home fans into delirium by sensationally lifting the World Cup for a second time in three years on a night of pulsating speedway action at the plush Smoczyk Stadium in Leszno. In front of a passionate 25,000 capacity crowd, the home nation overcame the spirited challenge from a youthful Danish side to clinch victory in an exceptionally tense final race decider. Holding a slender 1-point lead, Tomasz Gollob defeated Scott Nicholls and, crucially, Denmark's Hans N. Andersen in the concluding heat to collect the Ove Fundin Trophy, sending the speedway mad town of Leszno into frenzy in the process.

From the outset, there was an atmosphere to savour, as speedway's most devoted nation lapped up everything their side had to offer on a sun-drenched evening. The racing complemented the ambience wonderfully, with an array of breathtaking action served up on a track that was immaculately prepared. Quite simply, it was what speedway should be all about and was a fitting conclusion to the week of top-notch action that had preceded it.

Poland may have looked somewhat average in the Race-Off meeting, but they certainly made sure that they were flawlessly equipped for the big one, as they began the meeting in dominant fashion. Rumours that the Poles had spent the previous day locked away for a 9-hour testing session appeared to hold substance, as the home nation revelled in significantly enhanced straight line speed.

In contrast, Leigh Adams and his Australian troops mysteriously struggled to perform on a circuit on which they had excelled just two days earlier, as their heavily documented blend of youth and experience surprisingly failed to deliver. The Aussies were very much in touch during the first third of the meeting; indeed, after heat six, a mere 2 points was all that separated them from the leaders.

However, by around the half-way stage, it was clear that the 2007 World Cup had become a two-horse battle between Poland and Denmark, after Jason Crump had suffered an engine failure and clattered through the tapes in heat ten, whilst on a 'joker' outing. If Crump had been able to convert the double-points opportunity, then Australia would have been back in contention with the big two pace-setters out front. As it happened, Crump's misfortune inevitably led to heads dropping in the Aussie camp, as they began to lose touch with the leaders and became helplessly marooned in third spot.

Meanwhile, the lack-lustre British team huffed and puffed through the heats with little success, and failed to stamp any authority on the event. Scott Nicholls' outfit managed to collect a lowly 4 points after thirteen races and seemed to lack the sheer engine speed to successfully compete with the three sides around them.

Whilst the Brit's faltered, the Danes and Poles indulged in a fascinating ding-dong battle that went right down to the wire. The Danish side performed tenaciously to maintain the ferocious early pace set by the home nation and, despite trailing by 5 points at the mid-way stage, kept the meeting well and truly alive. The Danes even moved ahead by 3 points after heat eighteen, but the Poles kept their composure and, roared on by their fanatical home fans, collected overall victory by the narrowest of margins.

So, a deserved victory for Tomasz Gollob's Poland, who put on a tremendous show for their adoring fans. Just one week later, the squad received an invite to the palace of Polish President, Lech Kaczynski; an indication of the sheer popularity of the sport in the historic central European nation.

Chris Seaward

ROLL OF HONOUR

NOTE: Formerly known as the World Team Cup (1960-2000).

YEAR	FIRST	SECOND	THIRD	FOURTH
1960	Sweden	Great Britain	Czechoslovakia	Poland
1961	Poland	Sweden	Great Britain	Czechoslovakia
1962	Sweden	Great Britain	Poland	Czechoslovakia
1963	Sweden	Czechoslovakia	Great Britain	Poland
1964	Sweden	Soviet Union	Great Britain	Poland
1965	Poland	Sweden	Great Britain	Soviet Union
1966	Poland	Soviet Union	Sweden	Great Britain
1967	Sweden	Poland	Great Britain & Soviet Union	-
1968	Great Britain	Sweden	Poland	Czechoslovakia
1969	Poland	Great Britain	Soviet Union	Sweden
1970	Sweden	Great Britain	Poland	Czechoslovakia
1971	Great Britain	Soviet Union	Poland	Sweden
1972	Great Britain	Soviet Union	Poland	Sweden
1973	Great Britain	Sweden	Soviet Union	Poland
1974	England	Sweden	Poland	Soviet Union
1975	England	Soviet Union	Sweden	Poland
1976	Australia	Poland	Sweden	Soviet Union
1977	England	Poland	Czechoslovakia	Sweden
1978	Denmark	England	Poland	Czechoslovakia
1979	New Zealand	Denmark	Czechoslovakia	Poland
1980	England	USA	Poland	Czechoslovakia
1981	Denmark	England	West Germany	Soviet Union
1982	USA	Denmark	West Germany	Czechoslovakia
1983	Denmark	England	USA	Czechoslovakia
1984	Denmark	England	USA	Poland
1985	Denmark	USA	England	Sweden
1986	Denmark	USA	England	Sweden
1987	Denmark	England	USA	Czechoslovakia
1988	Denmark	USA	Sweden	England
1989	England	Denmark	Sweden	USA
1990	USA	England	Denmark	Czechoslovakia
1991	Denmark	Sweden	USA	England
1992	USA	Sweden	England	Denmark
1993	USA	Denmark	Sweden	England
1994	Sweden	Poland	Denmark	Australia
1995	Denmark	England	USA	Sweden
1996	Poland	Russia	Denmark	Germany
1997	Denmark	Poland	Sweden	Germany
1998	USA	Sweden	Denmark	Poland
1999	Australia	Czech Republic	USA	England
2000	Sweden	England	USA	Australia
2001	Australia	Poland	Sweden	Denmark
2002	Australia	Denmark	Sweden	Poland
2003	Sweden	Australia	Denmark	Poland
2004	Sweden	Great Britain	Denmark	Poland
2005	Poland	Sweden	Denmark	Great Britain
2006	Denmark	Sweden	Great Britain	Australia
2007	Poland	Denmark	Australia	Great Britain

WORLD UNDER-21 TEAM CUP 2007

FIRST SEMI-FINAL	3 JUNE, DEBRECEN, HUNGARY
GREAT BRITAIN 41	Daniel King 12; Edward Kennett 11; Lewis Bridger 10; James Wright 8; Ben Barker 0
CZECH REPUBLIC 37	Lubos Tomicek 14; Filip Sitera 10; Matej Kus 8; Hynek Stichauer 5; Adam Vandirek DNR
SWEDEN 32	Billy Forsberg 12; Simon Gustafsson 6; Robin Tornqvist 6; Ricky Kling 5; Thomas H. Jonasson 3
HUNGARY 9	Jozsef Tabaka 6; Roland Kovacs 2; Attila Lorincz 1 **NOTE**: The Hungarian side comprised three riders only.

SECOND SEMI-FINAL	3 JUNE, POZNAN, POLAND
POLAND 39	Karol Zabik 12; Maciej Piaszczynski 10; Mateusz Szczepaniak 9; Pawel Hlib 7; Marcin Jedrzejewski 1
DENMARK 31	Morten Risager 9; Nicolai Klindt 8; Kenneth Hansen 8; Patrick Hougaard 6; Klaus Jakobsen DNR
AUSTRALIA 30	Chris Holder 16; Troy Batchelor 10; Trevor Harding 4; Cory Gathercole 0; Robert Ksiezak 0
RUSSIA 20	Emil Sajfutdinov 12; Kiryl Filinov 3; Aleksandr Kosolapkin 3; Roman Kantiukov 1; Alexei Guzaev 1

FINAL	23 SEPTEMBER, ABENSBERG, GERMANY
POLAND 40	Krzysztof Buczkowski 11; Karol Zabik 10; Pawel Hlib 10; Mateusz Szczepaniak 9; Adrian Gomolski DNR
GREAT BRITAIN 36	Edward Kennett 14; Lewis Bridger 11; James Wright 6; Daniel King 5; Josh Auty DNR
CZECH REPUBLIC 30	Filip Sitera 11; Matej Kus 9; Lubos Tomicek 6; Hynek Stichauer 4; Martin Gavenda DNR
GERMANY 13	Richard Speiser 6; Max Dilger 4; Kevin Wölbert 3; Tobias Busch 0; Frank Facher 0

ROLL OF HONOUR

YEAR	FIRST	SECOND	THIRD	FOURTH
2005	Poland	Sweden	Denmark	Czech Republic
2006	Poland	Sweden	Denmark	Germany
2007	Poland	Great Britain	Czech Republic	Germany

WORLD UNDER-21 CHAMPIONSHIP 2007

QUALIFYING ROUND ONE; 23 APRIL, HERXHEIM, GERMANY

1st Chris Holder 14; 2nd Pawel Hlib 13; 3rd Martin Vaculik 12+3; Friedrich Wallner 12+2; Adrian Gomolski 11; Matej Kus 10; Frank Facher 8; Richard Speiser 7; Hynek Stichauer 6; Mark Stiekema 6; Manuel Novotny 6; Jannick de Jong 6; Jozsef Tabaka 4; Max Dilger 3; Attila Loerincz 1; Voldrih Matic 1.

QUALIFYING ROUND TWO; 12 MAY, MOTALA, SWEDEN

1st Morten Risager 13+3; 2nd Nicolai Klindt 13+2; 3rd Simon Gustafsson 13+1; Ricky Kling 11; Thomas H. Jonasson 11; Patrick Hougaard 10; Billy Forsberg 10; Kenneth Hansen 9; Dannie Soderholm 7; Viktor Bergstrom 6; Carl-Johan Raugstad 5; Robin Tornqvist 4; Klaus Jacobsen 2; Joni Keskinen 2; Teemu Lahti 1; Jari Makinen 1; Andreas Messing (Res) 1; Linus Eklof (Res) 1.

QUALIFYING ROUND THREE; 12 MAY, DONJI KRALJEVEC, CROATIA

1st Krzysztof Buczkowski 14; 2nd Jurica Pavlic 13; 3rd Maksims Bogdanovs 12; Lubos Tomicek 10; Marcin Jedrzejewski 10; Filip Sitera 10; Ben Barker 9; Andriy Karpov 8+3; Daniel King 8+2; Nikola Martinec 8+1; Igor Kononov 4; Davor Volk 4; Andrea Baroni 3; Matija Duh 2; Renato Cvetko 2; Vjaceslav Giruckis 1; Nikola Pigac (Res) 1; Jaroslav Polyuhovich (Res) 1.

QUALIFYING ROUND FOUR; 12 MAY, RYE HOUSE

1st Emil Sajfutdinov 13; 2nd Lewis Bridger 12+3; 3rd Danil Ivanov 12+2; Troy Batchelor 11; Tai Woffinden 11; William Lawson 10; Robert Ksiezak 9; Andrew Bargh 8; Kamil Brzozowski 7; Kenny Ingalls 5; Maciej Piaszczynski 4; Dale Facchini 4; Jeremy Diraison 3; Mathieu Tresarrieu 3; Stefan Kurz 3; Ramon Stanek 2; Steve Boxall (Res) 2; Adam Roynon (Res) 1.

FIRST SEMI-FINAL; 16 JUNE, VOJENS, DENMARK

1st Chris Holder 14; 2nd Edward Kennett 13; 3rd Morten Risager 12; Jurica Pavlic 10; Lewis Bridger 10; Simon Gustafsson 9; Kevin Wölbert 8; Filip Sitera 7+3; Adrian Gomolski 7+X; Billy Forsberg 6; Kenneth Hansen 6; William Lawson 6; Richard Speiser (Res) 5; Frank Facher 2; Matej Kus 1; Friedrich Wallner 1; Nicolai Klindt 0.

SECOND SEMI-FINAL; 17 JUNE, DAUGAVPILS, LATVIA

1st Emil Sajfutdinov 15; 2nd Kjastas Puodzhuks 12; 3rd Pawel Hlib 11; Karol Zabik 10; Ricky Kling 10; Thomas H. Jonasson 10; Lubos Tomicek 10; Danil Ivanov 8+3; Robert Ksiezak 8+2; Patrick Hougaard 6; Maksims Bogdanovs 5; Marcin Jedrzejewski 4; Martin Vaculik 4; Ben Barker 3; Krzysztof Buczkowski 3; Andrew Bargh 1.

WORLD UNDER-21 CHAMPIONSHIP FINAL 2007

9 SEPTEMBER, OSTROW, POLAND

1st   EMIL SAJFUTDINOV
2nd CHRIS HOLDER
3rd PAWEL HLIB
4th JURICA PAVLIC

RIDER	RACE SCORES					TOTAL
Emil Sajfutdinov	3	3	3	3	3	15
Chris Holder	2	3	3	3	3	14
Pawel Hlib	3	2	3	2	2	12
Jurica Pavlic	3	0	3	3	1	10
Karol Zabik	2	3	2	1	2	10
Thomas H. Jonasson	2	2	2	3	1	10
Danil Ivanov	3	1	1	0	3	8
Morten Risager	2	3	1	2	0	8
Filip Sitera	0	2	2	2	2	8
Lewis Bridger	1	2	2	R	1	6
Edward Kennett	0	1	1	R	3	5
Simon Gustafsson	1	0	0	2	2	5
Kjastas Puodzhuks	1	1	0	1	0	3
Ricky Kling	1	1	1	X	R	3
Lubos Tomicek	0	0	0	1	1	2
Kevin Wölbert	0	0	0	1	0	1

HEAT DETAILS

Ht 1:	Ivanov, Risager, Kling, Kennett, 65.00
Ht 2:	Sajfutdinov, Holder, Puodzhuks, Wölbert, 64.78
Ht 3:	Pavlic, Zabik, Bridger, Tomicek, 65.35
Ht 4:	Hlib, Jonasson, Gustafsson, Sitera, 65.15
Ht 5:	Risager, Sitera, Puodzhuks, Tomicek, 65.56
Ht 6:	Sajfutdinov, Jonasson, Ivanov, Pavlic, 64.28 (Track Record)
Ht 7:	Zabik, Hlib, Kling, Wölbert, 64.78
Ht 8:	Holder, Bridger, Kennett, Gustafsson, 64.44
Ht 9:	Sajfutdinov, Zabik, Risager, Gustafsson, 64.18 (Track Record)
Ht 10:	Hlib, Bridger, Ivanov, Puodzhuks, 66.19
Ht 11:	Holder, Jonasson, Kling, Tomicek, 65.19
Ht 12:	Pavlic, Sitera, Kennett, Wölbert, 65.47
Ht 13:	Jonasson, Risager, Wölbert, Bridger (ret), 65.33
Ht 14:	Holder, Sitera, Zabik, Ivanov, 65.81
Ht 15:	Pavlic, Gustafsson, Puodzhuks, Kling (ex, foul riding), 66.28
Ht 16:	Sajfutdinov, Hlib, Tomicek, Kennett (ret), 65.85
Ht 17:	Holder, Hlib, Pavlic, Risager, 65.11
Ht 18:	Ivanov, Gustafsson, Tomicek, Wölbert, 65.84
Ht 19:	Sajfutdinov, Sitera, Bridger, Kling (ret), 64.99
Ht 20:	Kennett, Zabik, Jonasson, Puodzhuks, 66.11

ROLL OF HONOUR

NOTE: Formerly known as the European Junior Championship (1977-1987).

YEAR	FIRST	SECOND	THIRD
1977	Alf Busk	Joe Owen	Les Collins
1978	Finn Jensen	Kevin Jolly	Neil Middleditch
1979	Ron Preston	Airat Faljzulin	Ari Koponen
1980	Tommy Knudsen	Tony Briggs	Dennis Sigalos
1981	Shawn Moran	Toni Kasper	Jiri Hnidak
1982	Toni Kasper	Mark Courtney	Peter Ravn
1983	Steve Baker	David Bargh	Marvyn Cox
1984	Marvyn Cox	Neil Evitts	Steve Lucero
1985	Per Jonsson	Jimmy Nilsen	Ole Hansen
1986	Igor Marko	Tony Olsson	Brian Karger
1987	Gary Havelock	Piotr Swist	Sean Wilson
1988	Peter Nahlin	Henrik Gustafsson	Brian Karger
1989	Gert Handberg	Chris Louis	Niklas Karlsson
1990	Chris Louis	Rene Aas	Tony Rickardsson
1991	Brian Andersen	Morten Andersen	Jason Lyons
1992	Leigh Adams	Mark Loram	Joe Screen
1993	Joe Screen	Mikael Karlsson (Max)	Rune Holta
1994	Mikael Karlsson (Max)	Rune Holta	Jason Crump
1995	Jason Crump	Dalle Anderson	Ryan Sullivan
1996	Piotr Protasiewicz	Ryan Sullivan	Jesper B. Jensen
1997	Jesper B. Jensen	Rafal Dobrucki	Scott Nicholls
1998	Robert Dados	Krzysztof Jablonski	Matej Ferjan
1999	Lee Richardson	Ales Dryml	Nigel Sadler
2000	Andreas Jonsson	Krzysztof Cegielski	Jaroslaw Hampel
2001	David Kujawa	Lukas Dryml	Rafal Okoniewski
2002	Lukas Dryml	Krzysztof Kasprzak	David Howe
2003	Jaroslaw Hampel	Chris Harris	Rafal Szombierski
2004	Robert Miskowiak	Kenneth Bjerre	Matej Zagar
2005	Krzysztof Kasprzak	Tomas Suchanek	Fredrik Lindgren
2006	Karol Zabik	Antonio Lindback	Christian Hefenbrock
2007	Emil Sajfutdinov	Chris Holder	Pawel Hlib

EUROPEAN CHAMPIONSHIP 2007

QUALIFYING ROUND; 1 MAY, STRALSUND, GERMANY

1st Karol Zabik 13+3; 2nd Lukas Dryml 13+2; 3rd Matej Ferjan 13+1; Christian Hefenbrock 11; Slawomir Drabik 11; Matthias Schultz 11; Tobias Kroner 9; Zdenek Simota 8; Fritz Wallner 7; Mariusz Staszewski 7; Jernej Kolenko 5; Mattia Carpanese 4; Izak Santej 4; Rene Schafer 2; Leonids Paura 2; Henk Bos 0.

QUALIFYING ROUND; 20 MAY, LVOV, UKRAINE

1st Zbigniew Suchecki 15; 2nd Renat Gafurov 14; 3rd Sebastian Ulamek 13; Sergey Darkin 11; Jozsef Tabaka 9; Andrey Karpov 9; Ales Dryml 9; Guglielmo Franchetti 9; Ronny Weis 8; Jaroslav Polyuhovich 6+3; Tomas Suchanek 6+2; Aleksandru Toma 3; Marko Vlah 3; Andrey Kobrin 2; Vladimir Marchuk (Res) 2; Fanel Popa 1; Rostislav Bandzi 0.

FIRST SEMI-FINAL; 17 JUNE, BLIJHAM, HOLLAND

1st Zbigniew Suchecki 12+3; 2nd Tomas Suchanek 12+2; 3rd Slawomir Drabik 12+1; Denis Gizatullin 10+3; Matej Ferjan 10+2; Mariusz Staszewski 10+1; Daniel Jeleniewski 9; Roman Ivanov 8; Tobias Kroner 8; Denis Sajfutdinov 6; Renat Gafurov 5; Jannick de Jong 5; Jernej Kolenko 4; Guglielmo Franchetti 4; Fritz Wallner 1.

SECOND SEMI-FINAL; 5 AUGUST, ESBJERG, DENMARK

1st Henrik Moller 14; 2nd Sebastian Alden 12+3; 3rd Nicolai Klindt 12+2; Kenneth Hansen 12+1; Henning Bager 12+0; Mads Korneliussen 11; Patrick Hougaard 10; Eric Andersson 8; Leon Madsen 7; Viktor Bergstrom 5; Jari Makinen 5; Carl Johan Raugstad 4; Tobias Johansson 3; Daniel Davidsson 2; Rune Sola 2; Tero Aarnio 1.

THIRD SEMI-FINAL; 18 AUGUST, GORICAN, CROATIA

1st Sebastian Ulamek 14; 2nd Jurica Pavlic 13; 3rd Lukas Dryml 12; Christian Hefenbrock 11; Ales Dryml 10; Lubos Tomicek 9; Jozsef Tabaka 9; Zdenek Simota 9; Vladimir Dubinin 7; Mathias Schultz 7; Ilya Bondarenko 6; Marat Gatyatov 5; Marko Vlah 3; Heinrich Schatzer 2; Ruslan Gatyatov 2; Nikola Pigac (Res) 1; Ronny Weis 0.

FINAL; 29 SEPTEMBER, WIENER-NEUSTADT, AUSTRIA

1st Jurica Pavlic 14; 2nd Sebastian Ulamek 13; 3rd Patrick Hougaard 11; Matej Ferjan 10; Zbigniew Suchecki 10; Denis Gizatullin 9; Lukas Dryml 9; Christian Hefenbrock 9; Manuel Hauzinger 7; Mariusz Staszewski 6; Sebastian Alden 6; Ales Dryml 5; Nicolai Klindt 5; Kenneth Hansen 5; Daniel Jeleniewski (Res) 1; Tomas Suchanek 0; Henrik Moller 0.

ROLL OF HONOUR

YEAR	FIRST	SECOND	THIRD
2001	Bohumil Brhel	Mariusz Staszewski	Krzysztof Cegielski
2002	Magnus Zetterstrom	Krzysztof Kasprzak	Rafal Szombierski
2003	Krzysztof Kasprzak	Slawomir Drabik	Magnus Zetterstrom
2004	Matej Zagar	Matej Ferjan	Hans N. Andersen
2005	Jesper B. Jensen	Ales Dryml	Kaj Laukkanen
2006	Krzysztof Jablonski	Grzegorz Walasek	Christian Hefenbrock
2007	Jurica Pavlic	Sebastian Ulamek	Patrick Hougaard

EUROPEAN UNDER-19 CHAMPIONSHIP 2007

FIRST SEMI-FINAL; 28 MAY, MISKOLC, HUNGARY

1st Jurica Pavlic 15; 2nd Maciej Piaszczynski 13; 3rd Grzegorz Zengota 12+3; Borys Miturski 12+2; Filip Sitera 11; Jozsef Tabaka 11; Frank Facher 8; Adrian Szewczykowski 8; Nikola Martinec 7; Henk Koonstra 6; Nicki Glanz 5; Maxime Mazeau 3; Matija Duh 3; Jeremy Diraison 3; Attila Lorincz 2; Henry van der Steen DNR.

SECOND SEMI-FINAL; 9 JUNE, SEINAJOKI, FINLAND

1st Nicolai Klindt 15; 2nd Linus Sundstrom 13+3; 3rd Thomas H. Jonasson 13+2; Patrick Hougaard 12; Anders Andersen 11; Klaus Jakobsen 10; Simon Gustafsson 9; Jonas Raun 6; Jari Makinen 6; Kalle Katajisto 5; Peter Juul Larsen 5; Linus Eklof 5; Robert Pettersson 4; Teemu Lahti 3; Markku Autio 2; Appe Mustonen 1.

THIRD SEMI-FINAL; 14 JULY, DAUGAVPILS, LATVIA

1st Martin Vaculik 14; 2nd Kevin Wölbert 14; 3rd Maksims Bogdanovs 13; Adam Kajoch 10; Tobias Busch 10; Artem Laguta 10; Matej Kus 9; Michal Mitko 8; Michal Lopaczewski 7; Oleg Bestchastnov 5; Vyacheslav Gieruckijs 4; Pavel Fuksa 4; Evgeny Karavackijs 4; Evgeny Petuhovs 4; Pawel Fleger 3; Andrey Kobrin 0. NOTE: Wolbert declined to run-off, handing first place to Vaculik.

FINAL; 19 AUGUST, CZESTOCHOWA, POLAND

1st Nicolai Klindt 14; 2nd Jurica Pavlic 11; 3rd Filip Sitera 10+3; Borys Miturski 10+2; Thomas H. Jonasson 10+1; Martin Vaculik 10+0; Artem Laguta 9; Kevin Wolbert 8; Adam Kajoch 7; Grzegorz Zengota 7; Tobias Busch 7; Maksims Bogdanovs 6; Patrick Hougaard 5; Linus Sundstrom 3; Anders Andersen 1; Maciej Piaszczynski 1.

ROLL OF HONOUR

YEAR	FIRST	SECOND	THIRD
1998	Rafal Okoniewski	Ales Dryml	Hans N. Andersen
1999	Rafal Okoniewski	Karol Malecha	Jaroslaw Hampel
2000	Lukas Dryml	Niels-Kristian Iversen	Zbigniew Czerwinski
2001	Lukasz Romanek	Daniel Davidsson	Rafal Kurmanski
2002	Matej Zagar	Kenneth Bjerre	Fredrik Lindgren
2003	Kenneth Bjerre	Janusz Kolodziej	Antonio Lindback
2004	Antonio Lindback	Karol Zabik	Morten Risager
2005	Karol Zabik	Kjastas Puodzhuks	Robert Pettersson
2006	Jurica Pavlic	Andrey Karpov	Lars Hansen
2007	Nicolai Klindt	Jurica Pavlic	Filip Sitera

RIDER INDEX
2007

The following is an A-Z list of riders who appeared in 2007, and includes all official meetings at Elite League, Premier League and Conference League level.

NOTE: The symbol II after a team's name differentiates between a club's Conference level and higher league side, when more than one team was operated in the same season.

ADAMS, Leigh Scott

DATE OF BIRTH: 28 April 1971, Mildura, Victoria, Australia.

BRITISH CAREER: (1989) Poole; (1990-92) Swindon; (1993-95) Arena-Essex; (1996) London; (1997-98) Swindon; (1999-00) King's Lynn; (2001-02) Oxford; (2003) Poole; (2004-07) Swindon.

MAJOR HONOURS: Australian Under-16 Champion: 1986; Australian Under-21 Champion: 1988, 1990, 1991, 1992; Victoria State Champion: 1989, 1990, 1991, 1992, 1994, 1995; Australian Champion: 1992, 1993, 1994, 1998, 2000, 2002, 2003, 2005, 2006; World Under-21 Champion: 1992; Commonwealth Champion: 1993; World Team Cup Champion: 1999; Czech Golden Helmet Champion: 1999, 2000, 2001, 2004; World Cup Champion: 2001, 2002.

GRAND PRIX: Challenge Champion: 1995, 1998; Scandinavian GP Champion: 2002, 2007; Slovenian GP Champion: 2003; Swedish GP Champion: 2004, 2007; Latvian GP Champion: 2007.

RIDER LINKS: Cousin of fellow rider Cory Gathercole.

ALLEN, Oliver (Olly) James

DATE OF BIRTH: 27 May 1982, Norwich, Norfolk.

BRITISH CAREER: (1997) Peterborough II; (1998) Mildenhall, Norfolk, Peterborough, Arena-Essex; (1999-01) Swindon; (2002) Swindon, Peterborough; (2003) Swindon, Wolverhampton; (2004) Swindon; (2005) King's Lynn, Swindon, Eastbourne; (2006-07) Coventry.

MAJOR HONOUR: Queensland State Champion: 2006.

RIDER LINKS: Son of former rider Dave Allen. Brother of fellow rider Tommy Allen.

ALLEN, Thomas (Tommy) David

DATE OF BIRTH: 4 September 1984, Norwich, Norfolk.

BRITISH CAREER: (2002) Mildenhall, Swindon II; (2003) Swindon, Swindon II; (2004) Rye House, Rye House II; (2005) Rye House, Swindon; (2006) Rye House, Belle Vue, Poole; (2007) Rye House, Swindon.

RIDER LINKS: Son of former rider Dave Allen. Brother of fellow rider Olly Allen.

ALLOTT, Adam Nick

DATE OF BIRTH: 19 March 1983, Stockport, Cheshire.

BRITISH CAREER: (1998) Norfolk, Buxton; (1999) Buxton, Sheffield; (2000) Sheffield, Owlerton; (2001) Sheffield; (2002) Sheffield II, Swindon, Somerset; (2003) Buxton, King's Lynn; (2004) King's Lynn; (2005) King's Lynn, Eastbourne, Workington, Stoke; (2006) Stoke II; (2007) King's Lynn.

RIDER LINKS: Son of former rider Nicky Allott. Great Nephew of former rider Tommy Allott. Grandson of former rider Guy Allott. Nephew of former riders Ian and Trevor Stead. Cousin of fellow rider Simon Stead.

ANDERSEN, Hans Norgaard

DATE OF BIRTH: 3 November 1980, Odense, Denmark.

BRITISH CAREER: (2001-02) Poole; (2003) Peterborough; (2004-05) Ipswich; (2006-07) Peterborough.

MAJOR HONOURS: World Cup Champion: 2006; Danish Champion: 2007.

GRAND PRIX: Scandinavian GP Champion: 2004; Danish GP Champion: 2006; Czech Republic GP Champion: 2006; Grand Final Champion: 2006.

ANDERSON, Scott

DATE OF BIRTH: 28 March 1975, Scunthorpe, North Lincolnshire.

BRITISH CAREER: (2007) Scunthorpe.

ANDERSSON, Eric

DATE OF BIRTH: 15 June 1984, St Dicka, Fors, Sweden.

BRITISH CAREER: (2006-07) Oxford.

ANDERSSON, Stefan Frederik

DATE OF BIRTH: 13 September 1971, Vastervik, Sweden.

BRITISH CAREER: (1994-98) Eastbourne; (1999) King's Lynn; (2000) Peterborough; (2001-02) Eastbourne; (2005) Oxford; (2007) Eastbourne.

MAJOR HONOUR: Nordic Champion: 1995.

ANDREWS, Darren Colin

DATE OF BIRTH: 19 January 1977, Banbury, Oxfordshire.

BRITISH CAREER: (1993) Coventry, Oxford; (1994) Coventry, Oxford, Mildenhall; (1995) Sittingbourne; (1996) Reading II; (1997) Long Eaton, Hull, Berwick, Oxford, Oxford II, Ryde; (2000) St Austell; (2001) Rye House; (2002) Mildenhall; (2003) Oxford, Oxford II, Carmarthen; (2004) Stoke II, Coventry II; (2005) Sittingbourne; (2007) Oxford II.

RIDER LINKS: Brother-in-law of fellow rider Paul Clews.

ARMSTRONG, Jon Thomas

DATE OF BIRTH: 1 August 1974, Manchester, Greater Manchester.

BRITISH CAREER: (1992-93) Belle Vue; (1994) Coventry; (1996) Buxton, Sheffield; (1997) Buxton, Belle Vue II, Swindon, Stoke; (1998) Newport, Newport II; (1999) Belle Vue, Stoke; (2000) Newport; (2001) Stoke; (2002) Buxton, Stoke; (2003) Stoke; (2004) Mildenhall, Belle Vue; (2005) Mildenhall, Peterborough; (2006) Mildenhall, Peterborough; (2007) Boston, Birmingham, Buxton.

MAJOR HONOUR: Amateur League Riders' Champion: 1997.

ASHWORTH, Richard (Ricky) David

DATE OF BIRTH: 17 August 1982, Salford, Greater Manchester.

BRITISH CAREER: (2001) Sheffield II; (2002) Sheffield, Sheffield II; (2003) Sheffield; (2004) Sheffield, Peterborough; (2005) Sheffield, Poole; (2006-07) Sheffield.

ATKIN, Anthony (Tony) Neville

DATE OF BIRTH: 8 April 1966, Wrexham, North Wales.

BRITISH CAREER: (1986) Stoke; (1994) Wolverhampton; (1995) Bradford; (1996) Sheffield, Wolverhampton, Buxton; (1997) Stoke; (1999-02) Stoke; (2003-07) Newport.

AUTY, Joshua (Josh) Liam

DATE OF BIRTH: 8 September 1990, Mirfield, West Yorkshire.

BRITISH CAREER: (2005-06) Scunthorpe; (2007) Redcar, Scunthorpe.

MAJOR HONOURS: British Under-15 Champion: 2004, 2005.

BAGER, Henning

DATE OF BIRTH: 18 February 1981, Esbjerg, Denmark.

BRITISH CAREER: (2001) Glasgow; (2002) Peterborough, Isle of Wight; (2003) Arena-Essex; (2004-05) Peterborough; (2006) Arena-Essex; (2007) Lakeside, Birmingham.

BALINSKI, Damian

DATE OF BIRTH: 5 August 1977, Leszno, Poland.

BRITISH CAREER: (2007) Swindon.

MAJOR HONOURS: World Cup Champion: 2007.

RIDER LINKS: Brother of former rider Dariusz Balinski. Uncle of fellow rider Damian Balinski [II], the son of Dariusz.

BARGH, Andrew Lawrence

DATE OF BIRTH: 15 April 1986, Napier, New Zealand.

BRITISH CAREER: (2005) Wimbledon, Mildenhall; (2006) Mildenhall II; (2007) Isle of Wight, Oxford II.

MAJOR HONOURS: New Zealand Under-21 Champion: 2005; New Zealand Champion: 2007.

RIDER LINKS: Nephew of former rider David Bargh.

BARKER, Benjamin (Ben) John

DATE OF BIRTH: 10 March 1988, Truro, Cornwall.

BRITISH CAREER: (2003) Oxford II, Trelawny II; (2004) Oxford II, Coventry II; (2005) Oxford II, Exeter; (2006) Somerset, Stoke II; (2007) Stoke.

BARKER, Dean

DATE OF BIRTH: 2 August 1970, Isleworth, Middlesex.

BRITISH CAREER: (1986) Eastbourne; (1987-88) Eastbourne, Cradley Heath; (1989) Eastbourne; (1990-92) Oxford; (1993-95) Eastbourne; (1997) Eastbourne; (1999-03) Eastbourne; (2004) Arena-Essex; (2005-07) Eastbourne.

RIDER LINKS: Brother of former rider Sean Barker.

BASEBY, Aaron Henry

DATE OF BIRTH: 31 May 1990, Pembury, Kent.

BRITISH CAREER: (2005-07) Sittingbourne.

RIDER LINKS: Brother of fellow rider Mark Baseby.

BASEBY, Mark Charles

DATE OF BIRTH: 28 February 1988, Pembury, Kent.

BRITISH CAREER: (2003) Stoke II, Swindon II; (2004) Rye House II, Sittingbourne; (2005) Sittingbourne; (2006) Mildenhall II; (2007) Sittingbourne, Mildenhall.

RIDER LINKS: Brother of fellow rider Aaron Baseby.

BATCHELOR, Troy Matthew

DATE OF BIRTH: 29 August 1987, Brisbane, Queensland, Australia.

BRITISH CAREER: (2005) King's Lynn, Eastbourne; (2006) King's Lynn, Coventry; (2007) Poole.

MAJOR HONOURS: Australian Under-16 Champion: 2003; Queensland State Champion: 2007.

BATES, Matthew (Mattie)

DATE OF BIRTH: 26 July 1989, Exeter, Devon.

BRITISH CAREER: (2004) Weymouth, Coventry II; (2005) Weymouth, Mildenhall; (2006) Plymouth; (2007) Oxford II.

BEATON HAMILTON, Gary

DATE OF BIRTH: 20 August 1986, Glasgow, Scotland.

BRITISH CAREER: (2002) Newport II, Newcastle II; (2003) Newcastle II, Wolverhampton II, Armadale; (2004-05) Armadale; (2006) Buxton, Cleveland; (2007) Cleveland.

RIDER LINKS: Nephew of former riders George, Bobby and Jim Beaton.

BEKKER, Byron Anthony

DATE OF BIRTH: 2 July 1987, Johannesburg, South Africa.

BRITISH CAREER: (2004) Newcastle [II]; (2005-07) Scunthorpe.

BELFIELD, Carl

DATE OF BIRTH: 1 September 1977, Stockport, Cheshire.

BRITISH CAREER: (2002) Buxton; (2004-07) Buxton.

BERGSTROM, Andreas

DATE OF BIRTH: 27 August 1978, Kroken, Sweden.

BRITISH CAREER: (2006-07) Berwick.

BETHELL, Jonathan

DATE OF BIRTH: 18 March 1973, Kendal, Cumbria.

BRITISH CAREER: (2003) Oxford II, Buxton; (2004) Buxton; (2005) Buxton, Workington; (2006) Buxton; (2007) Buxton, Stoke II.

BETSON, Daniel (Danny) Robert

DATE OF BIRTH: 11 January 1988, Eastbourne, East Sussex.

BRITISH CAREER: (2004) Mildenhall, Swindon II; (2005) Wimbledon; (2006) Rye House II; (2007) Oxford II.

RIDER LINKS: Nephew of former rider Scott Swain.

BIRD, Danny Lee

DATE OF BIRTH: 16 November 1979, Guildford, Surrey.

BRITISH CAREER: (1998-01) Isle of Wight; (2002-03) Isle of Wight, Ipswich; (2004) Reading, Ipswich; (2005) Reading; (2006) Glasgow; (2007) Reading.

BIRKINSHAW, James Alexander

DATE OF BIRTH: 6 March 1980, Sheffield, South Yorkshire.

BRITISH CAREER: (1996) Owlerton, Sheffield, Hull; (1997) Sheffield, Belle Vue II, Newcastle; (1998) Newcastle, St Austell; (1999) Workington, Edinburgh, Linlithgow, Stoke, Sheffield; (2000) Glasgow, Sheffield, Sheffield II; (2001) Newcastle, Sheffield II; (2002) Sheffield, Boston, Wolverhampton II; (2003) Sheffield; (2004) Sheffield, Buxton; (2005) Glasgow, Buxton, Newcastle; (2006) Boston, Berwick; (2007) Sheffield.

MAJOR HONOUR: Conference League Riders' Champion: 2002.

BJERRE JENSEN, Kenneth

DATE OF BIRTH: 24 May 1984, Esbjerg, Denmark.

BRITISH CAREER: (2002) Newcastle; (2003) Newcastle, Peterborough; (2004-06) Belle Vue; (2007) Peterborough.

MAJOR HONOURS: European Under-19 Champion: 2003; Danish Under-21 Champion: 2000, 2003, 2004, 2005.

BLACKBIRD, Lewis

DATE OF BIRTH: 21 February 1987, Peterborough, Cambridgeshire.

BRITISH CAREER: (2006) Sittingbourne; (2007) Oxford II.

RIDER LINKS: Son of former rider Carl Blackbird. Nephew of former riders Mark and Paul Blackbird.

BLAIR, Greg Sam Andrew

DATE OF BIRTH: 14 October 1990, Jedburgh, Scotland.

BRITISH CAREER: (2006-07) Cleveland.

BLAKE, Daniel (Dan) James

DATE OF BIRTH: 7 August 1988, Harlow, Essex.

BRITISH CAREER: (2004) Mildenhall; (2005-06) Sittingbourne; (2007) Plymouth, Oxford [II].

BOWEN, Luke Alex

DATE OF BIRTH: 26 January 1986, Harlow, Essex.

BRITISH CAREER: (2002) Rye House II, Carmarthen; (2003) Rye House II; (2004) Rye House II, King's Lynn II; (2005) Rye House II; (2006-07) Rye House, Rye House II.

RIDER LINKS: Son of former rider Kevin Bowen.

BOXALL, Steven (Steve) Shane

DATE OF BIRTH: 16 May 1987, Canterbury, Kent.

BRITISH CAREER: (2002-03) Rye House II; (2004-05) Rye House, Rye House II; (2006) Rye House; (2007) Rye House, Poole.

MAJOR HONOUR: Conference League Riders' Champion: 2005.

BOYCE, Craig

DATE OF BIRTH: 2 August 1967, Sydney, New South Wales, Australia.

BRITISH CAREER: (1988-90) Poole; (1991) Oxford; (1992-94) Poole; (1995) Swindon; (1996-98) Poole; (1999) Oxford; (2000) King's Lynn; (2001-02) Ipswich; (2003) Oxford, Poole (British League Cup only), Ipswich; (2004-05) Isle of Wight; (2006-07) Poole.

MAJOR HONOURS: New South Wales State Champion: 1991, 1993, 1994, 1995; Australian Champion: 1991, 1996, 1997; World Cup Champion: 2001.

BRADY, Ross Burns

DATE OF BIRTH: 17 February 1981, Winchburgh, Broxburn, Scotland.

BRITISH CAREER: (1997) Lathallan, Peterborough II; (1998) Mildenhall, Peterborough, Berwick; (1999-00) Edinburgh; (2001-02) Hull; (2003) Glasgow, Sheffield, Sheffield II; (2004) Hull; (2005) Edinburgh; (2006) Rye House; (2007) Newcastle.

RIDER LINKS: Son of former rider Alistair Brady.

BRAITHWAITE, Andrew (Andy) James

DATE OF BIRTH: 26 December 1989, Coventry, Warwickshire.

BRITISH CAREER: (2006) Plymouth, Buxton; (2007) Buxton.

BRANNEY, Craig Harry

DATE OF BIRTH: 31 July 1982, Whitehaven, Cumbria.

BRITISH CAREER: (2000) Ashfield; (2001) Workington, Buxton; (2002) Newcastle II, Hull; (2003) Newcastle, Newcastle II, Armadale; (2004) Oxford II, King's Lynn II; (2005) Hull, Oxford, Oxford II; (2006) Berwick; (2007) Workington.

RIDER LINKS: Brother of fellow rider John Branney.

BRANNEY, John James

DATE OF BIRTH: 7 November 1985, Whitehaven, Cumbria.

BRITISH CAREER: (2002) Rye House II, Newcastle II; (2003) Newcastle II, Wimbledon, Buxton; (2004) Newcastle II, King's Lynn II; (2005) Oxford II; (2006) Scunthorpe, Stoke II; (2007) Berwick, Stoke II, Workington.

RIDER LINKS: Brother of fellow rider Craig Branney.

BRIDGER, Lewis Alan

DATE OF BIRTH: 4 November 1989, Hastings, Sussex.

BRITISH CAREER: (2005) Weymouth; (2006-07) Eastbourne.

MAJOR HONOUR: British Under-18 Champion: 2006.

BROWN, Thomas (Tom) David

DATE OF BIRTH: 19 June 1984, Pontypool, South Wales.

BRITISH CAREER: (2000) Peterborough II, Newport II; (2001) Newport, Newport II; (2002) Workington, Newport II, Swindon II, Isle of Wight; (2003) Trelawny, Trelawny II; (2004) Stoke II, Berwick; (2005) Weymouth; (2006-07) Plymouth.

BRUNDLE, James Michael

DATE OF BIRTH: 15 December 1986, King's Lynn, Norfolk.

BRITISH CAREER: (2002) King's Lynn II, Mildenhall; (2003-04) King's Lynn, Mildenhall; (2005) King's Lynn; (2006) Mildenhall; (2007) King's Lynn, Boston.

BUCZKOWSKI, Krzysztof

DATE OF BIRTH: 30 April 1986, Grudziadz, Poland.

BRITISH CAREER: (2007) Reading.

MAJOR HONOURS: World Under-21 Team Cup Champion: 2006, 2007.

BUGEJA, Arlo Anthony

DATE OF BIRTH: 18 March 1986, Humbug Scrub, Adelaide, South Australia.

BRITISH CAREER: (2007) Redcar, Berwick.

BUNYAN, Jason Michael

DATE OF BIRTH: 9 March 1979, Milton Keynes, Buckinghamshire.

BRITISH CAREER: (1995) Poole; (1996) Eastbourne II; (1997) Oxford, Isle of Wight, Peterborough II; (1998) Isle of Wight; (1999-01) Ipswich; (2002) Reading; (2003) Coventry; (2004) Isle of Wight, Coventry; (2005-07) Isle of Wight.

MAJOR HONOURS: New Zealand Champion: 2004, 2005, 2006.

BURCHATT, Barry Peter

DATE OF BIRTH: 25 October 1987, Farnborough, Kent.

BRITISH CAREER: (2003) Newport II, Rye House II, Wimbledon; (2004-05) Rye House II; (2006) Rye House II, Mildenhall; (2007) Rye House II, Newport.

BURNETT, Paul Antony David

DATE OF BIRTH: 24 October 1981, Bradford, West Yorkshire.

BRITISH CAREER: (1997) Buxton, Belle Vue II, Western Warriors; (1998-04) Buxton; (2005) Scunthorpe, Mildenhall; (2006-07) Cleveland.

BURROWS, Dermot Mark (Buzz)

DATE OF BIRTH: 6 June 1964, Sheffield, South Yorkshire.

BRITISH CAREER: (1984) Scunthorpe; (1985) Edinburgh; (1986) Edinburgh; (1987) Middlesbrough; (1992) Glasgow, Middlesbrough; (1993) Middlesbrough; (1994) Buxton, Cleveland, Middlesbrough, Sheffield; Belle Vue, Coventry; (1995) Buxton, Long Eaton, Middlesbrough, Hull; (1996) Buxton; (1997-01) Stoke; (2002) Stoke, Belle Vue; (2003) Stoke II, Wimbledon; (2004-05) Wimbledon; (2007) Cleveland.

BURZA, Stanislaw (Stan)

DATE OF BIRTH: 26 September 1977, Tarnow, Poland.

BRITISH CAREER: (2006) Berwick, Oxford; (2007) Berwick, Coventry.

CAMPOS, Scott Dale

DATE OF BIRTH: 1 May 1989, Ipswich, Suffolk.

BRITISH CAREER: (2004) Mildenhall, Rye House II; (2005) Mildenhall, Boston; (2006) Boston; (2007) Oxford II.

CARPANESE, Mattia

DATE OF BIRTH: 5 November 1985, Padova, Italy.

BRITISH CAREER: (2007) Workington.

MAJOR HONOURS: Italian Under-21 Champion: 2005; Italian Champion: 2006.

CHRZANOWSKI, Tomasz

DATE OF BIRTH: 4 February 1980, Torun, Poland.

BRITISH CAREER: (2002) Poole; (2006-07) Swindon.

CLEWS, Paul Gordon

DATE OF BIRTH: 19 July 1979, Coventry, Warwickshire.

BRITISH CAREER: (1995) Coventry; (1996) Peterborough, Peterborough II, Coventry, Oxford, Anglian Angels; (1997) Skegness, Isle of Wight, Peterborough II, Coventry; (1998) Peterborough; (1999-03) Reading; (2004-06) Stoke; (2007) Newcastle.

RIDER LINKS: Brother-in-law of fellow rider Darren Andrews.

COCKLE, James Robert

DATE OF BIRTH: 26 May 1986, Edmonton, London.

BRITISH CAREER: (2001-03) Rye House II; (2004) Boston, Sheffield II, Reading, Glasgow; (2005) Glasgow, Sittingbourne, Boston; (2006) Glasgow; (2007) Sheffield, Scunthorpe.

COLES, Michael Timothy

DATE OF BIRTH: 11 August 1965, Exeter, Devon.

BRITISH CAREER: (1982-83) Exeter; (1984) Exeter, Weymouth; (1985-87) Exeter; (1988) Mildenhall; (1989-93) Edinburgh; (1994) Belle Vue; (1995) Oxford; (1996) Exeter; (1997) Exeter, King's Lynn; (1998-04) Exeter; (2005) Newport; (2006) Stoke, Plymouth; (2007) Berwick, Glasgow.

RIDER LINKS: Son of former rider Bob Coles.

COLLINS, Aidan

DATE OF BIRTH: 21 April 1982, Stockport, Greater Manchester.

BRITISH CAREER: (1998) Newport II; (1999) Buxton, Edinburgh; (2000) Glasgow, Ashfield; (2001) Glasgow; (2002) Buxton, Edinburgh; (2003-04) Workington; (2005) Mildenhall, Workington; (2006) Workington; (2007) Birmingham.

RIDER LINKS: Son of former rider Les Collins. Nephew of fellow rider Neil Collins. Nephew of former riders Peter, Phil and Steve Collins. Cousin of former rider Chris Collins.

COMPLIN, Lee

DATE OF BIRTH: 17 November 1984, Cowling, Yorkshire

BRITISH CAREER: (2001) Sheffield, Sheffield II; (2002) Sheffield, Belle Vue; (2007) Stoke.

COMPTON, Andre Neil

DATE OF BIRTH: 15 May 1977, Dewsbury, West Yorkshire.

BRITISH CAREER: (1993) Bradford, Newcastle; (1994) Stoke, Newcastle, Buxton; (1995) Hull, Buxton, Reading, Coventry, Belle Vue; (1996) Buxton, Bradford, Belle Vue; (1997) Newcastle, Berwick; (1998-99) Sheffield; (2000) Peterborough, Newcastle; (2001) Newcastle; (2002) Newcastle, Poole; (2003) Sheffield, Poole; (2004) Sheffield, Poole, Belle Vue; (2005-07) Sheffield.

MAJOR HONOUR: Premier League Riders' Champion: 2004.

RIDER LINKS: Brother of fellow rider Benji Compton.

COMPTON, Benjamin (Benji) Mark

DATE OF BIRTH: 17 September 1986, Tenerife, Spain.

BRITISH CAREER: (2002) Newcastle II; (2003) Sheffield II, Mildenhall; (2004) Buxton; (2005) Scunthorpe; (2006) Sheffield, Scunthorpe; (2007) Berwick, Scunthorpe, King's Lynn.

RIDER LINKS: Brother of fellow rider Andre Compton.

COOK, Harland Ashley

DATE OF BIRTH: 6 August 1988, Watford, Hertfordshire.

BRITISH CAREER: (2003) Rye House II; (2004) Rye House II, Coventry II; (2005-06) Rye House II; (2007) Rye House II, Sittingbourne.

COOPER, Paul Robert

DATE OF BIRTH: 7 June 1982, York, North Yorkshire.

BRITISH CAREER: (2003) Sheffield II; (2004) Oxford II, Sheffield II; (2005) Sheffield; (2006) Sheffield, Scunthorpe; (2007) Sheffield, Boston.

CORREY, Ronnie Dean

DATE OF BIRTH: 8 November 1966, Bellflower, California, USA.

BRITISH CAREER: (1987-93) Wolverhampton; (1995) Long Eaton; (1996-97) Wolverhampton; (1998-99) Belle Vue; (2000) Wolverhampton; (2004) Belle Vue; (2005) Wolverhampton; (2006) Swindon, Wolverhampton; (2007) Edinburgh.

MAJOR HONOURS: World Pairs Champion: 1992; World Team Cup Champion: 1992.

COTTHAM, Gary Dominic

DATE OF BIRTH: 13 September 1989, Eastbourne, East Sussex.

BRITISH CAREER: (2004-05) Rye House II; (2006) Rye House II, Sittingbourne; (2007) Rye House II.

RIDER LINKS: Son of former rider Gary Cottham [Senior].

COURTNEY, Jamie Mark

DATE OF BIRTH: 22 April 1988, Ashington, Northumberland.

BRITISH CAREER: (2003) Rye House II, Trelawny II; (2004) Swindon II, Isle of Wight, Oxford II; (2005) Oxford II, Workington; (2006) Rye House; (2007) Redcar, Cleveland.

RIDER LINKS: Son of former rider Mark Courtney. Nephew of former rider Sean Courtney. Brother of fellow rider Scott Courtney.

CROSS, Andre

DATE OF BIRTH: 12 June 1967, Norwich, Norfolk.

BRITISH CAREER: (2002-04) Wimbledon; (2005-07) Sittingbourne.

CRUMP, Jason Philip

DATE OF BIRTH: 6 August 1975, Bristol, Avon.

BRITISH CAREER: (1991) Poole; (1992) Peterborough; (1993) Swindon; (1994-95) Poole; (1996-97) Peterborough; (1998) Oxford; (1999) Peterborough; (2000-01) King's Lynn; (2002-06) Belle Vue; (2007) Poole.

MAJOR HONOURS: Australian Under-16 Champion: 1990; Australian Under-21 Champion: 1995; Queensland State Champion: 1995, 1997, 1998, 2001, 2004; Australian Champion: 1995, 2007; World Under-21 Champion: 1995; World Team Cup Champion: 1999; Elite League Riders' Champion: 1999, 2001, 2006; World Cup Champion: 2001, 2002; Czech Golden Helmet Champion: 2002, 2006; World Champion: 2004, 2006.

GRAND PRIX: British GP Champion: 1996, 1998, 2006; Swedish GP Champion: 2000, 2001, 2005, 2006; Polish GP Champion: 2001; Czech Republic GP Champion: 2002, 2003, 2004; Danish GP Champion: 2003, 2004; Scandinavian GP Champion: 2005; European GP Champion: 2006; Italian GP Champion: 2006.

RIDER LINKS: Son of former rider Phil Crump. Grandson of former rider Neil Street.

CUNNINGHAM, Glenn Arthur

DATE OF BIRTH: 10 June 1975, Bristol, Avon.

BRITISH CAREER: (1991-92) Oxford; (1993-96) Swindon; (1997) Reading; (1998) Peterborough; (1999) Swindon; (2000) Peterborough, Belle Vue; (2001) Newport; (2002) Somerset; (2003) Somerset, Eastbourne; (2004) Somerset, Swindon; (2005) Somerset; (2006) Somerset, Reading; (2007) Stoke.

MAJOR HONOUR: Premier League Riders' Champion: 1998.

DALLAWAY, Lewis Steven

DATE OF BIRTH: 26 February 1986, Walsall, West Midlands.

BRITISH CAREER: (2004) King's Lynn II; (2005) Newport II, Weymouth; (2006-07) Buxton.

DARKIN, Sergey

DATE OF BIRTH: 18 June 1973, Fergana, Uzbekistan.

BRITISH CAREER: (2001) Eastbourne; (2004) Coventry; (2005) Arena-Essex; (2007) Poole.

MAJOR HONOURS: Russian Champion: 2000, 2002.

DAVIDSSON, Jonas

DATE OF BIRTH: 7 August 1984, Motala, Sweden.

BRITISH CAREER: (2003) Reading; (2004) Oxford; (2005) Swindon; (2006) Poole; (2007) Reading.

MAJOR HONOURS: Finnish Under-21 Champion: 2002; Swedish Under-21 Champion: 2005.

RIDER LINKS: Son of former rider Jan Davidsson. Brother of fellow rider Daniel Davidsson.

DAY, Terry

DATE OF BIRTH: 26 February 1985, Poole, Dorset

BRITISH CAREER: (2002) Wimbledon; (2003) Newport II; (2006-07) Weymouth.

DENNIS, Richie William

DATE OF BIRTH: 16 April 1988, Boston, Lincolnshire.

BRITISH CAREER: (2003) Peterborough II; (2004) Boston, King's Lynn II; (2005-07) Scunthorpe.

DICKEN, Lee Charles

DATE OF BIRTH: 25 August 1978, Hull, East Yorkshire.

BRITISH CAREER: (1994) Buxton; (1995) Hull, Stoke, Peterborough; (1996) Hull, Owlerton, Sheffield; (1997-98) Hull; (1999) Hull, Exeter; (2000) Hull; (2001) Hull, Arena-Essex; (2002) Newport, Wolverhampton; (2003) Hull, Newcastle; (2004) Newcastle, Newcastle II, Glasgow; (2005) Hull, Sittingbourne, Newport, Newport II; (2006-07) Glasgow.

DOOLAN, Kevin

DATE OF BIRTH: 30 November 1980, Shepparton, Victoria, Australia.

BRITISH CAREER: (1999-00) Belle Vue; (2002) Berwick; (2003) Glasgow; (2004) King's Lynn; (2005) King's Lynn, Ipswich; (2006) King's Lynn, Eastbourne; (2007) Belle Vue.

DORE, Sam Benjamin

DATE OF BIRTH: 3 January 1987, Warragul, Victoria, Australia.

BRITISH CAREER: (2006) Stoke II; (2007) Stoke II, Newcastle.

DOYLE, Jason

DATE OF BIRTH: 6 October 1985, Newcastle, New South Wales, Australia.

BRITISH CAREER: (2005) Isle of Wight; (2006) Isle of Wight, Poole; (2007) Poole.

RIDER LINKS: Son of former junior rider Kevin Doyle.

DRYML, Ales

DATE OF BIRTH: 19 October 1979, Pardubice, Czech Republic.

BRITISH CAREER: (2000-02) Oxford; (2003) Belle Vue, Poole; (2004-05) Peterborough; (2006) Oxford. NOTE: Dryml did appear for Oxford in 2007, but only in the league. As such, this is not credited in his career record because the club closed down prematurely, with their record expunged from the league standings.

MAJOR HONOUR: German Under-21 Champion: 1998.

RIDER LINKS: Son of former rider Ales Dryml [Senior]. Brother of fellow rider Lukas Dryml.

DRYML, Lukas

DATE OF BIRTH: 16 April 1981, Pardubice, Czech Republic.

BRITISH CAREER: (2000-02) Oxford; (2003) Poole; (2004) Peterborough; (2005) Oxford, Peterborough; (2007) Peterborough.

MAJOR HONOURS: European Under-19 Champion: 2000; World Under-21 Champion: 2002; Czech Republic Champion: 2005.

RIDER LINKS: Son of former rider Ales Dryml [Senior]. Brother of fellow rider Ales Dryml.

DUFFILL, Jitendra

DATE OF BIRTH: 19 May 1981, Middlesbrough, Cleveland.

BRITISH CAREER: (1997) Lathallan; (1999) Glasgow, Berwick, Newcastle, Linlithgow, Mildenhall; (2000) Mildenhall; (2006-07) Cleveland.

DUNWORTH, Wayne

DATE OF BIRTH: 20 January 1967, Nottingham, Nottinghamshire.

BRITISH CAREER: (1984) Boston; (1986) Mildenhall; (2002) Boston, Carmarthen; (2003) Trelawny II, Boston, Peterborough II, Armadale; (2004) Boston, King's Lynn II; (2005) Boston; (2006) Weymouth; (2007) Boston.

EKBERG, Stefan

DATE OF BIRTH: 21 January 1972, Motala, Sweden.

BRITISH CAREER: (1994) Oxford; (1995) Eastbourne; (2005) Glasgow; (2007) Rye House.

ELLIOTT, Martin John

DATE OF BIRTH: 30 September 1970, Glasgow, Scotland.

BRITISH CAREER: (2004) Swindon II; (2006-07) Sittingbourne.

EMERSON, Martin

DATE OF BIRTH: 28 May 1984, Appleby, Westmorland, Cumbria.

BRITISH CAREER: (2006-07) Cleveland.

RIDER LINKS: Son of former rider Alan Emerson.

ERIKSSON, Freddie Ove

DATE OF BIRTH: 23 April 1981, Stockholm, Sweden.

BRITISH CAREER: (2001-02) King's Lynn; (2003) Ipswich; (2005-07) Oxford.

MAJOR HONOUR: Swedish Under-21 Champion: 2002.

EVANS, Barrie Charles

DATE OF BIRTH: 16 April 1984, King's Lynn, Norfolk.

BRITISH CAREER: (1999) Mildenhall; (2000-01) Arena-Essex, Mildenhall; (2002) Newport, Rye House II; (2003) Hull, Rye House II; (2004) Wimbledon, Newport; (2005-07) Stoke, Stoke II.

MAJOR HONOUR: Conference League Riders' Champion: 2003.

EZERGAILIS, Karlis Andrejs

DATE OF BIRTH: 8 April 1985, Melbourne, Victoria, Australia.

BRITISH CAREER: (2004) Newport II, Coventry II; (2005) Newport, Newport II; (2006) Newport II; (2007) Rye House II.

MAJOR HONOUR: Tasmanian Champion: 2005.

FELTON, Dean Graham

DATE OF BIRTH: 18 August 1969, Wolverhampton, West Midlands.

BRITISH CAREER: (1994) Buxton, Oxford, Ipswich; (1995-96) Buxton; (1997) Buxton, Stoke, Edinburgh, Skegness, Long Eaton, Shuttle Cubs; (1998) Stoke; (1999) Berwick, Glasgow; (2000) Buxton, Berwick; (2001) Stoke, Buxton; (2002-03) Carmarthen; (2004) Carmarthen, King's Lynn II; (2005) Buxton; (2006-07) Sittingbourne.

RIDER LINKS: Nephew of former rider Dave Harvey.

FILMER, Adam

DATE OF BIRTH: 26 September 1986, Maidstone, Kent.

BRITISH CAREER: (2005-07) Weymouth.

FISHER, Ryan Scott

DATE OF BIRTH: 7 September 1983, Riverside, California, USA.

BRITISH CAREER: (2002-03) Coventry; (2004) Oxford; (2007) Belle Vue.

FLINT, Gary George

DATE OF BIRTH: 5 May 1982, Ashington, Durham.

BRITISH CAREER: (1999) Berwick, Linlithgow, St Austell; (2000) Ashfield, Berwick; (2001) Buxton; (2002) Newcastle II; (2003) Buxton, Stoke II, Sheffield II; (2004) Sheffield II, Stoke II, Oxford II; (2005-07) Stoke II.

FORSBERG, Billy

DATE OF BIRTH: 13 May 1988, Norrkoping, Sweden.

BRITISH CAREER: (2007) Belle Vue.

RIDER LINKS: Grandson of former rider Dan Forsberg.

FRAMPTON, Jordan John

DATE OF BIRTH: 8 March 1985, Poole, Dorset.

BRITISH CAREER: (2004) Swindon II, King's Lynn II, Sheffield II; (2005) Sittingbourne; (2006) Plymouth, Mildenhall, Weymouth II; (2007) Somerset, Oxford II.

FRANC, Josef (Pepe)

DATE OF BIRTH: 18 January 1979, Caslav, Czech Republic.

BRITISH CAREER: (2001) Berwick; (2003-04) Berwick; (2005-07) Newcastle.

MAJOR HONOURS: Czech Republic Under-21 Champion: 1998, 1999, 2000.

FRY, Paul David

DATE OF BIRTH: 25 October 1964, Ledbury, Hereford & Worcestershire.

BRITISH CAREER: (1984) Newcastle, Cradley Heath, Arena-Essex; (1986-87) Cradley Heath; (1988) Stoke; (1989-90) Long Eaton; (1991) King's Lynn; (1992-96) Exeter; (1997-98) Newport; (1999) Stoke; (2000-02) Swindon; (2003) Swindon, Peterborough; (2004) Somerset, Belle Vue; (2005-06) Somerset; (2007) Mildenhall.

RIDER LINKS: Brother of former rider Mark Fry.

GATHERCOLE, Cory

DATE OF BIRTH: 2 December 1986, Irymple, Victoria, Australia.

BRITISH CAREER: (2007) Isle of Wight, Swindon.

MAJOR HONOURS: Western Australia State Champion: 2007; Victoria State Champion: 2007.

RIDER LINKS: Cousin of fellow rider Leigh Adams.

GIFFARD, Daniel James

DATE OF BIRTH: 10 November 1984, Eastbourne, East Sussex.

BRITISH CAREER: (2000) Rye House; (2001) Rye House; (2002) Isle of Wight, Rye House, Rye House II; (2003) Wimbledon, Eastbourne (British League Cup only), Stoke; (2004) Stoke, Stoke II, Weymouth; (2005) Weymouth, Hull; (2006) Redcar, Cleveland II; (2007) Redcar, Weymouth.

GIZATULLIN, Denis

DATE OF BIRTH: 11 March 1983, Oktyabrsky, Russia.

BRITISH CAREER: (2007) Eastbourne.

MAJOR HONOURS: Russian Under-21 Champion: 2002, 2004; Russian Champion: 2007.

GJEDDE, Charlie Rasmussen

DATE OF BIRTH: 28 December 1979, Holstebro, Denmark.

BRITISH CAREER: (1998) Swindon; (1999) Coventry, Wolverhampton; (2001) Reading; (2002) Swindon; (2003) Swindon, Oxford; (2004-05) Swindon; (2006) Reading; (2007) Swindon.

MAJOR HONOURS: Danish Under-21 Champion: 1995; World Cup Champion: 2006.

GLANZ, Nicki Jens

DATE OF BIRTH: 6 January 1990, Swindon, Wiltshire.

BRITISH CAREER: (2006) Newport II; (2007) Plymouth.

RIDER LINKS: Son of former rider Peter Glanz.

GOODY, Luke Steven

DATE OF BIRTH: 17 March 1990, Ashford, Kent.

BRITISH CAREER: (2006) Mildenhall II, Sittingbourne II; (2007) Sittingbourne.

GOMOLSKI, Adrian

DATE OF BIRTH: 29 April 1987, Gniezno, Poland.

BRITISH CAREER: (2007) Poole.

MAJOR HONOUR: World Under-21 Team Cup Champion: 2007.

RIDER LINKS: Son of former rider Jacek Gomolski.

GRANT, Alexander Robert (Rob)

DATE OF BIRTH: 10 June 1984, Newcastle-upon-Tyne, Tyne and Wear.

BRITISH CAREER: (1999) Linlithgow; (2000) Ashfield, Newcastle; (2001) Newcastle; (2002) Newcastle, Stoke; (2003) Berwick, Sheffield II, Stoke; (2004-05) Stoke, Stoke II; (2006) Stoke II; (2007) Berwick.

RIDER LINKS: Son of former rider Rob Grant. Grandson of former rider Alec Grant.

GRIEVES, James Robert

DATE OF BIRTH: 28 September 1974, Paisley, Scotland.

BRITISH CAREER: (1991-95) Glasgow; (1996-97) Wolverhampton; (1998) Wolverhampton, Berwick; (1999) Edinburgh; (2000-02) Glasgow; (2003-04) Glasgow, Wolverhampton; (2005) Newcastle, Wolverhampton; (2006) Newcastle; (2007) Redcar, Wolverhampton.

GUSTAFSSON, Simon

DATE OF BIRTH: 26 May 1990, Kumla, Sweden.

BRITISH CAREER: (2007) Eastbourne.

RIDER LINKS: Son of former rider Henrik Gustafsson.

HAIGH, David

DATE OF BIRTH: 12 December 1984, Whitehaven, Cumbria.

BRITISH CAREER: (2002) Newcastle II; (2003) Wimbledon, Newcastle II, Peterborough II; (2004) Newcastle II, Stoke II; (2006-07) Stoke (Conference League only).

HAINES, Joseph (Joe) Keir

DATE OF BIRTH: 4 September 1991, Bath, Somerset.

BRITISH CAREER: (2006) Cleveland; (2007) Scunthorpe.

MAJOR HONOUR: British Under-15 Champion: 2006.

HALL, Richard James

DATE OF BIRTH: 23 August 1984, Northallerton, North Yorkshire.

BRITISH CAREER: (2001) Newcastle; (2002) Newcastle, Newcastle II; (2003) Sheffield II, Coventry (British League Cup only), Boston; (2004) Sheffield, Sheffield II, Boston; (2005) Sheffield, Eastbourne; (2006-07) Peterborough.

HALSEY, Daniel John

DATE OF BIRTH: 15 September 1988, Aylesbury, Buckinghamshire.

BRITISH CAREER: (2005-07) Rye House II.

HAMILL, William (Billy) Gordon

DATE OF BIRTH: 23 May 1970, Arcadia, California, USA.

BRITISH CAREER: (1990-95) Cradley Heath; (1996) Cradley Heath + Stoke; (1997) Belle Vue; (1998-03) Coventry; (2005) Oxford; (2006-07) Wolverhampton.

MAJOR HONOURS: World Team Cup Champion: 1990, 1992, 1993, 1998; World Champion: 1996; AMA American Champion: 1999, 2001, 2002; SRA American Champion: 2002.

GRAND PRIX: Austrian GP Champion: 1995; Swedish GP Champion: 1996; Danish GP Champion: 1996; Challenge Champion: 1999; Czech Republic GP Champion: 2000, 2001; European GP Champion: 2000.

HANCOCK, Gregory (Greg) Alan

DATE OF BIRTH: 3 June 1970, Whittier, California, USA.

BRITISH CAREER: (1989-95) Cradley Heath; (1996) Cradley Heath + Stoke; (1997-01) Coventry; (2003-05) Oxford; (2006-07) Reading.

MAJOR HONOURS: World Pairs Champion: 1992; World Team Cup Champion: 1992, 1993, 1998; AMA American Champion: 1995, 1998, 2000, 2003, 2004, 2005, 2006; World Champion: 1997; Elite League Riders' Champion: 1997.

GRAND PRIX: British GP Champion: 1995, 2004; Czech Republic GP Champion: 1997; Polish GP Champion: 1997; Danish GP Champion: 2000; Challenge Champion: 2001; Australian GP Champion: 2002; Norwegian GP Champion: 2003; Latvian GP Champion: 2006.

HANSEN, Kenneth Kruse

DATE OF BIRTH: 19 October 1987, Herlev, Denmark.

BRITISH CAREER: (2007) Workington, Wolverhampton.

RIDER LINKS: Brother-in-law of former rider Lars Munkedal.

HARDING, Trevor Robert

DATE OF BIRTH: 1 November 1986, Subiaco, Western Australia.

BRITISH CAREER: (2002) Sheffield II, Carmarthen; (2003) King's Lynn, Boston; (2004) King's Lynn, King's Lynn II, Ipswich, Swindon II; (2005) Rye House II, Sheffield, Boston, Somerset, Eastbourne; (2006-07) King's Lynn, Eastbourne.

MAJOR HONOURS: Australian Under-16 Champion: 2002; Western Australia State Champion: 2005.

RIDER LINKS: Grandson of former rider Trevor Harding [Senior]. Brother of fellow rider Daniel Harding.

HARGREAVES, Jack

DATE OF BIRTH: 28 May 1988, Shrewsbury, Shropshire.

BRITISH CAREER: (2003) Wolverhampton II; (2004) Stoke II; (2005) Stoke, Stoke II; (2006) Redcar, Stoke II, Cleveland; (2007) Stoke, Stoke II, Redcar, Cleveland.

HARRIS, Christopher (Chris) Calvin

DATE OF BIRTH: 28 November 1982, Truro, Cornwall.

BRITISH CAREER: (1998) St Austell; (1999-00) Exeter; (2001) Trelawny; (2002-03) Trelawny, Peterborough; (2004-07) Coventry.

MAJOR HONOUR: British Champion: 2007.

GRAND PRIX: British GP Champion: 2007.

HARRISON, Russell (Rusty) Wade

DATE OF BIRTH: 11 October 1981, Elizebeth, Nr Adelaide, South Australia, Australia.

BRITISH CAREER: (2000) Glasgow; (2001-04) Workington; (2005) Edinburgh, Belle Vue; (2006) Edinburgh, Workington; (2007) Stoke.

MAJOR HONOURS: Australian Under-16 Champion: 1995, 1997; Australian Under-21 Champion: 2001; South Australia State Champion: 2003.

HART, Jerran

DATE OF BIRTH: 19 January 1991, Ipswich, Suffolk.

BRITISH CAREER: (2007) Sittingbourne.

HAUZINGER, Manuel

DATE OF BIRTH: 3 December 1982, Vienna, Austria.

BRITISH CAREER: (2005) Isle of Wight; (2006) Newcastle; (2007) Birmingham.

MAJOR HONOURS: Austrian Champion: 2002, 2005, 2006; Austrian/Croatian Champion: 2004; Argentine Champion: 2007.

HAVELOCK, Robert Gary

DATE OF BIRTH: 4 November 1968, Eaglescliffe, Yarm, Cleveland.

BRITISH CAREER: (1985) Middlesbrough, King's Lynn, Wolverhampton; (1986) Middlesbrough, Bradford; (1987-88) Bradford; (1990-97) Bradford; (1998) Eastbourne, Poole; (1999-02) Poole; (2003-04) Peterborough; (2005) Arena-Essex; (2006-07) Redcar.

MAJOR HONOURS: British Under-21 Champion: 1986; European Junior Champion: 1987; British Champion: 1991, 1992; Overseas Champion: 1992; World Champion: 1992; Premier League Riders' Champion: 1995.

RIDER LINKS: Son of former rider Brian Havelock.

HAWKINS, Ritchie Mark

DATE OF BIRTH: 9 November 1983, Peterborough, Cambridgeshire.

BRITISH CAREER: (2000) Sheffield II; (2001) Swindon, Sheffield II; (2002) Swindon, Swindon II; (2003) Swindon, Swindon II, Peterborough (British League Cup only); (2004) Mildenhall, Berwick; (2005) Somerset, Peterborough; (2006) Workington, Swindon; (2007) Somerset, Poole.

MAJOR HONOUR: British Under-21 Champion: 2004.

RIDER LINKS: Son of former rider Kevin Hawkins.

HEDLEY, Tom

DATE OF BIRTH: 7 January 1988, Mildura, Victoria, Australia.

BRITISH CAREER: (2007) Newport.

HEFENBROCK, Christian

DATE OF BIRTH: 15 May 1985, Liebenthal, Germany.

BRITISH CAREER: (2006) Wolverhampton; (2007) Lakeside, Peterborough.

MAJOR HONOURS: German Under-21 Champion: 2001, 2005; German Champion: 2006.

HENRY, Christian

DATE OF BIRTH: 20 February 1981, Sydney, New South Wales, Australia.

BRITISH CAREER: (2000) Edinburgh, Ashfield; (2001-02) Edinburgh; (2003) Glasgow; (2005-07) Newcastle.

HERNE, Jay Brett

DATE OF BIRTH: 22 September 1984, Campbell Town, Sydney, New South Wales, Australia.

BRITISH CAREER: (2007) Weymouth.

RIDER LINKS: Son of former rider Phil Herne. Brother of former rider Lee Herne.

HODGSON, Daniel (Danny) Lee

DATE OF BIRTH: 21 January 1982, Bradford, West Yorkshire.

BRITISH CAREER: (1998) Buxton; (1999) King's Lynn II; (2000) Buxton, Hull; (2001) Sheffield, Newport II, Somerset; (2003) Carmarthen; (2004) King's Lynn II; (2006-07) Buxton.

HODGSON, Russell (Rusty)

DATE OF BIRTH: 29 March 1981, Northallerton, North Yorkshire.

BRITISH CAREER: (2006) Cleveland; (2007) Redcar, Cleveland.

RIDER LINKS: Son of former rider Russ Hodgson. Grandson of former rider Frank Hodgson. Nephew of former rider Jack Hodgson.

HOLDER, Christopher (Chris)

DATE OF BIRTH: 24 September 1987, Appin, Sydney, New South Wales, Australia.

BRITISH CAREER: (2006-07) Isle of Wight.

MAJOR HONOURS: Australian Under-21 Champion: 2005, 2006, 2007; New South Wales State Champion: 2006, 2007.

RIDER LINKS: Brother of fellow rider James Holder.

HOPWOOD, Ben

DATE OF BIRTH: 13 March 1991, Salford, Greater Manchester.

BRITISH CAREER: (2006) Mildenhall II, Stoke II; (2007) Oxford II.

HOUGAARD, Patrick

DATE OF BIRTH: 23 May 1989, Fredericia, Denmark.

BRITISH CAREER: (2007) Reading.

HOWE, David Peter

DATE OF BIRTH: 1 March 1982, Leicester, Leicestershire.

BRITISH CAREER: (1997) Peterborough II; (1998) Peterborough, Norfolk; (1999-01) Peterborough; (2002-05) Wolverhampton; (2006) Oxford; (2007) Wolverhampton.

MAJOR HONOUR: British Under-21 Champion: 2000.

HUGHES, Kyle Richard

DATE OF BIRTH: 15 June 1989, Bath, Somerset.

BRITISH CAREER: (2004) Mildenhall; (2005) Oxford II; (2006) Boston; (2007) Oxford II.

HURRY, Paul William George

DATE OF BIRTH: 9 April 1975, Canterbury, Kent.

BRITISH CAREER: (1991) Arena-Essex; (1992-93) Peterborough; (1994-95) Arena-Essex; (1996) London; (1997) King's Lynn; (1998-99) Oxford; (2000) Eastbourne; (2001-02) Wolverhampton; (2003) Ipswich; (2004-06) Arena-Essex; (2007) Lakeside.

MAJOR HONOUR: British Under-21 Champion: 1994.

HURST, Samuel (Sam) Melvin

DATE OF BIRTH: 28 April 1989, Southampton, Hampshire.

BRITISH CAREER: (2004) Newport II, King's Lynn II; (2005) Newport II; (2006) Newport, Newport II; (2007) Weymouth.

IRVING, Kriss Jackson

DATE OF BIRTH: 3 April 1987, Whitehaven, Cumbria.

BRITISH CAREER: (2003) Newcastle II; (2004) Newcastle II, Stoke II; (2005-07) Stoke II.

RIDER LINKS: Nephew of former rider Greg Irving.

IRWIN, Nathan Christopher Terence

DATE OF BIRTH: 28 March 1983, Cuckfield, Sussex.

BRITISH CAREER: (1999) King's Lynn II; (2000) Peterborough II; (2002) Wimbledon; (2004) Weymouth, Swindon II; (2005-06) Boston; (2007) Weymouth.

RIDER LINKS: Nephew of former junior rider Nick Irwin.

ISHERWOOD, Gareth Andrew

DATE OF BIRTH: 28 November 1988, Manchester, Greater Manchester.

BRITISH CAREER: (2005) Stoke II; (2006-07) Stoke II, Buxton.

IVERSEN, Niels-Kristian Trochmann

DATE OF BIRTH: 20 June 1982, Esbjerg, Denmark.

BRITISH CAREER: (2001) King's Lynn; (2003) Newport, Oxford; (2004-05) Oxford; (2006-07) Peterborough.

MAJOR HONOURS: Danish Under-21 Champion: 2002; World Cup Champion: 2006.

GRAND PRIX: Grand Final Champion: 2007.

JAMES, Scott Terry

DATE OF BIRTH: 25 May 1984, Adelaide, South Australia.

BRITISH CAREER: (2002) Workington, Mildenhall; (2003) Mildenhall, Coventry (British League Cup only); (2005) Wimbledon, Workington; (2006) Buxton; (2007) Workington, Buxton.

JANKOWSKI, Lukasz

DATE OF BIRTH: 7 December 1982, Leszno, Poland

BRITISH CAREER: (2002) King's Lynn; (2007) Belle Vue.

NOTE: Jankowski made one British League Cup appearance for Oxford in 2003, but his inclusion in the side was later deemed ineligible.

RIDER LINKS: Son of former rider Roman Jankowski.

JANNIRO, Billy Mitchell

DATE OF BIRTH: 30 July 1980, Vallejo, California, USA.

BRITISH CAREER: (2001-04) Coventry; (2005) Peterborough, Coventry; (2006-07) Coventry.

MAJOR HONOUR: SRA American Champion: 2004.

JANSSON, Kim Patrik

DATE OF BIRTH: 30 October 1981, Gothenburg, Sweden.

BRITISH CAREER: (2002-07) Ipswich.

JENSEN, Jesper Bruun

DATE OF BIRTH: 14 October 1977, Esbjerg, Denmark.

BRITISH CAREER: (1997-03) Wolverhampton; (2004) Ipswich; (2005) Oxford, Peterborough; (2006) Peterborough; (2007) Oxford, Ipswich.

MAJOR HONOURS: Nordic Under-21 Champion: 1995; World Team Cup Champion: 1997; World Under-21 Champion: 1997; European Champion: 2005.

JIROUT, Mario

DATE OF BIRTH: 21 July 1976, Pardubice, Czech Republic.

BRITISH CAREER: (1995-97) Peterborough; (1999) Peterborough; (2001) Peterborough; (2002-03) Somerset; (2004) Newcastle; (2007) Mildenhall.

MAJOR HONOUR: Czech Republic Under-21 Champion: 1994.

RIDER LINKS: Son of former rider Jiri Jirout.

JOHNSON, Ashley

DATE OF BIRTH: 29 September 1984, Middlesbrough, Cleveland.

BRITISH CAREER: (2004) Newcastle II; (2005) Scunthorpe; (2006) Cleveland II; (2007) Newcastle, Cleveland.

JOHNSON, Benjamin (Ben)

DATE OF BIRTH: 17 December 1989, Manchester, Greater Manchester.

BRITISH CAREER: (2006-07) Boston.

JOHNSON, Brendan David

DATE OF BIRTH: 4 June 1992, Poole, Dorset.

BRITISH CAREER: (2007) Oxford II.

JOHNSON, Christopher (Chris) Simon

DATE OF BIRTH: 13 October 1987, Chichester, Sussex.

BRITISH CAREER: (2002) Wimbledon; (2003) Oxford II, Trelawny II, Isle of Wight; (2004) Isle of Wight, Swindon II, King's Lynn II; (2005) Reading, Rye House II, Mildenhall; (2006) Isle of Wight, Plymouth, Weymouth II; (2007) Isle of Wight.

JOHNSTON, Steven (Steve) Paul

DATE OF BIRTH: 12 October 1971, Kalgoorlie, Western Australia.

BRITISH CAREER: (1992) Sheffield; (1993) Sheffield, Long Eaton; (1994-96) Long Eaton; (1997) Ipswich; (1998-02) Oxford; (2003) Belle Vue; (2004) Swindon; (2005) Wolverhampton; (2006) Arena-Essex; (2007) Oxford, Coventry.

MAJOR HONOURS: Western Australia State Champion: 1993, 1996, 2004.

JONES, Steven Paul

DATE OF BIRTH: 27 September 1979, Gateshead, Tyne and Wear.

BRITISH CAREER: (1997) Lathallan; (1998) Edinburgh, Newcastle; (1999) Newcastle, Linlithgow; (2002-03) Newcastle II; (2004) Carmarthen; (2006-07) Cleveland.

JONSSON, Andreas Karl Rune

DATE OF BIRTH: 3 September 1980, Hallstavik, Sweden.

BRITISH CAREER: (1998-99) Coventry; (2001-05) Coventry; (2006) Arena-Essex; (2007) Lakeside.

MAJOR HONOURS: Swedish Under-21 Champion: 1998, 2000; World Under-21 Champion: 2000; World Cup Champion: 2003, 2004; Swedish Champion: 2006; Czech Golden Helmet Champion: 2007.

GRAND PRIX: Scandinavian GP Champion: 2006; Danish GP Champion: 2007; German GP Champion: 2007.

KARLSSON, Magnus Erik

DATE OF BIRTH: 28 December 1981, Gullspang, Sweden.

BRITISH CAREER: (2002) Edinburgh; (2003) Edinburgh, Wolverhampton; (2004) Hull, Wolverhampton; (2005-07) Wolverhampton.

RIDER LINKS: Son of former rider Gunnar Karlsson. Brother of fellow riders Peter Karlsson and Mikael Max.

KARLSSON, Peter Gunnar

DATE OF BIRTH: 17 December 1969, Gullspang, Sweden.

BRITISH CAREER: (1990) Wolverhampton; (1992-97) Wolverhampton; (1999) Wolverhampton; (2000) Peterborough; (2001) King's Lynn, Belle Vue; (2002-03) Wolverhampton; (2005) Peterborough; (2006-07) Wolverhampton.

MAJOR HONOURS: Nordic Under-21 Champion: 1989; Swedish Champion: 1989, 1991; World Team Cup Champion: 2000; World Cup Champion: 2003, 2004.

GRAND PRIX: Challenge Champion: 2000.

RIDER LINKS: Son of former rider Gunnar Karlsson. Brother of fellow riders Magnus Karlsson and Mikael Max.

KASPRZAK, Krzysztof

DATE OF BIRTH: 18 July 1984, Leszno, Poland.

BRITISH CAREER: (2003-06) Poole; (2007) Lakeside.

MAJOR HONOURS: European Champion: 2003; World Under-21 Champion: 2005; World Under-21 Team Cup Champion: 2005; World Cup Champion: 2007.

RIDER LINKS: Son of former rider Zenon Kasprzak. Brother of fellow rider Robert Kasprzak.

KATAJISTO, Kalle

DATE OF BIRTH: 24 April 1991, Varkaus, Finland.

BRITISH CAREER: (2007) Edinburgh.

KATT, Stephan

DATE OF BIRTH: 15 September 1979, Kiel, Germany.

BRITISH CAREER: (2003) Somerset; (2006-07) Somerset.

KENDREW, Guy

DATE OF BIRTH: 19 October 1987, Stokesley, Middlesbrough, Cleveland.

BRITISH CAREER: (2007) Stoke II.

KENNETT, Edward David

DATE OF BIRTH: 28 August 1986, Hastings, Sussex.

BRITISH CAREER: (2001) Rye House, Mildenhall; (2002-03) Rye House, Rye House II, Eastbourne; (2004) Eastbourne; (2005) Rye House, Poole; (2006) Rye House, Eastbourne; (2007) Poole.

MAJOR HONOURS: British Under-21 Champion: 2005, 2007.

RIDER LINKS: Son of former rider Dave Kennett. Nephew of former riders Gordon and Barney Kennett.

KERR, Christopher (Chris) Robert

DATE OF BIRTH: 28 June 1984, Grass Valley, California, USA.

BRITISH CAREER: (2006) Redcar; (2007) Redcar, Wolverhampton.

KESSLER, Robert (Robbie)

DATE OF BIRTH: 5 April 1973, Neuwied, Germany.

BRITISH CAREER: (1994) Sheffield; (1996-97) Sheffield; (1999) King's Lynn; (2000-01) Sheffield; (2002) Hull; (2003) Stoke; (2004) Stoke, Peterborough; (2005-06) Stoke; (2007) Stoke, Redcar, Rye House.

MAJOR HONOURS: German Under-21 Champion: 1992, 1993.

RIDER LINKS: Son of former rider Johann Kessler.

KING, Daniel (Danny) Robert

DATE OF BIRTH: 14 August 1986, Maidstone, Kent.

BRITISH CAREER: (2001) Peterborough II; (2002) Peterborough II, Swindon II; (2003) Peterborough II, Ipswich (British League Cup only), Reading, Mildenhall, Arena-Essex; (2004) Ipswich, Mildenhall; (2005) Rye House, Ipswich; (2006) Mildenhall, Ipswich; (2007) Peterborough.

MAJOR HONOUR: British Under-18 Champion: 2004.

RIDER LINKS: Brother of fellow rider Jason King.

KING, Jason Gary

DATE OF BIRTH: 13 April 1985, Maidstone, Kent.

BRITISH CAREER: (2000-01) Peterborough II; (2002) Swindon, Swindon II, Peterborough II; (2003) Arena-Essex, Peterborough II; (2004) Mildenhall, Rye House; (2005) Somerset, Newport; (2006-07) Mildenhall.

RIDER LINKS: Brother of fellow rider Daniel King.

KLING, Ricky

DATE OF BIRTH: 2 June 1987, Mallila, Sweden.

BRITISH CAREER: (2007) Lakeside.

NOTE: Kling also appeared for Oxford in 2007, but only in the league. As such, this is not credited in his career record because the club closed down prematurely, with their record expunged from the league standings.

RIDER LINKS: Son of former rider Anders Kling.

KOLODZIEJ, Janusz

DATE OF BIRTH: 27 May 1984, Tarnow, Poland.

BRITISH CAREER: (2003) Reading; (2006-07) Reading.

MAJOR HONOURS: Polish Under-21 Champion: 2004; Polish Champion: 2005; World Under-21 Team Cup Champion: 2005.

KORNELIUSSEN, Mads Klit

DATE OF BIRTH: 15 June 1983, Aalborg, Denmark.

BRITISH CAREER: (2003-04) Newport; (2005) Newport, Swindon; (2006-07) Swindon.

RIDER LINKS: Brother of former rider Tim Korneliussen.

KRAMER, Emil

DATE OF BIRTH: 14 November 1979, Mariestad, Sweden.

BRITISH CAREER: (2002) King's Lynn, Hull; (2003) Hull; (2004-05) Hull, Oxford; (2006-07) Somerset.

KRONER, Tobias (Tobi)

DATE OF BIRTH: 16 October 1985, Dohren, Nr Bremen, Germany.

BRITISH CAREER: (2005) Oxford; (2006-07) Ipswich.

KSIEZAK, Robert

DATE OF BIRTH: 15 January 1987, Pooraka, Adelaide, South Australia.

BRITISH CAREER: (2005) Edinburgh; (2006-07) Glasgow.

KUS, Matej

DATE OF BIRTH: 11 July 1989, Plzek, Czech Republic.

BRITISH CAREER: (2007) Berwick.

KYLMAKORPI, Joonas Nikolai

DATE OF BIRTH: 14 February 1980, Stockholm, Sweden.

BRITISH CAREER: (2001) Eastbourne; (2002) Ipswich; (2003) Arena-Essex, Eastbourne; (2004) Eastbourne; (2005) Peterborough, Coventry; (2006) Arena-Essex; (2007) Lakeside.

MAJOR HONOURS: Swedish Under-21 Champion: 1999; Nordic Under-21 Champion: 2001.

LAMBERT, Simon James

DATE OF BIRTH: 21 February 1989, Boston, Lincolnshire.

BRITISH CAREER: (2004) Boston, King's Lynn II; (2005) Boston; (2006) King's Lynn II, Boston; (2007) Boston.

LANHAM, Leigh Stefan

DATE OF BIRTH: 15 August 1977, Ipswich, Suffolk.

BRITISH CAREER: (1993) Ipswich, Arena-Essex; (1994-96) Ipswich; (1997) Exeter, Bradford, King's Lynn; (1998-99) Arena-Essex; (2001) Arena-Essex; (2002-03) Arena-Essex, Ipswich; (2004-06) Arena-Essex; (2007) Lakeside.

MAJOR HONOUR: British Under-21 Champion: 1997.

RIDER LINKS: Son of former rider Mike Lanham.

LAUKKANEN, Kaj Pekka

DATE OF BIRTH: 8 April 1975, Seinajoki, Finland.

BRITISH CAREER: (1995-96) Long Eaton; (1998) Glasgow; (1999-02) Belle Vue; (2003) Oxford; (2004) Belle Vue; (2007) Belle Vue, Edinburgh.

MAJOR HONOURS: Finnish Under-21 Champion: 1995; Finnish Champion: 1997, 1999, 2000, 2001, 2002, 2003, 2004, 2006; Nordic Champion: 2001.

LAWSON, William

DATE OF BIRTH: 27 February 1987, Perth, Perthshire, Scotland.

BRITISH CAREER: (2002) Newcastle II; (2003) Newcastle, Newcastle II; (2004) Newcastle, Newcastle II; (2005) Edinburgh, Armadale; (2006-07) Edinburgh, Wolverhampton.

MAJOR HONOUR: British Under-18 Champion: 2005.

LEE, Paul Kevin

DATE OF BIRTH: 21 March 1981, Nottingham, Nottinghamshire.

BRITISH CAREER: (1996) Peterborough II; (1997) Long Eaton, Shuttle Cubs, Peterborough, Coventry; (1998) Hull; (1999-00) Sheffield; (2001) Coventry; (2002) Swindon; (2003) Mildenhall; (2004) Mildenhall, King's Lynn; (2005) Peterborough, King's Lynn; (2007) King's Lynn.

LEGAULT, Kyle Patrick

DATE OF BIRTH: 30 May 1985, St Catharines, Ontario, Canada.

BRITISH CAREER: (2005-06) Sheffield; (2007) Mildenhall.

MAJOR HONOURS: Canadian Champion: 2003, 2004, 2006.

RIDER LINKS: Son of former rider Fred Legault.

LEGG, Billy Peter

DATE OF BIRTH: 6 September 1988, Swindon, Wiltshire.

BRITISH CAREER: (2003) Swindon II; (2004) Newport II, Mildenhall, Weymouth; (2005) Newport II; (2006) Newport, Newport II; (2007) Plymouth, Stoke II.

LEMON, Mark Ian John

DATE OF BIRTH: 12 February 1973, Bairnsdale, Victoria, Australia.

BRITISH CAREER: (1990) Poole; (1991) Poole, Middlesbrough; (1992) Middlesbrough, Long Eaton; (1996) Oxford; (1997-98) Poole; (1999) Eastbourne, Hull; (2000) Oxford; (2002) Oxford; (2003) Somerset, Belle Vue; (2004) Exeter, Poole; (2005) Exeter; (2006) Stoke, Reading; (2007) Reading.

MAJOR HONOURS: Victoria State Champion: 1993, 1996.

LEVERINGTON, Trent Ashley

DATE OF BIRTH: 13 May 1980, Brisbane, Queensland, Australia.

BRITISH CAREER: (2003) Glasgow, Armadale, Wolverhampton II; (2004) Buxton, Stoke; (2005) Glasgow; (2006) Stoke; (2007) Glasgow.

LINDBACK, Antonio

DATE OF BIRTH: 5 May 1985, Rio De Janeiro, Brazil.

BRITISH CAREER: (2003-06) Poole; (2007) Belle Vue.

MAJOR HONOURS: World Cup Champion: 2004; European Under-19 Champion: 2004; Swedish Under-21 Champion: 2006.

GRAND PRIX: Grand Final Champion: 2004.

LINDGREN, Jan Fredrik

DATE OF BIRTH: 15 September 1985, Orebro, Sweden.

BRITISH CAREER: (2003-07) Wolverhampton.

MAJOR HONOURS: Swedish Under-21 Champion: 2003, 2004.

RIDER LINKS: Son of former rider Tommy Lindgren.

LORAM, Mark Royston Gregory

DATE OF BIRTH: 12 January 1971, Mtarfa, Malta.

BRITISH CAREER: (1987) Hackney; (1988) Hackney, King's Lynn, Belle Vue, Reading, Swindon; (1989) Ipswich; (1990-94) King's Lynn; (1995-96) Exeter; (1997) Bradford; (1998) Wolverhampton; (1999-00) Poole; (2001) Peterborough; (2002-03) Eastbourne; (2004-05) Arena-Essex; (2006-07) Ipswich.

MAJOR HONOURS: British Under-21 Champion: 1988; National League Riders' Champion: 1989; Commonwealth Champion: 1994; British Champion: 1997, 1999, 2001; Overseas Champion: 1999; World Champion: 2000.

GRAND PRIX: Danish GP Champion: 1997; Swedish GP Champion: 1999.

LOUIS, Christopher (Chris)

DATE OF BIRTH: 9 July 1969, Ipswich, Suffolk.

BRITISH CAREER: (1988) Hackney, Wolverhampton, King's Lynn, Ipswich; (1989-02) Ipswich; (2004-07) Ipswich.

MAJOR HONOURS: World Under-21 Champion: 1990; British Champion: 1998, 2000.

RIDER LINKS: Son of former rider John Louis.

LOWE, Adam

DATE OF BIRTH: 17 February 1989, Leicester, Leicestershire.

BRITISH CAREER: (2005) Boston; (2006) Stoke II; (2007) Boston.

LYONS, Jason Rodney

DATE OF BIRTH: 15 June 1970, Mildura, Victoria, Australia.

BRITISH CAREER: (1990-91) Glasgow; (1992-03) Belle Vue; (2004) Poole, Newcastle; (2005) Belle Vue; (2006) Mildenhall; (2007) Birmingham.

MAJOR HONOURS: Victoria State Champion: 1997, 1998, 1999; Overseas Champion: 1998, 2001; South Australia State Champion: 1999; World Team Cup Champion: 1999; World Cup Champion: 2002.

RIDER LINKS: Son of former rider Rod Lyons.

MacDONALD, Grant

DATE OF BIRTH: 7 December 1979, Barrow-in-Furness, Cumbria.

BRITISH CAREER: (1996) Linlithgow, Cradley Heath + Stoke, Sheffield, London, Poole; (1997) Glasgow, Lathallan; (1998) Glasgow; (1999) Workington; (2000) Newcastle; (2001) Peterborough, Stoke, Newcastle; (2002) Glasgow; (2005) Wimbledon; (2007) Oxford II, King's Lynn.

McALLAN, David John

DATE OF BIRTH: 20 June 1980, Edinburgh, Scotland.

BRITISH CAREER: (1996) Berwick; (1997) Berwick, Berwick II, Sheffield; (1998) Berwick, Newcastle; (1999) Edinburgh, Linlithgow; (2000) Ashfield, Stoke; (2001) Berwick, Boston, Workington; (2002) Glasgow, Sheffield II; (2003-04) Glasgow, Boston; (2005) Sittingbourne, Edinburgh, Boston; (2006-07) Glasgow.

McDADE, Cal

DATE OF BIRTH: 25 April 1987, Glasgow, Scotland.

BRITISH CAREER: (2004) Swindon II; (2005) Armadale; (2006-07) Boston.

McGOWAN, Travis

DATE OF BIRTH: 13 January 1981, Mildura, Victoria, Australia.

BRITISH CAREER: (1999-00) King's Lynn; (2002) King's Lynn; (2003-05) Oxford; (2006-07) Reading.

MAJOR HONOURS: Australian Under-16 Champion: 1993; Australian Under-21 Champion: 1998, 2000, 2002; Victoria State Champion: 2001, 2002, 2003, 2004, 2005.

McKINNA, Adam Kenneth

DATE OF BIRTH: 17 August 1986, Crewe, Cheshire.

BRITISH CAREER: (2004-05) Armadale; (2006) Newcastle, Scunthorpe; (2007) Newcastle, Cleveland, Boston.

RIDER LINKS: Son of former rider Kenny McKinna. Nephew of former riders Charlie and Martin McKinna.

MADSEN, Tom Paarup

DATE OF BIRTH: 24 November 1977, Esbjerg, Denmark.

BRITISH CAREER: (1999) Berwick; (2000-02) King's Lynn; (2003) Ipswich, King's Lynn; (2004) King's Lynn, Oxford, Berwick; (2005) Oxford, Berwick; (2006) Belle Vue; (2007) Mildenhall.

MAKOVSKY, Michal

DATE OF BIRTH: 6 April 1976, Hradec Kralove, Czech Republic.

BRITISH CAREER: (2001-04) Berwick; (2005) Berwick, Oxford; (2006-07) Berwick.

MAJOR HONOUR: Czech Republic Champion: 1999.

MALLETT, Darren Carl

DATE OF BIRTH: 25 May 1986, Boston, Lincolnshire.

BRITISH CAREER: (2001) Somerset, Boston; (2002) Boston; (2003) Boston, King's Lynn; (2004) King's Lynn, King's Lynn II, Boston; (2005) Boston, King's Lynn; (2006-07) Boston.

RIDER LINKS: Son of former rider Dennis Mallett.

MARTIN, Sam Alan

DATE OF BIRTH: 8 February 1989, Bedford Park, Adelaide, South Australia.

BRITISH CAREER: (2004-05) Oxford II; (2006) Boston; (2007) Oxford II, Berwick.

RIDER LINKS: Son of former rider Mark Martin.

MASON, David Lee

DATE OF BIRTH: 20 December 1976, Crawley, West Sussex.

BRITISH CAREER: (1995) Sittingbourne, Reading, Arena-Essex, Swindon, Poole, Oxford; (1996) Sittingbourne, London, Reading; (1997) Arena-Essex; (1998) Newport, Stoke, Arena-Essex, Mildenhall; (1999) Swindon, Rye House; (2000) Rye House, Arena-Essex, Poole; (2001-03) Rye House; (2004-07) Weymouth.

MAJOR HONOUR: Conference League Riders' Champion: 2001.

MASON, Karl Lewis

DATE OF BIRTH: 4 March 1986, Hillingdon, London.

BRITISH CAREER: (2001) Buxton, Mildenhall, Somerset; (2002) Newport II; (2003) Newport, Newport II; (2004) Newport, Newport II, Coventry II; (2005) Newport, Newport II; (2006) Newport II; (2007) Newport, Weymouth.

MEAKINS, Gordon

DATE OF BIRTH: 18 March 1974, Aylesbury, Buckinghamshire.

BRITISH CAREER: (1999) King's Lynn II; (2000) Peterborough II; (2001) Buxton; (2002) Carmarthen; (2003) Carmarthen, Somerset (British League Cup only); (2004) Carmarthen; (2006) Weymouth II; (2007) Sittingbourne.

RIDER LINKS: Father of junior rider Scott Meakins. Son of former junior rider Nigel Meakins.

MEAR, Robert

DATE OF BIRTH: 12 January 1989, Welwyn Garden City, Hertfordshire.

BRITISH CAREER: (2004-07) Rye House II.

MELDRUM, David

DATE OF BIRTH: 6 October 1977, Berwick-upon-Tweed, Northumberland.

BRITISH CAREER: (1994-95) Berwick; (1996) Berwick, Eastbourne II; (1997) Berwick, Berwick II; (1998) Berwick, Buxton; (1999-01) Berwick; (2002) Somerset, Wimbledon; (2003) Berwick; (2004) Berwick, Newcastle, Newcastle II; (2005) Sittingbourne, Stoke; (2006) Berwick, Stoke II; (2007) Berwick.

RIDER LINKS: Nephew of former rider Andy Meldrum.

MESSING, Andreas

DATE OF BIRTH: 28 January 1987, Hallstavik, Sweden.

BRITISH CAREER: (2006) Arena-Essex; (2007) Lakeside.

MIEDZINSKI, Adrian

DATE OF BIRTH: 20 August 1985, Torun, Poland.

BRITISH CAREER: (2004) Eastbourne; (2006) Swindon.

NOTE: Miedzinski did appear for Oxford in 2007, but only in the league. As such, this is not credited in his career record because the club closed down prematurely, with their record expunged from the league standings.

MAJOR HONOURS: Polish Under-21 Champion: 2005; World Under-21 Team Cup Champion: 2006.

RIDER LINKS: Son of former rider Stanislaw Miedzinski.

MILLS, Christopher (Chris) William

DATE OF BIRTH: 29 March 1983, Chelmsford, Essex.

BRITISH CAREER: (2001) Arena-Essex; (2002) King's Lynn II, Wimbledon; (2003) Isle of Wight, Oxford II; (2004) Reading, Oxford II; (2005) Reading, Oxford, Oxford II, Somerset; (2006) King's Lynn, Reading; (2007) King's Lynn, Lakeside.

MISKOWIAK, Robert

DATE OF BIRTH: 21 November 1983, Rawicz, Poland.

BRITISH CAREER: (2005-07) Ipswich.

MAJOR HONOUR: World Under-21 Champion: 2004.

MOLLER, Henrik

DATE OF BIRTH: 3 September 1985, Fredericia, Denmark.

BRITISH CAREER: (2004) Peterborough; (2006) Edinburgh; (2007) Edinburgh, Birmingham.

NOTE: Moller also appeared for Oxford in 2007, but only in the league. As such, this is not credited in his career record because the club closed down prematurely, with their record expunged from the league standings.

MOORE, Andrew David

DATE OF BIRTH: 6 October 1982, Lincoln, Lincolnshire.

BRITISH CAREER: (1998) Skegness, Norfolk; (1999) Mildenhall, Sheffield; (2000) Sheffield, Sheffield II, Berwick; (2001) Sheffield, Sheffield II; (2002-03) Sheffield; (2004) Sheffield, Swindon, Eastbourne; (2005) Eastbourne; (2006) Eastbourne, Mildenhall; (2007) Swindon.

RIDER LINKS: Son of former junior rider Richard Moore.

MORRIS, Keiran

DATE OF BIRTH: 10 October 1988, Glasgow, Scotland.

BRITISH CAREER: (2005) Armadale; (2007) Boston.

MORRIS, Phillip (Phil) William

DATE OF BIRTH: 10 September 1975, Newport, Gwent, South Wales.

BRITISH CAREER: (1991-96) Reading; (1997) Stoke; (1998-03) Reading; (2004) Reading, Poole; (2005) Newcastle, Arena-Essex; (2006) Belle Vue; (2007) Newport, Reading, Birmingham.

MORTON, Raymond (Ray) Paul

DATE OF BIRTH: 19 June 1968, Peckham, London.

BRITISH CAREER: (1985-87) King's Lynn; (1988) Wimbledon, King's Lynn; (1989-90) Wimbledon; (1991-92) Reading; (1993) Poole; (1994-95) Reading; (1996) Reading, Hull; (1998) Isle of Wight; (1999) Hull; (2000-03) Isle of Wight; (2004) Isle of Wight, Arena-Essex; (2005) Poole, Exeter; (2006) Isle of Wight; (2007) Rye House.

NEATH, Christopher (Chris)

DATE OF BIRTH: 29 January 1982, Worcester, Hereford & Worcestershire.

BRITISH CAREER: (1998-99) Newport, Newport II; (2000-01) Newport; (2002-03) Swindon, Wolverhampton; (2004) Rye House, Wolverhampton; (2005-06) Rye House; (2007) Rye House, Lakeside, Reading.

NERMARK, Daniel Karl

DATE OF BIRTH: 30 July 1977, Karlstad, Sweden.

BRITISH CAREER: (2001-02) Wolverhampton; (2003) Ipswich; (2004) Wolverhampton; (2005) Edinburgh; (2006-07) King's Lynn.

RIDER LINKS: Son of former junior rider Anders Nermark.

NEWMAN, Kyle

DATE OF BIRTH: 14 December 1991, Poole, Dorset.

BRITISH CAREER: (2007) Weymouth.

RIDER LINKS: Son of former rider Keith Newman.

NICHOLLS, Scott Karl

DATE OF BIRTH: 16 May 1978, Ipswich, Suffolk.

BRITISH CAREER: (1994) Peterborough; (1995-98) Ipswich; (1999-00) Poole; (2001-04) Ipswich; (2005-07) Coventry.

MAJOR HONOURS: British Under-21 Champion: 1998, 1999; British Champion: 2002, 2003, 2005, 2006; Czech Golden Helmet Champion: 2005.

RIDER LINKS: Brother of former rider Shaun Nicholls.

NIEMINEN, Kauko Tapio

DATE OF BIRTH: 29 August 1979, Seinajoki, Finland.

BRITISH CAREER: (2002-05) Workington; (2006) Glasgow; (2007) Workington.

MAJOR HONOURS: Finnish Under-21 Champion: 1998, 1999, 2000.

NORRIS, David Michael

DATE OF BIRTH: 20 August 1972, Eastbourne, East Sussex.

BRITISH CAREER: (1988-89) Eastbourne; (1990-92) Ipswich; (1993) Ipswich, Eastbourne; (1994) Eastbourne; (1995) Reading; (1996-07) Eastbourne.

DUSHER-NORTON, Daniel (Danny)

DATE OF BIRTH: 27 August 1986, Boston, Lincolnshire.

BRITISH CAREER: (2001-02) Peterborough II; (2003) Peterborough (British League Cup only), Peterborough II, Armadale, Reading, Mildenhall; (2004) Oxford II, Reading; (2005) Scunthorpe; (2007) Cleveland.

OLIVER, John Francis

DATE OF BIRTH: 22 July 1987, Melbourne, Victoria, Australia.

BRITISH CAREER: (2003) Carmarthen, Buxton; (2004) King's Lynn II, Boston; (2006) King's Lynn, Boston; (2007) King's Lynn.

OSTERGAARD, Ulrich

DATE OF BIRTH: 19 April 1981, Odense, Denmark.

BRITISH CAREER: (2003) Eastbourne (British League Cup only); (2004) Eastbourne, Isle of Wight; (2005) Isle of Wight, Eastbourne, Swindon; (2006) Peterborough; (2007) Birmingham, Peterborough, Workington.

PARKER, Shane Andrew

DATE OF BIRTH: 29 April 1970, Adelaide, South Australia, Australia.

BRITISH CAREER: (1990-94) Ipswich; (1995-96) Middlesbrough; (1997-98) King's Lynn; (1999) Hull; (2000) King's Lynn, Belle Vue; (2001-02) Peterborough; (2003) King's Lynn, Peterborough; (2004-07) Glasgow.

MAJOR HONOURS: Australian Under-16 Champion: 1985; South Australia State Champion: 1991, 1994, 2001, 2002.

PARSONS, Joel Lewis

DATE OF BIRTH: 24 July 1985, Broken Hill, New South Wales, Australia.

BRITISH CAREER: (2003) Rye House II, Wimbledon; (2004) Rye House II, Hull, King's Lynn II; (2005) Hull, Mildenhall; (2006) Newport, Belle Vue; (2007) Sheffield, Belle Vue.

PEDERSEN, Bjarne

DATE OF BIRTH: 12 July 1978, Ryde, Denmark.

BRITISH CAREER: (2000-01) Newcastle; (2002) Poole; (2003) Poole, Newcastle; (2004-07) Poole.

MAJOR HONOURS: Danish Under-21 Champion: 1999; Danish Champion: 2004; Elite League Riders' Champion: 2004; World Cup Champion: 2006.

GRAND PRIX: European GP Champion: 2004.

PEDERSEN, Nicki

DATE OF BIRTH: 2 April 1977, Odense, Denmark.

BRITISH CAREER: (1998) Newcastle; (1999-00) Wolverhampton; (2001-02) King's Lynn; (2003) Oxford, Eastbourne; (2004-07) Eastbourne.

MAJOR HONOURS: Danish Under-21 Champion: 1997, 1998; Danish Champion: 2002, 2003, 2005, 2006; World Champion: 2003, 2007; Elite League Riders' Champion: 2005, 2007; World Cup Champion: 2006.

GRAND PRIX: European GP Champion: 2002, 2007; British GP Champion: 2003; Slovenian GP Champion: 2006, 2007; Polish GP Champion: 2006; Italian GP Champion: 2007; Czech Republic GP Champion: 2007.

RIDER LINKS: Brother of former rider Ronni Pedersen.

PHILLIPS, Glen Alan

DATE OF BIRTH: 22 November 1982, Farnborough, Kent.

BRITISH CAREER: (1999) Exeter, Isle of Wight, King's Lynn II; (2000) Isle of Wight, Somerset; (2001) Isle of Wight; (2002) Wimbledon, Reading; (2003-05) Isle of Wight; (2006) Somerset; (2007) Isle of Wight.

PICKARD, Jaimie

DATE OF BIRTH: 23 February 1990, Stourbridge, Worcestershire.

BRITISH CAREER: (2006-07) Plymouth.

PICKERING, Michael Philip

DATE OF BIRTH: 28 October 1982, Hull, East Yorkshire.

BRITISH CAREER. (1998) Buxton; (2000) Somerset; (2002) Newport II; (2003) Hull, Newcastle II; (2004) Newcastle II, King's Lynn II; (2005) Boston, Armadale; (2006) Scunthorpe; (2007) Cleveland.

RIDER LINKS: Son of former rider Phil Pickering.

PICKERING, Paul

DATE OF BIRTH: 15 February 1966, Hartlepool, Cleveland.

BRITISH CAREER: (1992) Middlesbrough; (1993) Middlesbrough, Bradford; (1994-96) Bradford; (1997) Reading; (1998-03) Stoke; (2004) Stoke, Ipswich; (2005) Stoke; (2007) Stoke.

PIJPER, Theo

DATE OF BIRTH: 11 February 1980, Dokkum, Holland.

BRITISH CAREER: (2002-06) Edinburgh; (2007) Wolverhampton, Edinburgh, Berwick.

PIPER, George David

DATE OF BIRTH: 3 August 1991, Kettering, Northamptonshire.

BRITISH CAREER: (2006) Weymouth; (2007) Weymouth, Oxford II.

POVAZHNY, Roman

DATE OF BIRTH: 23 October 1976, Togliatti, Russia.

BRITISH CAREER: (1999) Eastbourne; (2000) Oxford, Wolverhampton; (2001) Eastbourne; (2002) King's Lynn; (2004) Eastbourne, Arena-Essex; (2005) Arena-Essex; (2007) Eastbourne.

MAJOR HONOURS: Russian Under-21 Champion: 1997; Russian Champion: 2001

POWELL, Benjamin (Ben) Richard

DATE OF BIRTH: 29 November 1984, Helensvale, Gold Coast, Queensland, Australia.

BRITISH CAREER: (2002) Sheffield II; (2003) Carmarthen; (2004) Carmarthen, Coventry II, Boston; (2005) Boston, Rye House II; (2006) Rye House II, Mildenhall; (2007) Birmingham, Rye House II.

PRIEST, Luke Alex James

DATE OF BIRTH: 18 June 1985, Birmingham, West Midlands.

BRITISH CAREER: (2000) Ashfield, Owlerton; (2001) Sheffield II, Boston; (2002) Sheffield II; (2003) Sheffield II, Stoke II; (2004) Newport, Stoke II, Sheffield II; (2005) Stoke II; (2006) Stoke, Stoke II; (2007) Stoke II.

RIDER LINKS: Son of former rider John Priest.

PROTASIEWICZ, Piotr (Pepe)

DATE OF BIRTH: 25 January 1975, Zielona Gora, Poland.

BRITISH CAREER: (1998) King's Lynn; (2002-03) Peterborough; (2005-06) Ipswich.

NOTE: Protasiewicz did appear for Oxford in 2007, but only in the league. As such, this is not credited in his career record because the club closed down prematurely, with their record expunged from the league standings.

MAJOR HONOURS: World Under-21 Champion: 1996; World Team Cup Champion: 1996; Polish Champion: 1999; World Cup Champion: 2005.

GRAND PRIX: Challenge Champion: 1997; Grand Final Champion: 2003.

RIDER LINKS: Son of former rider Pawel Protasiewicz.

RAJKOWSKI, Michal

DATE OF BIRTH: 17 December 1984, Rawicz, Poland.

BRITISH CAREER: (2007) Newport.

RAUN, Jonas Lorenzen

DATE OF BIRTH: 22 August 1989, Haderslev, Denmark.

BRITISH CAREER: (2006) Peterborough; (2007) Newcastle.

REMPALA, Jacek (Jac)

DATE OF BIRTH: 16 February 1971, Tarnow, Poland.

BRITISH CAREER: (1992) Ipswich; (2006) Berwick, Coventry; (2007) Berwick.

RIDER LINKS: Brother of fellow riders Grzegorz and Marcin Rempala. Brother of former rider Tomasz Rempala

REMPALA, Marcin

DATE OF BIRTH: 20 November 1984, Tarnow, Poland.

BRITISH CAREER: (2007) Ipswich.

MAJOR HONOUR: World Under-21 Team Cup Champion: 2005.

RIDER LINKS: Brother of fellow riders Grzegorz and Jacek Rempala. Brother of former rider Tomasz Rempala

REYNOLDS, Joseph (Joe) Michael

DATE OF BIRTH: 20 March 1989, Wordsley, West Midlands.

BRITISH CAREER: (2004) Buxton; (2005) Buxton, Stoke II, Weymouth; (2006) Newport II; (2007) Sittingbourne.

RICHARDSON, Lee Stewart

DATE OF BIRTH: 25 April 1979, Hastings, Sussex.

BRITISH CAREER: (1995) Reading; (1996) Reading II, Poole; (1997) Reading, Peterborough, King's Lynn; (1998) Reading; (1999) Poole; (2000-03) Coventry; (2004) Peterborough; (2005-07) Swindon.

MAJOR HONOURS: World Under-21 Champion: 1999; Elite League Riders' Champion: 2003.

GRAND PRIX: Grand Final Champion: 2002.

RIDER LINKS: Son of former rider Colin Richardson. Nephew of former rider Steve Weatherley.

RICHARDSON, James Alan Scott

DATE OF BIRTH: 16 September 1988, Mirfield, West Yorkshire.

BRITISH CAREER: (2005-07) Scunthorpe.

RIDER LINKS: Son of former rider Derek Richardson.

RISAGER, Morten

DATE OF BIRTH: 30 September 1987, Arhus, Denmark.

BRITISH CAREER: (2004-06) Coventry; (2007) Coventry, Eastbourne.

ROBERTS, Jack Blain

DATE OF BIRTH: 27 October 1990, Stockport, Cheshire.

BRITISH CAREER: (2006-07) Buxton.

ROBERTSON, Jamie

DATE OF BIRTH: 8 October 1986, Berwick-upon-Tweed, Northumberland.

BRITISH CAREER: (2002) Newcastle II; (2003-04) Newcastle, Newcastle II; (2005) Newcastle, Oxford II; (2006) Newcastle; (2007) Workington, Berwick.

ROBSON, Stuart Anthony

DATE OF BIRTH: 8 November 1976, Sunderland, Tyne and Wear.

BRITISH CAREER: (1993-94) Newcastle, Edinburgh; (1995) Coventry; (1996) Coventry, Middlesbrough; (1997) Hull; (1998-02) Coventry; (2003) Coventry, Newcastle; (2004) Coventry; (2005-07) Rye House.

RIDER LINKS: Son of former rider John Robson. Brother of former rider Scott Robson.

ROYNON, Adam Wayne

DATE OF BIRTH: 30 August 1988, Barrow-in-Furness, Cumbria.

BRITISH CAREER: (2003) Swindon II, Armadale; (2004) Newcastle II, Mildenhall; (2005) Mildenhall, Boston, Glasgow; (2006) Buxton, Rye House; (2007) Rye House, Plymouth.

MAJOR HONOUR: Conference League Riders' Champion: 2006.

RIDER LINKS: Son of former rider Chris Roynon.

SANCHEZ, Emiliano Diebo

DATE OF BIRTH: 9 December 1977, Buenos Aires, Argentina.

BRITISH CAREER: (1999-01) Glasgow; (2002-03) Trelawny; (2004) Hull, Peterborough; (2005) Hull; (2006) Sheffield; (2007) Birmingham.

MAJOR HONOURS: Argentine Champion: 2000, 2001, 2002; Italian Champion: 2004, 2005.

SCHLEIN, Rory Robert

DATE OF BIRTH: 1 September 1984, Darwin, Northern Territory, Australia.

BRITISH CAREER: (2001-02) Edinburgh, Sheffield II; (2003-04) Edinburgh, Belle Vue; (2005-07) Coventry.

MAJOR HONOURS: Australian Under-16 Champion: 2000; Australian Under-21 Champion: 2003, 2004; South Australia State Champion: 2004, 2005, 2006, 2007.

RIDER LINKS: Son of former rider Lyndon Schlein.

SCHRAMM, Chris

DATE OF BIRTH: 30 May 1984, Maldon, Essex.

BRITISH CAREER: (2000) Peterborough II, Berwick, Arena-Essex; (2001-02) Peterborough II, Reading; (2003) Newport, Wimbledon, Peterborough II, Oxford II; (2004) Reading, Oxford II; (2005) Berwick, Peterborough; (2006) Newport; (2007) Newport, Ipswich.

SCREEN, Joseph (Joe)

DATE OF BIRTH: 27 November 1972, Chesterfield, Derbyshire.

BRITISH CAREER: (1989-93) Belle Vue; (1994-97) Bradford; (1998) Belle Vue; (1999) Hull; (2000-02) Eastbourne; (2003) Eastbourne, Belle Vue; (2004-07) Belle Vue.

MAJOR HONOURS: British Under-21 Champion: 1990, 1993; Division One Riders' Champion: 1992; World Under-21 Champion: 1993; British Champion: 1996, 2004.

SHIELDS, Adam Matthew

DATE OF BIRTH: 8 February 1977, Kurri-Kurri, New South Wales, Australia.

BRITISH CAREER: (2000-02) Isle of Wight; (2003) Isle of Wight, Eastbourne; (2004-06) Eastbourne; (2007) Lakeside.

MAJOR HONOURS: Australian Under-21 Champion: 1997; Premier League Riders' Champion: 2002; New South Wales State Champion: 2005.

RIDER LINKS: Nephew of former rider David Shields. Cousin of former rider Ben Shields.

SIMMONS, Nicholas (Nick) Steven John

DATE OF BIRTH: 24 July 1981, Leamington Spa, Warwickshire.

BRITISH CAREER: (1997) Shuttle Cubs, Ryde; (1998) Newport, Newport II, Isle of Wight, Exeter; (1999) Isle of Wight, Stoke, Newport II; (2000) Arena-Essex; (2001) Newport, Newport II, Somerset; (2002) Isle of Wight; (2003) Stoke, Mildenhall; (2004) Exeter, Weymouth; (2005) Exeter, Sittingbourne; (2006) Isle of Wight; (2007) Newport.

RIDER LINKS: Son of former junior rider Steve Simmons.

SIMOTA, Zdenek (Sam)

DATE OF BIRTH: 4 May 1985, Prachatice, Czech Republic.

BRITISH CAREER: (2005-07) Reading.

SKORNICKI, Adam

DATE OF BIRTH: 22 October 1976, Wolsztyn, Poland.

BRITISH CAREER: (2000-04) Wolverhampton; (2005) Wolverhampton, Arena-Essex; (2006) Oxford; (2007) Belle Vue.

SMART, Lee Mitchell

DATE OF BIRTH: 5 April 1988, Swindon, Wiltshire.

BRITISH CAREER: (2003) Swindon II, Stoke II; (2004) Mildenhall; (2005) Somerset, Weymouth, Mildenhall; (2006) Plymouth; (2007) Birmingham, Weymouth.

SMETHILLS, Lee Kenneth

DATE OF BIRTH: 30 March 1982, Bolton, Greater Manchester.

BRITISH CAREER: (1998) Mildenhall; (1999) Workington, Buxton, Rye House, Belle Vue, Newcastle; (2000) Workington, Buxton; (2001) Workington; (2002) Hull, Belle Vue; (2003) Exeter; (2004) Newcastle, Berwick; (2005) Exeter; (2006) Berwick, Wolverhampton, Rye House; (2007) Glasgow, Oxford II.

SMITH, Andrew (Andy)

DATE OF BIRTH: 25 May 1966, York, North Yorkshire.

BRITISH CAREER: (1982-88) Belle Vue; (1989-90) Bradford; (1991) Swindon; (1992-95) Coventry; (1996) Bradford; (1997) Coventry; (1998) Belle Vue, Swindon; (1999-01) Belle Vue; (2003) Oxford, Oxford II; (2004) Swindon; (2005) Belle Vue; (2006) Reading; (2007) Oxford, Reading.

MAJOR HONOURS: British Champion: 1993, 1994, 1995.

RIDER LINKS: Brother of former rider Paul Smith.

SMITH, Jamie Paul

DATE OF BIRTH: 20 July 1983, Peterborough, Cambridgeshire.

BRITISH CAREER: (1998) Norfolk; (1999) Eastbourne, Glasgow; (2000) Newcastle, Peterborough II, Hull, Somerset; (2001) Hull, Somerset; (2002) Hull; (2003) Swindon; (2004) Somerset, Coventry; (2005) Somerset; (2006) Somerset; (2007) Mildenhall, Stoke.

RIDER LINKS: Brother of former rider Darren Smith.

SMITH, Robert (Rob) William

DATE OF BIRTH: 18 February 1988, Eastbourne, East Sussex.

BRITISH CAREER: (2004) Mildenhall; (2005) Wimbledon; (2006) Plymouth; (2007) Boston, Plymouth.

RIDER LINKS: Brother of former junior rider Phil Smith.

SMOLINSKI, Martin

DATE OF BIRTH: 6 December 1984, Graefelfing, Nr Munich, Germany.

BRITISH CAREER: (2004-07) Coventry.

MAJOR HONOURS: German Under-21 Champion: 2003; German Champion: 2007.

SNEDDON, Derek

DATE OF BIRTH: 27 July 1982, Falkirk, Scotland.

BRITISH CAREER: (1998) Hull; (1999) Linlithgow, Isle of Wight; (2000) Ashfield, Edinburgh; (2001) Edinburgh, Glasgow; (2002) Newcastle; (2003) Edinburgh; (2004-05) Armadale; (2006-07) Edinburgh.

STANCL, Jiri (George)

DATE OF BIRTH: 19 August 1975, Prague, Czech Republic.

BRITISH CAREER: (1994-95) Sheffield; (1996-99) Wolverhampton; (2000) Coventry; (2002-04) Glasgow; (2005) Glasgow, Ipswich; (2006) Newcastle; (2007) Glasgow, Edinburgh.

MAJOR HONOUR: Czech Republic Under-21 Champion: 1993.

RIDER LINKS: Grandson of former rider Jiri Stancl [1]. Son of former rider Jiri Stancl [2].

STARKE, Paul Simon

DATE OF BIRTH: 18 November 1990, Hereford, Hereford & Worcestershire.

BRITISH CAREER: (2007) Buxton.

STEAD, Garry

DATE OF BIRTH: 5 January 1972, Holmfirth, West Yorkshire.

BRITISH CAREER: (1990-92) Stoke; (1993) Newcastle; (1994) Newcastle, Bradford; (1995) Bradford; (1996) Sheffield; (1997) Bradford; (1998) Wolverhampton; (1999-02) Hull; (2003) Hull, Eastbourne; (2004-05) Hull; (2006) Workington; (2007) Stoke.

STEAD, Simon Trevor

DATE OF BIRTH: 25 April 1982, Sheffield, South Yorkshire.

BRITISH CAREER: (1997) Peterborough II; (1998) Peterborough, Buxton; (1999-01) Sheffield; (2002) Sheffield, Peterborough; (2003-04) Workington, Wolverhampton; (2005-07) Belle Vue.

MAJOR HONOURS: British Under-21 Champion: 2001, 2002, 2003.

RIDER LINKS: Son of former rider Trevor Stead. Nephew of former rider Ian Stead. Cousin of fellow rider Adam Allott.

STEPHENS, Seemond Lee

DATE OF BIRTH: 9 August 1967, St Austell, Cornwall.

BRITISH CAREER: (1998) St Austell, Exeter, Sheffield, Swindon; (1999) Eastbourne, Swindon, St Austell; (2000-01) Exeter; (2002) Trelawny, Exeter; (2003) Exeter, Eastbourne; (2004-05) Exeter; (2006-07) Plymouth.

STEVENS, Jonathan (Jon) Richard Vernon

DATE OF BIRTH: 3 January 1983, Croydon, Surrey.

BRITISH CAREER: (2000) Rye House; (2001) Sheffield II; (2002-04) Wimbledon; (2007) Sittingbourne.

STODDART, Sean

DATE OF BIRTH: 20 January 1987, Edinburgh, Scotland.

BRITISH CAREER: (2003) Armadale, Trelawny II, Carmarthen II, Newcastle II; (2004) Armadale, Edinburgh; (2005) Armadale; (2006) Edinburgh, Boston; (2007) Newcastle, Boston, Cleveland.

STOJANOWSKI, Krzysztof

DATE OF BIRTH: 5 January 1979, Zielona Gora, Poland.

BRITISH CAREER: (2005) Isle of Wight; (2006) Isle of Wight, Swindon; (2007) Isle of Wight.

STONEHEWER, Carl Bryan

DATE OF BIRTH: 16 May 1972, Manchester, Greater Manchester.

BRITISH CAREER: (1988-89) Belle Vue; (1990) Wolverhampton; (1991-93) Belle Vue; (1994) Peterborough; (1995-96) Long Eaton; (1997) Long Eaton, King's Lynn, Peterborough, Coventry, Eastbourne; (1998) Sheffield; (1999-02) Workington; (2003) Workington, Belle Vue; (2004-05) Workington; (2007) Workington.

MAJOR HONOURS: Premier League Riders' Champion: 2000, 2001.

STONEMAN, Danny

DATE OF BIRTH: 22 April 1992.

BRITISH CAREER: (2007) Plymouth.

STRUDWICK, Lee

DATE OF BIRTH: 23 July 1988, Pembury, Kent.

BRITISH CAREER: (2005) Wimbledon; (2006-07) Rye House II.

RIDER LINKS: Cousin of junior rider Niall Strudwick.

SUCHANEK, Tomas

DATE OF BIRTH: 7 April 1984, Pardubice, Czech Republic.

BRITISH CAREER: (2003) King's Lynn (British League Cup only); (2005) Isle of Wight, Poole; (2006) Redcar, Wolverhampton; (2007) Somerset, Mildenhall.

MAJOR HONOURS: Czech Republic Under-21 Champion: 2002, 2003.

SUCHECKI, Zbigniew (Zibi)

DATE OF BIRTH: 21 July 1984, Gorzow, Poland.

BRITISH CAREER: (2007) Ipswich.

SUMMERS, Aaron

DATE OF BIRTH: 1 March 1988, Adelaide, South Australia.

BRITISH CAREER: (2007) Buxton, Edinburgh.

SWIDERSKI, Piotr

DATE OF BIRTH: 11 May 1983, Gostyn, Poland.

BRITISH CAREER: (2006-07) Peterborough.

SWIST, Piotr

DATE OF BIRTH: 20 June 1968, Gorzow, Poland.

BRITISH CAREER: (2005) Arena-Essex; (2007) Poole.

MAJOR HONOURS: Polish Under-21 Champion: 1987, 1988, 1989.

TACEY, Shaun James

DATE OF BIRTH: 27 November 1974, Norwich, Norfolk.

BRITISH CAREER: (1992) Ipswich; (1993) Ipswich, Arena-Essex; (1994-96) Coventry; (1997) King's Lynn, Isle of Wight, Bradford, Coventry; (1998-00) Coventry; (2001-02) Arena-Essex; (2003) King's Lynn, Coventry; (2005) Workington; (2006) Mildenhall, Arena-Essex, Poole; (2007) Mildenhall.

TAYLOR, Benjamin (Ben) Reece

DATE OF BIRTH: 7 November 1990, Dewsbury, West Yorkshire.

BRITISH CAREER: (2006-07) Buxton.

RIDER LINKS: Grandson of former rider Jack Hughes. Great nephew of former rider Arthur Wright.

TESSARI, Daniele

DATE OF BIRTH: 20 August 1984, Albaredo d-Adige, Italy.

BRITISH CAREER: (2006-07) Edinburgh.

MAJOR HONOUR: Italian Under-21 Champion: 2002.

THEOBALD, James Anthony

DATE OF BIRTH: 31 December 1985, Ashford, Kent.

BRITISH CAREER: (2002) Rye House II, Carmarthen; (2003) Rye House II, Sheffield II, Newport II, Peterborough II; (2004) Sittingbourne, Wimbledon, King's Lynn II; (2005) Sittingbourne; (2007) Sittingbourne.

THOMPSON, Mark

DATE OF BIRTH: 8 July 1979, Orsett, Essex.

BRITISH CAREER: (1996) Sittingbourne, Linlithgow, Mildenhall, Eastbourne II; (1997) Anglian Angels; (1998) Mildenhall, Newport, Stoke; (1999) King's Lynn II, Mildenhall, Newport II; (2000) St Austell, Arena-Essex; (2001) Peterborough II; (2002) King's Lynn II, Mildenhall; (2003) Boston, Peterborough (British League Cup only); (2004) Weymouth, Swindon II, King's Lynn II; (2005) Mildenhall; (2006) Mildenhall II, Sheffield; (2007) Mildenhall, Weymouth.

TOMICEK, Lubos

DATE OF BIRTH: 14 March 1986, Prague, Czech Republic.

BRITISH CAREER: (2003) Oxford (British League Cup only); (2004) Newcastle; (2005) Newcastle, Oxford; (2006) Oxford; (2007) Lakeside.

NOTE: Tomicek did appear for Oxford in 2007, but only in the league. As such, this is not credited in his career record because the club closed down prematurely, with their record expunged from the league standings.

RIDER LINKS: Grandson of former rider Lubos Tomicek [1]. Son of former rider Lubos Tomicek [2].

TOPINKA, Tomas

DATE OF BIRTH: 5 June 1974, Prague, Czech Republic.

BRITISH CAREER: (1993-95) King's Lynn; (1996) Oxford; (1997-98) King's Lynn; (1999) King's Lynn, Ipswich; (2001) Belle Vue; (2002) Coventry; (2003-04) King's Lynn; (2005) King's Lynn, Coventry; (2006-07) King's Lynn.

MAJOR HONOURS: Czech Republic Under-21 Champion: 1992; Czech Republic Champion: 1996, 2003; Czech Golden Helmet Champion: 1996.

TRESARRIEU, Mathieu

DATE OF BIRTH: 2 March 1986, Bordeaux, France.

BRITISH CAREER: (2002-03) Isle of Wight; (2005) Reading; (2006) Redcar, Oxford, Wolverhampton; (2007) Redcar.

MAJOR HONOURS: French Champion: 2002, 2007.

RIDER LINKS: Brother of fellow riders Sebastien and Stephane Tresarrieu.

TRUMINSKI, Sebastian

DATE OF BIRTH: 18 April 1980, Lublin, Poland.

BRITISH CAREER: (2007) Berwick, Newport.

TULLY, Andrew Bruce

DATE OF BIRTH: 26 May 1987, Douglas, Isle of Man.

BRITISH CAREER: (2003-05) Armadale; (2006) Scunthorpe; (2007) Edinburgh, Scunthorpe.

ULAMEK, Sebastian (Seba)

DATE OF BIRTH: 20 November 1975, Czestochowa, Poland.

BRITISH CAREER: (2000) Wolverhampton; (2002) King's Lynn; (2003-04) Oxford; (2005) Coventry; (2006-07) Swindon.

MAJOR HONOUR: Continental Champion: 2001.

VISSING, Claus

DATE OF BIRTH: 6 June 1986, Grindsted, Denmark.

BRITISH CAREER: (2007) Stoke.

WALDRON, Shane Ashley

DATE OF BIRTH: 26 October 1989, Swindon, Wiltshire.

BRITISH CAREER: (2005) Rye House II, Weymouth; (2006) King's Lynn, Plymouth; (2007) Plymouth, Boston.

WALKER, Simon Mark

DATE OF BIRTH: 19 February 1980, Bristol, Avon.

BRITISH CAREER: (2001) Newport II; (2002) Newport II, Swindon II; (2003) Swindon II, Trelawny II; (2004) Somerset, Swindon II, King's Lynn II; (2005) Boston, Somerset; (2006-07) Somerset.

WALLINGER, David

DATE OF BIRTH: 16 May 1984, York, North Yorkshire.

BRITISH CAREER: (2007) Cleveland.

RIDER LINKS: Son of former junior rider John Wallinger.

WARWICK, Daniel (Danny)

DATE OF BIRTH: 21 November 1983, Poole, Dorset.

BRITISH CAREER: (2002) Newport II; (2003) Newport II, Poole (British League Cup only); (2004) Weymouth, Swindon II, King's Lynn II; (2005) Newport II; (2006) Berwick, Weymouth; (2007) Somerset, Sittingbourne.

RIDER LINKS: Brother of former rider Carl Warwick.

WATSON, Craig

DATE OF BIRTH: 6 August 1976, Sydney, New South Wales, Australia.

BRITISH CAREER: (1997-99) Newport; (2000-01) Poole; (2002) Newport; (2003) Newport, Belle Vue; (2004-06) Newport; (2007) Poole, Glasgow.

MAJOR HONOUR: New South Wales State Champion: 2004.

WATT, David (Davey) John

DATE OF BIRTH: 6 January 1978, Townsville, Queensland, Australia.

BRITISH CAREER: (2001) Isle of Wight; (2002) Newcastle; (2003) King's Lynn, Poole; (2004) Rye House, Poole, Eastbourne; (2005) Eastbourne; (2006) Oxford; (2007) Eastbourne.

MAJOR HONOUR: Queensland State Champion: 2005.

WEBSTER, Timothy (Tim) Mark

DATE OF BIRTH: 26 May 1989, Walsall, West Midlands.

BRITISH CAREER: (2004) King's Lynn II; (2005) Weymouth, Scunthorpe; (2006) Newport II; (2007) Plymouth.

WERNER, Jeffrey Brent

DATE OF BIRTH: 15 April 1974, Los Angeles, California, USA.

BRITISH CAREER: (1995-97) Long Eaton; (1998) Newcastle; (1999-00) Workington; (2001) Eastbourne; (2002) Rye House; (2003) Rye House, Peterborough; (2004) Rye House, Belle Vue; (2005) Rye House, Oxford; (2006) Eastbourne, Mildenhall, Arena-Essex; (2007) Birmingham.

RIDER LINKS: Nephew of former rider Dubb Ferrell.

WESTACOTT, Jamie

DATE OF BIRTH: 9 April 1988, Newport, Gwent, South Wales.

BRITISH CAREER: (2003) Newport II, Stoke II; (2004) Newport II, Reading; (2005) Newport II; (2006) Plymouth; (2007) Weymouth, Plymouth.

WETHERS, Matthew James

DATE OF BIRTH: 30 May 1985, Adelaide, South Australia.

BRITISH CAREER: (2003) Armadale, Wolverhampton II, Edinburgh; (2004) Edinburgh, Armadale; (2005) Glasgow, King's Lynn, Edinburgh; (2006) Edinburgh, Poole; (2007) Edinburgh.

WILKINSON, Carl Adam

DATE OF BIRTH: 16 May 1981, Boston, Lincolnshire.

BRITISH CAREER: (1997) Peterborough II; (1998) Norfolk; (1999) King's Lynn II; (2000) Boston, Newcastle, Glasgow; (2001) Boston; (2002-03) Newport, Newport II; (2004) Newport; (2005) Boston, Berwick; (2006) Newport, Ipswich; (2007) Newcastle, Wolverhampton.

WILSON, Ben Ryan

DATE OF BIRTH: 15 March 1986, Sheffield, South Yorkshire.

BRITISH CAREER: (2001-02) Sheffield II; (2003) Sheffield, Sheffield II, Buxton; (2004) Sheffield, Sheffield II, Carmarthen; (2005) Sheffield; (2006) Sheffield, Wolverhampton; (2007) Sheffield, Belle Vue.

MAJOR HONOUR: British Under-21 Champion: 2006.

WOFFINDEN, Tai

DATE OF BIRTH: 10 August 1990, Scunthorpe, North Lincolnshire.

BRITISH CAREER: (2006) Scunthorpe, Sheffield; (2007) Rye House, Scunthorpe, Poole.

MAJOR HONOURS: Conference League Riders' Champion: 2007; British Under-18 Champion: 2007.

RIDER LINKS: Son of former rider Rob Woffinden.

WOODWARD, Cameron Jackson

DATE OF BIRTH: 8 January 1985, Mildura, Victoria, Australia.

BRITISH CAREER: (2003) Poole (British League Cup only); (2004-05) Edinburgh; (2006-07) Eastbourne.

MAJOR HONOUR: Victoria State Champion: 2006.

WRATHALL, Adam Mark Edward

DATE OF BIRTH: 27 November 1991, Blackpool, Lancashire.

BRITISH CAREER: (2007) Oxford II.

WRIGHT, Charles

DATE OF BIRTH: 26 October 1988, Stockport, Cheshire.

BRITISH CAREER: (2004-06) Buxton; (2007) Workington, Buxton.

RIDER LINKS: Grandson of former rider Jim Yacoby. Brother of fellow rider James Wright.

WRIGHT, James

DATE OF BIRTH: 13 June 1986, Stockport, Cheshire.

BRITISH CAREER: (2002) Buxton; (2003) Buxton, Belle Vue (British League Cup only); (2004) Workington, Buxton; (2005-07) Workington, Belle Vue.

MAJOR HONOURS: Conference League Riders' Champion: 2004; Premier League Riders' Champion: 2007.

RIDER LINKS: Grandson of former rider Jim Yacoby. Brother of fellow rider Charles Wright.

WRIGHT, Matthew Paul

DATE OF BIRTH: 19 November 1985, Harlow, Essex.

BRITISH CAREER: (2002) Boston, Mildenhall, Carmarthen, Wimbledon II; (2003) Mildenhall, Ipswich (British League Cup only); (2004-05) Wimbledon; (2006) Mildenhall, Mildenhall II; (2007) Boston.

ZAGAR, Matej

DATE OF BIRTH: 3 April 1983, Ljubljana, Slovenia.

BRITISH CAREER: (2003) Trelawny; (2004-07) Reading.

MAJOR HONOURS: Slovenian Champion: 2002, 2003, 2004, 2005, 2006, 2007; European Under-19 Champion: 2002; European Champion: 2004.

ZETTERSTROM, Hans Magnus

DATE OF BIRTH: 9 December 1971, Eskilstuna, Sweden.

BRITISH CAREER: (1996) Poole; (1998-99) Poole; (2000) Peterborough; (2001) Poole; (2002) Poole, Peterborough; (2003) Poole (British League Cup only); (2004) Poole; (2005-07) Somerset.

MAJOR HONOURS: European Champion: 2002; Premier League Riders' Champion: 2006.

ALSO AVAILABLE FROM METHANOL PRESS

Showered in Shale

One Man's Circuitous Journey Throughout the Country in Pursuit of An Obsession – British Speedway

"At the end of the month William Hill announces the shortlist for its sports book of 2006. If the author Jeff Scott's impulsively oddball doorstep is not already in pole position, then it jolly well should be."
FRANK KEATING, *Guardian*

"It's all here, in almost soap opera style proportions…this is British Speedway stripped bare, this is how it really is and some of it isn't pretty….many years into the future, historians will gladly hold this book to their bosom for its insight….. what the author has achieved - and it will be interesting to see how many people really take this on board - is that he's provided a book that will stand-up as a fly on the wall type narrative of where and what our sport really is in the early millennium. ….Showered in Shale is a quirky book, it's different and off-the-wall.
BRIAN BURFORD, *Speedway Star*

508 pages 409 Black & white photographs £20.00 Paperback

When Eagles Dared

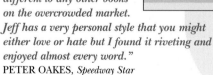

"A remarkable read and something completely different to any other books on the overcrowded market. Jeff has a very personal style that you might either love or hate but I found it riveting and enjoyed almost every word."
PETER OAKES, *Speedway Star*

172 pages 158 Black & white photographs £10.00 Paperback

Shifting Shale

2006 A Race Odyssey

"Nobody else writing about speedway at the moment can capture the speedway experience in the way that Scott can. As always, the beauty of his work is in the description of the minutiae"
ALLAN MELVILLE, *Speedway Plus*

"Makes marvellous, opinionated, reading…Jeff is a good listener, with a quick ear for a good quote, and his books are peppered – indeed at times salted — with the words of others, too"
DICK BARRIE

"Bill Brysonesque"
JIM HENRY, *Speedway Researcher*

354 pages 143 Black & white photographs £20.00 Paperback

Shale Britannia

A Sideways Glance at Speedway

"A brilliantly quirky book"
Big Issue

"A marvellously evocative book"
JOHN INVERDALE, *Daily Telegraph*

"Superbly produced. I found it absolutely fascinating"
PETER OAKES, *Speedway Star*

256 pages 245 colour photos £15.00 flexiback

**All available from
www.methanolpress.com**

MethanolPress